FAMILIAR
QUOTATIONS

FROM

GERMAN AND SPANISH AUTHORS

BY

CRAUFURD TAIT RAMAGE, LL.D

AUTHOR OF "NOOKS AND BY-WAYS OF ITALY" "BEAUTIFUL THOUGHTS
FROM LATIN AUTHORS" "BEAUTIFUL THOUGHTS FROM GREEK
AUTHORS" "BEAUTIFUL THOUGHTS FROM FRENCH
AND ITALIAN AUTHORS" ETC

*"Love of reading enables a man to exchange the wearisome hours of
life which come to every one for hours of delight."*

"Nous avons donné à penser."

LONDON

GEORGE ROUTLEDGE & SONS Limited

NEW YORK : E. P. DUTTON & CO

1904

REPUBLISHED BY GALE RESEARCH COMPANY, BOOK TOWER, DETROIT, 1968

This work also appeared under the
title *Beautiful Thoughts from
German and Spanish authors.*

Library of Congress Catalog Card Number 68–22043

TO THE

REV. JOHN DONALDSON, M.A.

THIS VOLUME IS INSCRIBED

AS A MARK OF ESTEEM AND RESPECT

FOR HIS CHARACTER

AS A CLERGYMAN AND A SCHOLAR

PREFACE.

THE favour with which my former volumes continue to
be received has induced me to prepare another and
final volume from sources which are little known in
this country. Germany and Spain abound in literary
treasures, which only require to be brought under notice
to be fully appreciated ; and my object has been to give
such specimens of " Beautiful Thoughts " from the
authors of these countries as may induce readers to
draw for themselves gold from mines comparatively
unwrought.

The writers of Germany are especially rich in senti-
ments which are of world-wide importance, and if I
have succeeded in making a collection of these thoughts,
I shall have accomplished the task which I set before
me. The philosophy of Fichte, the novels and dramas
of Goethe, Klopstock's bright imagination, the pleasing
epistolary correspondence of William von Humboldt,
Schleiermacher's religious mysticism, Schiller's immortal
works, the strange and often incomprehensible writings
of Paul Richter, have all been laid under contribution
to furnish materials for musing to the thoughtful mind.
Many authors little known have also been examined,
and pearls of value have occasionally been discovered
where they could have been least expected.

Spanish writers are perhaps less known than those of Germany, and much more could have been added, but enough will be found to show how rich Spain is in her literary treasures. Calderon's poetic fancy, the inimitable works of Cervantes, the poem of the Cid, of the Dance of Death, Garcilasso de la Vega, have all furnished specimens of Spain's peculiar mode of thinking.

As this volume completes the task which I had placed before me, I may be allowed to state that I am sensible how imperfectly I have filled up the picture which my imagination had bodied forth. My object in these volumes has been to address myself not merely to the thoughtful many but to the deep-thinking few, and it has been a gratification to me, in the midst of great labour, to know that my exertions have been appreciated by a wide circle of readers. The four volumes contain a larger mass of wisdom than has ever before been attempted to be brought together from the mighty minds of ancient and modern times. How much will be found there to refine, strengthen, delight, and teach, not merely the young but the thoughtful and educated ! They are, in fact, " Books of Wisdom ;" and I can speak freely on this point, as I assume no further merit than that of appreciating the wisdom and warming my heart with the sublime thoughts of noble natures.

All genius is akin, and many of these great thoughts are no doubt rather belonging to our humanity than peculiar to any individual. It is interesting, however, to trace the same idea through the writers of different ages and countries ; though I am not sure that even in cases where the influence of ancient writers is distinctly observable in those who follow them, whether it may not often be, because their thoughts are diffused through the air, so to speak, and breathed unconsciously by their successors. Those who take pleasure in tracing the similarity of thought that runs through writers of different ages, will find much in these volumes to assist their labours, and will be surprised at the diverse forms the same idea assumes in different minds.

In selecting from so wide a field, it is obvious that much must be omitted which would have been worthy of being recorded, but it is hoped that enough has been given to stimulate readers to go to the same sources and draw for themselves what may suit their peculiar bent of mind. There may be some things that may seem to be trifling and scarcely worthy of a place in such a volume, but these will often be found to be given as examples of "household words" that are in everybody's mouth in Germany. I refer more particularly to some expressions in Goethe and Schiller, which I have selected, not so much from their intrinsic worth, as because I knew them to be "winged words" used in common conversation in that country.

The German Index refers more particularly to Goethe and Schiller, as these authors are best known to English scholars, but the English Index is analytical and will furnish a complete key to the whole work. My former works have been largely used for illustrations ; the references are to subjects, which will be found in the Indexes, and not to pages. This plan I have been led to adopt, because my Latin volume is now out of print, and a new edition is passing through the press, and therefore I had no means of giving the page where the passage is cited. This, however, is an improvement, as the reference will suit any future edition of the works. I may state that the new edition of my Latin volume has had much new material added, and the illustrations from Greek, French, Italian, and German authors will, I trust, greatly enhance its value to scholars.

INDEX OF AUTHORS.

GERMAN.

CHRONOLOGICAL INDEX.

GERMAN AUTHORS.

SPANISH AUTHORS.

BEAUTIFUL THOUGHTS

FROM GERMAN AUTHORS.

—◆◆—

ARNDT.

Born A.D. 1769.   Died A.D. 1860.

Ernst Moritz Arndt was born, 1769, at Schoritz in the island of Rugen, and became Professor of Modern History at Bonn, where he died, 29th January 1860.

GOD MADE NO SLAVES.

Vaterlandslied.

Der Gott, der Eisen wachsen ließ,
Der wollte keine Knechte,
D'rum gab er Säbel, Schwert und Spieß
Dem Mann in seine Rechte.
D'rum gab er ihm den kühnen Muth,
Den Zorn der freien Rede,
Daß er bestände bis auf's Blut,
Bis in den Tod die Fehde.

The God, who made earth's iron, would create no slave ; therefore he gave the sabre, the sword, and the spear, for man's right hand.   Hence he imbued him with courage, lent accents of wrath to freedom's voice, that he might maintain the feud till death.

See (Lat.) Slavery ; (Gr.) Slave, no man born a, by nature.

ARNIM.

Born A.D. 1781.   Died A.D. 1831.

Ludwig Achim von Arnim was born, 1781, at Berlin; lived with Brentano, whose sister Bettina he married.   He spent his time between Berlin and his property at Wiepersdorf, where he died 1831.

A

WHAT WE OUGHT TO PRAY FOR.

Gebet.

Gieb Liebe mir und einen frohen Mund,
Daß ich dich, Herr der Erde, thue kund,
Gesundheit gieb bei sorgen freiem Gut,
Ein frommes Herz und einen festen Muth;
Gieb Kinder mir, die aller Mühe werth,
Verscheuch die Feinde von dem trauten Heerd;
Gieb Flügel dann und einen Hügel Sand,
Den Hügel Sand im lieben Vaterland,
Die Flügel schenk' dem abschiedsschweren Geist,
Daß er sich leicht der schönen Welt entreißt.

Give me love and contentment that I may proclaim thy glory, Lord of earth; give me health with competence, a pious heart, and a steadfast mind; give me children, worthy of all care; scare from my cheerful hearth the foe away; then give me wings, and one small hill of sand in my loved Fatherland, give wings to the soul so unwilling to flee, that it may easily tear itself from this beautiful world.

See (Lat.) Gods, prayer to; (Gr.) Pray for, what we ought to.

BÜRGER.

Born A.D. 1748.   Died A.D. 1794.

Gottfried Augustus Bürger, a celebrated poet, was born, 1748, at Wolmerswende, a village in the principality of Halberstadt, where his father was Lutheran minister. His early years were spent carelessly, and he was in his youth irregular in his habits, but his ballad of Leonora established his fame as a poet. His domestic life was an unhappy one, and he must have died in a state of the most abject poverty, if the government of Hanover had not relieved his necessities. He died the 8th June 1794.

WOMAN'S CUNNING.

Die Weiber von Weinsberg.

Doch wann's Matthä' am letzten ist,
Trotz Rathen, Thun, und Beten,
So rettet oft noch Weiberlist
Aus Aengsten und aus Nöthen.

Denn Pfaffentrug und Weiberlist
Gehn über Alles, wie ihr wißt.

Yet, when we are at our last gasp, notwithstanding the best of counsel, acting and praying, a woman's cunning often saves us from all our pain and sorrow. For the deceit of priests and the cunning of woman surpass everything, as you know.

See (Lat.) Woman full of wiles; (Gr.) Woman, deceit of.

THE PROMISE OF AN EMPEROR.

Die Weiber von Weinsberg.

Doch Conrad sprach: „Ein Kaiserwort
Soll man nicht drehn noch deuteln."

Then Conrad said, "An Emperer's word must not change nor quibble."

ALAS!

Die Weiber von Weinsberg.

O weh mir armen Korydon!

O, woes me, poor Corydon!

A SLANDEROUS TONGUE.

Trost.

Wenn dich die Lästerzunge sticht,
So laß dir dies zum Troste sagen:
Die schlechtsten Früchte sind es nicht,
Woran die Wespen nagen.

When the tongue of slander stings thee, let this be thy comfort:—
They are not the worst fruits on which the wasps alight.

See (Fr.) Slander.

THE DEAD.

Leonore.

Die Todten reiten schnell.
·   The dead ride swiftly.

GONE IS GONE.

Leonore.

„O Mutter, Mutter! Hin ist hin!
Verloren ist verloren!"

O mother, mother, gone is gone; the past shall ne'er return!
See (Lat.) Past time.

Rail not at Heaven's Will.

Leonore.

„Geduld! Geduld! Wenn's Herz auch bricht!
Mit Gott im Himmel hadre nicht!
Des Leibes bist du ledig;
Gott sey der Seele gnädig!"

Patience, patience; though thy heart breaks, rail not at Heaven's resistless will! and when thou leavest the body, God may be gracious to thy soul.

See **(Fr.)** Virtuous constancy ; (Lat.) Patience.

DINTER.

Fear not.

Fürchte nichts.

Gott ist, wo die Sonne glüht,
Gott ist, wo das Veilchen blüht,
Ist, wo jener Vogel schlägt,
Ist, wo dieser Wurm sich regt.
Ist kein Freund, kein Mensch bei dir,
Fürchte nichts! Dein Gott ist hier.

God is where the sun glows, God is where the violet blooms, is where yon bird is flapping its wings, is where this worm is moving. Though no friend, no man, be with thee, fear nothing! Thy God is here.

See **(Gr. Fr.)** God, omnipresence of.

ENGEL.

Born A.D. 1741.   Died A.D. 1802.

Alliances of the Soul.

Aus Engel's Philosoph für die Welt.

Traum des Galilei.

O sie sind süß, Viviani, die Verwandtschaften des Bluts, die schon selbst die Natur stiftet; aber wie viel süßer noch sind Verwandtschaften der Seele! Wie viel theurer und inniger, als selbst die Bruderliebe, sind die Bande der Wahrheit!

Blood-connection is sweet, and is what nature brings about; but how much sweeter are the alliances of the soul! How much dearer and more intimate than even brotherly love **are** the bonds of truth!

See (Gr.) Truth, force of.

FRIEDRICH EWALD.
Born A.D. 1730.

CONTRAST OF LIFE IN THE COUNTRY AND TOWN.

Der Landmann an den Städter.

Du schläfst auf weichen Betten, ich schlaf' auf weichem Klee;
Du siehest Dich im Spiegel, ich mich im stillen See;
Du wohnst in bangen Mauern, ich wohn' auf freier Flur;
Dir malen theure Maler, mir malet die Natur;
Du bist oft siech vom Schmausen, und ich bin stets gesund;
Dich schützt um Geld ein Schweizer, mich schützt mein treuer
     Hund;
Du trinkst gefärbte Weine und ich den klaren Quell;
Dein Auge blickt oft finster und meines stets so hell.
Sag an nun, reicher Städter, wer hat wohl von uns beiden,
Du, oder ich die meisten und auch die reinsten Freuden?

Thou sleepest on downy couches, I sleep on soft clover; thou beholdest thyself in a mirror, I in the still water; thou dwellest within anxious walls, I dwell in the open fields; expensive artists take thy portrait, nature paints me; thou art often sick from surfeiting, and I am always in the best health; a servant in rich livery attends on thee, my faithful dog protects me; thou drinkest rich wines, and I from the clear spring; thy eye looks often dark, and mine always clear. Say now, rich townsman, whether of us two, thou or I, has the most, and also the purest pleasures?

See (Lat. Gr.) Country life.

FICHTE.
Born A.D. 1762. Died A.D. 1814.

Johann Gottlieb Fichte, an eminent philosopher, was born at Rammenau, a village of Lusatia, on the 19th May 1762. He was the son of a ribbon-manufacturer, and put to school by a wealthy person in the neighbourhood, who was struck by his extraordinary genius. Theology became his favourite study, and after various

changes he obtained the appointment to the philosophical chair at
Jena, but was obliged to resign it for his heretical opinions. He
retired to Berlin, where he was received with great attention, and
occupied his time in giving private lectures and in composing his
various writings. When the university of Berlin was founded, he
obtained, through the interest of Humboldt, the situation of rector,
which secured him a comfortable subsistence. He died on the
29th January 1814.

GOD.

Ueber den Grund unseres Glaubens u. f. w. 1798. S. W., V, 187, 188.

Es ist ein Mißverständniß zu sagen, es sei zweifelhaft, ob ein
Gott sei, oder nicht. Es ist gar nicht zweifelhaft, sondern
das Gewisseste, was es gibt, ja der Grund aller andern Gewißheit, das einzig absolut gültige Objective, daß es eine moralische
Weltordnung gibt, daß jedem vernünftigen Individuum seine
bestimmte Stelle in dieser Ordnung angewiesen und auf seine
Arbeit gerechnet ist; daß jedes seiner Schicksale, Resultat ist
von diesem Plane; daß ohne ihn kein Haar fällt von seinem
Haupte, und in seiner Wirkungssphäre kein Sperling vom
Dache, daß jede wahrhaft gute Handlung gelingt, jede böse
sicher mißlingt, und daß denen, die nur das Gute recht lieben,
alle Dinge zum besten dienen müssen.

It is a mistake to say that it is doubtful whether there is a God
or not. It is not in the least doubtful, but the most certain thing
in the world, nay, the foundation of all other certainty—the only
solid absolute objectivity—that there is a moral government of the
world ; that to every rational being his determined place is assigned in this government, and his exertions are taken into account,
so that every part of his destiny is the result of this plan ; that
without him no hair falls from his head, and, within the sphere of
his working, no sparrow from the house-top ; that every good work
succeeds, and as certainly every bad deed miscarries ; and that to
those who love only what is good, all things must turn out for the
best.

NO REALLY EXISTING INDIVIDUAL CAN DIE.

Wissenschaftslehre. 1813. N. W., II, 158.

Ueber die Unsterblichkeit der Seele kann die Wissenschaftslehre nichts statuiren: denn es ist nach ihr keine Seele, und
kein Sterben oder Sterblichkeit, mithin auch keine Unsterblichkeit, sondern es ist nur Leben, und dieses ist ewig in sich

ſelber, und was Leben iſt, iſt ebenſo ewig wie dies: **alſo ſie**
hält es wie Jeſus: wer an mich glaubt, der ſtirbt nie, ſondern
es iſt ihm gegeben, das Leben zu haben in ihm ſelber.

As to the immortality of the soul the doctrine of science can
determine nothing; for there is according to it no soul, and **no**
dying or mortality, therefore, also, no immortality; but there is
only life, and this is eternal in itself, and whatever life is, it is just
eternal as this; therefore it affirms, as Jesus did, " whosoever believes in me, he never dies, but it is given to him to have life in
himself."

LIFE AFTER DEATH.
Brief. 1790. 2., I, 74, 95.

Das ſicherſte Mittel, ſich von einem Leben nach dem Tode zu
überzeugen, iſt das, ſein gegenwärtiges ſo zu führen, daß man
es wünſchen darf. Wer es fühlt, daß, wenn ein Gott iſt, er
gnädig auf ihn herabſchauen müſſe, den rühren keine Gründe
gegen ſein Daſein, und er bedarf keiner dafür. Wer ſo viel
für die Tugend aufgeopfert hat, daß er Entſchädigungen in
einem künftigen Leben zu erwarten hat, der beweiſt ſich nicht
und glaubt nicht die Exiſtenz eines ſolchen Lebens; er fühlt ſie.

The surest means to convince oneself of a life after death is so
to act in the present that one must wish it. Whoever feels that,
if there is a God, he must look graciously on him, seeks for no
reasons against his existence, and requires none. Whoever has
offered up so much for virtue, that he ought to expect indemni-
fications in a future life, such an one requires no proof of, nor
does he merely believe in, the existence of such a life; he feels it
within himself.

WHAT A FATE IS THAT OF MAN.
Briefe. 1790. 2., I, 88, 94.

O was iſt doch Menſchenſchickſal! So oft ich eine Geſchichte
unverſchuldeten Elends höre, verſtärkt ſich mein Blick in jene
Welt, wo alles gleich ſein, und wo die Arbeit des Mühevollen
herrlich enden wird. O könnte man doch allen Geplagten
dieſen Gedanken recht ſtark in ihr Herz rufen!

Oh, what a fate is that of man! As often as I hear of some
undeserved wretchedness, my thoughts rest on that world where
all will be made straight, and where the labours of the sorrowful
will end in joy. Oh, that we could call up in the hearts of the
afflicted such thoughts!

ALL DEATH IN NATURE IS BIRTH.

Beſtimmung des Menſchen. 1800. S. W., II, 315, 317.

Körperliche Leiden, Schmerz und Krankheit, wenn ſie mich treffen ſollten, werde ich nicht vermeiden können zu fühlen, denn ſie ſind Ereigniſſe meiner Natur, und ich bin und bleibe hienieden Natur; aber ſie ſollen mich nicht betrüben. Sie treffen auch nur die Natur, mit der ich auf eine wunderbare Weiſe zuſammenhänge, nicht mich ſelbſt, das über alle Natur erhabene Weſen. Das ſichere Ende alles Schmerzes und aller Empfänglichkeit für den Schmerz iſt der Tod; und unter allem, was der natürliche Menſch für ein Uebel zu halten pflegt, iſt es mir dieſer am wenigſten. Ich werde überhaupt nicht für mich ſterben, ſondern nur für andere—für die Zurückbleibenden, aus deren Verbindung ich geriſſen werde; für mich ſelbſt iſt die Todesſtunde Stunde der Geburt zu einem neuen herrlichern Leben.

Die Sonne gehet auf und gehet unter, und die Sterne verſinken und kommen wieder, und alle Sphären halten ihren Cirkeltanz; aber ſie kommen nie ſo wieder, wie ſie verſchwanden, und in den leuchtenden Quellen des Lebens iſt ſelbſt Leben und Fortbilden. Jede Stunde, von ihnen herbeigeführt, jeder Morgen und jeder Abend ſinkt mit neuem Gedeihen hinab auf die Welt; neues Leben und neue Liebe entträufelt den Sphären, wie die Thautropfen der Wolke, und umfängt die Natur, wie die kühle Nacht die Erde

Aller Tod in der Natur iſt Geburt, und gerade im Sterben erſcheint ſichtbar die Erhöhung des Lebens. Es iſt kein tödtendes Princip in der Natur, denn die Natur iſt durchaus lauter Leben, welches, hinter dem alten verborgen, beginnt und ſich entwickelt. Tod und Geburt iſt bloß das Ringen des Lebens mit ſich ſelbſt, um ſich ſtets verklärter und ihm ſelbſt ähnlicher darzuſtellen

Bodily sufferings, pains, and sickness, if they should be my fate, I would not care to avoid, since they are a part of my nature, and I am and remain here below nature; but they ought not to trouble me. Besides, they affect only nature, with which I am in close union, not myself—the being, that is superior to all nature. The certain end of all pains and of all susceptibility to pain is death;

and of all which the natural man is accustomed to regard as evil, to me this is the least. Then I shall not die for myself, but only for those surviving me, from whose company I shall be torn; for myself, the hour of death is the hour of birth to a new glorious life.

The sun sets and rises, the stars sink beneath the horizon and return again, and all the spheres continue in their circling dance; but they never come back exactly in the same state as they disappeared; and in the bright sources of life is life itself and its continuance. Every hour brought forward by them, every morning and every evening, sinks with new increase to the world; new life and new love thrill from the spheres, as the dewdrops trickle from the clouds, and embrace nature, as the cool night does the earth.

All death in nature is birth, and at the moment of death appears visibly the rising of life. There is no dying principle in nature, for nature throughout is unmixed life, which, concealed behind the old, begins again and develops itself. Death and birth is simply the circling of life in itself, in order to present itself ever more brightly and more like to itself.

HAPPINESS.

Aus Briefen. 1790. L., I, 58, 82, 94 fg.

Hienieden ist nicht das Land der Glückseligkeit; ich weiß es jetzt: es ist nur das Land der Mühe, und jede Freude, die uns wird, ist nur Stärkung auf eine folgende heißere Arbeit.

Wenn Sie sagen: am Hofe, und wenn ich selbst Premierminister würde, wäre kein wahres Glück, so reden Sie aus meiner Seele. Das ist unter dem Monde nirgends, beim Dorfpfarrer ebenso wenig als beim Premierminister. Der eine zählt Linsen, der andere Erbsen; das ist der ganze Unterschied. Glück ist nur jenseit des Grabes. Alles auf der Erde ist unbeschreiblich klein, das weiß ich: aber Glück ist's auch nicht, was ich suche; ich weiß, ich werde es nie finden.

Nicht Glückseligkeit ist der Zweck unsers Daseins, sondern Glückwürdigkeit.

Ich habe nur eine Leidenschaft, nur ein Bedürfniß, nur ein volles Gefühl meiner selbst, das: außer mir zu wirken. Je mehr ich handle, desto glücklicher scheine ich mir. Ist das auch Täuschung? Es kann sein, aber es liegt doch Wahrheit zum Grunde.

Here below is not the land of happiness; I know it now; it is only the land of toil, and every joy which comes to us is only to strengthen us for some greater labour that is to succeed.

When you say : At court, even if I were prime minister, there could be no real happiness, you speak as I would do. There is none under the moon, to the country parson just as little as to the prime minister. The one counts lentils, the other peas—that is the whole difference. Happiness is only on the other side of the grave. All on the earth is indescribably petty, *that* I know ; but happiness is not what I am in search of ; I know I shall not find it.

Happiness is not the end of our being, but being worthy of it.

I have only one passion, only one necessity, only one strong feeling, which is, to work on something external to myself. The more active I am, the more happy I appear to myself. Is this delusion? It may be so, but there is yet truth at the bottom.

See (Lat. Gr. Fr.) Happiness.

What Thou Lovest, that Thou Livest.
Religionslehre. 1806. S. W., V, 493.

Offenbare mir, was du wahrhaftig liebst, was du mit deinem ganzen Sehnen suchst und anstrebst, wenn du den wahren Genuß deiner selbst zu finden hoffst—und du hast mir dadurch dein Leben gedeutet. Was du liebst, das lebst du. Die angegebene Liebe ist dein Leben, und die Wurzel, der Sitz und der Mittelpunkt deines Lebens. Alle übrigen Regungen in dir sind Leben nur, inwiefern sie sich nach diesem einzigen Mittelpunkt hinrichten. Daß vielen Menschen es nicht leicht werden dürfte, auf die vorgelegte Frage zu antworten, indem sie gar nicht wissen, was sie lieben, beweist nur, daß diese eigentlich nichts lieben, und eben darum auch nicht leben, weil sie nicht lieben.

Reveal to me what thou really lovest, what thou seekest and strivest after with thy whole heart, that in which thou expectest to find real enjoyment of thyself, and thou hast revealed to me thereby thy whole life. What thou lovest, thou livest. The love which thou hast indicated is thy life, the root, purpose, and central point of thy life. All other emotions in thee are only life, so far as they are directed towards that special central point. That there may be many men who would not find it easy to answer the question I have asked, inasmuch as they know not what they love, only proves that such persons really love nothing, and thus have no life in them, because they do not love.

Can Not—Will Not.
Brief. 1791.

Der Mensch kann, was er soll; und wenn er sagt, er kann nicht, so will er nicht.

A man can do what he ought to do ; and when he says he *can*
not, he *will* not.

FREE-WILL.

Brief. 1791. L., I, 107.

Vollkommen bin ich von der Freiheit des Menschen überzeugt,
nur unter dieser Voraussetzung ist Pflicht, Tugend und über=
haupt eine Moral möglich. Es ist einleuchtend, daß aus der
Annahme der Nothwendigkeit aller menschlichen Handlungen
(Determinismus Spinoza's) sehr schädliche Folgen für die Gesell=
schaft fließen, daß das Sittenverderben der sogenannten höhern
Stände großentheils aus dieser Quelle entsteht, und daß es ganz
andere Gründe hat, als die Unschädlichkeit oder wohl gar Nütz=
lichkeit dieses Satzes, wenn jemand, der ihn annimmt, sich von
diesem Verderben rein erhält.

I am perfectly convinced of the free-will of men ; it is only under
this supposition that duty, virtue, and, above all, morality are possible. Let us admit the necessity of all human actions (the *determinismus* of Spinoza), and very baneful consequences for society
are the result ; the corruption of the manners of the so-called
higher classes springs in a great measure from this source ; and if
any one who believes in this principle keeps clear, it is caused by
some other reason than its innocuousness or utility.

See (Gr. Fr.) Free-will.

HYPOCRITES.

Brief. 1790. Leben, I, 41.

Frömmler setzen die Religion meist ins Aeußere, in Uebungen
der Andacht, zwecklos, maschinenmäßig und wie im Frondienst, an
Gott vollbracht, und haben unter anderm das charakteristische
Kennzeichen, daß sie sich angelegentlicher um die Gottesfurcht
anderer bekümmern, als um ihre eigene.

Hypocrites place religion chiefly in externals, in the outward
practices of devotion, objectless, like machines, and performed as
the service of thralls to God ; among other things, they have the
characteristic sign of being more alive to the religious life of others
than to their own.

See (Lat. Gr. Fr.) Hypocrites.

REAL AND IMAGINARY WANTS.

Französische Revolution. S. W, VI, 186.

Ein großes Heer unserer Bedürfnisse sind blos und einzig

Bedürfnisse der Einbildungskraft; wir bedürfen ihrer blos darum, weil wir ihrer zu bedürfen glauben, sie verschaffen uns keinen Genuß, wenn wir sie haben; ihr Bedürfniß macht sich blos durch die unangenehme Empfindung kund, wenn wir sie entbehren. Dinge dieser Art haben das ausschließende Kennzeichen, daß wir sie blos um anderer willen haben. Zu ihnen gehört alles, was zur Pracht gehört, die blos Pracht ist; alles, was zur Mode gehört, insofern es weder durch Schönheit noch durch Bequemlichkeit, noch durch irgend etwas vor Dingen der gleichen Art sich auszeichnet, als dadurch, daß es Mode ist.

A great number of our wants are simply special wants of the imagination ; we want them simply because we think that we want them ; they give us no enjoyment when we obtain them ; the want of them is only known by a disagreeable feeling when we are without them. Things of this kind have the exclusive mark, that we have them simply at the will of others. To them belongs all which belongs to pomp—that is, simple pomp ; everything which belongs to fashion, so far as it is distinguished neither by beauty, nor by convenience, nor by anything from things of the same kind, except merely that it is fashion.

PAUL FLEMMING.

Born A.D. 1609. Died A.D. 1640.

Paul Flemming was born in 1609 at Hartenstein, where his father was a Lutheran clergyman. He studied at Leipsic for the medical profession. In 1633 he accompanied an embassy sent by the Duke of Schleswig-Holstein to Moscow, and the following year he proceeded with the embassy sent by the same prince to Persia. On his return he determined to settle as physician at Hamburg, but was cut off at an early age in 1640.

WISDOM.

Weisheit.

Weisheit ist nicht, wie ihr denkt,
Eine Kunst, die zu erlernen ;
Weisheit kommt doch aus den Sternen
Sie ist's, die der Himmel schenkt,
Und nur Erdenkindern sendet,
Die sich vor zu ihm gewendet.

Vater! der du Aller bist,
Und um so viel mehr der Deinen,
Laß dein Himmelslicht mir scheinen,
Scheide Wahrheit von der List:
So wird aller Weisen Wissen
Meiner Einfalt weichen müssen.

Wisdom is not, as you think, an art which can be learned; wisdom comes from above. It is what Heaven sends, and only to children of the earth who turn themselves to it.

Father! thou who art Father of all, and so much more of thine, let thy heavenly light shine on me, separate truth from falsehood: thus must the knowledge of the wise yield to my simplicity.

See (Gr.) Wisdom of world of no value.

Enjoy the Present.

Lebenspflichten.

Wißt ihr, was wir morgen machen?
Heute laßt uns fröhlich seyn!
Trauern, Scherzen, Weinen, Lachen,
Ziehn bei uns bald aus, bald ein;
Wohl dem Manne; der vergnügt
Sich in sein Verhängniß fügt.

Know you what to-morrow may bring forth? To-day let us enjoy ourselves! Sorrows, joys, tears, and smiles go in and out before us. Happy the man who contentedly resigns himself to his fate.

Women.

Der beste Rath.

Wer Weibern trauet, pflügt die Winde
Und säet auf die wüste See,
Mißt des verborgnen Meeres Gründe,
Schreibt sein Gedächtniß in den Schnee.
Schöpft, wie die Schwestern ohne Liebe,
Das Wasser mit dem hohlen Siebe.

He who trusts women ploughs the wind, sows on the barren sea, finds not the bottom of the hidden ocean, writes his recollections in the snow, draws water, like the Danaides, with pitchers full of holes.

See (Lat. Gr. Fr.) Woman.

GEORGE FORSTER.

Born A.D. 1754. Died A.D. 1794.

Johann George Forster, born on the 20th November 1754 at Nassenhaben, near Dantzig, was son of the Lutheran minister of that poor village. He accompanied his father to Russia in 1765, invited by the Russian government to assist in forming a colony, but he was disappointed, and we next hear of him in England, giving private lessons in an educational establishment at Warrington. His father's reputation as a naturalist obtained him an appointment under Captain Cook in his second circumnavigation round the world. His son accompanied him, and was particularly employed in delineating the various objects of natural history which were discovered. On his return he settled in Paris, but in 1779 was appointed Professor of Natural History at Cassel, and in 1784 to a similar situation in the university of Wilna. He was next invited by the Elector of Mentz to accept the appointment of president in the university newly established in that city. He was unhappy in his domestic life, and resolved once more to leave Europe, but while he was preparing for a voyage to Thibet he died, 13th February 1794.

The Power of Fancy.

Collected Works.

Lebhaftigkeit des Geistes und Wärme der Empfindung führen uns bald über die Grenzen des Wirklichen hinaus, und was immer der Lieblingsgegenstand sei, womit sich unser intellectuelles Wesen beschäftigt, so idealisirt ihn unsere Phantasie.

A lively spirit and warm feelings soon carry us beyond the limits of the real; and, whatever may be the favourite subject on which our intellect is engaged, our fancy throws a halo around it.

Different Lives of Men.

Collected Works.

Einer geht seinen Weg ruhig, der Andere balgt sich durch die Welt, und Beide erreichen dasselbe Ziel.

One goes on his course calmly, another leads a struggling and bustling life, but both reach the same end.

Circumstances often make the Man.

Collected Works.

Wir glauben oft, etwas zu sein, was wir nur durch Umstände sind; ändern sich diese, dann fühlen wir unser Nichts.

We often think ourselves to be something, which we are only from circumstances, for should they change we feel ourselves to be nothing.

Mental Qualities.

Collected Works.

Wer kann den Menschen Eigenschaften geben, wozu sie den Keim nicht mit auf die Welt brachten?

Who can give qualities to men, when they have not brought the germ with them into the world?

Few Men of Original Genius.

Collected Works.

Es ist nicht Jedermanns Ding, etwas Neues zu sagen, zu schreiben, zu erfinden. Die liebe Mutter Natur hat dergleichen Genies gar sparsam ausgesäet, und wenn in einem Jahrhundert in einer Wissenschaft mehr als Einer aufsteht, so kann es für ein Wunder gelten. Allein Das, was nun einmal vorhanden ist, sammeln, ordnen, sieden und braten, sodaß es Diesem und Jenem gutschmeckt und leicht zu verdauen ist, dazu finden sich Leute genug, die in ihrer Art auch nicht umsonst geschaffen sind.

Every man cannot say, write, discover something new. Nature, that loving mother, has sown original genius of that sort very sparingly, and if in a century, on any special subject, more than one springs up, it may be regarded as a miracle. But to collect, arrange, boil, and roast what has once been brought forward, so that it may be well flavoured and easily digested by this man and that, plenty of people are found, who of their kind are not born in vain.

Fame.

Collected Works.

Nachruhm ist das eigentliche Erbe der wenigen Edeln. Oft zündet die Ehre, die man dem Andenken eines großen Mannes weihte, den Funken des Genius in einem andern Busen an. Mit einem Eifer, der alle Hindernisse besiegt, kämpft er dann um diesen Preis, der ihn so groß, so rein und göttlich dünkt; und wenn er am Ende seiner Laufbahn einen Blick in das Vergangene wirft, verläßt er diesen geschäftigen Schauplatz zufrieden, froh und mit dem festen Vertrauen, daß sein Beispiel

und der Ruhm feines Namens die wohlthätige Flamme fort=
pflanzen werde, fowie er fie zuerft empfing.   So wird der
Nachruhm gleichfam eine Schuld, welche die Nachwelt tilgen
muß; und ein Zeitalter, welches bei den Verdienften eines großen
Mannes fchweigt, verdient die Strafe, daß es feinen ihm ähn=
lichen Mann aus feiner Mitte hervorbringen fann.

Fame is the peculiar inheritance of the few noble.   The honour
which is devoted to the memory of a great man often lights up the
sparks of genius in another bosom.   With a zeal which overcomes
every obstacle he strives for a prize, which appears in his eyes so
great, so pure, and god-like; and if at the end of his course he throws
a glance over the past, he leaves this busy scene in full contentment, joyous and with the firm trust that his example and the
fame of his name will implant the living flame in some other breast
in the same way as he had received it.   This fame is as it were a
debt, which posterity must pay; and an age which passes over ir
silence the merits of the noble, deserves as a punishment that it
should not bring forth such an one in its midst.

INCOMPATIBLE THINGS.
Collected Works.

Was der Menfch fucht, das findet er; was er will, das fann
er; was er fich erbittet, das erlangt er;—nur muß er nicht
incompatible Dinge verlangen, nicht zugleich nach Norden und
nach Süden fegeln wollen.

What a man seeks, that he finds; what he wills, that he can;
what he prays for himself, that he attains;—only he must not
desire incompatible things, not wish to sail north and south at the
same moment.

EXAMPLE BETTER THAN PRECEPT.
Collected Works.

Es fördert das Gute nicht immer, wenn man es predigt.
Perlen find leicht weggeworfen, wenn die gute Lehre tauben
Ohren gepredigt wird.   Ich fange an, fehr deutlich überzeugt
zu werden, daß alles Sagen und Lehren zur Befferung der Welt
nichts beiträgt.   Es ift nur ein Heilmittel vorhanden, das ift:
Gutes thun, foviel an uns ift.   Beifpiel predigt beffer als
Lehre, und das, weil es foviel fchwerer ift.

Good is not always advanced by preaching.   Pearls are easily
thrown aside when good doctrine is preached to deaf ears.   I begin

We often think ourselves to be something, which we are only from circumstances, for should they change we feel ourselves to be nothing.

Mental Qualities.

Collected Works.

Wer kann den Menschen Eigenschaften geben, wozu sie den Keim nicht mit auf die Welt brachten?

Who can give qualities to men, when they have not brought the germ with them into the world?

Few Men of Original Genius.

Collected Works.

Es ist nicht Jedermanns Ding, etwas Neues zu sagen, zu schreiben, zu erfinden. Die liebe Mutter Natur hat dergleichen Genies gar sparsam ausgesäet, und wenn in einem Jahrhundert in einer Wissenschaft mehr als Einer aufsteht, so kann es für ein Wunder gelten. Allein Das, was nun einmal vorhanden ist, sammeln, ordnen, sieden und braten, sodaß es Diesem und Jenem gutschmeckt und leicht zu verdauen ist, dazu finden sich Leute genug, die in ihrer Art auch nicht umsonst geschaffen sind.

Every man cannot say, write, discover something new. Nature, that loving mother, has sown original genius of that sort very sparingly, and if in a century, on any special subject, more than one springs up, it may be regarded as a miracle. But to collect, arrange, boil, and roast what has once been brought forward, so that it may be well flavoured and easily digested by this man and that, plenty of people are found, who of their kind are not born in vain.

Fame.

Collected Works.

Nachruhm ist das eigentliche Erbe der wenigen Edeln. Oft zündet die Ehre, die man dem Andenken eines großen Mannes weihte, den Funken des Genius in einem andern Busen an. Mit einem Eifer, der alle Hindernisse besiegt, kämpft er dann um diesen Preis, der ihn so groß, so rein und göttlich dünkt; und wenn er am Ende seiner Laufbahn einen Blick in das Vergangene wirft, verläßt er diesen geschäftigen Schauplatz zufrieden, froh und mit dem festen Vertrauen, daß sein Beispiel und der Ruhm seines Namens die wohlthätige Flamme fort= pflanzen werde, sowie er sie zuerst empfing.   So wird der Nachruhm gleichsam eine Schuld, welche die Nachwelt tilgen muß; und ein Zeitalter, welches bei den Verdiensten eines großen Mannes schweigt, verdient die Strafe, daß es keinen ihm ähn= lichen Mann aus seiner Mitte hervorbringen kann.

Fame is the peculiar inheritance of the few noble.   The honour which is devoted to the memory of a great man often lights up the sparks of genius in another bosom.   With a zeal which overcomes every obstacle he strives for a prize, which appears in his eyes so great, so pure, and god-like; and if at the end of his course he throws a glance over the past, he leaves this busy scene in full content- ment, joyous and with the firm trust that his example and the fame of his name will implant the living flame in some other breast in the same way as he had received it.   This fame is as it were a debt, which posterity must pay; and an age which passes over in silence the merits of the noble. deserves as a punishment that it should not bring forth such an one in its midst.

INCOMPATIBLE THINGS.
Collected Works.

Was der Mensch sucht, das findet er; was er will, das kann er; was er sich erbittet, das erlangt er;—nur muß er nicht incompatible Dinge verlangen, nicht zugleich nach Norden und nach Süden segeln wollen.

What a man seeks, that he finds; what he wills, that he can; what he prays for himself, that he attains;—only he must not desire incompatible things, not wish to sail north and south at the same moment.

EXAMPLE BETTER THAN PRECEPT.
Collected Works.

Es fördert das Gute nicht immer, wenn man es predigt. Perlen sind leicht weggeworfen, wenn die gute Lehre tauben Ohren gepredigt wird.   Ich fange an, sehr deutlich überzeugt zu werden, daß alles Sagen und Lehren zur Besserung der Welt nichts beiträgt.   Es ist nur ein Heilmittel vorhanden, das ist: Gutes thun, soviel an uns ist.   Beispiel predigt besser als Lehre, und das, weil es soviel schwerer ist.

Good is not always advanced by preaching.   Pearls are easily thrown aside when good doctrine is preached to deaf ears.   I begin to be strongly convinced that it is not everything that is said and taught that conduces to the improvement of the world. There is only one remedy existing—that is, to do good as far as in us lies. Example preaches better than precept, and that too because it is so much more difficult.

OUR CONDUCT THROUGH LIFE.
Collected Works.

Es darf nicht die Frage sein: können wir Gutes stiften? können wir Mißbräuche abstellen? können wir Früchte unserer Bemühungen zur Wohlfahrt des Staats oder der Gesellschaft, in der wir zu wirken bestimmt sind, erleben? Nein, dies Alles hängt nicht von uns, hängt nicht von Menschen ab, es liegt im Rath der Götter beschlossen, im heiligen undurchdringlichen Dunkel des Schicksals verhüllt. Aber es kann und muß die Frage täglich aufgeworfen werden, ob wir heute thaten, was nach unserm Gefühl und Verstande das Beste schien, das Beste des Staats unter den Umständen, worin er, worin wir uns befanden, der Beste des einzelnen Menschen, mit dem wir besonders zu thun hatten; denn das Beste unsers eigenen Selbst, welches uns am nächsten angeht, ist Resultat dieser beiden und folgt unmittelbar daraus. Nicht was wir erzielt haben, sondern was wir mit Anwendung aller uns verliehenen Kräfte haben erzielen wollen, soll uns Beruhigung geben. Das Bewußtsein: „ich that, was ich vermochte," soll es nun einmal sein, was uns Trost und Zufriedenheit in allen Dingen gibt.

The question should not be, Can we lay the foundation of something good? Can we remedy abuses? Shall we see the fruit of our exertions in the well-being of the state or the society in which we are destined to work? No; all this depends not on ourselves, nor on man; it lies in the determinate counsel of God, concealed in the sacred and impenetrable darkness of fate. But the question can and must ever daily be, Whether we are doing to-day what, according to our feeling and understanding, appears the best—the best for the state under the circumstances in which it and we find ourselves, the best for individual men with whom we have particularly to do; since the best for ourselves, which concerns us nearest, is the result of both these, and follows immediately from it. Not what we have attained, but what we have wished to attain, with the earnest employment of all our powers, should give us comfort. The consciousness "I did what I could," should be what gives us comfort and contentment in all things.

B

A Man's Particular Vocation.

Collected Works.

Jeder muß selbst fühlen, was sein Beruf ist und wozu er Kräfte hat.

Every one must himself feel what is his particular vocation and what is his strength.

The Events of Life.

Collected Works.

Alles, was geschieht, hat seine Bestimmung vom Vorhergehenden und Beziehung aufs Zukünftige.

Everything which happens has its bent given by the events that have gone before, and is brought into relation with those that come after.

A Rational Soul and Moral Perfectibility.

Collected Works.

Alle haben eine vernünftige Seele, eine moralische Perfectibilität; diese Eigenschaften machen mir den ärmsten Bauer heilig und werth. Die moralische Vervollkommnung ist unsere Bestimmung und hier öffnet sich dem Schriftsteller ein unabsehbares Feld und eine große Ernte.

All men have a rational soul and moral perfectibility; it is these qualities which make the poorest peasant sacred and valued by me. Moral perfectibility is our destiny, and here are opened up to the historian a boundless field and a rich harvest.

Truth is the Message of all Great Men.

Collected Works.

Wahrheit war die Botschaft, die alle großen Männer an die Menschheit zu verkündigen hatten; Wahrheit, Verhältniß der Dinge untereinander und zu uns. Sie entledigten sich genau ihres Auftrags und brachten uns Wahrheit, das Kleinod des Weisen, das Schwert in eines Narren Hand. Doch Nutzen und Mißbrauch haben ihre Grenzen: die Aufklärung aber schreitet von Erfahrung zu Erfahrung in's Unbegrenzte fort. „Vielleicht erschöpft sie einst alle Verhältnisse des Menschen und bringt dann den Frieden des goldenen Zeitalters zurück?"

Diese harmlose Hoffnung, ein Stein der Weisen unsers Jahr=
hunderts, verdient wenigstens keinen Spott, so lange sie das
aufgesteckte Ziel bleibt, welches so viele Kräfte für das Be=
dürfniß des gegenwärtigen Augenblicks in Bewegung erhält
und einen Jeden anfeuert, in seiner Laufbahn nach der Voll=
kommenheit zu streben, die ihm erreichbar ist.   Wenn die
Verwegenheit in eine Zukunft zu schauen, die unsern Augen
geflissentlich entzogen ward, und Bestimmungen vorauszusagen,
welche sich aus den Prämissen der Erfahrung nicht folgern
lassen, mit Irrthum bestraft werden muß, so könnte wenigstens
keine Strafe unschädlicher und keine zugleich wohlthätiger sein
als diejenige, welche die Bilder der Phantasie benutzt, um den
Menschen an ein reelles Ziel zu geleiten. Ein solches Ziel ist
die subjective Vervollkommnung, welche nur durch eine voll=
kommnere Erkenntniß der Wahrheit erworben werden kann.

Truth was the message which all great men had to communicate to the human race; truth, the relation of things to one
another and to us. They discharged properly their commission,
and gave us truth, the jewel of the wise, the sword in the fool's
hand. What is useful and what is unprofitable have their limits,
but enlightenment of mind goes on from one experience to another
away to the infinite. "Does it not perhaps exhaust all the relations of man, and then bring back the peace of the golden age?"
Such a harmless hope as this, the philosopher's stone of our age,
deserves at least no ridicule, so long as it remains the end which
keeps in motion so many powers for the necessities of the present moment, and animates every one to strive in his course after
that perfection which is to be attained by him. If the audacity
to look into futurity, which is intentionally withdrawn from our
eyes, and to predict results which cannot be deduced from the
premises of experience, must be punished by falling into mistakes,
then no punishment could be more harmless, and none indeed
more salutary, than that which made use of the images of fancy
to direct men to a real end. Such an end is perfectibility, which
can only be attained by a more perfect knowledge of truth.

TRUE NOBILITY.

Collected Works.

Das ist ja wahrer Adel, wahre Erhabenheit unsers Geistes,
daß er über alles Leiden und über alle Bitterkeit durch in ihm
wohnende, ihm angeeignete Kraft zu siegen vermag.

That is true nobility, true elevation of soul, when man can rise

superior to any suffering and every pain by the indwelling powers
given to him.

THE MAN OF HIGH PRINCIPLE.
Collected Works.

Wer hundert mal moralisch handelt, ehe er einmal davon
spricht, das ist ein Mensch, den man segnen und herzen möchte.
Ich bin weit entfernt, ihn darum für fehlerfrei zu erklären;
das plus et minus und der Grad des Bestrebens nach Voll=
kommenheit und Tugend bestimmt aber den Werth des Men=
schen.

Whoso acts a hundred times with high moral principle before
he speaks once of it, that is a man whom one could bless and
clasp to one's heart. I am far from saying that he is on that
account free from faults, but the *plus et minus*, the degree of
striving after perfection and virtue, determines the value of the
man.

THE WISE.
Collected Works.

Der Weise sucht Weisheit — nicht leeres Wort — sondern
lebendige Gotteskraft, nahrhafte Lebensspeise, und wenn er sie
findet, wo die Welt sie nicht des Aufhebens würdigt, so ist des
Frohlockens in seiner Seele kein Ende.

The wise seek wisdom—no empty word but God's living power
—nutritious food; and if he finds it, where the world does not
deem it worthy of uplifting, there is no end of joy in his soul.

INDIVIDUAL ACTIONS.
Collected Works.

Je länger ich lebe und Erfahrungen mache, je mehr über=
zeuge ich mich, daß einzelne Handlungen weder für noch wider
die Menschen beweisen, — das Ganze muß hier entscheiden, weil
am Ende doch kein anderer Maßstab für den Charakter ist als
das Verhältniß des Willens zum Gewissen, oder Gefühl von
Recht und Unrecht, Gut und Böse. In einzelnen Fällen kann
das Gefühl sehr verschieden scheinen von Dem, was es gewöhn=
lich ist. — Es ist eine üble Angewohnheit, daß man sagt, Den
kann ich nicht leiden, Den hasse, Den verabscheue ich, Den bete
ich an; gerade als ob sie ganz böse oder gut wären; der

Liebenswürdigste ist Der, der sich selbst am vollkommensten beherrscht; denn das ist Gerechtigkeit gegen alle Mitmenschen

The longer I live and learn experience, the more I am convinced that individual actions prove nothing either for or against men; the whole life must be taken into account, for there is no other measure of character than the relation of the will to the conscience, or the feeling of right and wrong, good and evil. In individual cases the feeling may appear very different from that which it is in general. It is a bad habit to get into to say, "I cannot bear him, I hate him, I abhor him, I adore him," just as if they were completely bad or good; that man is most worthy of love who has the greatest control over himself, for that means justice to all our fellow-men.

PROSELYTISING SPIRIT.
Collected Works.

Von der Wahrheitsliebe ist der Bekehrungsgeist unzertrennlich, insofern er das Bestreben ist, Andere zu seiner Meinung zu gewinnen. Vom Wilden bis zum Großinquisitor, vom frommen Schwärmer bis zum Philosophen sind wir Alle Proselytenmacher; und was so tief in der menschlichen Natur gegründet ist, kann nicht an sich, kann nur durch den Gebrauch unrechtmäßiger Mittel sträflich sein.

The proselytising spirit is inseparable from the love of truth, inasmuch as it is a striving to win over others to our way of thinking. From savages to the Grand Inquisitor, from the pious enthusiast to the philosopher, we are all proselytisers; and that feeling, which is so deeply rooted in human nature, cannot be blamable in itself, but only through the use of improper means.

THE CONVERSION OF MEN.
Collected Works.

Es gibt nur zwei Wege, wie man auf die Ueberzeugung eines Menschen wirken kann: durch den Kopf und durch das Herz. Je heller und erleuchteter aber der Verstand, je reiner, edler und einfacher das Gefühl, desto fester steht die Ueberzeugung, desto schwerer wird es, eine andere an ihre Stelle zu setzen, desto wichtiger, erhabener, vollkommener müssen die Gründe sein, wodurch man eine Bekehrung bewerkstelligen will.

There are only two ways in which we can work for the conversion of men—through the head and through the heart. But the clearer and more enlightened the understanding, the purer, nobler, and simpler the feelings, so much stronger is the conviction, so much the more difficult is it to put another in our place, so much the more weighty, elevated, and perfect must the reasons be by which a conversion is brought about.

The Goal.
Collected Works.

Iſt es nicht eine ſehr richtige Bemerfung, daß man überall den Menſchen das Ziel weiter ſtecken müſſe, als ſie kommen können, damit ſie wenigſtens ſo weit kommen, als es ihnen möglich iſt.

Is it not a very proper remark that we should above all place the goal beyond the reach of men, in order that they may at least proceed as far as it is possible for their strength to carry them?

A Friend.
Collected Works.

Ein Freund iſt ein Weſen, das uns ganz trägt mit unſern Fehlern und Mängeln allen.

A friend is a being that is willing to bear with us in all our faults and failings.

Real Friends.
Collected Works.

Die wenigen Menſchen, die gleichförmig mit uns denken, ſind uns noch mehr noth als das ganze übrige Menſchengeſchlecht; ſie ſtärken und befeſtigen uns in unſern eigenen Grundſätzen.

The few men who think in common with us are much more necessary to us than the whole of the rest of mankind; they give strength and tone to our principles.

Self-Examination and Self denial.
Collected Works.

Selbſtprüfung und Selbſtverleugnung lehren, mit der menſch= lichen Natur nachſichtsvoll zu ſein, nicht zu viel von ihr zu fordern, feine Irregularitäten zu verzeihen, wenn nur Tugend im Ganzen, und mit ihr wahre Glückſeligkeit das Ziel bleibt; wir wiſſen, daß das höchſte, reinſte Glück, deſſen Menſchen auf Erden fähig ſein können, in Mittheilungen beſteht, in Liebe, die ſich ſelbſt in Andern empfindet und Anderer Wohl und Freude zum Ihrigen macht.

Self-examination and self-denial teach us to be indulgent to human nature, not to require too much from her, to forgive no irregularities, unless virtue on the whole, and with her true happiness, is the goal aimed at; we know that the brightest, purest happiness, of which men can be capable on earth, consists in social intercourse, in love which is felt for others, and makes the well-being and joy of others as its own.

A MAN WITHOUT PRETENSIONS.

Collected Works.

Die große, wirklich große Anzahl von Menschen, die mir Freundschaft und Liebe schenken, beweisen etwas für meinen Charakter und etwas für die Empfänglichkeit und angeborene Güte des Menschen überhaupt. Ich muß schließen, daß ich gefalle, weil ich ohne Prätension bin und Jedermann Wohl, Keinem Uebel wünsche; und da diese Denkungsart so sicher ist, den Beifall der Menschen zu gewinnen, so muß ich folgern, daß die Menschen im Grunde gute Geschöpfe und mit Wenigem zu befriedigen sind, daß Güte des Herzens immer den bleibendsten Eindruck auf sie macht und uneigennützig scheinende Liebe sie am tiefsten rührt. Folgere ich weiter, so sehe ich, daß mir die Vorsehung mit diesem Herzen und mit dieser Demuth wahrlich kein kleines Geschenk gemacht hat; sie trägt soviel zu meiner Glückseligkeit bei und lehrt mich, daß der größte Vortheil des Menschen ist, theilnehmend und liebevoll gegen die Welt zu sein.

The great, wonderfully great, number of men who offer me their friendship and love, proves something favourable for my character, and something also for the susceptible nature and innate goodness of men. It must be inferred that I please, because I am without pretensions, and everybody wishes me well, while I wish ill to no one—a disposition which is sure to win the goodwill of men. We must draw the inference from all this, that men are at bottom good creatures, and are easily pleased, that goodness of heart ever makes the most lasting impression on them, and unselfish love strikes deepest into their hearts. Moreover I infer, I see, that Providence has really made me no small gift by giving me this heart, this humility, as it contributes so much to my happiness, and teaches me that it is the greatest advantage to man that he should be indulgent and full of love to the world.

The Cause of Despotism.

Collected Works.

So lange es wahr bleiben wird, daß die größte Anzahl Menschen mehr sinnlich oder thöricht, als vernünftig leben und handeln, so lange wird Despotismus bleiben.

As long as it remains true that the greater part of mankind spend their lives rather in the pursuit of sensual pleasures and follies than like rational beings, so long will despotism be necessary.

How Men may become Free.

Collected Works.

Die Freiheit setzt etwas voraus, was sich noch nirgends fand, ein ganzes Volk oder wenigstens eine große Majorität von tugendhaften Menschen. Doch vermochte Trieb und sinnlicher Reiz immer unendlich mehr über die Menschen, im Ganzen genommen, als Raisonnement und einleuchtendste Wahrheit; noch immer führte die Welt Sittensprüche im Munde und handelte nach leidenschaftlichen Eindrücken; wenn es am besten ging, täuschten sich die guten Leute selbst und waren bei ihrer Menschenliebe so selbstsüchtig, bei ihrem Patriotismus so tyran= nisch, bei ihren Adlersblicken so blind, wenn es auf ihre Schwach= heiten und Lieblingsneigungen ankam, daß ich die Weisheit der Mönchsregel bewundere: „Sine res vadere sicut vadunt;“ d. h.: „Laß geschehen, was du nicht ändern kannst.“ Zur Vervollkommnung des Ganzen, wenn es je eine gibt, scheint mir in der That kein anderes Mittel übrig als das, mit Eifer unabläffig an fich felbft zu arbeiten. Dies sei das Geschäft aller Menschenfreunde, welches sie selbst treiben, und der ganzen, ganzen Welt, so laut sie nur immer reden können, empfehlen müffen. Ist die Welt erst tugendhaft, dann wird sie von selbst frei.

Freedom presupposes something, which is, however, never found: a whole people, or at least the greater part of them, to be virtuous. The passions and sensual feelings have ever much more power over men, taking them as a whole, than reason and the clearest truth. The world had indeed always in its mouth moral saws, yet acted on impressions dictated by passions; at the best, the good people deceived themselves, and were so selfish in their love of mankind, so tyrannical in their patriotism, so blind, eagle-eyed though they were, when it touched their weaknesses and favourite inclinations, that I admire the wisdom of the monk's saying: "Sine res vadere sicut vadunt"—"Let things go as they may." To bring everything to a state of perfection, if there is such a thing, it appears to me indeed that there are no other means than with diligence to work unceasingly on oneself. Let this be the business of all the friends of mankind, which they urge forward and which they press on the whole world so long as they have breath. If the world is once virtuous, then will it be free of itself.

Every One under some Control.
Collected Works.

Alles an uns Menschen ist erzwungen, ist nothwendige Folge der Einrichtung, die nicht von uns abhing, der Freie ist also nicht Derjenige, der von allem Zwang befreit ist, denn das ist kein Geschöpf, sondern der dem wenigsten Zwang, dem natürlichsten (wenn ich so sagen darf) allein gehorcht.

Everything in us men is forced, is the necessary result of a control which depends not on ourselves; the free, therefore, is not he who is free from all force, for there is no such creature, but he who is only under the least force, the most natural, if I may say so.

My Thoughts are my own Possession.
Collected Works.

Meine Meinungen sind mein Eigenthum; meine Handlungen können durch das Landesgesetz beschränkt werden.

My thoughts are my own possession; my acts may be limited by my country's laws.

Political Liberty.
Collected Works.

Es wäre Thorheit, den Menschen Freiheit zu geben oder nur zu wünschen, wenn sie Wilde dabei bleiben und ihre Anlagen zu moralischer Vollkommenheit nicht dadurch leichter ausgebildet werden sollten. Dies allein ist der Zweck, weswegen die politische Freiheit so wünschenswerth ist: denn ich glaube, es ist unwiderlegbar, daß nur in freien Staaten die Tugend allgemein werden kann. Allein was unser Individuum anbetrifft, uns haben die Verhältnisse, unter welchen wir in der Welt erschienen und fortlebten, zu einer Gattung von privilegirten Wesen gemacht, die nach jenem Zweck strebten, ohne die Hülfe einer freien Verfassung oder vielmehr durch die Hülfe einer nicht freien. Wir sind auch in Ketten und Kerkern frei, folglich haben wir weniger als uns unähnliche Menschen die Abwesenheit der politischen Freiheit zu beklagen.

It would be folly to give or even to wish for freedom to men if they still continue savages, and if their inclination to moral perfection is not thereby more easily cultivated. This alone is the end for which political liberty is worthy of being achieved, for I believe it to be undeniable, that only in free countries can virtue be generally diffused. But as to what belongs to us as individuals, the relations under which we appear, and continue to live in the world, have made us a kind of privileged beings, who are striving towards that end, without the assistance of a free constitution, or rather by the help of one not free. Even in chains and prisons we are free; therefore we have less reason to lament the absence of political liberty than men unlike to us.

No Perfect Happiness in the World.
Collected Works.

Es ist nicht das Loos des Menschen, in dieser Welt vollkommen glücklich zu sein: das Einzige, was uns übrig bleibt, ist, aus Dem, was wir erhalten und erreichen können, den besten Vortheil zu ziehen und so nützlich und glücklich zu sein, als unsere Lage zuläßt.

It is not the lot of men to be perfectly happy in this world; the only thing which remains to us is to make the best of what we receive and obtain, being as comfortable and happy as our circumstances allow.

True Happiness.
Collected Works.

Wahres Glück ist nach meiner Meinung jetzt: Alles zu genießen, was erlaubt ist — d. i. was mir selbst und Andern nicht schadet, sondern vielmehr zuträglich ist. Tugend werde ich immer nennen, mein Wohl ohne Nachtheil des Nächsten zu suchen, und das größte Wohl: Anderer Glück und Anderer Zufriedenheit genießen und befördern zu können.

True happiness is, in my opinion, to enjoy whatever is in our power—*i.e.*, what does not injure ourselves or others, but rather is beneficial. Virtue I shall ever call it to seek my weal without hurt to my neighbours ; and the greatest weal to be able to enjoy and further the happiness and contentment of others.

Much depends on our Organisation.
Collected Works.

Wir haben am Krankenbett ober sonst mit der Zeit erfahren' wie Vieles, wie Alles möcht' ich sagen, von unserer Organisa= tion abhängt, und wie unser Wohl und Wehe, unsere innigsten Gefühle des Schmerzes oder der Freude in der regen Kraft, wenigstens unsers Gehirns und unserer Nerven zu Hause sind.

We have to learn in sickness, or else in time, how much, I might say how everything, depends on our organisation, and how our weal and woe, our inmost feelings of joy or grief, arise from the activity of our brain and nerves.

Much must be left in the Hands of Fate.
Collected Works.

O es ist so Vieles, was wir der Hand des Schicksals geradezu überlassen müssen! Die Kunst besteht auch gar nicht darin, mit guten Karten ein Spiel zu gewinnen, sondern mit den Karten, so wie sie uns fallen, das Beste zu machen, was sich thun läßt.

Oh, many are the things that we must altogether leave in the hands of fate ! Our skill is not shown in winning the game with good cards, but to make the best of whatever cards are placed in our hands.

Misfortune is the Touchstone of Human Excellence.
Collected Works.

Wahr ist es, daß Unglück — wahres Unglück (nicht eingebil= detes, welches wir uns selbst schaffen) der größte Prüfstein der menschlichen Vortrefflichkeit ist, und daß eine eigene Gleich= müthigkeit und eine besondere Geistesstärke dazu gehört, um unbefangen auf die Welt zu wirken, wenn das Schicksal alle Quellen des Genusses abschneidet und selbst im Wirken uns die Hände bindet.

It is true that misfortune—real misfortune (not imaginary, which we create for ourselves), is the surest touchstone of human excellence, and that equanimity and strength of mind belong specially to it, to work without constraint on the world, when fate cuts off all our springs of enjoyment, and even binds our hands in working.

HAPPY CHILDREN MAKE HAPPY MEN.

Collected Works.

Glückliche Kinder geben glückliche Menschen! Alle Verstimmung des Charakters hat seinen wahrscheinlichen Grund in diesen frühen Eindrücken. Das Glück der Kinder ist das, wenn sie so wenig als möglich in ihrer Freude gestört werden. Wie leicht entwickeln sich da in ihnen alle guten Neigungen, und öffnen sie sich jedem menschlichen, sanften Gefühl. Harte und falsche Behandlung wirkt gerade das Gegentheil: sie verschließt. Die Begriffe, glaube ich, welche man blos erlernt, sind es nicht, die am wesentlichsten wirken auf den Charakter, sondern die man sich aneignet, weil die unmittelbare Beziehung auf unser Behagen sie uns wichtig machte. Richtige Begriffe können folglich auch die Einbildungskraft beschäftigen, deren Schöpfungen dadurch nur harmonischer werden. Aber nicht jede Phantasie ist rege und schöpferisch in gleichem Grade. Das allein weist dem Erzieher schon das verschiedene Betragen gegen beide an.

Happy children make happy men! All dissonance of character has its real foundation in these early impressions. The happiness of children depends much on their being as little as possible interfered with in their little joys. How quickly do their good inclinations unfold themselves! How open are they to every humane and gentle feeling! Harsh and erroneous treatment acts in the very opposite way; it shuts them up. It is not the ideas, I believe, that one learns, which really work on the character, but those which one makes his own, because the immediate bearing on our disposition is what makes them really important. Right ideas, therefore, may engage the imagination, whose creations become thereby only more harmonious. But every fancy does not act and create in the same degree. It is that alone which points out to the teachers the different treatment that is necessary.

GELLERT.

Born A.D. 1717. Died A.D. 1769.

Christian Fürchtegott Gellert was born, 1717, at Hainichen, near Freiberg, in Saxony, and died at Leipsic, 1769, as Professor of Philosophy.

POWERS DIFFERENT IN MEN.

Der Blinde und der Lahme.

Du haft das nicht, was Andre haben,
Und Andern mangeln deine Gaben;
Aus dieser Unvollkommenheit
Entspringet die Geselligkeit.

Wenn jenem nicht die Gabe fehlte,
Die die Natur für mich erwählte:
So wird er nur für sich allein
Und nicht für mich bekümmert sein.

Beschwer' die Götter nicht mit Klagen!
Der Vortheil, den sie dir versagen
Und jenem schenken, wird gemein;
Wir dürfen nur gesellig sein.

Thou hast not what others have, and others want what thou
hast got; out of this imperfect state of things springs the social
good of the world.

If the gifts which nature has bestowed on me did not fail my
neighbour, he would think of himself alone, and never waste a
thought on me. Plague not the gods with wailing! the advantages
which they deny to thee and give another are the common property
of both; we need but to be socially united.

CRITICS.

Der Maler.

Wenn deine Schrift dem Kenner nicht gefällt,
So ist es schon ein böses Zeichen:
Doch wenn sie gar des Narren Lob erhält,
So ist es Zeit, sie auszustreichen.

If thy writings please not the critics, it is no doubt an evil sign;
but when they are lauded to the skies by fools, it is time to blot
them out.

SALOMON GESSNER.

Born A.D. 1730.   Died A.D. 1788.

Salomon Gessner, a Swiss painter and poet, was born at Zurich
in 1730, where he spent the greater part of his life. His house
became the rendezvous of the leading artists and literary men of his

native town. His principal work is the " Death of Abel," which is based upon the narrative in the book of Genesis, reflecting the spirit of the Bible with wonderful closeness.

THE SUN.

The Death of Abel—Canto I.

Sey uns gegrüßt, du liebliche Sonne hinter den Cedern herauf! du gießest Farb' und Anmuth durch die Natur hin, und jede Schönheit lachet verjüngt uns wieder entgegen. Entweiche du Schlaf von jedem Aug', entfliehet, ihr flattern= den Träume, zu den Schatten der Nacht.

Hail, thou lovely sun, that risest behind the cedars! thou sheddest colour and grace over nature, and all that is beautiful laughs with renewed youth. Away, sleep, from every eye ; fly hence, ye flitting dreams, to the shades of night.

MAN NOT BORN TO MISERY.

The Death of Abel—Canto I.

Du bist nicht zum Elend geboren; der Herr ruft kein Geschöpfe aus dem Nichts zum Elend hervor. Zwar kann der Mensch elend seyn, bey seinem Glücke vorüber gehn, und elend seyn. Wenn die Vernunft unter dem ·Tumulte tobender Leiden= schaften und unreiner, unbeschränkter Begierden erliegt, dann wird der Mensch elend, und jedes anscheinende Glück ist trügen= des Elend. Dem Sturme kannst du nicht befehlen, daß er nicht tobe, und dem hinreißenden Strom nicht, daß er still stehe; aber deine Vernunft kannst du aus dem Dunkel hervor rufen, daß sie deine Seele erhelle; sie kann mächtig dem Tumulte befehlen, daß er schweige: sie kann jeden Wunsch, jede Begierde, jede aufschäumende Leidenschaft prüfen; dann schweigen die beschämten Leidenschaften, und die eiteln Wünsche und Begierden verschwinden wie Morgennebel vor der Sonne verschwinden.

Thou art not born to misery ; the Almighty never called any of his creatures into existence to render them unhappy ; yet man may be wretched from his own follies and vices : his reason may yield to the wild impulses of tumultuous passion ; then man is wretched, and every seeming good is perverted to misery. Thou canst not still the raging storm, nor stop the violent torrent, but thou mayest call on reason to dispel the darkness which clouds thy soul, and to hush thy tumultuous passions. She can put to the proof every wish, every desire and emotion, that rises in the mind. Shameless emotions, vain desires, then vanish like vapour before the rising sun.

Virtue.
The Death of Abel—Canto II.

Durch Tugend steigen wir empor zu der Seligkeit reiner Geister, zu paradiesischem Glücke; da hingegen jede unbesiegte, unreine Leidenschaft uns hinunterreißt, und in Labyrinthe schleppet, wo Unruh, Angst, Elend und Nachreu' auf uns lauren.

It is along the paths of virtue that we soar upwards to the blessed state of those pure spirits who dwell in paradise ; here, on the other hand, impure and unruly passions drag us down, and place us in a labyrinth where disquiet, anguish, misery, and remorse lie in wait to seize us.

Heavenly Spirits.
The Death of Abel—Canto II.

Worte sind zu schwach, die Schönheit des herrlichen Gesichtes zu sagen; wir sahen himmlische Jünglinge, unzählbar durch die Gegend zerstreut, schöner als Eva war, da sie neu geschaffen aus des Ewigen Händen hervorging, und mit lieblicher Stimme zu ihrer Umarmung mich weckte. Einige hießen die sanften Nebel aus der Erde hervorgehn und trugen sie auf schwebenden Flügeln empor, daß sanfter Thau zur Erde falle und erquickender Regen; dort ruheten andre bey sprudelnden Bächen, sorgetragend, daß ihre Quelle nicht versiege, damit den Gewächsen ihre feuchte Nahrung nicht entgehe. Viele waren auf den Triften zerstreut, und warteten des Wachsthumes der Früchte, oder bemalten aufkeimende Blumen mit der Farbe des Feuers oder des Abendroths, oder mit der Farbe des Himmels, und hauchten sie an, daß sie liebliche Gerüche zerstreuten; viele schwebten verschieden beschäftigt im Schatten der Haine. Von ihren glänzenden Flügeln zerstreuten sich sanfte Winde, die durch die Schatten säuselten, oder über Blumen sanft dahin fuhren, und dann auf schlängelnden Bächen oder kräuselnden Teichen sich kühlten. Einige ruheten von ihrer Arbeit und saßen in Chöre vertheilet im Schatten, und

fangen in die goldne Harfe zum Lobe des Höchsten, dem Ohre
der Sterblichen unhörbare Lieder. Viele wandelten auf unserm
Hügel, oder faßen im wirthschaftlichen Schatten unfrer Lauben,
und fahn mit himmlischer Freundlichkeit oft zu uns hin; aber
unfre Augen verdunkelten sich wieder und die entzückende Scene
verschwand.

Dieß find die Schutzgeister der Erde, so sprach der Engel.

Words are too weak to describe the beauty of the heavenly
spirits ; we saw hovering around us innumerable celestial youths
more beautiful than Eve when she first issued from the hand of her
Creator, and with her soft voice awoke me (Adam) to her embraces.
Some bade the light mists arise from the bosom of the earth, and
bearing them upwards on their shadowy wings, dispersed them in
balmy dews and gentle showers. Others reclined by the murmuring brooks, watching lest their pure springs should fail and the
flowers be deprived of their moisture. Many were scattered on the
meads, and tended the growth of fruits, or painted the opening
flowers with the ruddy glow of evening, or the rainbow's tints,
and breathing on them gave sweet perfume. Many were moving
around in the shade of the groves. They wafted gentle breezes
from their glittering wings, which, whispering through the groves,
or fanning the new-blown flowers, played upon the dimpled surface
of the brook or placid lake. Some rested from their labours, reclining in the cool shade, and sung on golden harps to the praise of
the Most High hymns unheard by mortal ears. Many hovered
round our hill, or sat in the hospitable shade of our bowers, looking
on with tenderest sympathy, but the shades of evening soon returned to our eyes, and the lovely scene vanished.

These are the guardian spirits of the earth, exclaimed the angel.

THE RETURN OF SPRING.

The Death of Abel—Canto II.

Da fing die Natur wieder an jugendlich zu lächeln, ein
fanftes Grün kleidete die Erde; ein buntes Gemische von Blumen schoß auf den Fluren empor und lachte der Sonn' entgegen;
Gefträuch' und Bäume glüheten in mannichfaltigem Schmuck,
und Freud' und Munterkeit herrscheten durch die ganze Natur.
So kam der frohe Morgen des Jahres, der blumichte Frühling
zur Erde zurück.

Nature smiled again in youthful beauty; the earth assumed
once more its robe of tender green ; the meads were again variegated with a thousand flowers, that expanded to meet the genial

beams of the sun. The thickets and groves were decked with innumerable blossoms, and joy and gladness reigned throughout all nature. Thus the gay morning of the year, delightful spring, returned to revive and cheer the earth.

Love.

Daphnis, Book III.

„Wer nicht liebt, der lebt im öden Winter, der ist wie ein träger Bach, der nicht rauschet; wie ein stummer Vogel, der nicht singt, und wie ein dürrer Baum, der nimmer blühet. O Amor! süßer Gott der Liebe!"

The man who has never felt the influence of love is like one who lives ever in gloomy winter, or he resembles a brook that never gives forth a pleasant murmur, a dumb bird that never sings, or a withered tree whose boughs never unfold a blossom to the sun. O Cupid! sweet god of love!

THE BEAUTY OF THE COUNTRY.

Idyls: Menalcas and Æschines.

Schöner ist der ungekünstelte schattichte Hain mit seinen gekrümmten Gängen; schöner sind die Wiesen mit den tausend= fältigen Blumen geschmückt; ich hab' auch Blumen um die Hütte gepflanzet; Majoran und Lilien und Rosen; und o wie schön sind die Quellen, wenn sie aus Klippen sprudeln, oder aus dem Gebüsche von Hügeln fallen, und dann durch blumichte Wiesen sich schlängeln! Nein, ich geh' nicht in die Stadt.

Oh, fairer is the simple shadowy dell with its winding paths, fairer the meadow, bright with a thousand blossoms! I have planted flowers, too, round my hut: marjoram and lilies and roses. Oh, how much fairer are our fountains, when they sparkle over the cliffs, or, bursting from the thick wood, rush down the hills and wind their mazy way through flowery meadows! No; I go not with thee to the town.

DOING GOOD.

Idyls: Mirtil and Daphne.

Denn wer am Morgen was Gutes beginnt, dem gelingt alles besser, und auf jeder Stunde wächst ihm Freude.

To those who do good in the morning every hour of the day brings pleasure; and for them peace and joy spring from every object around.

C

Sweet is the Recollection of a Benevolent Deed.

Idyls: Menalcas and Alexis.

Die schön aufgehende Sonne, das Abendroth, der volle Mond in einer hellen Nacht, schwellen unsern Busen vor Vergnügen; aber süßer, mein Sohn, süßer ist jene Freude noch.

The mild splendours of the rising sun, the ruddy glowing tints of evening, the moon's calm radiance in a serene night—all these swell our bosoms with pleasure; but sweeter, still sweeter, my son, is the recollection of a benevolent deed.

The Virtuous.

Idyls: Tityrus and Menalcas.

Denn, Sohn! der Segen ruhet bey der Hütte des Redlichen, und bey seiner Scheune. O Sohn! wer redlich ist, und auf die Götter traut, der wandelt nicht auf trügendem Sumpf. Wenn der Redliche opfert, dann steigt der Opferrauch hoch zum Olymp, und die Götter hören segnend seinen Dank und sein Flehen. Ihm singet die Eule nicht banges Unglück, und der traurig krächzende Nachtrabe; er wohnet sicher und ruht unter seinem freundlichen Dach; die freundlichen Hausgötter sehen des Redlichen Geschäfte, und hören seine freundlichen Reden, und segnen ihn.

My son, a blessing rests upon the hut of the virtuous and upon his fields. The righteous, who trusts in the gods, sinks not in deceitful bogs. When he offers sacrifices, the fragrant incense ascends Olympus, and the gods listen graciously to his prayers and supplications. The owl sings not to him of sorrow and misfortune; nor does the melancholy croaking night-raven disturb his slumbers. He dwells securely beneath his peaceful roof; the friendly household gods behold his benevolent deeds, they listen to his mild conversation, and bless him.

Active Employment makes the Time pass pleasantly.

Evander and Alcimna—Act I. sc. 1.

Die Tage kommen und gehen bey der Arbeit viel muntrer.

Days come and go much more pleasantly when our time is fully occupied.

Character of Women.

Evander and Alcimna—Act III. *sc.* 1.

Es ift doch den Mädchen wie angeboren, daß fie allem
gefallen wollen, was nur Augen hat.

It is, as it were, born in maidens that they should wish to
please everything that has eyes.

GLEIM.

Born A.D. 1719.   Died A.D. 1803.

John William Ludwig Gleim was born at Ermsleben, in Halberstadt, and studied at Halle (1738–1740), with the view of
devoting himself to the legal profession. He became secretary
to Prince William of Schwedt, and after his death he filled the
same office in the service of Prince Leopold of Dessau.   Latterly
he became a Canon in Halberstadt, where he lived for half-a-
century devoted to literary pursuits, being particularly happy
in lyric poetry and the simple descriptions of nature.   He died
in 1803.

Improvement of Time.

Benutzung der Zeit.

Pflücke Rosen, weil fie blühn,
Morgen ift nicht heut!
Keine Stunde laß entfliehn!
Morgen ift nicht heut.

Zu Genuß und Arbeit ift
Heut Gelegenheit.
Weißt du, wo du morgen bift?
Flüchtig eilt die Zeit.

Auffchub einer guten That
Hat fchon oft gereut.
Thätig leben ift mein Rath,
Flüchtig eilt die Zeit.

Gather roses while they blossom ; to-morrow is not to-day!
Allow no moment to escape ; to-morrow is not to-day.
To-day is the opportunity for enjoyment and work.   Knowest
thou where thou wilt be to-morrow? time flies swiftly away.

Procrastination of a good deed has often brought repentance: to work while it is called to-day is my advice: time flies swiftly away.

YOUTH.

Weiſe Benutzung der Jugend.

Wer die kurzen Roſentage
Seiner Jugend froh durchlebt
Und entfernt von Neid und Klage,
Gut zu werden ſich beſtrebt,
Der erfreut ſich noch der Jugend
Wenn des Lebens Winter naht,
Und Zufriedenheit und Tugend
Streuen Blumen ſeinem Pfad.
Ohne Furcht und ohne Grauen
Kann er vor- und rückwärts ſchauen.

He who lives happily through the short rose-days of his youth, and far away from envy and complaining strives to be good, still enjoys the days of his youth when the winter of life approaches, and contentment and virtue scatter flowers along his path. Without fear and without anxiety he can look before and behind.

THE HAND OF THE CREATOR.

Von der Eichel und dem Kürbiß.

Sohn, mit Weisheit und Verſtand
Ordnete des Schöpfers Hand
Alle Dinge. Sieh umher,
Keines ſteht von ohngefähr,
Wo es ſteht. Das Firmament,
Wo die große Sonne brennt,
Und der kleinſte Sonnenſtaub
Deines Athems leichter Raub,
Trat auf unſres Gottes Wort
Jegliches an ſeinen Ort.
Jedes Ding in ſeiner Welt
Iſt vollkommen; dennoch hält
Mancher Thor es nicht dafür
Und kunſtrichtert Gott in ihr.

My son, the hand of the Creator has ordered all things with wisdom and understanding. Look around : nothing stands by chance where it stands. The firmament where the great sun shines, and the smallest atom, the light vapour of thy breath, each at God's word assume their place. Everything is perfect in his world ; yet many a fool thinks not so, and criticises God in it.

GOETHE.

Born A.D. 1749. Died A.D. 1832.

John Wolfgang von Goethe, one of the most celebrated characters of Germany, was born A.D. 1749, in his father's house at Frankfort-on-the-Maine. His parents were of the middle class, and to his mother it was thought that he owed his intellectual advantages. He studied at Leipsic (1765) and at Strasburg (1770). It was in 1773 that he commenced his career as an author, making his maiden essay in *Götz von Berlichingen* and in the far-famed *Sorrows of Werther.* In 1775 he was invited by the Duke of Weimar to enter his service, and for upwards of fifty-five years his fortunes were bound up with those of the ducal house of Weimar. His life was quiet and uniform after this event, and he lived to see the family of his patron flourishing in his descendants to the fourth generation. On the morning of the 22d March 1832, after a six days' illness, which caused him no apparent suffering, he breathed away as if into a gentle sleep.

LIVE AND LET LIVE.

Faust, p. 5—*Prologue.*

Ich wünschte sehr der Menge zu behagen,
Besonders weil sie lebt und leben läßt.

I am very anxious to please the public, particularly as it lives and lets live.

THEY HAVE READ A TERRIBLE DEAL.

Faust, p. 5—*Prologue.*

Zwar sind sie an das Beste nicht gewöhnt,
Allein sie haben schrecklich viel gelesen.

Though they are not accustomed to the best, they have read a terrible deal.

Profit and Pleasure.

Faust, p. 5—Prologue.

Wie machen wir's, daß alles frisch und neu
Und mit Bedeutung auch gefällig sey?

How shall we manage, that all be fresh and new, pleasing and instructive at once?

See (Lat.) Profit and Pleasure.

The Genuine.

Faust, p. 6—Prologue.

Was glänzt, ist für den Augenblick geboren;
Das Aechte bleibt der Nachwelt unverloren.

What glitters is only for the moment, the genuine remains unchanged for aye.

Let there be Incident enough.

Faust, p. 7—Prologue.

Besonders aber laßt genug geschehn!
Man kommt zu schaun, man will am liebsten sehn
Wird Vieles vor den Augen abgesponnen,
So daß die Menge staunend gaffen kann.
Da habt ihr in der Breite gleich gewonnen,
Ihr seyd ein vielgeliebter Mann.
Die Masse könnt ihr nur durch Masse zwingen.
Ein jeder sucht sich endlich selbst was aus.
Wer Vieles bringt, wird manchem Etwas bringen;
Und jeder geht zufrieden aus dem Haus.

But, above all, let there be incidents enough! Men come to look; they come to feast their eyes; if much is spun off before their eyes, so that the wondering multitude may gaze, your reputation is made, you are a great favourite. You can only gain the mass by mass; then at last each picks out what he requires: who brings much suits the wants of many, and each from the house contented goes.

Madame de Sévigné says—"La Comédie des Visionaires nous réjouit beaucoup : nous trouvames que c'est la representation de tout le monde ; chacun a ses visions plus ou moins marquées."

The Poet.

Faust, p. 9 — Prologue.

Geh' hin und such' dir einen andern Knecht!
Der Dichter sollte wohl das höchste Recht,
Das Menschenrecht, das ihm Natur vergönnt,
Um deinetwillen freventlich verscherzen!
Wodurch bewegt er alle Herzen?
Wodurch besiegt er jedes Element?
Ist es der Einklang nicht, der aus dem Busen bringt,
Und in sein Herz die Welt zurücke schlingt?
Wenn die Natur des Fadens ew'ge Länge,
Gleichgültig drehend, auf die Spindel zwingt,
Wenn aller Wesen unharmon'sche Menge
Verdrießlich durch einander klingt:
Wer theilt die fließend immer gleiche Reihe
Belebend ab, daß sie sich rhythmisch regt?
Wer ruft das Einzelne zur allgemeinen Weihe,
Wo es in herrlichen Accorden schlägt?
Wer läßt den Sturm zu Leidenschaften wüthen?
Das Abendroth im ernsten Sinne glühn?
Wer schüttet allen schönen Frühlingsblüthen
Auf der Geliebten Pfade hin?
Wer flicht die unbedeutend grünen Blätter
Zum Ehrenkranz Verdiensten jeder Art?
Wer sichert den Olymp, vereinet Götter?
Des Menschen Kraft im Dichter offenbart.

Begone and choose another servant! What! shall the bard
wantonly sport away, for thy mean sake, the loftiest right, the
right of man, which Nature bestows on him? Whence masters
he every heart? whence bends he the elements beneath his
sway? Is it not the harmony which bursts from his breast and
sucks again the world back again into his heart? When Nature,
carelessly winding, whirls the unending threads of life upon her
spindle, when the jarring crowds of all beings mingle in harsh
strife, who, life-inspiring, quickens the unvarying round, that it
moves rhythmically? Who calls the individual to the general
consecration, to resound in noble unison with nature's chords?
Who bids the tempest rage in accord with passions?—the evening
red glow in the flush of thought? Who scatters spring's fairest

flowers on the loved one's path? Who twines from unmeaning green leaves a wreath for merits of all kinds? Who ensures Olympus?—associates gods? Man's lofty spirit revealed in the bard.

See (Lat. Gr.) Poet.

LIFE'S DEPTHS.

Faust, p. 9—Prologue.

Greift nur hinein in's volle Menschenleben!
Ein jeder lebt's, nicht vielen ist's bekannt,
Und wo ihr's packt, da ist's interessant.

Plunge boldly into the thick of life! each lives it, not to many is it known: and seize it where you will, it is interesting.

THE GROWING MIND.

Faust, p. 10—Prologue.

Wer fertig ist, dem ist nichts recht zu machen,
Ein Werdender wird immer dankbar sein.

Your finished gentleman you can never please; a **mind** that is forming will ever prove grateful.

OLD AGE.

Faust, p. 2—Prologue.

Das Alter macht nicht kindisch, wie man spricht,
Es findet uns nur noch als wahre Kinder.

Age makes us not childish, as some say; it finds us still only as true children.

WORDS ENOUGH—NOW DEEDS.

Faust, p. 11—Prologue.

Der Worte sind genug gewechselt,
Laßt mich auch endlich Thaten sehn.

Words enough have been interchanged; let us now at last see deeds.

THE GREATER AND THE LESSER LIGHT.

Faust, p. 12—Prologue.

Gebraucht das groß' und kleine Himmelslicht,
Die Sterne dürfet ihr verschwenden;

An Waſſer, Feuer, Felſenwänden,
An Thier und Vögeln fehlt es nicht.
So ſchreitet in dem engen Bretterhaus
Den ganzen Kreis der Schöpfung aus,
Und wandelt mit bedächt'ger Schnelle
Vom Himmel durch die Welt zur Hölle.

Use the greater and the lesser light of heaven; squander away the stars; in water, fire, rocks, birds and beasts, expend without end; thus bring the whole circle of creation within our narrow booth, and travel, with considerate speed, from heaven through the world to hell.

THE SUN EVER THE SAME.

Faust, p. 13—*Raphael.*

Die Sonne tönt nach alter Weiſe
In Bruderſphären Wettgeſang,
Und ihre vorgeſchrieb'ne Reiſe
Vollendet ſie mit Donnergang.

The sun chimes in, as in ancient time, with brother spheres in emulous song, and finishes his predestined course with thunder-march.

Thus Milton:—

" Such music (as 'tis said)
Before was never made."

MAN LIABLE TO ERROR.

Faust, p. 16—*The Lord.*

Es irrt der Menſch ſo lang' er ſtrebt.

So long as man strives, he is liable to error.

A GOOD MAN.

Faust, p. 16—*The Lord.*

Ein guter Menſch in ſeinem dunkeln Drange
Iſt ſich des rechten Weges wohl bewußt.

A good man, in his dark strivings, is still well aware of the right way.

All Things blend.

Faust, p. 21.

Wie alles sich zum Ganzen webt,
Eins in dem andern wirkt und lebt!
Wie Himmelskräfte auf und nieder steigen
Und sich die goldnen Eimer reichen!
Mit segenduftenden Schwingen
Vom Himmel durch die Erde dringen,
Harmonisch all' das All' durchklingen.

How all things weave themselves into the whole, one working and living into the other! How powers celestial ascend and descend, reaching each other the golden buckets! With rapture-breathing pinions press from heaven through earth, all sounding harmoniously through the All.

Coleridge says something to the same effect—

" And what if all of animated nature
Be but organic harps diversely framed,
That tremble into thought, as o'er them sweeps,
Plastic and vast, one intellectual breeze,
At once the soul of each, and God of all? "

The Loom of Time.

Faust, p. 24—Spirit.

So schaff' ich am sausenden Webstuhl der Zeit.
Thus I ply at the whizzing loom of time.

To Feel.

Faust, p. 25.

Wenn ihr's nicht fühlt, ihr werdet's nicht erjagen.
If feeling prompt not, you will not succeed by hunting after it.

Elocution.

Faust, p. 25— Wagner.

Allein der Vortrag macht des Redners Glück;
Ich fühl' es wohl, noch bin ich weit zurück.

But it is delivery that makes the orator's success: I feel that I am still far behind.

Good Sense and Sound Sense necessary in an Orator.

Faust, p. 26.

Es trägt Verstand und rechter Sinn
Mit wenig Kunst sich selber vor;
Und wenn's euch Ernst ist was zu sagen,
Ist's nöthig Worten nachzujagen?
Ja, eure Reden, die so blinkend sind,
In denen ihr der Menschheit Schnitzel kräuselt,
Sind unerquicklich wie der Nebelwind,
Der herbstlich durch die dürren Blätter säuselt.

Sound reason and good sense can be expressed with little art; and when you have anything to say in earnestness, is it necessary to search for words? Yes; your fine speeches, which are so sparkling, in which ye twist the shreds of human thought, are unrefreshing as the mist-wind, which whistles through the withered leaves of autumn.

See (Lat.) Man easily affected to grief or joy.

The Spirit of Former Times.

Faust, p. 26.

Verzeiht! es ist ein groß Ergötzen
Sich in den Geist der Zeiten zu versetzen,
Zu schauen, wie vor uns ein weiser Mann gedacht,
Und wie wir's dann zuletzt so herrlich weit gebracht.

Forgive me! It is delightful to transport oneself into the spirit of the past, to see how a wise man has thought before us, and to what a glorious height we have at last reached.

The Spirit of the Times is our own Spirit.

Faust, p. 27.

Was ihr den Geist der Zeiten heißt,
Das ist im Grund der Herren eigner Geist,
In dem die Zeiten sich bespiegeln.
Da ist's denn wahrlich oft ein Jammer!
Man läuft euch bei dem ersten Blick davon
Ein Kehrichtfaß und eine Rumpelkammer,
Und höchstens eine Haupt- und Staatsaction,

Mit trefflichen pragmatischen Maximen,
Wie sie den Puppen wohl im Munde ziemen!

What you call the spirit of the times is, in reality, your own spirit, in which the times are reflected as in a glass. And a very miserable exhibition it often is. One flies from it in dismay at the first glance! A rubbish-hole and a very lumber-room, and, at best, a mock-heroic play, full of fine pragmatical saws, such as suit well in the mouths of puppets!

WHAT IS CALLED KNOWING.

Faust, p. 27.

Ja was man so erkennen heißt!
Wer darf das Kind beim rechten Namen nennen?
Die wenigen, die was davon erkannt,
Die thöricht g'nug ihr volles Herz nicht wahrten,
Dem Pöbel ihr Gefühl, ihr Schauen offenbarten,
Hat man von je gekreuzigt und verbrannt.

Ay, what is knowledge among men? Who dares call the child by its true name? The few, who have known somewhat of these things, who foolishly did not keep a guard over their full hearts, who revealed their feelings and thoughts to the people—these, from time immemorial, have been crucified and burned.

Pascal says—" Il faut avoir une pensée de derrière et juger de tout par là, en parlant cependant comme le peuple."

See (Fr.) Fontanellè.

OUR FEELINGS GROW TORPID.

Faust, p. 29.

Die uns das Leben gaben, herrliche Gefühle,
Erstarren in dem irdischen Gewühle.

Our glorious aspirations, which give us life, grow torpid in the din of worldly bustle.

CARES OF LIFE.

Faust, p. 29.

Die Sorge nistet gleich im tiefen Herzen,
Dort wirket sie geheime Schmerzen,
Unruhig wiegt sie sich und störet Lust und Ruh;
Sie deckt sich stets mit neuen Masken zu,

Sie mag als Haus und Hof, als Weib und Kind erscheinen,
Als Feuer, Wasser, Dolch und Gift;
Du bebst vor allem, was nicht trifft,
Und was du nie verlierst, das mußt du stets beweinen.

Care straightway nestles in the deep heart of man, hatches undefined sorrows there, and rocking ceaselessly, scares away joy and rest; she is always putting on some new disguises; she may appear as house and land; as wife and child; as fire, water, dagger, and poison. Thou tremblest before anticipated ills, and still bewailest what thou never losest.

See (Lat. Fr.) Care.

Enjoy thy Inheritance.

Faust, p. 30.

Was du ererbt von deinen Vätern hast,
Erwirb es, um es zu besitzen.
Was man nicht nützt ist eine schwere Last;
Nur was der Augenblick erschafft, das kann er nützen.

Enjoy what thou hast inherited from thy sires if thou wouldst possess it; what we employ not is an oppressive burden; what the moment brings forth, that only can it profit by.

The Moonlight.

Faust, p. 31.

Warum wird mir auf einmal lieblich helle,
Als wenn im mächt'gen Wald uns Mondenglanz umweht?

Why is everything at once so lovely as when the moonlight plays round us in the forest gloom?

So Shakespeare says (*Merchant of Venice*, act v. sc. 1)—

" How sweet the moonlight sleeps upon that bank!"

Miracle the Pet Child of Faith.

Faust, p. 34.

Die Botschaft hör' ich wohl, allein mir fehlt der Glaube;
Das Wunder ist des Glaubens liebstes Kind.

I hear the message, but my faith is weak; miracle is the pet child of faith.

The Sabbath's Stilly Hours.

Faust, p. 31.

Sonst stürzte sich der Himmelsliebe Kuß
Auf mich herab, in ernster Sabbathstille;
Da klang so ahnungsvoll des Glockentones **Fülle,**
Und ein Gebet war brünstiger Genuß;
Ein unbegreiflich holdes Sehnen
Trieb mich durch Wald und Wiesen hinzugehn,
Und unter tausend heißen Thränen,
Fühlt' ich mir eine Welt entstehn.

In former days the kiss of heavenly love came over me in the Sabbath's stilly hour; then the deep-toned bell sounded so full of solemn power, and a yearning prayer was undefined enjoyment; a holy longing, indescribably sweet, drove me to wander through wood and plain; and amidst a thousand warm tears, I felt a world revealed within me.

So Shelley (*Hymn to Intellectual Beauty*):—

" While yet a boy I sought for ghosts, and sped
 Through many a listening chamber, cave, and **ruin,**
 And star-lit wood, with fearful steps pursuing
 Hopes of high talk with the departed dead."

To emerge from this Sea of Errors.

Faust, p. 45.

O glücklich! wer noch hoffen kann,
Aus diesem Meer des Irrthums aufzutauchen.
Was man nicht weiß, das eben brauchte man,
Und was man weiß, kann man nicht brauchen.

How happy he who can still hope to lift himself from this sea of error! What we know not, that we are anxious to possess, and cannot use what we know.

A Beautiful Sunset.

Faust, p. 45.

Betrachte, wie in Abendsonne-Gluth
Die grünumgebnen Hütten schimmern.
Sie rückt und weicht, der Tag ist überlebt,
Dort eilt sie hin und fördert neues Leben.
O daß kein Flügel mich vom Boden hebt,

Ihr nach und immer nach zu ſtreben!
Ich ſah' im ewigen Abendſtrahl
Die ſtille Welt zu meinen Füßen,
Entzündet alle Höhn, beruhigt jedes Thal,
Den Silberbach in goldne Ströme fließen.
Nicht hemmte dann den göttergleichen Lauf
Der wilde Berg mit allen ſeinen Schluchten;
Schon thut das Meer ſich mit erwärmten Buchten
Vor den erſtaunten Augen auf.
Doch ſcheint die Göttin endlich wegzuſinken;
Allein der neue Trieb erwacht.
Ich eile fort ihr ew'ges Licht zu trinken,
Vor mir den Tag, und hinter mir die Nacht,
Den Himmel über mir und unter mir die Wellen.
Ein ſchöner Traum, indeſſen ſie entweicht.
Ach! zu des Geiſtes Flügeln wird ſo leicht
Kein körperlicher Flügel ſich geſellen.

See how yon cottage homes with verdant green shimmer in the bright sunset! He bends and sinks—the day is now no more; there he hurries off and diffuses new life. Oh for a pinion to lift me from this earth, and to strive after, ever after him! Then should I see, in deathless evening beams, the stilly world at my feet—every height aglow—every vale reposing—the silver brooklets flowing into golden streams. The savage mountain, with all its dark defiles, would not then bar my godlike course. Already the ocean, with its warm bays, opes itself on my enraptured sight. Yet at length the god appears to sink: but the new impulse awakes. I hurry on to drink his quenchless light— the day before me and the night behind—the vaulted skies above and the waves below. A glorious dream, it vanished with the parting day. Alas, no bodily wing will so easily keep pace with the wings of the mind!

Spenser, in one of his sonnets, says—

" Oft when my spirit doth spread her bolder wings,
    In mind to mount up to the purer sky,
  It down is weighed with thought of earthly things,
  And clogged with burden of mortality."

Two Souls in Man.

Faust, p. 47.

Zwei Seelen wohnen, ach! in meiner Bruſt,
Die eine will ſich von der andern trennen;

Die eine hält in derber Liebeslust,
Sich an die Welt mit klammernden Organen;
Die andre hebt gewaltsam sich vom Dust
Zu den Gefilden hoher Ahnen.

Two souls, alas! are lodged in my breast—the one anxious to separate itself from the other: the one clings, with obstinate desire, to the world with organs like cramps of steel; the other raises itself with vehemence from the mist to the realms of an exalted ancestry.

Philippians i. 23: "For I am in a strait betwixt two, having a desire to depart and to be with Christ, which is far better."

A DOG WELL BROUGHT UP.

Faust, p. 49.

Fauſt.

Du haſt wohl Recht; ich finde nicht die Spur
Von einem Geiſt, und alles iſt Dreſſur.

Wagner.

Dem Hunde, wenn er gut gezogen,
Wird ſelbſt ein weiſer Mann gewogen.

Faust. You are right indeed; I find no traces of a spirit, and all is training—nothing more. *Wagner.* Even a wise man may become attached to a dog when he is well brought up.

In *Guy Mannering* (chap. xxii.) Scott says—

"A bonnie terrier that, sir—and a fell chield at the vermin, I warrant him—that is, if he's been weel entered, for it a' lies in that." "Really, sir," said Brown, "his education has been somewhat neglected, and his chief property is being a pleasant companion." "Ay, sir?—that's a pity, begging your pardon—it's a great pity that—beast or body, education should aye be minded."

MEN DERIDE WHAT THEY DO NOT UNDERSTAND.

Faust, p. 51.

Wir ſind gewohnt, daß die Menſchen verhöhnen,
Was ſie nicht verſtehn,
Daß ſie vor dem Guten und Schönen,
Das ihnen oft beſchwerlich iſt, murren.

We are accustomed to see men deride what they do not understand, and snarl at the good and beautiful because it lies beyond their sympathies.

The New Testament.

Faust, p. 51.

Wir lernen das Ueberirdische schätzen,
Wir sehnen uns nach Offenbarung,
Die nirgends würdiger und schöner **brennt,**
Als in dem neuen Testament.

We learn to treasure what is above this earth, we long for revelation, which nowhere burns more purely and more beautifully than in the New Testament.

A Travelling Scholar.

Faust, p. 55.

Das also war des Pudels Kern!
Ein fahrender Scolast? Der Casus macht mich lachen.

This, then, was the kernel of the poodle! a travelling scholar! Why, I needs must smile.

The Spirit that denies.

Faust, p. 55.

Ich bin der Geist der stets verneint!

I am the spirit that always denies.

The Devil.

Faust, p. 62.

Du bist noch nicht der Mann, den Teufel fest zu halten!

Thou art not yet the man to hold the devil!

The Devil is an Egotist.

Faust, p. 67.

Nein, nein! der Teufel ist ein Egoist
Und thut nicht leicht um Gottes Willen
Was einem Andern nützlich ist.

No, no! the devil is an egotist, and does not, for God's sake, what is useful to another.

Blood is a Peculiar Kind of Juice.

Faust, p. 71.

Blut ist ein ganz besondrer Saft.

Blood is quite a peculiar kind of juice.

The Infinite and Man.

Faust, p. 73.

Ich fühl's, vergebens hab' ich alle Schätze
Des Menschengeist's auf mich herbeigerafft,
Und wenn ich mich am Ende niedersetze,
Quillt innerlich doch keine neue Kraft;
Ich bin nicht um ein Haar breit höher,
Bin dem Unendlichen nicht näher.

I feel it ; in vain have I heaped upon my brain all the treasures of man's thought, and when I sit down at the end, no new-born power wells up within ; not a hair's-breadth is added to my height, nor am I a whit nearer the infinite.

Matthew vi. 27: "Which of you by taking thought can add one cubit to his stature?"

A Speculating Spirit.

Faust, p. 74.

Ich sag' es dir : ein Kerl, der speculirt,
Ist wie ein Thier auf dürrer Heide,
Von einem bösen Geist im Kreis herum geführt,
Und rings umher liegt schöne grüne Weide.

I tell you what ; a fellow that speculates is like a brute on a barren heath driven by an evil spirit round and round, while fair green pastures stretch everywhere beyond.

An Ardent Mind.

Faust, p. 75.

Ihm hat das Schicksal einen Geist gegeben,
Der ungebändigt immer vorwärts dringt,
Und dessen übereiltes Streben
Der Erde Freuden überspringt.

Fate has endowed him with a spirit which, unrestrained, still presses forward, and whose precipitate striving o'erleaps the joys of earth.

Shakespeare (*Macbeth*, act i. sc. 7) says—

> "I have no spur
> To prick the sides of my intent, but only
> Vaulting ambition, which o'erleaps itself,
> And falls on the other."

METHOD TEACHES TO GAIN TIME.

Faust, p. 77.

Gebraucht der Zeit, sie geht so schnell von hinnen,
Doch Ordnung lehrt euch Zeit gewinnen.

Make the most of time, it flies away so fast; yet method will teach you to win time.

CONFUSION IN THE HEAD.

Faust, p. 79.

Mir wird vor alle dem so dumm,
Als ging' mir ein Mühlrad im Kopf herum.

I am so confused by all this as if a mill-wheel were turning round in my head.

WHAT ONE HAS IN BLACK AND WHITE.

Faust, p. 79.

Denn was man schwarz auf weiß besitzt,
Kann man getrost nach Hause tragen.

For what one possesses in black and white, one can carry home in comfort.

LAWS.

Faust, p. 80.

Es erben sich Gesetz' und Rechte
Wie eine ew'ge Krankheit fort.

Laws and rights descend like an inveterate hereditary disease.

WORDS.

Faust, p. 80.

Im Ganzen — haltet euch an Worte:

Generally speaking, confine yourself to words !

WHERE IDEAS FAIL WORDS STEP IN.

Faust, p. 80.

Denn eben wo Begriffe fehlen,
Da stellt ein Wort zur rechten Zeit sich ein.

For there precisely where ideas fail, a word comes in most opportunely.

LEARN HOW TO MANAGE WOMEN.

Faust, p. 81.

Besonders lernt die Weiber führen;
Es ist ihr ewig Weh und Ach,
So tausendfach
Aus einem Punkte zu curiren.

Learn, above all, how to manage women ; their thousand Ahs ! and Ohs ! so thousand-fold, can be cured from a single point.

THE GREY AND GREEN OF LIFE.

Faust, p. 82.

Schüler.

Das sieht schon besser aus ! Man sieht doch wo und wie?

Mephistopheles.

Grau, theurer Freund, ist alle Theorie,
Und grün des Lebens goldner Baum.

Scholar. There's sense in that ! one sees the how and why ! *Mephistopheles.* Grey, my dearest friend, is all theory, and green he golden tree of life.

THE COMMON RACE OF MEN.

Faust, p. 88.

Mit wenig Witz und viel Behagen
Dreht jeder sich im engen Zirkeltanz,
Wie junge Katzen mit dem Schwanz.

With little wit and much self-complacency each turns round in his own small circle-dance, like young kittens playing with their tails.

A True German hates the French.

Faust, p. 94.

Ein echter deutscher Mann mag keinen Franzen leiden,
Doch ihre Weine trinkt er gern.

A true German cannot abide a Frenchman, but has a relish for
their wine.

Ravenous as Five Hundred Swine.

Faust, p. 95.

Uns ist ganz kanibalisch wohl,
Als wie fünfhundert Säuen!

We are quite as much cannibals as five hundred swine!

How to keep our Youth.

Faust, p. 99.

Mephistopheles.

Dich zu verjüngen giebt's auch ein natürlich Mittel;
Allein es steht in einem andern Buch,
Und ist ein wunderlich Capitel.

Faust.

Ich will es wissen.

Mephistopheles.

Gut! Ein Mittel, ohne Geld
Und Arzt und Zauberei zu haben!
Begieb dich gleich hinaus auf's Feld,
Fang' an zu hacken und zu graben,
Erhalte dich und deinen Sinn
In einem ganz beschränkten Kreise,
Ernähre dich mit ungemischter Speise,
Leb' mit dem Vieh als Vieh, und acht' es nicht für Raub,
Den Acker, den du erntest, selbst zu düngen;
Das ist das beste Mittel, glaub',
Auf achtzig Jahr' dich zu verjüngen!

Mephistopheles. There is also a natural method of renewing
youth, but the lesson is written in another book, and it is a strange
chapter. *Faust.* I should wish to know it. *Mephistopheles.*

Very well! to try a natural means without money, physician, or sorcery! go straight to the fields; begin to hack and delve; confine yourself and senses within a very contracted circle; support yourself upon the simplest fare; live among the beasts as a beast, and esteem it no robbery to dung the land you crop. That is the best way, believe me, to keep you young to eighty!

A Quiet Spirit works whole Years Long.

Faust, p. 100.

Ein stiller Geist ist Jahre lang geschäftig;
Die Zeit nur macht die feine Gährung kräftig.

A quiet spirit is busy at it for years; time only makes the subtle ferment strong.

The March of Intellect.

Faust, p. 106.

Auch die Cultur, die alle Welt beleckt,
Hat auf den Teufel sich erstreckt.

The march of intellect, too, which licks all the world into shape, has even reached the devil.

The Wicked remain.

Faust, p. 106.

Den Bösen sind sie los, die Bösen sind geblieben.

They are rid of the wicked one, but the wicked still remain.

The Way to deal with Witches.

Faust, p. 107.

Dieß ist die Art mit Hexen umzugehn.

This is the way to deal with witches.

A Downright Contradiction.

Faust, p. 108.

Denn ein vollkommner Widerspruch
Bleibt gleich geheimnißvoll für Kluge wie für Thoren.

For a downright contradiction still remains, alike mysterious both to fools and sages.

Words.

Faust, p. 109.

Gewöhnlich glaubt der Mensch, wenn er nur Worte hört,
Es müsse sich dabei doch auch was denken lassen.

Men usually believe when they hear words that there must be some thought in them.

Presents, and Success is sure.

Faust, p. 114.

Gleich schenken? Das ist brav! Da wird er reüssiren!

Presents so soon? That is famous! You are sure to succeed!

The Church.

Faust, p. 121.

Die Kirche hat einem guten Magen,
Hat ganze Länder aufgefressen,
Und doch noch nie sich übergessen;
Die Kirch' allein, meine lieben Frauen,
Kann ungerechtes Gut verdauen.

The Church has a good stomach; she has swallowed down whole countries, and has never known a surfeit; the Church alone, mv good women, can digest such ill-gotten wealth.

Reflections on the Moon.

Faust, p. 142.

Und steigt vor meinem Blick der reine Mond
Besänftigend herüber; schweben mir
Von Felsenwänden, aus dem feuchten Busch,
Der Vorwelt silberne Gestalten auf,
Und lindern der Betrachtung strenge Lust.

And when the clear moon, with its soothing beams, climbs up full in my view—from the wall-like rocks, out of the vapour-covered wood, the silvery forms of bygone ages hover up to me and soften the severe delight of earnest contemplation.

Coleridge, in his *Sibylline Leaves*, p. 65, says—

> "And he, with many feelings, many thoughts,
> Made up a meditative joy, and found
> Religious meanings in the forms of nature."

THE LOVE-SICK.

Faust, p. 145.

Die Zeit wird ihr erbärmlich lang;
Sie steht am Fenster, sieht die Wolken ziehn
Ueber die alte Stadtmauer hin.
Wenn ich ein Vöglein wär'! so geht ihr Gesang
Tage lang, halbe Nächte lang.
Einmal ist sie munter, meist betrübt,
Einmal recht ausgeweint,
Dann wieder ruhig, wie's scheint,
Und immer verliebt.

To her the hours seem miserably long ; she stands at the window looking at the clouds floating past over the ancient city-walls. "Were I a bird ! " so runs her song all the day and through half the night. One while she is gay, mostly cast down—one while fairly outwept ; anon she is tranquil, or so appears, and ever more love-sick.

Shelley, in his *Adonais*, says—

" As with no stain
She faded like a cloud that has outwept its rain."

HOMELY CARES.

Faust, p. 146.

Und seitwärts sie, mit kindlich dumpfen Sinnen,
Im Hüttchen auf dem kleinen Alpenfeld,
Und all' ihr häusliches Beginnen
Umfangen in der kleinen Welt.

And she, in her lowly cot, on the slope of a little mountain-field, lived with childlike simplicity, and all her homely cares embraced in that small world.

Rogers, in *Jacqueline*, says—

"Flies from her home, the humble sphere."

TWO LOVERS.

Faust, p. 150.

Und steigen freundlich blickend
Ewige Sterne nicht herauf?

Schau' ich nicht Aug' in Auge dir,
Und drängt nicht alles
Nach Haupt und Herzen dir,
Und webt in ewigem Geheimniß
Unsichtbar, sichtbar neben dir?
Erfüll' davon dein Herz, so groß es ist
Und wenn du ganz in dem Gefühle selig bist
Nenn' es dann wie du willst,
Nenn's Glück! Herz! Liebe! Gott!
Ich habe keinen Namen
Dafür! Gefühl ist alles;
Name ist Schall und Rauch,
Umnebelnd Himmelsgluth.

And do not the everlasting stars, beaming tenderly, climb on high? Are we not gazing into each other's eyes, and are not all nature's agencies thronging to thy head and heart, and weaving in eternal mystery, viewless, visibly about thee? Hence, fill thy heart, big as it is, and in the feeling when thou art wholly blest, then call it what thou wilt! Call it bliss! heart! love! God. I have no name for it—'tis feeling all. Name is but sound and smoke, shrouding the glow of heaven.

Moore, in *Lalla Rookh*, says—

> " When, full of blissful sighs,
> They sat and looked into each other's eyes."

Henry Taylor, in *Ion* (v. 2), says—

> "I have asked that dreadful question of the hills
> That look eternal ; of the flowing streams
> That lucid flow for ever ; of the stars,
> Amid whose fields of azure my raised spirit
> Hath trod in glory : all were dumb ; but now,
> While I thus gaze upon thy living face,
> I feel the love that kindles through its beauty
> Can never wholly perish ; we shall meet
> Again, Clemanthe !"

ODDITIES IN THE WORLD.

Faust, p. 152.

Es muß auch solche Käuze geben.

There must be, nevertheless, such strange oddities in the world.

An Antipathy.

Faust, p. 153.

Du haft nun die Antipathie!
Thou hast an antipathy, that is all.

A Man's Faith.

Faust, p. 154.

Die Mädels find doch sehr intereffirt,
Ob einer fromm und schlicht nach altem Brauch.
Sie denken, duckt er da, folgt er uns eben auch.

The girls are certainly much interested whether a man be pious and follows the old creed. They think, If he is pliant there, us too he will follow and obey.

Women take the Lead in Evil.

Faust, p. 174.

Denn, geht es zu des Bösen Haus,
Das Weib hat taufend Schritt voraus.

For, when we speed to the devil's house, woman takes the lead by a thousand steps.

The Trouble is Small, the Pastime Great.

Faust, p. 177.

Die Müh' ift klein, der Spaß ift groß.
The trouble is small, the pastime is great.

Witches' Wares.

Faust, p. 179.

Aufmerkfam blickt nach meinen Waaren;
Es fteht dahier gar mancherlei.
Und doch ift nichts in meinem Laden,
Dem keiner auf der Erde gleicht,
Das nicht einmal zum tücht'gen Schaden
Der Menfchen und der Welt gereicht.
Kein Dolch ift hier, von dem nicht Blut gefloffen,

Kein Kelch, aus dem sich nicht in ganz gesunden Leib,
Verzehrend heißes Gift ergossen,
Kein Schmuck, der nicht ein liebenswürdig Weib
Verführt, kein Schwert, das nicht den Bund gebrochen,
Nicht etwa hinterrücks den Gegenmann durchstochen.

Look attentively on my wares ; I have here a choice collection ;
and yet there is nothing among my store to which there is anything like on earth, which has not wrought some direful mischief
to mankind and the world. No dagger here from which blood
has not flowed ; no bowl which has not in some healthy frame
infused hot consuming poison ; no trinket that has not wrought
some woman's shame ; no sword which has not cut some sacred
tie, or stabbed behind the back an enemy.

MAN.

Faust, p. 195.

Der richtenden gefühllosen Menschheit!

To sentence-passing, unfeeling man!

BEAUTY WAS MY UNDOING.

Faust, p. 199.

Schön war ich auch, und das war mein Verderben.

I was fair, too, and that was my undoing.

MERIT AND FORTUNE UNITED.

Faust (Second Part), vol. XII. *p.* 20.

Wie sich Verdienst und Glück verketten,
Das fällt den Thoren niemals ein.

It never occurs to fools that merit and good fortune are closely
united.

THE WORLD A PARTICULARLY GREAT FOOL.

Faust (Second Part), vol. XII. *p.* 21.

Es bleibt doch endlich nach wie vor,
Mit ihren hunderttausend Possen,
Die Welt ein einz'ger großer Thor.

It remains, in short, in later times as before, that the world,
with its hundred thousand tricks, is a particularly great fool.

Law and Necessity.

Faust (Second Part), vol. XII. *p.* **49.**

Gefeß ift mächtig, mächtiger bie Noth.

Laws are powerful, necessity still more so.

Britons.

Faust (Second Part), vol. XII. *p.* 106.

Sinb Briten hier? Sie reifen fonft fo **viel,**
Schlachtfelbern nachzufpüren, Wafferfällen,
Geftürzten Mauern, claffifch bumpfen Stellen.

Are Britons here? They travel so much to examine fields of battle, waterfalls, ruined walls, classic spots of little note.

The Simple Joys of Early Youth.

Iphigenia in Tauris, I. 2. 33.

Sie war bahin,
Der Jugenb befte Freube, bas Gebeihn
Der erften Jahre.

The simple joys of early years were vanished, the best charm of youth.

Hannah More says—

"Oh, the joy
Of young ideas painted on the mind,
In the warm glowing colours fancy spreads
On objects not yet known, when all is new,
And all is lovely ! "

To Breathe is not to Live.

Iphigenia in Tauris, I. 2. 54.

Frei athmen macht bas Leben nicht allein.

To breathe freely alone is not to live.

A Useless Life.

Iphigenia in Tauris, I. 2. **63.**

Ein unnüß Leben ift ein früher Tob.

A useless life is only an early death.

The Far-seeing Mind.

Iphigenia in Tauris, I. 2. 92.

Das Wenige verschwindet leicht dem Blick
Der vorwärts sieht, wie viel noch übrig bleibt.

The little done vanishes from the sight of man, who looks forward to what is still to do.

The Modest and the Vain.

Iphigenia in Tauris, I. 2. 96.

Auch den, der wahren Werth zu stolz nicht achtet,
Wie den, der falschen Werth zu eitel hebt.

We blame equally him who is too proud to place a proper value on his own merit, and him who prizes too highly his spurious worth.

See (Fr.) Modest.

A Noble Man is led by Woman's Gentle Words.

Iphigenia in Tauris, I. 2. 161.

Ein edler Mann wird durch ein gutes Wort
Der Frauen weit geführt.

A noble man is led by woman's gentle words.

A Happy Home.

Iphigenia in Tauris, I. 3. 9.

Der ist am glücklichsten, er sey
Ein König oder ein Geringer, dem
In seinem Hause Wohl bereitet ist.

He is happiest, be he king or peasant, who finds peace in his home.

So J. H. Payne (*Home, sweet Home*) :—

"Mid pleasures and palaces though we may roam,
 Be it ever so humble, there's no place like home."

Kindness shown to the Wicked.

Iphigenia in Tauris, I. 3. 68.

Was man Verruchten thut wird nicht gesegnet.

The kindness which is shown to the wicked is not blessed.

To speak a Momentous Word calmly.

Iphigenia in Tauris, i. 3. 88.

Du ſprichſt ein großes Wort gelaſſen aus.

Thou speakest a word of great moment calml**y.**

The Weakness of the Human Race.

Iphigenia in Tauris, i. 3. 98.

Das ſterbliche Geſchlecht iſt viel zu ſchwach
In ungewohnter Höhe nicht zu ſchwindeln.

The mortal race of man is far too weak not to grow dizzy on
unwonted heights.

Noble Progenitors.

Iphigenia in Tauris, i. 3. 133.

Wohl dem, der ſeiner Väter gern gedenkt,
Der froh von ihren Thaten, ihrer Größe
Den Hörer unterhält, und ſtill ſich freuen♭
An's Ende dieſer ſchönen Reihe ſich
Geſchloſſen ſieht! Denn es erzeugt nicht gleich
Ein Haus den Halbgott noch das Ungeheuer;
Erſt eine Reihe Böſer oder Guter
Bringt endlich das Entſetzen, bringt die Freude
Der Welt hervor.

Happy he who remembers his progenitors with pride, who
relates with pleasure to the listener the story of their greatness,
of their deeds, and, silently rejoicing, sees himself linked to the
end of this goodly chain ! For the same house produces not a
demigod and monster. A line of good or bad brings either terrors
or joy to the world.

See (Fr.) Noble birth.

The Words of Heaven have not a Double Meaning.

Iphigenia in Tauris, xi. 1. 53.

Der Götter Worte ſind nicht doppelſinnig,
Wie der Gedrückte ſie im Unmuth wähnt.

The words of Heaven have not a double meaning, as the oppressed, in his despair, sometimes imagines.

Courage and Love.

Iphigenia in Tauris, II. 1. 107.

Und Luſt und Liebe ſind die Fittige
Zu großen Thaten.

Love and courage are the spirit's wings, raising to noble actions.

Future Deeds.

Iphigenia in Tauris, II. 1. 121.

Und künft'ge Thaten drangen wie die Sterne
Rings um uns her unzählig aus der Nacht.

And future deeds shone around us like the stars in countless numbers in the night.

The Popular Breath.

Iphigenia in Tauris, II. 1. 140.

Ich halte nichts von dem, der von ſich denkt
Wie ihn das Volk vielleicht erheben möchte.

I put no account on him who esteems himself just as the popular breath may chance to raise him.

The Gods know what is good for us.

Iphigenia in Tauris, III. 1. 177.

Wie man den König an dem Uebermaaß
Der Gaben kennt: denn ihm muß wenig ſcheinen
Was Tauſenden ſchon Reichthum iſt; ſo kennt
Man euch, ihr Götter, an geſparten, lang'
Und weiſe zubereiteten Geſchenken.
Denn ihr allein wißt, was uns frommen kann,
Und ſchaut der Zukunft ausgedehntes Reich,
Wenn jedes Abends Stern- und Nebelhülle
Die Ausſicht uns verdeckt. Gelaſſen hört
Ihr unſer Flehn, das um Beſchleunigung
Euch kindiſch bittet; aber eure Hand
Bricht unreif nie die goldnen Himmelsfrüchte;
Und wehe dem, der ungeduldig ſie
Ertrotzend ſaure Speiſe ſich zum Tod'
Genießt.

As we recognise the monarch by his bounteous gifts, for that is nothing to him which seems riches to others, so we know you, ye gods, by gifts long withheld, and wisely bestowed. For ye alone know what can profit us, viewing the extended realm of the future, while the starry or dim veil shrouds from us the prospect. Calmly ye listen to our prayers, when we petition like children for greater speed, but your hand plucks the golden fruit of heaven not unripe ; and woe to him who, impatiently forestalling the ripeness of the fruit, gathers death.

FALSEHOOD.

Iphigenia in Tauris, IV. 1. 37.

> O weh der Lüge ! Sie befreiet nicht,
> Wie jedes andre wahrgesprochne Wort
> Die Brust; sie macht uns nicht getrost, sie ängstet
> Den, der sie heimlich schmiedet, und sie kehrt,
> Ein losgedrückter Pfeil, von einem Gotte
> Gewendet und versagend, sich zurück
> Und trifft den Schützen.

Woe to falsehood! it relieves not the breast like words of truth ; it gives us no comfort, pains him who forges it, and, like an arrow directed by a god, flies back and wounds the archer.

Carlyle says—

"A lie should be trampled on and extinguished wherever found. I am for fumigating the atmosphere, when I suspect that falsehood, like pestilence, breathes around me."

THE COUNSEL OF A PRESENT FRIEND.

Iphigenia in Tauris, IV. 4. 93.

> Wie köstlich ist des gegenwärt'gen Freundes
> Gewisse Rede, deren Himmelskraft
> Ein Einsamer entbehrt und still verstuft.
> Denn langsam reift, verschlossen in dem Busen,
> Gedank' ihm und Entschluß ; die Gegenwart
> Des Liebenden entwickelte sie leicht.

How dear the sure counsel of a present friend, whose heavenly power failing, the lonely one sinks in silence. For earnest thought and resolution, locked within his breast, are slowly ripened ; the presence of the loved one soon warms them into being.

Rigid Scruples.

Iphigenia in Tauris, IV. 4. 120.

Zu ſtrenge Forb'rung iſt verborgner Stolz.

Scruples too rigid are nothing else but concealed pride.

A Conscience void of Offence.

Iphigenia in Tauris, IV. 4. 123.

Ganz unbefleckt genießt ſich nur das Herz.

Only the heart without a stain knows perfect ease.

No One is Righteous.

Iphigenia in Tauris, IV. 4. 127.

So wunderbar iſt dieß Geſchlecht gebildet,
So vielfach iſt's verſchlungen und verknüpft,
Daß Keiner in ſich ſelbſt, noch mit den Andern
Sich rein und unverworren halten kann.
Auch ſind wir nicht beſtellt uns ſelbſt zu richten;
Zu wandeln und auf ſeinen Weg zu ſehen,
Iſt eines Menſchen erſte, nächſte Pflicht:
Denn ſelten ſchätzt er recht was er gethan,
Und was er thut, weiß er faſt nicht zu ſchätzen.

So wonderfully is human nature formed, so involved and com-
plicate are its ties, that no one can hope to keep his spirit pure
and unperplexed in his walk through life; nor are we called upon
to judge ourselves; to pursue his course and walk with circum-
spection is the first and immediate duty of a man; for seldom
does he estimate rightly what he has done, nor yet what he does.

Necessity commands with Iron Hand.

Iphigenia in Tauris, IV. 4. 151.

       Die ehrne Hand
Der Noth gebietet, und ihr ernſter Wink
Iſt oberſtes Geſetz, dem Götter ſelbſt
Sich unterwerfen müſſen. Schweigend herrſcht
Des ew'gen Schickſals unberathne Schweſter.
Was ſie dir auferlegt, das trage: thu',
Was ſie gebeut.

E

The iron hand of Necessity commands, and her stern decree is supreme law, to which the gods even must submit. In deep silence rules the uncounselled sister of eternal fate. Whatever she lays upon thee, endure; perform whatever she commands.

See (Lat.) Fortune worshipped by all; (Gr.) Necessity.

All Mortal Things Decay.

Iphigenia in Tauris, IV. 5. 9.

Das beſte Glück, des Lebens ſchönſte Kraft,
Ermattet endlich.

The highest happiness, the purest joys of life, wear out at last.

The Gods rule Supreme.

Iphigenia in Tauris, IV. 5. 38.

Es fürchte die Götter
Das Menſchengeſchlecht!
Sie halten die Herrſchaft
In ewigen Händen,
Und können ſie brauchen
Wie's ihnen gefällt.

The children of men should dread the immortals! they hold in their hands eternal dominion, and can wield them as they choose.

Man easily accustomed to Slavery.

Iphigenia in Tauris, V. 2. 5.

Zur Sclaverei gewöhnt der Menſch ſich gut
Und lernet leicht gehorchen, wenn man ihn
Der Freiheit ganz beraubt.

Man is soon accustomed to slavery, and quickly learns submission, when he is quite deprived of freedom.

The Chance of Arms is uncertain.

Iphigenia in Tauris, V. 3. 63.

Das Loos der Waffen wechſelt hin und her;
Kein kluger Streiter hält den Feind gering.
Auch ohne Hülfe gegen Trutz und Härte
Hat die Natur den Schwachen nicht gelaſſen.

Sie gab zur Lift ihm Freude, lehrt' ihn Künste;
Bald weicht er aus, verspätet und umgeht.
Ja, der Gewaltige verdient, daß man sie übt.

The chance of arms is ever changing; no prudent warrior holds his foe in derision. Nature has not left the weak without aid against attack and harshness; she has given craft and wily cunning; quick he yields, delays, and escapes. Yea, the powerful deserve that they should be so treated.

HUMANITY IS HEARD BY ALL.

Iphigenia in Tauris, v. 3. 135.

Thoas.

Du glaubst es höre
Der rohe Scythe, der Barbar, die Stimme
Der Wahrheit und der Menschlichkeit, die Atreus,
Der Grieche, nicht vernahm?

Iphigenie.

Es hört sie jeder
Geboren unter jedem Himmel, dem
Des Lebens Quelle durch den Busen
Rein und ungehindert fließt.

Thoas. Thinkest thou that the savage Scythian will listen to the voice of truth and humanity, unheard by Atreus the Greek? *Iphigenia.* Every one hears it, under whatever clime he may be born, through whose breast flows the gushing stream of life, pure and unrestrained.

Bacon says—

"Our humanity were a poor thing but for the divinity that stirs within us."

·MAN RENOWNED IN SONG.

Iphigenia in Tauris, v. 6. 43.

Der rasche Kampf verewigt einen Mann:
Er falle gleich, so preiset ihn das Lied.

Rash combat often immortalises man; if he should fall, he is renowned in song.

A Noble Nature.

Torquato Tasso, I. 1. 59.

Ein edler Mensch zieht edle Menschen an
Und weiß sie fest zu halten, wie ihr thut.

A noble nature can alone attract the noble, and knows to retain
them as ye do.

The Good Man.

Torquato Tasso, I. 1. 80.

Die Stätte, die ein guter Mensch betrat,
Ist eingeweiht; nach hundert Jahren klingt
Sein Wort und seine That dem Enkel wieder.

The ground on which a good man treads is hallowed; when
centuries have passed, his words and his deeds are still re-echoed
to his children's children.

The Entranced Poet.

Torquato Tasso, I. 1. 159.

Sein Auge weilt auf dieser Erde kaum;
Sein Ohr vernimmt den Einklang der Natur;
Was die Geschichte reicht, das Leben giebt,
Sein Busen nimmt es gleich und willig auf:
Das weit Zerstreute sammelt sein Gemüth,
Und sein Gefühl belebt das Unbelebte.
Oft adelt er was uns gemein erschien,
Und das Geschätzte wird vor ihm zu nichts.
In diesem eignen Zauberkreise wandelt
Der wunderbare Mann, und zieht uns an
Mit ihm zu wandeln, Theil an ihm zu nehmen:
Er scheint sich uns zu nahn, und bleibt uns fern;
Er scheint uns anzusehn, und Geister mögen
An unsrer Stelle seltsam ihm erscheinen.

His eye scarcely lingers on this earth; his ear takes in the
melody of nature; what history offers and life presents, his bosom
promptly and with joy receives; his mind combines what is widely
scattered, and his quick feeling animates the dead. Oft he en-
nobles what we regard as common, and what is prized by others
is by him despised. The wondrous man moves in his own en-

chanted sphere, alluring us on to wander with him and partake his joy. He seems to approach us, and yet remains far off; he appears to look on us, and spirits often take our place before his mind's eye.

Tennyson thus sketches the poet :—

" The poet in a golden clime was born,
With golden stars above;
Dowered with the hate of hate, the scorn of scorn,
The love of love.
He saw through life and death, through good and ill,
He saw through his own soul;
The marvel of the everlasting will,
An open scroll,
Before him lay."

See (Lat. Gr. Fr.) Poet.

TIME IS NOT THE MEASURE OF A NOBLE WORK.

Torquato Tasso, I. 2. 41.

Laß ihn, mein Bruder! denn es ist die Zeit
Von einem guten Werke nicht das Maaß;
Und wenn die Nachwelt mit genießen soll,
So muß des Künstlers Mitwelt sich vergessen.

Leave him, my brother! for time alone is not the measure of a noble work; and if the coming age is to share our joy, the contemporaries of the artist must forget themselves.

THE EDUCATION OF A NOBLE SPIRIT.

Torquato Tasso, I. 2. 55.

Ein edler Mensch kann einem engen Kreise
Nicht seine Bildung danken. Vaterland
Und Welt muß auf ihn wirken. Ruhm und Tadel
Muß er ertragen lernen. Sich und andre
Wird er gezwungen recht zu kennen. Ihn
Wiegt nicht die Einsamkeit mehr schmeichelnd ein.
Es will der Feind — es darf der Freund nicht schonen;
Dann übt der Jüngling streitend seine Kräfte,
Fühlt was er ist, und fühlt sich bald ein Mann.

A noble spirit cannot develop his mental powers within a contracted circle. His fatherland and the world must work on his mind. Praise and blame he must learn to bear. Himself and others he must be forced to estimate properly. Solitude lulls him no more in delusive dreams. Opponents will not, friends dare not, spare. Then the youth striving puts forth his powers, knows what he is, and feels himself a man.

Talents are best nurtured in Solitude.

Torquato Tasso, I. 2. 66.

Es bildet ein Talent sich in der Stille,
Sich ein Charakter in dem Strom der Welt.

Talents are best nurtured in solitude ; character is best formed in the stormy billows of the world.

Mankind.

Torquato Tasso, I. 2. 72.

Die Menschen fürchtet nur wer sie nicht kennt,
Und wer sie meidet, wird sie bald verkennen.

He only fears man, who does not know them, and he who avoids them will soon misjudge them.

No One can lay aside his own Nature.

Torquato Tasso, I. 2. 85.

Laß uns, geliebter Bruder, nicht vergessen,
Daß von sich selbst der Mensch nicht scheiden kann.

Beloved brother, let us not forget that man can never lay aside his own nature.

See (Lat. Fr.) Nature, driven out, returns.

Friends.

Torquato Tasso, I. 3. 68.

Wer nicht die Welt in seinen Freunden sieht,
Verdient nicht, daß die Welt von ihm erfahre.

He who does not feel his friends to be the world to him, does not deserve that the world should hear of him.

The Gifts of Life.

Torquato Tasso, I. 3. 124.

Wer früh erwirbt, lernt früh den hohen Werth
Der holden Güter dieses Lebens schätzen ;

Wer früh genießt, entbehrt in seinem Leben
Mit Willen nicht, was er einmal besaß;
Und wer besitzt, der muß gerüstet seyn.

He who inherits in youth this life's sacred possessions, learns
early to prize their noble worth ; he who in youth enjoys them,
does not give up willingly what he has once possessed ; and he
who possesses them, must still be armed to guard them.

The Poet and Deeds of Fame.

Torquato Tasso, II. 1. 48.

Zwar herrlich ist die liebeswerthe That,
Doch schön ist's auch, der Thaten stärkste Fülle
Durch würd'ge Lieder auf die Nachwelt bringen.

Glorious in truth are deeds of high fame, yet noble it also is
to transmit the lofty grandeur of heroism to posterity through
worthy song.

See (Lat.) Poet forbids the brave to die.

Many Fair Gifts but without the Graces.

Torquato Tasso, II. 1. 197.

Doch — haben alle Götter sich versammelt,
Geschenke seiner Wiege darzubringen;
Die Grazien sind leider ausgeblieben,
Und wem die Gaben dieser Helden fehlen,
Der kann zwar viel besitzen, vieles geben,
Doch läßt sich nie an seinem Busen ruhn.

Alas! when all the gods assembled around his cradle to present
their gifts, the Graces were not there, and he to whom the favour
of these fair powers is wanting may indeed possess much and be
able to confer much, yet on his bosom we can never rest.

A Kind Purpose constrains us against our Will.

Torquato Tasso, II. 1. 216.

So liebenswürdig sie erscheinen kann,
Ich weiß nicht wie es ist, könnt' ich nur selten
Mit ihr ganz offen seyn, und wenn sie auch
Die Absicht hat, den Freunden wohlzuthun,
So fühlt man Absicht und man ist verstimmt.

Though she may appear so worthy of love, I know not how it is, I can rarely feel at ease in her presence; even when she has the intention to do a kind act to her friends, one feels her purpose and only those are constrained.

THE GOLDEN AGE.

Torquato Tasso, II. 1. 227.

Prinzeſſin.

Die goldne Zeit, die ihm von außen mangelt,
In ſeinem Innern wieder herzuſtellen,
So wenig der Verſuch gelingen will.

Taſſo.

O welches Wort ſpricht meine Fürſtin aus!
Die goldne Zeit, wohin iſt ſie geflohen?
Nach der ſich jedes Herz vergebens ſehnt!
Da auf der freien Erde Menſchen ſich
Wie frohe Heerden im Genuß verbreiteten;
Da ein uralter Baum auf bunter Wieſe
Dem Hirten und der Hirtin Schatten gab,
Ein jüngeres Gebüſch die zarten Zweige
Um ſehnſuchtsvolle Liebe traulich ſchlang;
Wo klar und ſtill auf immer reinem Sande
Der weiche Fluß die Nymphe ſanft umfing;
Wo in dem Graſe die geſcheuchte Schlange
Unſchädlich ſich verlor, der kühne Faun
Vom tapfern Jüngling bald beſtraft entfloh;
Wo jeder Vogel in der freien Luft,
Und jedes Thier, durch Berg und Thäler ſchweifend
Zum Menſchen ſprach: Erlaubt iſt was gefällt.

Prinzeſſin.

Mein Freund, die goldne Zeit iſt wohl vorbei:
Allein die Guten bringen ſie zurück;
Und ſoll ich dir geſtehen wie ich denke:
Die goldne Zeit, womit der Dichter uns
Zu ſchmeicheln pflegt, die ſchöne Zeit, ſie war,
So ſcheint es mir, ſo wenig als ſie iſt;

Und war sie je, so war sie nur gewiß
Wie sie uns immer wieder werden kann.
Noch treffen sich verwandte Herzen an
Und theilen den Genuß der schönen Welt:
Nur in dem Wahlspruch ändert sich, mein Freund,
Ein einzig Wort: Erlaubt ist was sich ziemt.

The Princess. The golden age, which exists no longer in the outward world, to restore within man's breast, is a vain attempt. *Tasso.* Oh, what a word my princess utters! The golden age,—ah! whither is it gone? Every heart in vain longs for it, then on the wide-extended earth men roamed, like joyous herds in silent delight; then an ancient tree gave its grateful shade on the flowery mead to the shepherd and shepherdess; a younger bush entwined lovingly its tender branches around confiding love, where clear and still, over sands for ever pure, the gentle brook encircled softly the nymph's fair form, where through the grass the scared serpent glided innoxious, and the daring fawn swiftly escaped from the bold youth; when every bird in the open vault of heaven and every living thing over hill and dale proclaimed to man, "What pleases, that is right." *Princess.* My friend, the golden age is indeed passed away; but the good can bring it back; and shall I tell you what I think?—The golden age, by which the bard is wont to charm us, that lovely age, was just as little then as it is now, and, did it ever exist, it was only as it might be now restored by ourselves. Congenial spirits still meet and enhance the enjoyment of this fair world; only in the motto change one single word, my friend, and say, "What is fitting, that is right."

See (Lat.) Golden age.

CONTRAST OF MEN AND WOMEN.

Torquato Tasso, II. 1. 276.

Nicht das! Allein ihr strebt nach fernen Gütern,
Und euer Streben muß gewaltsam seyn.
Ihr wagt es, für die Ewigkeit zu handeln,
Wenn wir ein einzig nah beschränktes Gut
Auf dieser Erde nur besitzen möchten,
Und wünschen, daß es uns beständig bleibe.
Wir sind von keinem Männerherzen sicher,
Das noch so warm sich einmal uns ergab.
Die Schönheit ist vergänglich, die ihr doch
Allein zu ehren scheint. Was übrig bleibt,
Das reizt nicht mehr, und was nicht reizt, ist todt.

Not so ! but ye (men) strive after distant objects, and that with violent efforts. Ye venture to act for eternity, while we (women) only seek one possession in narrow limits on this earth, and pray that it may be permanent. We are secure of no man's heart, however warm it may have been once towards us. Beauty is transient, which alone ye seem to honour. What remains no longer charms, and what does not charm is dead.

THE GREAT OF THIS EARTH.

Torquato Tasso, II. 1. 323.

So unterscheiden sich die Erdengötter
Vor andern Menschen, wie das hohe Schicksal
Vom Rath und Willen selbst der klügsten Männer
Sich unterscheidet. Vieles lassen sie,
Wenn wir gewaltsam Wog' auf Woge sehn,
Wie leichte Wellen, unbemerkt vorüber
Vor ihren Füßen rauschen, hören nicht
Den Sturm, der uns umsauf't und niederwirft,
Vernehmen unser Flehen kaum, und lassen,
Wie wir beschränkten armen Kindern thun,
Mit Seufzern und Geschrei die Luft uns füllen.

The gods of earth tower over other mortals, as supreme destiny rises above the counsel and will of the wisest men. When we see surge on surge roll on, they, like gentle billows, unheeded murmur at their feet ; the storm is unheard, which blusters and rushes around us ; they scarcely heed our prayers, and leave us, as we do helpless children, to fill the air with sighs and plaints.

VIRTUE AND LOVE CAN BE GAINED ONLY BY SELF-RESTRAINT.

Torquato Tasso, II. 1. 370.

Viele Dinge sind's,
Die wir mit Heftigkeit ergreifen sollen :
Doch andre können nur durch Mäßigung
Und durch Entbehren unser eigen werden.
So sagt man, sey die Tugend, sey die Liebe,
Die ihr verwandt ist. Das bedenke wohl !

There are many things that we may win with violence ; others can only become ours by moderation and self-restraint. So it is said is virtue, and love, which is allied to her. Think well of this !

Caution.

Torquato Tasso, II. 3. 14.

Wer wird die Klugheit tadeln? Jeder Schritt
Des Lebens zeigt, wie sehr sie nöthig sey;
Doch schöner ist's, wenn uns die Seele sagt,
Wo wir der feinen Vorsicht nicht bedürfen.

Who would find fault with caution? Every step of life shows
how much it is required ; yet nobler is it, if the soul tells us where
we may dispense with prudent foresight.

The Moderate.

Torquato Tasso, II. 3. 28.

Der Mäßige wird öfters kalt genannt
Von Menschen, die sich warm vor andern glauben,
Weil sie die Hitze fliegend überfällt.

The moderate is often called cold by men, who think themselves
more warm than other men, because a transient glow comes over
them.

Man's Inmost Nature.

Torquato Tasso, II. 3. 44.

Inwendig lernt kein Mensch sein Innerstes
Erkennen ; denn er mißt nach eignem Maaß
Sich bald zu klein und leider oft zu groß.
Der Mensch erkennt sich nur im Menschen, nur
Das Leben lehret jedem was er sey.

No man learns to know his inmost nature by introspection ; for
he rates himself sometimes too low, and often too high, by his own
measurement. Man knows himself only by comparing himself
with other men ; it is life that teaches him his genuine worth.

Love.

Torquato Tasso, II. 3. 76.

In Einem Augenblick gewährt die Liebe,
Was Mühe kaum in langer Zeit erreicht.

Love has power to give in a moment what toil can scarcely reach
in an age.

Good Will and Courage.

Torquato Tasso, II. 3. 101.

Der Wille lockt die Thaten nicht herbei;
Der Muth stellt sich die Wege kürzer vor,
Wer angelangt am Ziel ist, wird gekrönt,
Und oft entbehrt ein Würd'ger eine Krone.
Doch giebt es leichte Kränze, Kränze giebt es
Von sehr verschiedner Art; sie lassen sich
Oft im Spazierengehn bequem erreichen.

Good will does not always produce deeds; courage presents to itself the road shorter than it is; he who reaches the goal is crowned, and oft the most deserving is without a crown. Yet wreaths there are of very different kinds — light worthless wreaths; they are often easily reached in idly strolling.

Fortune.

Torquato Tasso, II. 3. 115.

Das Glück erhebe billig der Beglückte!

It is the fortunate that should extol fortune!

The Soul's Nobility.

Torquato Tasso, II. 3. 158.

Mich dünkt, hier ist die Hoheit erst an ihrem Platz,
Der Seele Hoheit! Darf sie sich der Nähe
Der Großen dieser Erde nicht erfreun?
Sie darf's und soll's. Wir nahen uns dem Fürsten
Durch Adel nur, der uns von Vätern kam;
Warum nicht durch's Gemüth, das die Natur
Nicht jedem groß verlieh, wie sie nicht jedem
Die Reihe großer Ahnherrn geben konnte.
Nur Kleinheit sollte hier sich ängstlich fühlen,
Der Neid, der sich zu seiner Schande zeigt:
Wie keiner Spinne schmutziges Gewebe
An diesen Marmorwänden haften soll.

Methinks here is nobility in its proper place, the soul's nobility! May she rejoice in the presence of this earth's great ones? We approach the prince only by nobility transmitted to us by our progenitors ; why should we not by genius, which Nature bestows only on few, as she gives not to every one a line of glorious ancestry ? Here littleness only should feel herself in a painful position, envy which shows itself to its shame, as the noisome web of no spider should attach itself to these marble walls.

So Thomson (*Coriolanus*, act iii. sc. 3) says —

> " Whoe'er amidst the sons
> Of reason, valour, liberty, and virtue,
> Displays distinguished merit, it is noble,
> Of nature's own creating."

See (Lat.) Genius the gift of Heaven.

CONTEMPT.

Torquato Tasso, II. 3. 191.

Kein Heiligthum heißt uns den Schimpf ertragen.

No sacred fane requires us to submit to contempt.

A GREAT SPIRIT IN A NARROW BREAST.

Torquato Tasso, II. 3. 199.

Welch hoher Geist in einer engen Brust!

What a mighty spirit in a narrow breast!

See (Lat.) Mighty souls.

THE RABBLE.

Torquato Tasso, II. 3. 201.

Es macht das Volk sich auch mit Worten Luft.

The rabble also vent their rage in words.

THE COWARD.

Torquato Tasso, II. 3. 207.

Der Feige droht nur, wo er sicher ist.

The coward only threatens when he is secure.

RASH YOUTH.

Torquato Tasso, II. 5. 3.

Beschränkt und unerfahren hält die Jugend

Sich für ein einzig auserwähltes Wesen,
Und Alles über Alle sich erlaubt.

Rash, inexperienced youth holds itself a chosen instrument, and allows itself unbounded license.

A GOD IN OUR BREAST.

Torquato Tasso, III. 2. 14.

Ach, daß wir doch dem reinen stillen Wink
Des Herzens nachzugehn, so sehr verlernen!
Ganz leise spricht ein Gott in unsrer Brust,
Ganz leise, ganz vernehmlich zeigt uns an,
Was zu ergreifen ist und was zu fliehn.

Alas, that we should be so unwilling to listen to the still and holy yearnings of the heart! A god whispers quite softly in our breast, softly yet audibly; tells us what we ought to seek and what to shun.

See (Lat.) God in our breast.

GRIEF.

Torquato Tasso, III. 2. 84.

Wer sich entschließen kann, besiegt den Schmerz.

He conquers grief who can take a firm resolution.

RENUNCIATION OF A JOY.

Torquato Tasso, III. 2. 124.

Nur halb ist der Verlust des schönsten Glücks,
Wenn wir auf den Besitz nicht sicher zählten.

The loss of a much-prized pleasure is only half felt when we have not regarded its tenure to be secure.

TO APPRECIATE THE NOBLE.

Torquato Tasso, III. 2. 185.

Das Edle zu erkennen ist Gewinnst,
Der nimmer uns entrissen werden kann.

To appreciate the noble is a gain which can never be torn from us.

THE EXCELLENT.

Torquato Tasso, III. 2. 188.

Zu fürchten ist das Schöne, das Fürtreffliche,
Wie eine Flamme, die so herrlich nützt,
So lange sie auf deinem Herde brennt,
So lang' sie dir von einer Fackel leuchtet,
Wie hold! wer mag, wer kann sie da entbehren?
Und frißt sie ungehütet um sich her,
Wie elend kann sie machen!

Thou hast to fear what is beautiful and excellent, like a flame
which aids thee nobly, so long as it blazes on thy hearth or gives
forth light from a torch. How lovely then! Who may or can be
without it? But if unheeded it spreads around, how miserable it
may make us!

THE SICKNESS OF THE HEART.

Torquato Tasso, III. 2. 197.

Die Krankheit des Gemüthes löset sich
In Klagen und Vertraun am leicht'sten auf.

The sickness of the heart is most easily got rid off by complaining and soothing confidence.

CHANGE.

Torquato Tasso, III. 2. 230.

Was ich besitze, mag ich gern bewahren:
Der Wechsel unterhält, doch nützt er kaum.

What I possess I would gladly retain; change amuses the mind,
yet scarcely profits.

THE PLEASURES OF THIS WORLD.

Torquato Tasso, III. 2. 249.

Wohl ist sie schön die Welt! In ihrer Weite
Bewegt sich so viel Gutes hin und her.
Ach, daß es immer nur um einen Schritt
Von uns sich zu entfernen scheint,
Und unsre bange Sehnsucht durch das Leben,
Auch Schritt vor Schritt, bis nach dem Grabe lockt!
So selten ist es, daß die Menschen finden,

Was ihnen doch bestimmt gewesen schien,
So selten, daß sie das erhalten, was
Auch einmal die beglückte Hand ergriff!
Es reißt sich los, was erst sich uns ergab,
Wir lassen los, was wir begierig faßten.
Es giebt ein Glück, allein wir kennen's nicht:
Wir kennen's wohl, und wissen's nicht zu schätzen.

Beauteous indeed is this world! In its wide domain many a joy floats around us. Alas! that they should appear ever only a step from us, and that our anxious yearning for them should allure us on through life, step by step, even to the grave. So seldom is it that men find what they think destined to them by Heaven; so seldom that they are able to retain what their hand had in an auspicious hour once grasped. What had come to them unsought tears itself away. We ourselves give up what we once seized with eagerness. There is a bliss, but we know it not; we know it indeed, but yet we prize it not.

The Poet.

Torquato Tasso, iii. 4. 58.

Denn ein Verdienst, das außerirdisch ist,
Das in den Lüften schwebt, in Tönen nur,
In leichten Bildern unsern Geist umgaukelt,
Es wird denn auch mit einem schönen Bilde,
Mit einem holden Zeichen nur belohnt;
Und wenn er selbst die Erde kaum berührt,
Berührt der höchste Lohn ihm kaum das Haupt.

For a service in itself divine, which floats in the air only in tuneful tones, charms us by evoking airy forms. Such service is only rewarded with some graceful form—with some sacred symbol; and if the bard scarcely touches the earth, the laurel, his highest reward, scarcely touches his brow.

Better to Hope than to Despair.

Torquato Tasso, iii. 4. 197.

Wir hoffen immer, und in allen Dingen
Ist besser hoffen als verzweifeln.

We always hope; and in all things it is better to hope than to despair.

Age.

Torquato Tasso, III. 4. 205.

Das Alter muß doch Einen Vorzug haben
Daß, wenn es auch dem Irrthum nicht entgeht,
Es doch sich auf der Stelle fassen kann.

Age must have this one advantage, that though it too is **not**
free from error, it yet can easily recover itself.

A Selfish Spirit.

Torquato Tasso, IV. 2. 79.

O glaube mir, ein selbstisches Gemüth
Kann nicht der Qual des engen Neids entfliehen.
Ein solcher Mann verzeiht dem andern wohl
Vermögen, Stand und Ehre; denn er denkt,
Das hast du selbst, das hast du wenn du willst,
Wenn du beharrst, wenn dich das Glück begünstigt.
Doch das, was die Natur allein verleiht,
Was jeglicher Bemühung, jedem Streben
Stets unerreichbar bleibt, was weder Gold,
Noch Schwert, noch Klugheit, noch Beharrlichkeit
Erzwingen kann, das wird er nie verzeihn.

Believe me, no selfish spirit can escape the torment of base
envy. Such a man pardons in others wealth, rank, and honour,
for he argues in this way : These thou hast thyself—these thou hast
if thou wilt—if thou persevere—if fortune favour thee. But that
which nature alone bestows—which always remains inaccessible
to every pain and effort—which can be procured neither by gold,
sword, forethought, nor perseverance, that he will never forgive.

An Absent Friend.

Torquato Tasso, IV. 2. 310.

Gar freundliche Gesellschaft leistet uns
Ein ferner Freund, wenn wir ihn glücklich wissen.

An absent friend gives us friendly company when we are well
assured of his happiness.

F

A Wounded Heart.

Torquato Tasso, IV. 4. 24.

Doch ein gekränktes Herz erholt sich schwer.

A wounded heart can with difficulty be cured.

"Make Hay while the Sun shines."

Torquato Tasso, IV. 4. 62.

Ein Tag der Gunst ist wie ein Tag der Ernte.
Man muß geschäftig seyn sobald sie reift.

The day of fortune is like a harvest-day, we must be busy when the corn is ripe.

Present Moments.

Torquato Tasso, IV. 4. 67.

Die Gegenwart ist eine mächt'ge Göttin.

The present moment is a powerful deity.

A Proof of True Friendship.

Torquato Tasso, IV. 4. 123.

Die wahre Freundschaft zeigt sich im Versagen
Zur rechten Zeit, und es gewährt die Liebe
Gar oft ein schädlich Gut, wenn sie den Willen
Des Fordernden mehr als sein Glück bedenkt.

True friendship shows itself by refusal at the right moment, and love often confers a baneful good when it consults the wish rather than the happiness of him that sues.

Disdaining the Voice of Poesy.

Torquato Tasso, V. 1. 19.

Und wer der Dichtkunst Stimme nicht vernimmt,
Ist ein Barbar, er sey auch wer er sey.

He who does not listen to the voice of poesy is a barbarian, be he who he may.

See (Lat.) Poet.

To Rule Oneself.

Torquato Tasso, V. 1. 46.

Wer seinen Geist so viel gebildet hat,
Wer jede Wissenschaft zusammengeizt,

Und jede Kenntniß, die uns zu ergreifen
Erlaubt ist, sollte der sich zu beherrschen
Nicht doppelt schuldig seyn? Und denkt er dran?

He who has formed his own mind so well—who has tried to
make every science and the whole range of human lore his own—
should he not be doubly bound to rule himself, and does he ever
think of it?

We are not allowed to enjoy Ourselves.

Torquato Tasso, v. 1. 51.

Wir sollen eben nicht in Ruhe bleiben!
Gleich wird uns, wenn wir zu genießen denken,
Zur Uebung unsrer Tapferkeit ein Feind,
Zur Uebung der Geduld ein Freund gegeben.

We cannot remain at rest! When we think of enjoying
ourselves a foe is sent us to try our valour, a friend to try our
patience.

An Intemperate Life.

Torquato Tasso, v. 1. 89.

Es ist gewiß, ein ungemäßigt Leben,
Wie es uns schwere, wilde Träume giebt,
Macht uns zuletzt am hellen Tage träumen.

It is certain that an intemperate life, as it produces wild
distempered dreams, makes us dream at last in open day.

Employ Men according to their peculiar Gifts.

Torquato Tasso, v. 1. 111.

Nicht alles dienet uns auf gleiche Weise;
Wer Vieles brauchen will, gebrauche Jedes
In seiner Art, so ist er wohl bedient.

All do not serve us in the self-same way; he who needs much
aid should use each according to his gift, and then he will be well
served.

The Toils of Life.

Torquato Tasso, v. 1. 119.

Wer weiß es nicht, mein Fürst? des Lebens Mühe
Lehrt uns allein des Lebens Güter schätzen.

Who knows not this, my prince?—The toils of life alone teach us to prize life's gifts.

See (Fr.) Labour, fruit of.

The Deepest Gulf in Ourselves.

Torquato Tasso, v. 2. 84.

Es liegt um uns herum
Gar mancher Abgrund, den das Schicksal grub;
Doch hier in unserm Herzen ist der tiefste,
Und reizend ist es sich hinab zu stürzen.

Around us many a gulf is yawning which has been dug by the hand of destiny ; yet here, in our own heart, is the deepest, and it is tempting to hurl oneself therein !

We deceive Ourselves willingly.

Torquato Tasso, v. 5. 51.

Allein wir selbst betrügen uns so gern,
Und ehren die Verworfnen, die uns ehren.
Die Menschen kennen sich einander nicht;
Nur die Galeerensklaven kennen sich,
Die eng' an Eine Bank geschmiedet keuchen;
Wo keiner was zu fordern hat und keiner
Was zu verlieren hat, die kennen sich;
Wo jeder sich für einen Schelmen giebt,
Und seines Gleichen auch für Schelmen nimmt.
Doch wir verkennen nur die Andern höflich,
Damit sie wieder uns verkennen sollen.

But we willingly deceive ourselves, and honour reprobates who honour us. Good men and true never know each other ; it is only galley-slaves that are blest with such knowledge, who, chained to a narrow plank, gasp for breath ; where none has aught to ask for, nor aught to lose—such know each other ; where every one avows himself a rascal, and holds his neighbour for a rascal too. But we courteously misjudge others in hopes that they will misjudge us in turn.

The Waves of the Sea.

Torquato Tasso, v. 5. 152.

Die mächtige Natur,
Die diesen Felsen gründete, hat auch

Der Welle die Beweglichkeit gegeben.
Sie sendet ihren Sturm, die Welle flieht
Und schwankt und schwillt und beugt sich schäumend über.
In dieser Woge spiegelte so schön
Die Sonne sich, es ruhten die Gestirne
An dieser Brust, die zärtlich sich bewegte.

All-mighty Nature, which has fixed these rocks, has also given its instability to the wave. She sends her storm ; the wave is driven, and rolls, and swells, and falls in billowy foam. On this very wave the sun mirrors his splendour ; the stars gently rest upon its bosom, which heaves softly.

Silence.

The Natural Daughter, i. 3. 34.

Es ist ein eigner, grillenhafter Zug,
Daß wir, durch Schweigen, das Geschehene,
Für uns und Andre, zu vernichten glauben.

It is a strange and fanciful idea to imagine that we may, by mere silence, destroy for ourselves and others what has actually happened.

Some Things not to be Spoken of.

The Natural Daughter, i. 3. 38.

Gar vieles kann, gar vieles muß geschehn,
Was man mit Worten nicht bekennen darf.

Very much can, much must happen, which we dare not acknowledge in words.

The Confusion of Different Classes of Society.

The Natural Daughter, i. 5. 119.

O diese Zeit hat fürchterliche Zeichen,
Das Niedre schwillt, das Hohe senkt sich nieder,
Als könnte Jeder nur am Platz des Andern
Befriedigung verworrner Wünsche finden,
Nur dann sich glücklich fühlen, wenn nichts mehr
Zu unterscheiden wäre, wenn wir alle,
Von einem Strom vermischt dahingerissen.

Oh, these times have fearful signs ! the low-born soar aloft, the noble sink below—as if each could only find contentment for his bewildered desires in the situation of another—could only then feel himself happy if there were no distinctive grades, if we all, mingled in one troubled stream, lost ourselves unperceived in the ocean.

A Purpose once made Known is no longer in thy Power.

The Natural Daughter, I. 5. 170.

Ein Vorſaß, mitgetheilt, iſt nicht mehr dein;
Der Zufall ſpielt mit deinem Willen ſchon;
Selbſt wer gebieten kann, muß überraſchen.

A resolution that is communicated is no longer within thy power ; thy intentions become now the plaything of chance ; he who would have his commands certainly carried out, must take man by surprise.

Man and Woman.

The Natural Daughter, I. 6. 92.

Der wichtigen Momente giebt's im Leben
Gar manche, die mit Freude, die mit Trauer
Des Menſchen Herz beſtürmen. Wenn der Mann
Sein Aeußeres, in ſolchem Fall, vergißt,
Nachläſſig oft ſich vor die Menge ſtellt,
So wünſcht ein Weib noch Jedem zu gefallen,
Durch ausgeſuchte Tracht, vollkommnen Schmuck,
Beneidenswerth vor andern zu erſcheinen.

Weighty moments there are in life, very many, that stir the depths of man's heart with joy and grief. If man on such occasions forgets his external appearance, and often presents himself to the world in careless guise, a woman wishes to please all, and by well-selected dress and gay attire, to excite the envy of her compeers.

Life.

The Natural Daughter, I. 6. 221

Das Leben iſt des Lebens Pfand; es ruht
Nur auf ſich ſelbſt und muß ſich ſelbſt verbürgen.

Life is the pledge of life ; it rests only on itself, and must give bail for its own existence.

SORROWS.

The Natural Daughter, II. 3. 17.

Ach! aus dem Glück entwickelt oft sich Schmerz.

Alas! sorrows are oft evolved from good fortune.

HAPPINESS.

The Natural Daughter, II. 5. 79.

Aus Mäßigkeit entspringt ein reines Glück.

Real and solid happiness springs from moderation.

So Pope (*Essay on Man*, Ep. iv. 1. 309)—

"Know then this truth (enough for man to know)—
'Virtue alone is happiness below.'"

See (Lat.) Happy man.

EXCESS OF SORROW.

The Natural Daughter, III. 1. 7.

Das Uebermaaß der Schmerzen löf'te sich
In der Natur balfam'schen Wohlthat auf.

Excess of sorrow is forgotten in sleep, that balmy blessing of nature.

So Shakespeare (*Macbeth*, act ii. sc. 1):—

"Methought I heard a voice cry, 'Sleep no more!
Macbeth does murder sleep!' the innocent sleep;
Sleep that knits up the ravelled sleave of care,
The death of each day's life, sore labour's bath,
Balm of hurt minds, great nature's second course,
Chief nourisher in life's feast."

THE MEMORY OF PAST SORROW.

Sorrows of Werther, 4th May.

Gewiß, du haft recht, Befter, der Schmerzen wären minder unter den Menschen, wenn fie nicht — Gott weiß, warum fie fo gemacht find! — mit fo viel Emfigkeit der Einbildungskraft fich beschäftigten, die Erinnerungen des vergangenen Uebels zurück zu rufen, eher als eine gleichgültige Gegenwart zu tragen.

My dear friend, thou art no doubt right, there would be far fewer sorrows among mankind, if men— God knows why they are so formed—made less use of their imaginations in recalling the memory of past sorrow than in bearing patiently their present lot.

MISUNDERSTANDINGS CAUSE MORE MISCHIEF THAN MALICE.

Sorrows of Werther, 4th May.

Und ich habe, mein Lieber, wieder bei diesem kleinen Geschäft gefunden, daß Mißverständnisse und Trägheit vielleicht mehr Irrungen in der Welt machen, als List und Bosheit. Wenigstens sind die beiden letzteren gewiß seltener.

My dear friend, I have again found in this trifling matter, that misunderstandings and neglect cause perhaps more mischief in the world than even malice and wickedness. At all events, the two latter more seldom occur.

PEOPLE OF PRETENCE.

Sorrows of Werther, 10th May.

Leute von einigem Stande werden sich immer in kalter Entfernung vom gemeinen Volke halten, als glaubten sie durch Annäherung zu verlieren; und dann giebt's Flüchtlinge und üble Spaßvögel, die sich herab zu lassen scheinen, um ihren Uebermuth dem armen Volke desto empfindlicher zu machen.

People of some position in the world keep themselves coldly aloof from the lower orders, as if they thought that they would lose their importance by a closer approach ; and then again there are silly idlers, and mere jesters, who seem to lower themselves to their level only to make poor people feel their impertinence more acutely.

ALL CANNOT BE EQUAL.

Sorrows of Werther, 10th May.

Ich weiß wohl, daß wir nicht gleich sind, noch seyn können; aber ich halte dafür, daß der, der nöthig zu haben glaubt, vom sogenannten Pöbel sich zu entfernen, um den Respect zu erhalten, eben so tadelhaft ist als ein Feiger, der sich vor seinem Feinde verbirgt, weil er zu unterliegen fürchtet.

I know very well that we are not all equal, nor can be so, but I maintain that he who thinks it necessary to keep aloof from the common people, that he may command respect, is as much to be blamed as a coward, who conceals himself from the enemy because he fears defeat.

The Human Race.

Sorrows of Werther, 17th May.

Es ist ein einförmiges Ding um das Menschengeschlecht. Die meisten verarbeiten den größten Theil der Zeit um zu leben und das Bißchen, das ihnen von Freiheit übrig bleibt, ängstigt.

The human race is a monotonous thing. The greater part labour the most of their time for mere subsistence, and the little remnant of time that is unemployed troubles them.

Nature and Rules.

Sorrows of Werther, 26th May.

Das bestärkte mich in meinem Vorsatze, mich künftig allein an die Natur zu halten. Sie allein ist unendlich reich, und sie allein bildet den großen Künstler. Man kann zum Vortheile der Regeln viel sagen, ungefähr was man zum Lobe der bürger= lichen Gesellschaft sagen kann. Ein Mensch, der sich nach ihnen bildet, wird nie etwas abgeschmacktes und schlechtes hervor= bringen, wie einer der sich durch Gesetze und Wohlstand modeln läßt, nie ein unerträglicher Nachbar, nie ein merkwürdiger Bösewicht werden kann; dagegen wird aber auch alle Regel, man rede was man wolle, das wahre Gefühl von Natur und den wahren Ausdruck derselben zerstören!

This strengthened me in my resolution to adhere for the future strictly to Nature. She alone is inexhaustibly rich, and can alone form the greatest masters. We may say much in favour of rules; as much too may be said in favour of the laws of society. A man who forms his taste upon them will never produce anything positively bad and disgusting, as a man who yields obedience to the laws and observes a becoming decorum will never be a thoroughly unbearable neighbour, nor a decided scoundrel; yet, say what you will of rules, they destroy the genuine feeling of nature, as well as its true expression.

Children.

Sorrows of Werther, 29th June.

Ja, lieber Wilhelm, meinem Herzen sind die Kinder am nächsten auf der Erde. Wenn ich ihnen zusehe, und in dem kleinen Dinge die Keime aller Tugenden, aller Kräfte sehe, die sie einmal so nöthig brauchen werden; wenn ich in dem Eigensinne künftige Standhaftigkeit und Festigkeit des Charakters, in dem Muthwillen guten Humor und Leichtigkeit, über die Gefahren der Welt hinzuschlüpfen, erblicke, alles so unverdorben, so ganz! — immer, immer wiederhole ich dann die goldenen Worte des Lehrers der Menschen: Wenn ihr nicht werdet wie eines von diesen! Und nun, mein Bester, sie, die unseres Gleichen sind, die wir als unsere Muster ansehen sollten, behandeln wir als Unterthanen. Sie sollen keinen Willen haben — Haben wir denn keinen? Und wo liegt das Vorrecht? — Weil wir älter sind und gescheidter! — Guter Gott von deinem Himmel! alte Kinder siehst du, und junge Kinder, und nichts weiter; und an welchen du mehr Freude hast, das hat dein Sohn schon lange verkündigt. Aber sie glauben an ihn, und hören ihn nicht, — das ist auch was altes — und bilden ihre Kinder nach sich.

Yes, my dear William, children are nearest my heart of anything on earth. When I look and observe in the little creatures the seeds of all those virtues and qualities which will hereafter be so necessary to them, when I mark in the self-willed all the future firmness and resolution of a noble character, in the petulant that good-humour and gaiety of temper, which will enable them to skim lightly over the dangers of life,—their whole nature simple and unpolluted!—then I call to mind the golden words of the Great Teacher of mankind, "If you become not like one of these." And now, my friend, these children, who are our equals, whom we ought to regard as ensamples, we treat as subjects. They are allowed no will of their own. And have we then none ourselves? And whence comes our exclusive privilege? Is it because we are older and more experienced? Good God! from thy heaven thou seest old children and young children, and no others; and in which thou hast most pleasure thy Son has long ago declared. But they believe in him. and hear him not—that also is an old story—and they bring up their children after their own image.

So Dryden (*All for Love*, prologue) says—

"Men are but children of a larger growth."

QUARRELLING.

Sorrows of Werther, 1st July.

Nun verdrießt mich nichts mehr, als wenn die Menschen einanber plagen, am meiften, wenn junge Leute in der Blüthe des Lebens, da fie am offenften für alle Freuden feyn könnten, einander die paar guten Tage mit Fraßen verderben, und nur erft zu fpät das Unerfeßliche ihrer Verfchwendung einfehen.

Nothing annoys me more than to see men torment each other, especially when young people, in the bloom of their age, at the time they are most alive to the pleasures of life, waste their few short days in quarrelling and disputes, only seeing their error when it is too late to repair it.

ILL-HUMOUR.

Sorrows of Werther, 1st July.

Oder, ift fie nicht vielmehr ein innerer Unmuth über unfere eigene Unwürdigkeit, ein Mißfallen an uns felbft, das immer mit einem Neide verknüpft ift, der durch eine thörichte Eitelfeit aufgeheßt wird?

Ill-humour is nothing more than an inward feeling of our own want of merit, a dissatisfaction with ourselves, which is always united with an envy that foolish vanity excites.

CHILDREN.

Sorrows of Werther, 6th July.

Wir follen es mit den Kindern machen, wie Gott mit uns, der uns am glücklichften macht, wenn er uns in freundlichem Wahne fo hintaumeln läßt.

We should treat children as God does us, who makes us happiest when he leaves us under the influence of innocent delusions.

THE FLOWERS OF LIFE.

Sorrows of Werther, 28th August.

Die Blüthen des Lebens find nur Erfcheinungen! Wie viele gehen vorüber, ohne eine Spur hinter fich zu laffen! wie wenige feßen Frucht an, und wie wenige diefer Früchte werden reif! Und doch find deren noch genug da; und doch — O mein Bruder! — können wir gereifte Früchte vernachläffigen, verachten, ungenoffen verfaulen laffen?

The flowers of life are only visionary! How many disappear

without leaving a trace behind them ! How few bear fruit, and when they do, how seldom does the fruit ripen ! And yet there are flowers enough ; and yet, my friend, how is it that we should allow the little that does ripen, to rot, decay, and perish unenjoyed?

APT TO COMPARE OURSELVES WITH OTHERS.

Sorrows of Werther, 20th October 1771.

Gewiß, weil wir doch einmal so gemacht sind, daß wir alles mit uns, und uns mit allem vergleichen, so liegt Glück oder Elend in den Gegenständen, womit wir uns zusammenhalten, und da ist nichts gefährlicher als die Einsamkeit. Unsere Ein= bildungskraft, durch ihre Natur gedrungen sich zu erheben, durch die phantastischen Bilder der Dichtkunst genährt, bildet sich eine Reihe Wesen hinauf, wo wir das unterste sind, und alles außer uns herrlicher erscheint, jeder andere vollkom= mener ist.

For nature has so constituted us, that we are always comparing ourselves with others, and making our happiness or misery depend on the objects that surround us. Therefore nothing is more dangerous than solitude ; then our imagination, impelled by nature to rise, and nourished by the wayward fancies of the poet, pictures to itself a chain of beings, of whom we are the lowest. All things appear more glorious than they really are, and all seem superior to us.

See (Lat.) Discontent of mankind.

WHO CAN ENDURE THE LAUGHTER OF FOOLS ?

Sorrows of Werther, 15th March.

Denn man rede von Selbstständigkeit, was man will, den will ich sehen, der dulden kann, daß Schurken über ihn reden, wenn sie einen Vortheil über ihn haben ; wenn ihr Geschwätze leer ist, ach, da kann man sie leicht lassen.

Say what you will of fortitude, will you point out to me the man who can submit with patience to the laughter of fools, when they have secured some advantage over him ? it is only when their silly talk is without foundation that we can easily endure it.

Goldsmith (*Deserted Village*, l. 121) says —

    " The watch-dog's voice that bayed the whispering wind,
      And the loud laugh that spoke the vacant mind."

WINE.

Goetz von Berlichingen, *Act* I. *p.* 11.

Der Wein erfreut des Menschen Herz, und die Freudigkeit ist die Mutter aller Tugenden. Wenn ihr Wein getrunken habt, seyd ihr alles doppelt was ihr seyn sollt, noch einmal so leicht denkend, noch einmal so unternehmend, noch einmal so schnell ausführend.

Wine rejoices the heart of man, and cheerfulness is the mother of every virtue. When thou hast drunk wine, thou art ever double what thou wouldst otherwise be—twice as full of ingenuity, twice as enterprising, twice as energetic.

See (Lat. Gr.) Wine.

A GOOD WIFE.

Goetz von Berlichingen, *Act* I. *p.* 14.

Wohl dem, der ein tugendsam Weib hat! deß lebt er noch eins so lange.

Happy the man who possesses a virtuous wife ; his life is doubled.

DEEP SHADES.

Goetz von Berlichingen, *Act* I. *p.* 24.

Wo viel Licht ist, ist starker Schatten.

Where there is much light, the shades are deepest.

EXPLANATIONS.

Goetz von Berlichingen, *Act* I. *p.* 28.

Ich bin ein Feind von Explicationen; man betrügt sich oder den Andern, und meist beide.

I am an enemy to long explanations ; they deceive either the maker or the hearer, generally both.

LAWS.

Goetz von Berlichingen, *Act* I. *p.* 31.

Der Menschen Leben ist kurz, und in Einer Generation kommen nicht alle Casus vor. Eine Sammlung solcher Fälle von vielen Jahrhunderten ist unser Gesetzbuch. Und dann ist der Wille und die Meinung der Menschen schwankend; dem däucht heute das recht, was der andere morgen mißbilliget; und so ist Verwirrung und Ungerechtigkeit unvermeidlich. Das alles bestimmen die Gesetze; und die Gesetze sind unveränderlich.

The life of man is short, and in one generation cases of every kind cannot occur. Our statute-book is made up of such cases gathered together during many centuries. But, then, the will and opinions of men vary ; to-day one man thinks right what to-morrow another thinks wrong, and thus confusion and injustice are unavoidable. Laws determine all such things absolutely, and laws are unchangeable.

The Independent Man.

Goetz von Berlichingen, Act i. *p.* **39.**

So gewiß ist der allein glücklich und groß, der weder zu herrschen noch zu gehorchen braucht, um Etwas zu seyn!

So certain is it that he alone is great and happy, who requires neither to command nor to obey, in order to secure his being of some importance in the world.

False Words.

Goetz von Berlichingen, Act ii. *p.* **53.**

Falsche Worte gelten zum höchsten, wenn sie Masken unsrer Thaten sind. Ein Vermummter, der kenntlich ist, spielt eine armselige Rolle.

False words are only of high value when they throw a veil over our actions. A discovered masquerader plays a pitiful part.

Women's Favour.

Goetz von Berlichingen, Act ii. *p.* **59.**

Das ist Weibergunst! Erst brütet sie, mit Mutterwärme, unsere liebsten Hoffnungen an; dann, gleich einer unbeständigen Henne, verläßt sie das Nest, und übergiebt ihre schon keimende Nachkommenschaft dem Tode und der Verwesung.

Such is the favour of women ! At first she fosters our dearest hopes with the affection of a mother ; then, like a giddy hen, she forsakes the nest, and gives over her still infant brood to death and disease.

THE MULTITUDE.

Goetz von Berlichingen, Act II. *p.* 60.

Die Menge schätzt nur den Widerschein des Verdienstes.

The multitude prize only the reflection of worth.

Roscommon (*Translated Verse*) says—

"The multitude is always in the wrong."

See (Lat. Gr. Fr.) Multitude.

FATE.

Goetz von Berlichingen, Act II. *p.* 62.

Ein Tag bringt den andern, und beim Schicksal steht das Zukünftige.

One day brings on another, and the future is dependent on fate.
See (Lat.) Future, man regardless of.

THE GREAT.

Egmont, Act I. *vol.* IX. *p.* 148.

O was sind wir Großen auf der Woge der Menschheit? Wir glauben sie zu beherrschen, und sie treibt uns auf und nieder, hin und her.

Oh, what are we great ones on the billows of life? We think to direct their course, and they drive us to and fro, hither and thither.

Rowe (*The Fair Penitent,* prologue) says—

"As if Misfortune made the throne her seat,
And none could be unhappy but the great."

THE MOB.

Egmont, Act II. *vol.* IX. *p.* 163.

Mir ist's bange, wenn's einmal unter dem Pack zu lärmen anfängt, unter dem Volk, das nichts zu verlieren hat. Die brauchen das zum Vorwande, worauf wir uns auch berufen müssen, und bringen das Land in Unglück.

I am always ill at ease when tumults arise among the mob—people who have nothing to lose. They use as a pretext that to which we also must appeal, and bring misery on the land.

To Live Merely for Life.

Egmont, Act II. *vol.* IX. *p.* 175.

Leb' ich nur um auf's Leben zu denken? Soll ich den gegenwärtigen Augenblick nicht genießen, damit ich des folgenden
gewiß sey? Und diesen wieder mit Sorgen und Grillen verzehren.

Do I live only to think of life? Shall I not enjoy the present
moment that I may be secure of the next? And must that, in its
turn, be wasted in anxieties and idle fears?

This is what Juvenal (*Sat.* viii. 84) says—

" Et propter vitam vivendi perdere causas."

The Sun-Steeds of Time.

Egmont, Act II. *vol.* IX. *p.* 177.

Wie von unsichtbaren Geistern gepeitscht, gehen die Sonnen-
pferde der Zeit mit unsers Schicksals leichtem Wagen durch;
und uns bleibt nichts als, muthig gefaßt, die Zügel festzuhalten,
und bald rechts bald links vom Steine hier, vom Sturze da,
die Räder wegzulenken. Wohin es geht, wer weiß es? Erinnert
er sich doch kaum, woher er kam.

As if spurred on by invisible spirits, the sun-steeds of time
hurry forward the light car of our destiny, and nothing remains to
us but with steady self-command to seize firmly the reins, and
now right, now left, to guide the wheels here from the rock,
there from the precipice. Whither he is hastening, who knows?
Whence he came, does any one consider?

Shakespeare (*Twelfth Night*, act v. sc. 1) says—

"Thus the whirligig of time brings in his revenges."

Imminent Danger.

Egmont, Act II. *vol.* IX. *p.* 184.

Bei so großer Gefahr kommt die leichteste Hoffnung in
Anschlag.

In imminent danger the faintest hope should be taken into
account.

A Dethroned King.

Egmont, Act III. *vol.* IX. *p.* 189.

Wer zu herrschen gewohnt ist, wer's hergebracht hat, daß jeden Tag das Schicksal von Tausenden in seiner Hand liegt, steigt vom Throne wie in's Grab. Aber besser so, als einem Gespenste gleich unter den Lebenden bleiben, und mit hohlem Ansehn einen Platz behaupten wollen, den ihm ein anderer abgeerbt hat, und nun besitzt und genießt.

He who is accustomed to rule, who has held daily the fate of thousands in his hands, descends from a throne as into a grave. But this is better than to linger a spectre among the living, and with hollow aspect try to maintain a position which another has inherited, and now possesses and enjoys.

See (Fr.) King, dethroned ; (Lat.) Slavery.

Children live only in the Present.

Egmont, Act III. *vol.* IX. *p.* 190.

Ihr Kinder seht nichts voraus, und überhorcht unsre Erfahrungen. Die Jugend und die schöne Liebe, alles hat sein Ende ; und es kommt eine Zeit, wo man Gott dankt wenn man irgendwo unterkriechen kann.

You children do not look before you, and give no ear to our experience. Youth and happy love all come to an end ; and there comes a time, when one thanks God, if one can find a corner anywhere to creep into.

The Rogue has everywhere the Advantage.

Egmont, Act IV. *vol.* IX. *p.* 200.

Der Schelm sitzt überall im Vortheil! Auf dem Armensünder-Stühlchen hat er den Richter zum Narren; auf dem Richterstuhl macht er den Inquisiten mit Lust zum Verbrecher.

The rogue has everywhere the advantage. In the dock he makes a fool of the judge ; on the bench he takes pleasure in convicting the accused.

Liberty.

Egmont, Act IV. *vol.* IX. *p.* 213.

Freiheit? Ein schönes Wort, wer's recht verstände. Was

n ollen Sie für Freiheit? Was ist des Freiesten Freiheit? —
Recht zu thun! — Und daran wird sie der König nicht hindern.
Nein! nein! sie glauben sich nicht frei, wenn sie sich nicht
selbst und andern schaden können.   Wäre es nicht besser abzu=
danken, als ein solches Volk zu regieren? Wenn auswärtige
Feinde drängen, an die kein Bürger denkt, der mit dem Nächsten
nur beschäftigt ist, und der König verlangt Beistand; dann
werden sie uneins unter sich, und verschwören sich gleichsam
mit ihren Feinden.   Weit besser ist's sie einzuengen, daß man
sie wie Kinder halten, wie Kinder zu ihrem Besten leiten kann.
Glaube nur, ein Volk wird nicht alt, nicht klug; ein Volk
bleibt immer kindisch.

Freedom? A fine word when rightly understood. What freedom would they have? What is the freedom of the most free?
To act rightly! And in that the king will not hinder them. No,
no! they think not themselves free, unless they have the power
to injure themselves and others. And is it not better to abdicate
than rule such a people? When foreign foes threaten the country,
the citizens, busy with their own private affairs, think nothing of
that, and when the king requires assistance, they are quarrelling
among themselves, and thus may be said to be conspiring with the
enemy. Far better is it to circumscribe their power, to treat them
as children, and guide them for their good. Trust me, a people
grows neither old nor wise ; a people remains always in its infancy.

THE WIDE OPEN COUNTRY MAN'S NATURAL ELEMENT.

Egmont, Act v. vol. ix. p. 224.

Unleidlich ward mir's schon auf meinem gepolsterten Stuhle,
wenn in stattlicher Versammlung die Fürsten, was leicht zu
entscheiden war, mit wiederkehrenden Gesprächen überlegten,
und zwischen düstern Wänden eines Saals die Balken der Decke
mich erdrückten.   Da eilt' ich fort, sobald es möglich war, und
rasch auf's Pferd mit tiefem Athemzuge.   Und frisch hinaus, da,
wo wir hingehören! in's Feld, wo aus der Erde dampfend jede
nächste Wohlthat der Natur, und durch die Himmel wehend,
alle Segen der Gestirne uns umwittern; wo wir, dem erd=
gebornen Riesen gleich, von der Berührung unsrer Mutter
kräftiger uns in die Höhe reißen; wo wir die Menschheit ganz,
und menschliche Begier in allen Adern fühlen; wo das Ver=

langen vorzudringen, zu besiegen, zu erhaschen, seine Faust zu brauchen, zu besitzen, zu erobern, durch die Seele des jungen Jägers glüht; wo der Soldat sein angebornes Recht auf alle Welt mit raschem Schritt sich anmaßt, und in fürchterlicher Freiheit wie ein Hagelwetter durch Wiese, Feld und Wald verderbend streicht, und keine Gränzen kennt, die Menschen= hand gezogen.

It used to be intolerable to me, when on my cushioned seat, in the solemn assembly of princes, some trivial matter had to be decided, that I found it overlaid with endless discussions ; the very rafters of the ceiling within the gloomy walls seemed as if they would choke me. Then I hurried forth, as quickly as possible, flinging myself upon my horse with deep-drawn breath. And then away to our natural element—the fresh fields, where, exhaling from the earth, all the richest treasures of nature are sent forth, and the stars shedding their blessings twinkle around us through the vault of heaven ; where we, like to earth-born giants, rise stronger from our mother's touch ; where we feel the energies of our manhood throb in every vein ; where the desire to overtake, to conquer, to capture, to use all his powers, glows through the soul of the young hunter ; where the warrior, with rapid stride, assumes to himself his inborn right to rule the world, and with terror-bringing license, sweeps like a desolating hailstorm over field and grove, careless of boundaries traced by the hand of man.

LIFE.

Egmont, Act v. *vol.* IX. *p.* 239.

Süßes Leben! schöne freundliche Gewohnheit des Daseyns und Wirkens! von dir soll ich scheiden!

Sweet life! thou fair familiar organisation of being and of activity ! must I part from thee?

THE DEAD STILL LIVE FOR US.

Egmont, Act v. *vol.* IX. *p.* 239.

Die Menschen sind nicht nur zusammen, wenn sie beisammen sind; auch der Entfernte, der Abgeschiedene lebt uns.

Men are not together only when they are with each other ; the distant, the departed, also live for us.

See (Lat.) Dead, life of the.

Man controlled by Destiny.

Egmont, Act v. vol. IX. *p.* 240.

Es glaubt der Mensch sein Leben zu leiten, sich selbst zu führen; und sein Innerstes wird unwiderstehlich nach seinem Schicksale gezogen.

Man supposes that he directs his life and governs his actions, when his existence is irretrievably under the control of destiny.

A Stupid Act.

Clavigo, Act III. *vol.* IX. *p.* 272.

Da macht wieder jemand einmal einen dummen Streich.

There some one for once does a silly act.

Passions.

Clavigo, Act IV. *vol.* IX. *p.* 277

Sind unsere Leidenschaften, mit denen wir in ewigem Streit leben, nicht schrecklicher, unbezwinglicher, als jene Wellen, die den Unglücklichen fern von seinem Vaterlande verschlagen!

Are not our passions, with which we are ever struggling, more fearful and invincible than those waves which drive the unfortunate far from their fatherland?

See (Fr.) Passions.

The Joys of the World.

Clavigo, Act IV. *vol.* IX. *p.* 278.

Nein, meine Liebe, glauben Sie, die besten Freuden der Welt sind nicht ganz rein; die höchste Wonne wird auch durch unsere Leidenschaften, durch das Schicksal unterbrochen.

No, my dear, trust me, the most fascinating pleasures of this world are not quite pure; the highest joys are destroyed by our passions and by destiny.

An Irresolute Man.

Clavigo, Act v. *vol.* IX. *p.* 289.

Es ist nichts erbärmlicher in der Welt, als ein unentschlossener Mensch, der zwischen zweien Empfindungen schwebt, gern beide vereinigen möchte, und nicht begreift, daß nichts sie vereinigen kann, als eben der Zweifel, die Unruhe, die ihn peinigen.

There is nothing more pitiable in the world than an irresolute man, oscillating between two feelings, who would willingly unite the two, and who does not perceive that nothing can unite them.

ONLY PLEASURES OF RARE OCCURRENCE ARE OF VALUE.

Wilhelm Meister, I. c. 4.

Er behauptete, nur ein seltenes Vergnügen könne bei den Menschen einen Werth haben, Kinder und Alte wüßten nicht zu schätzen, was ihnen Gutes täglich begegnete.

He used to maintain that none but pleasures of rare occurrence were really prized by men, that neither young nor old could set a due value on blessings which they tasted every day.

TO TURN THE FOLLY OF OTHERS TO OUR OWN ADVANTAGE.

Wilhelm Meister, I. c. 10.

Ich finde nichts vernünftiger in der Welt, als von den Thorheiten Anderer Vortheil zu ziehen.

Ich weiß nicht, ob es nicht ein edleres Vergnügen wäre, die Menschen von ihren Thorheiten zu heilen.

I know of nothing in the world more sensible than to turn the folly of others to our own advantage. I know not whether it is not a nobler pleasure to cure men of their follies.

THE WEB OF LIFE WOVEN OF NECESSITY AND CHANCE.

Wilhelm Meister, I. c. 17.

Das Gewebe dieser Welt ist aus Nothwendigkeit und Zufall gebildet; die Vernunft des Menschen stellt sich zwischen beide, und weiß sie zu beherrschen; sie behandelt das Nothwendige als den Grund ihres Daseyns; das Zufällige weiß sie zu lenken, zu leiten und zu nutzen, und nur, indem sie fest unerschütterlich steht, verdient der Mensch ein Gott der Erde genannt zu werden. Wehe dem, der sich von Jugend auf gewöhnt, in dem Nothwendigen etwas Willkürliches finden zu wollen, der dem Zufälligen eine Art von Vernunft zuschreiben möchte, welcher zu folgen sogar eine Religion sey. Heißt das etwas weiter, als seinem eignen Verstande entsagen und seinen Neigungen unbedingten Raum geben? Wir bilden uns ein, fromm zu seyn, indem wir ohne Ueberlegung hinschlendern, uns durch angenehme Zufälle determiniren lassen, und endlich dem Resultate eines solchen schwankenden Lebens den Namen einer göttlichen Führung geben.

The web of life is woven of necessity and chance ; reason stands between them, and knows how to rule them both, treating necessity as the groundwork of its being, and at the same time guiding and directing the operations of chance for its own purposes ; and only while this principle of reason stands steady and immovable, does man deserve to be called the god of this lower world. Woe, then, to him who has been accustomed from his youth to find in necessity something of arbitrary will, and to ascribe to chance a kind of reason which it seems a kind of religious duty to obey. What can we call this but a renouncing of our own understanding, and allowing unopposed sway to our own inclinations? We imagine that it is a kind of religious worship to move along without reflection, to let accidental circumstances that please us determine our conduct, and finally to bestow on the result of such a fluctuating life the appellation of providential guidance.

The Distance between Man's Wishes and Powers.

Wilhelm Meister, ii. c. 2.

Glücklich, wer den Fehlschuß von seinen Wünschen auf seine Kräfte bald gewahr wird !

Happy the man who early learns the wide chasm that lies between his wishes and his powers !

Mean and Pitiable Companions in Early Youth.

Wilhelm Meister, ii. c. 9.

Wer früh in schlechter unbedeutender Gesellschaft gelebt hat, wird sich, wenn er auch später eine bessere haben kann, immer nach jener zurücksehnen, deren Eindruck ihm, zugleich mit der Erinnerung jugendlicher, nur selten zu wiederholender Freuden, geblieben ist.

Whoever has spent his early years among low and mean companions, though he may at a later period have better society at his command, will ever look back with longing towards that which he enjoyed of old, which has left an impression on his mind, blended with the memory of his youthful joys, that can never reappear.

The Sad Fate of Man.
Wilhelm Meister, II. *c.* 13.

Wer nie fein Brod mit Thränen aß
Wer nie die kummervollen Nächte
Auf feinem Bette weinend faß,
Der kennt euch nicht, ihr himmlifchen Mächte.

> Who never ate his bread in sorrow,
> Who never spent the darksome hours
> Weeping and watching for the morrow,
> He knows ye not, ye gloomy Powers.

The Land where the Lemon-Trees Bloom.
Wilhelm Meister, III. *c.* 1.

Kennft du das Land, wo die Citronen blühn,
Im dunkeln Laub die Gold-Orangen glühn,
Ein fanfter Wind vom blauen Himmel weht,
Die Myrte ftill und hoch der Lorbeer fteht,
Kennft du es wohl?
Dahin! Dahin!
Möcht' ich mit dir, o mein Geliebter, ziehn.

> Know'st thou the land where the lemon-trees bloom?
> Where the gold-orange glows in the deep thicket's gloom
> Where a wind ever soft from the blue heaven blows,
> And the groves are of laurel, and myrtle, and rose?
> Know'st thou it?
> Thither, O thither,
> My dearest and kindest, with thee would I go!

The Development of our Powers.
Wilhelm Meister, III. *c.* 8.

Der Menfch kommt manchmal, indem er fich einer Entwicklung feiner Kräfte, Fähigkeiten und Begriffe nähert, in
eine Verlegenheit, aus der ihm ein guter Freund leicht helfen
könnte. Er gleicht einem Wanderer, der nicht weit von der

Herberge in's Waffer fällt; griffe jemand sogleich zu, riffe ihn an's Land, so wäre es um einmal naß werden gethan, anstatt daß er sich auch wohl selbst, aber am jenseitigen Ufer, heraus= hilft, und einen beschwerlichen weiten Umweg nach seinem be= stimmten Ziele zu machen hat.

It often happens to a man, when some development of his powers, capacities, and ideas is approaching, that he gets into a difficulty, from which a wise friend might easily deliver him. He is like a traveller who falls into the water at but a short dis- tance from the inn at which he means to rest; were any one to seize him then, and pull him to land, all is right, perhaps with a good wetting; but if, on the other hand, he struggles out him- self, it is often on the wrong side of the river, and he has then to make a wide and weary circuit to reach his intended destination.

BIRTH, RANK, AND FORTUNE CONSISTENT WITH GENIUS.
Wilhelm Meister, III. 9.

Geburt, Stand und Vermögen stehen in keinem Wider= spruch mit Genie und Geschmack, das haben uns fremde Nationen gelehrt, welche unter ihren besten Köpfen eine große Anzahl Edelleute zählen.

Birth, rank, and fortune are in no way incompatible with genius and taste, as foreign nations have taught us, having many noble- men on the list of their most distinguished authors.

SELF-ACCUSATIONS.
Wilhelm Meister, III. 10.

Er hatte zu wenig Kenntniß der Welt, um zu wissen, daß eben ganz leichtsinnige und der Befferung unfähige Menschen sich oft am lebhaftesten anklagen, ihre Fehler mit großer Frei= müthigkeit bekennen und bereuen, ob sie gleich nicht die mindeste Kraft in sich haben, von dem Wege zurück zu treten, auf den eine übermächtige Natur sie hinreißt.

He had too little knowledge of the world to perceive that per- sons of frivolous character, and little capable of improvement, often accuse themselves in the bitterest terms, acknowledging and deploring their failings with extreme candour, even when they are wholly destitute of strength of mind to turn back from the road along which the irresistible tendency of their nature is dragging them.

SHAKESPEARE.
Wilhelm Meister, III. 11.

Sie scheinen ein Werk eines himmlischen Genius zu seyn, der sich den Menschen nähert, um sie mit sich selbst auf die gelindeste Weise bekannt zu machen. Es sind keine Gedichte! Man glaubt vor den aufgeschlagenen, ungeheuren Büchern des Schicksals zu stehen, in denen der Sturmwind des bewegtesten Lebens saus't, und sie mit Gewalt rasch hin und wieder blättert.

They seem to be the productions of some heavenly genius, descending among men, to make them in the gentlest way acquainted with themselves. They are no mere poems! You would think that you were standing before the opened awful books of Fate, through which the whirlwind of most impassioned life was howling and tossing them fiercely to and fro.

MAN CAN ALWAYS PROCURE A SUBSISTENCE.
Wilhelm Meister, IV. 2.

Ich habe gesehen, so lange einer lebt und sich rührt, findet er immer seine Nahrung, und wenn sie auch gleich nicht die reichlichste ist. Und worüber habt ihr euch denn zu beschweren?

I have observed that as long as one lives and bestirs himself, he can always find food and raiment, though it may not be of the choicest description.

BLOCKHEADS ALONE INCAPABLE OF IMPROVEMENT.
Wilhelm Meister, IV. 19.

Stöcke allein sind die Unverbesserlichen, sie mögen nun aus Eigendünkel, Dummheit oder Hypochondrie ungelenk und unbiegsam seyn.

Blockheads alone are incapable of improvement, whether it be self-conceit, stupidity, or hypochondria, that makes them stiff and unguidable.

See (Fr.) Fool.

MAN WITH HIS HOPES REALISED.
Wilhelm Meister, IV. 19.

Der Mensch scheint mit nichts vertrauter zu seyn als mit seinen Hoffnungen und Wünschen, die er lange im Herzen nährt und bewahrt, und doch, wenn sie ihm nun begegnen, wenn sie sich ihm gleichsam aufdringen, erkennt er sie nicht und weicht vor ihnen zurück.

Man seems to be so well acquainted with nothing as with his own hopes and wishes, which he has long nourished and kept in his heart; yet when they meet us, when they, as it were, press forward to us -- then we recognise them not and recoil from them.

Neglect of our Relatives and Friends.

Wilhelm Meister, v. 1.

Er fühlte tief, wie unempfindlich man oft Freunde und Verwandte, so lange sie sich mit uns des irdischen Aufenthaltes erfreuen, vernachläßigt, und nur dann erst die Versäumniß bereut, wenn das schöne Verhältniß, wenigstens für dießmal, aufgehoben ist.

He deeply felt how negligent and careless we often are of our friends and relations, so long as they enjoy with us this earthly abode. and how we only then repent of our insensibility, when the pleasant union, at least on this side of time, has been severed.

A Change of Fortune without a Change of Feelings.

Wilhelm Meister, v. 1.

Der Mensch kann in keine gefährlichere Lage versetzt werden, als wenn durch äußere Umstände eine große Veränderung seines Zustandes bewirkt wird, ohne daß seine Art zu empfinden und zu denken darauf vorbereitet ist. Es giebt alsdann eine Epoche ohne Epoche, und es entsteht nur ein desto größerer Widerspruch, je weniger der Mensch bemerkt, daß er zu dem neuen Zustande noch nicht ausgebildet sey.

A man can scarcely be put in a more embarrassing position, than when a great change in his external circumstances takes place, while his thoughts and feelings have undergone no preparation for it. There is then an epoch without an epoch, and there arises only a greater contradiction, the less he feels that he has not been trained for this new mode of existence.

The Art of Reading.

Wilhelm Meister, v. 7.

Wie man von jedem Musicus verlange, daß er, bis auf einen

gewiſſen Grad, vom Blatte ſpielen könne, ſo ſolle auch jeder
Schauſpieler, ja jeder wohlerzogene Menſch, ſich üben, vom
Blatte zu leſen, einem Drama, einem Gedicht, einer Erzählung
ſogleich ihren Charakter abzugewinnen, um ſie mit Fertigkeit
vorzutragen. Alles Memoriren helfe nichts, wenn der Schauſpieler nicht vorher in den Geiſt und Sinn des guten Schrift-
ſtellers eingedrungen ſey; der Buchſtabe könne nichts wirken.

As you require of every musical performer that he should, to
some extent, be able to play at sight, so should every actor, nay,
every educated man, train himself to read from the book, catching
at once the spirit of any drama, poem, or tale, and exhibiting it
with grace and readiness. It will serve no good purpose to learn
a piece by heart, if the actor has not first penetrated into the spirit
and meaning of his author ; the mere letter will avail him nothing.

No Enjoyment is Transitory.
Wilhelm Meister, v. 10.

Aber kein Genuß iſt vorübergehend : denn der Eindruck, den
er zurückläßt, iſt bleibend, und was man mit Fleiß und Anſtren-
gung thut, theilt dem Zuſchauer ſelbſt eine verborgene Kraft
mit, von der man nicht wiſſen kann, wie weit ſie wirkt.

But no enjoyment is transitory ; the impression which it leaves
is lasting, and what is done with diligence and toil imparts to the
spectator a secret force, of which one cannot say how far the effect
may reach.

Wife a Gift from Heaven.
Wilhelm Meister, v. 10.

Wie das Weib dem Mann gegeben,
Als die ſchönſte Hälfte war,
Iſt die Nacht das halbe Leben,
Und die ſchönſte Hälfte zwar.

As his wife has been given to man as his best half, so night is
the half of life, and by far the better part of life.

United Exertions of Men and Circumstances.
Wilhelm Meister, v. 16.

Ueberhaupt iſt es leider der Fall, daß alles, was durch
mehrere zuſammentreffende Menſchen und Umſtände hervor-

gebracht werden soll, keine lange Zeit sich vollkommen erhalten kann. Von einer Theatergesellschaft, so gut wie von einem Reiche, von einem Cirkel Freunde, so gut wie von einer Armee, läßt sich gewöhnlich der Moment angeben, wenn sie auf der höchsten Stufe ihrer Vollkommenheit, ihrer Uebereinstimmung, ihrer Zufriedenheit und Thätigkeit standen; oft aber verändert sich schnell das Personal, neue Glieder treten hinzu, die Personen passen nicht mehr zu den Umständen, die Umstände nicht mehr zu den Personen; es wird alles anders, und was vorher ver= bunden war, fällt nunmehr bald auseinander.

In all circumstances it is unhappily the case that whatever is to be brought about by numerous co-operating exertions of men and circumstances cannot long continue perfect. This observation is applicable quite as much to a theatre as to a kingdom, to a circle of friends as to an army, that there is generally a precise moment, when it may be said that everything was standing on the highest pinnacle of perfection, harmony, contentment, and activity; but ere long, individuals change, new persons appear upon the stage, they are no longer suited to the circumstances, or the circum-stances to the persons; a general alteration takes place, and what was formerly united, quickly falls asunder.

How the Public act towards Men of Talent.

Wilhelm Meister, v. 16.

Das Publicum hat eine eigene Art, gegen öffentliche Men= schen von anerkanntem Verdienste zu verfahren; es fängt nach und nach an gleichgültig gegen sie zu werden, und begünstigt viel geringere aber neu erscheinende Talente; es macht an jene übertriebene Forderungen, und läßt sich von diesen alles gefallen.

The public has a peculiar mode of acting towards men of acknow-ledged merit; it begins by degrees to be indifferent towards them, and to favour talents which are new, though far inferior; it makes excessive demands of the former, and is satisfied with almost any thing from the latter.

Affecting Singularity.

Wilhelm Meister, v. 16.

Denn es bringt uns nichts näher dem Wahnsinn, als wenn

wir uns vor andern auszeichnen, und nichts erhält so sehr den gemeinen Verstand, als im allgemeinen Sinne mit vielen Menschen zu leben.

For nothing more exposes us to madness than affecting to make ourselves different from others, and nothing assists more to maintain our common sense than a life spent in the common way amidst general society.

MERE JUDGMENT REQUIRED FOR A UNIFORM KIND OF LIFE.

Wilhelm Meister, VII. 3.

Zu einer gewissen, gleichen, fortdauernden Gegenwart brauchen wir nur Verstand, und wir werden auch nur zu Verstand, so daß wir das Außerordentliche, was jeder gleichgültige Tag von uns fordert, nicht mehr sehen, und wenn wir es erkennen, doch tausend Entschuldigungen finden, es nicht zu thun. Ein verständiger Mensch ist viel für sich, aber für's Ganze ist er wenig.

For a certain equable and continuous mode of life, we require only judgment and we think of nothing more, so that we no longer discern what extraordinary things each unimportant day requires of us, and if we do discern them, we can find a thousand excuses for not doing them. A man of understanding is of importance to his own interests, but of little value for the general whole.

WE ARE SOON FORGOTTEN.

Wilhelm Meister, VII. 8.

Man kann die Erfahrung nicht früh genug machen, wie entbehrlich man in der Welt ist. Welche wichtige Personen glauben wir zu seyn! Wir denken allein den Kreis zu beleben, in welchem wir wirken; in unserer Abwesenheit muß, bilden wir uns ein, Leben, Nahrung und Athem stocken, und die Lücke, die entsteht, wird kaum bemerkt, sie füllt sich so geschwind wieder aus, ja sie wird oft nur der Platz, wo nicht für etwas besseres, doch für etwas angenehmeres.

We cannot too soon convince ourselves how easily we may be dispensed with in the world. What important personages we imagine ourselves to be! We think that we alone are the life of the circle in which we move; in our absence we fancy that life, existence, and breath will come to a general pause; and **alas!** the gap which we leave is scarcely perceptible, so quickly is it filled again; nay, it is often but the place, if not for something better, at least for something more agreeable.

ART IS LONG, LIFE IS SHORT.
Wilhelm Meister, VII. 9.

Die Kunst ist lang, das Leben kurz, das Urtheil schwierig, die Gelegenheit flüchtig. Handeln ist leicht, Denken schwer; nach dem Gedachten handeln, unbequem. Aller Anfang ist heiter, die Schwelle ist der Platz der Erwartung. Der Knabe staunt, der Eindruck bestimmt ihn, er lernt spielend, der Ernst überrascht ihn. Die Nachahmung ist uns angeboren, das Nachzuahmende wird nicht leicht erkannt. Selten wird das Treffliche gefunden, seltner geschätzt. Die Höhe reizt uns, nicht die Stufen; den Gipfel im Auge wandeln wir gern auf der Ebene. Nur ein Theil der Kunst kann gelehrt werden, der Künstler braucht sie ganz. Wer sie halb kennt, ist immer irre und redet viel; wer sie ganz besitzt, mag nur thun und redet selten oder spät. Jene haben keine Geheimnisse und keine Kraft, ihre Lehre ist wie gebackenes Brod, schmackhaft und sättigend für Einen Tag; aber Mehl kann man nicht säen, und die Saatfrüchte sollen nicht vermahlen werden. Die Worte sind gut, sie sind aber nicht das Beste. Das Beste wird nicht deutlich durch Worte. Der Geist, aus dem wir handeln, ist das Höchste. Die Handlung wird nur vom Geiste begriffen und wieder dargestellt. Niemand weiß, was er thut, wenn er recht handelt; aber des Unrechten sind wir uns immer bewußt. Wer bloß mit Zeichen wirft, ist ein Pedant, ein Heuchler oder ein Pfuscher. Es sind ihrer viel, und es wird ihnen wohl zusammen. Ihr Geschwätz hält den Schüler zurück, und ihre beharrliche Mittelmäßigkeit ängstigt die Besten. Des ächten Künstlers Lehre schließt den Sinn auf; denn wo die Worte fehlen, spricht die That. Der ächte Schüler lernt aus dem Bekannten das Unbekannte entwickeln, und nähert sich dem Meister.

Art is long, life short, judgment difficult, opportunity fleeting. To act is easy, to think is difficult; to act according to our thoughts is troublesome. Every beginning is agreeable; the threshold is the place of expectation. The boy is astonished, his impressions guide him, he learns as he plays, earnestness comes on him by surprise. Imitation is born with us, but what we ought to imitate is not easily discovered. The excellent is seldom found, more seldom prized.

The summit charms us, the steps to it do not : with the heights before our eyes, we like to linger in the plain. It is only a part of art that can be taught ; but the artist needs the whole. He who is only half instructed speaks much and is always wrong ; who knows it wholly is content with acting and speaks seldom or late. The former has no secrets and no force : his teaching is like baked bread, savoury and satisfying for a single day, but flour cannot be sown, and seed-corn ought to be ground. Words are good, but there is something better. The best is not to be explained by words. The spirit in which we act is the chief matter. Action can only be understood and represented by the spirit. No one knows what he is doing, while he is acting rightly, but of what is wrong we are always conscious. Whoever works with symbols only is a pedant, a hypocrite, or a burglar. There are many such, and they like to be together. Their babbling impedes the scholar, and their obstinate mediocrity annoys the best. The instruction of the genuine artist opens up the mind ; for where words fail, deeds speak. The genuine scholar learns from the known to unfold the unknown, and gradually approaches to being a master.

MEN VIRTUOUS WHEN FREE FROM PASSION.

Wilhelm Meister, VIII. 1.

Es erinnerte ihn dieser Zug an so viele Menschen, die höchst gerecht erscheinen, wenn sie ohne Leidenschaft sind und die Handlungen anderer beobachten.

This trait reminded him of the habits of men who appear scrupulously virtuous when free from passion, and merely looking at the conduct of their neighbours.

HOW WE SPEAK OF A CHILD.

Wilhelm Meister, VIII. 3.

Wenn man von einem Kinde redet, spricht man niemals den Gegenstand, immer nur seine Hoffnungen aus.

In speaking of a child, we never speak of what is present. but of what we hope for.

EDUCATION.

Wilhelm Meister, VIII. 3.

Er war, wenigſtens eine Zeit lang, überzeugt, daß die Erziehung ſich nur an die Neigung anſchließen müſſe; wie er jetzt denkt, kann ich nicht ſagen. Er behauptete: das erſte und letzte am Menſchen ſey Thätigkeit, und man könne nichts thun, ohne die Anlage dazu zu haben, ohne den Inſtinct, der uns dazu treibe. Man giebt zu, pflegte er zu ſagen, daß Poeten geboren werden, man giebt es bei allen Künſten zu, weil man muß, und weil jene Wirkungen der menſchlichen Natur kaum ſcheinbar nachgeäfft werden können; aber wenn man es genau betrachtet, ſo wird jede auch nur die geringſte Fähigkeit uns angeboren, und es giebt keine unbeſtimmte Fähigkeit. Nur unſere zweideutige, zerſtreute Erziehung macht die Menſchen ungewiß; ſie erregt Wünſche, ſtatt Triebe zu beleben, und anſtatt den wirklichen Anlagen aufzuhelfen, richtet ſie das Streben nach Gegenſtänden, die ſo oft mit der Natur, die ſich nach ihnen bemüht, nicht übereinſtimmen. Ein Kind, ein junger Menſch, die auf ihrem eigenen Wege irre gehen, ſind mir lieber, als manche, die auf fremdem Wege recht wandeln. Finden jene, entweder durch ſich ſelbſt, oder durch Anleitung, den rechten Weg, das iſt den, der ihrer Natur gemäß iſt, ſo werden ſie ihn nie verlaſſen, anſtatt daß dieſe jeden Augenblick in Gefahr ſind, ein fremdes Joch abzuſchütteln, und ſich einer unbedingten Freiheit zu übergeben.

He was convinced, at least for a time, that education ought to depend on the inclinations of the child; his present opinions I know not. He used to maintain that the first and last point was activity, and that we could accomplish nothing unless we were urged forward by a peculiar talent and instinct to the performance of our tasks. "You admit," he would say, "that men must be born poets; and this is admitted in regard to all professors of the fine arts, because you cannot help it, and because these workings of human nature can scarcely be aped with any appearance of plausibility. But when we examine closely, we shall find that even our slightest talents must be born with us, as there is no vague general capability in man. It is our ambiguous dissipating system of education which makes our lives unsuccessful; it awakens wishes, when it should be directing impulses, and instead of forwarding our real capacities, it turns our efforts towards objects with which our minds are generally in discord. I augur better of a child, a youth, who goes astray in a path of his own, than of many who never walk on strange paths. If the former, either by themselves or by the guidance of others, find the path suitable to their nature, they will never leave it ; while the latter are in constant danger of throwing off a foreign yoke and abandoning themselves to unrestricted license.

CIRCUMSTANCES FINISH THE WEB WHICH WE HAVE BEGUN.

Wilhelm Meister, VIII. 5.

Es giebt Augenblicke des Lebens, in welchen die Begeben= heiten, gleich geflügelten Weberschiffchen, vor uns sich hin= und wieder bewegen, und unaufhaltsam ein Gewebe vollenden, das wir mehr oder weniger selbst gesponnen und angelegt haben.

There are moments in life in which circumstances, like winged shuttles, move backward and forward before us, and ceaselessly finish the web, which we ourselves, more or less, have spun and put upon the loom.

A MISFORTUNE THAT IS SEEN.

Wilhelm Meister, VIII. 5.

Das Unglück, das wir mit Augen sehen, ist geringer, als wenn unsere Einbildungskraft das Uebel gewaltsam in unser Gemüth einsenkt.

Misfortune, upon which we look, is smaller than when our imagination sinks the misery down to the recesses of the soul.

MOST MEN LIMITED IN THEIR MINDS.

Wilhelm Meister, VIII. 5.

Die meisten Menschen, selbst die vorzüglichsten, sind nur beschränkt; jeder schätzt gewisse Eigenschaften an sich und andern; nur die begünstigt er, nur die will er ausgebildet wissen.

Most men, even the most accomplished, are of limited faculties ; every one sets a value on certain qualities in himself and others ; these alone he is willing to favour, these alone will he have culti- vated.

IN LOVE IT IS ALL RISK.

Wilhelm Meister, VIII. 7.

In der Liebe ist alles Wagestück. Unter der Laube oder

H

vor dem Altar, mit Umarmungen oder goldenen Ringen, beim Gesange der Heimchen oder bei Trompeten und Pauken, es ist alles nur ein Wagestück und der Zufall thut alles.

In love all is risk. In the grove or before the altar, in an embrace or a golden ring, by the chirping of a cricket or at the sound of trumpets and kettle-drums, it is all only a risk ; chance does it all.

Our Days are numbered.

Wilhelm Meister, VIII. 8.

Nach bestimmten Gesetzen treten wir in's Leben ein, die Tage sind gezählt, die uns zum Anblicke des Lichts reif machen, aber für die Lebensdauer ist kein Gesetz. Der schwächste Lebensfaden zieht sich in unerwartete Länge und den stärksten zerschneidet gewaltsam die Schere einer Parze, die sich in Widersprüchen zu gefallen scheint.

We enter into life according to fixed laws ; the days are numbered which are to make us ripe to see the light, but for the length of life there is no law. The weakest thread will draw itself out to an unexpected length, and the strongest is suddenly cut off by the scissors of Fate, who seems to take delight in contradictions.

The Difference of Men and Women.

Elective Affinities, I. 1.

Die Männer denken mehr auf das Einzelne, auf das Gegenwärtige, und das mit Recht, weil sie zu thun, zu wirken berufen sind ; die Weiber hingegen mehr auf das, was im Leben zusammenhängt, und das mit gleichem Rechte, weil ihr Schicksal, das Schicksal ihrer Familien, an diesem Zusammenhängende von ihnen gefordert wird.

Men think more on the immediate, the present : and properly enough, because it is their parts to act and work : women, on the other hand, more on how things hang together in life, and that too with equal right, because their fate and the fate of their families is bound up in this union ; and it is precisely this which is required of them.

Little Sacrifices.

Elective Affinities, I. 2.

Im Ganzen können wir Vieles aufopfern, aber uns im

Einzelnen herzugeben, ist eine Forderung, der wir selten ge=
wachsen si·d.

We can offer up much in the large, but to make sacrifices in
little things is what we are seldom equal to.

BUSINESS REQUIRES EARNESTNESS.

Elective Affinities, I. 4.

Das Geschäft verlangt Ernst und Strenge, das Leben
Willkür; das Geschäft, die reinste Folge, dem Leben thut eine
Inconsequenz oft Noth, ja sie ist liebenswürdig und erheiternd.
Bist du bei dem einem sicher, so kannst du in dem andern
desto freier seyn; anstatt daß bei einer Vermischung das
Sichre durch das Freie weggerissen und aufgehoben wird.

Business requires earnestness and strength of character, life
must be allowed more freedom ; business calls for the strictest
sequence, whereas in the conduct of life inconsecutiveness is often
necessary—nay, is charming and graceful. If thou art strict in
the first, thou mayest allow thyself more freedom in the second ;
while if thou mix them up, thou wilt find the free interfering
and breaking in upon the fixed.

AN AGREEABLE PERSON SHOWS THROUGH ALL DISGUISES.

Elective Affinities, I. 6.

Denn indem das Angenehme einer Person sich auch über
ihre Hülle verbreitet, so glaubt man sie immer wieder von
neuem und anmuthiger zu sehen, wenn sie ihre Eigenschaften
einer neuen Umgebung mittheilt

A pleasant character will appear under every disguise, but we
always imagine that it looks newer and more graceful when its
peculiarities are seen under some fresh drapery.

POWER OF HUMAN BEAUTY.

Elective Affinities, I. 6.

Denn wenn der Smaragd durch seine herrliche Farbe dem
Gesicht wohlthut, ja sogar einige Heilkraft an diesem edlen
Sinn ausübt; so wirkt die menschliche Schönheit noch mit
weit größerer Gewalt auf den äußern und inneren Sinn.

Wer fie erblickt, den kann nichts übles anwehen; er fühlt
fich mit fich felbft und mit der Welt in Uebereinſtimmung.

For as the emerald is refreshing to the eye by its pleasing hues
—nay, exercises, it is said, a wholesome effect on that noble
sense—so does human beauty operate still more powerfully on
the outward and inward sense. Whoever looks upon it cannot
be influenced by the breath of evil; he feels that he is in harmony
with himself and the world.

LIGHT AND SHADE.

Elective Affinities, I. 6.

Wo viel Licht ift, ift ſtarker Schatten.

Where there is much light, the shade is deep.

A SACRIFICE FOR AN AFTER ADVANTAGE.

Elective Affinities, I. 6.

Wie fchwer ift es, daß der Menfch recht abwäge, was man
aufopfern muß gegen das, was zu gewinnen ift! wie fchwer,
den Zweck zu wollen und die Mittel nicht zu verſchmähen!
Viele verwechſeln gar die Mittel und den Zweck, erfreuen fich
an jenen, ohne diefen im Auge zu behalten. Jedes Uebel foll
an der Stelle geheilt werden, wo es zum Vorſchein kommt, und
man bekümmert fich nicht um jenen Punkt, wo es eigentlich
feinen Urſprung nimmt, woher es wirkt. Deßwegen ift es ſo
fchwer, Rath zu pflegen, befonders mit der Menge, die im
Täglichen ganz verſtändig ift, aber felten weiter fieht als auf
morgen. Kommt nun gar dazu, daß der eine bei einer gemein-
ſamen Anſtalt gewinnen, der andre verlieren foll, da ift mit
Vergleich nun gar nichts auszurichten. Alles eigentlich gemein-
ſame Gute muß durch das unumſchränkte Majeſtätsrecht ge-
fördert werden.

How difficult it is to get men to balance a present sacrifice with
a future advantage! How hard to induce them to wish an end,
and not hesitate at the means! How many mingle together means
and ends, rejoicing in the first without having the other before
their eyes. Every evil is to be remedied at the place where it
makes its appearance, and yet man will not take the trouble to
examine the cause which produces it, or the remote effect that **is**

likely to result from it. This is the reason why it is so difficult to get advice listened to, especially by the many, who are sensible enough in matters from day to day, but can seldom see beyond the morrow ; and if it comes to a point where in some general arrangement one person will gain and another lose, it is impossible to induce them to strike a balance. All works of general advantage can only be carried out by an unlimited absolute authority.

To rest beside those whom we loved in Life.

Elective Affinities, II. 2.

Neben denen dereinst zu ruhen, die man liebt, ist die angenehmste Vorstellung, welche der Mensch haben kann, wenn er einmal über das Leben hinausdenkt. Zu den Seinigen versammelt werden, ist ein so herrlicher Ausdruck.

To rest hereafter at the side of those whom we love is the most charming thought which man can have, when he once extends his view beyond the limits of this world. What a noble expression is "to be gathered to his fathers ! "

The Red Thread.

Elective Affinities, II. 2.

Wir hören von einer besondern Einrichtung bei der englischen Marine. Sämmtliche Tauwerke der königlichen Flotte, vom stärksten bis zum schwächsten, sind dergestalt gesponnen, daß ein rother Faden durch das Ganze durchgeht, den man nicht herauswinden kann, ohne alles aufzulösen, und woran auch die kleinsten Stücke kenntlich sind, daß sie der Krone gehören.

Eben so zieht sich durch Ottiliens Tagebuch ein Faden der Neigung Anhänglichkeit, der alles verbindet und das Ganze bezeichnet.

We hear of a curious contrivance in the English naval service. All the ropes that are used in the Royal Navy, from the strongest to the weakest, are twisted in such a way that a red thread runs through them from end to end, which cannot be extracted without untwisting the whole, and by which the smallest pieces may be recognised as belonging to the Crown.

Just so is there drawn through Ottilie's diary a thread of attachment and affection, which connects it all together, and characterises the whole.

TIME WILL NOT ALLOW ITSELF TO BE CHEATED OF ITS RIGHTS.

Elective Affinities, II. 2.

Wenn man die vielen versunkenen, die durch Kirchgänger abgetretenen Grabsteine, die über ihren Grabmälern selbst zusammengestürzten Kirchen erblickt; so kann einem das Leben nach dem Tode doch immer wie ein zweites Leben vorkommen, in das man nun im Bilde, in der Ueberschrift eintritt und länger darin verweilt, als in dem eigentlichen lebendigen Leben. Aber auch dieses Bild, dieses zweite Daseyn verlischt früher oder später. Wie über die Menschen, so auch über die Denkmäler, läßt sich die Zeit ihr Recht nicht nehmen.

When we see the many dilapidated gravestones worn away by the footsteps of the congregation, and the churches themselves crumbled over them, we may imagine the life after death to be as it were a second life, into which a man enters in the figure or in the inscription, and lives longer there than when he was alive. But this figure too, this second existence, dies out sooner or later. Time will not allow itself to be cheated of its rights either over man or his monuments.

WE LIKE TO LOOK INTO THE FUTURE.

Elective Affinities, II. 4.

Wir blicken so gern in die Zukunft, weil wir das Ungefähre, was sich in ihr hin und her bewegt, durch stille Wünsche so gern zu unsern Gunsten heranleiten möchten.

We take pleasure in looking into the future, because we think that we may be able by our silent wishes to guide in our own favour what is undetermined in it, being moved this or that way.

SOCIETY.

Elective Affinities, II. 4.

Niemand würde viel in Gesellschaften sprechen, wenn er sich bewußt wäre, wie oft er die andern mißversteht.

No one would talk much in society if he were aware how oft he fails to understand others.

OPINIONS.

Elective Affinities, II. 4.

Jedes ausgesprochene Wort erregt den Gegensinn.

Every word a man utters calls forth an opposite opinion.

THE PLEASANTEST SOCIETY.

Elective Affinities, II. 4.

Die angenehmsten Gesellschaften sind die, in welchen ein heitere Ehrerbietung der Glieder gegen einander obwaltet.

The pleasantest society is that where the members feel a warm respect for each other.

THE SENSITIVE.

Elective Affinities, II. 4.

Der sinnliche Mensch lacht oft, wo nichts zu lachen ist. Was ihn auch anregt, sein inneres Behagen kommt zum Vorschein.

The sensitive man often laughs when there is nothing to laugh at. Whatever affects him, his inner nature comes to the surface.

WOMEN.

Elective Affinities, II. 5.

Der Umgang mit Frauen ist das Element guter Sitten.

The society of women is the element of good manners.

AN UNDERBRED CIVILIAN.

Elective Affinities, II. 5.

Niemand ist lästiger, als ein täppischer Mensch vom Civilstande. Von ihm könnte man die Feinheit fordern, da er sich mit nichts Rohem zu beschäftigen hat.

No one is more annoying than a rude clumsy civilian. From him one might expect delicacy of conduct, as he has no rough work to do.

SPECTACLES.
Elective Affinities, II. 5.

Es käme niemand mit der Brille auf der Nase in ein vertrauliches Gemach, wenn er wüßte, daß uns Frauen sogleich die Luft vergeht, ihn anzusehen und uns mit ihm zu unterhalten.

No one would come with spectacles on nose into a private confidential assembly, if he knew that at once we women lose all pleasure in looking at him, or listening to what he has to say.

BEHAVIOUR.
Elective Affinities, II. 5.

Das Betragen ist ein Spiegel, in welchem jeder sein Bild zeigt.

Behaviour is a mirror in which every one shows his image.

COURTESY OF THE HEART.
Elective Affinities, II. 5.

Es giebt eine Höflichkeit des Herzens; sie ist der Liebe verwandt. Aus ihr entspringt die bequemste Höflichkeit des äußern Betragens.

There is a courtesy of the heart; it is allied to love. From it springs the purest courtesy in the outward behaviour.

FOOLS AND MODEST PEOPLE ARE INNOCUOUS.
Elective Affinities, II. 5.

Thoren und gescheidte Leute sind gleich unschädlich. Nur die Halbnarren und Halbweisen, das sind die gefährlichsten.

Fools and modest people are alike innocuous. Only half-fools and half-wise are really dangerous.

OBLIGATIONS TO A FOOL.
Elective Affinities, II. 5.

Es ist was schreckliches um einen vorzüglichen Mann, auf den sich die Dummen was zu Gute thun.

There is something fearful in seeing a man of high character being under an obligation to a fool.

Spring.

Elective Affinities, II. 9.

So wiederholt sich denn abermals das Jahresmährchen von vorn. Wir sind nun wieder, Gott sey Dank! an seinem artig= sten Capitel. Veilchen und Maiblumen sind wie Ueberschriften oder Vignetten dazu. Es macht uns immer einen angenehmen Eindruck, wenn wir sie in dem Buche des Lebens wieder aufschlagen

So then the year is repeating its old story again. We are come once more, thank God ! to its most charming chapter. The violets and the mayflowers are as its inscriptions or vignettes. It always makes a pleasant impression on us, when we open again at these pages of the book of life.

Godless People.

Stella, Act I.

Die Leute, die keine Religion haben, haben keinen Gott und halten sich an keine Ordnung.

People that have no religion have no God, and are reckless of everything.

Who lives, loses.

Stella, Act I.

Ja, meine Liebe, wer lebt, verliert (aufstehend); aber er gewinnt auch.

Yes, my love, whosoever lives, loses (rising up), but he also wins.

Active Employment.

Stella, Act II.

Geschäftigkeit und Wohlthätigkeit sind eine Gabe des Him= mels, ein Ersatz für unglücklich liebende Herzen.

Active employment and kindly acts are gifts from heaven, a compensation for hearts that have been unfortunate in love.

THE PRESENCE OF THE MISERABLE.

Stella, Act III.

Die Gegenwart des Elenden ist dem Glücklichen zur Last,
und ach! der Glückliche dem Elenden noch mehr.

The presence of the wretched is a burden to the happy : and,
alas! the happy still more so to the wretched.

GOOD WILL BETTER THAN SUCCESS.

Stella, Act v.

Guter Wille ist höher als aller Erfolg.

Good will is of more value than the result that follows.

HEAR BOTH SIDES.

Truth and Poetry, I. *b.* 1, *vol.* XX. *p.* 17.

Eines Mannes Rede
Ist keines Mannes Rede :
Man soll sie billig hören Beede

One man's word is no man's word : we should quietly hear both
sides.

SELF-CONCEIT AND VANITY.

Truth and Poetry, I. *b.* 2, *vol.* II. *p.* 82.

So wahr ist es, daß alles, was den Menschen innerlich in
seinem Dünkel bestärkt, seiner heimlichen Eitelkeit schmeichelt,
ihm dergestalt höchlich erwünscht ist, daß er nicht weiter fragt,
ob es ihm sonst auf irgend eine Weise zur Ehre oder zur
Schmach gereichen könne.

So true is it that anything which confirms man in his self-
conceit, and flatters his secret vanity, is so highly desirable to
him, that he does not think it necessary to ask himself whether it
will in any way be for his honour and advantage.

CHILDREN.

Truth and Poetry, I. *b.* 2, *vol.* XX. *p.* 82.

Wüchsen die Kinder in der Art fort, wie sie sich andeuten, so
hätten wir lauter Genie's; aber das Wachsthum ist nicht bloß

Entwicklung; die verschiednen organischen Systeme, die den
Einen Menschen ausmachen, entspringen aus einander, folgen
einander, verwandeln sich in einander, verdrängen einander, ja
zehren einander auf, so daß von manchen Fähigkeiten, von
manchen Kraftäußerungen, nach einer gewissen Zeit, kaum eine
Spur mehr zu finden ist. Wenn auch die menschlichen Anlagen
im ganzen eine entschiedene Richtung haben, so wird es doch
dem größten und erfahrensten Kenner schwer seyn, sie mit Zuver-
lässigkeit voraus zu verkünden; doch kann man hinterdrein wohl
bemerken, was auf ein Künftiges hingedeutet hat.

If children were to grow up as is indicated in early years,
we would have many more geniuses; but growth is not mere
development; the various organic systems, which go to the formation of man, spring from each other, follow each other, change
into each other, push out each other, nay, consume each other;
so that, after a certain time, scarcely a trace of many mental
aptitudes and manifestations is to be found. Even when the
talents of a man have on the whole a very decided direction, yet
it is difficult for even the most experienced to fix upon it with
certainty, though one may afterwards easily point out what
might have predicted his future course of life.

THE PEACEFUL CITIZEN.

Truth and Poetry, I. b. 2, *vol.* XX. *p.* 83.

Der ruhige Bürger steht zu den großen Weltereignissen in
einem wunderbaren Verhältniß. Schon aus der Ferne regen
sie ihn auf und beunruhigen ihn, und er kann sich, selbst wenn
sie ihn nicht berühren, eines Urtheils, einer Theilnahme nicht
enthalten. Schnell ergreift er eine Partei, nachdem ihn sein
Charakter oder äußere Anlässe bestimmen.

The peaceful citizen stands in a wonderful relation to the great
events of the world. Already from a distance they rouse and
trouble him, and he cannot help, even when they do not touch
his interests, feeling an interest and sympathy with them.

NO ONE SATISFIED WITH THE COUNTERFEIT OF AN OBJECT.

Truth and Poetry, I. b. 4, *vol.* XX. *p.* 145.

Nicht leicht ist jemand mit dem Conterfei eines gegenwärtigen
zufrieden, und wie erwünscht ist uns jeder Schattenriß eines
Abwesenden oder gar Abgeschiedenen.

No one is easily satisfied with the counterfeit of an object still present, but how prized is every even shadowy likeness of one who is absent or departed !

Man always returns to Nature.

Truth and Poetry, i. b. 4, *vol.* xx. *p.* 153.

Der Menſch mag ſich wenden wohin er will, er mag unter⸗ nehmen was es auch ſey, ſtets wird er auf jenen Weg wieder zurückkehren, den ihm die Natur einmal vorgezeichnet hat.

A man may turn whither he chooses ; he may undertake whatever he may ; but he will always come back to the path which Nature has once prescribed to him.

Equality of all Conditions.

Truth and Poetry, i. b. 4, *vol.* xx. *p.* 181.

So entwickelte, ſo beſtärkte ſich in mir das Gefühl der Gleichheit, wo nicht aller Menſchen, doch aller menſchlichen Zuſtände, indem mir das nackte Daſeyn als die Haupt⸗ bedingung, das Uebrige alles aber als gleichgültig und zufällig erſchien.

Thus there was developed and strengthened in me the feeling of the equality, if not of all men, at least of all human conditions, while the chief point seemed to me to be mere existence, everything else being indifferent and accidental.

Every Bird has its Decoy

Truth and Poetry, i. b. 5, *vol.* xx. *p.* 196.

Für alle Vögel giebt es Lockſpeiſen, und jeder Menſch wird auf ſeine eigene Art geleitet und verleitet.

Every bird has its decoy, and every man is led and misled in his own peculiar way.

Mystifications an Amusement for Idle People.

Truth and Poetry, i. b. 5, *vol.* xx. *p.* 199.

Myſtificationen ſind und bleiben eine Unterhaltung für müßige, mehr oder weniger geiſtreiche Menſchen. Eine läß⸗ liche Bosheit, eine ſelbſtgefällige Schadenfreude ſind ein Genuß

für diejenigen, die fich weder mit fich felbft befchäftigen, **noch** nach außen heilfam wirfen fönnen.

Mystifications are, and will continue to be, an amusement for idle people, whether more or less clever. A pardonable wickedness, a self-complacent pleasure in the misfortunes of others, is an enjoyment for those who have neither resources in themselves, nor a wholesome mode of employing themselves in the world around

THE GREAT ARE BUT MEN.

Truth and Poetry, I. *b.* 5, *vol.* XX. *p.* 233.

Da die Großen nun auch einmal Menfchen find, fo denft fie der Bürger, wenn er fie lieben will, als feines Gleichen, und das fann er am füglichften, wenn er fie als liebende Gatten, als zärtliche Eltern, als anhängliche Gefchwifter, als treue Freunde fich vorftellen darf.

As the great are, after all, men, the citizen regards them as his equal, when he wishes to love them ; and that he can best do when he represents them to himself as loving husbands, tender parents, devoted brothers and sisters, and true friends.

YOUTH AND AGE.

Motto to Second Part.

Was man in der Jugend wünfcht, hat man im Alter die Fülle.

What one has wished for in youth, one has in abundance in old age.

PLANTS AND FLOWERS MAY FORM A DIARY FOR US.

Truth and Poetry, II. *b.* 6, *vol.* XXI. *p.* 11.

So fönnen uns Kräuter und Blumen der gemeinften Art ein liebes Tagebuch bilden, weil nichts, was die Erinnerung eines glücklichen Moments zurückruft, unbedeutend feyn fann; und noch jeßt würde es mir fchwer fallen, manches dergleichen, was mir aus verfchiedenen Epochen übrig geblieben, als werthlos zu vertilgen, weil es mich unmittelbar in jene Zeiten verfeßt, deren ich mich zwar mit Wehmuth, doch nicht ungern erinnere

Thus plants and flowers of the commonest kind can form a pleasing diary, because nothing which calls back to us the remembrance of a happy moment can be insignificant; and even now it causes me sorrow to destroy as worthless many of those things which have been kept by me from different epochs, because they carry me back at once to that time, which I remember with melancholy indeed, but not unwillingly.

CHILDREN PART FROM THEIR PARENTS.

Truth and Poetry, II. *b. 6, vol.* XXI. *p.* 32.

So lösen sich in gewissen Epochen Kinder von Eltern, Diener von Herren, Begünstigte von Gönnern los, und ein solcher Versuch, sich auf seine Füße zu stellen, sich unabhängig zu machen, für sein eigen Selbst zu leben, er gelinge oder nicht, ist immer dem Willen der Natur gemäß.

Thus at certain epochs children part from parents, servants from masters, dependants from patrons; and such an attempt, whether it be successful or not, to stand on one's own feet, to make oneself independent, to live for oneself, is always according to the dictates of nature.

MAN IS OF CONSEQUENCE ACCORDING AS HE ACTS.

Truth and Poetry, II. *b.* 7, *vol.* XXI. *p.* 75.

Denn nicht insofern der Mensch etwas zurückläßt, sondern insofern er wirkt und genießt, und andere zu wirken und zu genießen anregt, bleibt er von Bedeutung.

A man remains of consequence, not so much for anything he leaves behind him, as because he is energetic in life and enjoys it exciting others to activity and enjoyment.

THE GREATEST GOOD FORTUNE TO A CITY.

Truth and Poetry, II. *b.* 8, *vol.* XXI. *p.* 122.

Einer Stadt kann kein größeres Glück begegnen, als wenn mehrere, im Guten und Rechten gleichgesinnte, schon gebildete Männer daselbst neben einander wohnen.

No greater good can befall a city than when several educated men, thinking in the same way as to what is good and right, live together in it.

Time.

Truth and Poetry, ii. *b.* 8, *vol.* xxi. *p.* 162.

Die Zeit ist unendlich lang und ein jeder Tag ein Gefäß, in das sich sehr viel eingießen läßt, wenn man es wirklich aus- füllen will.

Time is incalculably long, and every day is a vessel into which very much may be poured, if one will really fill it up.

To take too much Care of Ourselves.

Truth and Poetry, ii. *b.* 8, *vol.* xxi. *p.* 164.

Freilich ist es eine langweilige und mitunter traurige Sache, zu sehr auf uns selbst und was uns schadet und nützt, Acht zu haben; allein es ist keine Frage, daß bei der wunderlichen Idiosynkrasie der menschlichen Natur von der einen, und bei der unendlichen Verschiedenheit der Lebensart und Genüsse von der andern Seite, es noch ein Wunder ist, daß das menschliche Geschlecht sich nicht schon lange aufgerieben hat. Es scheint die menschliche Natur eine eigene Art von Zähigkeit und Viel- seitigkeit zu besitzen, da sie alles, was an sie herankommt oder was sie in sich aufnimmt, überwindet, und wenn sie sich es nicht assimiliren kann, wenigstens gleichgültig macht.

It is indeed a wearisome, and, to say the truth, melancholy business, to consider too minutely what may injure our constitu- tion or do us good; but there is no doubt that with the strange idiosyncrasy of human nature on the one side, and the endless variety in the mode and enjoyment of life on the other, it is a wonder that the race of man has not long ago worn itself out. Human nature seems to possess a peculiar kind of toughness and many-sidedness, as it gets the better of anything which approaches it, or which it takes into itself; and though it may not be able to assimilate, it at least renders it indifferent.

Allowance to be made for Bad Health.

Truth and Poetry, ii. *b.* 10, *vol.* xxi. *p.* 234.

Dieser Fall kommt im Leben öfters vor, und man beachtet nicht genug die moralische Wirkung krankhafter Zustände, und beurtheilt daher manche Charaktere sehr ungerecht, weil man

alle Menschen für gesund nimmt und von ihnen verlangt, daß
sie sich auch in solchem Maaße betragen sollen.

This often takes place in life : we do not sufficiently take into
consideration the moral effects arising from sickly states of body,
and we therefore form an improper judgment of many characters,
because it is assumed that all men are healthy, and we require of
them that they shall conduct themselves accordingly.

JESTING ON A NAME NOT ALLOWABLE.

Truth and Poetry, II. *b.* 10, *vol.* XXI. *p.* 237.

Es war freilich nicht fein, daß er sich mit meinem Namen
diesen Spaß erlaubte; denn der Eigenname eines Menschen ist
nicht etwa wie ein Mantel, der bloß um ihn her hängt und an
dem man allenfalls noch zupfen und zerren kann, sondern ein
vollkommen paſſendes Kleid, ja wie die Haut ſelbſt ihm über
und über angewachſen, an der man nicht ſchaben und ſchinden
darf, ohne ihn ſelbſt zu verletzen.

It was not indeed polite to take the liberty of jesting on my
name ; for a man's name is not like a mantle, which merely hangs
about him, and which one perchance may safely twitch and pull,
but a perfectly fitting garment, which, like the skin, has grown
over and over him, at which one cannot rake and scrape without
injuring the man himself.

MAN HAS TIME ENOUGH FOR EVERYTHING.

Truth and Poetry, II. *b.* 10, *vol.* XXI. *p.* 233.

Man hat immer Zeit genug, wenn man sie gut anwenden
will.

One always has time enough, if one will apply it well.

FAULT.

Truth and Poetry, II. *b.* 10, *vol.* XXI. *p.* 241.

Man soll jedoch von eignen und fremden Fehlern niemals, am
wenigsten öffentlich reden, wenn man nicht dadurch etwas Nützliches zu bewirken denkt.

We should never speak, at least openly, of our own faults or
those of others, if we do not think thereby to effect some useful
purpose.

Trees.

Motto to Third Part.

Es ist dafür gesorgt, daß die Bäume nicht in den Himmel wachsen.

Care is taken that trees do not grow into the sky.

A Man born to Activity.

Truth and Poetry, III. *b.* 11, *vol.* XXII. *p.* 3.

Denn der zur Thätigkeit geborene Mensch übernimmt sich in Plänen und überladet sich mit Arbeiten. Das gelingt denn auch ganz gut, bis irgend ein physisches oder moralisches Hinderniß dazutritt, um das Unverhältnißmäßige der Kräfte zu dem Unternehmen in's Klare zu bringen.

For a man born for active life undertakes plans beyond his strength, and weighs himself down with labours. This is well enough, till some physical or moral impediment steps in, clearly showing the disproportion of the powers to the undertaking.

Presentiments.

Truth and Poetry, III. *b.* 11, *vol.* XXII. *p.* 6.

Alle Vorgefühle, wenn sie durch das Ereigniß bestätigt werden, geben dem Menschen einen höheren Begriff von sich selbst, es sey nun, daß er sich so zart fühlend glauben kann, um einen Bezug in der Ferne zu tasten, oder so scharfsinnig, um nothwendige aber doch ungewisse Verknüpfungen gewahr zu werden.

All presentiments, if they are confirmed by the event, give man a higher idea of himself, whether it be that, feeling a tender susceptibility of mind, he may believe himself to have a certain relation to the far distant, or that he is acute enough to perceive necessary but still uncertain associations.

Men have a Double Part to play in the World.

Truth and Poetry, III. *b.* 11, *vol.* XXII. *p.* 18.

Alle Menschen guter Art empfinden bei zunehmender Bildung, daß sie auf der Welt eine doppelte Rolle zu spielen haben,

I

eine wirkliche und eine ideelle, und in diesem Gefühl ist der Grund alles Edlen aufzusuchen. Was uns für eine wirkliche zugetheilt sey, erfahren wir nur allzu deutlich; was die zweite betrifft, darüber können wir selten in's Klare kommen. Der Mensch mag seine höhere Bestimmung auf Erden oder im Himmel, in der Gegenwart oder in der Zukunft suchen, so bleibt er deßhalb doch innerlich einem ewigen Schwanken, von außen einer immer störenden Einwirkung ausgesetzt, bis er ein für allemal den Entschluß faßt, zu erklären, das Rechte sey das, was ihm gemäß ist.

All men of a good disposition feel that, with increasing cultivation, they have a double part to play in the world—a real and an ideal—and in this feeling we have to search for everything noble. The real part that has been assigned us we feel only too strongly ; in respect to the second, we can seldom come to a clear understanding about it. Man may seek his higher destination on earth or in heaven, in the present or in the future, yet he remains on this account exposed within to a never-ending irresolution, to an influence from without that ever disturbs him, till he once for all adopts the resolution to declare that that is right which is suitable to himself.

Eminent Contemporaries.
Truth and Poetry, III. *b.* 11; *vol.* XXII. *p.* 33.

Denn vorzügliche mitlebende Männer sind den größeren Sternen zu vergleichen, nach denen, so lange sie nur über dem Horizont stehen, unser Auge sich wendet, und sich gestärkt und gebildet fühlt, wenn es ihm vergönnt ist, solche Vollkommenheiten in sich aufzunehmen.

For illustrious contemporaries may be likened to the greater stars, towards which, so long only as they remain above the horizon, our eye is turned, feels strengthened and cultivated, if it is allowed to take such perfections into itself.

The Highest Problem of any Art.
Truth and Poetry, III. *b.* 11, *vol.* XXII. *p.* 48.

Die höchste Aufgabe einer jeden Kunst ist, durch den Schein die Täuschung einer höheren Wirklichkeit zu geben.

The highest problem of any art is to cause by appearance the illusion of a higher reality.

Beautiful Thoughts.

Truth and Poetry, III. *b.* 11, *vol.* XXII. *p.* **54.**

Was man auch gegen solche Sammlungen sagen kann, welche die Autoren zerstückelt mittheilen, sie bringen doch manche gute Wirkung hervor. Sind wir doch nicht immer so gefaßt und so geistreich, daß wir ein ganzes Werk nach seinem Werth in uns aufzunehmen vermöchten. Streichen wir nicht in einem Buche Stellen an, die sich unmittelbar auf uns beziehen? Junge Leute besonders, denen es an durchgreifender Bildung fehlt, werden von glänzenden Stellen gar löblich aufgeregt, und so erinnere ich mich noch als einer der schönsten Epochen meines Lebens derjenigen, welche gedachtes Werk bei mir bezeichnete. Jene herrlichen Eigenheiten, die großen Sprüche, die treffenden Schilderungen, die humoristischen Züge, alles traf mich einzeln und gewaltig.

Whatever we may say against such collections, which present authors in a disjointed form, they nevertheless bring about many excellent results. We are not always so composed, so full of wisdom, that we are able to take in at once the whole scope of a work according to its merits. Do we not mark in a book passages which seem to have a direct reference to ourselves? Young people especially, who have failed in acquiring a complete cultivation of mind, are roused in a praiseworthy way by brilliant passages; and I myself remember as one of the finest epochs of my life, that which is marked by the aforesaid work (Dodd's *Beauties of Shakespeare*). Those noble peculiarities, those mighty thoughts, those wonderful descriptions, those humorist traits—all struck me singly and powerfully.

True Poetry.

Truth and Poetry, III. *b.* 11, *vol.* XXII. *p.* **55.**

Ich ehre den Rhythmus wie den Reim, wodurch Poesie erst zur Poesie wird, aber das eigentlich tief und gründlich Wirksame, das wahrhaft Ausbildende und Fördernde ist dasjenige, was vom Dichter übrig bleibt, wenn er in Prose übersetzt wird. Dann bleibt der reine vollkommene Gehalt, den uns ein blendendes Aeußere oft, wenn er fehlt, vorzuspiegeln weiß, und wenn er gegenwärtig ist, verdeckt. Ich halte daher, zum Anfang jugendlicher Bildung, prosaische Uebersetzungen für vortheil-

haſter als die poetiſchen: denn es läßt ſich bemerken, daß
Knaben, denen ja doch alles zum Scherze dienen muß, ſich am
Schall der Worte, am Fall der Sylben ergötzen, und durch eine
Art von parodiſtiſchem Muthwillen den tiefen Gehalt des edel=
ſten Werks zerſtören.

I respect rhythm as well as rhyme, by which poetry first becomes poetry ; but that which is peculiarly, deeply, and funda-
mentally efficient—that which is really permanent and furthering,
is that which remains of the poet when he is turned into prose.
Then remains the pure, perfect substance, which a dazzling exterior
often, when it fails, knows how to give a false appearance, and
when it is present, this exterior contrives to conceal. I consider,
therefore, prose translations more beneficial than poetical for the
commencement of youthful culture ; for it is to be remarked that
boys, to whom anything serves as a jest, take pleasure in the
sound of words, and the fall of syllables, and by a sort of parodis-
tical wantonness destroy the deep contents of the noblest work.

PATRIOTISM IN TIME OF PEACE.

Truth and Poetry, III. *b.* 12, *vol.* XXII. *p.* 107.

Im Frieden der Patriotismus eigentlich nur darin beſteht,
daß jeder vor ſeiner Thüre kehre, ſeines Amts warte, auch ſeine
Lection lerne, damit es wohl im Hauſe ſtehe.

In peace patriotism really consists only in this—that every one
sweeps before his door, minds his own business, also learns his
own lesson, that it may be well with him in his own house.

A NEW PASSION BEFORE THE OLD ONE IS QUITE EXTINCT.

Truth and Poetry, III. *b.* 13, *vol.* XXII. *p.* 139.

Es iſt eine ſehr angenehme Empfindung, wenn ſich eine neue
Leidenſchaft in uns zu regen anfängt, ehe die alte noch ganz
verklungen iſt. So ſieht man bei untergehender Sonne gern
auf der entgegengeſetzten Seite den Mond aufgehn und erfreut
ſich an dem Doppelglanze der beiden Himmelslichter.

It is a very pleasant feeling, when a new passion begins to be
felt within us, before the old one is quite gone. Thus we take
pleasure in seeing, as the sun sets below the horizon, the moon
rising on the opposite side, and we look with delight on the double
lustre of the two heavenly luminaries.

THE PROPER SPRINGS OF EARTHLY LIFE.

Truth and Poetry, III. *b.* 13, *vol.* XXII. *p.* 159.

Alles Behagen am Leben ist auf eine regelmäßige Wiederkehr der äußeren Dinge gegründet. Der Wechsel von Tag und Nacht, der Jahreszeiten, der Blüthen und Früchte, und was uns sonst von Epoche zu Epoche entgegentritt, damit wir es genießen können und sollen, diese sind die eigentlichen Triebfedern des irdischen Lebens. Je offner wir für diese Genüsse sind, desto glücklicher fühlen wir uns; wälzt sich aber die Verschiedenheit dieser Erscheinungen vor uns auf und nieder, ohne daß wir daran Theil nehmen, sind wir gegen so holde Anerbietungen unempfänglich: dann tritt das größte Uebel, die schwerste Krankheit ein, man betrachtet das Leben als eine ekelhafte Last.

The whole pleasure of life is dependent on the regular recurrence of external things. The vicissitude of night and day, the seasons of the year, blossoms and fruit, and whatever presents itself to the eye from epoch to epoch, so that we can and should enjoy it—these are the proper springs of earthly life. The more open we are to these enjoyments, the more happy we feel ourselves ; but if the change of these appearances roll up and down before us without our taking an interest in them, if we are insensible to such noble gifts of nature, then arises the greatest evil, the saddest disease—we regard life as a loathsome burden.

GIRLS AND YOUNG MEN

Truth and Poetry, III. *b.* 14, *vol.* XXII. *p.* 191.

Man liebt an dem Mädchen, was es ist, und an dem Jüngling, was er ankündigt.

Girls we love for what they are ; young men for what they promise to be.

TO WORK, MORALLY.

Truth and Poetry, III. *b.* 14, *vol.* XXII. *p.* 202.

Wer sittlich wirkt, verliert keine seiner Bemühungen : denn es gedeiht davon weit mehr, als das Evangelium vom Sämanne allzu bescheiden eingesteht.

He who works morally, loses none of his exertions ; for he gains much more than the Gospel too modestly claims for the sower.

FAITH AND KNOWLEDGE.

Truth and Poetry, III. *b.* 14, *vol.* XXII. *p.* 205.

Der Glaube sey ein großes Gefühl von Sicherheit für die Gegenwart und Zukunft, und diese Sicherheit entspringe aus dem Zutrauen auf ein übergroßes, übermächtiges und uner= forschliches Wesen. Auf die Unerschütterlichkeit dieses Zutrauens komme alles an; wie wir uns aber dieses Wesen denken, dieß hänge von unsern übrigen Fähigkeiten, ja von den Umständen ab, und sey ganz gleichgültig. Der Glaube sey ein heiliges Gefäß, in welches ein jeder sein Gefühl, seinen Verstand, seine Einbildungskraft, so gut als er vermöge, zu opfern bereit stehe. Mit dem Wissen sey es gerade das Gegentheil; es komme gar nicht darauf an, daß man wisse, sondern was man wisse, wie gut und wie viel man wisse. Daher könne man über das Wissen streiten, weil es sich berichtigen, sich erweitern und verengern lasse. Das Wissen fange vom Einzelnen an, sey endlos und gestaltlos, und könne niemals, höchstens nur träumerisch, zusam= mengefaßt werden, und bleibe also dem Glauben geradezu entgegengesetzt.

Faith is a deep feeling of security for the present and the future, and this security arises from the firm trust in an infinite, almighty, and incomprehensible Being. Everything flows from the tenacity of this assurance; but the way in which we think of this Being depends on our other faculties, or even on circumstances, and these may be quite indifferent. Faith is a holy vessel, into which every one is ready to pour his feelings, his understanding, his imagination, as completely as he can. With knowledge it is quite the reverse; with it the question is not whether we know but what we know, how much and how well we know. Hence it is that we may have disputes about knowledge, because it can be amended, widened, contracted. Knowledge begins with the par-ticular, is endless and formless, can never be all comprehended, at least only dreamily, and therefore remains the very opposite of Faith.

SELFISHNESS.

Truth and Poetry, III. *b.* 14, *vol.* XXII. *p.* 214.

Eben so viel Selbstgefälligkeit dazu gehöre, andern, die sich behaglich fühlen, wehe zu thun, als sich selbst oder seinen Freunden überflüssiges Gute zu erzeigen.

There is quite as much selfishness in giving pain to others, when we see them to be full of enjoyment, as in showing overflowing kindness to oneself and to one's friends.

To recall former Scenes.
Truth and Poetry, iii. b. 14, *vol.* xxii. *p.* 215.

Das, was man gedacht, die Bilder, die man gesehn, lassen sich in dem Verstand und in der Einbildungskraft wieder hervorrufen: aber das Herz ist nicht so gefällig, es wiederholt uns nicht die schönen Gefühle.

The thoughts we have had, the pictures we have seen, can be again called back before the mind's eye and before the imagination; but the heart is not so obliging; it does not reproduce its pleasing emotions.

To enjoy our Natural Gifts in Silence.
Truth and Poetry, iii. b. 15, *vol.* xxii. *p.* 255.

Wer sich aber an seinen Naturgaben nicht im Stillen erfreuen kann, wer sich bei Ausübung derselben nicht selbst seinen Lohn dahin nimmt, sondern erst darauf wartet und hofft, daß andere das Geleistete anerkennen und es gehörig würdigen sollen, der findet sich in einer übeln Lage, weil es nur allzu bekannt ist, daß die Menschen den Beifall sehr spärlich austheilen, daß sie das Lob verkümmern, ja wenn es nur einigermaßen thunlich ist, in Tadel verwandeln.

But he who is not able to enjoy his natural gifts in silence, and does not consider the mere exercise of them a sufficient reward, but expects and hopes that others will appreciate and acknowledge them, will generally find himself in an evil plight; for it is only too well known that men are very niggardly of their approbation, that they mingle gall with their praise, and, wherever it can be in any way done, turn it into blame.

Misfortunes never come Single.
Truth and Poetry, iv. b. 16, *vol.* xxii. *p.* 273.

Wie man zu sagen pflegt: daß kein Unglück allein komme, so läßt sich auch wohl bemerken, daß es mit dem Glück ähnlicher Weise beschaffen sey; ja auch mit andern Umständen, die sich auf eine harmonische Weise um uns versammeln; es sey nun, daß ein Schicksal dergleichen auf uns lege, oder daß der Mensch die Kraft habe, das, was zusammen gehört, an sich heranzuziehen.

What men usually say of misfortunes, that they never come alone, may with equal truth be said of good fortune ; nay, of other circumstances which gather round us in an harmonious way, whether it arise from a kind of fatality, or that man has the power of attracting to himself things that are mutually related.

On the Summit of Fortune One abides not long.

Truth and Poetry, iv. *b.* 17, *vol.* XXII. *p.* 317.

Es ist schon längst mit Grund und Bedeutung ausgesprochen: auf dem Gipfel der Zustände hält man sich nicht lange.

The old saying is expressed with depth and significance—" On the pinnacle of fortune man does not long stand firm."

Factitious Nobility.

Truth and Poetry, iv. *b.* 17, *vol.* XXII. *p.* 326.

Sondern anderwärts möcht' ich eine Quelle suchen, aus der ich einen besondern Abel schöpfte und nicht unter die wahnhaften Edelleute gezählt würde, zufrieden mit dem, was ich von meinen Voreltern empfangen; sondern daß ich zu jenen Gütern noch etwas selbst hinzugefügt hätte, was von mir auf meine Nach= kommen hinüberginge.

But I am anxious to seek a fountain, out of which I may draw a nobility that should be my own, a noble of nature's own creating, and not be merely mentioned among silly nobles, satisfied with what I have inherited from my ancestors, but that I should add something to the store, which may pass over from me to my posterity.

The Envious Ignoramus.

Truth and Poetry, iv. *b* 17, *vol.* XXII. *p.* 327.

Nicht allein ein Thor ist der Ungelehrte zu nennen, welcher den beneidet, der durch Kenntnisse sich hervorgethan, sondern unter die Elenden, ja unter die Elendesten zu zählen.

Not only is the ignorant man who envies him who has raised himself to eminence by his learning to be counted a fool, but to be reckoned a miserable wretch—yea, among the most miserable.

GENIUS.

Truth and Poetry, IV. *b.* 19, *vol.* XXII. *p.* 379.

Daß Genie diejenige Kraft des Menschen sey, welche, durch Handeln und Thun, Gesetz und Regel giebt.

Wenn einer zu Fuße, ohne recht zu wissen, warum und wohin, in die Welt lief, so hieß dieß eine Geniereise, und wenn einer etwas Verkehrtes ohne Zweck und Nutzen unternahm, ein Geniestreich.

Genius is that power of man which by deeds and actions gives laws and rules. When any one rushed into the world on foot without knowing precisely why or whither, it was called a journey of a genius; and when any one undertook some absurdity without aim or advantage, it was a stroke of genius.

SEEMING OBSCURITY IN STYLE.

Truth and Poetry, IV. *b.* 19.

Wer einem Autor Dunkelheit verwerfen will, sollte erst sein eigenes

Innere besuchen, ob es denn da auch recht hell ist. In der Dämmerung wird eine sehr deutliche Schrift unlesbar.

He who would reproach an author for obscurity should look into his own mind to see whether it is quite clear there. In the dusk the plainest writing is illegible.

GREAT MEN SELDOM FIND THEIR EQUALS AMONG THEIR CONTEMPORARIES.

Truth and Poetry, IV. *b.* 20, *vol.* XXII. *p.* 402.

Selten oder nie finden sich Gleichzeitige ihres Gleichen, und sie sind durch nichts zu überwinden, als durch das Universum selbst, mit dem sie den Kampf begonnen; und aus solchen Bemerkungen mag wohl jener sonderbare, aber ungeheure Spruch entstanden seyn: Nemo contra deum nisi deus ipse.

Seldom or never do great men find their equals among their contemporaries, and they cannot be overcome except by the universe itself, with which they commenced the strife ; it is from the observation of such a fact as this that the strange but most striking proverb has arisen—"No one can contend with God but God himself."

The Rich.

Hermann and Dorothea, c. 1. l. 15.

Denn Geben ist Sache des Reichen.

For to give is the business of the rich.

Man rejoices in the Misfortunes of his Neighbour.

Hermann and Dorothea, c. 1. l. 71.

So sind die Menschen fürwahr! und einer ist doch wie der andre,
Daß er zu gaffen sich freut, wenn den nächsten ein Unglück befället!
Läuft doch jeder, die Flamme zu sehn, die verderblich emporschlägt,
Jeder den armen Verbrecher, der peinlich zum Tode geführt wird.
Jeder spaziert nun hinaus, zu schauen der guten Vertriebnen
Elend, und niemand bedenkt, daß ihn das ähnliche Schicksal
Auch, vielleicht zunächst, betreffen kann, oder doch künftig.
Unverzeihlich find' ich den Leichtsinn; doch liegt er im Menschen.

So indeed are men! one is like the other; he takes pleasure when misfortune befalls his neighbour! Yea, every one runs to see the flames which have burst forth in fury; every one rushes to behold the poor wretch led sorrowful to death. Every one walks out to witness the afflictions of the exile; and no one thinks how the same fate may await him next, or at least on some future occasion. Such thoughtlessness I regard as unpardonable; yet it is in men.

Why Curiosity is implanted in the Breast of Man.

Hermann and Dorothea, c. 1. l. 86.

Ich table nicht gerne, was immer dem Menschen
Für unschädliche Triebe die gute Mutter Natur gab;
Denn was Verstand und Vernunft nicht immer vermögen, vermag oft
Solch ein glücklicher Hang, der unwiderstehlich uns leitet.

Lockte die Neugier nicht den Menschen mit heftigen Reizen,
Sagt! erführ' er wohl je, wie schön sich die weltlichen Dinge
Gegen einander verhalten? Denn erst verlangt er das Neue,
Suchet das Nützliche dann mit unermüdetem Fleiße;
Endlich begehrt er das Gute, das ihn erhebet und werth macht.
In der Jugend ist ihm ein froher Gefährte der Leichtsinn,
Der die Gefahr ihm verbirgt, und heilsam geschwinde die
      Spuren
Tilget des schmerzlichen Uebels, sobald es nur irgend vorbeizog.
Freilich ist er zu preisen, der Mann, dem in reiferen Jahren
Sich der gesetzte Verstand aus solchem Frohsinn entwickelt,
Der im Glück wie im Unglück, sich eifrig und thätig bestrebet;
Denn das Gute bringt er hervor und ersetzet den Schaden.

I am loth to blame what good Mother Nature certainly gave to
me for no evil end; for a lucky instinct, leading us on irresistibly,
often attains what neither understanding nor reason could ever
accomplish. Did not curiosity lure men forward with strong
attractions, tell me, how much could man have known of the
countless combinations of things? For he first longs for something new, then tries to attain the useful with unwearied efforts;
at last desires the good, which elevates and raises to renown. In
youth levity is his jocund guide, which veils his eyes to danger,
quickly razing the traces of the most bitter griefs the moment
they are passed. Highly to be praised is the man whose well-
poised mind in riper years releases him from such light conduct,
who in good and evil fortune is actively engaged, for he draws
good from evil.

ANTICIPATION OF EVIL WORSE THAN THE EVIL ITSELF.

Hermann and Dorothea, c. I. l. 160.

Denn es beschleichet die Furcht gar bald die Herzen der
      Menschen,
Und die Sorge, die mehr als selbst mir das Uebel verhaßt ist.

For fear surprises very often the heart of man, and care, which
is more hateful to me than the evil itself.

THE HAPPY.

Hermann and Dorothea, c. II. l. 50.

Der Glückliche glaubt nicht,
Daß noch Wunder geschehn; denn nur im Elend erkennt man

Gottes Hand und Finger, der gute Menschen zum Guten
Leitet. Was er durch Euch an uns thut, thu' er Euch selber.

The happy believe not in miracles, for it is only in misery that
they acknowledge God's hand and finger, which leads the good to
good. What he does through you to us he does himself.

Every Beginning is Difficult.

Hermann and Dorothea, c. II. l. 161.

        Nicht einen jeden betrifft es
Anzufangen von vorn sein ganzes Leben und Wesen;
Nicht soll jeder sich quälen, wie wir und andere thaten,
O, wie glücklich ist der, dem Vater und Mutter das Haus schon
Wohlbestellt übergeben, und der mit Gedeihen es ausziert!
Aller Anfang ist schwer, am schwersten der Anfang der Wirth-
    schaft.

It is not for every one to begin over again his whole life and
being; it is not every one that can toil and moil. Oh, how happy
he whose father and mother can make over the house well arranged
and in every way adorned! Every beginning is difficult; the most
difficult that of a domestic establishment.

Husband and Wife.

Hermann and Dorothea, c. II. l. 172.

Denn ein wackerer Mann verdient ein begütertes Mädchen.

For an active man deserves a maiden well tochered.

Man should not be like a Fungus.

Hermann and Dorothea, c. III. l. 9.

Soll doch nicht als ein Pilz der Mensch dem Boden entwachsen,
Und verfaulen geschwind an dem Platze, der ihn erzeugt hat,
Keine Spur nachlassend von seiner lebendigen Wirkung!

Man should not spring from the earth like a fungus, and rot
quickly on the spot where he rose, leaving no trace that he has
been.

Children.

Hermann and Dorothea, c. III. l. 47.

Denn wir können die Kinder nach unserm Sinne nicht formen;
So wie Gott sie uns gab, so muß man sie haben und lieben,

Sie erziehen auf's Beste und jeglichen laſſen gewähren.
Denn der eine hat die, die anderen andere Gaben;
Jeder braucht ſie, und jeder iſt doch nur auf eigene Weiſe
Gut und glücklich.

For we cannot form our children as we would wish ; as God has
given us them, so must we accept and love, educate them as we
best may, and rest content. For each has different gifts ; every
one is useful, but in his proper way.

The Germans and French.

Hermann and Dorothea, c. IV. l. 81.

Die Fluthen des Rheines
Schützen uns zwar; doch ach! was ſind nun Fluthen und Berge
Jenem ſchrecklichen Volke, das wie ein Gewitter daherzieht!
Denn ſie rufen zuſammen aus allen Enden die Jugend,
Wie das Alter, und dringen gewaltig vor, und die Menge
Scheut den Tod nicht; es bringt gleich nach der Menge die
    Menge.

The waters of the Rhine protect us no doubt, yet, alas ! what
are waters and mountains to that terror-bringing people, who rush
on like a thunderstorm? For they summon young and old from
every corner of their country, and press furiously forward, the
crowd shunning not death, but pressing man on man.

Boys ripen into Men.

Hermann and Dorothea, c. IV. l. 126.

Ein Tag iſt
Nicht dem anderen gleich. Der Jüngling reifet zum Manne;
Beſſer im Stillen reift er zur That oft, als im Geräuſche
Wilden ſchwankenden Lebens, das manchen Jüngling verderbt
    hat.

One day resembles not another; boys ripen into men, and ripen
better often under the shade than in a wild intoxicated world, the
bane of youth.

Marriages are made in Heaven.

Hermann and Dorothea, c. IV. l. 203.

Aber mir iſt es bekannt, und jetzo ſagt es das Herz mir:
Wenn die Stunde nicht kommt, die rechte, wenn nicht das rechte

Mädchen zur Stunde sich zeigt, so bleibt das Wählen im Weiten,
Und es wirket die Furcht, die falsche zu greifen, am meisten.

But it was known to me, and my heart now tells it me, till the
happy hour comes, till the right maiden appears at the hour, the
choice remains in abeyance; and there is always the fear that the
wrong maiden may be fixed on.

Improvement is a Duty.

Hermann and Dorothea, c. v. l. 6.

Ich weiß es, der Mensch soll
Immer streben zum Bessern; und, wie wir sehen, er strebt auch
Immer dem Höheren nach, zum wenigsten sucht er das Neue.
Aber geht nicht zu weit! Denn neben diesen Gefühlen
Gab die Natur uns auch die Lust zu verharren im Alten,
Und sich dessen zu freun, was jeder lange gewohnt ist.
Aller Zustand ist gut, der natürlich ist und vernünftig.
Vieles wünscht sich der Mensch, und doch bedarf er nur wenig;
Denn die Tage sind kurz, und beschränkt der Sterblichen
        Schicksal.
Niemals tadl' ich den Mann, der immer, thätig und rastlos
Umgetrieben, das Meer und alle Straßen der Erde
Kühn und emsig befährt und sich des Gewinnes erfreuet,
Welcher sich reichlich um ihn und um die Seinen herum häuft.

Right well I know that improvement is a duty, and as we see
man strives ever after a higher point, at least he seeks some
novelty. But beware! for with these feelings Nature has given
us also a desire to continue in the old ways, and to take pleasure
in that to which we have been accustomed. Every condition of
man is good which is natural and in accordance with reason.
Man's desires are boundless, but his wants are few. For his days
are short, and his fate bounded by a narrow span. I find no fault
with the man who, ever active and restless, crosses every sea, and
braves the rude extremes of every clime, daring and diligent in
pursuit of gain, rejoicing his heart and house by wealth.

An Instant decides the Fate of Man.

Hermann and Dorothea, c. v. l. 57.

Der Augenblick nur entscheidet
Ueber das Leben des Menschen und über sein ganzes Geschicke;

Denn nach langer Berathung ist doch ein jeder Entschluß nur
Werk des Moments, es ergreift doch nur der Verständ'ge das
Rechte.
Immer gefährlicher ist's, beim Wählen dieses und jenes
Nebenher zu bedenken und so das Gefühl zu verwirren.

An instant decides the life of man and his whole fate ; for after
lengthened thought the resolve is only the act of a moment ; it is
the man of sense that seizes on the right thing to be done ; it is
ever dangerous to linger in your selection on this and that, and
thus by your hesitation to get confused.

GIFTS FROM ON HIGH.

Hermann and Dorothea, c. v. l. 69.

Die Gaben
Kommen von oben herab in ihren eignen Gestalten.

Gifts come from on high in their own peculiar forms.

THE WISE MAN.

Hermann and Dorothea, c. v. l. 217.

Aber zerrüttet die Noth die gewöhnlichen Wege des Lebens,
Reißt das Gebäude nieder, und wühlet Garten und Saat um,
Treibt den Mann und das Weib vom Raume der traulichen
    Wohnung,
Schleppt in die Irre sie fort, durch ängstliche Tage und Nächte :
Ach ! da sieht man sich um, wer wohl der verständigste Mann sey,
Und er redet nicht mehr die herrlichen Worte vergebens.

But should evil times come, destroying the accustomed habits
of life—pulling down houses, uprooting gardens and fields of corn
—driving husband and wife from their beloved abode, and sending
them into the bleak world to spend sorrowing days and nights—
ah ! then we see who is the man that can " look before and after,"
and his words are then not in vain.

A BEAUTEOUS FORM.

Hermann and Dorothea, c. VI. l. 151.

Glücklich, wem doch Mutter Natur die rechte Gestalt gab !
Denn sie empfiehlet ihn stets, und nirgends ist er ein Fremdling

Jeder nahet sich gern, und jeder möchte verweilen,
Wenn die Gefälligkeit nur sich zu der Gestalt noch gesellet.

Happy on whom Mother Nature has conferred a beauteous form!
for it is always a passport, and nowhere is he looked on with
strange eyes. Every one receives him with delight, and every one
would welcome him, if manners correspond.

A Wandering Maiden.

Hermann and Dorothea, c. VII. l. 93.

Denn ein wanderndes Mädchen ist immer von schwankendem Rufe.

For a wandering maid is of doubtful reputation.

The Fate of Woman.

Hermann and Dorothea, c. VII. l. 114.

Dienen lerne bei Zeiten das Weib nach ihrer Bestimmung;
Denn durch Dienen allein gelangt sie endlich zum Herrschen,
Zu der verdienten Gewalt, die doch ihr im Hause gehöret.
Dienet die Schwester dem Bruder doch früh, sie dienet den
　　Eltern,
Und ihr Leben ist immer ein ewiges Gehen und Kommen,
Oder ein Heben und Tragen, Bereiten und Schaffen für andre.
Wohl ihr, wenn sie daran sich gewöhnt, daß kein Weg ihr zu
　　sauer
Wird, und die Stunden der Nacht ihr sind wie die Stunden
　　des Tages,
Daß ihr niemals die Arbeit zu klein und die Nadel zu fein dünkt,
Daß sie sich ganz vergißt, und leben mag nur in andern!
Denn als Mutter, fürwahr, bedarf sie der Tugenden alle,
Wenn der Säugling die Krankende weckt und Nahrung begehret
Von der Schwachen und so zu Schmerzen Sorgen sich häufen.
Zwanzig Männer verbunden ertrügen nicht diese Beschwerde,
Und sie sollen es nicht; doch sollen sie dankbar es einsehn.

　　The woman learns to serve by times to suit her fate; for by
having first learned to serve, she learns to govern in the domain
which belongs to her in the house. The sister must serve the
brother, parents; her life is an eternal coming and going, lifting
and carrying, preparing and getting things ready for others. Well
for her if she accustoms herself to such a life, so that no road is

too rough ; that the hours of night are to her the same as those of
the day, that no work seems too trifling, no needle too fine ; so
that, in fact, she forgets herself and lives only for others. For a
mother, certes, needs to possess every good quality ; the baby
wakes her in suffering and calls for food, and thus heavy cares
are heaped on sorrows. Not twenty men united could bear such
burdens, nor should they, but they should acknowledge woman's
worth.

IT IS WELL TO KNOW THE WHIMS OF A MASTER.

Hermann and Dorothea, c. VIII. l. 15.

Denn kennt jemand den Herrn, so kann er ihm leichter genug
   thun,
Wenn er die Dinge bedenkt, die jenem die wichtigsten scheinen,
Und auf die er den Sinn, den festbestimmten, gesetzt hat.

For it is an easier task to serve if one knows the character of
the master, can attend to the things which he considers most
important and on which he is most determined.

DEATH.

Hermann and Dorothea, c. IX. l. 46.

       Des Todes rührendes Bild steht,
Nicht als Schrecken dem Weisen, und nicht als Ende dem
   Frommen.
Jenen drängt es in's Leben zurück, und lehret ihn handeln;
Diesem stärkt es, zu künftigem Heil, im Trübsal die Hoffnung;
Beiden wird zum Leben der Tod. Der Vater mit Unrecht
Hat dem empfindlichen Knaben den Tod im Tode gewiesen.
Zeige man doch dem Jüngling des edel reifenden Alters
Werth, und dem Alter die Jugend, daß beide des ewigen Kreises
Sich erfreuen und so sich Leben im Leben vollende!

The soul-stirring image of death is no bugbear to the sage, and
is looked on without despair by the pious. It teaches the former
to live, and it strengthens the hope of the latter in salvation in the
midst of distress. Death is new life to both. The father should
not teach his sensitive son that death is death and nothing else ;
he should point out to youth the gain of noble ripening age, and
to the old the years of the young, so that both may rejoice in the
eternal circle—how this life ends in life that does not end !

The Firm in Will.

Hermann and Dorothea, c. IX. l. 303.

Aber wer fest auf dem Sinne beharrt, der bildet die Welt sich.
He who is firm in will moulds the world to himself.

"Cut your Coat according to your Cloth."

Proverbs, vol. III. *p.* 11.

Wer sich nicht nach der Decke streckt,
Dem bleiben die Füße unbedeckt.

He who does not stretch himself according to the coverlet finds
his feet uncovered.

Some People expect Everything to suit their Taste.

Proverbs, vol. III. *p.* 14.

Wer aber recht bequem ist und faul,
Flög' dem eine gebratne Taube in's Maul
Er würde höchlich sich's verbitten,
Wär' sie nicht auch geschickt zerschnitten.

But he who is idle and lazy, were a roast pigeon to fly into his
mouth, would be highly indignant if it were not also neatly cut
up into pieces.

Mode of Courtship.

Proverbs, vol. III. *p.* 14.

Der Mutter schenk' ich,
Die Tochter denk' ich.

I make presents to the mother, but I am thinking on the
daughter.

A Succession of Prosperous Days.

Proverbs, vol. III. *p.* 15.

Alles in der Welt läßt sich ertragen,
Nur nicht eine Reihe von schönen Tagen.

Everything in the world may be endured, except only a succession of prosperous days.

Every Man comes to an End.

Proverbs, vol. III. *p.* 19.

Der Mensch erfährt, er sey auch wer er mag,
Ein letztes Glück und einen letzten Tag.

Man, be he who he may, experiences a last piece of good fortune
and a last day.

He who serves the Public.

Proverbs, vol. III. *p.* 23.

Wer dem Publicum dient, ist ein armes Thier;
Er quält sich ab, niemand bedankt sich dafür.

He who serves the public is a poor animal ; he worries himself
to death, and no one thanks him for it.

He gives twice who gives quickly.

Proverbs, vol. III. *p.* 25.

Doppelt giebt, wer gleich giebt,
Hundertfach, der gleich giebt
Was man wünscht und liebt.

He gives doubly who gives quickly ; a hundred-fold, who gives
quickly what one wishes and likes.

Divide and Command.

Proverbs, vol. III. *p.* 31.

Entzwei' und gebiete! Tüchtig Wort,
Verein' und leite! Beßrer Hort.

Divide and command, a wise maxim ; unite and guide, a better.

Duty.

Maxims, vol. III. *p.* 141.

Was aber ist deine Pflicht? Die Forderung des Tages.

But what is your duty ?—The carrying on the affairs of the day
that lies before you.

How a Man must act in Life.

Maxims, vol. III. *p.* 142.

Jeder Mensch muß nach seiner Weise denken, denn er findet
auf seinem Wege immer ein Wahres, oder eine Art von Wahrem,
die ihm durch's Leben hilft; nur darf er sich nicht gehen lassen;
er muß sich controliren!

Every one must think in his own manner, for he finds on his
road always a truth or a kind of truth which helps him through
life ; only he must not let it have its own way, but control it.

The True.

Maxims, vol. III. *p.* 143.

Es ist nicht immer nöthig, daß das Wahre sich verkörpere;
schon genug, wenn es geistig umher schwebt und Uebereinstimmung bewirkt; wenn es wie Glockenton ernstfreundlich durch
die Lüfte wogt.

It is not always necessary that the true should take visible form ;
quite enough if, like a spirit, it hover about and produce harmony,
if it wave through the air in a friendly way like a peal of bells.

The Flute.

Maxims, vol. III. *p.* 145.

Blasen ist nicht flöten, ihr müßt die Finger bewegen.

To blow is not to play on the flute, you must move the fingers
to bring out the notes.

The Man of the Smallest Powers.

Maxims, vol. III. *p.* 145.

Der geringste Mensch kann complet seyn, wenn er sich inner-
halb der Gränzen seiner Fähigkeiten und Fertigkeiten bewegt;
aber selbst schöne Vorzüge werden verdunkelt, aufgehoben
und vernichtet, wenn jedes unerläßlich geforderte Ebenmaaß
abgeht. Dieses Unheil wird sich in der neuern Zeit noch öfter
hervorthun; denn wer wird wohl den Forderungen einer
durchaus gesteigerten Gegenwart und zwar in schnellster Bewegung, genugthun können?

The man of the least mental powers may be perfect if he move within the limits of his own capacities and abilities, but even the noblest advantages become obscured, annulled, and annihilated, when symmetry, that is so indispensable, is broken through. This mischief will still oftener appear in these present times ; for who will be able to satisfy the requirements of a present ever calling for more exertion and in the highest state of excitement?

MEN OF PRUDENT ENERGY.

Maxims, vol. III. *p.* 144.

Nur klugthätige Menschen, die ihre Kräfte kennen und sie mit Maaß und Gescheidtigkeit benutzen, werden es im Weltwesen weit bringen.

Only men of prudent energy, who know their own powers, and use them with moderation and discretion, will be successful in the world's affairs.

SELF-CONCEIT AND SELF-DEPRECIATION.

Maxims, vol. III. *p.* 144.

Ein großer Fehler: daß man sich mehr dünkt, als man ist und sich weniger schätzt, als man werth ist.

A great mistake—that we think ourselves greater than we are and value ourselves less than we deserve.

ENTHUSIASM.

Maxims, vol. III. *p.* 149.

Das Beste, was wir von der Geschichte haben, ist der Enthusiasmus, den sie erregt.

The best thing which we derive from history is the enthusiasm that it raises in us.

PECULIARITY.

Maxims, vol. III. *p.* 149.

Eigenthümlichkeit ruft Eigenthümlichkeit hervor.

One peculiarity calls up another.

Earnest-thinking Men.

Maxims, vol. III. *p.* 149.

Tief und ernstlich denkende Menschen haben gegen das Pub=
licum einen bösen Stand.

Deep and earnest-thinking men have a bad position in regard to
the public.

Superstition.

Maxims, vol. III. *p.* 149.

Der Aberglaube gehört zum Wesen des Menschen und
flüchtet sich, wenn man ihn ganz und gar zu verdrängen denkt,
in die wunderlichsten Ecken und Winkel, von wo er auf einmal,
wenn er einigermaßen sicher zu seyn glaubt, wieder hervortritt.

Superstition is natural to men, and takes refuge, when we
imagine that we have rooted it out, in the strangest nooks and
corners, from which it issues at once, when it thinks itself in any
way secure.

Hypocrites.

Maxims, vol. III. *p.* 153.

Deßwegen läßt sich bemerken, daß diejenigen, welche Fröm=
migkeit als Zweck und Ziel aufstecken, meistens Heuchler werden.

For this reason we may remark that those who make use of
devotion as a means and end, generally are hypocrites.

The Old.

Maxims, vol. III. *p.* 153.

Wenn man alt ist, muß man mehr thun, als da man jung
war.

When we are old, we must do more than when we were young.

Fortune.

Maxims, vol. III. *p.* 153.

Das höchste Glück ist das, welches unsere Mängel verbessert
und unsere Fehler ausgleicht.

The highest fortune is that which corrects our defects and
compensates our failings.

The Affairs of this World.

Maxims, vol. III. *p.* 156.

Es geschieht nichts Unvernünftiges, das nicht Verstand oder Zufall wieder in die Richte brächten; nichts Vernünftiges, das Unverstand und Zufall nicht mißleiten könnten.

There is nothing so irrational, which good sense or chance may not again set to rights; nothing so rational, which folly and chance may not utterly confound.

Wisdom.

Maxims, vol. III. *p.* 158.

Die Weisheit ist nur in der Wahrheit

Wisdom is only in truth.

A Mistake and a Falsehood.

Maxims, vol. III. *p.* 158.

Wenn ich irre, kann es jeder bemerken, wenn ich lüge nicht.

When I make a mistake every one can see it, when I tell a falsehood it is not so.

Enigmas in the World.

Maxims, vol. III. *p.* 159.

Ist denn die Welt nicht schon voller Räthsel genug, daß man die einfachen Erscheinungen auch noch zu Räthseln machen soll?

Is not the world sufficiently full of enigmas, that one must make simple appearances also to be enigmas?

A Hair throws its Shadow.

Maxims, vol. III. *p.* 159.

Das kleinste Haar wirft seinen Schatten.

The smallest hair throws its shadow.

How we would best know each other.

Maxims, vol. III. *p.* 161.

Man würde einander besser kennen, wenn sich nicht immer einer dem andern gleichstellen wollte.

We would better understand each other if we did not **wish to** compare ourselves with each other.

To Understand.

Maxims, vol. III. *p.* 161

Was man nicht versteht, besitzt man nicht.

What we do not understand, we do not possess.

A Happy Man.

Maxims, vol. III. *p.* 164.

Der ist der glücklichste Mensch, der das Ende seines Lebens mit dem Anfang in Verbindung setzen kann.

He is the happiest man who can place the end of his life in connection with the beginning.

Truth and Error.

Maxims, vol. III. *p.* 165.

Es ist so gewiß als wunderbar, daß Wahrheit und Irrthum aus Einer Quelle entstehen; deßwegen man oft dem Irrthum nicht schaden darf, weil man zugleich der Wahrheit schadet.

It is as certain as strange that truth and error spring from the same source, for which reason we ought often to do nothing against error, as we do at the same time injury to truth.

Not to think too much of Oneself.

Maxims, vol. III. *p.* 165.

Wer sich nicht zu viel dünkt, ist viel mehr als er glaubt.

He who does not think too much of himself is much more esteemed than he imagines.

Faith.

Maxims, vol. III. *p.* 167.

Der Glaube ist ein häuslich, heimlich Capital, wie es öffentliche Spar- und Hülfskassen giebt, woraus man, in Tagen der Noth, Einzelnen ihr Bedürfniß reicht; hier nimmt der Gläubige sich seine Zinsen im Stillen selbst.

Faith is a homely, private capital ; as there are public savings banks and poor funds, out of which in times of want we can relieve the necessities of individuals, so here the faithful take their coin in peace.

TRUTH.

Maxims, vol. III. *p.* 168.

Das Wahre ist eine Fackel, aber eine ungeheure; deßwegen suchen wir alle nur blinzend so daran vorbei zu kommen, in Furcht sogar uns zu verbrennen.

Truth is a torch, but a terrific one, therefore we all try to reach it with closed eyes lest we should be scorched.

HATRED AND ENVY.

Maxims, vol. III. *p.* 169.

Der Haß ist ein actives Mißvergnügen, der Neid ein passives; deßhalb darf man sich nicht wundern, wenn der Neid so schnell in Haß übergeht.

Hatred is an active feeling of disgust, envy a passive ; therefore we need not wonder that envy passes so quickly into hatred.

ERROR AND TRUTH.

Maxims, vol. III. *p.* 171.

Der Irrthum ist viel leichter zu erkennen, als die Wahrheit zu finden; jener liegt auf der Oberfläche, damit läßt sich wohl fertig werden; diese ruht in der Tiefe, danach zu forschen ist nicht jedermanns Sache.

It is much easier to perceive error than to find truth ; the former lies on the surface, so that it is easily got at ; the latter lies in the depth, which it is not every man's business to search for.

SUPERSTITION.

Maxims, vol. III. *p.* 172.

Der Aberglaube ist die Poesie des Lebens, deßwegen schadet's dem Dichter nicht, abergläubisch zu seyn.

Superstition is the poesy of life, so that it does not injure the poet to be superstitious.

THE MULTITUDE.

Maxims, vol. III. *p.* 173.

Die Menge kann tüchtige Menschen nicht entbehren, und die Tüchtigen sind ihnen jederzeit zur Last.

The multitude cannot do without clever people, and the clever are ever a burden to them.

THE LOWER ORDERS.

Maxims, vol. III. *p.* 173.

Wenn man von den Leuten Pflichten fordert und ihnen keine Rechte zugestehen will, muß man sie gut bezahlen.

If we require duties from the lower orders and will grant them no privileges, we must pay them well.

UPRIGHT AND UNBIASSED.

Maxims, vol. III. *p.* 174.

Aufrichtig zu seyn kann ich versprechen; unparteiisch zu seyn aber nicht.

I can promise to be upright, but not to be without bias.

INGRATITUDE.

Maxims, vol. III. *p.* 174.

Der Undank ist immer eine Art Schwäche. Ich habe nie gesehen, daß tüchtige Menschen wären undankbar gewesen.

Ingratitude is always a kind of weakness. I have never seen that clever men have been ungrateful.

THE MAN OF THE WORLD.

Maxims, vol. III. *p.* 175.

Eine Sammlung von Anekdoten und Maximen ist für den Weltmann der größte Schatz, wenn er die ersten an schicklichen Orten in's Gespräch einzustreuen, der letzten im treffenden Falle sich zu erinnern weiß.

A collection of anecdotes and maxims is the greatest of

treasures for the man of the world, for he knows how to intersperse conversation with the former in fit places, and to recollect the latter on proper occasions.

Men who never Err.

Maxims, vol. III. *p.* 175.

Es giebt Menschen die gar nicht irren, weil sie sich nichts Vernünftiges vorsetzen.

There are men who never err, because they never propose anything rational.

Time.

Maxims, vol. III. *p.* 176.

Die Zeit ist selbst ein Element.

Time itself is an element.

To know Little.

Maxims, vol. III. *p.* 179.

Eigentlich weiß man nur, wenn man wenig weiß; mit dem Wissen wächs't der Zweifel.

We know accurately only when we know little ; with knowledge doubt increases.

Different Feelings of Men.

Maxims, vol. III. *p.* 179.

Es giebt Menschen, die ihres Gleichen lieben und aufsuchen, und wieder solche, die ihr Gegentheil lieben und diesem nachgehn.

There are men who love and seek after those like to themselves, and again those who love their opposite and go after these.

A World of Delusion.

Maxims, vol. III. *p.* 180.

Wie in Rom außer den Römern noch ein Volk von Statuen war, so ist außer dieser realen Welt noch eine Welt des Wahns, viel mächtiger beinahe, in der die Meisten leben.

As in Rome, besides the Romans, there is a people of statues, so is there, besides this real world, also a world of fancy, much more powerful, in which most men dwell.

The Greeks.

Maxims, vol. III. *p.* 181.

Unter allen Völkerschaften haben die Griechen den Traum des Lebens am schönsten geträumt.

The Greeks more than all other people have dreamed the most beautiful dream of life.

Truth and Error.

Maxims, vol. III. *p.* 182

Die Wahrheit widerspricht unserer Natur, der Irrthum nicht, und zwar aus einem sehr einfachen Grunde: die Wahrheit fordert, daß wir uns für beschränkt erkennen sollen, der Irrthum schmeichelt uns, wir seyen auf ein oder die andere Weise unbegränzt.

Truth is opposed to our nature, error not, and that too for a simple reason : truth requires that we be confined within limits, error flatters us that we are not confined in any way.

The Age.

Maxims, vol. III. *p.* 183.

Zu allen Zeiten sind es nur die Individuen, welche für die Wissenschaft gewirkt, nicht das Zeitalter. Das Zeitalter war's, das den Sokrates durch Gift hinrichtete; das Zeitalter, das Hussen verbrannte; die Zeitalter sind sich immer gleich geblieben.

In all times it is only individuals who labour to advance knowledge, and not the ages in which they live. It was the age that executed Socrates by poison, the age that burned Huss ; ages have ever been the same.

To be Able to follow Good Advice.

Maxims, vol. III. *p.* 183.

Es ist eben als ob man es selbst vermöchte, wenn man sich guten Raths erholen kann.

It is the same as if one were able oneself, if one can accept good advice.

The Best Government.

Maxims, vol. III. *p.* 189.

Welche Regierung die beste sey? Diejenige, die uns lehrt, uns selbst zu regieren.

What government is the best? That which teaches us to govern ourselves.

Ignorance.

Maxims, vol. III. *p.* 191.

Es ist nichts schrecklicher, als eine thätige Unwissenheit.

There is nothing more frightful than a bustling ignorance.

The Old.

Maxims, vol. III. *p.* 191.

Der Alte verliert eins der größten Menschenrechte, er wird nicht mehr von seines Gleichen beurtheilt.

The old lose one of the greatest privileges of man, they are no longer judged by their contemporaries.

A Slave.

Maxims, vol. III. *p.* 203.

Niemand ist mehr Sklave, als der sich für frei hält, ohne es zu seyn.

No one is a greater slave than the man who considers himself free without being so.

Irish Character.

Maxims, vol. III. *p.* 203.

Dieser schnelle Wechsel von Ernst und Scherz, von Antheil und Gleichgültigkeit, von Leid und Freude soll in dem irländischen Charakter liegen.

This rapid change from seriousness to trifling, from sympathy to indifference, from joy to grief, must lie at the foundation of the Irish character.

No One a Hero to his Valet.

Maxims, vol. III. *p.* 204.

Es giebt, sagt man, für den Kammerdiener keinen Helden. Das kommt aber bloß daher, weil der Held nur vom Helden anerkannt werden kann. Der Kammerdiener wird aber wahrscheinlich Seinesgleichen zu schätzen wissen.

No one, it is said, is a hero to his own servant ; but that arises simply from the circumstance that a hero can only be known by heroes. The servant would probably be able to appreciate those like to himself.

See (Fr.) Men, few, are objects of admiration to their servants.

Those who are Indebted to us.

Maxims, vol. III. *p.* 205.

Begegnet uns jemand, der uns Dank schuldig ist, gleich fällt es uns ein. Wie oft können wir jemand begegnen, dem wir Dank schuldig sind, ohne daran zu denken.

If we meet with any one who is indebted to us, it immediately occurs to us—How often can we meet with those to whom we are indebted without thinking of it !

The Talkative.

Maxims, vol. III. *p.* 205.

Wer vor andern lange allein spricht, ohne den Zuhörern zu schmeicheln, erregt Widerwillen.

Whoever speaks long before others, without flattering his audience, excites opposition.

What shows the Character of a Man best.

Maxims, vol. III. *p.* 206.

Durch nichts bezeichnen die Menschen mehr ihren Charakter als durch das, was sie lächerlich finden.

Men show their character in nothing more clearly than by what they think laughable.

Two True Religions.

Maxims, vol. III. *p.* 217.

Es giebt nur zwei wahre Religionen, die eine die das Heilige, das in und um uns wohnt, ganz formlos, die andere die
es in der schönsten Form anerkennt und anbetet. Alles was
dazwischen liegt ist Götzendienst.

There are only two true religions—the one which acknowledges
and adores the holy, which dwells in and around us, quite without form ; the other adores it in its most beautiful forms. All
that lies between these is the service of God.

To Deceive.

Maxims, vol. III. *p.* 219.

Man wird nie betrogen; man betrügt sich selbst.

We are never deceived ; we deceive ourselves.

Imagination without Taste.

Maxims, vol. III. *p.* 220.

Es ist nichts fürchterlicher als Einbildungskraft ohne
Geschmack.

There is nothing more fearful than imagination without taste.

Modern Poets.

Maxims, vol. III. *p.* 222.

Neuere Poeten thun viel Wasser in die Dinte.

Modern poets mix much water with their ink.

Better to be employed.

Maxims, vol. III. *p.* 223.

Es ist besser das geringste Ding von der Welt zu thun, als
eine halbe Stunde für gering halten.

It is better to be doing the most insignificant thing in the
world than to reckon half an hour insignificant.

FOOLS.

Maxims, vol. III. *p.* 223.

Unter allem Diebsgefindel find die Narren die schlimmsten: fie rauben euch beides, Zeit und Stimmung.

Of all thieves fools are the worst; they rob you both of time and temper.

COURAGE AND MODESTY.

Maxims, vol. III. *p.* 223.

Muth und Bescheidenheit find die unzweideutigsten Tugenden; denn die find von der Art, daß Heuchelei fie nicht nachahmen kann; auch haben fie die Eigenschaft gemein, fich beide durch dieselbe Farbe auszudrücken.

Courage and modesty are the most unequivocal of virtues, for they are of a kind that hypocrisy cannot imitate ; they too have this quality in common, that they are expressed by the same colour.

DIFFICULTIES.

Maxims, vol. III. *p.* 226.

Die größten Schwierigkeiten liegen da, wo wir fie nicht fuchen.

The greatest difficulties lie where we are not looking for them.

LOVE OF TRUTH.

Maxims, vol. III. *p.* 229.

Das erfte und letzte, was vom Genie gefordert wird, ift Wahrheitsliebe.

The first and last thing which is required of genius is the love of truth.

THE MAN TRUE TO HIMSELF.

Maxims, vol. III. *p.* 229.

Wer gegen fich felbft und andere wahr ift und bleibt, befitzt die schönfte Eigenschaft der größten Talente.

He who is and remains true to himself and others possesses the finest quality of the greatest talents.

PREDESTINATION.

Maxims, vol. III. *p.* 232.

Frage.

Was ist Prädestination?

Antwort.

Gott ist mächtiger und weiser als wir, darum macht er es mit uns nach seinem Gefallen.

Ques. What is predestination? *Ans.* God is more powerful and wiser than we are, therefore he does with us according to his will.

THE MATURITY OF A NATION.

Maxims, vol. III. *p.* 236.

Ob eine Nation reif werden könne, ist eine wunderliche Frage. Ich beantworte sie mit Ja, wenn alle Männer als dreißigjährig geboren werden könnten. Da aber die Jugend vorlaut, das Alter aber kleinlaut ewig seyn wird, so ist der eigentlich reife Mann immer zwischen beiden geklemmt und wird sich auf eine wunderliche Weise behelfen und durchhelfen müssen.

Whether a nation can become ripe is a strange question. I answer with " Yes," if all men could be born thirty years of age. But as youth is too loud and age is ever too low in voice, thus the really mature man is always hemmed in between both, and must in a strange way resort to expedients, and help himself on his way.

THE PUBLIC LIKE A WOMAN.

Maxims, vol. III. *p.* 241.

Das Publikum will wie Frauenzimmer behandelt seyn: man soll ihnen durchaus nichts sagen als was sie hören möchten.

The public wishes itself to be managed like a woman : one must say nothing to it except what it likes to hear.

WE MUST BE EITHER AN ANVIL OR A HAMMER.

Grosscophta, 2.

Du mußt (herrschen und gewinnen,
Oder dienen und verlieren,

L

Leiden oder triumphiren,)
Amboß oder Hammer sein.

Thou must command and win, or serve and lose, suffer or
triumph, be an anvil or a hammer.

THE IGNORANT.

Maxims, vol. III. *p.* 277.

Unwiſſende werfen Fragen auf, welche von Wiſſenden vor
tauſend Jahren ſchon beantwortet ſind.

The ignorant start questions which have been already answered
thousands of years ago by the wise.

THE NIGHT COMES WHEN NO MAN CAN WORK.

Essex, p. 37.

Noch iſt es Tag, da rühre ſich der Mann,
Die Nacht tritt ein, wo Niemand wirken kann.

Still it is day, when man can exert himself; the night cometh,
when no man can work.

THE GODLIKE IN MAN.

Essex, p. 75.

Wär' nicht das Auge ſonnenhaft,
Die Sonn' könnt' es nie erblicken;
Läg' nicht in uns des Gottes eigne Kraft,
Wie könnt' uns Göttliches entzücken?

Were not the eye made to receive the rays of the sun it could
not behold the sun; if the peculiar power of God lay not in us,
how could the Godlike charm us?

HOW TO GAIN WOMAN.

Antworten bei einem geſellſchaftlichen Frageſpiel.

Geh' den Weibern zart entgegen,
Du gewinnſt ſie auf mein Wort,
Und wer raſch iſt und verwegen,
Kommt vielleicht noch beſſer fort.
Doch, wem wenig dran gelegen

Scheinet, ob er reizt und rührt,
Der beleidigt, der verführt.

If thou approachest women with tenderness thou winnest them with a word; and he who is bold and saucy comes off still better; but the man who seems to care little whether he charms and attracts is he who offends and who seduces.

THE GOOD LIES NEAR US.

Erinnerung.

Willst du immer weiter schweifen?
Sieh, das Gute liegt so nah.
Lerne nur das Glück ergreifen,
Denn das Glück ist immer da.

Willest thou ever roam abroad? See, what is good lies by thy side. Only learn to catch happiness, for happiness is ever by you.

APPEARANCE.

Du bist am Ende — was Du bist,
Setz' Dir Perrücken auf von Millionen Locken,
Setz' Deinen Fuß auf ellenhohe Socken,
Du bleibst doch immer — was Du bist.

Thou art after all *what thou art.* Deck thyself in a wig with a thousand locks; ensconce thy legs in buskins an ell high; thou still remainest just *what thou art.*

ANASTASIUS GRÜN.

Born A.D. 1806.

Anton Alexander, Count of Auersperg, better known by the name of Anastasius Grün, was born in 1806 at Laybach, in Austria; lives partly at Vienna and partly on his hereditary estates in Carinthia.

THE TEARS OF MAN.

Mannesthräne.

Mädchen, sahst du jüngst mich weinen?
Sieh, des Weibes Thräne dünkt
Mir der klare Thau des Himmels,
Der in Blumenkelchen blinkt.

Ob die trübe Nacht ihn weinet,
Ob der Morgen lächelnd bringt,
Stets doch labt der Thau die Blume,
Und ihr Haupt hebt sie verjüngt.

Doch es gleicht des Mannes Thräne
Edlem Harz aus Ostens Flur,
Tief in's Herz des Baums verschlossen,
Quillts freiwillig selten nur.

Schneiden musst du in die Rinde
Bis zum Kern des Marks hinein,
Und das edle Nass entträufelt
Dann so golden, hell und rein.

Maiden, didst thou see me weeping? Ah, the tears of woman
seem to me the pure dew of heaven, which glitters on the flowers.
Whether shed in the darkness of night, or in the smiling morning,
the dew always revives the flower, and refreshed, it raises its
head. But the tears of man resemble the precious gum of Araby,
concealed in the heart of the tree, seldom flowing freely. Thou
must make an incision in the bark to the very pith and marrow,
and the pure juice flows so clear, so pure and golden.

ANDREAS GRYPHIUS.

Born A.D. 1626. Died A.D. 1664.

Andreas Gryphius was born in 1626 at Glogau in Silesia, where
his father was an archdeacon. His life was devoted to literature.
He died in his native city in 1664.

THE GRAVE.

Der Todte an den Lebenden.

Hier ist der Gränzstein aller Macht,
Der Zielpunkt alles Strebens;
Kunst, Schönheit, Herrlichkeit und Pracht,
Sie trotzten hier vergebens.
Das Buch, der Pflug, das Schwert, der Stab,
Sucht unter Einem Staub' ein Grab.

Der Leib, das Haus, worin der Geist
Geherbergt so viel Jahre,

Der über Land und Meer gereist,
Liegt auf der Todtenbahre.
Was arm und reich, was gut und arg,
Was klein und groß, muß in den Sarg.

Here is the landmark of all power, the limit of all exertion; art, beauty, splendour, pomp—all resist in vain. Books, the plough, the sword, the staff of office, seek a grave under the same dust.

The body, the house in which the spirit dwelt so many years, which travelled over land and sea, lies on the bier. Rich and poor, good and bad, little and great, must enter into the coffin.

HAGEDORN.

Born A.D. 1708.   Died A.D. 1754.

Frederick von Hagedorn was born April 23, 1708, at Hamburg, where he died 1754.

ABUNDANCE.

Das Hühnchen und der Diamant.

Unglückfel'ger Ueberfluß,
Wo der nöthige Genuß
Unfern Schätzen fehlen muß.

Unhappy abundance, where real enjoyment attends not all the treasures which we hoard.

MAY MORNING.

Der Mai.

Der Nachtigall reizende Lieder
Ertönen und locken schon wieder
Die fröhlichsten Stunden in's Jahr.
Nun singet die steigende Lerche;
Nun klappern die reisenden Störche;
Nun schwatzet der gaukelnde Staar.

Wie munter sind Schäfer und Heerde!
Wie lieblich beblümt sich die Erde!
Wie lebhaft ist jetzo die Welt!
Die Tauben verdoppeln die Küsse;
Der Ent'rich besuchet die Flüsse;
Der lustige Sperling sein Feld.

The delightful strains of the nightingale resound and herald again the merriest hours of the year. Now sings the lark as it soars; now the wandering stork flaps its wings; now the chattering starlings appear.

How cheerful are shepherds and sheep! how lovely the earth blooms! how lively the world is now! the doves now double their kisses; the drakes visit the rivers; the sprightly sparrow the field.

The Pleasures of a Country Life.

Das Landleben.

In jährlich neuen Schätzen,
  Zeigt sich des Landmanns Glück,
Und Freiheit und Ergötzen
  Erheitern seinen Blick.

Verleumdung, Stolz und Sorgen,
  Was Städte sclavisch macht,
Das schwärzt nicht seinen Morgen,
  Das drückt nicht seine Nacht.

The happiness of the dweller in the country is shown in new treasures year by year, and freedom and delight make his countenance serene. Slander, pride, and cares, which enslave those who lead a town life, darken not his mornings, oppress not his nights.

VON HALLER.

The Inner Spirit of Nature.

The Falsehood of Human Virtue.

In's Inn're der Natur bringt kein erschaffner Geist,
Zu glücklich, wem sie noch die äuss're Schale weist.

Into the interior of nature no created spirit penetrates, too happy if he knows the outer shell.

HALM.

Two Souls, but one Heart.

Der Sohn der Wildniss.

Zwei Seelen und ein Gedanke.

Two souls, and one heart.

In one of the *rondeaux* of Villon we find—
  " Deux estions et n'avions qu'un cœur."

HEINE.

Born A.D. 1799.   Died A.D. 1856.

Heinrich Heine was born 1799 at Düsseldorf.   He spent the greater part of his life at Paris, where he was confined to his room by a disease of the spine from May 1848.   He died there in 1856.

MY HEART.

Du schönes Fischermädchen.

Mein Herz gleicht ganz dem Meere,
Hat Sturm und Ebb' und Flut,
Und manche schöne Perle
In seiner Tiefe ruht.

My heart resembles the ocean ! has storm, and ebb and flow ;
And many a beautiful pearl lies hid in its depths below.

AN OLD STORY.

Lyrishes Intermezzo, **39.**

Es ist eine alte Geschichte,
Doch bleibt sie immer neu.

It is an old story, yet remains ever new.

NO TALENT.

Atta Troll, c. **24.**

Kein Talent, doch ein Charakter.

No talent, but yet a character.

HERDER.

Born A.D. 1744.   Died A.D. 1803.

Johann Gottfried von Herder was the son of a schoolmaster in Mohrungen, East Prussia, and during his early years was subject to many difficulties.   The Bible and hymn-books taught him to read.   In his fifteenth year he was employed as amanuensis by the clergyman of the city, and continued for several years in this situation.   In his eighteenth year (1762) he became known to the surgeon of a Russian regiment, named Schwarzerloh, who was so much impressed with his abilities, that he offered to place him at a university, and train him to the medical profession. He entered the University of Königsberg, but soon relinquished the pursuit of medicine for the more congenial study of theology. Thus left to his own resources, he contrived to maintain himself during his university course. He became schoolmaster at Riga, and was at the same time licensed to preach. He was ordained in 1767, being as acceptable in the pulpit as in the class-room. He left Riga in 1769, and after spending some time in travelling, chiefly in France, and then as tutor to the Prince of Holstein, he accepted the office of Court Chaplain in Bükeburg, and member of the highest Ecclesiastical Court. After various changes, he obtained through Goethe, in 1776, a situation in Weimar, where he spent the remainder of his life, dying in 1803.

The Thinking Power within us.

Philosophy of History, p. 30.

Die Kraft, die in mir denkt und wirkt, ist ihrer Natur nach eine so ewige Kraft, als jene, die Sonnen und Sterne zusammenhält; ihr Werkzeug kann sich abarbeiten, die Sphäre ihrer Wirkung kann sich ändern, wie Erden sich abreiben und Sterne ihren Platz ändern; die Gesetze aber, durch die sie da ist und in andern Erscheinungen wieder kommt, ändern sich nie. Ihre Natur ist ewig, wie der Verstand Gottes, und die Stützen meines Daseyns (nicht meiner körperlichen Erscheinung) sind so fest, als die Pfeiler des Weltalls.

The power which thinks and works within us is, according to its nature, as never-dying as that which holds together suns and stars ; its organs may work themselves out, the sphere of its operations may change, as globes wear away and stars change their positions, but the laws, by which it is there and returns to other phases, change not. Its nature is eternal as the divine mind, and the supports of my being (not of my corporeal form) are as firm as the pillars of the universe.

What I am.

Philosophy of History, p. 31.

Wo und wer ich seyn werde, werde ich seyn, der ich jetzt bin, eine Kraft im System aller Kräfte, ein Wesen in der unabsehlichen Harmonie einer Welt Gottes.

Where and who I shall be, I shall be, that I am now, a power in the system of all powers, a being in the interminable harmony of a world of God.

WE LOVE OUR OWN.

Philosophy of History, p. 31.

Jeder liebt sein Land, seine Sitten, seine Sprache, sein Weib, seine Kinder, nicht weil sie die besten auf der Welt, sondern weil sie die bewährten Seinigen sind, und er in ihnen sich und seine Mühe selbst liebt. So gewöhnet sich Jeder auch an die schlechteste Speise, an die härteste Lebensart, an die roheste Sitte des rauhesten Klima und findet zuletzt in ihm Behaglichkeit und Ruhe.

Every one loves his own country, customs, language, wife, children, not because they are the best in the world, but because they are his established property, and he loves in them himself and the labour he has bestowed on them. Thus every one accustoms himself to the worst food, to the coarsest mode of living, to the rudest customs of the roughest climate, and finds at last comfort and peace in it.

HEALTH.

Philosophy of History, p. 99.

Lasset uns also die Vorsehung preisen, daß, da Gesundheit der Grund aller unsrer physischen Glückseligkeit ist, sie dieß Fundament so weit und breit auf der Erde legte.

Let us therefore praise Providence that, since health is the foundation of all our physical happiness, it has laid this foundation so far and wide on the earth.

See (Lat.) Health, good, is life. (Fr.) Without, life is not life.

EVERY LIVING THING REJOICES IN LIFE.

Philosophy of History, p. 101.

Jedes Lebendige freuet sich seines Lebens; es fragt und grübelt nicht, wozu es da sey? sein Daseyn ist ihm Zweck und sein Zweck das Daseyn. Kein Wilder mordet sich selbst, so wenig ein Thier sich selbst mordet; er pflanzt sein Geschlecht fort, ohne zu wissen, wozu er's fortpflanze und unterzieht sich auch unter dem Druck des härtesten Klima aller Müh' und Arbeit, nur damit er lebe. Dieß einfache, tiefe, unersetzliche Gefühl des Daseyns also ist Glückseligkeit, ein kleiner Tropfe aus jenem unendlichen Meer des Allseligen, der in Allem ist und sich in Allem freuet und fühlet.

Everything living rejoices in its life; it asks not nor racks its brain to find out how it is there; simple existence is its end, and its end is existence. No savage murders himself, as little does an animal; it propagates its species without knowing why it does so, and takes upon itself, under the pressure of the hardest climate, every trouble and labour only for mere existence. This simple, deep, inexpressible feeling of existence is happiness, a small drop out of that endless sea of the All-holy, which is in all, and rejoices and feels itself in all.

REVOLUTIONS.
Philosophy of History, p. 108.

Das Maschinenwerk der Revolutionen irrt mich also nicht mehr: es ist unserm Geschlecht so nöthig, wie dem Strom seine Wogen, damit er nicht ein stehender Sumpf werde. Immer verjüngt in seinen Gestalten, blüht der Genius der Humanität auf.

The working of revolutions, therefore, misleads me no more; it is as necessary to our race as its waves to the stream, that it may not be a stagnant marsh. Ever renewed in its forms, the genius of humanity blossoms.

THE CULTURE OF THE LOWER ORDERS
Philosophy of History, Part II. *p.* 20.

Die Cultur des Volks setzten sie in gute Sitten und nützliche Künste.

The culture of the lower orders they placed in good habits and useful arts.

MOTHER NATURE.
Philosophy of History, Part II. *p.* 27.

Große Mutter Natur, an welche Kleinigkeiten hast du das Schicksal unsres Geschlechts geknüpft! Mit der veränderten Form eines menschlichen Kopfs und Gehirns, mit einer kleinen Veränderung im Bau der Organisation und der Nerven, die das Klima, die Stammesart und die Gewohnheit bewirkt, ändert sich auch das Schicksal der Welt, die ganze Summe dessen, was allenthalben auf Erden die Menschheit thue und die Menschheit leide.

Great Mother Nature, to what trifles hast thou knit the fate of our race! With the altered form of a human head and brain, with a little change in the structure of the organisation and nerves, which the climate, the breed, and habits produce, the fate of the world also changes, the sum total of that which everywhere on earth man does, and humanity suffers.

EVERY EVIL WEARS ITSELF OUT.

Philosophy of History, Part II. *p.* 30.

Es ist ein hartes aber gutes Gesetz des Schicksals, daß, wie alles Uebel, so auch jede Uebermacht sich selbst verzehre.

It is a hard but good law of fate, that, as every evil, so every excessive power wears itself out.

BODY AND SPIRIT OF MAN.

Philosophy of History, Part II. *p.* 92.

Der Leib der Menschen ist eine zerbrechliche, immer erneuete Hülle, die endlich sich nicht mehr erneuen kann; ihr Geist aber wirkt auf Erden nur in und mit dem Leibe. Wir dünken uns selbstständig, und hangen von allem in der Natur ab; in eine Kette wandelbarer Dinge verflochten, müssen auch wir den Gesetzen ihres Kreislaufs folgen, die keine andre sind, als Entstehen, Seyn und Verschwinden. Ein loser Faden knüpft das Geschlecht der Menschen, der jeden Augenblick reißt, um von neuem geknüpft zu werden. Der flüggewordene Greis geht unter die Erde, damit sein Nachfolger ebenfalls wie ein Kind beginne, die Werke seines Vorgängers vielleicht als ein Thor zerstöre, und dem Nachfolger dieselbe nichtige Mühe überlasse, mit der auch Er sein Leben verzehrt. So ketten sich Tage: so ketten Geschlechter und Reiche sich aneinander. Die Sonne geht unter, damit Nacht werde und Menschen sich über eine neue Morgenröthe freuen mögen.

The body of man is a fragile, ever-renewed cover, which at last can no longer be renewed. But his spirit works on earth only in and with the body. We think ourselves self-existing, and yet are dependent on everything in nature; entwined in a chain of wonderful things, we must follow the laws of their succession, which are no other than beginning, existing, and ending. A loose thread binds the race of men, which breaks every moment, to be again renewed. The old man with his wisdom disappears in the grave, that his successor may begin as a child, may destroy perhaps like a fool the works of his predecessor, and leave to one who comes after him the same useless labour, with which he too consumes his life. Thus days are bound to each other; thus races and kingdoms are bound to each other. The sun sets, that night may come, and men may again rejoice over a new dawn.

NATIONS.
Philosophy of History, Part II. *p.* 93.

Die Nationen blühen auf und ab; in eine abgeblühete Nation kommt keine junge, geschweige eine schönere Blüthe wieder.

Nations blossom and fade; in a nation that has ceased to blossom, no young, much less a more beautiful budding again takes place.

WE WRITE AS ON THE WAVES OF THE SEA.
Philosophy of History, Part II. *p.* 95.

So bauen wir auf's Eis, so schreiben wir in die Welle des Meer's; die Welle verrauscht, das Eis zerschmilzt und hin ist unser Pallast, wie unsre Gedanken.

Thus we build on the ice, thus we write on the waves of the sea; the waves roaring pass away, the ice melts, and away goes our palace, like our thoughts.

THERE CAN BE NO SECOND HOMER.
Philosophy of History, Part II. *p.* 96.

Als Homer gesungen hatte, war in seiner Gattung kein zweiter Homer denkbar; jener hatte die Blüthe des epischen Kranzes gepflückt und wer auf ihn folgte, mußte sich mit einzelnen Blättern begnügen. Die griechischen Trauerspieldichter wählten sich also eine andere Laufbahn: sie aßen, wie Aeschylus sagt, vom Tisch Homers, bereiteten aber für ihr Zeitalter ein anderes Gastmahl.

When Homer had sung, we could expect no second Homer in his peculiar species of poetry; he had plucked the bloom of the epic crown, and whoever followed must be satisfied with the leaves only. The Greek tragic writers, therefore, chose another career; they ate, as Æschylus says, from the table of Homer, but prepared for the age in which they lived another kind of banquet.

Be Patient.

Der wiedergefundene Sohn.

Was die Schickung schickt, ertrage!
Wer ausharret, wird gekrönt.

What destiny sends, bear! Whoever perseveres will be crowned.

Thy Honour is Lost.

„Cid," Gesang 28.

Rückwärts, rückwärts, Don Rodrigo!
Deine Ehre ist verloren!
Rückwärts, rückwärts, stolzer Cid!

Back, back, Don Rodrigo! Thy honour is lost! Back, back, proud Cid!

The Soul of Man.

Der gerettete Jüngling.

Eine schöne Menschenseele finden
Ist Gewinn; ein schönerer Gewinn ist
Sie erhalten; und der schönst' und schwerste
Sie, die schon verloren war, zu retten.

To find a noble human soul is gain; it is nobler to keep it; and the noblest and most difficult is to save that which is already lost.

What closes the Heart of Man.

Der Wettstreit.

Gewalt und Härte macht verdrossen
Und läßt der Menschen Herz verschlossen.
Wo man oft lange widerstand,
Ein gutes Wort leicht Eingang fand.

Violence and harshness make men disgusted and close up their heart. Where there is long opposition, a kind word easily finds entrance.

FATE.

Die Schwestern des Schicksals.

Nenne nicht das Schicksal grausam,
Nenne seinen Schluß nicht Neid:
Sein Gesetz ist ew'ge Wahrheit,
Seine Güte Götterklarheit,
Seine Macht Nothwendigkeit.

Call not fate fearful, call not its determination envy; its law
is eternal truth, its goodness God's purity, its might is necessity.

THE BUTTERFLY.

Das Lied vom Schmetterling.

Liebes, leichtes, luft'ges Ding,
Schmetterling,
Das da über Blumen schwebet,
Nur von Thau und Blüten lebet,
Blüte selbst, ein fliegend Blatt,
Das mit welchem Rosenfinger
Wer bepurpurt hat?

War's ein Sylphe, der dein Kleid
So bestreut,
Dich aus Morgenduft gewebet,
Nur auf Tage dich belebet?
Seelchen, und dein kleines Herz
Pocht da unter meinem Finger,
Fühlet Todesschmerz.

Fleuch dahin, o Seelchen, sei
Froh und frei,
Mir ein Bild, was ich sein werde,
Wenn die Raupe dieser Erde
Auch wie du ein Zephyr ist
Und in Duft und Thau und Honig
Jede Blüte küßt!

Lovely, light, airy thing, thou butterfly, which **hovers over**
flowers, only lives on dew and blossoms, a blossom thyself, a flying
leaf, who has purpled thee with a rose's finger? Was it a **Sylph**

who besprinkled thy dress so, moulded thee of morning odours,
and animated thee only for a day? Little soul, and thy little
heart beats under my finger, and feels the pain of death.

Fly hence, O little soul! be joyful and free, an image to me
what I shall be, when (man) the chrysalis of earth becomes, like
thee, a Zephyr, and kisses every blossom in odour, dew, and honey.

THE SEA OF FORGETFULNESS.

Der Nachruhm.

Wir schwimmen in dem Strom der Zeit
Auf Welle Welle fort;
Das Meer der Allvergessenheit
Ist unser letzter Ort.

We sail on the stream of time from wave to wave; the sea of
forgetfulness is our last place.

THE WISE ALWAYS THE SAME

Zage nicht.

Unter wechselnden Gestalten
Steht erschaffend die Natur;
So geschäftig steht der Weise
In der Aenderungen Kreise,
Stürzet nicht, entweichet nur.

Nature appears ever young under many changing features; so
amid the vicissitudes of life the wise man stays unmoved, is never
thrown down, never yields.

FRIENDSHIP.

Denkspruch.

Wie der Schatten früh am Morgen,
Ist die Freundschaft mit den Bösen;
Stund' auf Stunde nimmt sie ab.
Aber Freundschaft mit den Guten
Wächset, wie der Abendschatten,
Bis des Lebens Sonne sinkt

As the shadow in early morning is friendship with the wicked;
it dwindles hour by hour. But friendship with the good increases,
like the evening shadows, till the sun of life sets.

A Real Friend.

Freundschaft.

Der Freund, der mir den Spiegel zeiget,
Den kleinsten Flecken nicht verschweiget,
Mich freundlich warnt, mich herzlich schilt,
Wenn ich nicht meine Pflicht erfüllt,
Der ist mein Freund,
So wenig er's auch scheint.

Doch wenn mich einer schmeichelnd preiset,
Mich immer lobt, mir Nichts verweiset,
Zu Fehlern gar die Hände beut
Und mir vergiebt, eh' ich bereut,
Der ist mein Feind,
So freundlich er auch scheint.

The friend who holds up before me the mirror, conceals not my smallest faults, warns me kindly, reproves me affectionately, when I have not performed my duty, he is my friend, however little he may appear so. Again, if a man flattering praises and lauds me, never reproves me, overlooks my faults and forgives them before I have repented, he is my enemy, however much he may appear my friend.

VON HIPPEL.

Born A.D. 1741. Died A.D. 1796.

Theodor Gottlieb von Hippel was born, 1741, at Gerdauen, in East Prussia, where his father was rector of a school. His talents were shown at an early age, and at fifteen he was sent to the University of Königsberg. After various changes he devoted himself to the legal profession, and rose to great eminence. He died at Königsberg in 1796.

THE GRAVE.

Grab und Tod.

Das Grab, Freunde, ist eine heilige Werkstätte der Natur! Ein Formzimmer; Tod und Leben wohnen hier beisammen, wie Mann und Weib. Ein Leib sind sie. Eins sind sie. Gott hat sie zusammen gefügt, und was Gott zusammenfügt, soll der Mensch nicht scheiden.

The grave, my **dear friend**, is a sacred workshop of nature! a **chamber** for the figure of the body; death and life dwell here together as man and wife. They are one body. They are in union; God has joined them together, and what God hath joined **together**, let no man put asunder.

CHRISTIAN VON HOFMANNSWALDAU.

Born A.D. 1618. Died A.D. 1679.

VANITY OF ALL THINGS.

Eitelfeit.

Was ist dieses Rund der Erden,
Als ein Tummelplatz voll Schein?
Helden, heute siegreich, werden
Morgen kaum noch Schatten seyn;
Seht, bey Kränzen, Thron und Siegen,
Fesseln, Band' und Ketten liegen!

What is this earth but a theatre full of vain show? heroes, to-day victorious, are to-morrow scarcely shadows; see chains, bonds, and fetters lie alongside crowns, thrones, and victories!

HÖLDERLIN.

Born A.D. 1770. Died A.D. 1843.

Frederick Hölderlin was born 1770 at Lauffen on the Neckar; studied at Tübingen, and spent many years as private tutor in various families, dying at Tübingen 1843, after living thirty-seven years in a state of mental derangement.

NATURE STILL AS LOVELY AS IN DAYS OF OLD.

Der Gott der Jugend.

Wie unter Tiburs Bäumen,
Wenn da der Dichter saß,
Und unter Götterträumen
Der Jahre Flucht vergaß,
Wenn ihn die Ulme fühlte,
Und wenn sie stolz und froh

M

Um Silberblüthen spielte,
Die Flut des Anio;

Und wie um Platons Hallen,
Wenn durch der Haine Grün,
Begrüßt von Nachtigallen,
Der Stern der Liebe schien,
Wenn alle Lüfte schliefen,
Und, sanft bewegt vom Schwan,
Cephisus durch Oliven
Und Myrtensträuche rann;

So schön ist's noch hienieden!
Auch unser Herz erfuhr
Das Leben und den Frieden
Der freundlichen Natur;
Noch blüht des Himmels Schöne,
Noch mischen brüderlich
In unsers Herzens Töne
Des Frühlings Laute sich.

As when the bard sat musing under the trees of Tibur, and, wrapt in dreams of heaven, forgot the flight of time, when the elms refreshed him, and when the waters of the Anio proudly there below played round the silver blossoms;

And as in Plato's bowers, when through the arbour's green, saluted by nightingales, the star of love was seen, when all the breezes slumbered, and, gently rippled by the swan, Cephisus through the olives and myrtle-bushes ran;

It is still here below as lovely ! our bosoms still feel the joys of life and the blessings of kind Nature ; still blooms Heaven's beauty, still in our bosoms the peaceful tones of spring mingle in harmony.

HÖLTY.

Born A.D. 1748. Died A.D. 1776.

Hölty, a poet of some celebrity, was the son of a clergyman of Mariensee in the kingdom of Hanover, being educated at the University of Göttingen, where he lived in terms of intimacy with Bürger, Voss, and the Stolbergs. His devotion to study undermined his constitution, and he died in the twenty-eighth year of his age. His poetical compositions are highly extolled, more particularly his lyric songs, which rival in popularity those of Bürger.

Truth and Uprightness.

Der alte Landmann.

Ueb' immer Treu und Redlichkeit bis an dein kühles Grab,
Und weiche keinen Finger breit von Gottes Wegen ab!
Dann wirst du, wie auf grünen Au'n, durch's Pilgerleben gehn;
Dann kannst du sonder Furcht und Grau'n dem Tod in's
     Antlitz sehn.

Dann wird die Sichel und der Pflug in deiner Hand so leicht;
Dann singest du beim Wasserkrug, als wär' dir Wein gereicht.
Dem Bösewicht wird alles schwer, er thue, was er thu';
Der Teufel treibt ihn hin und her und läßt ihm keine Ruh'.

Der schöne Frühling lacht ihm nicht, ihm lacht kein Aehrenfeld;
Er ist auf Lug und Trug erpicht und wünscht sich nichts als
     Geld.
Der Wind im Hain, das Laub am Baum saust ihm Entsetzen zu;
Er findet nach des Lebens Raum im Grabe keine Ruh'.

Practise ever truth and uprightness till the cold grave, and
deviate not a finger's breadth from God's ways! Then wilt thou,
as on a green meadow, go through thy pilgrimage of life; then
canst thou without fear and dread look death in the face.

Then will the sickle and the plough be light in thy hand; then
canst thou sing over the water-jug, as if it were filled with wine.
But to the scoundrel is everything full of trouble, do what he
may: the devil drives him to and fro, leaving him no rest.

The beautiful spring smiles not for him, the fields of corn wave
not with joy for him; he is a lover of lies and deceit, he cares for
nothing but gold; the wind in the wood, the leaf on the tree,
whisper horror to his heart; he finds no rest in the grave after
life is over.

A Country Life.

Das Landleben.

Wunderseliger Mann, welcher der Stadt entfloh!
Jedes Säuseln des Baums, jedes Geräusch des Bachs,
    Jeder blinkende Kiesel
      Predigt Tugend und Weisheit ihm.

Jedes Schattengesträuch ist ihm ein heiliger
Tempel, wo ihm sein Gott näher vorüberwallt,
    Jeder Rasen ein Altar,
      Wo er vor dem Erhabnen kniet.

Happy the man who has escaped from the town! Every whispering of the tree, every murmuring of the stream, every sparkling pebble, preaches to him virtue and wisdom.

Every shady grove is to him a holy temple, where his God waves nearer to him; every green sod an altar, where he kneels before the Lofty One.

TIME.

Der rechte Gebrauch des Lebens.

Wer hemmt den Flug der Stunden? Sie rauschen hin,
Wie Pfeile Gottes! Jeder Sekundenschlag
   Reißt uns dem Sterbebette näher,
     Näher dem eisernen Todesschlafe!

Dir blüht kein Frühling, wann du gestorben bist;
Dir weht kein Schatten, tönet kein Becherklang;
   Dir lacht kein süßes Mädchenlächeln,
     Strömet kein Scherz von des Freundes Lippe!

Noch rauscht der schwarze Flügel des Todes nicht!
Drum hasch die Freuden, eh' sie der Sturm verweht,
   Die Gott, wie Sonnenschein und Regen,
     Aus der vergeudenden Urne schüttet!

Who stops the flight of the hours? They rush on like the arrows of God! Every second stroke hurries us nearer to our deathbed, nearer to the iron sleep of death!

No spring blooms for thee, when thou art dead; no shadow is cast, no clanging of bowls, no pleasant smiles of maidens, no jests from the lips of friends!

As yet the black wings of death rustle not! Therefore seize pleasures, ere the storm carries them off, which God scatters like sunshine and rain from his urn!

LOVE.

Die Seligkeit der Liebenden.

Die Liebe macht zum Goldpallast die Hütte,
Streut auf die Wildniß Tanz und Spiel,
Enthüllet uns der Gottheit leise Tritte,
Gibt uns des Himmels Vorgefühl!

Love makes the hovel to be a golden palace, scatters dancing and play over the wilderness, uncovers to us the light traces of the Divinity, gives us a foretaste of heaven!

Enjoy the Present.

Lebenspflichten.

Rosen auf den Weg gestreut,
Und des Harms vergessen!
Eine kurze Spanne Zeit
Ward uns zugemessen.
Heute hüpft im Frühlingstanz
Noch der frohe Knabe;
Morgen weht der Todtenkranz
Schon auf seinem Grabe.

Wonne führt die junge Braut
Heute zum Altare;
Eh' die Abendwolke thaut,
Ruht sie auf der Bahre.
Gebt den Harm und Grillenfang,
Gebet ihn den Winden;
Ruht bei hellem Becherklang
Unter grünen Linden.

Strew the way with roses, forgetting every ill! a short span of time is measured out to us. To-day the frolicsome boy joins the dance in the spring-time of life; to-morrow the chaplet of the dead waves over his grave.

To-day sees the young bride conducted with joy to the altar; before the evening's dews are spread, she rests on her bier: give then grief and moping care to the wind that passes; beneath this beechen grove drain the jingling glasses.

Beautiful is God's Earth.

Aufmunterung zur Freude.

O wunderschön ist Gottes Erde,
Und werth, darauf vergnügt zu seyn!
Drum will ich, bis ich Asche werde,
Mich dieser schönen Erde freun!

Oh, wonderfully beautiful is God's earth, and worthy of being delighted in! therefore shall I, till I am changed into ashes, rejoice in this beautiful earth!

WILHELM VON HUMBOLDT.

Born A.D. 1767.   Died A.D. 1835.

Karl Wilhelm von Humboldt, a distinguished statesman and philologist, the elder brother of the illustrious traveller, was born at Potsdam 22d June 1767, where his father was chamberlain to the Princess of Prussia. He studied at the Universities of Frankfort-on-the-Oder and Göttingen. His early years were spent in strict seclusion, but he became Prussian minister in 1800 at the Papal Court. On his return he was appointed Minister of Public Instruction, and two years afterwards was sent ambassador to Vienna. For the next five years he was employed in all the great diplomatic transactions that took place, and it was he who in 1815 signed the treaty by which Saxony was compelled to abandon to Prussia a large portion of her territory. In 1818 he took part in the deliberations of the Congress of Aix-la-Chapelle, but on his return to Berlin he retired to private life, devoting himself to the pleasures of a literary life. He died 8th April 1835.

THE PAST.

To a Female Friend.   Letter I. 2.

Ich habe überdies eine große Liebe für die Vergangenheit. Nur was sie gewährt, ist ewig und unveränderlich, wie der Tod, und zugleich, wie das Leben, warm und beglückend.

I have, besides, a great love for the past. Only what refers to it is eternal and unchangeable like death, and at the same time warm and gladsome like life.

SOLITUDE.

To a Female Friend.   Letter I. 9.

Diese nun aber ist schon schöner, wenn man die Einsamkeit liebt, und wird schöner, wenn man dieser Liebe nachhängt.

If the mind loves solitude, it has thereby acquired a loftier character, and it becomes still more noble when the taste is indulged in.

THE LOVE OF EARLY ASSOCIATIONS.

To a Female Friend.   Letter I. 9.

Das gewiß wahr ist, daß ich unfähig wäre, je einen Menschen, der mir irgend nahe stand, zu vergessen oder aufzugeben, ich

verfolge vielmehr jede Spur, die aus der Vergangenheit übrig
ist. Jede solche Verbindung, ja jedes solches bloße Begegnen
hängt ja mit so vielen in einem zusammen und das Leben ist
schon ein solches Stück- und Flickwerf, daß man nicht genug
trachten kann, die zusammenhängenden Theile fester aneinander
zu knüpfen.

It is certainly true that I am unable to forget or give up any
one with whom I have been intimate ; far from this, I follow up
every trace that remains of the past. Every such tie, nay, every
accidental meeting, unites so many things together, and life is
such a medley and patchwork, that we can never sufficiently
labour to join the connecting links more and more closely to each
other.

A Letter.

To a Female Friend. Letter I. 9.

Ein Brief ist ein Gespräch unter Anwesenden und Entfernten.
Es ist seine Bestimmung, daß er nicht bleiben, sondern vergehen
soll, wie die Stimme verhallt.

A letter is a conversation between the present and the absent.
Its fate is that it cannot last, but must pass away like the sound
of the voice.

The Lot of Man.

To a Female Friend. Letter I. 9.

Ohne Kampf und Entbehrung ist kein Menschenleben, auch
das glücklichste nicht, denn gerade das wahre Glück baut sich
jeder nur dadurch, daß er sich durch seine Gefühle unabhängig
vom Schicksal macht.

The fate of no man, not even the happiest, is free from struggles
and privation ; for true happiness is only then attained, when by
the government of the feelings we become independent of all the
chances of life.

Difference between the Nature of Men and Women.

To a Female Friend. Letter I. 10.

Frauen sind darin glücklicher und unglücklicher als Männer,
daß ihre meisten Arbeiten von der Art sind, daß sie während
derselben meist an etwas ganz anderes denken können. Ich

würde es ein Glück nennen. Denn man kann ein ganz inneres Leben fast den ganzen Tag fortführen, ohne in seinen Arbeiten oder in seinem Berufe dabei zu verlieren oder gestört zu werden. Es ist das auch wohl ein Hauptgrund, warum wenigstens viele Frauen die Männer in allem übertreffen, was zur tiefern und feinern Kenntniß seiner selbst und anderer führt. Allein wenn jene innern Gedanken nicht beglückend, oder wenn sie wenigstens das nicht rein und unvermischt sind, sondern niederschlagend und beunruhigend dabei, so ist allerdings die Gefahr größer, welche die innere Ruhe bedroht; da Männer in ihren Geschäften selbst, auch wider ihren Willen, Zerstreuung und Abziehung von einem das Innere einnehmenden Gedanken finden.

Women are in this respect more fortunate, and yet more unfortunate, than men—that most of their employments are of such a nature that they may at the same time be thinking of quite different things. I would pronounce this to be a lucky circumstance, for one may almost the whole day continue a train of deep thought without the slightest interruption to work, or being in any way distracted in our labours. This is no doubt one of the chief reasons why many women surpass men in everything which requires deep thought and a more subtle knowledge of ourselves and others. But when, on the other hand, these inner thoughts are not of a pleasant nature, or at least not in a pure and unmixed degree, but partly depressing and disquieting, then the danger is certainly greater, and more likely to destroy the inward peace; whereas men, in their business itself, and even against their will, find distraction and relief from inward troubles and vexations.

HAPPINESS AND UNHAPPINESS IN LIFE.

To a Female Friend. Letter 1. 10.

Das Glück vergeht und läßt in der Seele kaum eine flache Spur zurück und ist oft gar kein Glück zu nennen, da man dauernd dadurch nicht gewinnt. Das Unglück vergeht auch (und das ist ein großer Trost), läßt aber tiefe Spuren zurück, und wenn man es wohl zu benutzen weiß, heilsame, und ist oft ein sehr hohes Glück, da es läutert und stärkt. Dann ist es eine eigene Sache im Leben, daß, wenn man gar nicht an Glück und Unglück denkt, sondern nur an strenge, sich nicht schonende Pflichterfüllung, das Glück sich von selbst, auch bei entbehrender, mühevoller Lebensweise einstellt. Dies habe ich oft bei Frauen in sehr unglücklichen ehelichen Verhältnissen erlebt, die aber lieber untergingen, als ihre Stelle verlassen wollten.

Happiness passes away, leaving hardly the slightest trace behind, indeed can scarcely be called happiness, since nothing lasting is gained. Unhappiness also passes away (and that is a great comfort), but leaves deep traces behind; and if we know how to improve them, of a most wholesome nature, and is often the cause of the highest happiness, as it purifies and strengthens the character. Then, again, in life it is worthy of special remark, that when we are not too anxious about happiness and unhappiness, but devote ourselves to the strict and unsparing performance of duty, then happiness comes of itself—nay, even springs from the midst of a life of troubles, and anxieties, and privations. This I have often observed in the case of women who have been married unhappily, but who would rather sink into the grave than abandon the position in which fate has placed them.

FRIENDSHIP AND LOVE.

Letter I. 12.

Freundschaft und Liebe bedürfen des Vertrauens, des tiefsten und eigentlichsten, aber bei großartigen Seelen nie der Vertraulichkeiten.

Friendship and love require the deepest and most entire confidence, but souls of a high character demand not communications of a familiar nature.

TRIALS AND REVERSES OF LIFE.

Letter I. 15.

Es kommt nicht auf die äußere Ursache an, von welcher der Schmerz oder die Widerwärtigkeit entsteht, und der Himmel hat Schmerz und Widerwärtigkeit so weise vertheilt, daß der äußerlich noch so vorzüglich Begünstigte darum keinen Augenblick hindurch freier ist von Anlässen und Ursachen innern Schmerzes.

Sorrows and reverses spring up independently of external circumstances, and Heaven has dealt them out so wisely to man, that those who are to outward appearance most highly favoured by fortune, are yet not on that account more exempt from the causes that originate inward pain.

Firmness in the Trials of Life.

Letter I. 15.

Eine gewiſſe Stärke bedarf der Menſch in allen, auch den glücklichſten Verhältniſſen des Lebens, vielleicht kommen ſogar Unfälle, wie Sie jetzt einen erfahren, um dieſelbe zu prüfen und zu üben, und wenn man nur den Vorſatz faßt, ſie anzuwenden, ſo kehrt bald auch ſelbſt dadurch Heiterkeit in die Seele zurück, die ſich allemal freut, pflichtgemäße Stärke geübt zu haben.

Man stands in need of a certain degree of firmness in all the circumstances of life, even those that appear most fortunate; and when painful events occur, such as you now experience, they are perhaps sent only to try and prove us; and if we have the resolution to hold fast in our hour of trial, from this very firmness itself serenity soon returns to the mind, which always feels satisfaction in acting conformably to duty.

The Beauty of the Heavens.

Letter I. 17.

Der Anblick des Himmels hat überhaupt unter allen Umſtänden einen unendlichen Reiz für mich, bei ſternenhellen wie bei dunkeln Nächten, bei heiterm Blau wie bei ziehenden Wolken oder dem traurigen Grau, worin ſich das Auge verliert, ohne etwas darin zu unterſcheiden.

The appearance of the heavens has under all circumstances a never-ending charm for me, in the clear starlight as well as in dark nights, in the soft blue as well as in the cloudy or dark-grey sky, in which the eye loses itself, without being able to distinguish anything.

Life.

Letter I. 17.

Mir iſt überhaupt das Klagen über Wetter fremd, und ich kann es an andern nicht ſonderlich leiden. Ich ſehe die Natur gern als eine Macht an, an der man die reinſte Freude hat, wenn man ruhig mit allen ihren Entwickelungen fortlebt und die Summe aller als ein Ganzes betrachtet, in dem es nicht gerade darauf ankommt, ob jedes einzelne erfreulich ſei, wenn

nur der Kreislauf vollendet wird. Das Leben mit der Natur
auf dem Lande hat vorzüglich darin seinen Reiz für mich, daß
man die Theile des Jahres vor seinen Augen abrollen sieht.
Mit dem Leben ist es nicht anders, und es scheint mir daher
immer auf's mindeste eine müßige Frage, welches Alter, ob
Jugend oder Reife, oder sonst einen Abschnitt man vorziehen
möchte. Es ist immer nur eine Selbsttäuschung, wenn man
sich einbildet, daß man wahrhaft wünschen könnte in einem zu
bleiben. Der Reiz der Jugend besteht gerade im heitern und
unbefangenen Hineinstreben in das Leben, und er wäre dahin,
wenn es einem je deutlich würde, daß dies Streben nie um eine
Stufe weiter führt, etwa wie das Treten der Leute, die in
einem Rade eine Last in die Höhe heben. Mit dem Alter ist
es nicht anders, es ist im Grunde, wo es schön und kräftig
empfunden wird, nichts anderes als ein Hinaussehen aus
dem Leben, ein Steigen des Gefühls, daß man die Dinge
verlassen wird, ohne sie zu entbehren, indem man doch zugleich
sie liebt und mit Heiterkeit auf sie hinblickt und mit Antheil in
Gedanken bei ihnen verweilt.

The complaint about the weather is to me specially strange,
and I cannot endure it well in others. I like to look upon Nature
as a mighty power, imparting the purest joy, when we live
tranquilly with her in all her developments, and consider the
sum of all these as one great whole, in which we are not to think
whether any individual portion is pleasing if only the great general
ends are accomplished. For me the peculiar charm of a country life
in the society of Nature consists in this, that we see the different
seasons of the year roll past our eyes. It is just the same with
life ; and it has therefore always appeared to me an idle question,
to say nothing more, what period of life has the greatest attractions—youth or manhood, or any other portion of time. It is
ever only self-deception when we imagine that we would really
wish to continue in any one particular period. The charm of
youth just consists in the joyous and unrestrained anticipations
of life, and all these would vanish whenever it was evident to
any one that he was ever striving and never advancing a step,
very much like people condemned to the treadmill. With age it
is just the same ; when clearly and powerfully understood, it is
nothing else than a *looking beyond this life,* a stage in our course,
a feeling that we must leave all things without being able to dispense with them, loving meanwhile, and looking with cheerfulness
on all we are leaving, as a scene in which we are interested, and
on which our thoughts still love to linger.

Proper Views of Religion.

Letter I. 17.

Die Religion wird oft nicht in ihrer wahren Größe gefühlt und von einem niedern Standpunkt aus genommen. Wer Gott selbst nur in Rücksicht auf sich dient, um wieder dafür Schutz, Hülfe und Segen von ihm zu erhalten, um gleichsam von ihm zu fordern, daß er sich um jedes einzelne Lebensschicksal kümmern soll, der macht doch wieder sich zum Mittelpunkt des Alls. Wer aber die Größe und väterliche Güte Gottes so mit bewundernder Anbetung und mit tiefer Dankbarkeit in sein Gemüth aufgenommen hat, daß er alles von selbst zurückstößt, was nicht mit der reinsten und edelsten Gesinnung übereinstimmt wie der Gedanke, daß, was Pflicht und Tugend von ihm fordern, zugleich der Wille des Höchsten und die Forderung der von ihm gegründeten Weltordnung ist, der hat die wahrhaft religiöse und gewiß tugendhafte Gesinnung.

We often find that religion is not understood in its true greatness, but that man looks at it from a lower point of view. He who worships God only on selfish principles, that he may receive protection, aid, and blessing in return, and who demands, as it were, that he should concern himself about the petty fate of every individual, such a one makes himself the central point of the whole universe; whereas he who thoroughly comprehends the greatness and fatherly goodness of God, receiving the idea with admiring devotion and deep thankfulness, so that he removes from his mind everything that does not accord with the purest and noblest conceptions; as, for instance, the thought that what duty and virtue require of him is at the same time the will of the Most High, and necessary for the proper regulation of the affairs of the world; such a man possesses a truly religious and virtuous mind.

We ought to resist Pain.

Letter I. 19.

Wenn ein Mann dem Schmerze Herrschaft über sich einräumt, wenn er ihn ängstlich meidet, über den unvermeidlichen klagt, flößt er eher Nichtachtung als Mitleid ein. So vieles muß in einer Frau anders sein als im Manne. Einer Frau geziemt es sehr wohl, und scheint natürlich in ihr, sich an ein anderes Wesen anzuschließen. Der Mann muß gewiß auch das Vermögen daʒu beſiʒen, aber wenn es ihm ʒum Bedürfniß würde, ſo wäre es ſicher ein Mangel oder eine Schwäche ʒu nennen. Ein Mann muß immer ſtreben, unabhängig in ſich daʒuſtehen.

When a man allows pain to get the mastery over him, when he is anxious to avoid it on all occasions, and is ever moaning over what is unavoidable, then he becomes an object of contempt rather than pity. It is not so in the case of a woman. In a woman it is becoming enough, and seems natural, that she lean upon another being. The man ought certainly to possess the power of endurance ; but if he fail, it must be regarded as a want or weakness. A man ought ever to strive to stand on his own independent bottom.

A Weak Man.

Letter i. 19.

Ein Mann, der ſich durch Schwächen verführen, hinreißen läßt, kann gut, in andern Punkten recht liebenswürdig ſein, er iſt aber kein Mann, ſondern ein Mittelding ʒwiſchen beiden Geſchlechtern.

The man who allows himself to be deceived and carried away by his own weakness may be a very amiable person in other respects, but he cannot be called a man—only a sort of intermediate being between the two sexes.

On Asking and Giving Advice.

Letter i. 22.

Es iſt aber wahr, daß ich nichts davon halte, Rath ʒu fragen noch ʒu ertheilen. Gewöhnlich wiſſen die Fragenden ſchon, was ſie thun wollen, und bleiben auch dabei. Man kann ſich von einem andern über mancherlei, auch über Convenienʒ, Pflicht aufklären laſſen, aber entſchließen muß man doch ſich ſelbſt.

It is true, however, that I lay very little stress either upon asking or giving advice. Generally speaking, they who ask advice know what they wish to do, and remain firm to their intentions. A man may allow himself to be enlightened on various points, even upon matters of expediency and duty, but, after all, he must determine his course of action for himself.

Education.

Letter i. 26.

Man muß ſich die Erʒiehung ja nicht blos und immer als

eine birefte Leitung zu verständiger Haltung, gutem Character und hinlänglichem Reichthum von Kenntnissen denken. Sie wirft oft weit mehr als ein Zusammenfluß von Umständen, deren beabsichtigte Wirkung ganz vereitelt wird, die aber durch den Streit gegen die Individualität des zu Erziehenden in ihm bewirkt, was die birefte Einwirkung nie vermocht hätte. Denn das Resultat der Erziehung hängt ganz und gar von der Kraft ab, mit der der Mensch sich auf Veranlassung oder durch den Einfluß derselben selbst bearbeitet.

We must now simply regard education as a direct guide to propriety of conduct, a good character, and a pretty fair amount of knowledge. It effects often much more by the bringing together a number of influences, the intended result of which may indeed be frustrated, but which produces by the conflict with the individuality of the person being educated, that which the direct influences could never have brought about: for the result of any system of education depends entirely upon the power that a man possesses of applying the influences brought to bear upon him to the ends of self-culture, or whether he allows himself to be moulded by them.

THE ESSENTIAL FEATURES OF A MAN'S NATURE CANNOT BE CHANGED.

Letter I. 26.

Es ist immer meine Meinung gewesen, daß sich der Mensch, wenn man das Wesentliche seines Charafters nimmt, nicht eigentlich ändert. Er legt Fehler ab, vertauscht auch wohl Tugenden und gute Gewohnheiten gegen schlechte, allein seine Art zu sein, ob mehr nach der Außenwelt oder mehr nach innen gekehrt, ob heftig oder sanft, ob in die Tiefe der Ideen eingehend oder auf der Oberfläche verweilend, ob mit kühnerm oder festem Entschluß in's Leben eingreifend oder Schwäche verrathend, bleibt gewiß von der Kindheit bis in den Tod die nämliche.

It has ever been my opinion that the essential features of a man's nature cannot be changed; he may give up errors—he may change from virtuous and good habits to vicious courses; but the natural bent of his disposition, whether devoted to active employment or inward contemplation—whether impetuous or gentle—whether penetrating to the hidden depths of things, or resting satisfied with superficial views—whether acting in the affairs of life with a firm and powerful grasp or with weakness—ever remains from childhood to death the same.

Difficult Problems.

Letter I. 26.

Die Zulassung des Bösen in der Welt, die Straflosigkeit der Lasterhaften, sowie das Unglück der Guten in der Welt, sind von jeher Aufgaben gewesen, die der Mensch bald so, bald anders in der Weltregierung zu lösen versucht hat.

The permission of the wicked in the world, the impunity of the vicious, as well as the misfortunes of the good, are some of those problems which man has tried to solve, sometimes this way, sometimes that, in considering the government of the world.

On what Happiness depends.

Letter I. 27.

Mir kommt es immer vor, daß die Art, wie man die Ereignisse des Lebens nimmt, ebenso wichtigen Antheil an unserm Glück und Unglück hätten, als diese Ereignisse selbst. Den eigentlich frohen, heitern Genuß kann man sich allerdings nicht geben, er ist eine Gabe des Himmels. Aber man kann viel dazu thun, das Unangenehme, dessen für jeden das Leben immer viel herbeiführt, ruhiger aufzunehmen, muthiger zu tragen, besonnener abzuwehren oder zu vermindern. Man kann wenigstens vermeiden, sich unnöthige und ungegründete Besorgniß und Unruhe zu erregen.

I am more and more convinced that our happiness or unhappiness is much more dependent on the way that we meet the events of life than upon the nature of these events themselves. The joyous cheerful temper a man cannot exactly give himself, for that is the gift of Heaven ; but we can do much in preparing ourselves to encounter with tranquillity, to bear courageously, and by prudent forethought to turn aside or lessen, the many sorrows which the chances of life, more or less, bring upon all. One may at least avoid bringing on oneself unnecessary and groundless ares and troubles.

Bulwarks against the Evils of Life.

Letter I. 28.

Ergebung in das, was geschehen kann, Hoffnung und Vertrauen, daß nur dasjenige geschehen wird, was heilsam und gut ift, und Standhaftigkeit, wenn etwas Widerwärtiges eintrifft, find alles, was man dem Schickfale entgegenstellen kann.

Resignation to whatever may happen, hope and trust that only that will happen which is good and beneficial, and firmness when adversity overtakes us : these are the only efficient bulwarks that we can raise against destiny.

THE INSCRUTABLE DECREES OF GOD.

Letter I. 30.

Mir ift es immer als das ficherfte Mittel vorgekommen, fich in inniger Demuth auf die unerforfchliche, aber fichere Weisheit der göttlichen Rathfchläge und auf die natürliche Betrachtung zu befchränken, daß wir in diefem Leben nur einen fo furzen Theil des menfchlichen Dafeins überfehen, daß derfelbe gar fein Urtheil über das Ganze zuläßt.

To me it has always appeared to be best to bow with heartfelt humility to the inscrutable but unerring counsels of Heaven, and to remember that we can only in this life see a small portion of man's existence, and therefore can form no judgment of the whole.

DIFFERENT IDEAS OF HAPPINESS AND UNHAPPINESS.

Letter I. 31.

Ihr Ausdruck, daß es fcheine, als ob die Gottheit nur ihren Segen in reine Gefäße ergieße, hat mir ungemein gefallen. Der Menfch vermag diefen Segen, wenn er ihm entfteht, nicht herbeizuzaubern. Daß diefer Segen wirklich mit den Menfchen zufammenhängt auf unfichtbare und geheimnißvolle Weife, das glaube ich mit Ihnen. Aber die Begriffe von Glück und Unglück find felbft bei denen, die richtige Ideen zu haben pflegen, fo unbeftimmt und fo irrig, daß ich von früh an immer geftrebt habe, mir darüber ganz klar zu werden, und wie ich dahin gelangt bin, habe ich gefühlt, daß man des Glückes, bis auf einen gewiffen Grad wenigftens, immer ficher ift, fowie man fich von den äußern Umftänden unabhängig macht, fowie man lernt Freude aus allem Erfreulichen in Menfchen und Dingen zu ziehen, aber in Menfchen und Dingen nichts eigentlich zu bedürfen.

Your expression that "it appears as if God would only pour his blessings into pure vessels," pleases me exceedingly. If a man be without this blessing, he cannot charm it towards him. I agree with you in thinking that this blessing is given to man in a mysterious way which we cannot see. But the ideas attached to the words happiness and unhappiness are of so vague and undetermined a nature, even in the minds of those who usually entertain correct views and opinions, that I have from early youth endeavoured to get clear conceptions upon this subject ; and the conclusion at which I have arrived is, that man is ever sure to enjoy a certain amount of happiness at least, if he render himself independent of external circumstances—if he learn to draw happiness from every event of a pleasing nature, whether relating to man or things, at the same time maintaining his independence of both sources.

When Merit for an Act ceases.

Letter I. 31.

Gewiß hat man seinen Lohn dahin, indem alles Verdienst aufhört, wenn man der Folgen wegen etwas thut.

All merit ceases the moment we perform an act for the sake of its consequences. Truly in this respect " we have our reward."

Harmony in the Inner Nature of Man.

Letter I. 34.

Indem die Vorsehung die Schicksale der Menschen bestimmt, ist auch das innere Wesen des Menschen dabei in Einklang gebracht. Es ist eine solche Harmonie hierin, wie in allen Dingen der Natur, daß man sie auch gegenseitig aus einander ohne höhere Fügung erklären und herleiten könnte. Gerade dies aber beweist um so klarer und sicherer diese höhere Fügung, die jener Harmonie das Dasein gegeben.

Since it is Providence that determines the fates of men, their inner nature is thus brought into unison. There is such harmony, as in all things of nature, that one might explain the whole without referring to a higher Providence. But this only proves the more clearly and certainly this higher Providence, which has given existence to this harmony.

Life regarded as a Sea.

Letter I. 35.

Man kann sich aber doch nicht entschlagen, das Leben wie

ein Gewässer zu betrachten, durch das man sein Schiff mehr oder minder glücklich durchbringt, und da ist es ein natürliches Gefühl, lieber den kürzern als den längern Raum vor sich zu haben. Diese Ansicht des Lebens, als eines Ganzen, als einer zu durchmessenden Arbeit, hat mir immer ein mächtiges Mittel geschienen, dem Tode mit Gleichmuth entgegenzugehen. Betrachtet man dagegen das Leben nur stückweise, strebt man nur einen fröhlichen Tag dem andern beizugesellen, als könne das nun so in alle Ewigkeit fortgehen, so gibt es allerdings nichts Trostloseres, als an der Grenze zu stehen, wo der Faden auf einmal abgebrochen wird.

We cannot get rid of the idea that life must be regarded as an ocean, through which we are to conduct our bark more or less successfully, and then it is a natural feeling that we should contemplate with more satisfaction the short distance than the long voyage. This idea of viewing life as a whole, as a work to be got through, has ever appeared to me to be a powerful reason why we should regard death with indifference. On the other hand, if we look at life in detached portions, we have only to strive to associate one happy day with another, as if this would continue for an eternity ; and then nothing can be more void of a comfortable feeling than to find ourselves standing on the brink of that bourn at which the thread of life must be at once snapped.

INVESTIGATIONS INTO EARLY TIMES.

Letter I. 35.

Von früh an hat mich das Alterthum aber angezogen, und es ist auch eigentlich das, was mein wahres Studium ausmacht. Wo der Mensch noch seinem Entstehen näher war, zeigt sich mehr Gedanken und Gefühlen, wie in dem Ausdrucke, den er beiden lieh.

Investigations into early times charmed me at an early period of my life, and it is this which now constitutes my real study. When man was nearer to the dawn of his existence, he showed more heroism and simplicity of character, more depth and artlessness in his thoughts and emotions, as also in the language in which he clothed them.

THE POWER OF TIME.

Letter I. 36.

Wie groß die Macht der Zeit ist, so entfremdet sie doch nie,

auch nach so lange nicht mehr unmittelbar angeklungenen Ge=
fühlen, dem Gemüthe ganz; in diesen gibt es vielmehr auch im
wirklichen Dasein etwas, das man mit Recht zeitlos nennen
kann.

However great the power of time may be, yet it never entirely
obliterates the remembrance and influences of the past; even
though the mind may have long remained unoccupied by the
emotions immediately produced by those events. With all its
changes, it is time itself which has given that which may be
regarded as true existence, and which may be justly said to be
independent even of time.

In what Respect arises.

Letter I. 36.

Die Ehrerbietung, die das Kind den Aeltern, und überhaupt
jeder dem innerlich Höhern, dem er nahe kommt, schuldig ist,
und die jedem gutgearteten und weichgebildeten Gemüth so leicht
darzubringen wird, gründet sich mehr auf ein oft mehr geahntes
als deutlich in Handlungen erfanntes Wesen, auf ein Etwas,
das vielleicht nicht einmal zur völligen Ausbildung gekommen
ist, aber in Mienen, Geberden und dem Ganzen des Charakters
durchscheint.

That respect which the child owes to his parents, and every
man to those of higher intellectual power with whom he may
come in contact, and which every well-regulated and well-disposed
mind so readily pays, is much oftener founded upon an imaginary
worth than upon a distinct and actual experience of its existence
—upon a something, which may not perhaps have attained perfect
development, but which shines forth in the carriage, gestures,
and whole character.

Resignation and Contentment.

Letter I. 36.

Ergebung und Genügsamkeit sind es vor allem, die sicher
durch das Leben führen. Wer nicht Festigkeit genug hat zu
entbehren und selbst zu leiden, kann sich nie vor schmerzlichen
Empfindungen sicher stellen, ja er muß sich sogar selbst we=
nigstens die zu rege Empfindung dessen, was ihn ungünstig
trifft, zuschreiben.

It is resignation and contentment that are best calculated to lead us safely through life. Whoever has not sufficient power to endure privations, and even suffering, can never feel that he is armour-proof against painful emotions—nay, he must attribute to himself, or at least to the morbid sensitiveness of his nature, every disagreeable feeling he may suffer.

To Fight against Men and Gods.

Letter I. 36.

Gegen Menschen und gegen Schickfale ist es nicht blos die edelste und sich selbst am meisten ehrende, sondern auch die am meisten auf dauernde Ruhe und Heiterkeit berechnete Gemüthsstimmung, nicht gegen sie zu streiten, sondern sich, wo und wie es nur immer das Verhältniß erlaubt, zu fügen, was sie geben, als Geschenk anzusehen, aber nicht mehr zu verlangen, und am wenigsten mißmuthig über das zu werden, was sie verweigern.

To set ourselves against men and fate is not a disposition of mind which is the noblest, and which does honour to us, nor is it that which is likely to procure us the greatest amount of tranquillity and cheerfulness. We ought rather to try to accommodate ourselves, so far as it is possible, to circumstances, to look on all that fate bestows upon us as a gift, being careful not to desire more, and least of all to be dissatisfied because all our desires are not gratified.

The Noblest Feelings often lead to a Disastrous Issue.

Letter I. 37.

Es zeigt sich recht oft, daß die besten, edelsten, aufopferndsten Gefühle gerade die sind, die in unglückliche Schickfale führen, Es ist, als würden durch eine höhere, weise Führung die äußern Geschicke absichtlich in Zwiespalt mit den innern Empfindungen gebracht, damit gerade die letztern einen höhern Werth erlangen, in höherer Reinheit glänzen und dem, der sie hegt, eben durch Entbehrung und Leiden theurer werden sollten. So wohlthätig die Vorsehung waltet, so kommt es ihr nicht immer auf das Glück der Menschen an. Sie hat immer höhere Zwecke und wirkt gewiß vorzugsweise auf die innere Empfindung und Gesinnung.

It is often found that those feelings which are best, noblest, and most self-denying, are exactly those which lead to a disastrous issue. It is as if, by the command of a higher and wiser Power, man's fate were intentionally brought into variance with his inner feelings, in order that the latter might acquire a higher value, shine with greater purity, and thus become more precious by the very privations and sufferings to him who cherishes such feelings. However benevolent may be the intentions of Providence, they do not always advance the happiness of the individual. Providence has always higher ends in view, and works in a pre-eminent degree on the inner feelings and disposition.

TIME.

Letter I. 38.

Die Zeit ist das Wichtigste im menschlichen Leben; denn was ist die Freude nach dem Verfliegen der Zeit? und das Tröstliche, denn der Schmerz ist ebenso nichts nach ihrem Verfließen, sie ist das Gleis, in dem wir der letzten Zeit entgegenwallen, die dann zum Unbegreiflichen führt. Mit diesem Fortschreiten verbindet sich eine reißende Kraft, und sie reift mehr und wohlthätiger, wenn man auf sie achtet, ihr gehorcht, sie nicht verschwendet, sie als das größte Endliche ansieht, in der alles Endliche sich wieder auflöst.

Time is the most important thing in human life—for what is pleasure after the departure of time? and the most consolatory, since pain, when pain has passed, is nothing. Time is the wheel-track, in which we roll on towards eternity, conducting us to the Incomprehensible. In its progress there is a ripening power, and it ripens us the more and the more powerfully, when we duly estimate it, listen to its voice, do not waste it, but regard it as the highest finite good, in which all finite things are resolved.

LIFE IS AN ADVANCING TOWARDS ANNIHILATION.

Letter I. 44.

Daß alles Leben nur ein der scheinbaren Vernichtung Entgegengehen ist, wird einem nie so klar als in dem regel-mäßigen Wechsel der Jahreszeiten. Die ganze Pflanzenwelt nun mit so harmlos zuversichtlicher Freude in's Leben treten zu sehen, als ahnte sie gar nicht das winterliche Ersterben, hat

ebenſo etwas tief Rührendes wie das Leben eines noch feine
Gefahren ahnenden Kindes.

That all life is only an advancing towards apparent annihilation
can be nowhere so clearly seen as in the regular succession of the
seasons. To behold the whole vegetable world starting forth into
life with innocent unsuspecting joy, as if it did not once anticipate
its wintry death, contains something as deeply affecting as the life
of a child, who as yet has not dreamt of danger.

The Power of Fancy.

Letter I. 46.

Die bloße Wirklichkeit wäre unendlich arm ohne den Reiz
der Einbildung, die freilich ſo gut eitle Schrecken als leere
Hoffnungen in ihrem Schoß trägt, aber doch viel häufiger,
wenn ſie auch Täuſchungen mit ſich führt, ihnen ſchmeichelnd
liebliche als zurückſchreckende Farben leiht.

The mere reality of life would be inconceivably poor without
the charm of fancy, which brings in its bosom, no doubt, as many
vain fears as idle hopes, but lends much oftener to the allusions it
calls up a gay flattering hue than one which inspires terror.

The Idea of a Devil.

Letter I. 47.

Der Gedanke einer verfolgenden Macht würde mir immer
fremd ſein. Ich habe mich niemals mit den Vorſtellungen
vertragen können, die eines ſolchen, allem Guten feindſeligen,
am Böſen Gefallen findenden Weſens Daſein annehmen. Im
Neuen Teſtamente halte ich die dahin einſchlagenden Stellen
nur für bildliche, ſich an die Vorſtellungen des Judenthums
anſchließende Ausdrücke für das Böſe, das der Menſch, auch
wenn er gut iſt und ſich ganz ſchuldlos glaubt, doch immer in
ſich zu bekämpfen hat.

The thought of a persecuting power has always appeared quite
strange to me. I have never been able to endure the idea, which
admits the existence of a being inimical to all good and taking
pleasure in everything evil. In the New Testament I consider
such passages merely figurative, expressions connected with the
representations of Judaism for the evil, which man, even if he is
good and believes himself quite innocent, has yet ever to fight
against.

We are the Creatures of Time.

Letter I. 48.

Sehr natürlich, da er selbst das Geschöpf der Zeit ist, da seine Schicksale auf ihr wie auf einem immer wogenden Meere schweben, da er nie weiß, ob er sich der Gegenwart sicher vertrauen darf, und ob nicht eine trügerische Zukunft seiner wartet.

We are both the creatures of time; our fate rests upon it as upon an ever-agitated sea, as we never know whether we can safely trust the present, or whether a deceitful future may not yet be awaiting us.

Free-will and Necessity.

Letter I. 49.

Indeß ist es eine schöne Eigenschaft im Menschen, und ein ihm von dem Schöpfer ausschließlich vor den übrigen Erdengeschöpfen eingeräumter Vorzug, daß er immer fühlt, daß er durch den Gedanken und durch den Entschluß jeden körperlichen Einfluß, wie stark er sein möge, hemmen und beherrschen kann. Es sagt dem Menschen eine innere Stimme, daß er frei und unabhängig ist, sie rechnet ihm das Gute und das Böse an, und aus der Beurtheilung seiner selbst, die immer stärker und strenger sein muß als die anderer, muß man jene ganz körperlichen Einflüsse völlig hinweglassen. Es sind zwei verschiedene Gebiete, das der Abhängigkeit und das der Freiheit, und durch den bloßen Verstand läßt sich der Streit beider nicht lösen. In der Welt der Erscheinungen sind alle Dinge dergestalt verkettet, daß man, wenn man alle Umstände bis auf die kleinsten und entferntesten immer genau wüßte, beweisen könnte, daß der Mensch in jedem Augenblick gezwungen war so zu handeln, wie er gehandelt hat. Dabei hat er aber doch immer das Gefühl, daß er, wollte er in das hemmende Rad greifen und sich von dieser ihn umstrickenden Verkettung losmachen, es vermöchte. In diesem Gefühl seiner Freiheit liegt seine Menschenwürde.

It is a beautiful attribute of our nature, a privilege granted to man exclusively, and before all the other creatures of this world, that he ever feels that he can by forethought and determination

control and govern every physical influence, however mighty it may
be. An inward voice proclaims to him that he is free and independent ; it imputes to him good and evil, and in the judgments
which he passes on himself, which must always be more severe and
strict than those of others, he must entirely throw out of sight all
physical influences. Man is subject to two distinct laws, that of
dependence and that of freedom, and the conflict is not to be settled
by the mere understanding. In the visible world all things seem
to be so connected together, that, if we were acquainted with all
possible circumstances—the most minute and most remote—it
looks as if we could show that man at any moment could not
avoid acting exactly as he did. And yet there is always the feeling within us, that if we did but will it, we could grasp the
revolving wheel, and free ourselves from the chain that binds us
to it. In this consciousness of his freedom lies the true dignity of
man.

Every Man the Maker of his own Fortune.

Letter I. 49.

Es ift eine ſprichwörtliche Redensart, daß jeder ſich das
ſeinige ſchafft, und man pflegt das ſo zu nehmen, daß er es ſich
durch Vernunft oder Unvernunft gut oder ſchlecht bereitet.
Man kann es aber auch ſo verſtehen, daß, wie er es aus den
Händen der Vorſehung empfängt, er ſich ſo hineinpaßt, daß es
ihm doch wohl darin wird, wie viel Mängel es darbieten möge.

It is a proverbial expression that every man is the maker of his
own fortune, and we usually regard it as implying that every man,
by his folly or wisdom, prepares good or evil for himself. But we
may view it in another light—namely, that we may so accommodate
ourselves to the dispensations of Providence as to be happy in our
lot, whatever may be its privations.

See (Lat.) Man, every, maker of his own fortune.

The Starry Heavens.

Letter I. 56.

Aber der bloße Gedanke, daß ſie ſo außer und über allem Irdiſchen ſind ; das Gefühl, daß alles Irdiſche davor ſo verſchwindet,
daß der einzelne Menſch gegen dieſe in den Luftraum verſtreuten
Welten ſo unendlich unbedeutend iſt, daß ſeine Schickſale, ſein
Genießen und Entbehren, worauf er einen ſo kleinlichen Werth
legt, wie nichts gegen dieſe Größe verſchwinden; dann daß die
Geſtirne alle Menſchen und alle Zeiten des Erdbodens ver-

knüpfen, daß sie alles gesehen haben von Anbeginn an, und
alles sehen werden, darin verliere ich mich immer in stillem
Vergnügen beim Anblick des gestirntem Himmels. Gewiß ist
es aber auch ein wahrhaft erhabenes Schauspiel, wenn in der
Stille der Nacht, bei ganz reinem Himmel, die Gestirne,
gleichsam wie ein Weltenchor, herauf= und herabsteigen, und
gewissermaßen das Dasein in zwei Theile zerfällt. Der eine
Theil, wie dem Irdischen angehörend, in völliger Stille der
Nacht verstummt, und nur der andere heraufkommend in aller
Erhabenheit, Pracht und Herrlichkeit. Dann wird der gestirnte
Himmel, aus diesem Gesichtspunkte angesehen, gewiß auch von
moralischem Einfluß. Wer, der sich gewöhnt hat in dergleichen
Empfindungen und Ideen zu leben, und oft darin zu verweilen,
könnte sich leicht auf unmoralischen Wegen verirren? Wie
entzückt nicht schon der einfache Glanz dieses wundervollen
Schauspiels der Natur?

But the simple thought that the stars are far beyond and above
everything earthly—the feeling that everything earthly in comparison fades from the view, and that man himself is utterly
insignificant when contrasted with those worlds scattered over
the firmament, while his fate, his enjoyments, and wants are as
nothing—then again that the stars bind together all men and all
periods of the world's history, as they have seen all from the
beginning of time, and will see all that shall come hereafter ;—
when I meditate on all these things, I lose myself in serene
delight while contemplating the starry heavens. Certainly it is a
truly sublime spectacle, when in the stillness of the night, in an
unclouded sky, the stars, like the world's choir, rise and set, and as
it were divide existence into two portions :—the one, belonging to
the earthly, is silent in the perfect stillness of night, whilst the other
alone comes forth in sublimity, pomp, and majesty. Viewed
in this light the starry heavens truly exercise a moral influence
over us ; and who can readily stray into the paths of immorality,
if he has been accustomed to live amidst such thoughts and feelings, and frequently to dwell upon them? How are we entranced
by the simple splendours of this wonderful drama of nature?

TASTE FOR SCULPTURE.

Letter I. 54.

Wenn man Sinn für die Schönheit einer Bildsäule hat, so
gehört das zu den reinsten, edelsten und schönsten Genüssen, und

man entbehrt die Gestalten sehr ungern, an denen sich das Vergnügen, wie unzähligemal man sie sieht, immer erneuert, ja steigert.

A taste for sculpture belongs to the best, purest, and noblest of **our enjoyments**; and we feel most reluctant to be separated from those forms, from which, however often **we** contemplate them, we derive renewed and indeed heightened pleasure.

Sleep of the Innocent and Guilty contrasted.

Letter I. 55.

Aber der Schlaf ist auch charakteristisch. Wie reizend in holder Unschuld sind Kinder, wie engelgleich in ihrer blühenden Farbe! Wie bange und quälend ist der Schlaf und der Ausdruck des Gesichts eines nicht schuldlosen Gewissens.

Even sleep is characteristic. How charming are children in their lovely innocence! how angel-like their blooming hue! how painful and anxious is the sleep and expression in the countenance of the guilty!

The Close of Life.

Letter I. 56.

Ich scheue das Alter nicht, und den Tod habe ich, durch eine sonderbare innere Stimmung, vielleicht von meiner Jugend an, nicht als eine so rein menschliche Begebenheit angesehen, daß sie einen, der über Menschenschicksale zu denken gewohnt ist, unmögliche betrüben kann, sondern eher als etwas Erfreuliches. Jetzt ist meine Rechnung mit der Welt längst abgeschlossen. Ich verlange vom langen Leben weiter nichts, ich habe keine weitaussehenden Pläne, nehme jeden Genuß dankbar aus der Hand des Geschickes, würde es aber sehr thöricht finden, daran zu hängen, daß das noch lange so fortdauere. Meine Empfindungen sind doch eigentlich der Kreis, in dem ich lebe und den ich genieße, von außen bedarf ich kaum etwas, und diese Gedanken und Empfindungen sind zu sehr mein, als daß ich sie nicht mit mir hinübernehmen sollte. Niemand kann den Schleier wegziehen, den die Vorsehung gewiß mit tiefer Weisheit über das Jenseits gezogen hat.

I do not dread old age, and death I have, from a peculiarity of my constitution and from my youth, been accustomed to regard not simply as an event in human life but as something joyous. Such an occurrence cannot possibly excite feelings of regret in one who has meditated deeply on the destiny of man. My reckoning with the world has long been closed—I have nothing more to look for from length of life—I have no deep-laid plans extending to a distant futurity. I take any enjoyments gratefully from the hand of Providence, but would think it foolish to be so dependent upon them as to expect them to be of long continuance. My feelings are the precise central point in which I stand, and where my enjoyments are placed ; from anything external to myself I can derive no pleasure, and those thoughts and feelings are so peculiarly my own that I cannot imagine that they should not go with me. No one, however, can raise the veil which Providence has with profound wisdom drawn over the world beyond the grave.

THE IDEA OF A MISFORTUNE.

Letter I. 57.

Die Vorstellung eines Unglücks ist noch immer etwas ganz anderes als das Unglück selbst, wenn es mit der furchtbaren Gewißheit seiner Gegenwart eintritt. Man muß daher auf nichts so wenig vertrauen und an nichts so unablässig arbeiten als an seiner Seelenstärke und seiner Selbstbeherrschung, die beide die einzigen sichern Grundlagen des irdischen Glücks sind.

The idea we form of a misfortune is ever somewhat different from the misfortune itself, when it appears in all its frightful certainty. We must trust in nothing so little, and must labour for nothing so unceasingly, as for the strengthening of our soul and for self-government, both of which are the only sure foundations of earthly happiness.

WHAT LIES IN THE NATURE OF THINGS.

Letter I. 58.

Was in der Natur der Dinge liegt und das Schicksal herbeiführt, darüber wäre es thöricht und unmännlich zugleich, seine Ruhe und sein inneres Gleichgewicht zu verlieren.

What lies in the nature of things and is dependent on fate, it would be silly and unmanly to lose one's rest and inward equilibrium in thinking of it.

TEMPERATE HABITS.

Letter I. 58.

Es ist unglaublich, wie viel es thut, wenn der ganze Körper in einer steten und immer unterbrochen fortgesetzten Ordnung bleibt und von dem Wechsel der Eindrücke frei ist, der doch immer die körperlichen Functionen mehr oder weniger stört. Durchgängige Mäßigkeit ist gewiß doch am Ende dasjenige, was den Körper am längsten erhält und am sichersten vor Krankheit bewahrt.

It is incredible how important it is that the corporeal frame should be kept under the influence of constant. continuous. and unbroken order, and free from the impressions of vicissitude, which always more or less derange the corporeal functions. After all, it is continued temperance which sustains the body for the longest period of time, and which most surely preserves it free from sickness.

MAN.

Letter I. 60.

Der Mensch ist einmal überall der Mittelpunkt, und jeder Mensch bleibt doch am Ende allein, sodaß nur, was in ihm war und aus ihm ausgeht, auf ihn Wichtigkeit ausübt. Wie der Mensch im Leben auf Erden mitempfindend, wirksam, theilnehmend, immer sich gesellig entwickelnd ist, so macht er den größern Weg, der über die Grenzen der Irdischkeit hinausreicht, doch allein, und keiner kann ihn da begleiten, wenn auch freilich in allen Menschen die Ahnung liegt, jenseit des Grabes die wiederzufinden, die verangegangen sind, und die um sich zu versammeln, die nach uns übrig bleiben. Kein gefühlvoller Mensch kann dieser Ahnung, ja dieses sichern Glaubens entbehren, ohne einen großen Theil seines Glücks und gerade den edelsten und reinsten, aufzugeben.

Man is, above all, the central point of human action. and each man remains at last alone, so that what was in him and went forth from him is alone important. Man, during his life on earth, sympathising and active, is ever associated in his feelings with others ; yet he treads alone the more important path, which leads over the confines of the earthly state ; no one can accompany him there, though in every man there is the presentiment, that beyond the grave he will find again those who have gone before him, and will

there gather around him again those whom he leaves behind. No
man of affectionate feeling can be without this anticipation, yea,
this firm belief, without giving up a large portion of his happiness,
and that the purest and noblest.

Motives of Actions alone to be regarded.
Letter I. 61.

Die erbärmlichsten Menschen sind die, die nichts über sich
vermögen, nicht können, was sie wollen, und die, welche selbst,
indem sie tugendhaft sind, niedrige Motive haben, Rücksichten
auf Glück und Zufriedenheit, Furcht vor Gewissensbissen oder
gar vor künftigen Strafen. Es ist recht gut und nützlich,
wenn die Menschen auch nur aus diesen Gründen nicht sündigen,
aber wer auf Gesinnung und Seelenzustand sieht, kann daran
keinen Gefallen haben. Das Edle ist nur dann vorhanden,
wenn das Gute um des Guten willen geschieht, entweder als
selbst erkanntes und empfundenes Gesetz aus reiner Pflicht, oder
aus dem Gefühl der erhabenen Würde und der ergreifenden
Schönheit der Tugend. Nur diese Motive beweisen, daß
wirklich die Gesinnung selbst groß und edel ist, und nur sie
wirken auch wieder auf die Gesinnung zurück.

The men most to be pitied are those who have no command
over themselves, who cannot do what they would, and who, even
whilst they are performing virtuous deeds, do so from mean
motives, from regard to happiness and mental satisfaction, fear of
the reproaches of conscience, or else of future punishment. This
is all very well and useful, supposing that man cannot be kept in
the straight path by any other motives, but he who looks inwardly
to the heart and soul can derive no satisfaction from such conduct.
True nobility only exists when the good is sought for its own
sake, either as a recognised law of pure duty, or from the feeling
of the lofty dignity and constraining beauty of virtue. It is only
these motives that show the disposition to be great and noble,
and these alone react upon the character.

Providence does not favour Individuals.
Letter I. 67.

Die Vorsehung begünstigt gewiß nicht einzelne, sondern die
tiefe Weisheit ihrer Rathschläge dehnt sich auf die Zurecht-
weisung und Veredlung aller aus.

Providence certainly does not attend merely to the interests of individuals, but the profound wisdom of its counsels extends to the right ordering and betterment of all.

THE SEA.

Letter I. 68.

Es ist ein so hübscher Gedanke, daß, wie weit auch die Ufer von einander entfernt sind, die Welle, die mir die Füße bespült, in kurzer Zeit am gegenüberstehenden Gestade sein kann.

It is a beautiful thought, that however far one shore may be from another, the wave that ripples over my foot will in a short time be on the opposite strand.

SUNDAYS AND HOLIDAYS.

Letter I. 70.

Es gibt nichts so Selbstisches und Herzloses, als wenn Vornehme und Reiche mit Mißfallen oder wenigstens mit einem gewissen verschmähenden Ekel auf Sonn= und Feiertage zurück= blicken. Selbst die Wahl des siebenten Tages ist gewiß die weiseste, welche hätte gefunden werden können. So willkürlich es scheint und bis auf einen Punkt auch sein mag, die Arbeit um einen Tag zu verkürzen oder zu verlängern, so bin ich überzeugt, daß die sechs Tage gerade das wahre, den Menschen in ihren physischen Kräften und in ihrem Beharren in ein= förmiger Beschäftigung angemessene Maß ist. Es liegt noch etwas Humanes auch darin, daß die zur Arbeit dem Menschen behülflichen Thiere diese Ruhe mit genießen.

There is nothing so selfish and heartless as the displeasure, or at least the kind of contemptuous aversion, with which men of distinction and wealth sometimes regard Sundays and holidays. Even the choice of the seventh day is certainly the wisest which could have been made. However it may seem to lie, and in one respect really may lie, within the power of the will to shorten or lengthen the usual period of labour, I am thoroughly convinced that the six days are the really true, fit, and adequate measure of time for work, whether as regards the physical strength of man or his perseverance in a uniform occupation. There is also some- thing humane in the arrangement, by which those animals which assist man in his work rest along with him.

TREES.

Letter I. 71.

Die Bäume haben darin etwas so Schönes und Anziehendes, auch für die Phantasie, daß, da sie ihren Ort nicht verändern können, sie Zeugen aller Veränderungen sind, die in einer Gegend vorgehen, und da einige ein überaus hohes Alter erreichen, so gleichen sie darin geschichtlichen Monumenten und haben doch ein Leben, sind doch wie wir entstehend und vergehend, nicht starr und leblos wie Fluren und Flüsse, von denen sonst das im vorigen Gesagte in gleichem Maße gilt. Daß man sie jünger und älter und endlich nach und nach dem Tode zugehend sieht, zieht immer näher und näher an sie an.

Trees have about them something beautiful and attractive even to the fancy, since they cannot change their places, are witnesses of all the changes that take place around them ; and as some reach a great age, they become, as it were, historical monuments, and like ourselves they have a life, growing and passing away—not being inanimate and unvarying like the fields and rivers. One sees them passing through various stages, and at last step by step approaching death, which makes them look still more like ourselves.

WORK AS NECESSARY AS EATING AND SLEEPING.

Letter I. 73.

Das Arbeiten ist, meinem Gefühl nach, dem Menschen so gut ein Bedürfniß als Essen und Schlafen. Selbst diejenigen, die gar nichts thun, was ein vernünftiger Mensch Arbeit nennen würde, bilden sich doch ein, etwas zu thun. Einen Müßiggänger, der es seiner Meinung nach wäre, gibt es wohl nicht auf der Welt.

Work, according to my feeling, is as much of a necessity to man as eating and sleeping. Even those who do nothing which to a sensible man can be called work, still imagine that they are doing something. The world possesses not a man who is an idler in his own eyes.

THE LITTLE INFLUENCE OF STATE AFFAIRS ON PRIVATE HAPPINESS.

Letter I. 79.

Alles, was man Staats- und Weltbegebenheiten nennt hat

in allen äußern Dingen die größte Wichtigkeit, stiftet und vernichtet im Augenblick das Glück, oft das Dasein von Tausenden; aber wenn nun die Welle des Augenblicks vorübergerauscht ist, der Sturm sich gelegt hat, so verliert sich, ja so verschwindet oft spurlos ihr Einfluß. Viele andere ganz geräuschlos die Gedanken und Empfindung stimmende Dinge sind da oft weit mehr von tiefem und dauerndem Einfluß. Der Mensch kann sich überhaupt sehr frei halten von allem, was nicht unmittelbar in sein Privatleben eingreift, und dies ist eine sehr weise Einrichtung der Vorsehung, weil so das individuelle Glück unendlich mehr gesichert ist.

Everything that regards statesmanship and the interest of the world is in all outward respects of the greatest importance; it creates and destroys in a moment the happiness, even the very existence, of thousands, but when the wave of the moment has rushed past, and the storm has abated, its influence is lost, and even frequently disappears without leaving a trace behind. Many other things that are noiselessly influencing the thoughts and feelings often make far deeper and more lasting impressions on us. Man can for the most part keep himself very independent of all that does not trench on his private life—a very wise arrangement of Providence, since it gives a much greater security to human happiness.

EARNESTNESS IN LIFE.
Letter I. 81.

Der Ernst und selbst der größte des Lebens ist etwas sehr Edles und Großes, aber er muß nicht störend in das Wirken im Leben eingreifen. Er bekommt sonst etwas Bitteres, das Leben selbst Verleidendes.

Earnestness in life, even when carried to an extreme, is something very noble and great, but it must not be allowed to disturb the common business of life, else it will produce bitterness, producing injurious effects.

HOME.
Letter I. 89.

Das Haus und die Sachen darin haben mir denselben erfreuenden Anblick als sonst gemacht. Es spricht einen immer, wenn man auch gerade unmittelbar vorher Großes und Schönes gefehen hat, mit heimlicher und zur Heiterkeit **stimmender** Freundlichkeit an.

My house and the things in it have always something pleasant to me. There is always a something about home which addresses us with a friendly air, and touches the heart, even after having just come from direct intercourse with objects that are great and beautiful.

THE COURSE OF NATURE.

Letter II. 3.

So geht die Natur ihren ewigen Gang fort und kümmert sich nicht um den in ihrer Mitte vergänglichen Menschen. Mag auch das Schmerzhafteste und Zerreißendste begegnen, mag es sogar eine unmittelbare Folge ihrer eigenen gewöhnlichen Umwandelungen oder ihrer außerordentlichsten Revolutionen sein, sie verfolgt ihre Bahn mit eiserner Gleichgültigkeit, mit scheinbarer Gefühllosigkeit.

Diese Erscheinung hat, wenn man eben vom Schmerz über ein schon geschehenes Unglück, oder von Furcht vor einem drohenden ergriffen ist, etwas wieder schmerzlich Ergreifendes, die innere Trauer Vermehrendes, etwas, das schaudern und starren macht. Aber sowie der Blick sich weiter wendet, sowie die Seele sich zu allgemeinen Betrachtungen sammelt, sowie also der Mensch zu der Besonnenheit und Ergebung zurückkehrt, die seiner wahrhaft würdig sind, dann ist gerade dieser ewige, wie an ihr Gesetz gefesselte Gang der Natur etwas unendlich Tröstendes und Beruhigendes. Es gibt dann doch auch hier schon etwas Festes, „einen ruhenden Pol in der Flucht der Erscheinungen", wie es einmal in einem Schiller'schen Gedichte sehr schön heißt. Der Mensch gehört zu einer großen, nie durch einzelnes gestörten noch störbaren Ordnung der Dinge, und da diese gewiß zu etwas Höherm und endlich zu einem Endpunkte führt, in dem alle Zweifel sich lösen, alle Schwierigkeiten sich ausgleichen, alle früher oft verwirrt und im Widerspruch klingenden Töne sich in Einen mächtigen Einklang vereinigen, so muß auch er mit eben dieser Ordnung zu dem gleichen Punkte gelangen.

Nature goes forward in her never-ending course, and cares nothing for the race of man that is ever passing before her.

Whatever may be the painful and distressing events that happen, either in the direct course of her accustomed revolutions, or by some apparent deviation, she still goes on her way with stern indifference and apparent insensibility. Whether we suffer from some present sorrow, or from the fear of one impending, this thought has something deeply painful, which increases the bitterness of the inward grief—something that makes us pause and shudder. But when we extend our view—when the soul loses itself in universal contemplation—when man turns to reflection and resigns himself to the inevitable, a course alone worthy of him, then the eternal, unchangeable order of Nature has a comforting and peaceful influence. It even gives us here a resting-place, "a stationary pole-star amidst the flight of meteors," as has been beautifully expressed in a song of Schiller's. Man belongs to a great order of things not easily disturbed or thrown into confusion; and as this certainly leads to something higher, and at length to a point in which all doubts shall be resolved, all difficulties smoothed, and all the jarring tones of contradiction and discordance joined in one mighty harmony—*he* must also in this order attain to this point.

Memory of the Past.

Letter II. 3.

Die Vergangenheit und die Erinnerung haben eine unendliche Kraft, und wenn auch schmerzliche Sehnsucht daraus quillt, sich ihnen hinzugeben, so liegt darin doch ein unaussprechlich süßer Genuß. Man schließt sich in Gedanken mit dem Gegenstande ab, den man geliebt hat, und der nicht mehr ist, man kann sich in Freiheit und Ruhe überall nach außen hinwenden, hülfreich und thätig sein, aber für sich fordert man nichts, da man alles hat, alles in sich schließt, was die Brust noch zu fühlen vermag

The past and the remembrance of it have a never-ending power, and if painful longings arise to give ourselves up to it, it has yet an inexpressible charm. We can shut ourselves up in thought with those whom we have loved and lost—we can turn away in peace and freedom from all that is external, and though still active and beneficent, for ourselves we ask nothing, for everything that the heart has the power to enjoy is within our breast.

The Path of Life.

Letter II. 4.

Die zusammen die Lebensbahn gehen, müssen sich an einem

Punkte ſcheiden; es iſt glücklicher, wenn die Zwiſchenzeit **ſehr kurz** iſt, in der ſie einander folgen. Allein aller Verluſt von Jahren iſt kurz gegen die Ewigkeit. In mir geht jetzt nichts anderes vor, als daß mein Inneres ſich ungekünſtelt, unabſichtlich, ohne durch Vorſätze oder Maximen geleitet zu ſein, blos ſich ſeinem Gefühl überlaſſend, mit der Lebens= oder Schickſals= periode in's Gleichgewicht ſetze, in die ich unglücklicherweiſe früher getreten bin, als es der gewöhnliche Gang des Lebens erwarten ließ. An einem ſolchen Gleichgewichte darf es dem Menſchen, meiner Empfindung nach, nie fehlen, das Streben danach ſollte ihm wenigſtens immer eigen ſein. Das Setzen in's Gleichgewicht wird oft nur dadurch erreicht, daß man viel Schmerz, phyſiſchen und moraliſchen, in ſein Daſein mit auf= nimmt, aber es beſteht darin die wahre Demüthigung unter die Fügung des Geſchickes, die ich mir immer als die erſte und höchſte Pflicht des Menſchen betrachte.

Those who go along the path of life together must separate at some point; it is well when the interval at which they follow each other is very short. But every period of years is short in comparison of eternity. As for myself, I care now for nothing else except that my inward being, simple and undisguised, without being led by prejudices or maxims, yielding only to its feelings, should place itself in unison with that period of life on which I have unluckily entered sooner than the usual course of life might have led me to expect. Such a state, in my opinion, no man need fear to attain, but there must be much striving after it. It is, indeed, often attained only after much physical and moral suffering, but in this there is a lesson of humility under the hand of God, which I have ever regarded as the best and highest duty of man.

MAN AS INDIVIDUALS AND IN THE MASS.

Letter II. 7.

Was iſt der einzelne in dem Strome der Weltbegebenheiten? Er verſchwindet darin nicht blos, wie ein Atom gegen eine unermeßliche, alles mit ſich fortreißende Kraft, ſondern auch in einem höhern, edlern Sinne. Denn dieſer Strom wälzt ſich doch nicht, einem blinden Zufall hingegeben, gedankenlos fort, **er** eilt doch einem Ziele zu, und ſein Gang wird von allmächtiger und allweiſer Hand geführt. Allein der einzelne erlebt das Ziel nicht, das erreicht werden ſoll, er genießt, wie ihn **der Zufall,**

worunter ich nur hier eine in ihren Gründen nicht erforschbare
Fügung verstehe, in die Welt wirft, einen größern oder kleinern
Theil des schon in der That erreichten Zweckes, wird dem noch
zu erreichenden oft hingeopfert, und muß das ihm dabei ange=
wiesene Werk oft plötzlich und in der Mitte der Arbeit verlassen.
Er ist also nur Werkzeug, und scheint nicht einmal ein wichtiges,
da, wenn der Lauf der Natur ihn hinwegraft, er immer auf
der Stelle ersetzt wird, weil es ganz widersinnig zu denken
wäre, daß die große Absicht der Gottheit mit den Welt=
begebenheiten durch Schicksale schwacher einzelner auch nur um
eine Minute könnte verspätet werden.   In den Weltbegeben=
heiten handelt es sich um ein Ziel, es wird eine Idee verfolgt,
man kann es sich wenigstens, ja man muß es sich so denken.
Im Laufe der körperlichen Natur ist das anders.   Man kann
da nichts anderes sagen, als daß Kräfte entstehen und so lange
auslaufen, als ihr Vermögen dauert.   So lange man bei
einzelnen stehen bleibt, scheint darin ein Mensch gar sehr von
andern verschieden, verschieden an Thätigkeit, Gesundheit und
Lebensdauer. Sieht man aber auf eine Masse von Geschlech=
tern, so gleicht sich das alles aus.

What is the individual in the stream of this world's events?
He disappears in it, not merely like an atom in an immeasurable,
all-absorbing power, but in a higher, nobler spirit. For this stream
does not rush on thoughtlessly, led by blind chance, but pursues
its distinct end, guided in its course by an almighty and all-wise
hand. But the individual does not live to see the attainment of
this end ; he enjoys a greater or less share of success as chance
wills it, by which I merely mean an uninvestigated providence ;
he will often be sacrificed in the attainment, and must frequently
leave his work suddenly, and in the midst of his labours. He is
therefore only an instrument, and does not appear to be even
a powerful one ; as, when the course of nature sweeps him away,
his place is ever filled up, for it would be absurd to suppose that
the great objects of the Creator could be for a moment delayed
by any circumstance in the life of a weak individual. In the
events of the moral world there is an aim—there is an idea pursued—one can at least, nay, one must think so in reference to
himself. In the order of the material nature it is otherwise.
One can only say that powers arise and run their course as
long as they are permitted. As long as one looks at a single
individual, he appears different from other men—different in
ability, health, length of life, &c. ; but if we look at a mass of
living beings, they appear all alike.

OLD AGE.

Letter II. 9.

Es ist eine große Weisheitsregel im Leben, nicht zu gesund und zu frei von Unbequemlichkeiten des Alters und körperlichen Zufällen sein zu wollen. Es ist viel besser, das, was nur beschwert, nicht aber zu sehr hindert, mit Geduld zu ertragen, und noch besser, sich über die unangenehme Empfindung, die es erregt, wegzusetzen.

It is a very wise rule in life not to be too anxious about health, or to be entirely free from the inconveniences and bodily ailments of old age. It is far better to submit with patience to what is merely annoying, but does not altogether confine us, and still bet er to treat with indifference the uncomfortable feelings which such a state of body calls up.

PEACE IS THE NATURAL TONE OF A WELL-REGULATED MIND.

Letter II. 12.

Die Ruhe ist die natürliche Stimmung eines wohlgeregelten, mit sich einigen Herzens. Aeußere Ereignisse können sie bedrohen und das ruhigste Gemüth aus den Angeln heben. Ein großes weicht zwar auch da nicht, allein obgleich es Frauen gibt, welche diese Stärke mit der größten und lebendigsten Regsamkeit der Empfindung und der Einbildungskraft verbinden, so kann man das bewundern, aber nicht fordern. In einem Manne aber ist es Pflicht, es läßt sich verlangen, und er verliert gleich bei allen richtig Urtheilenden an Achtung, wie hierin in ihm ein Mangel sichtbar wird.

Peace is the natural tone of a well-regulated mind at one with itself. External circumstances may assume a threatening aspect, and unhinge for a time the most stoical disposition, but a truly noble soul yields not ; and there are even women who unite such firmness with the greatest and liveliest activity of mind and vigour of imagination. This we may admire, though we must not expect often to find it in them. But in man it is an imperative duty, and he loses in the eyes of the right-thinking all title to respect when he shows a deficiency in this quality.

The Future and the Present.

Letter ii. 13.

Man muß die Zukunft abwarten und die Gegenwart genießen oder ertragen.

We must wait for the future, and enjoy or bear the present.

Evangelical Churches.

Letter ii. 14.

Unsere evangelischen Kirchen werden viel zu sehr als Orte, die zum Predigen bestimmt sind, angesehen, und auf die religiöse Erhebung des Gemüths im Gebet und Nachdenken wird zu wenig gedacht.

Our evangelical churches are too much regarded as places for preaching, and too little thought as intended for the religious elevation of the mind by prayer and meditation.

Death.

Letter ii. 15.

Tod ist nichts als ein Wort. Erst die eigene Empfindung kann sagen, was in der Wirklichkeit diesem Worte zum Grunde liegt. Der Anblick der Sterbenden gibt wenig dazu. Was man an ihnen sieht, geht blos dem Tode vorher. Mit ihm selbst tritt für uns die starre Besinnungslosigkeit ein. Ob dies aber auch für sie so ist, und sie erst wieder später und anders erwachen? das ist's, was man zu wissen wünschte, und was unmöglich ist zu erfahren.

Death is only a word. Experience alone can first tell us what is the true meaning of the word. The appearance of the dying tells us nothing. What we see is merely the prelude to death. A dull unconsciousness is what strikes us. Whether this be so— how and when the spirit wakes to life again—this is what we wish to know, and which never can be known till it is experienced.

Life regarded as a Casket.

Letter ii. 15.

Es ist eine sehr schöne Stelle Ihres letzten Briefes, worin Sie sagen, daß Sie das Leben als ein Gefäß ansehen, in das man so viel Köstliches hineinlegen kann, als man innerlich in sich besitzt. Es ist das ein ungemein glücklicher Ausdruck. Der Mensch kann das Leben zu dem machen, was er will, und ihm für sich selbst und andere so viel Werth geben, als er Kraft hat es zu thun. Freilich versteht sich das von selbst nur in sittlich=geistiger Hinsicht, da der Mensch die äußern Umstände nicht in seiner Gewalt hat, und nur über sein Geistiges und Moralisches, über dieses aber ganz gebieten kann.

That is a very beautiful expression in your last letter, in which you say that you regard life as a casket, in which we can lay up all the spiritual treasures that we possess. It is indeed a remarkably happy idea. In fact, man can make of life what he will, and give as much value to it for himself and others as he has power given him. This, however, is to be understood merely in a spiritual sense, as man has not external circumstances in his own power, but over his spiritual and moral nature he has entire control.

How Happiness is procured.
Letter II. 16.

Das Glücklichsein, sich innerlich Glücklichfühlen ist keine Gabe des Schicksals und kommt nicht von außen. Man muß es sich, wenn es dauernd sein soll, immer selbst erkämpfen. Das ist aber auch tröstend, denn man kann es auch immer erkämpfen. Aeußerlich immer oder nur größtentheils glücklich, immer gesund, wohlhabend durch sich, gelingend in seinen Wünschen kann selbst Gott nicht den Menschen machen; denn er hat die Menschen mit großer Weisheit in die Bedingungen der Welt gesetzt, und die erlauben das nicht immer. Aber innerlich glücklich kann er immer machen, denn dazu hat er uns die Kraft in's Herz gelegt: die Erhebung zu ihm, die Bewunderung seiner, die Liebe zu ihm, das Vertrauen auf ihn, alle die Empfindungen, durch welche sein Friede über uns kommt.

To be happy and to feel inward happiness is not the gift of fate, and comes not from the circumstances in which we are placed. We must reach it by our own exertions if it is to remain. But then it is comforting to think that it is always within our own power. God himself cannot make a man happy in his external circumstances, or at least only to a certain extent, nor yet can he make him always prosperous and successful in his aims; for God has with supreme wisdom placed men in the midst of ever-changing events, and these do not admit of men being always happy. **But inwardly happy he can always make him,** for he has given us this power in our heart—the yearning for him, the admiration, love, **and trust in him ;** in fact, all those feelings by which his peace comes to us.

MAN CAN DO MUCH FOR HIMSELF.

Letter II. 17.

Die Erfahrung wird Ihnen bestätigen, was ich Ihnen oft sagte, daß man doch sehr viel dazu thun kann. Gott hätte den Menschen nicht das erregbare, leichtbewegliche, dem Gram und dem Schmerz so zugängliche Gemüth gegeben, wenn er nicht zugleich darein hätte die Kraft legen wollen, diese Gefühle zu beherrschen und diesen Schmerz zu besiegen. Er gibt nichts unmittelbar, er will immer, daß der Mensch durch eigene Kraft seinen Segen erlange, man kann nicht sagen erwerbe oder verdiene, denn das Menschliche kann nicht auf diese Weise an das Göttliche reichen. Alles, auch was Gott gibt, muß doch ebenso durch den Menschen und sein eigenes Thun gehen, als wäre es einzig und allein sein Werk. Es ist mit dem Samenkorn, das im Grund aus dem Herzen geistige Frucht trägt, ebenso als mit demjenigen, welches aus der Erde emporschießt, oder wenigstens auf ganz ähnliche Weise. Die Frucht wird auch nicht unmittelbar von Gott, ja nicht einmal von der Natur gegeben, sie muß alle Zustände durchgehen, welche sie nach und nach zur Reife bringen, und wenn der Mensch auch unter dem glücklichsten Himmel und in dem am meisten günstigen Boden derselben gewiß sein will, muß er selbst seine Mühe und den Schweiß seiner Stirn daranwenden. Noch viel mehr aber ist das der Fall bei der Frucht des Geistes und des Herzens, allein die Sicherheit ist da auch unendlich größer.

Experience will convince you, what I have often said, that man can do much for himself. God would not have given him a disposition so easily excited and so easily moved to sorrow and grief, if he had not bestowed at the same time a strength of mind to control these feelings, and to get the better of this grief. He gives nothing directly ; he ever wills that man should merit his blessing by his own exertions ; we cannot say *earn* and *deserve*, for the *human* can never in this way attain the *heavenly.* All, too, that God gives must pass through man and his own exertions, as if it were his own peculiar work. It is with the seed which produces the fruit of the Spirit precisely as with that which springs from the earth, or at least in quite a similar way. The seed is not immediately from God or from nature : it must go through all the processes necessary to bring it by degrees to maturity ; and if man, under the most favourable sky and the most fruitful soil, wishes to be secure of his harvest, he must bestow his labour and the " sweat of his brow." This is still more the case with the fruit of the Spirit and of the heart, but the certainty of the harvest is still greater.

ALL THINGS ARE IN CHANGE.

Letter II. 18.

Die Dinge der Welt sind in ewigem Steigen und Fallen und in unaufhörlichem Wechsel, und dieser Wechsel muß Gottes Wille sein, da er weder der Macht noch der Weisheit die Kraft verliehen hat, ihn aufzuhalten und ihm zum Stillstand zu bringen. Die große Lehre ist auch hier, daß man seine Kräfte in solchen Zeiten doppelt anstrengen muß, um seine Pflicht zu erfüllen und das Rechte zu thun, daß man aber für sein Glück und seine innere Ruhe andere Dinge suchen muß, die ewig unentreißbar sind.

The things of the world are ever rising and falling, and in unceasing change. This change must be in accordance with the will of God, as he has given to man neither the power nor the wisdom to control it and bring it to a close. The great lesson to be learned in such cases is, that man must strengthen himself doubly to perform his duty, and do what is right, seeking his happiness and inward peace in objects which cannot be taken away from him.

SORROW.

Letter II. 18.

Der Kummer, der nach Hülfe und Trost verlangt, ist nicht der höchste und kommt nicht aus dem Tiefsten des Herzens.

The sorrow which calls for help and comfort is not the greatest, nor does it come from the depths of the heart.

HOW ENJOYMENT ARISES.

Letter II. 19.

Der Genuß entsteht durch die Thätigkeit; beide sind aber immer verbunden. Es gibt allerdings auch Genuß, der wie

eine reine Himmelsgabe uns zuströmt. Den kann man aber
nicht suchen, und es ist beklagenswerth, wenn sich die Sehnsucht
auf einen solchen heftet. Aber der große Genuß, das große
Glück, das wahrhaft durch keine Macht entreißbare, liegt in
der Vergangenheit und in der gewissen Betrachtung, daß das
Glück zwar ein großes, schätzenswürdiges Gut, aber daß doch
die Bereicherung der Seele durch Freude und Schmerz, die
Erhöhung aller edeln Gefühle der wahre und letzte Zweck,
übrigens alles in der Welt wechselnd und seiner Natur nach
vergänglich ist. Durch diese Ansicht versinkt das Leben in der
Vergangenheit nicht in ein dumpfes Brüten über vergangene
Freuden oder empfundene Leiden, sondern verschlingt sich in die
innere Thätigkeit, welche das Gemüth in der Gegenwart
beschäftigt.

Enjoyment arises from activity of mind; both are ever united.
There is indeed also an enjoyment which streams in upon us as
a pure gift of Heaven. Such, however, we should not seek after;
it is to be regretted when an anxious longing for this arises. But
the great enjoyment, the great happiness, that which cannot be
torn from us by any power, lies in the past and in the thought
that happiness is indeed a great and precious good, but yet the
improvement of the soul by joys and griefs, the development of
noble feelings, is the true and only end of existence; whereas
everything else in the world is ever changing, and in its nature
transient. According to this view, life in the past sinks not into
a stupid brooding over past pleasures or sorrows that have been
felt, but is united closely with the mental activity which employs
itself on the present.

RELIGION IMPLANTED IN THE VERY NATURE OF MAN.

Letter II. 19.

Die Religion selbst ist in der Natur des Menschen ein-
gepflanzt. Die christliche ist durch besondere Anordnung von
oben in die Welt gekommen. Es ist doch aber dem Menschengeschlecht, in Rücksicht auf sie, die Freiheit nicht genommen,
vielmehr im höchsten Grade gelassen worden, da gerade
Religionsgefühle nur durch das freieste Herausgeben aus dem
Innern, Werth haben. So ist sie angenommen und zurück-
gestoßen worden, bis sie endlich überall gesiegt hat. Allein in
die Herzen der Menschen aufgenommen, gestaltet sie sich

anders und anders, nach den Eigenthümlichkeiten des Geistes und Charakters derer, die sich zu ihr bekennen. Schon an den Aposteln, also gleich im ersten Anfange, sieht man das. Die Lehre gestaltet sich anders in Johannes wie in Petrus. In der Folge entstanden dann auch wirkliche Spaltungen. Es mischten sich Leidenschaften und weltliche Absichten ein. So entstand Entweihung und Mißbrauch. Immer aber sieht man in dieser Religionsgeschichte Göttliches neben Irdischem, immer das Eine, Ewige und Unsterbliche, wie eine Sonne Licht und Wärme anziehen, aber bald mehr, bald minder durch den Schleier des Irdischen verhüllt.

Religion is implanted in the very nature of man. The Christian religion has come down from above by the special will of God. It has, however, not deprived man of freedom on this point, but rather has conferred it on him in a still higher degree; just because religious feelings have their true value according as they spring freely and spontaneously from man's inner nature. Thus it has been received and pushed on till everything has yielded to it. But when it has been received into the hearts of men, it produces different effects according to the peculiar spirit and character of each. Already we see this take place among the Apostles, and therefore from the very earliest days of the Christian religion. See the difference between John and Peter. In the end there arose real dissensions. Passions and worldly views got mixed up. Thus profanity and abuses were the result. But still we always see in these religious disputes the godlike alongside of the earthly —ever the One, Eternal, and Immortal giving light and warmth as the sun, but overcast, sometimes more, sometimes less, by the clouds of the earthly.

CHEERFULNESS.

Letter II. 23.

Die Froheit ist wie ein Sonnenglanz des Lebens. Er wird keinem ganz und beständig zu Theil, und das Wort selbst umfaßt auch wieder eine Menge von Graden und Abstufungen. Die Summe von allem dem ist doch, daß der Mensch sich zuletzt immer aus seinem Innern und Aeußern einen Seelenzustand bildet, der ihm eigenthümlich ist, und das Gleis wird, in dem sein Leben fortgleitet. Es liegt darin eine große Wohlthat der Vorsehung. Denn das innere Streben nach Harmonie und Seelenerhebung gewinnt und behält doch immer die Oberhand.

Cheerfulness is, as it were, the sunny ray of life. This is the constant portion of none, and the word itself comprehends also a multitude of degrees and modifications. The sum of all is this —that man, ever from inward and outward circumstances, forms for himself a nature which is peculiar to him, and is the track on which his life glides. This is a beneficent arrangement of Providence, for no struggle after harmony and elevation is ever without effect.

PROPER PRIDE.
Letter II. 23.

Der Stolz, den man wirklich nicht aufgeben soll, bleibt jedem rechtlich Gesinnten dennoch. Diesen sollte man aber nicht Stolz, sondern richtig abgewägtes Selbstgefühl nennen. Es ist eigentlich dies die Erhebung des Gemüths, welche daraus entsteht, daß es fühlt, das eine würdige Idee sich mit ihm vereinigt, sich seiner bemächtigt hat. Der Mensch ist da eigentlich stolz auf die Idee, auf sich nur insofern, als die Idee Eins mit ihm geworden ist.

There is a pride which belongs to every rightly-constituted mind, though it is scarcely to be called pride, but rather a proper estimate of self. It is, properly speaking, the elevation of mind which arises when we feel that we have mastered some noble idea and made it our own. Man is proud of the idea only so far as he feels that it has become part of himself.

MATURITY FOR DEATH.
Letter II. 33.

Es ist ein wichtiges Naturgesetz, das man nicht aus den Augen lassen darf, ich meine das der Reife zum Tode. Der Tod ist kein Abschnitt des Daseins, sondern blos ein Zwischenereigniß, ein Uebergang aus einer Form des endlichen Wesens in die andere. Beide Zustände, hier und jenseits, hängen alle genau zusammen, ja sie sind unzertrennlich mit einander verbunden, und der erste Moment des Dort kann sich nur wahrhaft anschließen, wenn der des Scheidens von hier, nach der freien Entwickelung des Wesens, wahrhaft der letzte gewesen ist. Diesen Moment der Reife zum Tode, oder der Unmöglichkeit hier weiter zu gedeihen, kann keine menschliche Klugheit berechnen, kein inneres Gefühl anzeigen. Dies zu versuchen, wäre nur eine eitle Vermessenheit menschlichen Stolzes. Nur der, welcher das ganze Wesen zu durchschauen und zu erkennen im Stande ist, kann dies, und ihm die Stunde anheimzustellen, und seiner Bestimmung auch nicht einmal durch heftige Wünsche entgegenzukommen, ist Gebot und Pflicht der Vernunft.

There is an important law of nature which should never be lost sight of, I mean that of our maturity for death. Death is not a cutting off of being, but a transition, a passing from one form of being to another. Both conditions, here and hereafter, so depend on each other, and are so inseparably connected, that the first moment *there* can only commence with the last moment *here*, when the perfect development of the being is completed. No human wisdom can calculate, no inward feeling can show, the moment of this maturity for death, or the impossibility of advancing farther; to attempt this would be the vain presumption of human pride. He only who is in a position to penetrate and understand our whole being can do this; and it is the dictate alike of duty and of wisdom to commit the hour to Him, and never to oppose our impatient wishes to his will.

MANY TERRORS ARE ONLY IMAGINARY.

Letter II. 33.

Viele Schrecknisse sind es größtentheils nur in der Einbildung. Selbst in vielen und wahren Krankheiten fügt diese bei Leuten, die furchtsam und ängstlich sind, noch vieles hinzu. Die Unruhe, die gewisse Krankheiten mit sich führen, mindert sich, wenn man ihr moralische Ruhe entgegensetzt. Mit dem positiven Schmerz ist es allerdings anders; aber auch da kann man viel thun. Ueberhaupt gewinnt man sehr, wenn man die Krankheit nicht wie ein Leiden ansieht, sondern als eine Arbeit, die man durchmachen muß. Denn es ist gewiß, daß der Kranke viel zur Aufrechthaltung seiner Kräfte und zu seiner Heilung beitragen kann.

Many terrors are in a great measure only in the imagination. Even in many real illnesses it adds much when people are timid and of anxious minds. The restlessness which certain diseases bring with them is lessened if we are able to counteract them by peace of mind. With positive pain it is otherwise, but even with it much may be done. Above all, much is gained if we regard sickness not as a state of suffering, but as a labour which must be got over. For no one can doubt but that the patient can contribute much to the restoration of his strength and to his own recovery.

The Sea.

Letter II. 36.

Wie das Meer in seiner erhabenen Einförmigkeit immer die mannichfaltigsten Bilder vor die Seele führt und die verschieden= artigsten Gedanken erweckt, so ist mir erst jetzt bei den an= haltenden heftigen Stürmen recht sichtbar geworden, welche schmeichelnde Freundlichkeit das Meer gerade in seiner größten Furchtbarkeit hat. Die Welle, die, was sie ergreift, verschlingt, kommt wie spielend an, und selbst den tiefen Abgrund bedeckt lieblicher Schaum. Man hat darum oft das Meer treulos und tückisch genannt, es liegt aber in diesem Zuge nur der Charakter einer großen Naturkraft, die sich, um nach unserer Empfindung zu reden, ihrer Stärke erfreut und sich um Glück und Unglück nichts kümmert, sondern den ewigen Gesetzen folgt, welchen sie durch eine höhere Macht unterworfen ist.

As the sea in its sublime uniformity ever brings manifold images before the soul, and calls up a variety of thoughts, it became quite evident to me, from violent continuous storms, what flatter- ing gentleness the sea has in its greatest terrors. The sea, which swallows up what it seizes, advances with playfulness and covers the deep abyss with white foam. The sea has been called deceit- ful and treacherous, but there lies in this trait only the character of a great natural power which, to speak according to our own feelings, renews its strength, and, without reference to joy or sorrow, follows eternal laws which are imposed by a higher Power.

Man judges with his own Preconceived Ideas.

Letter II. 37.

Der Mensch beurtheilt die Dinge lange nicht so sehr nach dem, was sie wirklich sind, als nach der Art, wie er sie sich denkt und sie in seinen Ideengang einpaßt.

Man is apt to judge of things not so much by their intrinsic worth, as by their agreement with his own preconceived ideas.

Man rebels against Anything out of the ordinary Course of Nature.

Letter II. 37.

Durch etwas, was der Mensch einmal in seine Ordnung und

in die Reihe der gewöhnlichen Naturereigniffe aufgenommen hat, läßt er fich, ohne eben zu murren, vom Schickfal und fogar von Menfchen plagen. Nur das Außerordentliche ift ihm, wenn es verletzend ift, unangenehm und widrig. Es gefellt fich auch eine moralifche Idee hinzu. Das Außerordentliche ift, oder erfcheint vielmehr als eine Ungerechtigkeit des Himmels.

Man reconciles himself to almost any event, however trying, if it happens in the ordinary course of nature. It is the extraordinary alone that he rebels against. There is a moral idea associated with this feeling, for the extraordinary is, or at least appears to be, something like an injustice of Heaven.

TIME IS ONLY AN EMPTY SPACE.

Letter II. 42.

Die Zeit ift nur ein leerer Raum, dem Begebenheiten, Gedanken und Empfindungen erft Inhalt geben. Da man aber weiß, das fie, wenn man auch viel einzelnes davon kennt, diefen Inhalt freudvoll und leidvoll für empfindende Menfchen getragen hat, fo ift fie an fich immer das Herz ergreifend. Auch ihr ftilles und heimliches Walten hat etwas magifch Anziehendes. Der Tag, an dem einem ein großes Unglück begegnet, ift eine lange Reihe von Jahren ungeahnt an einem vorbeigegangen, und ebenfo ftill und unbekannt fchreitet der an uns vorüber, an dem uns ein Unglück unwandelbar bevorfteht. Denkt man aber der Folge der Zeit nach, fo verliert man fich darin wie in einem Abgrund. Es ift nicht Anfang noch Ende. Ein großer Troft liegt aber im Wandel, da er immer an ein höchftes Gefetz, an einen ewig lenkenden Willen in unverrückter Ordnung erinnert. Das Erkennen diefer Ordnung ift in allen Welteinrichtungen, bei der Hinfälligkeit der menfchlichen Natur und der fcheinbar oft regellos zermalmenden Gewalt der Elemente, etwas fehr Beruhigendes.

Time is only an empty space, first acquiring meaning from the events, thoughts, and feelings with which we fill it. But as we know that this meaning has come fraught with joy and sorrow to many sensitive natures, our own hearts cannot but be affected by it. Its quiet, secret power, too, has a magical charm. The day on which a great misfortune has befallen us is, after a long course of years, passed unnoticed, and then, too, unknown to us is the approach of one on which a calamity inevitably awaits us. If we reflect deeply on the consequences of time, we lose ourselves as in an abyss. There is neither beginning nor end. A great comfort lies, however, in contemplating the course of life, as it ever reminds us of a sublime law—an eternal controlling power—an immutable order. There is something very tranquillising in the knowledge of this order in all the affairs of the world, in the frailty of human nature, and in the apparently uncontrolled destructive power of the elements.

Good Recitation.

Letter II. 42.

Zum guten Hersagen gehört aber unendlich viel: zuerst freilich nur Dinge, die jede gute Erziehung jedem geben kann, richtiges Verstehen des Sinnes, eine gute, deutliche, von Provinzialfehlern freie Aussprache; aber dann freilich Dinge, welche nur angeboren werden, ein glückliches, schon in sich seelenvolles Organ, ein feiner musikalischer Sinn für den Fall des Silbenmaßes, ein wahrhaft dichterisches Gefühl, und hauptsächlich ein Gemüth, in dem alle menschlichen Empfindungen rein und stark widerklingen.

But for good recitation many things are necessary: first, of course, what only a good education can give to any one, a clear conception of the meaning, and a good, distinct pronunciation, free from provincialisms; and then what is innate: a happily-constituted, sensitive organisation, a fine musical ear for the intonation, a genuine poetic feeling, and a mind in which all the human affections exist in strength and purity.

The Grand Course of Human Destiny.

Letter II. 46.

Wie auch die sogenannten großen politischen Angelegenheiten stehen mögen, die einzelnen Menschen und Familien gehen ihren Weg mit geringer Störung fort, streben sich ihre Lage besser und gewinnreicher zu machen, benutzen die Mittel, welche die Zeit in sich immer vermehrenden Maßen dazu an die Hand gibt, und vermehren diese Mittel selbst dadurch, daß sie dieselben benutzen. Dies ist ein sehr tröstender Gedanke, und der große Gang der Schicksale des Menschengeschlechts zeigt sich darin viel weniger abhängig von fremder Willkür und Zufall, als es beim ersten Anblick erscheint.

In whatever way the so-called great political affairs of the world may go, individuals and families proceed on their course with little interruption, endeavour to better their condition, and to improve the means which time puts more and more into their hands, and to increase those means so as to improve their position in society. This is a very consoling reflection, and the grand course of human destiny thus shows itself to be much less dependent on foreign will and chance than appears at first sight.

POSTHUMOUS FAME.

Letter II. 47.

Auch erscheint immermehr, was zur Charakterisirung der damals merkwürdigsten Personen dient. In den Urtheilen über sie wirkt noch die Stimmung mit fort, welche sie im Leben hervorbrachten; allein nach und nach tritt eine andere Stimmung ein, bis sich endlich das bildet, was man den bleibenden Nachruhm nennt. Die Menschen werden in diesem gewissermaßen zu Schattengestalten. Vieles, was sie an sich tragen, erlischt, und das Uebrigbleibende wird nun zu einer ganz andern Erscheinung. Dabei wird noch, was man von ihnen weiß, nach dem Geiste der jedesmaligen Zeit aufgenommen. So ungewiß steht es um das Bild, das auch die größten Menschen hinterlassen, und um die Geschichte!

As time advances more things appear, which enable the world to judge of the characters of remarkable men. In our judgments of them at first we are influenced by the opinions which their contemporaries held respecting them, but gradually another opinion arises, on which at last what is called posthumous fame is built up. Men in this way become in a certain degree like phantoms. Much which belongs to them vanishes, and what remains assumes quite a different aspect. Therefore what we know of them will be received according to the spirit of the existing time. So uncertain is the image which even the greatest men leave behind them in history.

CHEERFULNESS CANNOT BE FORCED.

Letter II. 49.

Die Heiterkeit läßt sich nicht erzwingen, und der Mensch hat nicht viel mehr Gewalt über seinen innern Wolkenhimmel als über den äußern. Indeß darf man doch nicht ganz dabei müßig bleiben, und muß auch hier die allgemeine Pflicht üben, auf sich wachsam sein und an sich arbeiten.

Cheerfulness cannot be forced, and man has not much more power over the clouds that overshadow his mind than over those that darken the sky. Meanwhile man ought not to be altogether inactive, but must labour at his daily duties, and be watchful over himself.

PRAYER.
Letter II. 50.

Die Gebete sind größtentheils für die Andacht der einzelnen bestimmt. Wenn aber der einzelne betet, bedarf er keiner Formel. Er ergießt sich viel natürlicher in von ihm selbst gewählten und verknüpften Gedanken vor Gott, und bedarf kaum der Worte. Die rechte innige Andacht weiß von keinem andern als von einem aus ihr selbst hervorgegangenen Gebet.

Prayer is intended to increase the devotion of the individual, but if the individual himself prays he requires no formula—he pours himself forth much more naturally in self-chosen and connected thoughts before God, and scarcely requires words at all. Real inward devotion knows no prayer but that arising from the depths of its own feelings.

THE CHARACTERISTIC OF OLD AGE.
Letter II. 51.

Es liegt in dem Alter selbst, daß man diese Flüchtigkeit der Zeit beschleunigt findet. Je weniger man zu Stande bringt, desto kürzer scheint sie.

It is a characteristic of old age to find that time passes on with accelerated pace. The less one accomplishes in a given time, the shorter does the retrospect appear.

GODLIKE THOUGHTS.
Letter II. 52.

Das ist das, was der Mensch nie genug an der Vorsehung bewundern und wofür er nie dankbar genug sein kann, daß sie die wahrhaft göttlichen Gedanken, die, auf denen unser innerstes Dasein ruht, bald im Geiste ganzer Völker und Zeiten, bald in einzelnen Menschen weckt und durchbrechen läßt.

One cannot enough wonder or be thankful to Providence that from time to time he awakens in the spirits of a whole people, or of individuals, those truly godlike thoughts on which our inner being reposes.

KANT.

Born A.D. 1724. Died A.D. 1804.

Immanuel Kant, the founder of modern German philosophy, and one of the most profound thinkers of the eighteenth century, was born at Königsberg, A.D. 1724, where his father was a poor but respectable citizen. After receiving his early education in his native town he devoted himself to the clerical profession, was appointed to an office in the Library of Königsberg, and in 1770 exchanged it for a professorship. Here he continued to employ himself in philosophical pursuits till his death in 1804.

Everything with a Beginning has an End.

Aus der Allgemeinen Naturgeschichte und Theorie des Himmels (1755).

Man darf nicht erstaunen, selbst in dem Großen der Werke Gottes, eine Vergänglichkeit zu verstatten. Alles, was endlich ist, was einen Anfang und Ursprung hat, hat das Merkmal seiner eingeschränkten Natur in sich; es muß vergehen, und ein Ende haben. Die Dauer eines Weltbaues hat, durch die Vortrefflichkeit ihrer Errichtung, eine Beständigkeit in sich, die unsern Begriffen nach, einer unendlichen Dauer nahe kommt. Vielleicht werden tausend, vielleicht Millionen Jahrhunderte sie nicht vernichten; allein, weil die Eitelkeit, die an den endlichen Naturen haftet, beständig an ihrer Zerstörung arbeitet; so wird die Ewigkeit alle mögliche Perioden in sich halten, um durch einen allmählichen Verfall den Zeitpunkt ihres Unterganges doch endlich herbei zu führen.

We must not be surprised to find that even the mightiest works of God come to an end. Everything with an end, beginning, and origin, has the mark of its circumscribed nature in itself. The duration of a universe has, by the excellence of its construction, a permanence in itself, which, according to our ideas, comes near to an endless duration. Perhaps thousands, perhaps millions of centuries will not bring it to an end ; but while the perishableness which adheres to evanescent natures is always working for their destruction, so eternity contains within itself all possible periods, so as to bring at last by a gradual decay the moment of its departure.

Richness of Nature.

Wir dürfen aber den Untergang eines Weltgebäudes nicht als einen Verlust der Natur bedauern. Sie beweiset ihren Reichthum in einer Art von Verschwendung, welche, indem einige Theile der Vergänglichkeit den Tribut bezahlen, sich durch unzählige neue Zeugungen in dem ganzen Umfange ihrer Vollkommenheit unbeschädet erhält. Welch' eine unzählige Menge Blumen und Insecten zerstöret ein einziger kalter Tag; aber wie wenig vermisset man sie, ohnerachtet es herrliche Kunstwerke der Natur und Beweisthümer der göttlichen Allmacht sind; an einem andern Orte wird dieser Abgang mit Ueberfluß wiederum ersetzet. Der Mensch, der das Meisterstück der Schöpfung zu seyn scheinet, ist selbst von diesem Gesetze nicht ausgenommen. Die Natur beweiset, daß sie eben so reich, eben so unerschöpflich in Hervorbringung des trefflichsten unter den Kreaturen, als des geringschätzigsten, ist und das selbst deren Untergang eine nothwendige Schattirung in der Mannigfaltigkeit ihrer Sonnen ist, weil die Erzeugung derselben ihr nichts kostet. Die schädlichen Wirkungen der angesteckten Luft, die Erdbeben, die Ueberschwemmungen, vertilgen ganze Völker von dem Erdboden; allein es scheinet nicht, daß die Natur dadurch einigen Nachtheil erlitten habe. Auf gleiche Weise verlassen ganze Welten und Systeme den Schauplatz, nachdem sie ihre Rolle ausgespielet haben. Die Unendlichkeit der Schöpfung ist groß genug, um eine Welt, oder eine Milchstraße von Welten, gegen sie anzusehen, wie man eine Blume, oder ein Insect, in Vergleichung gegen die Erde, ansiehet. Indessen, daß die Natur mit veränderlichen Auftritten die Ewigkeit auszieret, bleibt Gott in einer unaufhörlichen Schöpfung geschäftig, den Zeug zur Bildung noch größerer Welten zu formen.

We must not lament the disappearance of a universe as a loss which Nature sustains. She shows her richness in a kind of prodigality, which, while some parts pay the tribute of evanescence, preserves it uninjured by unnumbered new generations in the circle of her complete whole. What numberless flowers and insects a single cold day destroys, but how little they are missed, though they are splendid specimens of Nature's labours, and of God's almighty workmanship! In some other part this deficiency is made up by excessive superfluity. Man, who seems to be the masterpiece of creation, is no exception to this law. Nature shows that she is quite as rich, as inexhaustible, in the production of the noblest as of the meanest of her creatures, and that their destruction is but a necessary shading in the variety of her suns, because their production costs her nothing. The injurious effects of tainted air, earthquakes, deluges, cause all nations to disappear from the surface of the earth, but it does not seem that Nature has thereby suffered a loss. In the same way whole worlds and systems leave the stage after they have played out their parts. The boundless extent of creation is so large that it can look at a world or a galaxy of worlds in the same way as we compare a flower or insect with the world around us. While Nature adorns eternity with ever-changing appearances, God remains actively employed in ceaselessly creating materials for the formation of still greater worlds.

KLOPSTOCK.

Born A.D. 1724. Died A.D. 1803.

Friedrich Gottlieb Klopstock, born at Quedlinburg in Prussian Saxony, was educated first at the grammar-school of that town, and afterwards at the Schulpforte near Naumburg. In 1745 he devoted himself to the study of theology at Jena, commencing the first canto of his "Messiah." The first three cantos appeared in the periodical called the "Bremische Beiträge" in 1748, and excited great attention. Both in Switzerland and Denmark they met with a favourable attention, and Klopstock was invited to Copenhagen by the minister Bernstorff, with a small pension to finish the poem. Setting out in 1751, he travelled through Brunswick and Hamburg, and in the latter city he met with Meta Moller, whom he married in 1754. From 1759 to 1766 he resided alternately at Brunswick, Quedlinburg, and Blankenberg, and afterwards at Copenhagen. He finished the "Messiah" in Hamburg. He died in 1803, when his body was buried with great pomp and solemnity in the presence of a large multitude.

Soft Winds.

The Messiah, I. 53.

Ringsum nahmen ihn Palmen in's Kühle. Gelindere Lüfte, Gleich dem Säuseln der Gegenwart Gottes, umflossen sein Antlitz.

Palms around received him in their shade. Soft winds, like whisperings announcing the presence of the Deity, breathed round his face.

The Eternal Father and Son.

The Messiah, i. 146.

Indem die Ewigen sprachen,
Ging durch die ganze Natur ein ehrfurchtsvolles Erbeben.
Seelen, die jetzo wurden, noch nicht zu denken begannen,
Zitterten, und empfanden zuerst. Ein gewaltiger Schauer
Faßte den Seraph, ihm schlug sein Herz, und um ihn lag wartend,
Wie vor dem nahen Gewitter die Erde, sein schweigender Welt-
kreis.

While the Eternal Beings spoke a reverential shudder passed
through the whole of nature. Souls which had just received the
breath of life, but not yet the power of speech, trembled and felt
unknown sensations. A solemn awe came over the Seraph,
thrilling through his heart, while he lay silent and expecting, like
the earth when it waits in solemn pause the coming thunder.

Heaven's Far Verge.

The Messiah, i. 195.

Unterdeß eilte der Seraph zum äußersten Schimmer des Him-
mels
Wie ein Morgen empor. Hier füllen nur Sonnen den Umkreis;
Und, gleich einer Hülle gewebt aus Strahlen des Urlichts,
Zieht sich ihr Glanz um den Himmel herum. Kein dämmern-
der Erdkreis
Naht sich des Himmels verderbendem Blick. Entfliehend und
ferne
Geht die bewölkte Natur vorüber. Da eilen die Erden
Klein, unmerkbar dahin, wie unter des Wanderers Fuße
Niedriger Staub, von Gewürme bewohnt, aufwallet, und hin-
sinkt.

Meanwhile, the Seraph, bright as the dawn's first ray, reached
heaven's far verge. Here suns only circle in an eternal round,
and, like a raiment woven of rays of purest ether, send their
lustre through the heaven. No opaque orbs are there to deface
its fair appearance. Planets involved in clouds roll far away.
There globes whirl, small and unnoticed, as grains of dust, moved
by worms, rise and fall beneath some wandering foot.

THE EFFECT OF MAN'S FALL.
The Messiah, I. 215.

Die ſtillen Gebirge,
Wo noch die Spur des Ewigen war; die rauſchenden Haine,
Welche vordem das Säuſeln der Gegenwart Gottes beſeelte;
Selige, friedſame Thäler, ſonſt von der Jugend des Himmels
Gern beſucht; die ſchattigen Lauben, wo ehmals die Menſchen
Ueberwallend von Freuden und ſüßen Empfindungen weinten,
Daß Gott ewig ſie ſchuf; die Erde trug des Fluches
Laſten jetzt, war ihrer vordem unſterblichen Kinder
Großes Grab.

The lonely hills, which yet bore the traces of the Almighty ;
the breathing groves, whose whispering voice had oft confessed
the presence of the Deity ; the holy and peaceful valleys formerly
visited with delight by the youth of heaven ; the shady bowers
where once men, overflowing with pleasure and sweet feelings,
shed rapturous tears because God had made them immortal—all
earth now bore the burden of the curse—was one wide grave to
her once deathless children.

POLAR REGIONS.
The Messiah, I. 596.

Niemals hat noch ein Auge, von kleineren Himmeln umgränzet,
Dieſe Gefilde geſehn, die in nächtlicher Stille ruhen
Unbewohnt, und wo von des Menſchen Stimme kein Laut tönt,
Wo ſie keinen Todten begruben, und keiner erſtehn wird.

No eye of man has viewed these grim fields which lie silent as
night and uninhabited, and where no sound of human voice breaks
the repose, where no dead are buried, and none can rise.

THE WINTER'S SUN.
The Messiah, I. 606.

Wie zu der Zeit, wenn der Winter belebt, ein heiliger Feſttag
Ueber beſchneiten Gebirgen nach trüben Tagen hervorgeht;
Wolfen und Nacht entfliehen vor ihm, die beeiſten Gefilde,
Hohe durchſichtige Wälder entnebeln ihr Antlitz und glänzen.

As at the time when winter reigns, a bright day shines over the
snow-clad mountains after gloomy weather, clouds and darkness
vanish, the icy plains and lofty leafless woods slowly emerge and
sparkle brightly.

The Earth's Abyss.

The Messiah, I. 613.

Nun wandelt der Seraph
In der Erd' Abgründen. Da wälzten sich Ozeane
Ringsum, langsamer Flut, zu menschenlosen Gestaden.
Alle Söhne der Ozeane, gewaltige Ströme
Flossen, wie Ungewitter sich aus den Wüsten heraufziehn,
Tiefauftönend ihm nach. Er ging, und sein Heiligthum zeigte
Sich ihm schon in der Nähe. Die Pfort', erbauet von Wolken,
Wich ihm aus, und zerfloß vor ihm, wie in himmlische Schimmer.
Unter dem Fuße des Eilenden zog sich flüchtige Dämmrung
Wallend weg. Nah' hinter ihm an den dunkeln Gestaden
Blieb es in seinem Tritte zurück, wie wehende Flammen.
Und der Unsterbliche war zu der Engelversammlung gekommen.

Now the Seraph plunged deep down into the earth's abyss.
There oceans rolled their slow and heavy waves to lonely shores.
All the sons of ocean, mighty rivers, poured their streams down
with deafening roar, as the tempest rushes o'er the desert. He
went on, and at length appeared his bright abode. The gates, built
of clouds, yielded, melting away before him in heavenly splendour.
Beneath his feet pale twilight faded, while behind him, over the
gloomy shores, a brilliant track followed like quivering flames;
and now the Seraph reached the assembly of the immortals.

Infant Spirits.

The Messiah, I. 673.

Auch die Seelen, die zarten, nur sprossenden Leibern entflohen,
Sammelten sich um den Seraph herum. Sie flohen noch
    sprachlos,
Mit der Kindheit zärtlichem Weinen. Ihr schüchternes Auge
Hatte kaum staunend erblickt der Erde kleine Gefilde;
Darum durften sie sich auf der Welten furchtbaren Schauplatz,
Noch ungebildet, so bald hervorzutreten nicht wagen.
Ihre Beschützer geleiten sie zu sich, und lehren sie reizend,
Unter beseelender Harfen Klang', in lieblichen Liedern:
Wie, und woher sie entstanden; wie groß die menschliche Seele
Von dem vollkommensten Geiste gemacht sei; wie jugendlich
    heiter

Sonnen und Monde nach ihrer Geburt zu dem Schöpfer
gekommen.

Tender souls, too, who had flown from opening life, gathered
round the Seraph. Their timid eyes scarcely, with wondering
gaze, had seen the narrow bounds of earth, whose fearful theatre
they dared not tread; their guardian angel guided them, teaching
them on heavenly harps and with lovely hymns to sing how and
whence they sprung, how bright and noble man's immortal soul
had come from his Maker's hand, how beauteous in early brilliancy
the sun and moon shot forth their rays.

THE SEPULCHRES.

The Messiah, II. 98.

Also sagt' er, und näherte sich den Gräbern der Todten.
Unten am mitternächtlichen Berge waren die Gräber
In zusammengebirgte zerrüttete Felsen gehauen.
Dicke, finsterverwachsene Wälder verwahrten den Eingang,
Vor des fliehenden Wanderers Blick. Ein trauriger Morgen
Stieg, wenn der Mittag schon sich über Jerusalem senkte,
Dämmernd noch in die Gräber mit kühlem Schauer hinunter.

Thus he spoke, approaching the sepulchres of the dead. Deep
beneath the shade of dark overhanging hills and precipitous rocks
the sepulchres were hewn. Thick tangled woods concealed the
entrance from the passing traveller's gaze. A dim twilight arose
when noon blazed over Jerusalem, scarcely shooting a cold and
quivering gleam over the sepulchres.

SATAN.

The Messiah, II. 171.

Ich bin Satan, antwortet' ein zorniges tiefes Gebrüll, bin
König der Welt, die oberste Gottheit unsclavischer Geister,
Die mein Ansehn etwas erhabnerem, als den Geschäften
Himmlischer Sänger bestimmt. Dein Ruf, o sterblicher Seher,
Denn Maria wird wohl Unsterbliche niemals gebähren!
Dieser dein Ruf drang, wer du auch bist, zu der untersten Hölle.
Selber ich verließ sie, sei stolz ob meiner Heraufkunft!
Dich von himmlischen Sklaven verkündigten Retter zu sehen.

"I am Satan," roared a deep and angry growl, "king of the
world, monarch of those free spirits, to whom I give something

more noble than to chant heaven's songs. Thy fame, O mortal
prophet, for Mary never bare anything immortal, this thy fame,
whoever thou art, has reached hell's lowest depths. I myself am
come (well may it swell thy pride) to see thee who art announced
by heaven's servile host man's Saviour."

Approach to Hell.

The Messiah, II. 246.

Jeßo hatt' er sich schon bei den äußersten Weltgebäuden
Stürmisch heruntergesenkt. Unermeßliche dämmernde Räume
Thaten vor ihm wie unendlich sich auf. Die nennt er den
    Anfang
Weiterer Reiche, die Satan durchherrscht! Hier sah er von
    ferne
Flüchtigen Schimmer, so weit die letzten Sterne der Schöpfung
Noch das unendliche Leere mit sterbendem Strahle durchirrten.
Doch hier sah er die Hölle noch nicht. Die hatte die Gottheit
Ferne von sich, und ihren Geschöpfen, den seligen Geistern,
Weiter hinunter in ewige Dunkelheit eingeschlossen.
Denn in unserer Welt, dem Schauplatz ihrer Erbarmung,
War kein Raum für Orte der Qual. Der Ewige schuf sie
Furchtbar, zu dem Verderben, zu seinem strafenden Endzweck
Weit hinreichend, vollkommen. In drei erschrecklichen Nächten
Schuf er sie, und verwandte von ihr sein Antlitz auf ewig.

Already he had furious plunged headlong down to the farthest
orbit of the universe. There lay stretched before him a boundless
shadowy void. This was the verge of those wide-spread realms
over which Satan reigned! Here he saw from far a glimmering;
to this point the last stars of creation penetrated through the vast
abyss with faint and dying rays. Hell yet in view appeared not.
Amid eternal gloom had God, far from himself and his holy
creatures, fixed its dismal bounds. For in our world, the theatre of
mercy, there was no place found for everlasting woe. The Eternal
formed it tremendous, fearfully fit to fulfil its purpose, well suited
for punishment and pain. The work was ended in three dreadful
nights, and then he turned away his face from it for ever.

Infernal Princes,

The Messiah, II. 397.

Also versammelten sich der Hölle Fürsten zu Satan.

Wie Eilande des Meers aus ihren Sitzen gerissen,

Rauschten sie hoch, unaufhaltsam einher. Der Pöbel der Geister

Floß mit ihnen unzählbar, wie Wogen des kommenden Weltmeers

Gegen den Fuß gebirgter Gestade, zum Thron des Empörers.

Tausendmal tausend Geister erschienen. Sie gingen, und sangen

Eigene Thaten, zur Schmach und unsterblichen Schande ver=
    urtheilt.

Unterm Getös gespaltner, sie hatten Donner gespalten!

Dumpfer, entheiligter Harfen, verstimmt zu den Tönen des
    Todes,

Sangen sie's her. So rauschen in mitternächtlicher Stunde

Grimmige Schlachten von tödtenden, und von sterbenden
    Streitern

Furchtbar umher, wenn brausend auf ehernen Wagen der
    Nordwind

Gegen sie fährt, und gebrüllt von dem Wiederhall ihr Gebrüll
    wird.

Round Satan the infernal princes thus gathered. Like islands
uptorn from their ocean-seats, they moved proudly and restless.
With them flocked countless hosts of meaner rank round the rebel
throne, as waves of the flowing tide beat the foot of some high
rock-bound shore. Thousands on thousands of spirits press on.
They advanced and sung their own exploits of shame and lasting
scorn. On the chords of broken harps, split by heaven's red
thunder, hoarse and unhallowed, they shrieked the cries of death.
So resounds at midnight's hour the din of battle, the last shrieks
of dying warriors, fearful, when in his brazen car the northern
blast sweeps o'er the scene of conflict, and conveys to distant
echo war's tremendous roar.

GOD AN IDLE DREAM.

The Messiah, II. 413.

Sein schrecklicher Führer,

Gog, war darunter, erhabner als all' an Gestalt, und an Unsinn.

Daß das alles ein Traum, ein Spiel sei irrer Gedanken,

Was es im Himmel gesehen, Gott, erst Vater, dann Richter,

Das zu wähnen, reizt' es sich, krümmt' es sich, wand es sich
    wüthend.

Gog, its fearful leader, was there, eminent in stature as in frenzy. The fiend madly writhed, and strove to think that all in heaven—God, first Father, then awful Judge—were mere idle dreams, fancy's sport.

Thought on Thought.

The Messiah, II. 828.

So drängten Gedanken,
Andre Gedanken, wie Wogen des Meers, wie der Ozean drängte,
Als er von drei Welten dich, fernes Amerika, losriß.

Thought on thought pressed o'er his soul, like those ocean-waves which tore thee, distant America, from the three continents.

The Immortal in the Calmness of Strength.

The Messiah, v. 112.

Ihm kam in das Antlitz
Durch die Himmel entgegen ein tausendstimmiger Sturmwind.
Da erklang's um die goldenen Achsen, da flog ihm das Haupthaar
Und das Gewand, wie Wolken, zurück. Mit der Ruhe der Stärke,
Stand der Unsterbliche da! In der hochgehobenen Rechte
Hielt er ein Wetter empor. Bei jedem erhabnen Gedanken
Donnert' er aus dem Wetter hervor.

He met the stormy breeze which, with a roar of thousand voices, rushed impetuous by. His golden axles rung; his hair and robes streamed back like clouds. The Immortal stood with the calmness of strength. In his uplifted right hand he grasped a tempest. As thought sublime succeeded thought, the thunder broke from the stormy mass.

The Dying.

The Messiah, v. 190.

Ihm schwindet das Antlitz der Erd' und des Himmels
Tief in die Nacht. Er höret nicht mehr die Stimme des Menschen,
Noch die zärtliche Klage der Freundschaft. Er selbst kann nicht reden;
Kaum noch mit bebender Zunge den bangen Abschied stammeln;
Athmet tiefer herauf; und kalter ängstlicher Schweiß läuft
Ueber sein Antlitz; das Herz schlägt langsam, dann steht's,
dann stirbt er!

In der liebenden Mutter Arm, die gern mit ihr stürbe,
Und nicht sterben kann, stirbt die Tochter. Umfaßt von dem
    Vater,
Und an das Herz gedrückt, stirbt, ach der Jüngling, im Aufblühn,
Seines Vaters einziger Sohn.

The face of heaven and earth vanishes darkly in night. He
hears no more the voice of man, nor the tender plaints of friendship. He cannot himself speak; scarce his faltering tongue
articulates the last farewell; with deeper heave he strives to
breathe; cold dews bathe painfully his brow; his labouring heart
throbs slow, then ceases—he is dead! So in loving mother's arms,
who would willingly die with her and cannot die, a beloved
daughter sinks. Pressed to a father's heart, the only son thus
fades away in youth.

A Fair Lady.
The Messiah, VI. 229.

Dort, an ein Marmorgeländer gebückt, stand unter den Frauen
Portia, jugendlich schön, das Weib Pilatus des Römers.
Aber ihr Geist war nicht jung. Die Blume blühte, mit
    Früchten,
Wie die Mutter der Gracchen, die ausgearteten Römer
Zu bereichern: allein in dem ernsten Rathe der Wächter
War Roms Untergang, und kein Erretter beschlossen.

There, leaning on a marble balustrade, stood among her women
the fair young Portia, wife of the Roman Pilate. But her spirit
was not young. The flower promised noble fruit, as the mother
of the Gracchi tried to improve the degenerate Romans, but in
the councils of heaven Rome's doom was pronounced, and none
could save her.

The Angel of Death.
The Messiah, VI. 303.

Also droht' ihm der Todesengel, und zog auf der Stirne
Zorn, wie Wolken, zusammen. Vom hohen treffenden Auge
Strömet' er Rache. Sein Haupthaar sank in Locken der Nacht
    gleich
Auf die Schultern, es stand sein Fuß, wie ein ruhender Fels da!
Aber noch schlug der Verderber ihn nicht. Er ließ nur die
    Stimme
Seiner Schrecken, ließ den Todeston um sich rauschen.

The angel of death looked with threatening eyes upon him, and on his brow hung wrath like thick clouds. From his flashing eye the fire of vengeance darted. His locks, black like midnight, streamed over his shoulders. He stood like a firm rock there! but yet he smote not. He only allowed a thrill of terror and the voice of death to sound around him.

THE DYING CHRISTIAN.
The Messiah, VI. 409.

Also stehn um den sterbenden Christen, mit bleichen Gedanken,
Und mit halber Freude, die gern sich freute, die Haufen
Niedriger Spötter, und athmen leis', und stammeln Erwartung:
Auch ihm wird der muthige Traum vom unsterblichen Leben,
Wie er selber, vergehn. Er bekennt's noch! Aber der Weise
Betet für sie, und für sich, und lächelt die Gräber vorüber.

Thus round the couch of some dying Christian, pale with doubt, yet with a kind of ill-assured joy, stand a knot of sceptics, murmuring lowly and stammering forth their expectations! now surely his bold dream of immortality, like himself, will fade away. But he holds fast. The wise man pours out a prayer for them, himself, and smiles over the grave.

THE DEITY.
The Messiah, VI. 512.

O du, der erste der Götter!
Der die Welt aus Nächten erschuf, und dem Menschen ein Herz
    gab!
Wie dein Name auch heißt, Gott! Jupiter! oder Jehovah!
Romulus, oder Abrahams Gott! nicht einzelner Menschen,
Nein! du Aller Vater und Richter!

O thou above all gods supreme! who broughtest the world out of darkness, and gavest man a heart to feel! by whatsoever name thou art addressed, God, Father, or Jehovah; the God of Romulus or of Abraham; not the God of one man but the Father and Judge of all!

ARTIFICE.
The Messiah, VII. 46.

Jetzo, voll von den heißen Entschlüssen, ein luftig Gewebe,
Leicht zu entweben, hätte Gott nur Winke gesendet!

Now full of fell thoughts, a web of flimsy artifice, easy to unravel had God but breathed upon it.

A Lone Traveller.

The Messiah, VII. 203.

So hört ein Verirrter

Stimmen im einſamen Walde voll Nacht, wenn über den Bergen
Meilenferne Gewitter die Ceder der Wolf' entſtürzen.

As some lone traveller, in the solitary forest's gloom benighted, hears moans, when over the mountains from afar the whirlwind's voice sweeps over the cedars.

Socrates.

The Messiah, VII. 416.

Sokrates leidet nicht mehr von den Böſen!   Elyſium iſt nicht,
Noch die Richter am nächtlichen Strom.   Das waren nur
   Bilder
Schwacher, irrender Züge.   Dort richtet ein anderer Richter,
Leuchten andere Sonnen, als die in Elyſiums Thale!
Sieh, es zählet die Zahl, und die Wagſchal' wägt, und das
   Maß mißt
Alle Thaten!   Wie krümmen alsdann der Tugenden höchſte
Sich in das kleine! wie fliegt ihr Weſen verſtäubt in die Luſt
   aus!
Einige werden belohnt; die meiſten werden vergeben!
Mein aufrichtiges Herz erlangte Vergebung.

Socrates has to suffer no more pain from the wicked.   Elysium exists not, nor the judge on the dark streams of Tartarus.   These were but tales of erring fiction.   Yet there *is* a Judge! there *are* more brilliant suns than in the vales of Elysium.   See, the count is reckoned, and the scale weighs every action—and they all fall short.   How shrinks then the pride of virtue?   How flies the balance in the air?   Some have reward; most are forgiven; my upright heart has earned me forgiveness.

God.

The Messiah, VII. 460.

Er, der dieſe wandelnden Himmel ſo leicht, wie den Sprößling,
Der dort keimet, erſchuf, der hier dem Menſchen ein Leben

Voller Müh, voll fliehender Freud', und fliehendes Schmerzes
Gab, daß sie nicht vergäßen den Werth der höhern Seele,
Und es fühlten, daß über dem Grab' Unsterblichkeit wohne!
Er, Er ist nur Einer! Er heißt Jehovah! der Schöpfer
Und der Richter der Welt! des ersten unter den Menschen,
Adams Gott; dann vieler von Adams Söhnen; dann Abrams,
Unseres Vaters. Allein die Art, auf die wir ihm dienen,
Ist den Frommen bei uns, wie sehr auch die Stolzen sich aufblähn,
Dennoch dunkel. Doch hat sie der Ewige selber geboten!
Und er kennet sie, wird sie enthüllen! enthüllet sie jetzt schon!

The God who created these fair heavens with the same facility
as yon green sapling : he who hath bestowed on man a life of toil,
of transient joys and fleeting pains, that he might not forget the
higher worth of his enduring soul, and might feel that immortality waited for him beyond the grave,—he, he is one only God!
his mighty name Jehovah! earth's Creator and Judge! adored
by Adam, first of men, and Adam's sons; then by Abraham, our
father. But the rites by which we serve him are obscure and
dark even to our wisest men. Yet God himself prescribed our
sacred types, and will in time disclose their purport.

WINGED WORDS.
The Messiah, VII. 636.

Geflügelte Worte

Sprach er zu ihnen, dann sandt' er sie unter das weichende Volk
aus
Und sie vertheilten sich schnell. So fleußt von dem Becher des
Todfeinds
Gift, und jeder Tropfen entzündet den Tod.

He whispered low winged words to them, then sent them among
the yielding crowd, with whom they mingled by separate paths.
Thus poison flows from the goblet of the murderer, and each dis-
tilling drop conveys a separate death.

THE HURRICANE.
The Messiah, VII. 660.

So stehn, wenn der geschmetterte Wald vor dem wilden Orkane
Auf vielmeiligen Bergen die langen Rücken herunter
Liegt, noch einsame Cedern, und tragen die bebende Wolke.

So when forests sink on the wild mountains before the hurri-
cane, with firmer root some cedars lift their solitary heads
unshaken amid the troubled sky.

Deeds of lowly Virtue contrasted with Ostentation.

The Messiah, VII. 496.

Alſo wird durch den Sturm in dem tiefen Walde das Rufen
Eines hülfloſen Kindes zu leiſem Laute. So ſchwindet,
Vor des Hohen rauſchender That, des Weiſen beſcheidne.

Thus the cry of some helpless infant is drowned by the storm
which bellows through the forest ; thus deeds of lowly virtue fade
before the glare of lofty ostentation.

A Storm.

The Messiah, VIII. 139.

Aber wie zwei Gewitter, die an zwo Alpen herunter
Dunkel kommen, (ein ſtärkerer Sturm tönt ihnen entgegen,
Wird ſie verſtreun!) wie die in ihrem Schooße den Donner
Fliegend reizen, damit er die krummen Thäler durchbrülle ;
Alſo rüſten ſich wider Eloa die Stolzen zur Antwort.

But as two storm-clouds, which collect darkly on two Alpine
heights (a fiercer tempest roaring against them will dissipate
them), from their bosom send forth the angry thunders which
rush through the winding vale ; so stood the fiends with threatening aspect against Eloa.

The Swell of Heaving Ocean.

The Messiah, IX. 25.

Selbſt der läſternden Menge
Ungeſtüm legte ſich, wie an dem unbeſtürmten Geſtade
Endlich das Weltmeer ruht.

Even the loud din of the blaspheming crew had dropped to
silence, as the angry swell of heaving ocean sinks into repose upon
some level shore.

An Earthquake.

The Messiah, IX. 473.

So, wenn die Erde bebt, und gerichtbelaſteter Städte

Q

Eine, nun Eine der großen Verbrecherinnen, verurtheilt,
Mit der Sinkenden sinkt, so winseln dann mit dem schnellen
Dumpfen Donnerschlage der unterirdischen Rache
Todesstimmen herauf! Noch Einmal bebet die Erde,
Und noch Einmal ertönen mit ihr entheiligte Tempel,
Stürzende Marmorhäuser, und ihrer zu sichern Bewohner
Todesstimmen! Es flieht der bleiche rufende Wandrer!

Thus, when earth heaves, and wreaking vengeance on some
guilty city, one of the greatest culprits sinks with its sinking
inhabitants, then piercing shrieks of death mingle with the thun-
dering roar of subterranean vengeance. Earth shakes again, and
now once more the agonising cries of the too secure inhabitants
mix with the crash of profane temples and marble palaces. The
affrighted traveller flies.

JUDAS.

The Messiah, IX. 707.

Wende, Todter, dich! komm! Ich führe dich jetzt zu der Hölle,
Deiner ewigen Wohnung! So sprechen Donner, so sprach es
Mit zerschmetternder Stimme der Todesengel, und eilte.
Und schon näherten sie der Hölle sich, hörten von ferne
Ihr Getöse, das an der äußersten Schöpfung Gestade
Brüllend schlug, und unter den nächsten Sternen verhallte.
In dem Raume, den Gott ihr in dem Unendlichen abmaß,
Wälzt sie sich, keiner Ordnung gehorsam, auf und nieder,
Keinem Gesetz der langsamen, oder schnellen Bewegung,
Fleugt sie eilend einher; so hatte Gott ihr geboten,
Ihrer Bewohner neue Verbrechen, durch wildere Flammen,
Durch geschärftere Pfeile des ewigen Todes, zu rügen!

"Now, spectre, turn and come! I lead thee now to hell, thine
everlasting home!" So spoke the thunder, so spoke with dread
voice the angel of death, and flew on. And now they approached
towards hell. and heard from far her sullen roar, which broke with
hollow sound on the outermost shores of creation, and echoed
faint over the nearest stars. Through that dark void, which amid
unmeasured space God has allotted her, hell rolls wildly, obedient
to no order, up and down, in slow or swift progression, without
law. Such is her hard doom, to torture her guilty inhabitants
with more raging flames and sharper darts of death.

ENTRANCE TO HELL.
The Messiah, IX. 727.

Lägen Gebirge darin, sie würden den furchtbaren Eingang
Nicht ausfüllen; sie würden nur rauher ihn machen! Obaddon
Bleibt hier stehn mit dem Todten. Es führet kein Weg zu
    der Hölle
Schreckenden Tiefen. Es wälzen sich nah' bei der Pforte die
    Felsen
Unabsehlich hinab, durch träufelndes Feuer gespaltet,
Sprachlos, schwindelnd, bleich, mit weit vorquellendem Auge,
Blickt das Entsetzen hinunter. Der göttlichen Rache Vollender
Stand an diesem Grab', hier schläft der Tod nicht! mit dir still,
Judas Ischariot, du Verräther!

Mountains lay within, but they would not have filled the horrid
chasm; they would only have made it more terrific. Here stood
Obaddon with the guilty shade. No pathway leads to hell's tremendous gulf. Close by the gate her rocky sides, deep cleft with
molten fire, descend abrupt in viewless precipice. Speechless,
dizzy, pale, with staring eye-balls, stands Terror at the brink. The
dread minister of Heaven's vengeance stood over this grave; here
Death never sleeps. With thee, Judas, thou traitor! Death never
sleeps.

THE THRONE OF THE ALMIGHTY.
The Messiah, X. 15.

Von dem Throne, der sonst, die hellste sichtbare Schönheit,
Leuchtete, nun in schreckenerschaffende Nächte gehüllt stand,
Einsam stand, um den jetzt kein Unsterblicher feierte;
Außer, daß von der weit hinbebenden untersten Stufe
Knieend, mit betendem Auge, mit banggerungenen Händen,
Starr vor Erwartung, der erste der Todesengel emporsah:
Von dem Throne schaute, mit ungewendetem Antlitz,
Auf den göttlichen Sündeversöhner Jehovah herunter.
Durch die helleren Stäubchen, die Sonnen, die dunklern, die
    Erden,
Durch die verstummte Natur; mit Blicken, von dem nur ver-
    standen,
Dem nur gefühlt, auf den sie vom Auge des Ewigen strömten,
Schaut er hinab.

The eternal throne, which was wont to stand in purest beauty visible to the eye, now rose darkly involved in gloomy shades, in lonely silence, round which no immortals now raised their hallelujahs, save that on its extremest step, kneeling with supplicating eye, with folded hands clasped in terror, in silent expectation, Death's chief angel waited ; Jehovah still gazed on his sin-atoning Son with unaverted look. His divine eye penetrated through the suns, those lucid specks of dust, through the opaquer planets, through the tracts of silent nature, with a glance comprehended by none save by him on whom it rested.

CONGENIAL SOULS IN LIFE'S SHORT PILGRIMAGE.

The Messiah, XIV. 67.

So nahn oft Pilger nach Salem,
Deren Seelen sich gleich, und für einander gemacht sind,
Sich in diesem Leben, und fehlen sich dennoch. In Salem
Sehn sie sich erst, verwundernd, daß sie sich hier nicht gefunden.

Thus often pilgrims, on their way towards heaven, whose souls are like and made for each other, approach, yet miss, till at length in heaven they greet, amazed that on the earth they had never met.

A STORM.

The Messiah, XIV. 659.

Wie ein Sturm, der beginnt, mit gehaltner Stärke noch wehet,
Noch den kühleren Wald nicht ganz füllt; Stille ruhet
Noch in seinen Thalen, noch liegen blässere Schatten,
Ganz ist die Sonne noch nicht von des Sturmes Wolken umnachtet!

Even as a rising storm, with strength yet curbed, only blows gently, nor fills the cool woods ; silence still sleeps in the vales, shadows still float palely; the sun is not yet wholly dimmed by the clouds of the storm.

THE STORM.

The Messiah, XIV. 665.

So reißt sich
Durch den Wald der stärkere Sturm. Die Bäume des Waldes
Zittern, rauschen mit Ungestüm alle, beugen sich alle,
Vor dem herrschenden Sturm, der Donnerwolken, und Fluten
Himmelstürzender Meere von Berge treibet zu Berge!

So sweeps the storm through the forest in fury. The shivering trees bend low; all yield to the mighty blast, to the thunder-clouds, while sheets of rain are driven from hill to hill.

SOLITUDE.

The Messiah, XIV. 863.

Einen Becher der Freuden hat in der Rechte, der Linken
Einen wüthenden Dolch die Einsamkeit; reicht dem Beglückten
Ihren Becher, dem Leidenden reicht sie den wüthenden Dolch hin!

Solitude holds a cup sparkling with bliss in her right hand, a raging dagger in her left; to the blest she offers her goblet, but stretches towards the wretch the ruthless steel.

A SIGHING BROOK.

The Messiah, XV. 338.

Aber jetzo ergriff die Unbekannte die Harfe,
Und wie ein fernherweinender Bach, wenn vor dem Gewitter
Todesstille den Wald beherrscht, erklangs in den Saiten
Um die sinkende Hand der grabverlangenden Freundin.

But the unknown now took the harp, and, like a far-sighing brook, when a death-like stillness reigns through the forest ere the tempest comes, her languid hand swept o'er the chords as if to invoke her friend, whom the grave contains.

THE HUES OF RUDDY EVE.

The Messiah, XV. 769.

Denn die Schönheit der Abendröthe glänzt' auf der Wang' ihr,
Und ihr Lächeln im Blick.

For the hues of ruddy eve began to shine over her cheek; its smile danced in her eye.

LIGHT AS A SUMMER LEAF.

The Messiah, XV. 821.

Und sie erhob sich, leicht wie ein Laub, das Athmen der Luft hebt.

She rose light as a summer's leaf, which the breath of the zephyr raises.

The Music of Human Voices.

The Messiah, xv. 979.

Und die Stimme des Menschen, vor allen Saiten und Erzen
Unerschöpflich, die mächtigste Herrscherin über die Herzen.

The tones of human voices mightier than strings or brass to
move the soul.

Man's Life.

An Gott.

Das Leben gleichet gegen die Ewigkeit,
Dem schnellen Hauche, welcher dem Sterbenden
Entfließt; mit ihm entfloß die Seele,
Die der Unendlichkeit ewig nachströmt!

Man's life, when compared with eternity, is but like the passing
breath breathed by the dying; with it the spirit flees, and
streameth on to eternity, endless soaring.

KRUMMACHER.

Born A.D. 1767.   Died A.D. 1845.

Frederick Adolf Krummacher was born at Tecklinburg in West-
phalia in 1767, and after many changes became a clergyman at
Bremen, where he died in 1845.

Finish what we have to do.

Ein gutes Mittel sich von schwerer Arbeit frei zu machen.

Der sagte mir immer, so lange man ein schweres Geschäft
vor sich habe, würde man niemals recht vergnügt. Deswegen
müsse man es frisch angreifen, so käme es bald zu Ende, und
wenn es zu Ende sei, habe man immer darüber eine große
Freude.

He always said to me, So long as you have a difficult business
before you, you will never feel satisfied. Therefore you must set
about it, and finish it off; and when you have finished it, then
great pleasure is felt.

KULMAN.

Born A.D. 1808. Died A.D. 1825.

Elizabeth Kulman was born at St. Petersburg 1808, and died there 9th November 1825. She wrote poetry in Russian, German, and Italian, being acquainted with eleven languages, eight of which she spoke.

THE IMPOSSIBLE IS POSSIBLE.

Talent und Kunst.

Schwer ist's, doch nicht unmöglich,
Wie vieles in der Welt.
Unmögliches wird möglich,
Wenn es an Muth nicht fehlt.

It is difficult, but not impossible, as much that is on earth. The impossible becomes possible when courage spurs us on.

DEATH.

An meinen Arzt.

Was hold im Lenze blühte,
Fällt vor dem Herbst oft ab;
Denn ihre Zeit hat Blüthe,
Und seine Zeit das Grab.

What bloomed so sweetly in spring oft fades before autumn. There is one time for the blossom, another for the tomb.

LESSING.

Born A.D. 1729. Died A.D. 1781.

Gotthold Ephraim Lessing, the son of a clergyman of Camenz in Saxony, was educated at the school of Meissen, where he received the surname of "Admirable," from the distinguished position which he held in the school. Thence he was sent to the University of Leipsic, where his parents wished him to study theology. This, however, did not suit his taste, and conceiving a passion for the drama, he gave himself up to the amusements of life. To soothe his mother's anxieties he laid his comic studies aside, and returned to the university with the view of studying medicine, but his old passion broke out anew. At the request of

his parents he resided for some time at Wittemberg with his
brother, who was studying for the Church. After various literary
attempts, which were not successful, in 1759 appeared the
"Letters on Literature," which formed an epoch in German
literature. He was passionately fond of gambling, and he was
often seen over the faro-table in the utmost state of excitement.
In 1769 he went to Hamburg as director of the theatre; and at
last was appointed Librarian of the Wolfenbüttel Library, at
a salary of £90 per annum, with a free house and firewood. Here
he died 1781.

THE HEART.

Minna von Barnhelm, II. 1.

Das Herz, gnädiges Fräulein? Man traue doch ja seinem
Herzen nicht zu viel. Das Herz redet uns gewaltig gern nach
dem Maule. Wenn das Maul eben so geneigt wäre, nach dem
Herzen zu reden, so wäre die Mode längst aufgekommen, die
Mäuler unterm Schloffe zu tragen.

The heart, my dear young lady? We should not trust the
heart too much. The heart speaks to us very gladly, as our
mouth expresses itself. If the mouth were as much inclined to
speak the feelings of the heart, it would have been the fashion
long ago to put a padlock on the mouth.

THE GOOD QUALITIES WHICH WE POSSESS.

Minna von Barnhelm, II. 1.

Man spricht selten von der Tugend, die man hat; aber desto
öfter von der, die uns fehlt.

One seldom speaks of the virtues which one has; but much
oftener of that which fails us.

A GRATEFUL THOUGHT TO HEAVEN.

Minna von Barnhelm, II. 3.

Ein einziger dankbarer Gedanke gen Himmel ist das voll-
kommenste Gebet!

A single grateful thought towards heaven is the most perfect
prayer.

A Happy Being.

Minna von Barnhelm, II. 3.

Ich bin glücklich! und fröhlich! Was kann der Schöpfer lieber sehen, als ein fröhliches Geschöpf!

I am happy and joyous! What can the Creator see with greater pleasure than a happy creature?

The Beautiful.

Minna von Barnhelm, II. 3.

Wenn wir schön sind, sind wir ungeputzt am schönsten.

When we are beautiful, we are most beautiful when unadorned.

Thomson (*Autumn,* l. 204) says—

"Loveliness
Needs not the foreign aid of ornament,
But is, when unadorned, adorned the most."

See (Lat.) Dress, simplicity of. (Fr.) Unadorned.

Joy.

Minna von Barnhelm, II. 3.

Die Freude macht drehend, wirblicht.

Joy makes us giddy and unable to stand.

A Keepsake.

Minna von Barnhelm, II. 5.

So was erinnert Einen manch Mal, woran man nicht gern erinnert seyn will. Darum schafft man's aus den Augen.

Thus something reminds us many a time of that which we would rather not be reminded of. Therefore we put it out of sight.

Laughing.

Minna von Barnhelm, III. 5.

Was haben Sie denn gegen das Lachen? Kann man denn nicht auch lachend sehr ernsthaft seyn? Lieber Major, das Lachen erhält uns vernünftiger, als der Verdruß.

What have you to say against laughing? Can we not while

laughing be very serious! Laughing keeps us more rational than sadness caused by vexation.

See (Lat.) Laugh and be wise.

The Heart.

Minna von Barnhelm, v. 4.

Wo das Herz reden darf, braucht es keiner Vorbereitung.

Where the heart dare speak, it requires no preparation.

Painting has its Limits.

Emilia Galotti, i. 4.

Ich bitte, Prinz, daß Sie die Gränzen unserer Kunst erwägen wollen. Vieles von dem Anzüglichsten der Schönheit liegt ganz ausser den Gränzen derselben.

I beg, Prince, that you would consider the limits of our art. Much of the most attractive qualities of beauty lie quite beyond its limits.

Art must Flatter.

Emilia Galotti, i. 4.

Auch ist es in der That nicht mehr geschmeichelt, als die Kunst schmeicheln muß. Die Kunst muß malen, wie sich die plastische Natur, — wenn es eine giebt — das Bild dachte: ohne den Abfall, welchen der widerstrebende Stoff unvermeidlich macht; ohne das Verderb, mit welchem die Zeit dagegen ankämpfet.

It is not in reality more flattered than art must flatter. Art must paint, as plastic nature—if there is one—conceived the original idea, without the abatements rendered unavoidable by the resisting material, without the injury sustained from the effects of time.

The Difficulties of a Painter.

Emilia Galotti, i. 4.

Ha! daß wir nicht unmittelbar mit den Augen malen! Auf dem langen Wege, aus dem Auge durch den Arm in den Pinsel, wie viel geht da verloren!

Ah! would that we could at once paint with the eyes! In the long way from the eye through the arm to the pencil, how much is lost!

A Painter.

Emilia Galotti, I. 4.

Oder meynen Sie, Prinz, daß Raphael nicht das größte malerische Genie gewesen wäre, wenn er unglücklicher Weise ohne Hände wäre geboren worden? Meynen Sie, Prinz?

But think you, Prince, that Raphael would not have been the greatest genius, as a painter, even though he had unluckily been born without hands? Think you so, Prince?

Pride and Poverty.

Emilia Galotti, I. 6.

Mit euren ersten Häusern! — in welchen das Ceremoniel, der Zwang, die Langeweile, und nicht selten die Dürftigkeit herrschet.

With your first houses! in which ceremonial, constraint, ennui, and often poverty, reigns.

Allow the Devil to catch you by a Hair.

Emilia Galotti, II. 3.

Ha! Laß Dich den Teufel bei Einem Haare fassen; und Du bist sein auf ewig! Ich Unglücklicher!

Ha! let the devil catch you by a hair, and thou art his for ever! Unhappy I!

The Gift of Prayer.

Emilia Galotti, II. 6.

Die Gabe zu beten, ist nicht immer in unserer Gewalt.

The gift of prayer is not always in our power.

The Lover and the Husband.

Emilia Galotti, II. 6.

Wisse, mein Kind, daß ein Gift, welches nicht gleich wirket, darum kein minder gefährliches Gift ist. Was auf den Liebhaber feinen Eindruck macht, kann ihn auf den Gemahl machen. Dem Liebhaber könnt' es fogar fchmeicheln, einem fo wichtigen Mitbewerber den Rang abzulaufen. Aber wenn er ihm den nun ein Mal abgelaufen hat: ah! mein Kind, — fo wird aus dem Liebhaber oft ein ganz anderes Gefchöpf. Dein gutes Geftirn behüte Dich vor diefer Erfahrung.

Know, my child, that a poison, though it does not work, is not a less dangerous poison. What makes no impression on the lover, may make it on the husband. The lover it may flatter to carry off the prize from a powerful competitor. But when he has once gained it—ah! my child!—the lover becomes quite another being. Thy good star keep thee from learning this by experience.

THE ADVICE OF A FOOL.

Emilia Galotti, III. 1.

Wenn der Rath eines Thoren ein Mal gut ift, fo muß ihn ein gefcheuter Mann ausführen.

If the advice of a fool is once good, a sensible man must carry it out.

INDIFFERENCE INSTEAD OF LOVE.

Emilia Galotti, IV. 3.

Gleichgültigfeit! Gleichgültigfeit an die Stelle der Liebe? —Das heißt, Nichts an die Stelle von Etwas. Den lernen Sie, nachplauberndes Hofmännchen, lernen Sie von einem Weibe, daß Gleichgültigfeit ein leeres Wort, ein bloßer Schall ift, dem nichts, gar nichts entfpricht. Gleichgültig ift die Seele nur gegen das, woran fie nicht denkt; nur gegen ein Ding, das für fie fein Ding ift. Und nur gleichgültig für ein Ding, das fein Ding ift — das ift fo viel, als gar nicht gleichgültig.

Indifference! indifference in the place of love? that means nothing in the place of something. Wherefore, prattling courtier, learn from a woman that indifference is an empty word, a mere sound, expressing nothing. The soul is indifferent only towards that about which it does not think; only towards a thing which for it is nothing. And only indifferent for a thing which is nothing—that is as much as not indifferent.

Accident.

Emilia Galotti, iv. **3.**

Nichts unter der Sonne ist Zufall;—am wenigsten das, wovon die Absicht so klar in die Augen leuchtet.

Nothing under the sun is accident—least of all that of which the intention is so very clear.

To lose One's Senses.

Emilia Galotti, iv. 7.

Wer über gewisse Dinge den Verstand nicht verlieret, der hat keinen zu verlieren.

He who loses not his senses in certain things has no senses to lose.

A Young Head on Old Shoulders.

Emilia Galotti, v. 2,

Nichts verächtlicher als ein brausender Jünglingskopf mit grauen Haaren!

Nothing more contemptible than a young head full of fury with grey hairs.

The Man regardless of Law.

Emilia Galotti, v. 4.

Wer kein Gesetz achtet, ist eben so mächtig, als wer kein Gesetz hat.

He who disregards law is quite as powerful as he who is bound by no law.

Woman.

Emilia Galotti, v. 7.

Ich hab' es immer gesagt: das Weib wollte die Natur zu ihrem Meisterstücke machen.

I have always said it—Nature meant to make woman as its masterpiece.

God rewards the Good in this Life.

Nathan, i. 2.

Denn Gott lohnt Gutes, hier gethan, auch hier noch.

For God rewards good done in this world, even here also.

A Pious Hypocrite.

Nathan, I. 2.

Begreifſt du aber,
Wie viel andächtig ſchwärmen leichter, als
Gut handeln iſt? wie gern der ſchlaffſte Menſch
Andächtig ſchwärmt, um nur, — iſt er zu Zeiten
Sich ſchon der Abſicht deutlich nicht bewußt —
Um nur gut handeln nicht zu dürfen?

But understandest thou how much easier it is to be a pious
visionary than to act an honest part in life? how willingly the
worst of men is a pious enthusiast only—at times he is himself
not really aware of his motives—that he may not require to act
an honest part?

Medicine, not Poison, I offer.

Nathan, I. 2.

Es iſt Arznei, nicht Gift, was ich dir reiche.

It is medicine, not poison, I offer you.

The Will and not the Gift.

Nathan, I. 5.

Denn der Wille
Und nicht die Gabe macht den Geber.

For the will and not the gift makes the giver.

Every Land bears Good Men.

Nathan, II. 5.

Weiß,
Daß alle Länder gute Menſchen tragen.

Know that all lands bear good men.

The Vulgar Herd.

Nathan, II. 5.

Nathan.

Nur das Gemeine
Verkennt man ſelten.

Tempelherr.
Und das Seltene
Vergißt man schwerlich. — Nathan, ja,
Wir müssen, müssen Freunde werden.

Nathan. It is only the common herd, of which we seldom mis-
apprehend the character. *Templar.* And then the exception we
forget with difficulty.—Nathan, yes, we must, must be friends.

A PAUL PRY.

Nathan, II. 8.

Der Blick des Forschers fand
Nicht selten mehr, als er zu finden wünschte.

The eye of the Paul Pry often finds more than he wished to find.

IMAGES DEEPLY IMPRINTED ON THE MIND.

Nathan, II. 8.

Wie solche tiefgeprägte Bilder doch
Zu Zeiten in uns schlafen können, bis
Ein Wort, ein Laut sie weckt!

How can such deeply-imprinted images sleep in us at times,
till a word, a sound, awake them?

TO BORROW.

Nathan, II. 9.

Borgen ist
Viel besser nicht als betteln.

To borrow is not much better than to beg.

See (Fr.) Borrow.

THE TRUE BEGGAR.

Nathan, II. 9.

Der wahre Bettler ist
Doch einzig und allein der wahre König!

The true beggar is the only king above all comparison.

THE MOMENTS.

Nathan, III. 1.

Wie viel Augenblicke
Sind aber schon vorbei! — Ach nun; wer denkt
An die verflossenen?

But how many moments are already past! Ah! who thinks of those that are past?

HEAVEN'S WAYS.

Nathan, III. 1.

Sperre dich, so viel du willst!
Des Himmels Wege sind des Himmels Wege.

Resist as much as thou wilt; Heaven's ways are Heaven's ways.

A WOMAN.

Nathan, III. 4.

Was hätt' ein Weiberkopf erdacht, das er
Nicht zu beschönen wüßte?

What could a woman's head contrive, which she would not know to excuse?

STORIES.

Nathan, III. 6.

Nicht die Kinder bloß speist man
Mit Mährchen ab.

It is not children only that one amuses with stories.

HE WHO KNOWS MUCH.

Nathan, IV. 2.

Wer viel weiß,
Hat viel zu sorgen.

He who knows much has much to care for.

REAL AND APPARENT CHARACTER.

Nathan, V. 4.

Doch was man ist, und was
Man seyn muß in der Welt, das paßt ja wohl
Nicht immer.

What a man is, and what he ought to be in the world, do not always correspond.

SUSPICION AND MISTRUST.

Nathan, v. 8.

Argwohn folgt auf Mißtraun!

Suspicion follows close on mistrust.

LICHTWER.

Born A.D. 1719. Died A.D. 1782.

Magnus Gottfried Lichtwer was born 1719 at Wurzen, and died at Halberstadt 1782, in the service of Prussia as a judge.

BLINDFOLD ZEAL.

Die Katzen und der Hausherr.

Blinder Eifer schadet nur.

Blindfold zeal can do but harm.

MOLESCHOTT.

FLOWERS ARE AIR-WOVEN CHILDREN OF LIGHT.

Licht und Leben, p. 29.

Blumen, Blätter, Früchte sind also aus Luft gewebte Kinder des Lichts.

Flowers, leaves, fruit, are therefore air-woven children of light.

There is also an analogous idea in Rückert's fine poem, "Die sterbende Blume" ("The Dying Flower"), so beautifully translated by Professor Blackie. It occurs in the eighth verse :—

„Wie aus Duft und Glanz gemischt
Du mich schufst, dir dank' ich's heut."

"As thou hast created me of mingled air and glitter, I thank thee for it."

This seems to have been adapted by G. H. Lewes (*Seaside Studies,* ed. 1860, p. 248) thus :—

"Bright April showers
Will bid again the fresh green leaves expand;
And May, light floating in a cloud of flowers,
Will cause thee to rebloom with magic hand."

R

MICHAELIS.

Born A.D. 1746. Died A.D. 1772.

PITY THE WRETCHED.

Die Biene und die Taube.

Erbarmt euch willig fremder Noth!
Du gibst den Armen heut dein Brod,
Der Arme kann dir's morgen geben.

Be willing to pity the misery of the stranger! Thou givest to-day thy bread to the poor, to-morrow the poor may give it to thee.

MÖSER.

Born A.D. 1720. Died A.D. 1794.

Justus Möser was born at Osnabrück in 1720, where his father was president of the Consistorial Court. He studied at the University of Jena and Göttingen, and became a member of the legal profession. He was appointed by his countrymen "advocatus patriæ," to defend their rights; serving his country for many years in various capacities. He died in 1794.

ENNUI AND LABOUR.

Die Spinnstube,

eine Osnabrückische Geschichte.

Ich habe auch die Welt gesehen, und nach einer langen Erfahrung gefunden, daß lange Weile unser größter Feind, und eine nützliche Arbeit unsere dauerhafteste Freundin sei.

I have also seen the world, and after long experience have discovered that ennui is our greatest enemy, and remunerative labour our most lasting friend.

MÜLLNER.

Schuld, Act II. *sc.* 5.

Wer erklärt mir, Gerindur,
Diesen Zwiespalt der Natur?

Who explains to me, Gerindur, this discord of nature?

NOVALIS.

Born A.D. 1772.   Died A.D. 1801.

Frederick von Hardenberg, or, as he called himself, Novalis, was the eldest son of the Baron von Hardenberg, who had charge of the manufactory of salt in Saxony, being born, 1772, on the family property in the province of Mansfeld.   After a dangerous illness in his ninth year his mental faculties suddenly awoke, and he discovered that he was possessed of wonderful talents.   Poetry became a mere recreation, and he pursued the sciences with zeal, and more particularly history.   He studied at Jena, and afterwards attended with his brother the University of Leipsic, and also Wittenberg, where he became acquainted with Frederick Schlegel and Fichte, who exercised an important influence on his future life.   The death of his betrothed was a sad blow, and he lived ever afterwards as in a dream.   He died at an early age, 1801, at the moment when his philosophical genius and his rich poetical talents had excited the highest hopes among his countrymen.   He left little else than fragments ; an imperfect romance — "Henry von Oefterdingen ;" "Hymns to the Night ;" and numerous fragments of thoughts.

Fragments.

FRIENDSHIP, LOVE, AND PIETY.

Freundſchaft, Liebe und Pietät ſollten geheimnißvoll behandelt werden.   Man ſollte nur in ſeltnen vertrauten Momenten davon reden, ſich ſtillſchweigend darüber einverſtehen.   Vieles iſt zu zart um gedacht, noch mehres um beſprochen zu werden.

Friendship, love, and piety should be treated in private.   We should only speak of them on rare and confidential moments, have a silent understanding regarding them.   There is much in respect to them that is too tender to be thought of, still more to be talked about.

THE EVENTS OF LIFE.

Alle Zufälle unſers Lebens ſind Materialien, aus denen wir machen können, was wir wollen.   Wer viel Geiſt hat, macht viel aus ſeinem Leben.   Jede Bekanntſchaft, jeder Vorfall wäre für den durchaus Geiſtigen erſtes Glied einer unendlichen Reihe, Anfang eines unendlichen Romans.

All the events of our life are materials, out of which we may make what we will.   He who has much spirit makes most of his life.   Every piece of knowledge, every occurrence, might be, for the truly spiritual, the first part of an infinite series, the commencement of an endless romance.

The Artist.

Derjenige wird nie als Darfteller etwas leiften, der nichts weiter darftellen mag, als feine Erfahrungen, feine Lieblings= gegenftände, der es nicht über fich gewinnen kann, auch einen ganz fremden, ihm ganz unintereffanten Gegenftand, mit Fleiß zu ftudiren und mit Muße darzuftellen. Der Darfteller muß alles darftellen können und wollen. Dadurch entfteht der große Stil der Darftellung, den man mit Recht an Göthe fo fehr bewundert.

He will never accomplish anything as an artist who can represent nothing except his own experiences, his favourite objects; who cannot prevail on himself to study with diligence, and represent with care, objects that are foreign to his taste, and even quite uninteresting to him. The artist must be able and willing to represent everything. From this arises the great style of the artist which is so much and so justly admired in Goethe.

Sickness.

Krankheiten, befonders langwierige, find Lehrjahre der Lebenskunft und der Gemüthsbildung. Man muß fie durch tägliche Bemerkungen zu benutzen fuchen. Ift denn nicht das Leben des gebildeten Menfchen eine beftändige Aufforderung zum Lernen? Der gebildete Menfch lebt durchaus für die Zukunft; fein Leben ift Kampf, feine Erhaltung und fein Zweck Wiffenfchaft und Kunft. — Je mehr man lernt, nicht mehr in Augenblicken, fondern in Jahren u. f. w. zu leben, defto edler wird man.

Sicknesses, particularly if they are of long continuance, are years of apprenticeship for the art of living, and the forming of the mind. We must endeavour to make use of them by daily observations. Is not, then, the life of the well-educated man a constant effort to acquire learning? The educated man lives in that way for the future; his life is a battle; his food, and the object at which he aims, is knowledge and art. The more we learn to live, not only in the passing time, but in years, the nobler we become.

Spring.

Es find nicht die bunten Farben, die luftigen Töne und die

warme Luft, die uns im Frühling so begeistern, es ist der stille weissagende Geist unendlicher Hoffnungen, ein Vorgefühl vieler frohen Tage, des gedeihlichen Daseyns so mannichfaltiger Naturen, die Ahndung höherer ewiger Blüten und Früchte, und die dunkle Sympathie mit der gesellig sich entfaltenden Welt.

It is not the variegated colours, the cheerful sounds, and the warm breezes, which enliven us so much in spring; it is the quiet prophetic spirit of endless hopes, a presentiment of many joyful days, of the happy existence of such manifold natures, the anticipation of higher everlasting blossoms and fruits, and the secret sympathy with the world that is developing itself.

NATURE.

Die Natur ist eine Aeolsharfe, ein musikalisches Instrument, dessen Töne wieder Tasten höherer Saiten in uns sind.

Nature is an Æolian harp, a musical instrument, whose tones are the re-echo of higher strings within us.

OPITZ.

Born A.D. 1597.   Died A.D. 1639.

Martin Opitz was born in 1597 at Bunzlau in Silesia, where his father was a councillor. He studied at the University of Frankfort, and devoted his life, against his father's wishes, to literature. The troubles of his country induced him to proceed to Denmark, where he spent some time. He became professor of philosophy at Weissenburg, but never remained long in any employment. He was cut off by the plague at Dantzic in 1639.

MAN NEVER RETURNS.
Wiederkehr.

Schlüpft die Blume Winters gleich
In das kalte Erdenreich,
Sehen wir sie doch im Lenzen
Nochmals auf den Auen glänzen;
Täglich sinkt die Sonn' in's Meer,
Hebt sich fröhlich morgen wieder:
Legt der Mensch in's Grab sich nieder,
Er kommt nimmer zu uns her.

The flowers of winter glide at once into the cold earth, yet we
see them again bloom in spring in the meadows; the sun sinks
day by day into the sea, and again rises joyful in the morning;
man lays himself down in the grave and never returns to us.

JEAN PAUL F. RICHTER.

Born A.D. 1763.   Died A.D. 1825.

Jean Paul Friedrich Richter was born 21st March 1763 at Wun-
siedel in Bavaria, where his father was schoolmaster and organist.
At first he studied for the Church, but his peculiar religious ideas
unfitted him for that profession, and he resolved to devote himself
to literature.   He lived with his mother for some time in great
poverty.   In 1786 he became tutor in a family, but was rendered
miserable by the disposition of his pupil and the narrowness of his
employer.   However, he struggled gradually into notice by the
publication of his various works, and in 1801 formed a matri-
monial engagement, which turned out to be a happy one.   After
various changes he settled at Bayreuth, where he spent the rest
of his life, diversifying it only by short annual tours to visit his
scattered friends.   He died 14th November 1825.

CHILDLIKE LOVE.

Titan, Cycle 1.

Dieſes Sehnen war nicht kindliche Liebe — dieſe gehörte ſeinen
Pflegeeltern an, weil kindliche nur gegen ein Herz entſteht,
woran wir lange lagen, und das uns gleichſam mit den erſten
Herzblättern gegen kalte Nächte und heiße Tage beſchirmte.

This longing was not filial love—*that* belonged to his foster-
parents—for childlike love can only spring up toward a heart
whereon we have long reposed, and which has protected us, as it
were, with the first heart's-leaves against cold nights and hot days.

THE FIRST JOURNEY.

Titan, Cycle 1.

Die erſte Reiſe, zumal wenn die Natur nichts als weißen
Glanz und Orangenblüten und Kaſtanienſchatten auf die lange
Straße wirft, beſchert dem Jüngling das, was oft die letzte
dem Mann' entführt — ein träumendes Herz, Flügel über die
Eisſpalten des Lebens und weit offne Arme für jede Menſchen-
bruſt.

The first journey, especially when nature throws over the long road nothing but bright radiance—orange-blossoms, and chestnut-shadows, gives to the youth what the last journey often takes away from the man—a dreaming heart, wings for the ice-chasms of life, and wide-spread arms for every human breast.

WHAT NATURE DOES FOR MAN.

Titan, Cycle 1.

Hohe Natur! wenn wir dich sehen und lieben, so lieben wir unsere Menschen wärmer, und wenn wir sie betrauern oder vergessen müssen, so bleibst du bei uns und ruhest vor dem nassen Auge wie ein grünendes abendrothes Gebirge. Ach vor der Seele, vor welcher der Morgenthau der Ideale sich zum grauen kalten Landregen entfärbet hat — und vor dem Herzen, dem auf den unterirdischen Gängen dieses Lebens die Menschen nur noch wie dürre gekrümmte Mumien auf Stäben in Katakomben begegnen — und vor dem Auge, das verarmt und verlassen ist und das kein Mensch mehr erfreuen will — und vor dem stolzen Göttersohne, den sein Unglaube und seine einsame, menschenleere Brust an einen ewigen unverrückten Schmerz anschmieden — — vor allen diesen bleibst du, erquickende Natur, mit deinen Blumen und Gebirgen und Katarakten treu und tröstend stehen, und der blutende Göttersohn wirft stumm und kalt den Tropfen der Pein aus den Augen, damit sie hell und weit auf deinen Vulkanen und auf deinen Frühlingen und auf deinen Sonnen liegen!

Mighty Nature! when we see and love thee, we love our fellow-men more warmly ; and when we must pity or forget them, thou still remainest with us, and reposest before the tearful eye like a green ridge of mountains in the evening red. Alas! before the soul, in whose sight the morning dew of its ideals has faded to a cold, grey drizzle—and before the heart, which, in the subterranean passages of this life, meets no longer men, but only dry, crooked-up mummies on crutches in catacombs—and before the eye, which is impoverished and forsaken, and which no human creature will any longer gladden—and before the proud son of the gods, whom his unbelief and his lonely bosom, emptied of humanity, rivet down to an eternal, unchangeable anguish ; before all these thou remainest, quickening Nature, with thy flowers, and mountains, and cataracts, a faithful comforter ; and the bleeding son of the gods, cold and speechless, dashes the drop of anguish from his **eyes,** that they may rest, far and clear, on thy volcanoes, and on thy springs, and on thy suns!

The Naturalness of Children.

Titan, Cycle 2.

Sie hatten jene heitere Unbefangenheit der Kinder, der Künstler und der südlichen Völker, die nur den Honigbehälter der Minute ausnascht; und daher fanden sie an jeder anfallenden Welle, an jedem Zitronenspalier, an jeder Statue unter Blüten, an jedem rückenden Wiederschein, an jedem fliehenden Schiffe mehr als eine Blume, die den gefüllten Kelch weiter unter dem warmen Himmel aufmachte, anstatt daß es uns unter unserm kalten wie den Bienen geht, vor denen Maifröste die Blumen verschließen.—O die Insulaner thun Recht. Unser größter und längster Irrthum ist, daß wir das Leben, d. h. seinen Genuß, wie die Materialisten das Ich, in seiner Zusammensetzung suchen, als könnte das Ganze oder das Verhältniß der Bestandtheile uns etwas geben, das nicht jeder einzelne Theil schon hätte. Besteht denn der Himmel unsers Daseyns, wie der blaue über uns, aus oder matter Luft, die in der Nähe und im Kleinen nur ein durchsichtiges Nichts ist und die erst in der Ferne und im Großen blauer Aether wird? Das Jahrhundert wirft den Blumensamen deiner Freude nur aus der porösen Säemaschine von Minuten; oder vielmehr an der seligen Ewigkeit selber ist keine andere Handhabe als der Augenblick. Das Leben besteht nicht aus 70 Jahren, sondern die 70 Jahre bestehen aus einem fortwehenden Leben, und man hat allemal gelebt und genug gelebt, man sterbe, wenn man will.

They had that serene naturalness of children, artists, and southern people, which is only from the honey-cup of the moment ; and, accordingly, they found in every dashing wave, in every citron-frame, in every statue among blossoms, in every dancing reflection, in every darting ship, more than one flower which opened its full cup wider under the warm sky ; whereas with us, under our cold one, it fares as with the bees, against whom the frosts of May shut the flowers up. Oh, the islanders are right! Our greatest and most lasting error is, that we look for life— that is, its happiness—as the materialists look for the soul, in the combination of parts—as if the whole, or the relation of its component parts, could give us anything which each individual part had not already. Does, then, the heaven of our **existence**, like the blue one over our heads, consist of mere empty air, which, when near to and in little, is only a transparent nothing, and which only in the distance and in gross becomes blue ether? The century casts the flower-seeds of thy joy only from the porous sowing-machine of minutes; or, rather, to the blest eternity itself there is no other handle than the instant. It is not that life consists of seventy years, but that seventy years consist of a continuous life; and one has lived at all events, and lived enough, die when one may.

PLEASURES ARE LIKE PINE-APPLES.
Titan, Cycle 3.

Freuden von ausnehmendem Geschmack wie Ananas haben das Schlimme, daß sie wie Ananas das Zahnfleisch bluten machen.

Pleasures of high flavour, like pine-apples, have the misfortune that, like pine-apples, they make the gums bleed.

LIFE IS LIKE THE OLIVE.
Titan, Cycle 3.

Ist das Leben wie eine Olive, eine bittere Frucht, so greife nur beide scharf mit der Presse an, sie liefern das süßeste Oel.

If life, like the olive, is a bitter fruit, then grasp both with the press and they will afford the sweetest oil.

MEN ONLY TO BE SUBDUED BY MEN.
Titan, Cycle 5.

Nur durch Menschen besiegt und übersteigt man Menschen, nicht durch Bücher und Vorzüge. Man muß nicht seinen Werth auslegen, um die Menschen zu gewinnen, sondern man muß sie gewinnen, und dann erst jenen zeigen. Unglück ist nichts wie Unverstand, und nicht sowohl durch Tugend als durch Verstand wird man furchtbar und glücklich.

Only through men are men subdued and surpassed, not by books and superior qualities. One must not display his worth in order to gain men, but gain them first, and then, and not till then, show his worth. There is no calamity like ignorance; and not so much by virtue as by understanding is man made formidable and fortunate.

Vanity, Libertinism, and Idleness.

Titan, Cycle 9.

Mir wenigstens der Egoismus, die Libertinage und das Müßiggehen gewiß bleiben und sitzen; denn diese Schwämme und Moose säete das Schicksal so weit, als es konnte, in die höhern Stände hinauf, weil sie in den niedern und breitern zu sehr ausgegriffen und sie ausgesogen hätten — welches das Muster derselben Vorsicht gewesen zu seyn scheint, aus der die Schiffe den Teufelsdreck, den sie aus Persien holen, stets oben an den Mastbaum hängen, damit sein Gestank nicht die Fracht des Schiffraums besudle.

At least vanity, libertinism, and idleness, will stay and sit for their likeness; for fate has sown these mushrooms and mosses as high as possible among the upper classes, because in the lower and broader they would have spread too much, and sucked them dry— which seems to be the pattern of that same foresight by which ships always have their asafœtida, which they bring from Persia, hanging overhead on the mast, in order that its stench may not contaminate the freight on deck.

Hedgehog-like Souls and free Hearts.

Titan, Cycle 10.

Nur weiche Blattwickler= und Igel=Seelen ringeln und krempen sich vor jedem Finger in sich zusammen; unter dem offnen Kopfe hängt gern ein offnes Herz.

Only weak, caterpillar, and hedgehog-like souls curl and crumple up into themselves at every touch ; under the free brain beats gladly a free heart.

The Season of Childhood.

Titan, Cycle 10.

In jener kindlichen Zeit, wo die Seele auf der Regenbogen= brücke der Phantasie trocknes Fußes über die Lachen und Mauern der untern Erde wegschreitet.

That very season of childhood, when the soul, on the rainbow bridge of fancy, glides along, dry-shod, over the walls and ditches of this lower earth.

Days never to be Forgotten.

Titan, Cycle 12.

Aus der Kindheit — ach aus jedem Alter — bleiben unserm Herzen oft Tage unvergänglich, die jedes andere vergessen hätte.

Childhood—ah yes ! every age—often leaves behind in our hearts imperishable days, which every other heart had forgotten.

Wordsworth (*To a Butterfly*) says—

"Sweet childish days that were as long
As twenty days are now."

Posts of Honour.

Titan, Cycle 16.

Jede Ehrensäule erhebt das Herz eines Mannes, den man daraufstellt, über den Brodem des Lebens, über die Hagelwolken der Drangsale, über den Frostnebel der Verdrießlichkeit und über die brennbare Luft des — Zorns.

Every post of honour lifts the heart of a man who is placed on it above the vapour of life, the hail-clouds of calamity, the frosty mists of discontent, and the inflammable air of wrath.

Men full of Love and Hatred.

Titan, Cycle 16.

Es müßte Unsterbliche rühren, wenn sie die beladnen, vom Schicksal und von der Schuld oft so weit auseinander gehaltnen Menschen sähen, wie sie, gleich der Valisnerie,* sich vom sumpfigen Boden abreißen und aufsteigen in ein schöneres Element, und wie sie nun in der freiern Höhe den Zwischenraum ihrer Herzen überwinden und zusammenkommen. — Aber es muß auch Unsterbliche schmerzen, wenn sie uns unter dem schweren Gewitter des Lebens gegeneinander auf dem Schlachtfelde der Feindschaft ausgerückt erblicken, unter doppelten Schlägen, und so tödtlich getroffen vom fernen Schicksal und von der nahen Hand, die uns verbinden sollte!

---

* Die weibliche Valisnerie liegt zusammengerollt unten im Wasser, aus welchem sie mit der Blumenknospe aufsticht. um im Freien zu blühen; die männliche macht sich dann vom zu kurzen Stengel los und schwimmt mit ihrem trocknen Blütenstaube der erstern zu.

It must touch immortals when they see men, the heavy-laden, and often held so widely asunder by fate or fault, how, like the Valisneria,* they will tear themselves away from the marshy bottom, and ascend into a fairer element; and then, in the freer upper air, how they will conquer the distance between their hearts and come together. But it must also pain immortals when they behold us, under the violent *tempests* of life, arrayed against each other on the *battlefield* of enmity, under double blows, and so mortally smitten, at once by remote destiny and by that nearer hand which should bind up our wounds!

* The female Valisneria lies rolled up under the water, out of which it lifts its bud to bloom in the open air; the male then loosens itself from the too short stalk and swims to her with its dry blossom-dust.

THE MORNING-REDNESS OF LIFE.

Titan, Cycle 20.

Ach, wir haben es alle einmal gewußt, wir wurden alle einmal von der Morgenröthe des Lebens gefärbt! . . . . O warum achten wir nicht alle ersten Regungen der menschlichen Natur für heilig, als Erstlinge für den göttlichen Altar? Es gibt ja nichts Reineres und Wärmeres als unsere erste Freundschaft, unsere erste Liebe, unser erstes Streben nach Wahrheiten, unser erstes Gefühl für die Natur; wie Adam, werden wir erst aus Unsterblichen Sterbliche; wie Aegypter werden wir früher von Göttern als Menschen regiert;—und das Ideal eilet der Wirklichkeit, wie bei einigen Bäumen die weichen Blüten den breiten rohen Blättern, vor, damit nicht diese sich vor das Stäuben und Befruchten jener stellen.

Ah! we have all once known it, we have all once been tinged with the morning-redness of life! . . . . Oh, why do we not regard all first stirrings of human emotion as holy, as firstlings for the altar of God? There is truly nothing purer and warmer than our first friendship, our first love, our first striving after truths, our first feeling for nature. Like Adam, we are made mortals out of immortals; like Egyptians, we are governed earlier by gods than by men; and the ideal foreruns the reality, as with some trees, the tender blossoms anticipate the broad, rough leaves, in order that the latter may not set before the dusting and the fructifying of the former.

LOVING EMOTIONS.
Titan, Cycle 22.

Alle liebenden Empfindungen gehen, wie Gewächse, bei gewitterhafter Luft des Lebens schneller in die Höhe.

All loving emotions, like plants, shoot up most rapidly in the tempestuous atmosphere of life.

MEN LIKE BULLETS.
Titan, Cycle 26.

Die Menschen gehen wie Schießkugeln weiter, wenn sie abgeglättet sind.

Men, like bullets, go farthest when they are smoothest.

GREAT AND INTELLECTUAL MEN.
Titan, Cycle 29.

Je kräftiger und geistreicher und größer zwei Menschen sind, desto weniger vertragen sie sich unter Einem Deckenstück, wie große Insekten, die von Früchten leben, ungesellig sind (z. B. in jeder Haselnuß sitzt nur Ein Käfer), indeß die kleinen, die nur von Blättern zehren, z. B. die Blattläuse, nesterweise beisammenkleben.

The more powerful and intellectual, and great too, men are, so much the less can they bear each other under one ceiling; as great insects which live on *fruits* (for example, in every hazel-nut there sits only one chafer), whereas the little ones, which only live on *leaves* (for instance the leaf-lice), cleave together nest-wise.

THE EMPTY-BRAINED AND INQUISITIVE.
Titan, Cycle 31.

Er stäubte sogleich mit der Kleie von leeren schnellen unähnlichen Fragen um sich und eilte stets; denn er hatte fast noch mehr Langweile, als er machte, wie sich überhaupt für keinen das Leben so widrig verlängert, als für den, der es verkürzet.

He immediately began to dust about him with the bran of empty, rapid, disconnected questions, and was always in a hurry;

for he suffered almost more ennui than he caused ; as, in general,
there is no one with whom life drags so disagreeably as with him
who tries to make it shorter.

EASIER TO FLATTER THAN TO PRAISE.
Titan, Cycle 34.

Es ist dem Menschen leichter und geläufiger, zu schmeicheln
als zu loben.

It is easier and handier for men to flatter than to praise.

CENTURIES PAST AND FUTURE.
Titan, Cycle 34.

In den Jahrhunderten vor uns scheint uns die Menschheit
heranzuwachsen, in denen nach uns abzuwelken, in unserm herrlich blühend aufzuplatzen : so scheinen uns nur die Wolken
unsers Scheitelpunktes gerade zu gehen, die einen vor uns
steigen vom Horizonte herauf, die andern hinter uns ziehen
gekrümmt hinab.

In the centuries before us humanity appears to us to be growing
up ; in those which come after us, to be fading away ; in our own,
to burst forth in glorious bloom : thus do the clouds, only when
in our zenith, seem to move straight forward ; those in front of
us come up from the horizon, the others behind us sail downward
with foreshortened forms.

IN OLD AGE HOPE CEASES.
Titan, Cycle 34.

Das Alter ist nicht trübe, weil darin unsre Freuden, sondern
weil unsre Hoffnungen aufhören.

What makes old age so sad is, not that our joys, but that our
hopes cease.

Solomon (*Ecclesiastes* xii. 5) says—" Desire shall fail."

OLD AGE OF WOMEN.
Titan, Cycle 34.

Das Alter der Weiber ist trüber und einsamer als das der
Männer : darum schont in jenen die Jahre, die Schmerzen und

das Geſchlecht! — Ueberhaupt gleicht das Leben oft dem Fang-
Baume mit aufwärtsgerichteten Stacheln, an welchem der Bär
leicht hinauf zum Honig-Köder klettert, wovon er aber unter
lauter Stichen wieder zurückrutſchet.

The old age of women is sadder and more solitary than that of
men ; spare, therefore, in them their years, their sorrows, and
their sex ! In fact, life often resembles the trap-tree, with its
thorns directed upwards, on which the bear easily clambers up to
the honey-bait, but from which he can slide down again only
under severe stings.

POVERTY AND IMPOVERISHMENT.
Titan, Cycle 34.

Habt Mitleiden mit der Armuth, aber noch hundertmal
mehr mit der Verarmung! Nur jene, nicht dieſe macht Völker
und Individuen beſſer.

Have compassion on poverty, but a hundred times more on
impoverishment! Only the former, not the latter, makes nations
and individuals better.

LOVE.
Titan, Cycle 34.

Die Liebe vermindert die weibliche Feinheit und verſtärkt
die männliche.

Love lessens woman's delicacy and increases man's.

NOBLE PRIDE.
Titan, Cycle 34.

Es gibt einen gewiſſen edlen, durch welchen mehr als durch
Beſcheidenheit Verdienſte heller glänzen.

There is a certain noble pride through which merits shine
brighter than through modesty.

A MIGHTY WILL.
Titan, Cycle 36.

In ihm wohnte ein mächtiger Wille, der blos zur Dienerſchaft
der Triebe ſagte: es werde! Ein ſolcher iſt nicht der Stoizis-
mus, welcher blos über innere Miſſethäter oder Hämlinge

ober Kriegsgefangene ober Kinder gebeut, sondern es ist
jener genialisch-energische Geist, der die gesunden Wilden unsers
Busens bingt und bändigt, und der königlicher zu sich, als der
spanische Regent zu andern, sagt: Ich, der König!

There dwelt in him a mighty will, which merely said to the
serving company of impulses, Let it be! Such a will is not
stoicism, which rules merely over internal *malefactors*, or *knaves*,
or *prisoners of war*, or *children*, but it is that genially energetic
spirit which conditions and binds the healthy *savages* of our
bosoms, and which says more royally to itself than the Spanish
regent to others: I, the king.

The Beloved.
Titan, Cycle 36.

Aber in der heiligern Zeit des Lebens wird das Bild der
geliebtesten Seele nicht im Sprach- und Vorzimmer, sondern
im dunkeln stillen Oratorium aufgehangen; nur mit Geliebten
spricht man von Geliebten.

But in the holier season of life the image of the most beloved
soul is hung, not in the parlour and antechamber, but in the dim,
silent oratory; only with loved ones do we speak of loved ones.

Coming Events.
Titan, Cycle 38.

Gewisse Leute sind den ganzen Tag schon im Voraus voll
Aerger für irgend eine Zukunft, gleich dem Uzinphosphor, der
immer unter dem Mikroskope kocht, oder den Eisenhütten, worin
jeden Tag Feuer auskommt.

Certain people keep themselves all day long full of vexation
beforehand, for some coming event or other, like urinal phosphate,
which always boils under the microscope, or forges, wherein every
day fire breaks out.

A Character.
Titan, Cycle 39.

Betrachte das kalte, aber kecke und schneidend-geschliffne Auge,
dessen Winkel eine offne Blechscheere oder aufgestellte Falle
scheinen — die rothe Nase und den harten lippenlosen Mund,
dessen röthliche Krebsscheere sich abgewetzt zusammenzwickt in
das aufgestülpte Kinn und die ganze stämmige feste Figur.

Examine the cold, but impudent and cutting, sharply-ground **eye,** whose corners resemble a pair of open tinman's shears, or a trap set—the red nose, and the hard lipless mouth, whose reddish crab's-claw, worn off by whetting, pinches together—the cocked-up chin, and the whole stocky, firm figure.

What Impression is caused by the Wicked.
Titan, Cycle 39.

Verdammt! neben gewiſſen Geſichtern krümmen und mauſern ſich die Seelenſchwingen, wie neben Adlerkielen Schwanen= und Taubenfedern zerfallen; allen ſchuldloſen Gefühlen in der ſo geräumigen Bruſt Albano's wurd' es ſo unruhig und eng wie einem Taubenfluge, in deſſen Schlag man einen Iltisſchwanz geworfen.

Furies! in the neighbourhood of certain faces the pinions of the soul crumple up and mew themselves, as swans' and pigeons' feathers are crushed before eagles' quills; it was as uncomfortable and close for all the innocent feelings in such a roomy breast as Albano's, as it is to a flock of pigeons, into whose cot some one has thrown the tail of a polecat.

Refreshing at Times to give some Men a Drubbing.
Titan, Cycle 39.

Es gibt Menſchen und Zeiten, wo einen rechtſchaffenen Mann nichts mehr erquicken könnte als — Prügel, die er gäbe.

There are men and times at which and with whom nothing could be more refreshing to an honest man than to give them a sound drubbing.

Men are like Sheep in some Things.
Titan, Cycle 40.

Die Menſchen, in Rückſicht der Zeremonien, Moden und Geſetze, gleich einem Zug Schafe, insgeſammt, wofern man nur den Leithammel über einen Stecken ſetzen laſſen, an der Stelle des Stabes, den man nicht mehr hinhält, noch aus Vorſicht aufſpringen; — und die meiſten und höchſten Sprünge im Staate thun wir ohne den Stecken.

Men, in respect to ceremonies, modes, and laws, like a flock of sheep, will, in a body, provided the bell-wether can only be got to leap over a pole, continue to leap carefully over the same place when the pole has been taken away ; and the most and highest leaps in the state are those we make without the pole.

WHAT FANCY ACCOMPLISHES.

Titan, Cycle 43.

Denn der Reiz und sogar Vorzug der Aehnlichkeit und Kopie ist so groß, daß sogar einer, der einem gleichgültigen Wesen ähnlich sieht, uns lieber wird, wie das Echo eines leeren Rufs, blos weil hier wie in der nachahmenden Kunst die Vergangenheit und Abwesenheit eine durch die Phantasie durchscheinende Gegenwart wird.

For the charm, and even preferableness, of resemblance and copy is so great, that one who looks like even an indifferent person becomes more dear to us, like the echo of an empty sound, merely because, in this case as in the imitative art, the past and absent, shining through the fancy, become a present.

RIPENING LOVE.

Titan, Cycle 46.

Die werdende Liebe ist die stillste ; die schattigen Blumen in diesem Frühlinge meiden, wie die im andern, das Sonnenlicht.

Ripening love is the stillest; the shady flowers in this spring, as in the other, shun sunlight.

THOUGHTS OF THE DEAD.

Titan, Cycle 47.

Wem die heiligen Todten gleichgültig sind, dem werden es die Lebendigen auch.

To whomsoever the holy dead are of no consequence, to him the living are so too.

MAN IS EASILY FORGOTTEN.

Titan, Cycle 47.

Dir fiel es auf's Herz, wie leicht der Mensch vergessen wird, er liege in der Urne oder in der Pyramide — und wie man unser unsterbliches Ich wie einen Schauspieler für abwesend ansieht.

ſobald es nur in der Kuliſſe ſteht und nicht auf der Bühne unter den Spielern poltert.

It sank into thy heart, how easily man is forgotten, whether he lies in the urn or in the pyramid ; and how our immortal self is regarded like an actor, as *absent*, so soon as it is once behind the scenes, and frets and fumes no longer among the players on the stage.

Our Birthdays like Feathers in the Broad Wing of Time.

Titan, Cycle 47.

Oft zählt' ich am Geburtstage die wachſenden Jahre ab, die Federn im breiten Flügel der Zeit, und bedachte das Ver= rauſchen der Jugend: da ſtreckt' ich weit die Hand noch einem Freunde aus, der bei mir im Charons Nachen, worin wir geboren werden, ſtehen bliebe, wenn vor mir die Jahreszeiten des Lebens am Ufer vorüberlaufen mit Blumen und Blättern und Früchten, und wenn auf dem langen Strome das Menſchen= geſchlecht in tauſend Wiegen und Särgen hinunterſchießet.

Ach nicht das bunte Ufer fliehet vorüber, ſondern der Menſch und ſein Strom; ewig blühen die Jahreszeiten in den Gärten des Geſtades hinauf und hinab, aber nur wir rauſchen einmal vor den Gärten vorbei und kehren nicht um.

Often have I reckoned up on my birthday the increasing years— the feathers in the broad wing of time—and thought upon the sounding flights of youth ; then I stretched my hand far out after a friend who should stick by me in the Charon's skiff wherein we are born, when the seasons of life's year glide by along the shore before me, with their flowers, and leaves, and fruits ; and when, on the long stream, the human race shoots downwards in its thousand cradles and coffins.

Ah, it is not the gay, variegated shore that flies by, but man and his stream ; for ever bloom the seasons in the gardens up and down along the shore ; only *we* sweep by once for all before the garden, and never return.

Friendship.

Titan, Cycle 48.

Die Freundſchaft hat Stufen, die am Throne Gottes durch alle Geiſter hinaufſteigen bis zum unendlichen; nur die Liebe iſt erſättlich und immer dieſelbe und wie die Wahrheit ohne brei Vergleichungsgrade und ein einziges **Wesen** füllet ihr Herz.

Friendship has steps which lead up on the throne of God, through all spirits, even to the Infinite ; only love is satiable, and like truth admits no three degrees of comparison ; and a single being fills the heart.

THE INCOMING AND OUTGOING OF LIFE.

Titan, Cycle 59.

Nicht nur der Ein- und Ausgang des Lebens ist vielfach überschleiert, auch die kurze Bahn selber; wie um ägyptische Tempel, so liegen Sphinxe um den größten Tempel, und anders als bei der Sphinx löset das Räthsel nur der, welcher stirbt.

Not only the incoming and the outgoing of life are hidden with a manifold veil, but even the short path itself; as around Egyptian temples, so around the greatest of all temples, sphinxes lie, and reversing the case as it was with the sphinx, he only solves the riddle who dies.

JEALOUSY.

Titan, Cycle 61.

Und nun sog sich die Kröte der Eiferfucht, die im lebendigen Baume lebt und wächst, ohne sichtbaren Eingang und Ausgang, in seinem warmen Herzen fest.

And now the toad of jealousy, which lives and grows in the living tree without any visible way in or out, nursed itself to full size in his warm heart.

A FEMALE HEART.

Titan, Cycle 63.

Indeß gleicht ein weibliches Herz oft dem Marmor; der geschickte Steinmetz thut tausend Schläge, ohne daß der parische Block nur in die Linie eines Sprunges reiße; aber auf einmal bricht er auseinander eben in die Form, die der geschickte Steinmetz so lange hämmernd verfolgte.

However, a female heart is often like marble ; the cunning stonecutter strikes a thousand blows without the Parian block showing the line of a crack, but all at once it breaks asunder into the very form which the cunning stonecutter has so long been hammering after.

THE TIME OF YOUTH.
Titan, Cycle 64.

Fühlt' er unbeschreiblich ſtark und ſüß, daß die holde Jugend-
zeit unſer Welſch- und Griechenland iſt voll Götter, Tempel
und Luſt — ach und welches ſo oft Gothen mit Tatzen durch-
ſtreifen und ausleeren.

He felt with indescribable strength and sweetness that the
lovely time of youth is our Italy and Greece, full of gods, temples,
and bliss ; and which, alas! so often Goths and Vandals stalk
through, and strip with their talons.

CREATION-DAYS OF NATURE.
Titan, Cycle 64.

Es gibt zwiſchen den Alltags-Tagen des Lebens — wo der
Regenbogen der Natur uns nur zerbrochen und als ein unförmlicher bunter Klumpe am Horizont erſcheint — zuweilen einige
Schöpfungstage, wo ſie ſich in eine ſchöne Geſtalt rundet und
zuſammenzieht, ja wo ſie lebendig wird und wie eine Seele uns
anſpricht.

There are sometimes between the everyday days of life, when
the rainbow of nature appears to us only broken up, and as a
misshapen, motley mass on the horizon, certain creation-days,
when she rounds and contracts herself into a fair form—nay,
when she becomes alive and speaks to us like a soul.

LIFE'S WAVES.
Titan, Cycle 64.

Die Woge und der Tropfe im unendlichen Meere des Lebens
verfloſſen untheilbar mit den Strömen und Strudeln, welche
darin gingen.

The wave and the drop in the endless sea of life flowed away
in indivisible union with the streams and whirlpools which it bore
onwards.

LOVE CANNOT BE CONCEALED FROM WOMEN.
Titan, Cycle 64.

Sie hatte Albano's Liebe leicht erlauſcht, weil überall den

Weibern alles leichter zu verdecken ist, sogar der Haß, als sein Gegentheil.

She had easily detected Albano's love, because everything is easier to disguise from women—even hatred, than its opposite.

MAIDENS AS DOVES OF PASSAGE.
Titan, Cycle 65.

Ich habe oft das schöne leichte Nomaden-Leben der Mädchen in ihren arkadischen Lebens-Abschnitten bewundert mit Neid; leicht flattern diese Flugtauben in eine fremde Familie und nähen und lachen und besuchen da mit der Tochter des Hauses ein oder zwei Monate lang, und man hält das Kopulirreis für einen Familienzweig; — hingegen wir Stubentauben werden schwer versetzt und einheimisch und reiten meistens nach einigen Tagen wieder zurück.

I have often admired with envy the fine, light, nomadic life of maidens in their Arcadian life-segments ; easily do these *doves of passage* flutter into a strange family, and sew, and laugh, and visit there, with the daughters of the house, one or two months, and one takes the ingrafted shoot for a family twig ; on the other hand, we *household pigeons* are inhabitive and hard to transplant, and generally after a few days journey back again.

FANCY AND SICKNESS.
Titan, Cycle 66.

Phantasie und Krankheit sind die Eltern des luftigen Würgengels, der wie ein taubes Wetterleuchten sengend über alle Blüten der Jugend fliegt.

Fancy and sickness are the parents of the air-born destroying angel, who flies scorching, like a dumb heat-lightning, over all the blossoms of youth.

WHAT FATE DOES TO MAN.
Titan, Cycle 66.

Da sprach er edel von der Wüstenei des Lebens und vom Schicksal, das den Menschen wie den Vesuv zum Krater ausbrenne und dann wieder kühle, Auen darein säe und ihn wieder mit Feuer fülle — und vom einzigen Glück des hohlen Lebens, von der Liebe, und von der Verletzung, wenn das Geschick mit seinen Winden eine Blume reibend hin und her bewege und dadurch die grüne Rinde an der Erde durchschneide.

Nobly he spoke of life's wilderness, and of fate which burns out man, like Vesuvius, into a crater, and then again sows cool meadows therein, and fills it again with fire ; and of the only blessedness of this hollow life—love ; and of the injury inflicted, when fate with its winds sways and rubs a flower to and fro, and thereby cuts through the green skin against the earth.

A LOVING MAIDEN.
Titan, Cycle 71.

Ein liebendes Mädchen wird unbewußt kühner.

A loving maiden grows unconsciously more bold.

THE STAR OF LOVE.
Titan, Cycle 71.

Das Herz bedarf zu seinem Himmel nicht viel Platz und nicht viel Sterne daran, wenn nur der der Liebe aufgegangen.

The heart needs not for its heaven much space, nor many stars therein, if only the star of love has arisen.

A CONVULSIVE SMILE.
Titan, Cycle 80.

Der alte Ehemann verbreitete über sein Gesicht jenes zuckende Lächeln, das bei einigen Menschen der Zuckung des Korkholzes ähnlicht, welche das Anbeißen des Fisches ansagt.

The old bridegroom diffused over his face that convulsive smile which, with some men, resembles the convulsive quiver of the cork when it announces the bite of the fish.

REMEMBRANCES LAST LONGER THAN PRESENT REALITY.
Titan, Cycle 81.

Erinnerungen dauern länger als Gegenwart, wie ich Blüten

viele Jahre konserviret habe, aber keine Früchte. Ja, es gibt zarte weibliche Seelen, die sich nur in den Blüten des Wein= gartens der Freude berauschen, wie andere erst in den Beeren des Weinbergs.

Remembrances last longer than present reality, as I have con-served blossoms many years, but never fruits. Yes, there are tender female souls which intoxicate themselves only among the blossoms of the vineyard of joy, as others do only with the berries of the vinehill.

The Wound of Conscience.
Titan, Cycle 82.

O die Wunde des Gewissens wird keine Narbe, und die Zeit fühlt sie nicht mit ihrem Flügel, sondern hält sie blos offen mit ihrer Sense.

Oh, the wound of conscience is no scar, and Time cools it not with his wing, but merely keeps it open with his scythe.

What happens when Women wish to carry a Point.
Titan, Cycle 91.

Wenn Weiber etwas durchsetzen wollen, so werden sie, sobald die Hindernisse immer wiederkehren, am Ende blind und wild und wagen Alles.

When women wish to carry a point, and find hindrances con-stantly recurring, they grow at last blind and wild, and dare anything and everything.

The Wormwood of Conscience.
Titan, Cycle 93.

Der Wermuth des Gewissens verbittert sogar den Schmerz.

The wormwood of conscience embitters even sorrow.

Rome by Night.
Titan, Cycle 103.

Er stand an der Granitschale gegen das Colifeo gekehrt, dessen Gebirgsrücken hoch in Mondlicht stand, mit den tiefen Klüften, die ihm die Sense der Zeit eingehauen — scharf standen

die zerriſſenen Bogen von Nero's goldnem Hauſe wie mörde=
riſche Hauer darneben. — Der palatiniſche Berg grünte voll
Gärten und auf zerbrochnen Tempel=Dächern nagte der
blühende Todtenkranz aus Epheu, und noch glühten lebendige
Ranunkeln um eingeſenkte Kapitäler. — Die Quelle murmelte
geſchwätzig und ewig, und die Sterne ſchaueten feſt herunter
mit unvergänglichen Strahlen auf die ſtille Wahlſtatt, worüber
der Winter der Zeit gegangen, ohne einen Frühling nachzu=
führen — die feurige Weltſeele war aufgeflogen und der kalte
zerſtückte Rieſe lag umher, auseinandergeriſſen waren die
Rieſen=Speichen des Schwungrads, das einmal der Strom der
Zeiten ſelber trieb. — Und noch dazu goß der Mond ſein Licht
wie ätzendes Silberwaſſer auf die nackten Säulen und wollte
das Coliſeo und die Tempel und alles auflöſen in ihre eignen
Schatten!

He stood on the granite margin turning toward the Colosseum,
whose mountain-ridges of wall stood high in the moonlight, with
the deep gaps which had been hewn in them by the scythe of
Time.   Sharply stood the rent and jagged arches of Nero's golden
house hard by, like murderous cutlasses.   The Palatine hill lay
full of green gardens, and on crumbling temple-roofs the blooming
death-garland of ivy was gnawing, and living ranunculæ still
glowed around sunken capitals.   The fountain murmured bab-
blingly and eternally, and the stars gazed steadfastly down with
imperishable rays upon the still battlefield, over which the winter
of time had passed without bringing after it a spring ; the fiery
soul of the world had flown up, and the cold, crumbling giant lay
around ; torn asunder were the gigantic spokes of the fly-wheel
which once the very stream of ages drove.   And in addition to all
this, the moon shed down her light, like eating silver-water, upon
the naked columns, and would fain dissolve the Colosseum, and
the temples, and all, into their own shadows!

THE SUBLIME.

Titan, Cycle 104.

Steht nur einmal das Erhabne wirklich da, ſo verſchlingt
und vertilgt es eben ſeiner Natur nach alle kleinen Zierden um
ſich her.

When the sublime once really appears, it then, by its very nature,
absorbs and annihilates all little circumstantial ornaments.

WHAT YOUTH APPRECIATES BEST.
Titan, Cycle 104.

Daß überall der Jüngling gleich den Völkern das Erhabene besser empfinde und leichter finde als das Schöne, und daß der Geist des Jünglings vom Starken zum Schönen reife, wie der Körper desselben vom Schönen zum Starken.

That youth, like nations, always more easily found, and better appreciated, the sublime than the beautiful, and that the spirit of the young man ripened from strength to beauty, as his body ripens from beauty to strength.

AN ABSORBING IDEA IN MAN SHUTS OUT LOVE.
Titan, Cycle 104.

Die Weiber begreifen nicht genug, daß die Idee, wenn sie den männlichen Geist erfüllt und erhebt, ihn dann vor der Liebe verschließe und die Personen verdränge, indeß bei Weibern alle Ideen leicht zu Menschen werden.

Women do not sufficiently comprehend that an idea, when it fills and elevates man's mind, shuts it against love, and crowds out persons ; whereas with women all ideas easily become human beings.

MAN EXCITED TO EXERTION BY EXAMPLE.
Titan, Cycle 105.

O wer kann sich unwürdig und zusehend hinlegen vor die herrliche Bewegung der Welt? — Die Geister der Heiligen, der Helden, der Künstler, gehen dem lebendigen Menschen nach und fragen zornig : was bist Du?

Oh, who can stretch himself out in inglorious ease and contemplation before the magnificent stirring of the world? The spirits of saints, of heroes, of artists, follow after the living man, and ask indignantly, "What art thou?"

THE BATTLEFIELD.
Titan, Cycle 105.

Wo ist denn weiter auf der Erde die Stelle als auf dem Schlachtfeld, wo alle Kräfte, alle Opfer und Tugenden eines ganzen Lebens, in Eine Stunde gedrängt, in göttlicher Freiheit zusammenspielen mit tausend Schwester=Kräften und Opfern? Wo sind denn allen Kräften, von dem schnellsten Scharfblick an bis zu allen körperlichen Fertigkeiten und Abhärtungen, von der höchsten Großmuth und Ehre an bis auf die weichste Thräne herab, von jeder Verachtung des Körpers an bis zur tödtlichen Wunde hinauf, so alle Schranken aufgethan für einen wetteifernden Bund? Wiewohl eben darum der Spielraum aller Götter auch dem Larventanz aller Furien frei steht.

Where else on earth than on the battlefield is the place to be found in which all energies, all offerings, and virtues of a whole life, crowded into an hour, play together in divine freedom with thousand sister powers and offerings? Where else do all faculties—from the most rapid sharp-sightedness even to all bodily capacities of despatch and of endurance, from the highest magnanimity down to the tenderest pity, from all contempt of the body even up to the mortal wound—find the lists so freely open for a covenant-rivalry? although, for the very same reason, the play-room of all the gods stands open also to the masked dance of all the furies.

CRITICISM.
Titan, Cycle 105.

Die Kritik nimmt oft dem Baume Raupen und Blüthen mit einander.

Criticism often takes from the tree caterpillars and blossoms together.

JOYS AND SORROWS.
Titan, Cycle 105.

Die Rose blüht nicht ohne Dornen. Ja; wenn nur aber nicht die Dornen die Rose überlebten!

The rose does not bloom without thorns. True; but would that the thorns did not outlive the rose!

INTOXICATION OF MULTITUDE BY MULTITUDE.
Titan, Cycle 105.

Freiheit werde an Einem Tage so wenig gewonnen als ver= loren; wie schwache Individuen im Rausche gerade ihr Gegen=

theil wären, so geb' es auch wohl einen Rausch der Menge durch die Menge.

Freedom was as little gained as lost in a day; as weak individuals in a state of intoxication were exactly the opposite of themselves, so too there was a sort of intoxication of the multitude by multitude.

SELFISHNESS OF MAN.
Titan, Cycle 106.

Das sei so recht menschlich und üblich, fremde Schmerzen ungemein zu beklagen und redlich mitzufühlen, sie aber ohne Anstand zu schärfen, sobald das Geringste gethan werden solle.

That it is so really human and common to bewail the pains of others immoderately, and sympathise with them sincerely, and yet ungraciously to sharpen them so soon as the smallest thing must be done.

SUNRISE FROM ST. PETER'S DOME.
Titan, Cycle 107.

Plötzlich stand der Sonnengott auf dem schönen Gebirg, er richtete sich auf im Himmel und riß das Netz der Nacht vor der bedeckten Erde weg; da brannten die Obelisken und das Coliseum und Rom von Hügel zu Hügel, und auf der einsamen Campagna funkelte in vielfachen Windungen die gelbe Riesenschlange der Welt, die Tiber — alle Wolken zerliefen in die Tiefen des Himmels und goldnes Licht rann von Tusculum und von Tivoli, und von Nebenhügeln in die vielfarbige Ebene, an die zerstreueten Villen und Hütten, in die Zitronen- und Eichenwälder — im tiefen Westen wurde wieder das Meer wie am Abend, wenn es der heiße Gott besucht, voll Glanz, immer von ihm entzündet und sein ewiger Thau.

All at once the sun-god stood upon the fair ridge; he stood erect in heaven, and rent away the network of night from the covered earth; then burned the obelisks and the Colosseum, and Rome from hill to hill, and on the solitary Campagna sparkled in manifold windings the yellow giant snake of the world—the Tiber; all clouds dissipated themselves into the depths of heaven, and golden light ran from Tusculum and from Tivoli, and from the vinehills into the many-coloured plains, over the scattered villas and cottages, into the citron and oak groves; low in the far west the sea was again as at evening, when the hot god visits it, full of splendour, ever kindled by him, and became his eternal dews.

How a Man portrays his Character most vividly.
Titan, Cycle 110.

Nie zeichnet der Mensch den eignen Charakter schärfer als in seiner Manier, einen fremden zu zeichnen.

Never does a man portray his own character more vividly than in his manner of portraying another.

How a Man's Powers degenerate.
Titan, Cycle 110.

Entweder große Menschen (versetzte er) oder große Zwecke muß ein Mensch vor sich haben, sonst vergehen seine Kräfte, wie dem Magnet die seinigen, wenn er lange nicht nach den rechten Welt-Ecken gekehrt gelegen.

"A man must have," he replied, "either great men or great objects before him, otherwise his powers degenerate, as the magnet's do when it has lain for a long time without being turned towards the right corners of the world."

Individuality.
Titan, Cycle 111.

Individualität ist überall zu schonen und zu ehren als Wurzel jedes Guten.

Individuality is everywhere to be spared and respected as the root of everything good.

Sunset over the Pontian Islands.
Titan, Cycle 112.

Die Sonne stand schon zu einem großen Goldschild gewachsen, vom Himmel gehalten, über den Ponzischen Inseln und vergoldete das Blau derselben — die weiße Krone aus Felsen-Stacheln, Kapri, lag in Glut, und von Sorrento's bis Gaeta's Küsten war den Welt-Mauern dämmerndes Gold angeflogen — die Erde rollte mit ihrer Axe wie mit einer Spielwelle nahe an

der Sonne und schlug aus ihr Strahlen und Töne — seitwärts
lagerte sich versteckt der Riesen-Bote der Nacht auf das Meer,
der unendlich Schatte des Epomeo.

Jetzt berührte die Sonne ihr Meer und ein goldner Blitz
zitterte durch den nassen Aether umher — und sie wiegte sich
auf tausend feurigen Wellen-Flügeln — und sie zuckte und hing
liebesbrünstig, liebeglühend an dem Meere, und das Meer sog
brennend alle ihre Glut — Da warf es, als sie vergehen wollte,
die Decke eines unendlichen Glanzes über die erblassende
Göttin — — Dann wurd' es still auf der Welt — eine bewegliche Abendröthe überfloß mit Rosen-Oel alle Wogen — die
heiligen Untergangs-Inseln standen verklärt — die fernsten
Küsten traten heran und zeigten ihr Roth der Entzückung —
auf allen Höhen hingen Rosenkränze — der Epomeo glühte bis
zum Aether hinauf und auf dem ewigen Wolkenbaum, der aus
dem hohlen Vesuv aufwächset, verglomm im Gipfel der letzte
dünne Glanz.

The sun stood already, big as a great golden shield held from
heaven, above the Pontian islands, and gilded their blue; the
white, rocky crown of thorns, Capri, lay in glowing light, and
from Sorrento's coasts to Gaeta's, glimmering gold had shot up
along the walls of the world ; the earth rolled with her axis as
with a music-barrel, near the sun, and struck from the great
luminary rays and tones ; sidewards lay in ambush the giant
messenger of night, camped on the sea, the immense shadow of
Epomeo.

At this moment the sun touched the sea, and a golden lightning
darted trembling round through the humid ether—and he cradled
himself on a thousand fiery wave-wings, and he quivered and
hung, burning and glowing with love, on the sea—and the sea,
burning, drank all his glow. Then it threw, as if he was about
to pass away for ever, the veil of an infinite splendour over the
pale-growing god. Then it became still on the earth ; a floating
evening-redness overflowed with rose-oil all the waves—the holy
islands of sundown stood transfigured—the remotest coasts drew
near and showed their redness of delight—on all heights hung
rose-garlands—Epomeo glowed upward, even to the ether, and on
the eternal cloud-tree, which grows up out of the hollow Vesuvius,
went out on the summit the last thin glimmering of splendour.

THE GREAT EPIC GREEK FEATURE.

Titan, Cycle 114.

Immer dieselbe große durch dieß erhabene Land ziehende

ewige griechiſche Verſchmelzung des Ungeheuren mit dem
Heitern, der Natur mit den Menſchen, der Ewigkeit mit der
Minute. — Landhäuſer und eine lachende Ebene gegenüber der
ewigen Todesfackel — zwiſchen alten heiligen Tempelſäulen geht
ein luſtiger Tanz, der gemeine Mönch und der Fiſcher — die
Glut-Blöcke des Bergs thürmen ſich als Schutzwehr um Wein-
gärten und unter dem lebendigen Portici wohnt das hohle todte
Herkulanum — in's Meer ſind Lavaklippen gewachſen, und in die
Blumen ſchwarze Sturmbalken geworfen.

Ever the same great epic Greek feature running through this
sublime land (Italy)—the same blending of the monstrous with
the beautiful, of nature with men, of eternity with the moment;
country-houses and a laughing plain opposite to the eternal death-
torch (Vesuvius); between old holy temple-columns goes a merry
dance—the common monk and fisherman ; the glowing blocks of
the mountain tower up as a bulwark around vineyards, and
beneath the living Portici dwells the hollow, dead Herculaneum ;
lava-cliffs have grown out into the sea, and dark battering-rams
lie cast among the flowers.

VESUVIUS.

Titan, Cycle 114.

Im Veſuv ſei der Stall der unaufhörlich polternden Don-
nerpferde.

In Vesuvius was the stall of the incessantly-stamping thunder-
clouds.

THE CRATER OF VESUVIUS.

Titan, Cycle 114.

Endlich fand ich den Schlund dieſes Feuerlands, ein großes
glühendes Dampf-Thal wieder mit einem Berg — eine Land-
ſchaft von Kratern, eine Werkſtätte des jüngſten Tags — voll
zerbrochner Welt-Stücken, gefrorner geborſtener Höllenflüſſe —
ein ungeheuerer Scherbenberg der Zeit — aber unerſchöpflich,
unſterblich wie ein böſer Geiſt, und unter dem kalten reinen
Himmel ſich ſelber zwölf Donnermonate gebärend.

At last I found the throat of this land of fire—a great glowing
smoke-valley, containing another mountain within it—a land-
scape of craters, a workshop of the last day, full of fragments
of worlds, of frozen, burst hell-floods—an enormous potsherd of

time, but inexhaustible, immortal as an evil spirit, and under the cold, pure heaven, bringing forth to itself twelve thunder-months

EVERY NATURE PUTS FORTH ITS OWN FRUIT.
Titan, Cycle 116.

Es gibt nichts erbärmlicheres als einen Menschen, der sich durch dieß oder das zeigen will, was ihm selber groß, selten und ohne Verhältniß zu seinem Wesen vorkommt, und ihm daher gar nicht angehört. Jede Natur treibt ihre eigne Frucht und kann es nicht anders; aber ihr Kind kann ihr niemals groß erscheinen, sondern immer nur klein und gerecht.

There is nothing more pitiable than a man who will show himself by this or that which appears to himself great, rare, and without relation to his being, and therefore does not belong to him at all. Every nature puts forth its own fruit, and cannot do otherwise; but its child can never seem great to it, but always only small, or just as it should be.

LOOKING BACK UPON ONE'S YOUTH.
Titan, Cycle 117.

Der Mensch sieht bewegt in die tiefe Zeit hinunter, wo seine Lebensspindel fast noch nackt ohne Faden umlief; denn sein Anfang gränzt näher als die Mitte an sein Ende, und die aus- und einschiffende Küste unsers Lebens hängt in's dunkle Meer.

Man looks with emotion into the far, low-lying time, when the spindle of his life ran round as yet almost naked without threads; for his beginning borders more nearly upon his end than the middle, the outward-bound and the homeward-bound coasts of our life hang over into the dark sea.

A REAL HATRED IN A GOOD HEART.
Titan, Cycle 120.

Hart und schauerlich tritt, wie ein neues wunderbares Raubthier hinter dem Gitter, zum erstenmal ein rechter, wenn auch waffenloser Haß, vor ein gutes Herz.

With a hard and horrible aspect, like a new and extraordinary beast of prey behind the grating, does a real though unarmed hatred present itself for the first time before a good heart.

EVERY MAN HAS A RAINY CORNER OF HIS LIFE.

Titan, Cycle 123.

Jeder Menſch (ſagt' er erzürnt) hat eine Regen=Ecke ſeines Lebens, aus der ihm das ſchlimme Wetter nachzieht.

"Every man," said he, angrily, "has a rainy corner of his life, out of which foul weather proceeds, and follows after him."

A SECRET.

Titan, Cycle 123.

Wer den kleinſten Theil eines Geheimniſſes hingibt, hat den andern nicht mehr in der Gewalt.

He who gives up the smallest part of a secret has the rest no longer in his power.

VOLUPTUARIES.

Titan, Cycle 125.

Lüſtlinge halten es unter vielen edlen Frauen, gedrückt von deren vielſeitigen ſcharfen Beobachtungen, nie lange aus, obwohl leichter bei einer allein, weil ſie dieſe zu verſtricken hoffen.

Voluptuaries can never hold out long among *many* noble women, tormented as they are by their many-sided, sharp observations, although they can more easily with one, because they hope to ensnare her.

MUSIC.

Titan, Cycle 125.

Daß ſie alle an Muſik gewöhnte, dieſen rechten Mondſchein in jedem Lebens=Dunkel; „ohne Poeſie und Kunſt (ſetzte ſie dazu) vermooſe und verholze der Geiſt im irdiſchen Klima."

That she trained all to music—that real moonlight in every gloomy night of life. "Without poesy and art," she added, "the spirit grows weary and wooden in this earthly clime."

CHEERFULNESS ON THE FACE.

Titan, Cycle 125.

Nichts ſchöneres gebe es als Heiterkeit auf einem alten Geſicht,

T

und unter Landleuten sei sie immer das Zeichen eines wohl und fromm geführten Lebens.

There is nothing more beautiful than cheerfulness on an old face ; and among country people it is always the sign of a well-egulated and pious life.

The Country Man.
Titan, Cycle 125.

Nur der Landmann allein ist so glücklich (sagte sie), daß er in allen arkadischen Verhältnissen seiner Kindheit fortlebt. Der Greis sieht nichts um sich als Geräthschaften und Arbeiten, die er auch als Kind gesehen und getrieben. Endlich geht er jenen Garten drüben hinauf und schläft aus.

"Only the country man is so fortunate," said she, "as to live on in all the Arcadian relations of his childhood. The old man sees nothing around him but implements and labours, which as a child he also saw and plied. At last he goes up into that garden (the churchyard), and sleeps it out."

God's Acre.
Titan, Cycle 125.

Dort ist der einzige Ort (sagte Idoine), wo der Mensch mit sich und andern einen ewigen Frieden schließet, sagte so schön zu mir ein französischer Geistlicher.

"There is the only place," said Idoine, "where man concludes an eternal peace with himself and others, as a French clergyman so beautifully said to me."

Echo from a Churchyard.
Titan, Cycle 125.

Nun gab das Echo — das Mondlicht des Klangs — wieder Töne wie Todtenlieder aus dem Todten=Chor; und es war, als sängen die vereinigten Schatten sie in ihrer stillen Woche unter der Erde nach, als regte sich der Leichenschleier auf der weißen Lippe und aus den letzten Höhlen tönte ein hohles Leben wieder. Das Singen hörte auf, Alphörner fingen auf den Bergen an. Da ging wieder das Nachspiel des Tonspiels feurig herüber, als spielten die Abgeschiednen noch hinter der

Bruſtwehr des Grabhügels und kleideten ſich ein in Nachklänge. Alle Menſchen tragen Todte oder Sterbende in der Bruſt; auch die drei Jungfrauen; Töne ſind ſchimmernd zurückflatternde Gewänder der Vergangenheit und erregen damit das Herz zu ſehr.

Now did the echo, the moonlight of sound, give back tones like dirges from the funeral choir ; and it was as if the united shades of the departed sang them over in their holy-week under the ground—as if the corpse-veil stirred on the white lip, and out of the last hollows sounded again a hollow life. The singing ceased ; Alpine horns began on the mountains, then the echo of the concert came over again in enchanting tones, as if the departed still played behind the breastwork of the grave-mound, and rehabited themselves in echoed tones. All men bear dead or dying ones in their breast ; so did the three maidens. Tones are the garments of the past fluttering back with a glimmer, and they excite the heart too much thereby.

A Busied Heart.

Titan, Cycle 125.

Ein beſchäftigtes Herz iſt wie ein umgeſchwungenes Gefäß mit Waſſer; man halt' es ſtill, ſo fließet es über.

A busied heart is like a vessel of water swung round ; hold it still and it runs over.

Love without Marriage.

Titan, Cycle 125.

Die Liebe ohne Ehe gleicht einem Zugvogel, der ſich auf einen Maſtbaum ſetzt, der ſelber zieht, ich lobe mir einen hübſchen grünen Wurzelbaum, der da bleibt und ein Neſt annimmt.

Love without marriage is like a bird of passage, who seats himself upon a mast which itself moves along. I praise, for my part, a fine green rooted tree which stays there, and admits a nest.

Some Men like Glass.

Titan, Cycle 135.

Viele Menſchen gleichen dem Glas, glatt und geſchliffen und ſtumpf, ſo lange als man ſie nicht zerbricht, dann verflucht ſchneidend und jeder Splitter ſticht.

Many men resemble glass—smooth, and slippery, and flat, so long as one does not break them, but *then* cursedly cutting, and every splinter stings.

A Free Soul never grows Old.

Titan, Cycle 140.

O nur eine freie Seele wird nicht alt!

Oh, only a free soul never grows old!

Time has Delicate Little Waves.

Titan, Cycle 140.

Die Zeit hat weiche, kleine Wellen, aber am Ende wird doch der eckigste, schärffte Kiesel darin glatt und stumpf.

Time has delicate little waves, but the sharpest-cornered pebble, after all, becomes smooth and blunt therein at last.

The Fates and Furies.

Titan, Cycle 140.

Die Parzen und Furien ziehen auch mit verbundnen Händen um das Leben, wie die Grazien und die Sirenen.

The Fates and Furies, too, glide with linked hands over life, as well as the Graces and Sirens.

Actions give Strength to Life.

Titan, Cycle 145.

Nur Thaten geben dem Leben Stärke, nur Maß ihm Reiz.

Only actions give life strength, only moderation gives it a charm.

What is the Charm of Domestic Discourse.

Hesperus, 1.

Aber dieses Wiederholen der alten Geschichte ist eben der schönste Reiz des häuslichen Gesprächs. Wenn wir süße Gedanken uns selber oft ohne Langweile wiederholen können, warum soll sie nicht auch der andere öfters in uns erwecken dürfen?

But this repetition of the old story is just the fairest charm of domestic discourse. If we can often repeat to ourselves sweet thoughts without ennui, why shall not another be suffered to awaken them within us still oftener?

SPRING.

Hesperus, 1.

Der Frühling, der Raphael der Norderde, ftand ſchon draußen und überdeckte alle Gemächer unſers Vatikans mit feinen Gemälden.

Spring, the Raphael of the northern earth, stood already out of doors, and covered all apartments of our Vatican with his pictures.

THE WISE MAN AND THE FOOL.

Hesperus, 2.

Es ift auf der Erde ſchwer, Tugend, Freiheit und Glück zu erwerben, aber es ift noch ſchwerer, ſie auszubreiten; der Weiſe bekömmt alles von ſich, der Thor alles von andern. Der Freie muß den Sklaven erlöſen, der Weiſe für den Thoren denfen, der Glückliche für den Unglücklichen arbeiten.

It is hard in this world to win virtue, freedom, and happiness, but still harder to diffuse them. The wise man gets everything from himself, the fool from others. The freeman must release the slave—the philosopher think for the fool—the happy man labour for the unhappy.

TO EXPLAIN ONESELF GUARDEDLY.

Hesperus, 2.

Denn wenn ſich jemand verſteckt erklärt, ſo ift nichts un= höflicher als eine neue — Frage.

For when any one explains himself guardedly, nothing is more uncivil than to put a new question.

FEATHERS OF LOVE.

Hesperus, 3.

War's einem ſolchen Herzen wie ſeinem, das in den Federn der Liebe wiegend hing, noch nöthig, daß es in jedem zerſägten Fenſterſtock, in jedem glatten Pflaſterſteinchen, in jeder vom

Regen gebohrten vertieften Arbeit auf dem Hausthürstein seine Knabenjahre musivisch abgebildet sah, und daß er in denselben Gegenständen Alter und Neuheit genoß?

To a heart like his, that hung rocking in the feathers of love, was there any need that it should see in every notched window-sill, in every smooth pavement-pebble, in every round hole drilled by the rain in the door-step, his boyhood's years mosaically pictured, and that he should enjoy in the same objects age and novelty?

Hood says, somewhat to the same effect—

> " My spirit flew in feathers then,
> That is so heavy now."

WORDS WINGED BY VIRTUE.
Hesperus, 4.

Blos Worte, von Tugend und Empfindung beflügelt, sind die Bienen, die den Samenstaub der Liebe in solchen Fällen von einer Seele in die andre tragen. Eine solche bessere Liebe aber wird vom kleinsten unmoralischen Zusatz vernichtet; wie könnte sie sich zusammensetzen und heraufläutern in einem besubelten Herzen, das der Hochverrath gegen einen Freund erfüllte?

Only words winged by virtue and sensibility are the bees which, in such cases, carry the pollen of love from one soul into another. But such a love, of the better kind, is annihilated by the least immoral alloy. How could it form and filter up in a defiled heart, filled with high treason against a friend?

FALSEHOOD.
Hesperus, 4.

Je mehr Schwäche, je mehr Lüge; die Kraft geht gerade; jede Kanonenkugel, die Höhlen oder Gruben hat, geht krumm. Schwächlinge müssen lügen.

The more weakness, the more falsehood; strength goes straight; every cannon-ball that has in it hollows and holes goes crooked. Weaklings must lie.

BROTHERS AND SISTERS.
Hesperus, 4.

Nichts ist fataler als ein Nest, worin lauter Brüder oder

lauter Schwestern sitzen; gemischt zu einer bunten Reihe muß das Nest seyn, Brüder und Schwestern nämlich schichtweise gepackt, so daß ein ehrlicher pastor fido kommen und nach dem Bruder fragen kann, wenn er blos nach der Schwester aus ist; und so muß auch die Liebhaberin eines Bruders durchaus und noch nöthiger eine Schwester haben, deren Freundin sie ist, und die der Henkel und Schaft am Bruder wird.

Nothing is more annoying than a nest in which there sit none but brothers or none but sisters; the nest must be shaken up into a mixed and motley gradation—that is to say, of brothers and sisters packed in layers, so that an honest *pastor fido* can come and ask after the brother, when he is only on the look-out for the sister; and so too must the girl who loves a brother, absolutely and by stronger necessity, have a sister, whose friend she is, and who may be hook and handle to the brother.

The Conversation of Fine People.

Hesperus, 4.

Feinen Leuten war, die (trotz der spitzigsten Verhältnisse) dem Gespräche vier Schmetterlingflügel geben, damit er — als Gegenspiel der klebenden Raupe, die sich in jedem Dorn aufspießet — ohne Getöse und in kleinen Bogen über Stacheln fliege und nur auf Blüten falle.

Fine people who, despite the most angular relations, give to conversation four butterflies' wings, that it may, in contrast to the clinging caterpillar, who impales himself on every thorn, fly without noise, and in little curves, over all prickles, and alight only on blossoms.

Good and Bad Men.

Hesperus, 4.

Gute Menschen können sich leichter in schlimme hineindenken, als diese in jene.

Good men can more easily see into bad ones than the latter can into the former.

Life on the Wing.

Hesperus, 4.

Nein, unter diesem Leben im Flug sollte doch das Ding, das

ſo prestissimo hinſchießt aus einem Regenſchauer in den andern
und von Gewölke zu Gewölke, doch nicht in Einem fort den
Schnabel auffperren zum Gelächter.

No; amidst this life on the wing, a thing which darts so *prestissimo* out of one rain-shower into another, and from cloud to cloud,
should not keep its bill open on the stretch for one continued peal
of laughter.

There is a beautiful passage in Bede's "History," where the
Northumbrian prince compares man's life to the flight of the
swallow through the lighted hall from darkness to darkness.

MAN'S LIFE.

Hesperus, 4.

Der Menſch hat hier dritthalb Minuten, eine zu lächeln —
eine zu ſeufzen — und eine halbe zu lieben; denn mitten in
dieſer Minute ſtirbt er.

Man has here two and a half minutes—one to smile, one to sigh,
and half a one to love; for in the midst of this minute he dies.

THE GRAVE.

Hesperus, 4.

Aber das Grab iſt nicht tief, es iſt der leuchtende Fußtritt
eines Engels, der uns ſucht. Wenn die unbekannte Hand den
letzten Pfeil an das Haupt des Menſchen ſendet; ſo bückt er
vorher das Haupt und der Pfeil hebt blos die Dornenkrone von
ſeinen Wunden ab.*

* Vielleicht eine Anſpielung auf das für die Phantaſie liebliche
Mährchen, daß in Neapel ein Crucifix, da darin Alphons 1439 belagert
wurde, den Kopf vor einer Kanonkugel neigte, die alſo nur die Dornenkronenahm — *Voyage d'un François*, t. vi. p. 303.

But the grave is not deep, it is the gleaming footmark of an
angel who seeks us. When the unknown hand sends the last
arrow at the head of man he bends, and the arrow merely takes
off the crown of thorns from his wounds.*

* An allusion, perhaps, to the legend, so lovely to the fancy, that a
crucifix in Naples, when Alfonso was besieged there in 1439, bowed its
head before a cannon-ball, which consequently took off only the crown of
thorns.

WHAT THE GOOD OF A STATE CONSISTS OF.

Hesperus, 6.·

Das Glück eines Staates, wie eines Menschen, besteht nicht im Reichthum, sondern im Gebrauche des Reichthums, nicht in seinem kaufmännischen, sondern moralischen Werthe — daß die Ausscheurung des alterthümlichen Sauerteigs und unsre meisten Institutionen und Novellen und Edicte nur die fürstlichen Gefälle, nicht die Moralität zu erhöhen suchten, und daß man begehre, die Laster und die Unterthanen brächten, wie die alten Juden, ihre Opfer nur in Einer Stadt, nämlich in der Residenzstadt, daß die Menschheit von jeher sich die Nägel nur an den nackten Händen, nicht an den verhüllten Füßen, die oft darüber selber herunterkamen, beschnitten habe — daß Aufwand= und Prachtgesetze den Fürsten selber noch nöthiger wären, wenigstens den höchsten Ständen, als den tiefsten — daß **Rom** seinen vielen Feiertagen viel von seiner Vaterlandliebe verdanke.

The good of a state, as of a man, consisted not in riches, but in the use of riches—not in its commercial, but in its moral worth ; that the sweeping out of the ancient leaven, and most of our institutions, and pandects, and edicts, had for their objects only to enhance princely incomes, not morality ; and that one wanted to have vices and subjects, like the old Jews, bring their offerings only in one city—namely, the residence city ; that humanity, from time immemorial, had cut its nails only on its bare *hands*, not on its covered *feet*, which often themselves decayed on that account ; that economical and sumptuary laws were still more needful to princes themselves, at least to the highest classes, than to the lowest ; that Rome owed to her many holidays much of her patriotism.

THE SHELL OF HOURS THAT HAVE FLOWN AWAY.

Hesperus, 6.

Die Menschen behalten einen fremden Lebenslauf besser, als den eignen: wahrhaftig, wir achten eine Geschichte, die einmal die unsrige war, und welche die Hülse der verflognen Stunden ist, viel zu wenig, und doch werden die Zeittropfen, durch die wir schwimmen, erst in der Ferne der Erinnerung zum Regen= bogen des Genusses. Die Männer wissen, wann alle Kaiser geboren und alle Philosophen gestorben sind — die Weiber wissen aus der Chronologie blos das, wann ihre Männer, die ihre Regenten und klassischen Autoren sind, beides thaten.

Mankind keep the run of another's life better than of their own; truly we make altogether too little account of a history which once was ours, and which is the shell of hours that have flown away, and yet the drops of time, through which we swim, do only in the distance of memory form the rainbow of enjoyment. Men know when all emperors were born, and all philosophers died; women know by reckoning time only this—when their husbands, who are *their* regents and classic authors, underwent both.

Example.
Hesperus, 6.

Nicht das Geschrei, sagt ein chinesischer Autor, sondern der Aufflug einer wilden Ente treibt die Heerde zur Folge und zum Nachfliegen.

"Not the cry, but the flight of a wild duck," says a Chinese author, "leads the flock to fly and follow."

A Day full of Hopes.
Hesperus, 6.

Ach! diesen schönen stillen Tag faßte ein goldner Horizont der unendlichen Hoffnung ein und ein Ring aus Morgenroth. — Jetzo ist der Tag dahin, und der Horizont hinab, und blos das Gerippe noch da: der Gitterstuhl.

Ah! this tranquil and lovely day was set in a golden horizon of infinite hope, and a ring of morning-red. Now the day is gone, and the horizon sunk, and only the skeleton remains there—the latticed pew.

The Morning, Noonday, and Evening of Life.
Hesperus, 6.

Aber wenn wir schon jetzt in den Mittagstunden des Lebens so denken und seufzen: wie wird uns nicht am Abend, wo der Mensch seine Blumenblätter zusammenlegt und unfenntlich wird wie andre Blumen, am Abend, wo wir unten am Horizont in Westen stehen und auslöschen, wird uns da nicht, wenn wir uns umwenden und den kurzen mit ertretenen Hoffnungen

bebeckten Weg überschauen, wird dann uns der Garten der
Kindheit, der in Often, tief an unserm Aufgange und noch
unter einem alten blaffen Rothe liegt, nicht noch holder an=
blicken, noch magischer anschimmern, aber auch noch weicher
machen? — Und darauf legt sich der Mensch nicht weit vom
Grabe nieder auf die Erbe, und hofft hienieden nicht mehr.

But if we now, even in the noonday hours of life, think and
sigh thus, how much more at evening, when man folds up his
flower-leaves, and becomes undistinguishable like other flowers—
at evening, when we stand low in the western horizon, and go
out—then, when we turn round and survey the short road
strewed with trampled-out hopes—oh! then, how much more
sweetly will it not look upon us—the garden of childhood lying
in the east, low down near the place of our rising, and still
suffused with an old, pale redness—how much more magically
will it gleam on us, and yet how much more will it affect us to
tenderness! And thereupon man lays himself down on the earth
not far from the grave, and hopes here below no more.

VIGOROUS MEN AND COLD NATURES.
Hesperus, 7.

Die Jahre geben den stürmischen überkräftigen Menschen
eine schönere Harmonie des Herzens, aber den verfeinerten
kalten Menschen nehmen sie mehr, als sie geben; jene Kraft=
herzen gleichen den englischen Gärten, die das Alter immer
grüner, voller, belaubter macht; hingegen der Weltmann
wird, wie ein französischer, durch die Jahre mit ausgedorrten
und entstellten Aesten überdeckt.

Years give to stormy, over-vigorous men a finer harmony of the
heart, but from refined, cold natures they take more than they
give. Those strong hearts resemble English gardens, which age
always makes greener, fuller, more leafy ; whereas the man of the
world, like a French one, is covered by years with dried-up and
disfigured boughs.

THE JOY OF A MOTHER.
Hesperus, 7.

In der Natur ist keine Freude so erhaben=rührend, als die
Freude einer Mutter über das Glück eines Kindes.

No joy in nature is so sublimely affecting as the joy of a mother
at the good fortune of a child.

The Setting Sun.

Hesperus, 7.

In die Wolfen floß das Abend=Blut der verfinkenden Sonne, wie in's Meer das Blut feiner in der Tiefe fterbenden Riefen. Das lockere Gewölke langte nicht zu, den Himmel zu decken; es fchwamm um den Mond herum, und ließ fein bleiches Silber aus den Schlacken blicken.

The evening-blood of the sinking sun flowed into the clouds, as into the sea sinks the blood of its giants dying in its depths. The porous cloud did not avail to hide the heavens; it swam round about the moon, and let her pale silver glisten from amidst the slags.

Thoughts.

Hesperus, 8.

Gedanken vielleicht, die aber wie Feldmäuse der Seele unter die Füße fpringen und fich wie Ottern anlegen.

Thoughts perhaps, which, however, like field-mice of the soul, leap under the feet, and stick like adders.

A Scholar.

Hesperus, 8.

Ein Gelehrter hat feine lange Weile.

A scholar has no ennui.

Our Study.

Hesperus, 8.

In diefer Brautkammer des Geiftes (das find unfere Studir= ftuben), in diefem Konzertfaal der fchönften aus allen Zeiten und Plätzen verfammelten Stimmen, hinderten ihn die äftheti= fchen und philofophifchen Luftbarfeiten faft an ihrer Wahl.

In this bridal-chamber of the mind (such are our study-chambers), in this concert-hall of the finest voices gathered from all times and places—the æsthetic and philosophical enjoyments almost overpowered his faculty of choice.

The Seasons of Life.

Hesperus, 9.

Ach die Zeiten der Liebe rollen nicht zurück, sond.rn etwa weiter hinab.

Ah! the seasons of life roll not back, but onward, downward, for ever.

Secret Grief.

Hesperus, 12.

Denn die Wunden, die aufgedeckt werden können, sind nicht tief; der Schmerz, den ein menschenfreundliches Auge finden, eine weiche Hand lindern kann, ist nur klein. — Aber der Gram, den der Freund nicht sehen darf, weil er ihn nicht nehmen kann, dieser Gram, der zuweilen in's beglückte Auge in Gestalt eines plötzlichen Tropfens aufsteigt, den das weg= gewandte Angesicht vertilgt, hängt überdeckt schwerer und schwerer am Herzen, und zieht es endlich los und fällt mit ihm unter die heilende Erde hinab: so werden die Eisenkugeln an den über dem Meer gestorbnen Menschen angeknüpft und sie sinken mit ihm schneller in sein großes Grab.

For those wounds which can be disclosed are not deep; that grief which a humane eye can discover, a soft hand alleviate, is but small; but the woe which a friend must not see, because he cannot take it away—that woe which sometimes rises into the eye in the midst of blessedness, in the form of sudden trickle which the averted face smothers,—this hangs in secret more and more heavily on the heart, and at last breaks it, and goes down with it under the healing sod. So are iron balls tied to man when he dies on the sea, and they sink with him more quickly into his vast grave.

The Greatest Hatred is Quiet.

Hesperus, 12.

Der größte Haß ist, wie die größte Tugend und die schlimm= sten Hunde, still.

The greatest hatred, like the greatest virtue and the worst dogs, is quiet.

The really Modest.

Hesperus, 12.

Wenn jemand bescheiden bleibt, nicht beim Lobe, sondern beim Tadel, dann ist er's.

When any one remains modest, not after praise but after censure, then he is really so.

Passion.

Hesperus, 12.

Die Leidenschaft macht die besten Beobachtungen und die elendesten Schlüsse. Sie ist ein Fernrohr, dessen Feld desto heller, je enger es ist.

Passion makes the best observations and the most wretched conclusions. It is a telescope, whose field is so much the brighter as it is narrower.

How One learns Taciturnity best.

Hesperus, 12.

Man lernt Verschwiegenheit am meisten unter Menschen, die keine haben — und Plauderhaftigkeit unter Verschwiegenen.

One learns taciturnity best among people who have none, and loquacity among the taciturn.

Self-Knowledge is the Road to Virtue.

Hesperus, 12.

Wenn Selbstkenntniß der Weg zur Tugend ist: so ist Tugend noch mehr der Weg zur Selbstkenntniß. Eine gebesserte gereinigte Seele wird von der kleinsten moralischen Giftart wie gewisse Edelsteine von jeder andern trübe, und jetzo nach der Besserung merkt sie erst, wie viele Unreinigkeiten sich noch in allen Winkeln aufhalten.

If self-knowledge is the road to virtue, so is virtue still more the road to self-knowledge. An amended and purified soul is darkened by the least moral poison, as certain precious stones are by every other; and now, after the amendment, one observes for the first time how many impurities still lurk in all corners.

MELODY OF A SONG FROM CHILDHOOD.

Hesperus, 13.

Sie zog tief in sein Herz hinein, wie die Melodie eines Liedes, das aus der Kindheit heraufklingt.

It went deep into his heart, like the melody of a song that sounds up from childhood.

THE WHOLE CREATION ONLY AN ÆOLIAN HARP.

Hesperus, 14.

Da es nur wenige Seelen gibt, die wissen, wie weit die Harmonie der äußern Natur mit unserer reicht, und wie sehr das ganze All nur Eine Aeolsharpe ist, mit längern und kürzern Saiten, mit langsamen und schnellern Bebungen, vor einem göttlichen Hauche ruhend.

As there are but few souls that know how far the harmony of outward nature with our own reaches, and in how very great a degree the whole creation is but an Æolian harp, with longer or shorter strings, with slower and swifter vibrations—passive before a divine breath.

Coleridge (*The Æolian Harp*) says—

> " And what if all of animated nature
> Be but organic harps diversely framed,
> That tremble into thought as o'er them sweeps,
> Plastic and vast, one intellectual breeze,
> At once the soul of each and god of all?"

THE RELIGIOUS AND WORLDLY MAN CONTRASTED.

Hesperus, 14.

Wie verschieden ist ein Spaziergang mit einem frommen Menschen, und einer mit einer gemeinen Weltseele! Die Erde kam ihm heilig vor, erst aus den Händen des Schöpfers entfallen — ihm war, als ging' er in einem über uns hängenden überblumten Planeten. Emanuel zeigte ihm Gott und die Liebe überall abgespiegelt, aber überall verändert, im Lichte, in den Farben, in der Tonleiter der lebendigen Wesen, in der Blüte und in der Menschenschönheit, in den Freuden der Thiere, in den Gedanken der Menschen und in den Kreisen der Welten;

— denn entweder ift alles ober nichts fein Schattenbild; — fo malt die Sonne ihr Bild auf alle Wefen, groß im Weltmeere, bunt in Thautropfen, flein auf die Menfchen-Netzhaut, als Nebenfonne in die Wolfe, roth auf den Apfel, filbern auf den Strom, fiebenfarbig in den fallenden Regen und fchimmernd über den ganzen Mond und über ihre Welten.

How different is a walk with a religious man from one with a vulgar, worldly soul! The earth appeared to him holy, just fallen from the hands of the Creator ; it was to him as if he were walking in a planet hanging over us, and clothed with flowers. Emanuel showed him God and love everywhere mirrored, but everywhere transformed—in the light, in colours, in the scale of living creatures, in the blossom, and in human beauty, in the pleasures of animals, in the thoughts of men, and in the circles of worlds, for either everything or nothing is his shadow. So the sun paints its image on all creatures—great in the ocean, many-coloured in the dewdrop, small on the human retina, as mock-sun on the cloud, red on the apple, silvery on the stream, seven-coloured in the falling rain, and gleaming over the whole moon, and over all its other worlds.

What is Noblest in Man conceals itself.

Hesperus, 14.

Das Höchfte und Edelfte im Menfchen verbirgt fich und ift ohne Nutzen für die thätige Welt (wie die höchften Berge feine Gewächfe tragen), und aus der Kette fchöner Gedanken können fich nur einige Glieder als Thaten ablöfen.

What is highest and noblest in man conceals itself, and is without use for the practical world (as the highest mountains bear no herbage) ; and out of the chain of fine thoughts only some members can be detached as actions.

Sorrows are like Thunder-Clouds.

Hesperus, 14.

Die Leiden find wie die Gewitterwolfen: in der Ferne fehen fie fchwarz aus, über uns faum grau.

Sorrows are like thunder-clouds—in the distance they look black, over our heads hardly grey.

THE DREAM OF LIFE WHEN IT IS OVER.

Hesperus, 14.

Wie traurige Träume eine angenehme Zukunft bedeuten: so werd' es mit dem so oft quälenden Traume des Lebens seyn, wenn er aus sei.

As sad dreams betoken a glad future, so may it be with the so-often-tormenting dream of life when it is over.

STRONG FEELINGS HOLD SWAY ONLY UP TO A CERTAIN HOUR.

Hesperus, 14.

Alle unsere starken Gefühle regieren wie die Gespenster nur bis auf eine gewisse Stunde, und wenn ein Mensch immer zu sich sagte: diese Leidenschaft, dieser Schmerz, diese Entzückung ist in drei Tagen gewiß aus deiner Seele heraus: so würd' er immer ruhiger und stiller werden.

All our strong feelings, like ghosts, hold sway only up to a certain hour; and if a man would always say to himself, This passion, this grief, this rapture, will in three days certainly be gone from this soul—then would he become more and more tranquil and composed.

SPRING RENEWS EVERYTHING EXCEPT MAN.

Hesperus, 14.

Vergeblich sah ich den heitern Frühling an, der jeden Tag neue Farben, neue Mücken, neue Blumen aus der Erde zieht — ich wurde nur betrübter, da er alles verjüngt, aber den Menschen nicht.

In vain did I look upon the sparkling spring, which draws every day new colours, new insects, new flowers, out of the earth. I only grew sadder, since it makes everything young, but not man.

Michael Bruce says—

" Now spring returns, but not to me returns
The vernal joy my better years have known."

PERFECT SINCERITY COMPORTS ONLY WITH VIRTUE.

Hesperus, 14.

Aber die vollendete Aufrichtigkeit steht nur der Tugend an:

U

ber Menſch, in bem Argwohn unb Finſterniß iſt, leg' immer
ſeinem Buſen Nachtſchrauben unb Nachtriegel an, ber Böſe
verſchon' uns mit ſeiner Leichenöffnung, unb wer keine Himmel;
thür' an ſich zu öffnen hat, laſſe bas Höllenthor zu !

But perfect sincerity comports only with virtue. Let the man
in whom suspicion and darkness dwell by all means apply to his
bosom night-screws and night-bolts—let the bad man spare us his
opening of coffins ; and whoso has no heaven's door about him to
open, let him keep the hell-gate shut!

THE EARTH OF OUR CHILDHOOD.
Hesperus, 15.

Gleichwohl war ihm bie Erbe ein geliebter Ort, eine ſchöne
Wieſe zu unſern erſten Kinberſpielen, unb er hing bieſer Mutter
unſers erſten Lebens noch mit ber Liebe an, womit bie Braut
ben Abenb voll kinblicher Erinnerungen an ber Bruſt ber
geliebten Mutter zubringt, eh' ſie am Morgen bem Herzen bes
Bräutigams entgegen zieht.

And yet the earth was to him a beloved place, a fair meadow
for the earliest plays of childhood ; and he still hung upon the
mother of our first life with the love wherewith the bride spends
the evening, full of childish remembrances. on the bosom of her
beloved mother, before on the morrow she goes to meet the
bridegroom of her heart.

A SECRET TOLD TO THE FAIR SEX.
Hesperus, 16.

Kenner ſagen, jebes Geheimniß, bas man einer Schönen
ſage, ſei ein Heftpflaſter, bas mit ihr zuſammenleime unb bas
oft ein zweites Geheimniß gebäre.

Connoisseurs say that every secret he tells to one of the fair
sex is a sticking-plaster, which attaches him to her, and often
begets a second secret.

THE SWEETEST MINUTES OF A VISIT.
Hesperus, 16.

Die ſchönſten Minuten in einem Beſuche ſinb bie, bie ſein
Enbe wieber verſchieben ; bie allerſchönſten, wenn man ſchon
ben Stock ober ben Fächer in ber Hanb hat, unb boch nicht
geht.

The sweetest minutes of a visit are those which once more postpone its close; the sweetest of all, those in which one already has cane or fan in hand, and yet does not go.

IMMORAL NIGHT-LIFE.

Hesperus, 16.

Denn unmoralisches Nachtleben macht Züge und Farbe noch widerlicher als das längste Krankenlager.

For immoral night-life makes features and complexion still more repulsive than the longest confinement to the sick-bed.

LEAVE-TAKING.

Hesperus, 16.

Kalte selbstsüchtige und bequeme Personen vermeiden das Abschiednehmen, so wie unpoetische von zu heftigen Empfindungen; weibliche hingegen, die sich alle Schmerzen durch Sprechen, und poetische, die sich alle durch Phantasiren mildern, suchen es.

Cold, self-seeking, comfortable persons avoid leave-taking, just as unpoetic ones of too intense sensibilities do ; women, on the contrary, who alleviate all their sorrows by talking, and people of poetic temperaments, who relieve all theirs by fantasying, court it.

BUSINESS-PEOPLE AND COURT-PEOPLE.

Hesperus, 17.

Geschäftsleute bekümmern sich um keinen Gesprächs- und keinen Briefstyl; aber bei Hofleuten ist die Zunge die Pulsader ihres welken Lebens, die Spiral- und Schwungfeder ihrer Seelen; alle sind geborne Kunstrichter, die auf nichts als Wendung, Ausdruck, Feuer und Sprache sehen.

Business-people never trouble themselves about any conversational or epistolary style : but with court-people the tongue is the artery of their withered life, the spiral-spring and flag-feather of their souls; they are all born critics, who look at nothing but fine turns, expression, fire, and speech.

TOO MUCH LAUGHING.

Hesperus, 19.

Niemand wird tiefer traurig, als wer zu viel lächelt.

No one is more profoundly sad than he who laughs too much.

Sleep and Death.

Hesperus, 20.

Der lange Schlaf des Todes schließt unsere Narben zu, und der kurze des Lebens unsere Wunden. Der Schlaf ist die Hälfte der Zeit, die uns heilt.

The long sleep of death closes our *scars,* and the short sleep of life our *wounds.* Sleep is the half of time which heals us.

Childhood and Old Age.

Hesperus, 20.

An den Menschen sind vorn und hinten, wie an den Büchern, zwei leere weiße Buchbinderblätter — Kindheit und Greisenalter.

There are in man, in the beginning and at the end, as in books, two blank bookbinder's leaves—childhood and old age.

Fools at Great Parties.

Hesperus, 21.

Ueberhaupt, so oft ich Narren in großen Partieen studiren wollte, sah ich mich ordentlicher Weise nach einer großen Schönheit um; — diese umfassen sie wie Wespen eine Obstfrau.

In fact, whenever I have wanted to study fools at great parties, I have always looked round regularly for a great beauty; they gather round such a one like wasps around a fruit-woman.

The Echo of the Nest-Life.

Hesperus, 22.

Der Wiederhall des zweiten Lebens, die Stimme unserer bescheidnen, schönern, frömmern Seele wird nur in einem vom Kummer verdunkelten Busen laut, wie die Nachtigallen schlagen, wenn man ihren Käfig überhüllt.

The echo of the nest-life, the voice of our modest, fairer, holier soul, is audible only in a sorrow-darkened bosom, as the nightingales warble when one veils their cage.

The Voice of the Beloved comes back after Death.

Hesperus, 23.

Leser, wenn das, was du liebtest, lange verschwunden ist aus

der Erde oder aus deiner Phantasie, so wird doch in Trauer=
stunden die geliebte **Stimme** wiederkommen und alle deine
alten Thränen mitbringen, und das trostlose Herz, das sie
vergossen hat!

Reader, when that which thou lovedst has long vanished from
the earth or from thy fancy, then will nevertheless the beloved
voice come back, and bring with it all thy old tears, and the dis-
consolate heart which has shed them!

WHAT CHILLS THE NOBLEST PARTS OF THE INNER MAN.
Hesperus, 23.

Nichts erkältet mehr die edelsten Theile des innern Men=
schen, als Umgang mit Personen, an denen man keinen Antheil
nehmen kann.

Nothing chills the noblest parts of the inner man more than
intercourse with persons in whom we cannot take any interest.

A WORLDLY LIFE.
Hesperus, 24.

Und da er bedachte, daß das Weltleben alles Große **am**
Menschen wegschleife, wie das Wetter an Statuen und Leichen=
steinen die **erhabnen Theile** wegnagt.

And as he bethought himself that a worldly life grinds down
all the greatness in man, as the weather gnaws away from statues
and gravestones precisely the *relieved* parts.

MAN AND NATURE.
Hesperus, 24.

Der Mensch hält sein Jahrhundert oder sein Jahrfunfzig
für die Kulmination des Lichts, für einen Festtag, zu welchem
alle andre Jahrhunderte nur als Wochentage führen. Er
kennt nur zwei goldne Zeitalter, das am Anfang der Erde, das
am Ende derselben, worunter er nur seines denkt; die Geschichte
findet er den großen Wäldern ähnlich, in deren Mitte Schweigen,
Nacht= und Raubvögel sind, und deren Rand blos Licht und
Gesang erfüllen. — Allerdings dienet mir alles; aber ich diene
auch allem. Da **es** für die Natur, die **bei ihrer Ewigkeit**

feinen Zeitverluſt, bei ihrer Unerſchöpflichkeit keinen Kraftver=
luſt kennt, kein anderes Geſetz der Sparſamkeit gibt, als das
der Verſchwendung — da ſie mit Eiern und Samenkörnern
eben ſo gut der Ernährung als der Fortpflanzung dient
und mit einer unentwickelten Keim=Welt eine halbe entwickelte
erhält — da ihr Weg über keine glatte Kegelbahn, ſondern über
Alpen und Meere geht : ſo muß unſer kleines Herz ſie mißver=
ſtehen, es mag hoffen oder fürchten; es muß in der Aufklärung
Morgen= und Abendröthe gegenſeitig verwechſeln; es muß
im Vergnügen bald den Nachſommer für den Frühling, bald
den Nachwinter für den Herbſt anſehen. Die moraliſchen
Revolutionen machen uns mehr irre, als die phyſiſchen, weil
jene ihrer Natur nach einen größern Spiel= und Zeitraum
einnehmen, als dieſe — und doch ſind die finſtern Jahrhunderte
nichts als eine Eintauchung in den Schatten des Saturns,
oder eine Sonnenfinſterniß ohne Verweilen.

Man regards his century or his half-century as the culmination
of light, as a festal-day, to which all other centuries lead only as
week-days. He knows only two golden ages—the one at the
beginning of the world, and the one at the end of it—by which
he understands only his own ; he finds history to be like great
woods, in the middle of which are silence, night-birds, and birds
of prey, and whose borders only are filled with light and music.
Certainly all things serve me ; but I too serve all. As Nature,
who in her eternity knows no loss of time, in her inexhaustible-
ness no loss of power, has no other law of frugality assigned her
than that of prodigality — as she, with eggs and seed-corns,
ministers equally well to nourishment and to propagation, and
with an undeveloped germ-world sustains half a developed one—
as her way leads over no smooth bowling-alley, but over alps and
seas ; our little heart must needs misunderstand her, whether in
its hopes or in its fears—it must, as it becomes enlightened,
reciprocally interchange morning and evening red—it must, in its
contentment, now regard after-summer as spring, and now after-
winter as autumn. Moral revolutions mislead us more than
physical, because the former, according to their nature, occupy
a greater play-room and space of time than the latter ; and yet
the Dark Ages are nothing but a dipping into the shadow of
Saturn, or an eclipse of the sun of short duration.

WHAT INEQUALITY OF CULTURE CAUSES.

Hesperus, 24.

Nicht die Ungleichheit der Güter am meiſten — denn dem

Reichen hält die Stimmen- und Fäuste-Mehrheit der Armen die Wage — sondern die Ungleichheit der Kultur macht und zertheilt die politischen Druckwerke und Druckpumpen.

Not inequality of goods, for the majority of voices and fists on the part of the poor balances in the scale the power of the rich, but inequality of culture does most to create and distribute the political fly-presses and forcing-pumps.

THE EARTH IS GREAT, BUT THE HEART THAT RESTS
UPON IT IS STILL GREATER.

Hesperus, 25.

Die Erde ist groß — aber das Herz, das auf ihr ruht, ist noch größer als die Erde, und größer als die Sonne . . . Denn es allein denkt den größten Gedanken.

The earth is great, but the heart which rests upon it is still greater than the earth, and greater than the sun. . . . For it alone thinks the greatest thought.

THE CLOSE OF DAY.

Hesperus, 25.

Plötzlich ging es vom Sterbebette der Sonne kühl wie aus einem Grabe daher. Das hohe Luftmeer wankte, und ein breiter Strom, in dessen Bette Wälder niedergebogen lagen, brauste durch den Himmel die Laufbahn der Sonne zurück. Die Altäre der Natur, die Berge, waren wie bei einer großen Trauer schwarz überhüllt. Der Mensch war vom Nebelgewölke auf die Erde eingesperrt und geschieden vom Himmel. Am Fuße des Gewölkes leckten durchsichtige Blitze, und der Donner schlug dreimal an das schwarze Gewölbe. Aber der Sturm richtete sich auf und riß es auseinander; er trieb die fliegenden Trümmer des zerbrochenen Gefängnisses durch das Blau, und warf die zerstückten Dampfmassen unter den Himmel hinab — und noch lange braust' er allein über die offne Erde fort, durch die lichte gereinigte Ebene. . . . Aber über ihm, hinter dem weggerissenen Vorhang glänzte das Allerheiligste, die Sternen- nacht.

Suddenly there came forth a coolness from the deathbed of the sun as from a grave. The high sea of the air undulated, and a

broad stream, in whose bed woods lay prostrate, came roaring
back through the heaven, along the path by which the sun had
departed. The altars of nature, the mountains, were veiled in
black as at a great mourning. Man was fastened down to the
earth by the mist-cloud, and separated from heaven. Transparent lightnings licked at the foot of the cloud, and the thunder
smote three times at the black arch. But the storm upreared
itself and rent it asunder ; it drove the flying ruins of the shattered
prison through the blue, and flung the dismembered masses of
vapour down below the sky ; and for a long time it still continued
to roar alone over the open earth, through the bright and cleansed
plain. . . . But above it, behind the curtain which it had torn
aside, glistened the all-holiest, the starry night.

THE INFINITE.

Hesperus, 25.

Denn der Unendliche hat in den Himmel seinen Namen in
glühenden Sternen gesäet, aber auf die Erde hat er seinen
Namen in sanften Blumen gesäet.

For the Infinite has sowed his name in the heavens in burning
stars, but on the earth he has sowed his name in tender flowers.

GOD.

Hesperus, 25.

Wer erblickt und erhält denn uns kleine Menschen aus
Staub ? — Du, Allgütiger, erhältst uns, du, Unendlicher, du, o
Gott, du bildest uns, du siehest uns, du liebest uns — O Julius,
erhebe deinen Geist und fasse den größten Gedanken des
Menschen ! Da wo die Ewigkeit ist, da wo die Unermeßlichkeit
ist, und wo die Nacht anfängt, da breitet ein unendlicher Geist
seine Arme aus und legt sie um das große fallende Welten=All,
und trägt es und wärmt es. Ich und du, und alle Menschen,
und alle Engel und alle Würmchen ruhen an seiner Brust, und
das brausende schlagende Welten= und Sonnenmeer ist ein
einziges Kind in seinem Arm. Er siehet durch das Meer
hindurch, worin Korallenbäume voll Erden schwanken, und sieht
an der kleinsten Koralle das Würmchen kleben, das ich bin, und
er gibt dem Würmchen den nächsten Tropfen, und ein seliges
Herz, und eine Zukunft, und ein Auge bis zu ihm hinauf —
ja, o Gott, bis zu dir hinauf, bis an dein Herz.

Who then sees and sustains us little mortals made of dust?
Thou, all-gracious One, sustainest us—thou, infinite One, thou, O
God, thou formest us, thou seest us, thou lovest us. O Julius!
raise thy spirit and grasp the greatest thought of man! There
where eternity is—there where immensity is, and where night
begins—there an Infinite Spirit spreads out its arms and folds
them around the great falling universe of worlds, and bears it,
and warms it. I and thou, and all men, and all angels, and all
worms, rest on his bosom ; and the roaring, beating sea of worlds
and suns is an only child in his arms. He sees away through the
ocean, wherein coral-trees full of earths sway to and fro, and sees
the little worm that cleaves to the smallest coral, which is I—and
he gives the worm the nearest drop, and a blissful heart, and
a future, and an eye to look up even to himself—**yea, O God,**
even up to thee, even to thy heart!

GOD.

Hesperus, 25.

Gott ist die Ewigkeit, Gott ist die Wahrheit, Gott ist die
Heiligkeit — er hat nichts, er ist alles — das ganze Herz fasset
ihn, aber kein Gedanke; und Er denkt nur uns, wenn
wir ihn denken. — — Alles Unendliche und Unbegreifliche im
Menschen ist sein Wiederschein; aber weiter denke dein
Schauder nicht. Die Schöpfung hängt als Schleier, der aus
Sonnen und Geistern gewebt ist, über dem Unendlichen, und
die Ewigkeiten gehen vor dem Schleier vorbei, und ziehen ihn
nicht weg von dem Glanze, den er verhüllet.

God is eternity—God is truth—God is holiness. He has nothing,
he is all, the whole heart conceives him, but no thought ; and **we**
are only his thought when he is ours. All that is infinite and
incomprehensible in man is his reflection ; but beyond this let not
the awe-stricken thought go. Creation hangs as a veil, woven out
of suns and spirits, over the Infinite, and the eternities pass by
before the veil, and draw it not away from the splendour which
it hides.

WORLDLINGS MAINTAIN A UNIFORM DEMEANOUR.

Hesperus, 26.

Die Weltleute hingegen behaupten ein immer gleiches Betragen, weil sie es nie nach fremden Verdiensten, sondern nach
eignen Absichten abformen.

Worldlings, on the contrary, maintain always a uniform demeanour, because they never shape it after other people's merits, but according to their own designs.

THE HEART OF A GOOD WOMAN.
Hesperus, 29.

O vor wem das liebevolle zugedrückte Herz eines guten Weibes aufginge : wie viel bekämpfte Zärtlichkeit, verhüllte Aufopferungen und stumme Tugenden würd' er darin ruhen sehen !

Oh, if the loving, closed heart of a good woman should open before a man, how much controlled tenderness, how many veiled sacrifices and dumb virtues would he see reposing therein!

THE CANCER OF JEALOUSY.
Hesperus, 30.

Der eifersüchtige Krebs auf der Brust ist nie ganz zu schneiden, wenn ich großen Heilkünstlern glauben soll.

The cancer of jealousy on the breast can never wholly be cut out, if I am to believe great masters of the healing art.

VAIN MEN.
Hesperus, 35.

Eitle erliegen dem Lächerlichen, dem der Sonderling trotzt; und jene hassen, diese suchen ihre Ebenbilder.

Vain men succumb to the ridiculous, which the whimsical man defies ; and the former hate, the latter seek their likenesses.

WHAT MAKES LOVE SWEET AND TENDER.
Hesperus, 35.

Nichts macht die Liebe süßer und zarter als ein kleines Reifen und Frieren vorher, so wie die Weintrauben durch einen Frost vor der Lese dünnere Schalen und bessern Most gewinnen.

Nothing makes love sweeter and tenderer than a little previous scolding and freezing, just as the grape-clusters acquire by a frost before vintage thinner skins and better must.

Individual Man and the Race of Man.

Hesperus, 35.

Der Sterbliche hält sich hier für ewig, weil das Menschen=
geschlecht ewig ist; aber der fortgestoßene Tropfe wird mit dem
unversiegenden Strome verwechselt; und keimten nicht immer
neue Menschen nach, so würde jeder die Flüchtigkeit seiner
Lebensterzie tiefer empfinden.

Mortal man regards himself as eternal here because the human
race is eternal; but the propelled drop is confounded with the
inexhaustible stream; and were it not that new human creatures
always spring up after us, each one would feel more deeply the
fleetingness of his second life.

Rest.

Hesperus, 38.

O Ruhe, du sanftes Wort! — Herbstflor aus Eden! Mond=
schein des Geistes! Ruhe der Seele, wann hältst du unser
Haupt, daß es still liege, und unser Herz, daß es nicht klopfe?
Ach eh' jenes bleich und dieses starr ist, so kommst du oft und
gehst du oft und nur unten bei dem Schlafe und bei dem Tode
bleibest du, indeß oben die Stürme, die Menschen mit den größ=
ten Flügeln, gleich Paradiesvögeln, am meisten umherwerfen!

O Rest! thou soft word! autumnal flower of Eden! Moonlight
of the spirit! Rest of the soul, when wilt thou hold our head
that it may be still, and our heart that it may cease beating?
Ah! ere the one grows pale and the other stiff, thou comest often
and goest often, and only down below with sleep and with death
thou abidest; whereas above, men with the greatest wings, like
birds of paradise, are whirled about most of all by the storms.

Flowers of Gladness.

Hesperus, 44.

Denn von den zertretenen Freudenblumen auf dem Lebens=
wege wehet Wohlgeruch auf die jetzige Stunde herüber, wie
ziehende Heere oft aus Steppen den Wohlgeruch zerquetschter
Kräuter ausschicken.

For from the crushed flowers of gladness on the road of life a sweet **perfume** is wafted over to the present hour, as marching armies **often** send out from heaths the fragrance of trampled plants.

WAYS TO BECOME HAPPY.

Quintus Fixlein : To my Friends.

Ich konnte nie mehr als drei Wege, glücklicher (nicht glücklich) zu werden, auskundschaften. Der erste, der in die Höhe geht, ist: so weit über das Gewölfe des Lebens hinauszubringen, daß man die ganze äußere Welt mit ihren Wolfsgruben, Beinhäusern und Gewitterableitern von weitem unter seinen Füßen nur wie ein eingeschrumpftes Kindergärtchen liegen sieht. — Der zweite ist: gerade herabzufallen in's Gärtchen und da sich so einheimisch in eine Furche einzunisten, daß, wenn man aus seinem warmen Lerchennest heraussieht, man ebenfalls keine Wolfsgruben, Beinhäuser und Stangen, sondern nur Aehren erblickt, deren jede für den Nestvogel ein Baum, und ein Sonnen= und Regenschirm ist. — Der dritte endlich — den ich für den schwersten und klügsten halte — ist der: mit den beiden andern zu wechseln.

I could **never** find out more than three ways to become happier (not happy). The **first**, rather a high one, is this : to soar so far above the clouds of life that one sees the whole external world, with its wolf-dens, charnel-houses, and thunder-rods, down far beneath us, shrunk into a child's little garden. The second is— merely to sink down into this little garden, and there to nestle yourself so snugly in some little furrow, that when you look out of your warm lark-nest you likewise can perceive no wolf-dens, charnel-houses, and poles, but only blades, every one of which, for the nest-bird, is a tree, and sun-screen, and rain-screen. The third, finally, which I regard as the hardest and cunningest, **is** that of alternating with the other two.

THE MAN WITH A GREAT PURPOSE AND FIXED IDEA.

Quintus Fixlein : To my Friends.

Der Held — der Reformator — Brutus — Howard — der Republikaner, den bürgerliche Stürme — das Genie, das artistische bewegen — kurz jeder Mensch mit einem großen Entschluß oder auch nur mit einer perennirenden Leidenschaft (und wär' es die, den größten Folianten zu schreiben), alle diese

bauen ſich mit ihrer innern Welt gegen die Kälte und Glut
der äußern ein, wie der Wahnſinnige im ſchlimmern Sinn:
jede fixe Idee, die jedes Genie und jeden Enthuſiaſten wenigſtens periodiſch regiert, ſcheidet den Menſchen erhaben von
Tiſch und Bett der Erde, von ihren Hundsgrotten und Stech-
dornen und Teufelsmauern — — gleich dem Paradiesvogel
ſchläft er fliegend, und auf den ausgebreiteten Flügeln ver-
ſchlummert er blind in ſeiner Höhe die untern Erdſtöße und
Brandungen des Lebens im langen ſchönen Traume von ſeinem
idealiſchen Mutterland.

The hero—the reformer—your Brutus—your Howard—your
republican, whom civic storm—your genius, whom poetic storm
impels; in short, every man with a great purpose, or even with
a continuous passion (were it but that of writing the largest
folios); all these men defend themselves by their internal world
against the frosts and heats of the external, as the madman in
a worse sense does; every fixed idea, such as rules every genius
and every enthusiast, at least periodically, separates and raises
a man above the bed and board of this earth—above its dog's
grottoes, buckthorns, and devils' walls; like the bird of paradise
he slumbers flying; and on his outspread pinions oversleeps unconsciously the earthquakes and conflagrations of life in his long
fair dream of his ideal motherland.

Looking back to the Years of Childhood.

Quintus Fixlein: Third Letter-Box.

Nun nahm er den Schnee der Zeit von dem Wintergrün der
Erinnerung hinweg und ſah die ſchönen Jahre ſeiner Kindheit
aufgedeckt, friſch, grün und duftend vor ſich darunter ſtehen.

And now he shook away the snow of time from the winter-green
of memory, and beheld the fair years of his childhood uncovered,
fresh, green, and balmy, standing afar off before him.

Great Changes make us Younger.

Quintus Fixlein: Fourth Letter-Box.

Große Veränderungen verjüngen — in Aemtern, Ehen, Reiſen
— weil man das Leben allezeit von der letzten Revolution an
datirt, wie die Franzoſen von der ihrigen an.

Great changes—in offices, marriages, travels—make us younger; we always date our history from the last revolution, as the French have done from theirs.

MEN ARE NOTCHED LONG BEFORE FELLING.
Quintus Fixlein : Fifth Letter-Box.

Alter und Leiden hatten an ihr schon dem Tode die ersten Einschnitte vorgezeichnet, daß er wenig Müle brauchte, sie ganz zu fällen; denn den Menschen geht es wei den Bäumen, die lange vor dem Umsägen eingekerbet werden, damit ihnen der Lebenssaft entfließe.

Age and sufferings had already marked out the first incisions for death, so that he required but little effort to cut her down; for it is with men as with trees, they are notched long before felling, that their life-sap may flow out.

TRIFLES ARE THE PROVENDER OF LOVE.
Quintus Fixlein : Fifth Letter-Box.

Inzwischen sind Geringfügigkeiten die Proviantbäckerei der Liebe;—die Finger sind die elektrischen Auslader eines an allen Fibern glimmenden Feuers;—Seufzer sind Leittöne konvergirender Herzen und das allerschlimmste und stärkste dabei ist ein Unglück: denn die Flamme der Liebe schwimmt, wie die von Naphtha, gern auf Thränenwasser.

At the same time trifles are the provender of love—the fingers are electric discharges of a fire sparkling along every fibre ; sighs are the guiding tones of two approximating hearts ; and the worst and most effectual thing of all in such a case is some misfortune ; for the flame of love, like that of naphtha, likes to swim on water.

LOVE DIES OFTENER OF EXCESS THAN HUNGER.
Quintus Fixlein : Eighth Letter-Box.

Die Liebe stirbt wie die Menschen öfter am Uebermaß als am Hunger; sie lebt von Liebe, aber sie gleicht den Alpenpflanzen, die sich vom Einsaugen der nassen Wolken ernähren, und die zu Grunde gehen, wenn man sie besprengt.

Love, like men, dies oftener of excess than of hunger ; it lives

on love, but it resembles those Alpine flowers, which feed themselves by suction from the wet clouds and die if you besprinkle
them.

WOMAN.

Quintus Fixlein : Eleventh Letter-Box.

Wahrlich, ein Mann muß nie über die mit einer Ewigkeit
bedeckte Schöpfungminute der Welt nachgesonnen haben, der
nicht eine Frau, deren Lebensfaden eine verhüllte unendliche
Hand zu einem zweiten spinnt, und die den Uebergang vom
Nichts zum Seyn, von der Ewigkeit in die Zeit verhüllt, mit
philosophischer Verehrung anblickt, — aber noch weniger muß
ein Mann je empfunden haben, dessen Seele vor einer Frau in
einem Zustande, wo sie einem unbekannten ungesehenen Wesen
noch mehr aufopfert als wir dem bekannten, nämlich Nächte,
Freuden und oft das Leben, sich nicht tiefer und mit größerer
Rührung bückt als vor einem ganzen singenden Nonnen-
Orchester, auf ihrer Sarawüste ; und schlimmer als beide ist
einer, dem nicht seine Mutter alle anderen Mütter verehrung-
würdig macht.

In truth, a man must never have reflected on the creation-
moment, when the universe first rose from the bosom of an eternity, if he does not view with philosophic reverence a woman,
whose thread of life a secret, all-wondrous hand is spinning to
a second thread, and who veils within her the transition from
nothingness to existence, from eternity to time ; but still less can
a man have any heart of flesh, if his soul, in presence of a woman,
who, to an unknown, unseen being, is sacrificing more than we
will sacrifice when it is seen and known—namely, her nights, her
joys, often her life—does not bow lower, and with deeper emotion,
than in presence of a whole nun-orchestra on their Sahara-desert ;
and worse than either is the man for whom his own mother has
not made all other mothers venerable.

THE DUSK OF DOWN-GONE DAYS.

Quintus Fixlein : Fourteenth Letter-Box.

Der Kranke erkannte den Augenblick diese vorragenden
Spitzen einer im Strome der Zeit untergegangnen Frühling-
welt, diesen Halbschatten, diese Dämmerung versunkner Tage
— diese Brand- und Schädelstätte einer himmlischen Zeit, die

wir nie vergeſſen, die wir ewig lieben und nach der wir noch auf dem Grab zurückſehen.

The sick man recognised in a moment these projecting peaks of a spring-world sunk in the stream of Time—these half-shadows, this dusk of down-gone days—this conflagration and Golgotha of a heavenly time, which none of us forgets, which we love for ever and look back to, even from the grave.

Wordsworth (*Nutting*) says—

" One of those heavenly days that cannot die."

WISDOM AND MORALITY.

Levana : Preface.

Weisheit, Sittlichkeit ſind kein Ameiſenhaufen abgetrennter zuſammentragender Thätigkeiten, ſondern organiſche Eltern der geiſtigen Nachwelt, welche bloß der weckenden Nahrung bedürfen. Wir kehren die Unwiſſenheit der Wilden, welche Schießpulver ſäeten, anſtatt es zu machen, bloß um, wenn wir etwas zuſammenſetzen wollen, was ſich nur entfalten läßt.

Wisdom and morality are no ants' colonies of separate, co-operating workmen, but organic parents of the mental future, which only require animating nourishment. We merely reverse the ignorance of the savages, who sowed gunpowder instead of making it, when we attempt to compound what can only be developed.

OLD THOUGHTS.

Levana : Preface.

Es iſt gut, in den neueſten Büchern alte Gedanken zu ſagen, weil man die alten Werke, worin ſie ſtehen, nicht lieſ't; von manchen Wahrheiten müſſen, wie von fremden Muſterwerken, in jedem Jahrfunfzig neue Ueberſetzungen gegeben werden.

It is good to respect old thoughts in the newest books, because the old works, in which they stand, are not read. New translations of many truths, as of foreign standard works, must be given forth every half-century.

TEACHERS.

Levana : Preface.

Hier ſind Erzieher die Horen, welche die Himmelsthüren öffnen oder ſchließen.

Here teachers are the hours who open or close the gates of heaven.

The Words of a Father in the Privacy of Home.
Levana: Preface.

Das heimliche häusliche Wort, das der Vater seinen Kindern sagt, wird nicht vernommen von der Zeit; aber wie in Schall=gewölben, wird es an dem fernen Ende laut und von der Nachwelt gehört.

The words that a father speaks to his children in the privacy of home are not heard by the world, but, as in whispering-galleries they are clearly heard at the end and by posterity.

The World of Childhood.
Levana, chap. I. s. 1.

In der Kinderwelt sieht die ganze Nachwelt vor uns, in die wir, wie Moses in's gelobte Land, nur schauen, nicht kommen; und zugleich erneuert sie uns die verjüngte Vorwelt, hinter welcher wir erscheinen mußten; denn das Kind der feinsten Hauptstadt ist ein geborner Otaheiter und der einjährige Sanskülotte ein erster Christ, und die letzten Kinder der Erde famen mit dem Paradiese der ersten Eltern auf die Welt.

In the world of childhood all posterity stands before us, upon which we, like Moses upon the Promised Land, may only gaze, but not enter; and at the same time it renews for us the ages of the young world, behind which we must appear; for the child of the most civilised capital is a born Otaheitan, and the one-year-old Sansculotte a first Christian, and the last children of the earth came upon the world with the paradise of our first parents.

Deeds and Books.
Levana, chap. I. s. 1.

Denn womit wir sonst noch auf die Welt — mit Thaten und Büchern — wirken können, dieß findet immer schon eine bestimmte und erhärtete und schon unsers Gleichen; nur aber mit dem Erziehen säen wir auf einen reinen weichen Boden entweder Gift oder Honigkelche; und wie die Götter zu den ersten Menschen, so steigen wir (physisch und geistig den Kindern zu Riesen) zu den Kleinen herab, und ziehen sie groß oder — klein. Es ist rührend und erhaben, daß jetzt vor dem Erzieher die großen Geister und Lehrer der nächsten Nachwelt als Säuglinge

X

feines Milchglaſes kriechen — daß er künftige Sonnen als
Wandelſternchen an ſeinem Laufband führt.

For deeds and books, the means by which we have hitherto
been able to work upon the world, always find it already defined
and hardened, and full of people like ourselves ; only by education can we sow upon a pure soft soil the seeds of poison or of
honey-bearing flowers ; and as the gods to the first men, so do we,
physical and spiritual giants to children, descend to these little
ones and form them to be great or small. It is a touching and mighty
thought that now, before their educator, the great spirits and
teachers of our immediate posterity creep, as the sucklings of his
milk-store—that he guides future suns like little wandering stars
in his leading-strings.

EARLY YEARS.

Levana, chap. I. *s.* 2.

Denn wiewohl ihr die Kraft des Genius nicht brechen und
richten könnt — je tiefer das Meer, deſto ſteiler iſt uns die
Küſte — : ſo könnt ihr doch im einweihenden wichtigſten Jahrzehend des Lebens, im erſten, unter dieſem Erſtgeburtthore
aller Gefühle, die gelagerte Löwenkraft mit allen zarten Gewohnheiten des ſchönen Herzens, mit allen Banden der Liebe
umgeben und überſtricken.

For though you might not be able to break or bend the power
of genius—the deeper the sea, the more precipitous the coast—
yet in the most important initiatory decade of life, in the first, at
the opening dawn of all feelings, you might surround and overlay
the slumbering lion-energies with all the tender habits of a gentle
heart, and all the bands of love.

WHAT A SYSTEM OF EDUCATION MUST PROVIDE FOR.

Levana, chap. I. *s.* 2.

Wiewohl eine Erziehlehre zuerſt genialer Weſen gedenken
muß, da dieſe, ſo ſelten ſie auch aufgehen, doch allein die Welt-
geſchichte regieren, als Heerführer entweder der Seelen oder der
Körper oder beider: ſo würde jene gleichwohl einer praktiſchen
Anweiſung, wie man ſich zu verhalten habe, falls man das
große Loos gewinne, zu ähnlich lauten, wenn ſie nicht die
Mehrheit der Mittelgeiſter, welche ja die Zukunft bilden, auf
die ein großer wirken kann, extenſiv eben ſo wichtig finden
wollte, als einen genialen intenſiv.

Although a system of education must, in the first instance, **pro-**vide for the beings endowed with genius—since these, though they seldom arise, yet alone rule the world's history, either as leaders of souls or of bodies, or of both ; yet would such a system **too** much resemble a practical exposition of how to conduct one-self in case of winning the great prize, if it did not observe that the multitude of mediocre talents, on which a great one can act, are quite as important in the **mass** as the man of genius is in the individual.

THE GREAT MASS OF THE PEOPLE EVER THE SAME.

Levana, chap. II. *s.* 7.

Kein Volklehrer bleibt sich so gleich, als das lehrende Volk. Die Geister zu Maſſen eingeſchmolzen, büßen von freier Bewe= gung — welche Körper gerade durch Maſſe zu gewinnen ſcheinen, z. B. die Weltkörper vielleicht das Körper=All — etwas ein, und rücken nur als ſchwerfällige Koloſſe auf alten, eiſern über= legten Gleiſen beſſer fort. Denn ſo ſehr auch Heirathen, Alter, Tödten und Haſſen ſich bei dem Einzelweſen dem Geſetze der Freiheit unterwerfen ; ſo kann man doch über ein ganzes Volk Geburt= und Sterbliſten machen, und man kann heraus= bringen, daß im Kanton Bern (nach Mad. Staël) die Zahl der Eheſcheidungen, wie in Italien die der Ermordungen, von Jahrzehend zu Jahrzehend dieſelbe iſt. — Muß nun nicht auf einer ſolchen immer und gleich wirkenden Lebenswelt der kleine Menſch wie auf einer fliegenden Erde fortgetragen werden, wo die einzelnen Richtungen, die der Erzieher geben kann, nichts vermögen, weil ſie noch dazu ſelber erſt auf ihr den Richtwinkel unbewußt empfangen ? — Daher ſäen eben, trotz aller verſchiedenen Re= und Informatoren, Völker wie Wieſen, ſich ſelber aus zu gleichem Schmelz ; daher behauptet ſogar in Reſidenzen, wohin ſich alle Lehrbücher und Lehrmeiſter und ſelber Eltern aller Arten ziehen, der Geiſt ſich unverändert feſt.

No teacher of the people continues so uniformly one with him-self as the people that are taught. Minds molten into masses lose nothing of their free movements, which bodies, for instance that of the world, perhaps that of the universe, seem to gain by their very massiveness, and, like a heavy colossus, to move all the more easily along the old, iron-covered track. For however much marriages, old age, deaths, and enmities, are in the individual case

subject to the law of freedom, yet in a whole nation lists of births
and deaths can be made—by which it may be shown that in the
Canton of Berne (according to Madame de Staël) the number of
divorces, as in Italy that of murders, is the same from year to
year. Must not now the little human being, placed on such an
eternally and ever similarly acting world, be borne, as upon a
flying earth, where the only directions that a teacher can give
avail nothing, because he has first unconsciously received his line
of movement upon it? Thence, in spite of all reformers and in-
formers, nations, like meadows, reach ever a similar verdure;
thence, even in capital cities, where all school-books and school-
masters, and even parents of every kind, educate, the spirit maintains itself unalterably the same.

Repetition is the Mother of Study.

Levana, chap. II. *s.* 7.

Die Wiederholung ist die Mutter — nicht bloß des Studirens,
auch der Bildung. Wie der Freskomaler, so gibt der Erzieher
dem nassen Kalke Farben, die immer versiegen, und die er von
neuen aufträgt bis sie bleiben und lebendig blühen.

Repetition is the mother, not only of study, but also of education. Like the fresco-painter, the teacher lays colours on the wet
plaster which ever fade away, and which he must ever renew until
they remain and brightly shine.

Everything has an Influence on a Man's Eternity.

Levana, chap. III. *s.* 17.

So gewiß es folglich ist, daß kein Mensch einen Spaziergang
machen kann, ohne davon eine Wirkung auf seine Ewigkeit nach
Hause zu bringen — so gewiß jedes Spornrad, jeder Himmel-
und Orden-Stern, Käfer, Fußstoß, Handschlag sich in uns so
gut eingräbt, als in den Granitgipfel ein leiser Thaufall und
das Bestreifen einer Nebelwolke — so gewiß ist wieder auf der
andern Seite die Behauptung nöthig: „jedes nur so und so
stark, nach gestrigem, heutigem und morgendem Verhältniß."

Hence it is certain that no man can take a walk without bringing home an influence on his eternity; every spur, every star of
heaven and of knighthood, every beetle, every trip or touch of
hand, as certainly engraves itself upon us as the gentle dewdrop
or the hanging of a mist affects the granite mountains; but just

as certainly, on the other hand, is this assertion necessary—
that the strength of every impression depends on our condition
yesterday, to-day, and to-morrow.

When should be the First Seeds of Education.

Levana, chap. III. *s.* 17.

Wie Wirthschafter im Nebel am fruchtbarsten zu säen
glauben, so fällt ja die erste Aussaat in den ersten und dicksten
Nebel des Lebens.

As farmers believe it most advantageous to sow in mist, so the
first seeds of education should fall in the first and thickest mist
of life.

Conversion.

Levana, chap. III. *s.* 17.

Es gibt Menschen, die sich tief bis an die Gränzstunde hinein
besinnen, wo ihnen zum erstenmal das Ich plötzlich aus dem
Gewölke wie eine Sonne vorbrach und wunderbar eine be-
strahlte Welt aufdeckte.

Das Leben, besonders das sittliche, hat Flug, dann Sprung,
dann Schritt, dann Stand; jedes Jahr läßt sich der Mensch
weniger bekehren, und einen bösen Sechziger dient weniger ein
Missionar als ein Autodafé.

There are men who can remember far back to the bounding-
hour of existence, in which their self-consciousness suddenly
burst through the clouds like a sun, and wonderfully revealed a
beaming universe. Life, especially moral life, has a flight, then a
leap, then a step, then a halt; each year renders a man less easy
to convert, and a missionary can effect less on a wicked sexa-
genarian than an auto-da-fé.

What forms Character.

Levana, chap. III. *s.* 17.

Nur einzelne rühren uns im späten Leben, wie im frühesten,
formend an, die Menge geht als fernes Heer vorüber. Ein
Freund, ein Lehrer, eine Geliebte, ein Klub, eine Wirthstafel,
ein Sitzungtisch, ein Haus in unsern Zeiten, sind dem Einzel-
wesen die einwirkende Nation und der Nationalgeist, indeß die
übrige Menge an ihm spurlos abgleitet.

Only some few in later as in early life affect the formation of our characters; the multitude passes by like a distant army. One friend, one teacher, one beloved, one club, one dining-table, one work-table, one house, are in our age the nation and national spirit influencing the individual—while the rest of the crowd passes him without leaving a trace behind.

The Character of the Individual.

Levana: Second Fragment, chap. II. *s.* 29.

Aber leider sind drei Dinge schwer zu finden und zu geben: einen Charakter haben — einen zeichnen — einen errathen; und vor dem gewöhnlichen Erzieher scheint eine Unart schon eine Unnatur — ein Höcker, ein Leib und Pockengruben feste Theile des Gesichts.

But, alas! three things are very difficult to discover and to impart: to have a character—to draw one—to guess one. To ordinary teachers a naughty trick seems a wicked nature—a pimple or a pock-mark as parts of the countenance.

How Every One regards his own Life.

Levana: Second Fragment, chap. III. *s.* 32.

Denn der Mensch ist eng und arm; seine Sterndeuterei der Zukunft — ein bloßes entweder Potenziiren oder Depotenziiren der Gegenwart — sieht bloß ein Mondviertel am Himmel, das mit ihm ab- oder zunimmt, keine Sonne. Jeder hält sein Leben für die Neujahrnacht der Zeit, und mithin, wie der Aber- gläubige, seine — aus Erinnerungen zusammengehefteten — Träume darin für Prophezeihungen auf's ganze Jahr. Daher trifft stets — nicht etwa das prophezeihete Gute und Böse, oder das Gegentheil davon, sondern — etwas Anderes ein, das die Weissagungen und ihre Gegenstände, wie ein Meer die Ströme, aufnimmt und auflöset in den Wogen-Kreis. Denn in der Minute, wo du in deiner Wüste weissagest, fliegt der feine Samenstaub einer Eiche auf die Erde, und wird nach einem Jahrhundert ein Hain.

For man is feeble and poor; his star-reading of the future, a mere strengthening or weakening of the present, sees only a crescent-moon in the sky, which waxes and wanes in unison with him, but no sun. Every one regards his own life as the new-year's eve of time, and also, like the superstitious, his dreams, woven from memories, as prophecies for the year. Thence there always comes, not the foretold good or evil, nor yet its opposite, but something quite different, which receives the prophecies and their objects as an ocean does the rivers, and resolves them into the circle of its waves. For in the moment when you are prophesying in the desert, the fine seed-pollen of an oak falls upon the earth, and in a century grows up to be a forest.

The Word "God" directs the Eyes of Men upwards.

Levana : Second Fragment, chap. III. *s.* 34.

So lange das Wort Gott in einer Sprache noch dauert und tönt: so richtet es das Menschenauge nach oben auf. Es ist mit dem Ueberirdischen, wie mit der Sonne, welche in einer Verfinsterung, sobald auch nur der kleinste Rand von ihr noch unbedeckt leuchten kann, stets den Tag forterhält, und sich selber gerundet in der dunkeln Kammer abmalt.

So long as the word God endures in a language will it direct the eyes of men upwards. It is with the Eternal as with the sun, which, if but its smallest part can shine uneclipsed, prolongs the day, and gives its rounded image in the dark chamber.

The Sin-Stains of the Past.

Levana : Second Fragment, chap. III. *s.* 34.

So wie in der Vergangenheit die Irrthümer der Völker, ungleich den Dekorationsgemälden, verzerrter und unförmlicher sich ausdehnen, weil die Ferne uns ihre feinern und wahren Ausfüllungen entzieht: so stellen sich umgekehrt die schwarzen Schandflecken der Vergangenheit, z. B. der römischen, spartischen, gemildert und gerundet dar, und, wie an einen Mond, fällt an die Gegenwart der höckerige Erdschatte der Vorzeit rund und durchsichtig hinauf.

As in past ages the errors of nations, unlike decorative paintings, seem very distorted and shapeless, because distance hides from us their finer and true completeness ; so, on the other side, the black sin-stains of the past, of the Roman and Spartan for example, show softened and rounded, and as on a moon, the high rugged shadow of the past falls round and transparent on the present.

THE USE OF AFFLICTION.

Levana: Second Fragment, chap. III. *s.* 35.

Da Lebensarten Denkweisen, und umgekehrt Meinungen Handlungen erzeugen — und Kopf und Herz, wie körperlich, so geistig, gegenseitig einander entweder befruchten oder lähmen: — so hat das Schicksal, sobald beide zugleich zu heilen sind, nur Eine, aber lange Kur, die Ekel= und Vipernkur der Qual. Wenn Unglück Menschen läutert, warum nicht Völker? Frei= lich — und darum sieht man es weniger ein — wenn dort Wunden und Schalttage bessern, so hier erst Schlachtfelder und Schalt= jahrhunderte, und Geschlechter müssen trüb und blaß zu Unter= lagen froher hinuntersinken.

Since modes of life beget modes of thought, and opinions actions, and head and heart, spiritually as well as physically, mutually improve or injure each other, so has fate, when both are to be healed at once, only one cure, and that a long one—the harsh viper-like cure of affliction. If sorrow purifies men, why not nations? Certainly, and it is for this reason that men perceive it less, if wounds and fast-days improve the one, battlefields and centuries of penance do the other—and generations must sink sadly and sorrowfully to destruction.

John Brown (*Barbarossa*, Act v. sc. 3) says—

> "Now let us thank the Eternal Power; convinced
> That Heaven but tries our virtue by affliction,
> That oft the cloud that wraps the present hour
> Serves but to brighten all our future days."

WHAT IS RELIGION?

Levana: Second Fragment, chap. IV. *s.* 37.

Was ist nun Religion? — Sprecht die Antwort betend aus: der Glaube an Gott; denn sie ist nicht nur der Sinn für das Ueberirdische und das Heilige, und der Glaube an's Unsichtbare, sondern die Ahnung dessen, ohne welchen kein Reich des Unfaß= lichen und Ueberirdischen, kurz kein zweites All nur denkbar wäre. Tilgt Gott aus der Brust, so ist alles, was über und hinter der Erde liegt, nur eine wiederholende Vergrößerung derselben; das Ueberirdische wäre nur eine höhere Zahlenstufe des Mechanismus, und folglich ein Irdisches.

What then is religion? prayerfully pronounce the answer. The belief in God; for it is not only a sense for the holy, and a belief in the invisible, but a presentiment of it, without which no kingdom of the Incomprehensible were conceivable. Efface God from the heart, and everything which lies above as below the earth is only a recurring enlargement of it; that which is above the earth would become only a higher grade of mechanism, and consequently earthly.

RELIGION IS THE LEARNING OF GOD.

Levana : Second Fragment, chap. IV. *s.* 37.

Religion ift anfangs Gottlehre, daher der hohe Name Gott= gelehrter — recht ift fie Gottfeligkeit. Ohne Gott ift das Ich einfam durch die Ewigkeiten hindurch; hat es aber feinen Gott, fo ift es wärmer, inniger, fefter vereinigt, als durch Freund= fchaft und Liebe. Ich bin dann nicht mehr mit meinem Ich allein. Sein Urfreund, der Unendliche, den er erkennt, der eingeborne Blutfreund des Innerften, verläßt es fo wenig als das Ich fich felber; und mitten im unreinen oder leeren Ge= wühl der Kleinigkeiten und der Sünden, auf Marktplatz und Schlachtfeld fteh' ich mit zugefchloffener Bruft, worin der All= höchfte und Allheiligfte mit mir fpricht, und vor mir als nahe Sonne ruht, hinter welcher die Außenwelt im Dunkel liegt. Ich bin in feine Kirche, in das Weltgebäude, gegangen und bleibe darin felig=andächtig fromm, werde auch der Tempel dunkel oder kalt, oder von Gräbern untergraben. Was ich thue oder leide, ift kein Opfer für Ihn, fo wenig, als ich mir felber eines bringen kann; ich liebe Ihn bloß, Ich mag ent= weder leiden, oder nicht. Vom Himmel fällt die Flamme auf den Opfer=Altar und verzehrt das Thier, aber die Flamme und der Priefter bleiben. Wenn mein Urfreund etwas von mir verlangt, fo glänzt mir Himmel und Erde, und ich bin felig, wie er; wenn er verweigert, fo ift Sturm auf dem Meer, aber es ift mit Regenbogen überdeckt, und ich kenne wohl die gute Sonne darüber, welche keine Wetter=, nur lauter Sonnen= feiten hat. Nur böfen lieblofen Geiftern gebietet ein Sitten= gefetz, damit fie nur erft beffer werden und darauf gut. Aber das liebevolle Anfchauen des Urfreundes der Seele, der jenes Gefetz erft befeelt und unüberfchwenglich macht, verbannt nicht bloß den böfen Gedanken, der fiegt, fondern auch den andern,

ber nur verfucht. Wie doch über dem höchsten Gebirge noch
hoch der Abler schwebt, so über der schwer ersteigbaren Pflicht
die rechte Liebe.

Religion is, in the beginning, the learning of God ;—hence the
great name divine, one learned about God,—truly religion is the
blessedness arising from a knowledge of God.   Without God we
are lonely through eternity ; but if we have God, we are more
warmly, more intimately, more steadfastly united than by friendship and love.   I am then no longer alone with my spirit.   Its great
first Friend, the Everlasting, whom it recognises, the inborn Friend
of its innermost soul, will abandon it as little as it can do itself,
and in the midst of the impure or empty whirl of trifles and of
sins, on the market-place, and the battlefield, I stand with
closed breast, in which the Almighty and All-holy speaks to me,
and reposes before me like a near sun, behind which the outer
world lies in darkness.   I have entered into his church, the
temple of the universe, and remain therein blessed, devout, pious,
even if the temple should become dark, cold, or undermined by
graves.   What I do, or suffer, is as little a sacrifice to him as I
can offer one to myself.   I love him whether I suffer or not.   The
flame from heaven falls on the altar of sacrifice, and consumes the
beast, but the flame and the priest remain.   If my great Friend
demand something from me, the heaven and the earth seem glorious
to me, and I am happy as he is ; if he deny me anything, it is a
storm on the ocean, but it is spanned by rainbows, and I recognise
above it the kindly sun, which has no tempestuous sides but only
sunshiny ones.   A code of morality only rules bad, unloving souls,
in order that they may first become better and afterwards good.
But the loving contemplation of the soul's first Friend, who
abundantly animates those laws, banishes not merely the bad
thoughts which conquer, but those also which tempt.   As the
eagle flies high above the highest mountains, so does true love
above struggling duty.

A RELIGIOUS MAN.

Levana : Second Fragment, chap. II. *s.* 38.

Wer aber Religion hat, findet eine Vorsehung mit nicht
mehr Recht in der Weltgeschichte, als in seiner Familien-
geschichte; den Regenbogen, der sich auf Höhen als blühender
Zirkel in den Himmel hängt, schafft dieselbe Sonne im Thautropfen einer niedrigen Blume nach.

He who possesses religion finds a providence not more truly in
the history of the world than in his own family history ; the rain-

bow, which hangs a glistering circle in the heights of heaven, is also formed by the same sun in the dewdrop of a lowly flower.

Everything Holy is before what is Unholy.

Levana : Second Fragment, chap. II. s. 38.

Alles Heilige ist früher, als das Unheilige; Schuld setzt Unschuld voraus, nicht umgekehrt; es werden Engel, aber nicht gefallne, geschaffen. Daher kommt eigentlich der Mensch nicht zum Höchsten hinauf, sondern immer von da herab und erst dann zurück empor; und nie kann ein Kind für zu unschuldig und gut gehalten werden.

Everything holy is before what is unholy; guilt presupposes innocence, not the reverse; angels, but not fallen ones, were created. Hence man does not properly rise to the highest, but first sinks gradually down from it, and then afterwards rises again: a child can never be considered too innocent and good.

How a Child is to be taught Religion.

Levana : Second Fragment, chap. II. s. 38.

Das Erhabene ist die Tempelstufe zur Religion, wie die Sterne zur Unermeßlichkeit. Wenn in die Natur das Große hereintritt, der Sturm, der Donner, der Sternenhimmel, der Tod: so spricht das Wort Gott vor dem Kinde aus. Ein hohes Unglück, ein hohes Glück, eine große Uebelthat, eine Edelthat sind Baustätten einer wandernden Kinderkirche.

The sublime is the temple-step of religion, as the stars are of immeasurable space. When what is mighty appears in nature— a storm, thunder, the starry firmament, death—then utter the word God before the child. A great misfortune, a great blessing, a great crime, a noble action, are building-sites for a child's church.

Fear should not create the God of Childhood.

Levana : Second Fragment, chap. II. s. 38.

Nur keine Furcht erschaffe den Gott der Kindheit; sie selber ist vom bösen Geiste geschaffen; soll der Teufel der Großvater Gottes werden?

Let not fear create the God of childhood; fear was itself created by a wicked spirit; shall the devil become the grandfather of God?

Living Religion.

Levana : Second Fragment, chap. II. *s.* 38.

Nicht durch die Lehrsätze, sondern durch die Geschichten der
Bibel keimet lebendige Religion auf; die beste christliche
Religionlehre ist das Leben Christi, und dann das Leiden und
Sterben seiner Anhänger, auch außerhalb der heiligen Schrift
erzählt.

Living religion grows not by the doctrines, but by the narratives
of the Bible ; the best Christian religious doctrine is the life of
Christ; and after that, the sufferings and deaths of his followers,
even those not related in Holy Writ.

The Wild Flowers gathered in our Youth.

Levana : Third Fragment, chap. I. *s.* 42.

Und wer hat nicht an sich meine Erfahrung gemacht, daß
oft ein ländlicher Blumenstrauß, welcher uns als Kindern im
Dorf ein Lustwald gewesen, in späten Mannjahren und in der
Stadt durch seine alten Düfte unnennbare Zurückentzückungen
in die göttliche Kindheit gegeben, und wie er, gleich einer
Blumengöttin, uns in das erste umfassende Aurorengewölfe der
ersten dunkeln Gefühle hineingehoben?

And who is there who has not experienced in himself—what I
have done—that often a nosegay of wild flowers, which was to us,
as village children, a grove of pleasure, has in after-years of manhood, and in the town, given us by its old perfume an indescribable transport back into godlike childhood? and how, like a
flower-goddess, it has raised us into the first embracing Aurora-
clouds of our first dim feelings?

The Joys and Sorrows of Children.

Levana : Third Fragment, chap. II. *s.* 43.

Freilich sind alle Schmerzen der Kinder nur kürzeste Nächte,
wie ihre Freuden nur heißeste Tage ; und zwar beides so sehr,
daß in der spätern, oft wolken- und sternlosen Lebenszeit sich
der aufgerichtete Mensch nur alter Kinderfreuden sehnsüchtig
erinnert, indeß er der Kinderschmerzen ganz vergessen zu haben
scheint.

Certainly all the sorrows of children are but shortest nights, as their joys are but hottest days ; and both so much so, that in the later, often clouded and starless, time of life, the matured man only longingly remembers his old childhood's pleasures, while he seems altogether to have forgotten his childhood's griefs.

BEWARE OF FRIGHTENING CHILDREN.

Levana: Third Fragment, chap. II. *s.* 43.

Eltern, bedenkt also, daß jeder Kindheit-Ruprecht, wenn er Jahrzehende lange an der Kette gelegen, davon sich losreißet, und sich über den Menschen herwirft, so bald er ihn auf dem Krankenlager findet. Der erste Schreck ist desto gefährlicher, je jünger er fällt; später erschrickt der Mensch immer weniger; der kleine Wiegen= und Betthimmel des Kindes wird leichter ganz verfinstert, als der Sternenhimmel des Mannes.

Parents, consider then that every childhood's Rupert,* even though it has lain chained for tens of years, yet breaks loose and gains mastery over the man so soon as it finds him on a sick-bed. The first fright is the more dangerous, the sooner it happens ; as the man grows older he is less and less easily frightened : the little cradle or bed-canopy of the child is more easily quite darkened than the starry heaven of the man.

* Rupert is the name given in Germany to the fictitious being employed to frighten children into obedience.

HAPPINESS DANCES IN THE CHILD.

Levana: Third Fragment, chap. IV. *s.* 55.

Im Kinde tanzt noch die Freude, im Manne lächelt oder weint sie höchstens. Der reife Mensch darf durch den Tanz nur die Schönheit der Kunst, nicht sich und seine Empfindung, ausdrücken; Liebe würde sich dadurch zu roh, Freude zu laut und zu keck, vor der ernsten Nemesis gebärden.—Im Kinde leben noch Leib und Seele in den Flitterwochen einträchtig, und der freudigen Seele hüpfet noch der lustige Körper nach, bis später beide von Tisch und Bett sich scheiden und endlich ganz verlassen; der leise Zephyr der Zufriedenheit dreht später die schwere metallne Fahne nicht mehr zu seinem Zeiger um.

In the child happiness dances ; in the man, at most, it only smiles or weeps. The mature man can in dancing only express the beauty of the art, not himself or his emotions ; love would thereby comport itself too rudely, joy too loudly and boldly, before the stern Nemesis.　In the child, body and soul still live united in their honeymoon, and the active body dances after the happy soul ; until afterwards both separate from bed and board, and at last entirely leave one another.　In later times the light zephyrs of contentment cannot turn the heavy metal standard to point its curse.

A Child's Tears.

Levana : Third Fragment, chap. VIII. *s.* 66.

Wenn Rubens durch einen Strich ein lachendes Kind in ein weinendes verkehrte: so thut die Natur diesen Strich eben so oft an dem Urbilde; nie zieht ein Kindauge, wie die Sonne, leichter Wasser, als in dem heißen Wetter der Lust.

As Rubens by one stroke converted a laughing into a crying child, so nature frequently makes this stroke in the original : a child's eye, like the sun, never draws water so readily as in the hot temperature of pleasure.

Mothers.

Levana : Fourth Fragment, chap. II. *s.* 78.

Aber ihr Mütter, und besonders ihr in den höhern und freiern Ständen, denen das Geschick das Lasttragen der Haus= haltung erspart, die es mit einem heitern grünen Erziehgarten für eure Kinder umgibt, wie könnt ihr lieber die Langweile der Einsamkeit und der Geselligkeit erwählen, als den ewigen Reiz der Kinderliebe, das Schauspiel schöner Entfaltung, die Spiele geliebtester Wesen, das Verdienst schönster und längster Wir= kung? Verächtlich ist eine Frau, die Langweile haben kann, wenn sie Kinder hat.

But you mothers, and especially you in the higher and less busy classes, whose fortune spares you the heavy burden of careful housekeeping, and surrounds you with a cheerful green garden for the education of your children,—how is it that you can prefer the tedium of solitude and society to the enduring charms of your children's love—to the drama of their fair development—to the sports of the best-beloved beings—to the reward of the most de- lightful and lasting influence? That woman is despicable, who, having children, ever feels ennui.

The Child never forgets his Mother.

Levana: Fourth Fragment, chap. II. *s.* 78.

Nie, nie hat eines je seiner rein= und rechterziehenden Mutter vergessen. Auf den blauen Bergen der dunkeln Kinderzeit, nach welchen wir uns ewig umwenden und hinblicken, stehen die Mütter auch, die uns von da herab das Leben gewiesen; und nur mit der seligsten Zeit zugleich könnte das wärmste Herz vergessen werden. Ihr wollt recht stark geliebt seyn, Weiber, und recht lange und bis in den Tod: nun so seyd Mütter eurer Kinder.

Never, never has one forgotten his pure, right-educating mother. On the blue mountains of our dim childhood, towards which we ever turn and look, stand the mothers, who marked out to us from thence our life; the most blessed age must be forgotten ere we can forget the warmest heart. You wish, O woman! to be ardently loved, and for ever, even till death. Be, then, the mothers of your children.

Resemblance between Women and Children.

Levana: Fourth Fragment, chap. III. *s.* 79.

Dieselbe unzersplitterte Einheit der Natur — dasselbe volle Anschauen und Auffassen der Gegenwart — dieselbe Schnelligkeit des Witzes — der scharfe Beobachtung=Geist — die Heftigkeit und Ruhe — die Reizbarkeit und Beweglichkeit — das gutmüthige schnelle Uebergehen vom Innern zum Aeußern, und umgekehrt, von Göttern zu Bändern, von Sonnenstäubchen zu Sonnen= systemen — die Vorliebe für Gestalten und Farben, und die Erregbarkeit, setzen die körperliche Nähe beider Wesen mit einer geistigen fort. Gleichsam zum Gleichniß werden daher die Kinder anfangs weiblich gekleidet.

The same unbroken unity of nature—the same clear perception and understanding of the present—the same sharpness of wit, the keen spirit of observation, ardour and quietness, excitability and easily-raised emotions—the ready quick passage from the inward to the outward, and conversely, from gods to ribbons, from motes in the sunbeam to solar system—the admiration of forms and colours, and excitability, carry out by a mental alliance the physical alliance of the two beings. Hence, to use an appropriate simile, children are in the first instance in women's habits.

For what Purpose Nature sent Women into the World.

Levana: Fourth Fragment chap. III. *s.* 81.

Mit diesem Brautschatz der Liebe schickte die Natur die Frauen in's Leben, nicht etwa, wie Männer oft glauben, damit sie selber von jenen so recht durch und durch, von der Sohle bis zur Glatze, liebgehabt würden, sondern darum, damit sie — was ihre Bestimmung ist — Mütter wären, und die Kinder, denen Opfer nur zu bringen, nicht abzugewinnen sind, lieben könnten.

Nature sent women into the world with this bridal dower of love, not, as men often think, that they altogether and entirely love them from the crown of their head to the sole of their feet, but for this reason, that they might be, what their destination is— mothers, and love children, to whom sacrifices must ever be offered, and from whom none are to be obtained.

The Maiden and the Matron.

Levana: Fourth Fragment, chap. III. *s.* 85.

Wahrlich eine kräftige und rein erzogene Jungfrau ist eine so poetische Blume der matten Welt, daß jedem der Anblick, diese Prunkblüthe einige Jahre nach den Flitterwochen mit welkgelben gekrümmten Blättern in unbegossenen Blumenscherben nieder= hängen zu sehen, wehe thun müßte, sobald er nur darauf als ein Dichter schaute, wenn er folglich im Schmerze über die Dienstbarkeit und Knechtgestalt des menschgewordenen Lebens, über den Unterschied der Frau von Jungfrau lieber das Tödt= lichste wünschte; so daß er die Jungfrau lieber noch mit ihrem Knospenkranze von Rosen, mit ihrer Zärte, ihrer Unkunde der Lebens=Schärfen, ihrem Traum=Abrisse eines heiligen Edens lieber, sag' ich, in die Gottesacker=Erde, als in die Lebens=Heide schicken würde. — Thu' es doch nicht Dichter; die Jungfrau wird ja Mutter, und gebärt die Jugend und das Eden wieder, das ihr entflogen ist; auch zur Mutter fliegt einstmals eines zurück, aber ein schöneres; und so lasse, was ist!

Certainly a wisely and purely educated maiden is so poetic a flower of this dull world, that the sight of this glorious blossom hanging some years after the honeymoon, with yellow faded leaves, in un- watered beds, must grieve any man who beholds it with a poet's eye; and who must, consequently, in sorrow over the common usefulness and servitude of the merely human life, over the difference between the virgin and the matron, utter the deadliest wishes; yes, I say, he would rather send the virgin, with her wreath of rosebuds, her tenderness, her ignorance of the sufferings of life, her dream-pictures of holy Eden, into the graveyard of earth, which is God's field, than into the waste places of life. Yet, do it not, poet; the virgin becomes a mother, and again gives birth to the youth and the Eden which have fled from her; and to the mother herself they return, and fairer than before; and so let it be as it is.

WOMAN IS ALL HEART.

Levana: Fourth Fragment, chap. IV. *s.* 88.

Die Frau fühlt sich, aber sieht sich nicht; sie ist ganz Herz, und ihre Ohren sind Herz-Ohren. Sich selber und was dazu gehört, nämlich Gründe anzuschauen, wird ihr zu sauer. Vielleicht ließ deßwegen die alte Rechtsgelehrsamkeit den Schwur früher einem Manne, als einer Frau, abnehmen, hingegen die Folter früher dieser, als jenem, anthun. Gründe verändern und bewegen den festen Mann leichter, als die weiche bewegliche Frau, so wie der Blitz leichter durch feste Körper geht, als durch die leichte Luft.

A woman feels, but does not see herself; she is all heart— her very ears are ears of the heart. To observe herself, and what pertains thereunto, viz., reasons, is too disagreeable for her. Perhaps it was on this account that our ancient jurisprudence sooner relieved a man than a woman from an oath, but applied the torture sooner to him than to her. Reasons change and affect the firm man more easily than the weak versatile woman, as lightning passes better through solid bodies than through the thin air.

FEELINGS AND PRINCIPLES.

Levana: Fourth Fragment, chap. IV. *s.* 88.

Gefühle als leichte Truppen fliehen und kommen, dem Siege der Gegenwart folgend; Begriffe aber bleiben als Linientruppen unverrückt, und stehen bei.

Feelings come and go like light troops following the victory of the present; but principles, like troops of the line, are undisturbed, and stand fast.

Y

The Higher Worth of Women than of Men.

Levana : Fourth Fragment, chap. IV. *s.* 89.

Je reiner das Goldgefäß, desto leichter wird es verbogen; der höhere weibliche Werth ist leichter einzubüßen, als der männliche.

The purer the golden vessel the more readily is it bent ; the higher worth of women is sooner lost than that of men.

What produces Vanity.

Levana : Fourth Fragment, chap. IV. *s.* 96.

Vorzüge, welche wie Blumen auf der Oberfläche liegen, und immer prangen, machen leicht eitel ; daher Weiber Witzköpfe, Schauspieler, Soldaten durch Gegenwart, Gestalt und Anzug es sind; indeß andere Vorzüge, die wie Gold in der Tiefe ruhen, und sich nur mühsam offenbaren, Stärke, Tiefsinn, Sittlichkeit, bescheiden lassen und stolz.

Charms which, like flowers, lie on the surface and always glitter, easily produce vanity ; hence women, wits, players, soldiers, are vain, owing to their presence, figure, and dress.   On the contrary, other excellences, which lie down like gold, and are discovered with difficulty—strength, profoundness of intellect, morality—leave their possessors modest and proud.

Cheerfulness and Peevishness.

Levana : Fourth Fragment, chap. IV. *s.* 97.

Lachende Heiterkeit wirft auf alle Lebens-Bahnen Tages-Licht; der Mißmuth weht seinen bösen Nebel in jede Ferne ; der Schmerz macht zerstreuter und verworrener, als der sogenannte Leichtsinn.

Laughing cheerfulness throws sunlight on all the paths of life. Peevishness covers with its dark fog even the most distant horizon. Sorrow causes more absence of mind and confusion than so-called levity.

Two Different Worlds.

Levana : Fifth Fragment, chap. I. *s.* 100.

Wenn Sie Ihren Zögling zwischen zwei ganz verschiedenen

Welten hin= und herzuführen haben, aus der einen in die andere, aus jener ächtgroßen, auf welcher nur Seelen=Adel, Charakter, große Zwecke, und große Blicke, und Verächter der Zeit und Lust, und Menschen der Ewigkeit standen und galten, und wo ein Epaminondas, Sokrates, Cato in ihren Katakomben, als aus ewigen delphischen Höhlen, sprachen und riethen, wo der Ernst, und der Mensch, und Gott, alles wog — aus dieser heraus in jene scheingroße Welt, worin alles Große und Vergangene leicht, alles Leichte und Gegenwärtige bedeutend genommen wird, wo alles Sitte, nicht Pflicht ist.

If you have to conduct your pupil through two totally different worlds, out of the one into the other—out of that really great world in which only nobility of soul, character, great principles, and comprehensive views, are valued—where only the despisers of pleasure and the passing hour, the men of eternity, stand— where an Epaminondas, a Socrates, a Cato, still speak from their tombs, and deliver oracles as from an everlasting Delphic cavern —where earnestness of purpose and man and God bring all things into life ; out of this into that world of sham greatness in which all that is great and departed is little esteemed, and what is trifling and present is alone held important—where everything is custom and nothing duty.

PRINCE ALBERT.

Levana : Fifth Fragment, chap. I. s. 100.

Ich wüßte keine ehrwürdigere Gruppe, als einen fürstlichen Vater unter seinen Söhnen, ihnen die hohen Kron=Gesetze strenge einprägend, die er selber erfüllte.

I can imagine no more honourable group than a royal father among his sons, earnestly instilling into them the high laws of the kingly office which he himself religiously observed.

UPRIGHT MINDS ARE LIKE STRAIGHT ROADS.

Levana : Fifth Fragment, chap. I. s. 100.

Gerade Seelen scheinen, wie gerade Alleen, dem Auge nur die halbe Größe zu haben, im Vergleich mit denen, die sich künstlich winden ; aber die ganze findet man durch näheres Eingehen in sie.

Upright minds are like straight roads, which seem to the eye scarce half so long as those which wind artfully about; but their true length is found by nearer examination.

Variety of mere Nothings.

Levana: Fifth Fragment, chap. I. *s.* 100.

Weil Verſchiedenheit des Nichts mehr ergötzt, als Einerleiheit des Etwas.

Because variety of mere nothings gives more pleasure than uniformity of something.

JOHANN RIST.

Born A.D. 1607.   Died A.D. 1667.

Self-Conquest.

Heldenſtärke.

Schwer iſt's, gleich dem Babelvolke,
Zinnen bis gen Himmel baun,
Schwer, wie Dädalus die Wolke
Ueberfliegen ſonder Graun;
Schwer iſt's, Löwenmütter binden:
Schwerer, ſelbſt zu überwinden.

Der iſt überall zu loben,
Der ſein eigner Meiſter iſt!
Schreclos bei des Unglücks Toben
Und verkappter Neider Liſt'
Ob er heute ſtirbt, ob morgen,
So geſchicht's doch ohne Sorgen.

It is difficult, like the people of Babel, to build towers to heaven —difficult, like Dædalus, to fly above the clouds without feeling horror—it is difficult to bind the mother of the young lion—more difficult still to conquer our passions.

He is to be praised above all who is his own master! who is fearless amidst the raging of misfortune and the artifices of the envious. Whether he dies to-day or to-morrow, he dies without anxiety.

SALIS.

Born A.D. 1762.   Died A.D. 1834.

Johann Gaudenz von Salis-Seewis was born A.D. 1762 in his father's castle of Bothmar, near Malans in Graubündten, and acted as captain in the Swiss Guards at Versailles till the French Revolution. Latterly his life was spent in Paris, Rouen, and Arras. He died at Malans, January the 28th, 1834.

THE GRAVE.

Das Grab.

Das Grab ist tief und stille
Und schauderhaft sein Rand;
Es deckt mit schwarzer Hülle
Ein unbekanntes Land.

Das Lied der Nachtigallen
Tönt nicht in seinem Schooß;
Der Freundschaft Rosen fallen
Nur auf des Hügels Moos.

Verlaßne Bräute ringen
Umsonst die Hände wund;
Der Waise Klagen dringen
Nicht in der Tiefe Grund.

Doch sonst an keinem Orte
Wohnt die ersehnte Ruh:
Nur durch die dunkle Pforte
Geht man der Heimath zu.

Das arme Herz, hienieden
Von manchem Sturm bewegt,
Erlangt den wahren Frieden
Nur, wo es nicht mehr schlägt.

The grave is deep and still, and fearful is its brink ; it covers with a dark mantle an unknown land.

The song of the nightingale sounds not in its bosom ; the roses of friendship fall only on the moss of the hillock.

Forsaken brides in vain wring their hands ; the wailings of the orphan penetrate not the depths of the ground.

Yet in no other place dwells the longed-for rest ; only through its dark portals man goes to his home.

The poor heart, tormented here below by many a storm, only attains true peace where it no longer beats.

Man's Wisdom appears in his Actions.

Ermunterung.

Handelt! durch Handlungen zeigt sich der Weise,
Ruhm und Unsterblichkeit sind ihr Geleit.
Zeichnet mit Thaten die schwindenden Gleise
Unserer flüchtig entrollenden Zeit.
Den uns umschliessenden Zirkel beglücken,
Nütze so viel, als ein Jeder vermag.
O das erfüllet mit stillem Entzücken,
O das entwölket den düstersten Tag!

Muthig! Auch Leiden, sind einst sie vergangen,
Laben die Seele, wie Regen die Au'!
Gräber, von Trauer-Cypressen umhangen,
Malet bald stiller Vergissmeinnicht Blau.
Freunde, wir sollen, wir sollen uns freuen,
Freud' ist des Vaters erhab'nes Gebot,
Freude der Unschuld kann niemals gereuen,
Lächelt durch Rosen dem nahenden Tod.

Act! the wise are known by their actions—fame and immortality are ever their attendants. Mark with deeds the vanishing traces of swift-rolling time. Let us make happy the circle around us—be useful as much as we may. For that fills up with soft rapture, that dissolves the dark clouds of the day!

Courage! even sorrows, when once they are vanished, quicken the soul as rain the valley! Soon will the graves, overshadowed by the cypresses, be covered by the silent forget-me-not's blue. Friends, let us then rejoice and be cheerful ; joy is the command of the Father on high ; the pleasures of innocence can never bring repentance—they smile amid roses when death draweth nigh.

SCHEFER.

Born A.D. 1784. Died A.D. 1862.

Leopold Schefer was born, 1784, at Muskau, where he spent most of his life on his own property, and where he died 1862.

WHAT THOU DOST IS DONE FOR ETERNITY.

Aus: Laienbrevier.

Denn wiſſe, was du auch gethan, du thuſt
Es auf Zeitlebens in Erinnerung;
Die gute That klingt hell den Himmel an
Wie eine Glocke, ja er wird zum Spiegel,
In dem du aufſchauend ſelig dich erblickſt.

For know, whatever thou doest thou dost through life's never-dying memory; good deeds ring clear through heaven like a bell—yea, shine like a mirror, in which thou mayest behold thyself with joy.

LIVE IN PURITY.

Lebe rein, mein Kind, dies ſchöne Leben,
Rein von allem Fehl und böſem Wiſſen,
Wie die Lilie lebt in ſtiller Unſchuld,
Wie die Taube in des Haines Wipfeln;
Daſs du, wenn der Vater niederblicket,
Seiſt ſein liebſtes Augenmerk auf Erden,
Wie des Wandrers Auge unwillkürlich
An den ſchönen Abendſtern ſich heftet;
Daſs du, wenn die Sonne dich einſt löſet,
Eine reine Perl' ihr mögeſt zeigen,
Daſs dein Denken ſei wie Duft der Roſe,
Daſs dein Lieben ſei wie Licht der Sonne,
Wie des Hirten Nachtgeſang dein Leben,
Wie ein Ton aus ſeiner ſanften Flöte.

Live in purity, my child, through this fair life, pure from every vice and evil knowledge, as the lily lives in silent innocence, as the turtle-dove amid the branches, that thou, when the Father downward gazes, mayest be his beloved object on earth, as the eye of the unconscious wanderer gazes on the lovely star of even; that thou, when the sun dissolves thee, mayest show thyself a pearl of purest whiteness—that thy thoughts may be like roses' perfume—that thy love may be like a glowing sunbeam, and thy life like shepherd's song of evening—like the tones his flute pours forth so softly.

SCHILLER.

Born A.D. 1759.   Died A.D. 1805.

John Christopher Frederick von Schiller was born at Marbach, a small town in the duchy of Wirtemberg, A.D. 1759, the same year as Robert Burns, and about ten years before Napoleon. His father, Casper Schiller, was in the military service of the Duke of Wirtemberg, and continued to serve his serene highness in various capacities during a long life. To his mother it is thought that Schiller owed the preternatural endowments of his intellect. She was of humble origin—the daughter of a baker, but rich in the gifts of the heart and understanding. Schiller passed a happy childhood with his pious parents. He received his education at Stuttgard, and became M.D. in 1780. His writings, more particularly "The Robbers," gave offence to the Duke of Wirtemberg, and after much petty persecution he fled to Mannheim, where he became acquainted with Dalberg, the director of a theatre. This connection aided in determining the subsequent direction of Schiller's talents; and his "Fiesco," his "Intrigue and Love," his "Don Carlos," and his "Maria Stuart," followed within a short period of years. Finally he brought out his "Wallenstein," an immortal drama, and, beyond all competition, the nearest in point of excellence to the dramas of Shakespeare. In 1799 he was appointed to the chair of Civil History in Jena, but his health had been gradually undermined by his own negligence, sitting up through the night and defrauding his wasted frame of all natural and restorative sleep. He died on the 9th May 1805.

JOY.

An die Freude. St. 4.

Freude heißt die starke Feder
 In der ewigen Natur.
Freude, Freude treibt die Räder
 In der großen Weltenuhr.
Blumen lockt sie aus den Keimen,
 Sonnen aus dem Firmament,
Sphären rollt sie in den Räumen,
 Die des Sehers Rohr nicht kennt.

Joy is the mainspring in the whole round of everlasting Nature; joy, joy moves the wheels of the great timepiece of creation; she it is that loosens flowers from their buds, suns from the firmament; she that rolls spheres in distant space, seen not by the glass of the astronomer.

JOY.

An die Freude. St. 5.

Aus der Wahrheit Feuerspiegel
Lächelt sie den Forscher an.

Zu der Tugend steilem Hügel
Leitet sie des Dulders Bahn.
Auf des Glaubens Sonnenberge
Sieht man ihre Fahnen wehn,
Durch den Riß gesprengter Särge
Sie im Chor der Engel stehn.

Joy smiles on the toil of the investigator of truth from her
bright mirror; she leads the patient on his way to the steep
heights of virtue; we see on Faith's refulgent mountain her
banners wave aloft; through the opening of the grave joy pervades
the choir of angels.

I WAS BORN IN ARCADIA.

Resignation. St. 1.

Auch Ich war in Arkadien geboren.

I too was born in Arcadia.

This is the motto which Goethe chose for his *Travels in Italy.*
It is a very common saying or citation in Germany.

THE MAY OF LIFE ONLY BLOOMS ONCE.

Resignation. St. 2.

Des Lebens Mai blüht einmal und nicht wieder.

The May of life only blooms once, and never a second time.

THE WORLD'S DOOMSDAY.

Resignation. St. 17.

Die Weltgeschichte ist das Weltgericht.

The world's history is the world's judgment-doom.

ETERNITY GIVES NOTHING BACK.

Resignation. St. 18.

Was man von der Minute ausgeschlagen,
Gibt keine Ewigkeit zurück.

Eternity gives nothing back of the minute that has struck.

TRUTH AND BEAUTY.

Die Götter Griechenlands. St. 6.

Aus der schlechtesten Hand kann Wahrheit mächtig noch wirken;
Bei dem Schönen allein macht das Gefäß den Gehalt.

Truth can work powerfully, even when directed by the worst hand ; but in the case of the beautiful it is the vessel that makes the contents.

THE BEAUTIFUL.

Die Götter Griechenlands. St. 6.

Damals war nichts heilig, als das Schöne.

In days of yore nothing was holy but the beautiful.

THE FAITHLESS.

Die Ideal. St. 1.

So willst du treulos von mir scheiden.

So will'st thou, faithless one, leave me.

YOUTH FLIES SWIFTLY.

Der Jüngling am Bache. St. 1.

An der Quelle saß der Knabe,
  Blumen wand er sich zum Kranz.
Und er sah sie fortgerissen
  Treiben in der Wellen Tanz.
Und so fliehen meine Tage,
  Wie die Quelle, rastlos hin!
Und so bleichet meine Jugend,
  Wie die Kränze schnell verblühn.

The youngster sat by the brook, plaiting a wreath of flowers, when he saw them torn from his hand and carried dancing down the stream : so fly away my days in restlessness, like the waters, and so my youth is blanched, as the flowers quickly lose their bloom.

ROOM ENOUGH IN THE SMALLEST COT FOR LOVERS.

St. 4.

Raum ist in der kleinsten Hütte
Für ein glücklich liebend Paar.

In the smallest cot there is room enough for a loving pair.

EVERY BEAUTIFUL GIFT OF HEAVEN IS EVANESCENT.

Die Gunst des Augenblicks. St. 8.

Wie im hellen Sonnenblicke
Sich ein Farbenteppich webt,

Wie auf ihrer bunten Brücke
    Iris durch den Himmel schwebt.

So ist jede schöne Gabe
    Flüchtig wie des Blitzes Schein;
Schnell in ihrem düstern Grabe
    Schließt die Nacht sie wieder ein.

As in a bright sun-blink a prismatic carpet is woven, while Iris moves through the heaven up her parti-coloured bridge, so evanescent is every fair gift like the lightning's gleam ; quick in her dark grave the night again envelops them.

Shakespeare says—

> " And ere a man hath power to say 'Behold ! '
> The jaws of darkness do devour it up ;
> So quick bright things come to confusion."

LIFE.

An die Freunde. St. 1.

Wir, wir leben! Unser sind die Stunden,
Und der Lebende hat Recht.

We, we live ! Ours are the hours, and the living have their claims.

THE POET'S FANCY.

An die Freunde. St. 4.

Größres mag sich anderswo begeben,
Als bei uns in unserm kleinen Leben;
Neues — hat die Sonne nie gesehn.
Sehn wir doch das Große aller Zeiten
Auf den Brettern, die die Welt bedeuten,
Sinnvoll still an uns vorübergehn.
Alles wiederholt sich nur im Leben,
Ewig jung ist nur die Phantasie.
Was sich nie und nirgends hat begeben,
Das allein veraltet nie!

Greater scenes may be elsewhere passing than on our narrow sphere ; anything new the sun has never seen. We see pass quickly before our mind's eye, at the poet's bidding, the great of all time on the stage of the world. Everything on earth repeats itself, fancy only has perpetual May ; what has never and nowhere been, that alone never grows old.

Fame is the Noblest of Human Possessions.

Das Siegesfest. St. 9.

Von des Lebens Gütern allen
Ist der Ruhm das höchste doch;
Wenn der Leib in Staub zerfallen,
Lebt der große Name noch.

Of all the possessions of this life fame is the noblest; when the body has sunk into the dust the great name still lives.

Drink and Forget the Bitters of Life.

Das Siegesfest. St. 11.

Trink' ihn aus, den Trank der Labe,
Und vergiß den großen Schmerz!
Wundervoll ist Bacchus Gabe,
Balsam für's zerrißne Herz.

Quaff it off, the drink of forgetfulness, and forget your tragic sorrows; wondrous is the gift of Bacchus, balm for the shattered soul.

Death is a Blessing to Mortals.

Klage der Ceres. St. 4.

Mütter die aus Pyrrha's Stamme
Sterbliche geboren sind,
Dürfen durch des Grabes Flamme
Folgen dem geliebten Kind;
Nur was Jovis Haus bewohnet,
Nahet nicht dem dunkeln Strand,
Nur die Seligen verschonet,
Parcen, eure strenge Hand.

Mothers, who are born of the mortal race of Pyrrha, can follow their beloved through the flames of the pile. Only those who dwell in Jove's palace are banished from the darksome strand. Ye Fates! your heavy hand spares only the heavenly deities.

Nature revives in Spring.

Klage der Ceres. St. 9.

Führt der gleiche Tanz der Horen
Freudig nun den Lenz zurück,

Wird das Todte neu geboren
Von der Sonne Lebensblick.
Keime, die dem Auge starben
In der Erde kaltem Schooß,
In das heitre Reich der Farben
Ringen sie sich freudig los.

When the measured dance of the hours brings back the happy smile of Spring, the buried dead is born again in the life-glance of the sun. The germs, which perished to the eye within the cold breast of the earth, spring up with joy in the bright realm of day.

THE CRANES OF IBYCUS.

Die Kraniche des Ibykus. St. 20.

Sieh' da, sieh' da, Timotheus,
Die Kraniche des Ibykus!

See there, see there, Timotheus, the cranes of Ibycus!

FRIENDSHIP.

Die Bürgschaft. St. 20.

Ich sey, gewährt mir die Bitte,
In eurem Bunde der Dritte.

Let me be, grant my prayer, the third of your band of love.

TEMPT NOT HEAVEN.

Der Taucher. St. 16.

Da unten aber ist's fürchterlich,
Und der Mensch versuche die Götter nicht.

But down there it is fearful, and man must not tempt the gods.

THE TERRIFIC GAME.

Der Taucher. St. 19.

Laßt, Vater, genug seyn das grausame Spiel!

Cease, father, the grim game has been played enough!

A FEELING BREAST.

Der Taucher. St. 21.

Unter Larven die einzig fühlende Brust.

Amidst horrible faces the only feeling breast.

WHAT IS THE TUMULT?

Der Kampf mit dem Drachen.

Was rennt das Volk, was wälzt sich dort
Die langen Gassen braufend fort?

Why runs the people, why rush they roaring through the streets!

PLUCK NOT THE FORBIDDEN FRUIT OF PLEASURE.

Das Ideal und das Leben. St. 2.

Wollt ihr schon auf Erden Göttern gleichen,
Frei seyn in des Todes Reichen,
Brechet nicht von seines Gartens Frucht!
An dem Scheine mag der Blick sich weiden;
Des Genuffes wandelbare Freuden
Rächet schleunig der Begierde Flucht.

If you wish to be like to the gods on earth, to be free in the realms of the dead, pluck not the fruit from the garden! in appearance it may glisten to the eye: but the perishable pleasure of possession quickly avenges the curse of curiosity.

LIFE MOVES ON IN SPITE OF US.

Das Ideal und das Leben. St. 5.

Mächtig, selbst wenn eure Sehnen ruhten,
Reißt das Leben euch in seine Fluten,
Euch die Zeit in ihren Wirbeltanz.

Even though your desires are satisfied, life hurries you forward on its flood, and the dancing surge of Time whirls you downward.

PLEASING THE MANY.

Das Ideal und das Leben. St. 5.

Kannst Du nicht Allen gefallen durch deine That und dein
    Kunstwerk,
Mach' es Wenigen recht; Vielen gefallen ist schlimm.

If thou canst not please every one through all thy labour and art-work, do what contents the few; pleasing the many is bad.

Victory crowns the Strong.

Das Ideal und das Leben. St. 5.

Wenn es gilt, zu herrschen und zu schirmen,
Kämpfer gegen Kämpfer stürmen
Auf des Glückes, auf des Ruhmes Bahn,
Da mag Kühnheit sich an Kraft zerschlagen,
Und mit krachendem Getös die Wagen
Sich vermengen auf bestäubtem Plan.
Muth allein kann hier den Dank erringen,
Der am Ziel der Hippodromes winkt,
Nur der Starke wird das Schicksal zwingen,
Wenn der Schwächling untersinkt.

If it be worth thy while to strive and fight, breast to breast on the road to fortune and to fame, where strength and valour are found, and where the cars with whirling thunder roll along the dusty plain, courage alone can here secure the prize which beckons you on towards the winning-post; in life victory only crowns the strong, while the feeble sinks in the struggle.

The Patriot's Blood.

Der Spaziergang, l. 99.

Von eurem Blute begossen
Grünet der Oelbaum, es keimt lustig die köstliche Saat.

From your blood the olive blooms and the precious seed springs lustily.

Art is nourished by Freedom.

Der Spaziergang, l. 122.

Von der Freiheit gesäugt wachsen die Künste der Lust.

Art draws its aliment from Freedom's breast.

The Eagle.

Der Spaziergang, l. 147.

Im einsamen Luftraum
Hängt nur der Adler und knüpft an das Gewölke die Welt.

The eagle, his calm wings unfurled,
Lone-halting in the solitary air,
Knits to the vault of heaven this ball—the world!

The Sun of Homer shines upon us still.

Der Spaziergang, l. 163.

Aber jugendlich immer, in immer veränderter Schöne
    Ehrst du, fromme Natur, züchtig das alte Gesetz
Immer dieselbe, bewahrst du in treuen Händen dem Manne,
    Was dir das gaukelnde Kind, was dir der Jüngling vertraut,
Nährest an gleicher Brust die vielfach wechselnden Alter;
    Unter demselben Blau, über dem nämlichen Grün
Wandeln die nahen und wandeln vereint die fernen Geschlechter,
    Und die Sonne Homers, siehe! sie lächelt auch uns.

But ever youthful, O bounteous Nature! thou honourest in ever-changing beauty, discreetly, one ancient law! Ever the same, thou hoardest in faithful hands for the man what the frolicsome boy or the youth has intrusted to thee. Thou nurturest at thy breasts impartially the many-changing ages; beneath the self-same blue vault, over the self-same green, eternally wander all races of men, near or distant, brother-like! Ah, see! the sun of Homer smiles upon us still!

Thought and Reflection are necessary.

Das Lied von der Glocke. St. 2.

Zum Werke, das wir ernst bereiten,
Geziemt sich wohl ein ernstes Wort;
Wenn gute Reden sie begleiten,
Dann fließt die Arbeit munter fort
So laßt uns jetzt mit Fleiß betrachten,
Was durch die schwache Kraft entspringt;
Den schlechten Mann muß man verachten,
Der nie bedacht, was er vollbringt.

Surely an earnest word is due to the work which the earnest hand prepares; when sweet discourse accompanies it, labour ever prospers there. So let us ponder with caution what is to spring from our flagging powers; for vile the wretch who never reflects on the business in which he is employed.

Oh, that Love were Eternal!

Das Lied von der Glocke. St. 5.

O zarte Sehnsucht, süßes Hoffen,
Der ersten Liebe goldne Zeit,

Das Auge steht den Himmel offen,
Es schwelgt das Herz in Seligkeit;
O daß sie ewig grünen bliebe,
Die schöne Zeit der jungen Liebe!

O tender longing! sweet hope! the golden time of first love—the eye sees the heaven open while the heart is silent in blissfulness.

Oh! that the year were ever vernal!
And lovers' youthful dreams eternal!

THE STERN AND THE MEEK ARE WELL JOINED.

Das Lied von der Glocke.   St. 7.

Denn, wo das Strenge mit dem Zarten,
Wo Starkes sich und Mildes paarten,
Da gibt es einen guten Klang.
Drum prüfe, wer sich ewig bindet,
Ob sich das Herz zum Herzen findet!
Der Wahn ist kurz, die Reu' ist lang.
Lieblich in der Bräute Locken
Spielt der jungfräuliche Kranz,
Wenn die hellen Kirchenglocken
Laden zu des Festes Glanz.
Ach! des Lebens schönste Feier
Endigt auch den Lebensmai,
Mit dem Gürtel, mit dem Schleier
Reißt der schöne Wahn entzwei.

For where the strong is betrothed to the weak, where the stern is joined to the meek, the tone it gives is clear and strong. Therefore let those who would unite themselves for aye pause and consider whether the heart flows in one to the heart, love-delighted. Illusion is brief, repentance long. Lovely in the bride's hair the bridal wreath plays when the church-bell invites to the love-feast. Alas! with that sweetest holiday life's young May is over for thee. With the zone that thou unbindest the sweet illusion vanishes too.

FIRE.

Das Lied von der Glocke.   St. 11.

Wohlthätig ist des Feuers Macht,
Wenn sie der Mensch bezähmt, bewacht.

Of wondrous use is the might of flame when man can watch and tame it.

Z

A Father's Joy in seeing his Family saved.

Das Lied von der Glocke. St. **13.**

Ein süßer Trost ist ihm geblieben,
Er zählt die Häupter seiner Lieben,
Und sieh! ihm fehlt kein theures Haupt.

A sweet joy remains to him; he tells his beloved children o'er, and, lo! not one is missing from that store.

Labour is Renown.

Das Lied von der Glocke. St. **19.**

Arbeit ist des Bürgers Zierde,
Segen ist der Mühe Preis;
Ehrt den König seine Würde,
Ehret uns der Hände Fleiß.

Labour is the ornament of the citizen; the reward of toil is when you confer blessings on others: his high dignity confers honour on the king; be ours the glory of our hands.

The Results of Freedom and Equality.

Das Lied von der Glocke. St. 23.

Freiheit und Gleichheit! hört man schallen;
Der ruh'ge Bürger greift zur Wehr,
Die Straßen füllen sich, die Hallen,
Und Würgerbanden ziehn umher.
Da werden Weiber zu Hyänen
Und treiben mit Entsetzen Scherz:
Noch zuckend, mit des Panthers Zähnen,
Zerreißen sie des Feindes Herz.
Nichts Heiliges ist mehr, es lösen
Sich alle Bande frommer Scheu;
Der Gute räumt den Platz dem Bösen,
Und alle Laster walten frei.

"Freedom and Equality!" are the words we hear: the peaceful citizen rushes to arms; the streets, the halls, are filled, and murderous bands swarm around. The hyena-shapes that once were women jest with the horrors they survey. While still palpitating, with panther's teeth they rend their enemy's heart. Holy things are known no more—all the bands of awe and reverence are burst. The wicked reign—the good retire—and universal crime is law.

Man in Error is Terrible.

Das Lied von der Glocke. St. 23.

Gefährlich ist's, den Leu zu wecken,
Verderblich ist des Tigers Zahn;
Jedoch der schrecklichste der Schrecken,
Das ist der Mensch in seinem Wahn.

It is dangerous to wake the lion from his sleep, terrific are the fangs of the tiger, but worse than both united is man in his delirious fury.

The Power of Song.

Die Macht des Gesanges. St. 4.

So rafft von jeder eiteln Bürde,
Wenn des Gesanges Ruf erschallt,
Der Mensch sich auf zur Geisterwürde
Und tritt in heilige Gewalt;
Den hohen Göttern ist er eigen,
Ihm darf nichts Irdisches sich nahn,
Und jede andre Macht muß schweigen,
Und kein Verhängniß fällt ihn an;
Es schwinden jedes Kummers Falten,
So lang des Liedes Zauber walten.

So song, like fate itself, is given
  To scare the idler thoughts away,
To raise the human to the holy,
  To wake the spirit from the clay!
One with the gods, the bard: before him
  All things unclean and earthly fly:
Hushed are all meaner powers, and o'er him
  The dark fate swoops unharming by:
And while the Soother's magic measures flow,
Smoothed every wrinkle on the brows of Woe!

Honour to Women.

Würde der Frauen. St. 1.

Ehret die Frauen! sie flechten und weben
Himmlische Rosen in's irdische Leben,
Flechten der Liebe beglückendes Band,
Und in der Grazie züchtigem Schleier

Nähren sie wachsam das ewige Feuer
Schöner Gefühle mit heiliger Hand.

Honour to women ! they twine and weave the roses of heaven into the life of man ; it is they that unite us in the fascinating bonds of love ; and, concealed in the modest veil of the Graces, they cherish carefully the external fire of delicate feeling with holy hands.

This has been caricatured into the following words :—

„Ehret die Frauen, sie flechten und weben
Wollene Strümpfe für's irdische Leben."

POWER OF WOMAN OVER MAN.

Würde der Frauen. St. 7.

Aber mit sanft überredender Bitte
Führen die Frauen den Scepter der Sitte,
Löschen die Zwietracht, die tobend entglüht,
Lehren die Kräfte, die feindlich sich hassen,
Sich in der lieblichen Form zu umfassen,
Und vereinen, was ewig sich flieht.

But with soft persuasive prayers woman wields the sceptre of the life which she charmeth : she lulls the discord which roars and glows—teaches the fierce powers which hate each other like fiends to embrace in the bonds of love—and draws together what are for ever flying asunder.

THE CHILD HAS INSTINCTS OF HEAVEN.

Thekla. St. 6.

Wage du zu irren und zu träumen :
Hoher Sinn liegt oft in kind'schem Spiel.

Oh, dare to err and to dream ; deep meaning often lies in the instinct of the child.

THE WORLD DARKENS WHAT IS BRIGHT.

Das Mädchen von Orleans. St. 3.

Es liebt die Welt, das Strahlende zu schwärzen,
Und das Erhabne in den Staub zu ziehn.

The world loves to darken what is bright, and to drag each loftier thought in the dust.

The Beautiful soon passes away.

Nenie. L. 11.

Siehe, da weinen die Götter, es weinen die Göttinnen alle,
  Daß das Schöne vergeht, daß das Vollkommene stirbt.
Auch ein Klaglied zu seyn im Mund der Geliebten, ist herrlich,
  Denn das Gemeine geht klanglos zum Orkus hinab.

Tears are shed by every god and goddess that the beautiful is past, that the perfect dies away ; yet noble is the voice of wailing for those whom we love, for the base go to Pluto unlamented and unmourned.

Man Free by Birthright.

Die Worte des Glaubens. St. 2.

Der Mensch ist frei geschaffen, ist frei,
  Und würd' er in Ketten geboren.

Man has been created free—is free by birthright, even though he may have been born in chains.

A Childlike Mind.

Die Worte des Glaubens. St. 3.

Und was kein Verstand der Verständigen sieht,
  Das übet in Einfalt ein kindlich Gemüth.

A childlike mind in its simplicity practises that science of good to which the wise may be blind.

There is a God.

Die Worte des Glaubens. St. 4.

Und ein Gott ist, ein heiliger Wille lebt,
  Wie auch der menschliche wanke ;
Hoch über der Zeit und dem Raume webt
  Lebendig der höchste Gedanke,
Und ob Alles in ewigem Wechsel kreis't,
  Es beharret im Wechsel ein ruhiger Geist.

And there is a God ; a holy will is active, however much the human will rocks to and fro ; high over time and space a sublime thought is woven, and though everything is in labour and change an immutable Spirit continues amidst all this change.

Bulwer thus translates it :—

  " And a God there is ! over space, over time,
    While the human will rocks like a reed to and fro,

Lives the will of the Holy—a purpose sublime,
  A thought woven over creation below ;
Changing and shifting the all we inherit,
But changeless through all one Immutable Spirit ! "

How anything Noble can be performed.

Breite und Tiefe.   St. 2.

Wer etwas Treffliches leisten will,
Hätt' gern was Großes geboren,
Der sammle still und unerschlafft
Im kleinsten Punkte die höchste Kraft.

Whoever wishes to perform something noble, if he would produce some great work, collects quietly and perseveringly the mightiest powers into the smallest space.

The Division of Ranks.

Unterschied der Stände.

Adel ist auch in der sittlichen Welt.   Gemeine Naturen
Zahlen mit dem, was sie thun, edle mit dem, was sie sind.

There is a nobility also in the moral world.   Common natures pay with that which they do, noble with that which they are. Bulwer thus translates this :—

  "Yes, in the moral world, as ours, we see
  Divided grades—a soul's nobility ;
  By deeds their titles commoners create,
  The loftier order are by birthright great."

Wisdom.

Wissenschaft.

Einem ist sie die hohe, die himmlische Göttin, dem Andern
Eine tüchtige Kuh, die ihn mit Butter versorgt.

To one it is the mighty, heavenly goddess, to another it is an excellent cow, that furnishes him with butter.

Kant and his Commentators.

Kant und seine Ausleger.

Wie doch ein einziger Reicher so viele Bettler in Nahrung
Setzt !   Wenn die Könige baun, haben die Kärrner zu thun.

How many starvelings one rich man can nourish !
When monarchs build the rubbish-carriers flourish.

HOPE.

Hoffnung.

Es reden und träumen die Menschen viel
  Von bessern künftigen Tagen;
Nach einem glücklichen, goldenen Ziel
  Sieht man sie rennen und jagen.
Die Welt wird alt und wird wieder jung,
  Doch der Mensch hofft immer Verbesserung.

Die Hoffnung führt ihn in's Leben ein,
  Sie umflattert den fröhlichen Knaben,
Den Jüngling locket ihr Zauberschein,
  Sie wird mit dem Greis nicht begraben;
Denn beschließt er im Grabe den müden Lauf,
Noch am Grabe pflanzt er — die Hoffnung auf.

Es ist kein leerer schmeichelnder Wahn,
  Erzeugt im Gehirne des Thoren.
Im Herzen kündet es laut sich an:
  Zu was Besserm sind wir geboren,
Und was die innere Stimme spricht,
Das täuscht die hoffende Seele nicht.

We children of men, we speak and dream
  Of future halcyon days ;
On some beloved and lovely theme
  We fix our steadiest gaze ;
The world grows old and young while we
Still hope this future good to see.

Gay Hope springs with us to life and light,
  And boyhood's by her illumed ;
The youth she enraptures with delight,
  With the old she's not entombed ;
For when we rest within the grave,
Even o'er its dust her flow'rets wave.

Hers is no flatt'ring empty show
  In the brain of folly bred,
For well our conscious bosoms know
  For glory they are made ;
And what this secret voice declares,
The future in fruition shares.

Destiny.

Shakespeare's Schatten, l. 35.

Das große, gigantische Schicksal,
Welches den Menschen erhebt, wenn es den Menschen zermalmt!

Vast, colossal Destiny, which raises man to fame, though it may also grind him to powder !

Seeming and Reality.

An Goethe, als er den Mahomet von Voltaire auf die
Bühne brachte. St. 6.

Der Schein soll nie die Wirklichkeit erreichen,
Und siegt Natur, so muß die Kunst entweichen.

Seeming will never reach reality ; and if nature gets the better, art must give way.

Freedom only in the Land of Dreams.

Der Antritt des neuen Jahrhunderts. St. 9.

Freiheit ist nur in dem Reich der Träume,
Und das Schöne blüht nur im Gesang.

Freedom is only in the land of dreams, and the beautiful only blooms in song.

The Child in the Cradle.

Das Kind in der Wiege.

Glücklicher Säugling! dir ist ein unendlicher Raum noch die
Wiege,
Werde Mann und dir wird eng die unendliche Welt.

Happy child ! the cradle is still to thee a vast space ; become a man, and the boundless world will be too small to thee.

It is the Heart that makes us Sons and Brothers.

The Robbers, I. 1.

Nicht Fleisch und Blut, das Herz macht uns zu Vätern und
Söhnen.

It is not flesh and blood, it is the heart that makes us fathers and sons.

What Nature has given.
The Robbers, I. 1.

Nein! nein! ich thu' ihr Unrecht. Gab sie uns doch Erfindungsgeist mit, setzte uns nackt und armselig an's Ufer dieses großen Oceans, Welt — Schwimme, wer schwimmen kann, und wer plump ist, geh' unter!

No, no! I do Nature injustice; she gave inventive faculty, and set us naked and helpless on the shore of this great ocean—the world; swim those who can—the heavy may go to the bottom.

The Man who fears nothing.
The Robbers, I. 1.

Wer nichts fürchtet, ist nicht weniger mächtig, als der, den Alles fürchtet.

The man who fears nothing is not less powerful than he who is feared by every one.

The Present Generation.
The Robbers, I. 2.

Da krabbeln sie nun, wie die Ratten auf der Keule des Herkules.

The present generation are like rats crawling about the club of Hercules.

Thus Shakespeare (*Julius Cæsar*, i. 2) says—

> "We petty men
> Walk under his huge legs and peep about."

Sweet to be lulled to Death by a Son's Prayers.
The Robbers, II. 2.

Wie süß ist's, eingewiegt zu werden in den Schlaf des Todes von dem Gebet eines Sohnes — das ist Wiegengesang.

How pleasant it is to be lulled into the sleep of death by a son's prayer—that is the true requiem!

The Honest Man and the Rogue.
The Robbers, II. 3.

Denn siehst du, ich pfleg' immer zu sagen: einen honneten

Mann kann man aus jedem Weidenstoßen formen, aber zu einem Spißbuben will's Grüß'.

Then observe that I used always to say that an honest man you may form of windlestraws, but to make a rogue you must have grist.

Feeling of Power.

The Robbers, II. 3.

Ich fühle eine Armee in meiner Fauſt.

I feel an army in my fist.

The Drama of Life.

The Robbers, III. 2.

Bruder — ich habe die Menſchen geſehen, ihre Bienenſorgen und ihre Rieſenprojecte — ihre Götterpläne und ihre Mäuſe= geſchäfte, das wunderſeltſame Wettrennen nach Glückſeligkeit; — dieſer dem Schwung ſeines Roſſes anvertraut — ein anderer der Naſe ſeines Eſels — ein dritter ſeinen eigenen Beinen; dieſes bunte Lotto des Lebens, worein ſo Mancher ſeine Unſchuld und — ſeinen Himmel ſeßt, einen Treffer zu haſchen, und — Nullen ſind der Auszug — am Ende war kein Treffer darin. Es iſt ein Schauſpiel, Bruder, das Thränen in deine Augen lockt, wenn es dein Zwerchfell zum Gelächter kißelt.

Brother, I have watched men : their insect cares and giant pro-jects—their godlike plans and their mouselike employments—their eager race after happiness ; this one trusting to the swift-ness of his horse—another to the nose of his ass—a third to his own legs ; this chequered lottery of life, on which so many stake their innocence and heaven to snatch a prize, and—blanks are all they draw ; for they find to their disappointment that there was no prize in the wheel. It is a drama, brother, which might bring tears into your eyes, while it burst your sides with laughter.

The Remorse of the Wicked.

The Robbers, III. 2.

Alles hinausgegangen, ſich im friedlichen Strahl des Früh= lings zu ſonnen — warum ich allein die Hölle ſaugen aus den Freuden des Himmels? — Daß Alles ſo glücklich iſt, durch den

Geift des Friedens Alles so verschwistert! — Die ganze Welt
eine Familie und ein Vater dort oben — Mein Vater nicht -
ich allein der Verstoßene, ich allein ausgemustert aus den Reihen
der Reinen — mir nicht der süße Name Kind — nimmer mir der
Geliebten schmachtender Blick — nimmer, nimmer des Busen-
freundes Umarmung. (Wild zurückfahrend.) Umlagert von
Mördern — von Nattern umzischt — angeschmiedet an das Laster
mit eisernen Banden — hinausschwindelnd in's Grab des Verderbens auf des Lasters schwankendem Rohr — mitten in den
Blumen der glücklichen Welt ein heulender Abbadonna!

Daß ich wiederkehren dürfte in meiner Mutter Leib! daß ich
ein Bettler geboren werden dürfte! — Nein; ich wollte nicht
mehr, o Himmel — daß ich werden dürfte wie dieser Taglöhner
einer! — O ich wollte mich abmüden, daß mir das Blut von den
Schläfen rollte — mir die Wollust eines einzigen Mittagsschlafs
zu erkaufen — die Seligkeit einer einzigen Thräne.

Es war eine Zeit, wo sie mir so gern flossen — o ihr Tage
des Friedens! du Schloß meines Vaters — ihr grünen schwär-
merischen Thäler! O all' ihr Elyssiums-Scenen meiner Kindheit! — werdet ihr nimmer zurückkehren — nimmer mit köstlichem Säuseln meinen brennenden Busen kühlen? — Traure
mit mir, Natur! — Sie werden nimmer zurückkehren, nimmer
mit köstlichem Säuseln meinen brennenden Busen kühlen. —
Dahin; dahin! unwiederbringlich!

See! all things are gone forth to bask in the peaceful beam of
the spring; why must I inhale alone the torments of hell out of
the joys of heaven? That all should be so happy, all so married
together by the spirit of peace! The whole world one family, its
Father above; that Father not mine! I alone the castaway! I
alone struck out from the company of the just! for me no child
to lisp my name; never for me the languishing look of one whom
I love! never! never the embracing of a bosom friend! Encircled
with murderers—serpents hissing around me—riveted to vice with
iron bonds—rushing down to the gulf of perdition on the eddy-
ing torrent of wickedness—amid the flowers of the glad world a
howling Abaddon! Oh, that I might return into my mother's
womb, that I might be born a beggar! I would never more—O
Heaven! that I could be as one of these day-labourers. Oh! I
would toil till the blood ran down from my temples to buy myself
the pleasure of one noontide sleep—the blessing of a single tear.
There was a time, too, when I could weep—O ye days of peace!

thou castle of my father! ye green, lovely valleys! O all ye Elysian scenes of my childhood! will ye never come again—never with your balmy sighing cool my burning bosom! Mourn with me, Nature! They will never come again—never cool my burning bosom with their balmy sighing! They are gone! gone! and may not return!

WE LIVE TO DIE IN SORROW.

The Robbers, IV. 2.

Alles lebt, um traurig wieder zu sterben. Wir interessiren uns nur darum, wir gewinnen nur darum, daß wir wieder mit Schmerzen verlieren.

We all live that we may die in sorrow. We devote our thoughts, and only win the things of this world to part with them in sorrow.

MAN IS MADE OF FILTH.

The Robbers, IV. 2.

Der Mensch entsteht aus Morast, und watet eine Weile im Morast, und macht Morast, und gährt wieder zusammen in Morast, bis er zuletzt an den Schuhsohlen seines Urenkels unfläthig anklebt. Das ist das Ende vom Lied—der morastige Cirkel der menschlichen Bestimmung.

Man is made of filth—wades a while in filth—produces filth—and sinks back again into filth, till at last it sticks to the boots of his own posterity. That is the burden of the song—the filthy cycle of human fate.

So Shakespeare (*Hamlet*, act v. sc. 1) says—"To what base uses we may return, Horatio! Why may not imagination trace the noble dust of Alexander till he find it stopping a bung-hole?"

EXTERNAL FORMS ARE THE TRAPPINGS OF THE MIND.

The Robbers, IV. 5.

Außendinge sind nur der Anstrich des Mannes—Ich bin mein Himmel und meine Hölle.

Outward things are only the trappings of the man. I am my own heaven and hell.

THE DESTINIES OF MANKIND ARE BALANCED.

The Robbers, v. 1.

Sehet zu, das Schickſal der Menſchen ſtehet unter ſich in fürchterlich ſchönem Gleichgewicht. Die Wagſchale dieſes Lebens ſinkend, wird hochſteigen in jenem, ſteigend in dieſem, wird in jenem zu Boden fallen. Aber was hier zeitliches Leiden war, wird dort ewiger Triumph; was hier endlicher Triumph war, wird dort ewige unendliche Verzweiflung.

Observe, the fates of men are balanced with wonderfully nice adjustments. The scale of this life, if it sinks, rises there, while if it rises here, it will sink to the ground there. What was here temporary affliction, will be there eternal triumph ; what was here temporary triumph, will be there eternal and ever-enduring despair.

JEALOUSY.

Fiesco, I. 1.

O der alles vergrößernden Eiferſucht!

O jealousy ! thou magnifier of trifles !

WHEN DOES A JEST LOSE ITS POINT?

Fiesco, I. 7.

Der Spaß verliert Alles, wenn der Spaßmacher ſelber lacht.

The jest loses its point when the wit is the first to laugh.

THE YOUTHFUL ARTIST CANNOT AT FIRST COMPREHEND THE DESIGN OF THE MASTER.

Fiesco, I. 9.

Ich dächte doch, das Gewebe eines Meiſters ſollte künſtlicher ſeyn, als dem flüchtigen Anfänger ſo geradezu in die Augen zu ſpringen.

I thought that it was not for the eye of the youthful artist to take in at once the vast design of the master.

THE PERJURIES OF MEN.

Fiesco, II. 3.

Einen Meineid! Hör auf! Ihr ermüdet den Griffel

Gottes, der fie niederfchreibt. Männer! Männer! wenn eure
Eide zu fo viel Teufeln würden, fie könnten Sturm gegen den
Himmel laufen, und die Engel des Lichts als Gefangene weg-
führen.

A false oath! Cease! Men! men! ye would tire the very pen
of the recording angel to write them down. If your violated oaths
were turned into devils, you might storm heaven itself, and lead
away the angels of light as prisoners.

THE WIND OF ACCIDENT.

Fiesco, II. 5.

Was der Ameife Vernunft mühfam zu Haufen fchleppt, jagt
in einem Hui der Wind des Zufalls zufammen.

What reason, like the careful ant, draws laboriously together,
the wind of accident collects in one brief moment.

THE MULTITUDE.

Fiesco, II. 7.

Der blinde, unbeholfene Koloß, der mit plumpen Knochen
anfangs Gepolter macht, Hohes und Niederes, Nahes und
Fernes mit gähnendem Rachen zu verfchlingen droht, und
zuletzt — über Zwirnfäden ftolpert?

The blind, unwieldy monster, which at first rattles its heavy
bones, threatening to swallow high and low, the near and distant
with gaping jaws, at last—stumbles over a thread.

ART THE RIGHT HAND OF NATURE.

Fiesco, II. 17.

Kunft ift die rechte Hand der Natur. Diefe hat nur
Gefchöpfe, jene hat Menfchen gemacht.

Art is the right hand of Nature. The latter has only given us
being, the former has made us men.

THE LAMP OF GENIUS.

Fiesco, II. 17.

Das Licht des Genie's bekam weniger Fett, als das Licht
des Lebens.

The lamp of genius burns away quicker than the lamp of life.

Different Degrees of Guilt.

Fiesco, III. 2.

Es ist schimpflich, eine volle Börse zu leeren — es ist frech, eine Million zu veruntreuen, aber es ist namenlos groß, eine Krone zu stehlen. Die Schande nimmt ab mit der wachsenden Sünde.

It is base to filch a purse – daring to embezzle a million, but it is great beyond measure to steal a crown. The sin lessens as the guilt increases.

The Thoughts of One climbing to a Throne.

Fiesco, III. 2.

Zu stehen in jener schrecklich erhabenen Höhe — niederzuschmollen in der Menschlichkeit reißenden Strudel, wo das Rad der blinden Betrügerin Schicksale schelmisch wälzt — den ersten Mund am Becher der Freude — tief unten den geharnischten Riesen Gesetz am Gängelbande zu lenken — schlagen zu sehen unvergoltene Wunden, wenn sein kurzarmiger Grimm an das Geländer der Majestät ohnmächtig poltert — die unbändigen Leidenschaften des Volks, gleich so viel strampfenden Rossen, mit dem weichen Spiele des Zügels zu zwingen — den emporstrebenden Stolz der Vasallen mit Einem — Einem Athemzug in den Staub zu legen, wenn der schöpferische Fürstenstab auch die Träume des fürstlichen Fiebers in's Leben schwingt!

To stand on that fearfully giddy height—to look down on the boiling vortex of the human race, where blind deceitful Fortune on her wheel is ever turning—to quaff early draughts of pleasure —to hold with firm hand in leading strings that armed giant law, while she strives with fruitless efforts against the might of majesty—to curb the turbulent passions of the people with playful rein, as if they were so many untamed horses—with a breath, a single breath, to restrain the rising pride of vassals, while the creative sceptre of the prince can embody even his wildest dreams of fancy!

The Stage of Life.

Fiesco, III. 2.

Nicht der Tummelplatz des Lebens — sein Gehalt bestimmt seinen Werth.

It is not the mere stage of life that stamps the value on us, but the manner in which we act our part.

Thunder.

Fiesco, III. 2.

Zerstücke den Donner in seine einfachen Sylben, und du wirst Kinder damit in den Schlummer singen; schmelze sie zusammen in einen plötzlichen Schall, und der monarchische Laut wird den ewigen Himmel bewegen.

Spread out the thunder into its single tones, and it becomes a lullaby for children ; pour it forth together in *one* quick peal, and the royal sound shall move the heavens.

The Moor has done his Work.

Fiesco, III. 4.

Der Mohr hat seine Arbeit gethan, der Mohr kann gehen.

The Moor has done his work – the Moor may go.

The Iron and Silken Cord.

Fiesco, III. 5.

Ketten von Stahl oder Seide — es sind Ketten.

The iron chain and the silken cord, both equally are bonds.

Many have died better than Thou.

Fiesco, III. 5.

Fahre wohl, Doria, schöner Stern!
　　　Auch Patroklus ist gestorben,
　　　Und war mehr als du.

Farewell, Doria, beauteous star !
　　　Patroclus to the shades is gone,
　　　And he was more than thou.

See Homer (*Il.* xxi. 106).

Novelty loses its Zest.

Fiesco, III. 10.

Sehen Sie, die beste Neuigkeit verliert, sobald sie Stadt= mährchen wird.

Observe, the prettiest novelty palls upon the taste **when it** becomes the town-talk.

THE WAY TO WOO A MAID.

Love and Intrigue, I. 2.

Einem Liebhaber, der den Vater zu Hülfe ruft, trau' ich — erlauben Sie — keine hohle Haselnuß zu. Ist er was, so wird er sich schämen, seine Talente durch diesen altmodischen Canal vor seine Liebste zu bringen — Hat er's Courage nicht, so ist er ein Hasenfuß, und für den sind keine Louisen gewachsen — — Da! hinter dem Rücken des Vaters muß er sein Gewerb' an die Tochter bestellen. Machen muß er, daß das Mädel lieber Vater und Mutter zum Teufel wünscht, als ihn fahren läßt, — oder selber kommt, dem Vater zu Füßen sich wirft und sich um Gotteswillen den schwarzen gelben Tod oder den Herzeinzigen ausbittet. — Das nenn' ich einen Kerl! das heißt lieben! und wer's bei dem Weibsvolk nicht so weit bringt, der soll — — auf seinem Gänsekiel reiten.

A lover who calls for the assistance of a father in his love affairs —with your permission—is not worth a doit. If there be anything in him he will blush to approach his beloved in this old-fashioned style. If he have not the courage, he is a mere milksop, and for him no Louisas are brought into the world. No! he must carry on his affairs with the daughter behind the back of the father, and so manage that the maiden would wish father and mother at Old Nick rather than give him up—or else that she come, and, throwing herself at her father's feet, implore death or the beloved of her heart. That's the fellow for me! That's what I call love ; and he who can't bring matters to this point with women folks may stick the goose-feather in his cap.

VIRTUE.

Love and Intrigue, II. 6.

Ehrfurcht befiehlt die Tugend auch im Bettlerkleid!

Virtue commands respect even in a beggar's garb!

THE ENTHUSIAST.

Love and Intrigue, III. 1.

Zwang **erbittert** die Schwärmer immer, aber bekehrt sie nie.

Opposition always inflames the enthusiast, never converts him.

2 A

THE WORM OF CONSCIENCE.

Love and Intrigue, v. 1.

Nur der Gewiſſenswurm ſchwärmt mit der Eule. Sünder und böſe Geiſter ſcheuen das Licht.

The worm of conscience only rambles with the owl; the light is shunned by none but sinners and evil spirits.

THE DRINK IS BAD.

Love and Intrigue, v. 7.

Die Limonade iſt matt wie deine Seele — Verſuche!

The lemonade is bad as thy soul—Taste it!

JUSTICE.

Demetrius, I. 1.

Es iſt die große Sache aller Staaten
Und Thronen, daß geſcheh', was Rechtens iſt,
Und Jedem auf der Welt das Seine werde;
Denn da, wo die Gerechtigkeit regiert,
Da freut ſich Jeder, ſicher ſeines Erb's,
Und über jedem Hauſe, jedem Thron
Schwebt der Vertrag wie eine Cherubswache.

It is the most important concern of every state and throne that justice should prevail, and all men in the world should have their own; for there where justice rules every one enjoys his property secure, and over every house and every throne law watches with an angel's eye.

THE MULTITUDE AND THE FEW.

Demetrius, I. 1.

Die Mehrheit?

Was iſt die Mehrheit? Mehrheit iſt der Unſinn;
Verſtand iſt ſtets bei Wen'gen nur geweſen.
Bekümmert ſich um's Ganze, wer nichts hat?
Hat der Bettler eine Freiheit, eine Wahl?
Er muß dem Mächtigen, der ihn bezahlt,
Um Brod und Stiefel ſeine Stimm' verkaufen.
Man ſoll die Stimmen wägen, und nicht zählen;

Der Staat muß untergehn, früh oder spät,
Wo Mehrheit siegt und Unverstand entscheidet.

Majority? What does that mean? sense has ever been centred in the few; what cares he who has nothing for the general weal? Has the beggar choice or liberty? He must sell his vote to the great ones, who pay him, for bread and raiment. Votes should be weighed, not counted. That state must sooner or later go to wreck where numbers sway and ignorance decides.

Customs.

Demetrius, I. 1.

Nicht fremder Brauch gedeiht in einem Lande.

Strange customs do not thrive in a foreign soil.

The Statue.

Demetrius, II. 1.

Du gleichst der unbeweglichen Gestalt,
Wie sie der Künstler in den Stein geprägt,
Um ewig fort dasselbe zu bedeuten.

Thou art like some motionless statue, which has been carved in stone by sculptor's chisel, and ever keeps the same unalterable mien.

The Pleasant Days are now over.

Don Carlos, I. 1. 1.

Die schönen Tage in Aranjuez
Sind nun zu Ende.

The pleasant days of Aranjuez are now gone.

Tennyson (*Poems*) says—

" Break, break, break,
    At the foot of thy crags, O sea!
    But the tender grace of a day that is dead
    Will never come back to me."

See (Lat.) Sweet meetings.

The Future.

Don Carlos, I. 1. 44.

O wer weiß,
Was in der Zeiten Hintergrunde schlummert?

Who knows what slumbering woes the future may have in store?

Tale-Bearers.

Don Carlos, I. 1. 73.

Doch hab' ich immer sagen hören, daß
Geberdenspäher und Geschichtenträger
Des Uebels mehr auf dieser Welt gethan,
Als Gift und Dolch in Mörders Hand nicht konnten.

Yet have I ever heard it said that spies and tale-bearers have done more mischief in this world than poisoned bowl or the assassin's dagger.

Times long past.

Don Carlos, I. 2. 47.

Du sprichst von Zeiten, die vergangen sind.

Thou speakest of times that long have passed **away.**

A Beautiful Idea.

Don Carlos, I. 2. 55.

O, der Einfall
War kindisch, aber göttlich schön! Vorbei
Sind diese Träume.

Oh, the idea, though only that of a child, was yet divinely fair! Those dreams are past.

The Pangs of Conscience.

Don Carlos, I. 2. 190.

Sprich mir von allen Schrecken des Gewissens,
Von meinem Vater sprich mir nicht.

Tell me of all the torturing pangs of conscience, but speak not to me of my father.

Great Souls.

Don Carlos, I. 4. 152.

Doch große Seelen dulden still.

Great souls suffer in silence.

The Sun sets not in my Dominions.

Don Carlos, I. 6. 58.

Ich heiße
Der reichste Mann in der getauften Welt;
Die Sonne geht in meinem Staat nicht unter.

I am called the richest monarch in Christendom. The sun never sets in my dominions.

The Mortal Point.

Don Carlos, I. 6. 65.

Hier ist die Stelle, wo ich sterblich bin.
This is the point in which I feel I am mortal.

Fear.

Don Carlos, I. 6. 68.

Wenn ich einmal zu fürchten angefangen,
Hab' ich zu fürchten aufgehört.

For the moment that my fear begins I have ceased to fear.
Shakespeare (*Othello*, iii. 3)—
" To be once in doubt
Is once to be resolved."

I defy the World with Thee.

Don Carlos, I. 9. 97.

Arm in Arm mit dir,
So fordr' ich mein Jahrhundert in die Schranken.
Arm in arm with thee, I dare defy the whole world into the lists.

A Tear.

Don Carlos, II. 2. 50.

Wer ist das?
Durch welchen Mißverstand hat dieser Frembling
Zu Menschen sich verirrt? — Die ewige
Beglaubigung der Menschheit sind ja Thränen;

Sein Aug' ist trocken, ihn gebar kein Weib—
O, zwingen Sie die nie benetzten Augen,
Noch zeitig Thränen einzulernen, sonst,
Sonst möchten Sie's in einer harten Stunde
Noch nachzuholen haben.

Who is this man? By what mistake of nature has he thus
strayed among mankind? Tears are the ever-enduring proof of
humanity; whose eye is dry was never born of woman. Oh, force
the eye that has never been moistened to learn in time the science
of tears, else in some dark hour you will have to find such relief.

A SON.

Don Carlos, II. 2. 90.

Wie entzückend
Und süß ist es, in einer schönen Seele
Verherrlicht uns zu fühlen, es zu wissen,
Daß unsre Freude fremde Wangen röthet,
Daß unsre Angst in fremden Busen zittert,
Daß unsre Leiden fremde Augen wässern! —
Wie schön ist es und herrlich, Hand in Hand
Mit einem theuern, vielgeliebten Sohn
Der Jugend Rosenbahn zurück zu eilen,
Des Lebens Traum noch einmal durchzuträumen!
Wie groß und süß, in seines Kindes Tugend
Unsterblich, unvergänglich fortzudauern,
Wohlthätig für Jahrhunderte! — Wie schön,
Zu pflanzen, was ein lieber Sohn einst erntet,
Zu sammeln, was ihm wuchern wird, zu ahnen,
Wie hoch sein Dank einst flammen wird!

What rapture of delight there is in feeling ourselves reflected
in the beauteous soul of another—to know that our joys gladden
another's cheek—our sorrows bring anguish to another's bosom—
that our grief causes tears to flow from another's eyes! How
beautiful, how glorious it is, hand in hand with a dear beloved
child, to tread once more the rosy paths of youth, and dream o'er
again life's fond illusions! How great, how sweet, to live through
endless ages immortal in the virtues of a son! How sweet to plant
what a son shall reap, to gather what will increase his store, anticipating how high his thanks will one day rise!

A Man's Insignificance.

Don Carlos, II. 5. 57.

Werd' ich das
In meines Nichts durchbohrendem Gefühle?

I am condemned by my own conscious insignificance.

Difficult to know Mankind.

Don Carlos, II. 10. 25.

Schwer zu unterscheiden,
Noch schwerer zu ergründen sind die Menschen.

It is difficult to understand men, but still more hard to know them thoroughly.

Restraints to be borne.

Don Carlos, II. 10. 91.

Des Zwanges ungewohnt, womit man Zwang
Zu kaufen sich bequemen muß.

Unaccustomed to those strict restraints to which one must submit who would govern others.

General Belief.

Don Carlos, III. 4. 54.

Doch freilich gibt es Fälle, wo der Glaube
Des Volks, und wär' er noch so unerwiesen,
Bedeutend wie die Wahrheit wird.

Yet there are occasions when the general belief of the people, even though it be groundless, works its effect as sure as truth itself.

A Virtuous Name.

Don Carlos, III. 4. 60.

Guter Name
Ist das kostbare, einz'ge Gut, um welches
Die Königin mit einem Bürgerweibe
Wetteifern muß.

A virtuous name is the precious only good for which queens and peasants' wives must contest together.

Truth.

Don Carlos, III. 4. 124.

Treue!

Die Treue warnt vor drohenden Verbrechen,
Die Nachgier spricht von den begangenen.

Truth! truth warns of threatening danger; it is malice that speaks only of the past.

Chance in Life.

Don Carlos, III. 9. 13.

Und was

Ist Zufall anders, als der rohe Stein,
Der Leben annimmt unter Bildners Hand?
Den Zufall gibt die Vorsehung — zum Zwecke
Muß ihn der Mensch gestalten.

What else is chance but the rude stone which receives its life from the sculptor's hand? Providence gives us chance—and man must mould it to his own designs.

The Spaniard.

Don Carlos, III. 10. 23.

Stolz will ich den Spanier.

Proud I wish the Spaniard to be.

Rage for Innovation.

Don Carlos, III. 10. 121.

Die lächerliche Wuth

Der Neuerung, die nur der Ketten Last,
Der sie nicht ganz zerbrechen kann, vergrößert,
Wird mein Blut nie erhitzen.

The ridiculous rage for innovation, which only increases the weight of the chains it cannot break, shall never fire my blood!

The Churchyard's Peace.

Don Carlos, III. 10. 220.

Die Ruhe eines Kirchhofs!

A churchyard's peace.

See (**Lat.**) Peace they call it.

ENTHUSIAST.

Don Carlos, III. 10. **277.**

Sonderbarer Schwärmer!

Enthusiast most strange!

THE CREATOR.

Don Carlos, III. 10. 292.

Er — der Freiheit

Entzückende Erscheinung nicht zu stören —
Er läßt des Uebels grauenvolles Heer
In seinem Weltall lieber toben — ihn,
Den Künstler, wird man nicht gewahr, bescheiden
Verhüllt er sich in ewige Gesetze!
Die sieht der Freigeist, doch nicht ihn. Wozu
Ein Gott? sagt er: die Welt ist sich genug!
Und keines Christen Andacht hat ihn mehr,
Als dieses Freigeists Lästerung gepriesen.

God, that he may not mar the fair appearance of free will,
permits the frightful ravages of evil to waste his beautiful
domains. The great Creator we behold not; he veils himself
within his own eternal laws. The sceptic sees their operation,
but he beholds not him. "Wherefore a God?" he cries, "the
world itself suffices for itself." And the piety of no Christian
has praised him more than does this sceptic's blasphemy.

MAN MUST NOT ATTEMPT TO GUIDE THE HELM OF DESTINY.

Don Carlos, IV. 21. 32.

Wer ist der Mensch, der sich vermessen will,
Des Zufalls schweres Steuer zu regieren
Und doch nicht der Allwissende zu seyn?

Who is the mortal who will presume to rule the difficult helm
of destiny if he be not the Almighty?

MAN MUST REVERENCE THE DREAMS OF YOUTH.

Don Carlos, IV. 21. 106.

Sagen Sie

Ihm, daß er für die Träume seiner Jugend

Soll Achtung tragen, wenn er Mann seyn wird,
Nicht öffnen soll dem tödtenden Insekte
Gerühmter besserer Vernunft das Herz
Der zarten Götterblume — daß er nicht
Soll irre werden, wenn des Staubes Weisheit
Begeisterung, die Himmelstochter, lästert.

Tell him, in manhood he must still revere the dreams of early youth, nor open the heart's all-tender flower to the canker-worms of boasted reason; that he must not be led astray when the wisdom of the dust blasphemes enthusiasm, the daughter of heaven.

TRUTH.

Don Carlos, IV. 21. 186.

Die Wahrheit ist vorhanden für den Weisen,
Die Schönheit für ein fühlend Herz.

Truth is created for the sage, beauty for the feeling heart.

LIFE IS LOVELY.

Don Carlos, IV. 21. 233.

O Gott, das Leben ist doch schön!

O God! how lovely still is life!

DUTY.

Don Carlos, V. 11. 108.

Cardinal, ich habe
Das meinige gethan. Thun Sie das Ihre.

Cardinal, I have done my part. Go now and do yours.

These are the last words of the king when he gives over his son to the Inquisition.

EVIL SPIRITS.

Mary Stuart, I. 4. 107.

Es gibt böse Geister,
Die in des Menschen unverwahrter Brust
Sich augenblicklich ihren Wohnplatz nehmen,
Die schnell in uns das Schreckliche begehn,
Und zu der Höll' entfliehend das Entsetzen
In dem befleckten Busen hinterlassen.

There are evil spirits who suddenly fix their abode in man's unguarded breast, causing us to commit devilish deeds, and then hurrying back to their native hell, leave behind the stings of remorse in the poisoned bosom.

DEEP MEANING IN ANCIENT CUSTOMS.
Mary Stuart, I. 7. 131.

Ein tiefer Sinn wohnt in den alten Bräuchen.

A deep meaning often lies in ancient customs.

THE PUBLIC EVER ON THE SIDE OF THE UNHAPPY.
Mary Stuart, I. 8. 43.

O, auch die heilige Gerechtigkeit
Entflieht dem Tadel nicht. Die Meinung hält es
Mit dem Unglücklichen, es wird der Neid
Stets den obsiegend Glücklichen verfolgen.

Oh, even holy justice cannot escape the voice of censure. Opinion is ever on the side of the unfortunate ; envy always will pursue the laurelled conqueror.

THE VOICE OF NUMBERS.
Mary Stuart, II. 3. 81.

Nicht Stimmenmehrheit ist des Rechtes Probe.

The voice of the majority is no proof of justice.

THE JUDGMENT OF THE MULTITUDE.
Mary Stuart, II. 3. 86.

Wie sich
Die Neigung anders wendet, also steigt
Und fällt des Urtheils wandelbare Wege.

As inclination changes, thus ebbs and flows the unstable tide of public judgment.

THE SUNNY SIDE OF LIFE.
Mary Stuart, II. 3. 136.

Nicht seine Freudenseite kehrte dir
Das Leben zu.

Life did not present to thee its sunny side.

The Worst is known of Me.

Mary Stuart, III. 4. 207.

Das Aergste weiß die Welt von mir, und ich
Kann sagen, ich bin besser als mein Ruf.

The world knows the worst of me, and I can say that I am
better than my fame.

The Fickle Multitude.

Mary Stuart, IV. 11. 14.

Die wankelmüth'ge Menge,
Die jeder Wind herumtreibt! Wehe dem,
Der auf dies Rohr sich lehnet!

The fickle multitude, which veers with every wind! Woe to
him who leans on such a reed!

The Pious Wish.

Mary Stuart, V. 7. 17.

Beruhige dein Herz. Dem Himmel gilt
Der feurig fromme Wunsch statt des Vollbringens.
Tyrannenmacht kann nur die Hände fesseln,
Des Herzens Andacht hebt sich frei zu Gott,
Das Wort ist todt, der Glaube macht lebendig

Compose your heart : the ardent pious wish is prized in heaven
as high as the performance. The power of tyrants can only bind
the hands, the devotion of the heart rises free to God ; the word
is dead, it is faith that gives it life.

Everything passing away.

The Ghost-Seer : Letter IV. *vol.* X. *p.* 225.

Ist nicht alles Flucht um mich herum? Alles stößt sich und
drängt seinen Nachbar weg, aus dem Quell des Daseyns einen
Tropfen eilend zu trinken, und lechzend davon zu gehen. Jetzt
in dem Augenblicke, wo ich meiner Kraft mich freue, ist schon
ein werdendes Leben an meine Zerstörung angewiesen. Zeigen
Sie mir etwas, das dauert, so will ich tugendhaft seyn.

Is not everything passing away around me? Every one is pressing on and pushing his neighbour aside, hastily to drink a few drops from the fountain of life and to depart still thirsty. At this very moment, while I am rejoicing in my strength, some being is waiting to start into life at my dissolution. Show me anything which endures, and I will become a virtuous man.

THE BEFORE AND AFTER.

The Ghost-Seer : Letter IV. *vol.* X. *p.* 226.

Was mir vorherging und was mir folgen wird, sehe ich als zwei schwarze und undurchdringliche Decken an, die an beiden Gränzen des menschlichen Lebens herunter hangen, und welche noch kein Lebender aufgezogen hat. Schon viele hundert Generationen stehen mit der Fackel davor, und rathen und rathen, was etwa dahinter seyn möchte. Viele sehen ihren eigenen Schatten, die Gestalten ihrer Leidenschaft, vergrößert auf der Decke der Zukunft sich bewegen, und fahren schaudernd vor ihrem eigenen Bilde zusammen. Dichter, Philosophen und Staatenstifter haben sie mit ihren Träumen bemalt, lachender oder finsterer, wie der Himmel über ihnen trüber oder heiterer war ; und von weitem täuschte die Perspective. Auch manche Gaukler nützten diese allgemeine Neugier, und setzten durch seltsame Vermummungen die gespannten Phantasien in Erstaunen. Eine tiefe Stille herrscht hinter dieser Decke. Keiner, der einmal dahinter ist, antwortet hinter ihr hervor ; Alles was man hörte, war ein hohler Wiederschall der Frage, als ob man in eine Gruft gerufen hätte. Hinter diese Decke müssen alle, und mit Schaudern fassen sie sie an, ungewiß, wer wohl dahinter stehe, und sie in Empfang nehmen werde ; quid sit id, quod tantum perituri vident. Freilich gab es auch Ungläubige darunter, die behaupteten, daß diese Decke die Menschen nur narre, und daß man nichts beobachtet hätte, weil auch nichts dahinter sey, aber um sie zu überweisen, schickte man sie eilig dahinter.

What went before me and what will follow me I regard as two impenetrable curtains which hang down at the two extremities of human life, and which no living man has yet drawn aside. Many hundreds of generations have already stood before them with their torches, guessing anxiously what lies behind. On the curtain of

Futurity many see their own shadows—the forms of their passions enlarged and put in motion; they shrink in terror at this image of themselves. Poets, philosophers, and founders of states, have painted this curtain with their dreams—more smiling or more dark, as the sky above them was cheerful or gloomy; and their pictures deceive the eye when viewed from a distance. Many jugglers, too, make profit of this our universal curiosity by their strange mummeries; they have set the outstretched fancy in amazement. A deep silence reigns behind this curtain; no one once within it will answer those he has left without; all you can hear is a hollow echo of your question, as if you shouted into a chasm. To the other side of this curtain we are all bound; men grasp hold of it as they pass, trembling, uncertain who may stand within it to receive them; *quid sit id, quod tantum morituri vident.* Some unbelieving people there have been who have asserted that this curtain did but make a mockery of men, and that nothing could be seen because nothing was behind it; but to convince these people the rest have seized them and hastily pushed them in.

ART IS DIFFICULT OF ACQUIREMENT.

Prolog, l. 40.

Schwer ist die Kunst, vergänglich ist ihr Preis.

The acquirement of art is difficult, its reward is transient.

THE MAN WHO HAS SATISFIED THE BEST OF HIS TIME.

Prolog, l. 48.

Denn wer den Besten seiner Zeit genug
Gethan, der hat gelebt für alle Zeiten.

For he who has given satisfaction to the best of his time has lived for all ages.

THE MIND OF MAN.

Prolog, l. 59.

Im engen Kreis verengert sich der Sinn
Es wächst der Mensch mit seinen größern Zwecken.

The mind is contracted within a narrow circle; man expands it with his mightier objects.

A SOLDIER'S LIFE IN WAR.

Wallenstein's Camp, v. 18.

Heute da, Herr Vetter, und morgen dort,

Wie einen der rauhe Kriegesbesen
Fegt und schüttelt von Ort zu Ort.

To-day here, to-morrow there, my kinsman, as the war-broom
sweeps and scatters us from place to place.

WHAT DIFFERENT BED-FELLOWS WE MEET IN LIFE.

Wallenstein's Camp, v. 59.

Was man nicht alles für Leute kennt!
Und wie die Zeit von dannen rennt.

What different people does one meet in life! How time moves
on with a ceaseless flow!

Shakespeare says (*Tempest*, act ii. sc. 2)—

" Misery acquaints a man with strange bed-fellows."

HOW THE PROPER TONE IS LEARNED.

Wallenstein's Camp, VI. 27.

Der feine Griff und der rechte Ton,
Das lernt sich nur um des Feldherrn Person.

Erster Jäger.

Sie bekam euch übel, die Lektion.
Wie er räuspert und wie er spuckt,
Das habt ihr ihm glücklich abgeguckt.

The clever knack and the proper tone are only acquired by those
at the General's side. *First Yager.* The lesson has been wofully
thrown away upon you. How he hawks and spits; that you have
copied in the cleverest way.

LIVE AND LET LIVE.

Wallenstein's Camp, VI. 106.

Sein Spruch war: leben und leben lassen.

The General's saying was ever : " Live and let live."

MIGHT MAKES RIGHT.

Wallenstein's Camp, VI. 144.

Es ist hier wie in den alten Zeiten,
Wo die Klinge noch alles that bedeuten.

It is here as in times of old, where the sword is what rules.
See (Lat., Gr.) Might makes right.

THE WILL OF MAN MAKES HIS FORTUNE.

Wallenstein's Camp, VII. 25.

Des Menschen Wille, das ist sein Glück.

Man's will, that shapes his fortune.

Milton (*Paradise Lost*, b. i. l. 106) speaks of the " unconquerable will."

See (Lat.) Wise man, maker of his own fortune.

VICE FOLLOWED BY WOE.

Wallenstein's Camp, VIII. 47.

Auf das Unrecht, da folgt das Uebel,
Wie die Thrän' auf den herben Zwiebel,
Hinter dem U kommt gleich das W,
Das ist die Ordnung in A B C.

Close upon vice follows woe, as the onion causes the tear to flow :
The W duly succeeds the V : this is the order as in A B C.

See (Lat.) Wickedness its own punishment.

LET THEM GO, THE RAILERS.

Wallenstein's Camp, X. 13.

Laß sie gehen ! sind Tiefenbacher,
Gevatter Schneider und Handschuhmacher !

Let them go ! They are of Tiefenbach's corps, the railers. a
glorious train of glovers and tailors !

THE FATE OF A SOLDIER.

Wallenstein's Camp, XI. 262.

Das Schwert ist kein Spaten, kein Pflug,
Wer damit ackern wollte, wäre nicht klug.
Es grünt uns kein Halm, es wächst keine Saat,
Ohne Heimath muß der Soldat
Auf dem Erdboden flüchtig schwärmen,
Darf sich an eignem Herd' nicht wärmen

The sword is no delving-tool nor plough ; he who **would till**
with **it is** not wise.   For us neither grass nor grain **grows :** without **a home** must the soldier go, a changeful wanderer, **and can**
warm himself at no home-lit hearth.

To Succeed in the World One must bestir Oneself.

Wallenstein's Camp, XI. 290.

> Will einer in der Welt was erjagen,
> Mag er sich rühren und mag sich plagen ;
> Will er zu hohen Ehren und Würden,
> Bück' er sich unter die goldnen Bürden ;
> Will er genießen den Vatersegen,
> Kinder und Enkelein um sich pflegen,
> Treib' er ein ehrlich Gewerb' in Ruh.

If a man wish to make his way in the world, he must bestir
himself and work his brains ; if he wish to rise to honour and
place, he must bend his back to the golden load.   If he prefer to
enjoy the delights of home, with children and grandchildren round
his knees, let him follow an honest trade in peace.

PLAGUE TAKE THE FELLOWS !

Wallenstein's Camp, XI. 325.

> Schad' um die Leut' !   Sind sonst wackre Brüder.
> Aber das denkt wie ein Seifensieder.

Plague take the fellows !—they are brave, I know :
They haven't a soul 'bove a soap-boiler's though.

He who would Win must face Death.

Wallenstein's Camp, XI. *Chor.*

> Und setzet ihr nicht das Leben ein,
> Nie wird euch das Leben gewonnen seyn.

If you do not dare to die, never will you win the prize.

You come Late.

Piccol. I. 1. 1.

> Spät kommt ihr — doch ihr kommt !

You come late, yet you come !

The Difference between a Soldier and a Peaceful Citizen.

Piccol. I. 2. 60.

Mit Unterſchied, Herr Graf! Die einen füllen
Mit nützlicher Geſchäftigkeit den Beutel,
Und andre wiſſen nur ihn brav zu leeren.
Der Degen hat den Kaiſer arm gemacht;
Der Pflug iſt's, der ihn wieder ſtärken muß.

Here is the difference, sir:—The one fills with profitable
industry the purse; the others know well to empty it. The
sword has made the Emperor poor; the plough it is that must
furnish him with resources.

See (Gr.) War, calamities of.

War is a Rough Game.

Piccol. I. 2. 100.

Es iſt der Krieg ein roh gewaltſam Handwerk.
Man kommt nicht aus mit ſanften Mitteln, alles
Läßt ſich nicht ſchonen.

War is a rough violent trade : one cannot always succeed by
soft means : everything cannot be spared.

Cowper (*The Task*, b. v.) says—

"But war's a game, which, were their subjects wise,
Kings would not play at."

What is the Short and Long of this Harangue?

Piccol. I. 2. 150.

Was iſt der langen Rede kurzer Sinn?

What is the short meaning of this long harangue?

Men's Words often bolder than their Deeds.

Piccol. I. 3. 57.

Verzagen wir auch nicht zu früh, mein Freund!
Stets iſt die Sprache kecker als die That,
Und mancher, der in blindem Eifer jetzt
Zu jedem Aeußerſten entſchloſſen ſcheint,
Find't unerwartet in der Bruſt ein Herz.

Let us not despair too soon, my friend. Men's words are ever bolder than their deeds, and many a one, who now appears resolute to meet every extremity with eager zeal, will on a sudden find in their breast a heart which he wot not of.

DISSIMULATION IS FOREIGN TO AN INGENUOUS MIND.

Piccol. I. 3. 104.

Ich muß ihn seiner Unschuld anvertrauen,
Verstellung ist der offnen Seele fremd;
Unwissenheit allein kann ihm die Geistesfreiheit
Bewahren, die den Herzog sicher macht.

I must trust him to his own innocence : dissimulation is foreign to an ingenuous soul. Ignorance alone can keep alive the cheerful air that makes the Duke secure.

SOME MEN BORN TO COMMAND.

Piccol. I. 4. 27.

Er ist nun einmal nicht gemacht, nach andern
Geschmeidig sich zu fügen und zu wenden,
Es geht ihm wider die Natur, er kann's nicht.
Geworden ist ihm eine Herrscherseele,
Und ist gestellt auf einen Herrscherplatz.
Wohl uns, daß es so ist! Es können sich
Nur wenige regieren, den Verstand
Verständig brauchen — Wohl dem Ganzen, findet
Sich einmal einer, der ein Mittelpunkt
Für viele Tausend wird, ein Halt; — sich hinstellt,
Wie eine feste Säul', an die man sich
Mit Lust mag schließen und mit Zuversicht.
So einer ist der Wallenstein.

He is not made to bend and cringe in flattery to others; it goes against his nature; he can't do it. There is in him a commanding spirit; well for us it is so! There exist few fit to rule themselves, few that use their understandings intelligently. Then well for the whole when there is found a man who is the central point, the pause, for many thousands — who stands fixed like a firm-built column, round which all may press with joy and confidence. Such a man is Wallenstein.

The Right Man in the Right Place.

Piccol. I. 4. 48.

Jedwedem zieht er seine Kraft hervor,
Die eigenthümliche, und zieht sie groß,
Läßt jeden ganz das bleiben, was er ist,
Er wacht nur drüber, daß er's immer sey
Am rechten Ort; so weiß er aller Menschen
Vermögen zu dem seinigen zu machen.

He draws forth every latent energy, that which is peculiar in
each, and does it thoroughly, leaving to each all that nature has
made them ; he watches also that every man be in his right place ;
thus he knows to mould the powers of all to his own end.

Power of Ancient Customs and Laws.

Piccol. I. 4. 82.

Mein Sohn, laß uns die alten, engen Ordnungen
Gering nicht achten! Köstlich unschätzbare
Gewichte sind's, die der bedrängte Mensch
An seiner Dränger raschen Willen band;
Denn immer war die Willkür fürchterlich —
Der Weg der Ordnung, ging er auch durch Krümmen,
Er ist kein Umweg. Grad aus geht des Blitzes,
Geht des Kanonballs fürchterlicher Pfad —
Schnell auf dem nächsten Wege langt er an,
Macht sich zermalmend Platz, um zu zermalmen.
Mein Sohn! die Straße, die der Mensch befährt,
Worauf der Segen wandelt, diese folgt
Der Flüsse Lauf, der Thäler freien Krümmen,
Umgeht das Weizenfeld, den Rebenhügel,
Des Eigenthums gemeßne Gränzen ehrend —
So führt sie später, sicher doch zum Ziel.

My son, let us not speak disparagingly of old narrow ordinances.
They are weights of priceless value, which down-trodden man has
tied to the vehement will of their oppressors ; for at all times has
unshackled will been a cause of fearful sorrow. The way of ancient
ordinance, though it may wind circuitously, is yet no devious
path. Straight onward goes the lightning's path, straight the
fearful path of the cannon-ball. Straight it goes the shortest

way, shattering that it may reach and shattering what it reaches. My son, the road along which the human being travels, that on which blessing comes and goes, follows the river's course, the playful windings of the valleys, curves round the cornfields, the hills of vines, honouring the sacred bounds of property; and thus secure, though late, leads to the end.

THERE IS SOMETHING HIGHER THAN THE WARRIOR'S EXCELLENCE.

Piccol. I. 4. 102.

Es gibt
Noch höhern Werth, mein Sohn, als kriegerischen;
Im Kriege selber ist das letzte nicht der Krieg.
Die großen, schnellen Thaten der Gewalt,
Des Augenblicks erstaunenswerthe Wunder,
Die sind es nicht, die das Beglückende,
Das ruhig, mächtig Daurende erzeugen.

My son, there exists a higher than the warrior's excellence. In war itself war is the end that is aimed at. The vast and sudden deeds of violence, the striking wonders of the moment, these are not they that generate the calm, the blissful, and the enduring mighty.

THE VIOLET.

Piccol. I. 4. 119.

Den blut'gen Lorbeer geb' ich hin mit Freuden
Für's erste Veilchen, das der März uns bringt,
Das duft'ge Pfand der neuverjüngten Erde.

Most gladly would I give the blood-stained laurel for the first violet which March brings us, the fragrant pledge of the new-fledged year.

DIFFERENCE BETWEEN REAL AND PRETENDED COURTESY.

Piccol. II. 2. 20.

Würdig und voll Anstand
War das Benehmen — aber an die Stelle
Huldreich vertraulicher Herablassung
War feierliche Förmlichkeit getreten.
Ach! und die zarte Schonung, die man zeigte,
Sie hatte mehr vom Mitleid als der Gunst.

The reception was respectful and full of courtesy, but in the place of condescending confidential kindness, there was only ceremonial formality. Alas! the tenderness which they showed had more of pity than of favour.

There is a Turning-point in the Affairs of Men.

Piccol. ii. 6. 66.

O! nimm der Stunde wahr, eh' sie entschlüpft.
So selten kommt der Augenblick im Leben,
Der wahrhaft wichtig ist und groß. Wo eine
Entscheidung soll geschehen, da muß Vieles
Sich glücklich treffen und zusammenfinden —
Und einzeln nur, zerstreuet zeigen sich
Des Glückes Fäden, die Gelegenheiten,
Die nur in einen Lebenspunkt zusammen
Gedrängt, den schweren Früchteknoten bilden,
Sieh, wie entscheidend, wie verhängnißvoll
Sich's jetzt um dich zusammenzieht!

Oh, seize the moment ere it slip from you. Seldom comes the moment in life, which is really sublime and weighty. When a great decision must be come to, then must many things come together, and meet at the same moment, and single threads of fate must show themselves, those circumstances, which have been woven in one potent web, pressing together to an important life's point, see how decisive and full of important events they are!

Numbers give Courage.

Piccol. ii. 6. 83.

Die hohe Fluth ist's, die das schwere Schiff
Vom Strande hebt — und jedem Einzelnen
Wächst das Gemüth im großen Strom der Menge.

It is the high tide that strands the loaded vessel – and each individual's spirit rises in the great stream of multitudes.

A Clever Idea.

Piccol. ii. 7. 236.

Wär' der Gedank' nicht so verwünscht gescheidt,
Man wär' versucht, ihn herzlich dumm zu nennen.

Were the idea not cursedly clever, one might have been induced to call it gloriously silly.

Our Starting-point is soon forgotten.

Piccol. III. 1. 62.

Doch, wißt ihr, in der Hitze des Verfolgens
Verliert man bald den Anfang aus den Augen.

Thou knowest that in the ardour of pursuit men soon forget the goal from which they started.

The Happy numbers not the Hours.

Piccol. III. 3. 73.

Da rann kein Sand, und keine Glocke schlug.
Es schien die Zeit dem Ueberseligen
In ihrem ew'gen Laufe stillzustehen.

Then ran no sand, then struck no hours for us; it appeared as if time, in our excess of happiness, stood still in its eternal course.

When does the Game of Life look Cheerful?

Piccol. III. 4. 50.

Das Spiel des Lebens sieht sich heiter an,
Wenn man den sichern Schatz im Herzen trägt.

The game of life looks more cheerful when one carries in one's heart the inalienable treasure.

Fable is the World of Love.

Piccol. III. 4. 115.

Die Fabel ist der Liebe Heimathwelt,
Gern wohnt sie unter Fern, Talismanen,
Glaubt gern an Götter, weil sie göttlich ist.
Die alten Fabelwesen sind nicht mehr,
Das reizende Geschlecht ist ausgewandert;
Doch eine Sprache braucht das Herz, es bringt
Der alte Trieb die alten Namen wieder,
Und an dem Sternenhimmel gehn sie jetzt,
Die sonst im Leben freundlich mit gewandelt;

Dort winken sie dem Liebenden herab,
Und jedes Große bringt uns Jupiter
Noch diesen Tag, und Venus jedes Schöne.

Fable is Love's world; delightedly he dwells among fays and talismans, delightedly believes in deities, being himself divine. The old fabulous beings are no longer here, the beauteous race has vanished, yet still the heart needs a language; still the old instinct brings back the old names, and to yon starry world they now are gone—those who once used to share this earth with man as with a friend; to the lover down here they beckon, and even at this day it is Jupiter who brings whatever is great, and Venus who brings everything that is fair!

I HAVE LIVED AND HAVE LOVED.

Piccol. III. 7. 9.

Ich habe genossen das irdische Glück,
Ich habe gelebt und geliebet.

I have enjoyed the happiness of this world, I have lived and have loved.

WOMAN BELONGS NOT TO HERSELF

Piccol. III. 8. 66.

Das Weib soll sich nicht selber angehören,
An fremdes Schicksal ist sie fest gebunden.
Die aber ist die Beste, die sich Fremdes
Aneignen kann mit Wahl, an ihrem Herzen
Es trägt und pflegt mit Innigkeit und Liebe.

The woman must not belong to herself; she is bound to alien destinies. But she performs her part best who can take freely of her own choice the alien to her heart, can bear and foster it with sincerity and love.

THE VOICE OF FATE.

Piccol. III. 8. 82.

Der Zug des Herzens ist des Schicksals Stimme.
Fate hath no voice but the heart's impulses.

WINE.

Piccol. IV. 7. 42.

Der Wein erfindet nichts, er schwatzt's nur aus.
Wine invents nothing; it only tattles.

We tremble often at a Fancy.

Piccol. v. 1. 105.

Ich weiß, daß man vor leeren Schrecken zittert;
Doch wahres Unglück bringt der falsche Wahn.

I know that we often tremble at an empty terror; yet the false
fancy brings a real misery.

The World soils us.

Piccol. v. 1. 197.

Mein bester Sohn! Es ist nicht immer möglich,
Im Leben sich so kinderrein zu halten,
Wie's uns die Stimme lehrt im Innersten.
In steter Nothwehr gegen arge List
Bleibt, ach das redliche Gemüth nicht wahr —
Das eben ist der Fluch der bösen That,
Daß sie, fortzeugend, immer Böses muß gebären.

My dearest son! it is not always possible to preserve our infant
purity in the world, as the voice of conscience teaches us in our
inmost heart. In constant alarm against the wiles of the wicked,
the honest heart remains not always pure. This is the curse of
every evil deed—that, propagating still, it brings forth evil.

The Power of Time.

Wallenstein's Death, I. 3. 32.

Doch zittre vor der langsamen,
Der stillen Macht der Zeit.

But think with terror on the slow, the quiet power of time.

Dally not with the Devil.

Wallenstein's Death, I. 3. 64.

Verflucht, wer mit dem Teufel spielt!

Accursed he who dallies with the devil!

Necessity.

Wallenstein's Death, I. 4. 45.

Ernst ist der Anblick der Nothwendigkeit.

Nicht ohne Schauder greift des Menschen Hand
In des Geschicks geheimnißvolle Urne.

Stern is the on-look of necessity. Not without a shudder may the hand of man grasp the mysterious urn of destiny.

AN ANCIENT THRONE NOT EASILY SHAKEN.

Wallenstein's Death, I. 4. 56.

Du willst die Macht,
Die ruhig, sicher thronende erschüttern,
Die in verjährt geheiligtem Besitz,
In der Gewohnheit festgegründet ruht,
Die an der Völker frommen Kinderglauben
Mit tausend zähen Wurzeln sich befestigt.

Thou wouldst shake power on an ancient consecrated throne, which rests on long holy possession, fast fixed in custom—which is bound by a thousand tough and stringy roots to the people's pious nursery-faith.

MAN IS THE CREATURE OF CUSTOM.

Wallenstein's Death, I. 4. 70.

Ein unsichtbarer Feind ist's, den ich fürchte,
Der in der Menschenbrust mir widersteht,
Durch feige Furcht allein mir fürchterlich —
Nicht was lebendig, kraftvoll sich verkündigt,
Ist das gefährliche Furchtbare. Das ganz
Gemeine ist's, das ewig Gestrige,
Was immer war und immer wiederkehrt,
Und morgen gilt, weil's heute hat gegolten!
Denn aus Gemeinem ist der Mensch gemacht,
Und die Gewohnheit nennt er seine Amme.
Weh dem, der an den würdig alten Hausrath
Ihm rührt, das theure Erbstück seiner Ahnen!
Das Jahr übt eine heiligende Kraft;
Was grau für Alter ist, das ist ihm göttlich.
Sey im Besitze, und du wohnst im Recht,
Und heilig wird's die Menge dir bewahren.

It is a foe invisible which I fear—an enemy in the human breast which opposes me—by its coward fear alone made fearful to me;

not that which, full of life, instinct with power, makes known its
present being ; that is not the perilously formidable. Oh, no! it
is the common, the quite common, the thing of an eternal yesterday, which ever was and evermore returns—sterling to-morrow
for it was sterling to-day ; for man is made of the wholly common,
and custom is his nurse. Woe then to them who lay irreverent
hands on his old house-furniture, the dear inheritance from his
forefathers! For time consecrates, and what is grey with age
becomes religion. Be in possession, and thou hast the right, and
sacred will the many guard it for thee.

THE COMMANDING INTELLECT SHOULD BE KING.

Wallenstein's Death, I. 5. 26.

Und stets der Herrschverständigste, beliebt' ihm
Zu sagen, sollte Herrscher seyn und König.

And always it pleased him to say, the commanding intellect
should have the command and be king.

THE WORLD GOVERNED BY SELF-INTEREST.

Wallenstein's Death, I. 6. 40.

Denn nur vom Nutzen wird die Welt regiert.
For the world is only governed by self-interest.

EVERY EVENT IS THE DECISION OF GOD.

Wallenstein's Death, I. 7. 32.

Denn aller Ausgang ist ein Gottesurtel.
For all event is God's arbitrement.

WHEN DANGER IS AT HAND THE GIANT-SPIRIT IS CALLED FOR.

Wallenstein's Death, I. 7. 145.

Doch wenn das Aeußerste ihm nahe tritt,
Der hohle Schein es nicht mehr thut, da fällt
Es in die starken Hände der Natur,
Des Riesengeistes, der nur sich gehorcht,
Nichts von Verträgen weiß.

It is at the approach of extreme danger, when a hollow puppet can accomplish nothing, that power falls into the mighty hands of Nature, of the spirit giant-born, who listens only to himself, and knows nothing of compacts.

Every Man should act in Consistence with Himself.

Wallenstein's Death, I. 7. 159.

Denn Recht hat jeder eigene Charakter,
Der übereinstimmt mit sich selbst; es gibt
Kein andres Unrecht, als den Widerspruch.

For every individual character is in the right that is in strict consistence with itself. Self-contradiction is the only wrong.

Every Crime has its own Avenging Angel.

Wallenstein's Death, I. 7. 211.

Nicht hoffe, wer des Drachen Zähne sä't,
Erfreuliches zu ernten. Jede Unthat
Trägt ihren eignen Rache-Engel schon,
Die böse Hoffnung, unter ihrem Herzen.

Let him that sows the serpent's teeth not hope to reap a joyous harvest. Every crime has, in the moment of its perpetration, its own avenging angel—dark misgivings at the inmost heart.

Powers of Destiny are Jealous.

Wallenstein's Death, I. 7. 221.

Denn eifersüchtig sind des Schicksals Mächte.
Voreilig Jauchzen greift in ihre Rechte.
Den Samen legen wir in ihre Hände,
Ob Glück, ob Unglück aufgeht, lehrt das Ende.

For the Powers of Destiny are jealous. Shouts before victory encroach on their rights; we place the seeds in their hands, the end tells us whether for good or bad.

Youth is Hasty in Words.

Wallenstein's Death, II. 2. 99.

Schnell fertig ist die Jugend mit dem Wort.

Youth is too hasty in words.

Universal Blessings.

Wallenstein's Death, ii. 2. 110.

Was die Göttlichen uns senden
Von oben, sind nur allgemeine Güter;
Ihr Licht erfreut, doch macht es keinen reich,
In ihrem Staat erringt sich kein Besitz.
Den Edelstein, das allgeschätzte Gold,
Muß man den falschen Mächten abgewinnen,
Die unterm Tage schlimmgeartet hausen.
Nicht ohne Opfer macht man sie geneigt,
Und keiner lebet, der aus ihrem Dienst
Die Seele hätte rein zurückgezogen.

What the Powers divine send us from above are only blessings common to all the world; their light rejoices us, yet it makes no man rich—in their eternal realm no property is possessed. The jewel, the all-valued gold, we win from the deceiving powers, depraved in nature, that dwell beneath the daylight. Not without sacrifices are they made propitious, and there lives no soul on earth that ever retired unsullied from their service.

Great Moments in the Life of Man.

Wallenstein's Death, ii. 3. 59.

Es gibt im Menschenleben Augenblicke,
Wo er dem Weltgeist näher ist, als sonst,
Und eine Frage frei hat an das Schicksal.

There exist moments in the life of man when he is nearer to the Spirit of the world than is usual, and possesses freely the power of questioning his destiny.

There is no Chance.

Wallenstein's Death, ii. 3. 106.

Es gibt keinen Zufall;
Und was uns blindes Ohngefähr nur dünkt,
Gerade das steigt aus den tiefsten Quellen.

There is no such thing as chance; and what seems to us merest accident springs from the deepest source of destiny.

Man's Thoughts grow by certain Laws.

Wallenstein's Death, II. 3. 116.

Des Menschen Thaten und Gedanken, wißt!
Sind nicht, wie Meeres blind bewegte Wellen.
Die innre Welt, sein Mikrokosmus, ist
Der tiefe Schacht, aus dem sie ewig quellen.
Sie sind nothwendig, wie des Baumes Frucht,
Sie kann der Zufall gaukelnd nicht verwandeln.
Hab' ich des Menschen Kern erst untersucht,
So weiß ich auch sein Wollen und sein Handeln.

Know that the human being's thoughts and deeds are not like ocean-billows, blindly moved. The inner world, his microcosmos, is the deep shaft, out of which they spring eternally. They grow by certain laws, like the tree's fruit—juggling chance cannot change them. Have I the human kernel first examined? Then I know his future will and actions.

Gratitude from the House of Austria.

Wallenstein's Death, II. 6. 55.

Dank vom Haus Oestreich!

Gratitude from the house of Austria!

This expression was applied to Austria, 3d December 1850, by the Prussian deputy, Von Vincke, in the Prussian Chambers, and received with great applause.

Man an Imitative Animal.

Wallenstein's Death, III. 4. 9.

Der Mensch ist ein nachahmendes Geschöpf,
Und wer der Vorderste ist, führt die Heerde.

Man is an imitative creature, and whoever is foremost leads the herd.

To Build on a Narrow Basis.

Wallenstein's Death, III. 4. 123.

O mein Gemahl! Sie bauen immer, bauen
Bis in die Wolken, bauen fort und fort
Und denken nicht dran, daß der schmale Grund
Das schwindelnd schwanke Werk nicht tragen kann.

O my husband! you are ever building, building to the clouds, still building higher, and never reflecting that the poor narrow basis cannot sustain the giddy tottering column.

THE UNTHINKING MAN.

Wallenstein's Death, III. 7. 42.

Ja, der verdient betrogen sich zu sehn,
Der Herz gesucht bei dem Gedankenlosen
Mit schnell verlöschten Zügen schreiben sich
Des Lebens Bilder auf die glatte Stirne,
Nichts fällt in eines Busens stillen Grund,
Ein muntrer Sinn bewegt die leichten Säfte,
Doch keine Seele wärmt das Eingeweide.

Yea, he deserves to find himself deceived who seeks a heart in the unthinking man! With quickly-erased marks the forms of life impress their characters on the smooth forehead; nought sinks into the bosom's silent depth; quick sensibility moves the light fluids, yet no soul warms the inner frame.

I KNOW MY PAPPENHEIMERS.

Wallenstein's Death, III. 15. 52.

Daran erkenn' ich meine Pappenheimer.

Therein I recognise my Pappenheimers.

SECRECY IS FOR THE HAPPY.

Wallenstein's Death, III. 18. 10.

Das Geheimniß
Ist für die Glücklichen, das Unglück braucht,
Das hoffnungslose, keinen Schleier mehr,
Frei, unter tausend Sonnen kann es handeln.

Secrecy is for the happy—misery, hopeless misery, needs no veil; under a thousand suns it dares act openly.

CUNNING AND CONFIDENCE.

Wallenstein's Death, III. 18. 86.

Denn Krieg ist ewig zwischen List und Argwohn,
Nur zwischen Glauben und Vertraun ist Friede.

Wer das Vertraun vergiftet, o der mordet
Das werdende Geschlecht im Leib der Mutter!

For eternal war exists between cunning and suspicion, only
between faith and confidence is there peace. Whoever poisons
confidence, he murders future generations in the womb of their
mother!

RAGE HEARS NO LEADER.

Wallenstein's Death, III. 20. 16.

Dem tauben Grimm, der keinen Führer hört.

Deep remorseless rage, that hears no leader.

THE HUMAN BEING MAY NOT BE TRUSTED TO SELF-GOVERNMENT.

Wallenstein's Death, IV. 2. 40.

Denn um sich greift der Mensch, nicht darf man ihn
Der eignen Mäßigung vertraun. Ihn hält
In Schranken nur das deutliche Gesetz,
Und der Gebräuche tiefgetretne Spur.

For man spreads his wings—he cannot be trusted to self-government. He can only be kept in the road of faith and duty by
the clear and written law, and the deep-trod footmarks of ancient
custom.

WE OUGHT TO LISTEN TO OUR OWN HEART.

Wallenstein's Death, IV. 8. 70.

Seyd edelmüthig!
Das Herz und nicht die Meinung ehrt den Mann.

Be noble-minded! Our own heart, and not other men's opinions
of us, forms our true honour.

MAN IS GREAT OR LITTLE BY HIS OWN WILL.

Wallenstein's Death, IV. 8. 77.

Ein jeder gibt den Werth sich selbst. Wie hoch ich
Mich selbst anschlagen will, das steht bei mir.
So hoch gestellt ist keiner auf der Erde,
Daß ich mich selber neben ihm verachte.
Den Menschen macht sein Wille groß und klein.

Every man stamps his value on himself. The price we challenge for ourselves is given us. There does not live on earth the man, be his station what it may, that I despise myself compared with him. Man is made great or little by his own will.

DISTANT EVILS ARE MAGNIFIED.

Wallenstein's Death, IV. 9. 82.

Das gegenwärt'ge Unglück trägt sich leicht,
Doch grauenvoll vergrößert es der Zweifel
Und der Erwartung Qual dem weit Entfernten.

The misfortune that is before us is easily borne, the mists of doubt magnify evils to a shape of horror.

MISERY.

Wallenstein's Death, IV. 11. 30.

Frei geht das Unglück durch die ganze Erde!

Misery travels free through the whole earth!

THE PILGRIM COUNTS NOT THE DISTANCE.

Wallenstein's Death, IV. 11. 33.

Zählt der Pilger Meilen,
Wenn er zum fernen Gnadenbilde wallt?

Does the pilgrim count the miles when he travels to some distant shrine of hope?

THE HOPE OF THE NOBLE.

Wallenstein's Death, IV. 12. 26.

Das ist das Loos des Schönen auf der Erde!

That is the lot of the noble upon earth!

NO PANG IS PERMANENT WITH MAN.

Wallenstein's Death, V. 3. 55.

Verschmerzen werd' ich diesen Schlag, das weiß ich,
Denn was verschmerzte nicht der Mensch! Vom Höchsten
Wie vom Gemeinsten lernt er sich entwöhnen,
Denn ihn besiegen die gewalt'gen Stunden.

2 C

I shall grieve down this blow, of that I am conscious ; for **what** does not man grieve down? From the highest as from the **vilest** thing he learns to wean himself, for the strong hours conquer him.

The Fisherman's Boat.

Wallenstein's Death, v. 4. 40.

Mein Fürst! Mit leichtem Muthe knüpft der arme Fischer
Den kleinen Nachen an im sichern Port,
Sieht er im Sturm das große Meerschiff stranden.

My Prince! with light heart the poor fisherman moors his little boat in a secure port; and sees the lofty ship stranded amid the storm.

Hope.

Wallenstein's Death, v. 4. 64.

Dem Unglück ist die Hoffnung zugesendet.
Furcht soll das Haupt des Glücklichen umschweben,
Denn ewig wanket des Geschickes Wage.

Hope is sent to the unfortunate ; fear hovers round the head **of** the prosperous—for the scales of fate are ever unsteady.

The Long Sleep of Death.

Wallenstein's Death, v. 5. 85.

Gut' Nacht, Gordon!
Ich denke einen langen Schlaf zu thun.

Good night, Gordon! I think to make a long sleep of it.

Easy to advise in the Port.

Wilhelm Tell, I. 1. 146.

Vom sichern Port läßt sich's gemächlich rathen.

When safe in the port it is easy to advise.

I do but what I may not leave undone.

Wilhelm Tell, I. 1. 166.

       Landsmann, tröstet ihr
Mein Weib, wenn mir was Menschliches begegnet,
Ich hab' gethan, was ich nicht lassen konnte.

Herdsman, do thou console my wife if aught of ill befall me ; I only do what I may not leave undone.

WHEN WILL DELIVERANCE COME TO THIS LAND?

Wilhelm Tell, I. 1. 193.

Gerechtigfeit des Himmels!
Wann wird der Retter fommen tiefem Lande?

Righteous Heaven! when will deliverance come to this land?

This was constantly in the mouths of the Germans when they were oppressed by the French.

GOD NEVER DESERTS THE BRAVE.

Wilhelm Tell, I. 2. 132.

Dem Muthigen hilft Gott!

God helps the brave!

See (Lat.) Fortune favours the brave.

PEACE AND QUIETNESS.

Wilhelm Tell, I. 3. 74.

Die schnellen Herrscher sind's, die furz regieren.
— Wenn sich der Föhn erhebt aus seinen Schlünden
Löscht man die Feuer aus, die Schiffe suchen
Eilends den Hafen, und der mächt'ge Geist
Geht ohne Schaden, spurlos, über die Erde.
Ein Jeder lebe still bei sich daheim;
Dem Friedlichen gewährt man gern den Frieden.

Impetuous rulers have the shortest reigns. When the impetuous south wind rises from its chasms men cover up their fires, the ships in haste make for the harbour, and the mighty spirit sweeps over the earth, leaving no trace behind. Let every man live quietly at home. Peace is rarely denied to the peaceful.

THE EYE.

Wilhelm Tell, I. 4. 138.

O eine edle Himmelsgabe ist
Das Licht des Auges — Alle Wesen leben

Bom Lichte, jedes glückliche Geschöpf —
Die Pflanze selbst kehrt freudig sich zum Lichte.

Oh, the eye's light is a noble gift of Heaven. All beings live
from light, each fair created thing—the very plants turn with a
joyful transport to the light.

I am the Last of my Race.

Wilhelm Tell, II. 1. 100.

Ich bin der letzte meines Stamms — Mein Name
Endet mit mir.

I am the last of all my race. My race ends with me.

Fatherland.

Wilhelm Tell, II. 1. 163.

An's Vaterland, an's theure, schließ dich an,
Das halte fest mit deinem ganzen Herzen.
Hier sind die starken Wurzeln deiner Kraft.

Cling to the land, the dear land of thy sires—grapple to that
with thy whole heart and soul; here are the strong roots of thy
power.

A New Race is springing up.

Wilhelm Tell, II. 1. 195.

Es lebt ein anders denkendes Geschlecht!

A race is springing up that think not as their fathers thought
before.

One Heart, one Race.

Wilhelm Tell, II. 1. 258.

Wir sind ein Volk, und einig wollen wir handeln.

We are all one people, and will act shoulder to shoulder.

Force is a Fearful Thing.

Wilhelm Tell, II. 2. 382.

Schrecklich immer,
Auch in gerechter Sache, ist Gewalt.
Gott hilft nur dann, wenn Menschen nicht mehr helfen.

Even in a righteous cause force is a fearful thing; God only
helps when men can help no more.

WE SWEAR TO BE A NATION OF TRUE BROTHERS.

Wilhelm Tell, II. 2. 510.

Wir wollen seyn ein einzig Volk von Brüdern,
In keiner Noth uns trennen und Gefahr.

We swear to be a nation of true brothers, never to part in danger or in death.

THE CAUTIOUS MAN.

Wilhelm Tell, III. 1. 72.

Wer gar zu viel bedenkt, wird wenig leisten.

He that is over-cautious will do little.

EXCESSIVE RIGOUR MISSES ITS AIM.

Wilhelm Tell, III. 3. 184.

Zu weit getrieben,
Verfehlt die Strenge ihres weisen Zwecks,
Und allzustraff gespannt zerspringt der Bogen.

Rigour pushed too far is sure to miss its aim, however good, as the bow snaps that is bent too stiffly.

MAN IS LIKE A BALL.

Wilhelm Tell, IV. 1. 59.

Der Sturm ist Meister, Wind und Welle spielen
Ball mit dem Menschen.

The storm is master. Man is like a ball tossed betwixt the winds and billows.

BE UNITED.

Wilhelm Tell, IV. 2. 158.

Seyd einig — einig — einig.

Be one—be one—be one.

THE OPPORTUNITY IS GOOD.

Wilhelm Tell, IV. 3. 1.

Durch diese hohle Gasse muß er kommen;

Es führt kein andrer Weg nach Küßnacht — Hier
Vollend' ich's — Die Gelegenheit ist günstig.

Here through this deep defile he needs must pass; there leads
no other road to Kussnacht; here I finish it—the opportunity is
good.

This soliloquy of Tell is a passage used in the schools of Germany
for declamation.

THY SAND IS RUN.

Wilhelm Tell, IV. 3. 7.

Mach deine Rechnung mit dem Himmel, Vogt!
Fort mußt du, deine Uhr ist abgelaufen.

Now balance thine account with Heaven! Thou must away
from earth—thy sand is run.

THE MILK OF HUMAN KINDNESS.

Wilhelm Tell, IV. 3. 23.

In gährend Drachengift hast du
Die Milch der frommen Denkart mir verwandelt.

The milk of human kindness thou hast turned to rankling poison
in my breast.

THERE IS A GOD TO PUNISH.

Wilhelm Tell, IV. 3. 37.

Es lebt ein Gott zu strafen und zu rächen.
There is a God to punish and avenge.

NO PEACE NEAR WICKED NEIGHBOURS.

Wilhelm Tell, IV. 3. 124.

Es kann der Frömmste nicht im Frieden bleiben,
Wenn es dem bösen Nachbar nicht gefällt.

The most peaceful dwells not in peace if wicked neighbours hinder.

REVENGE IS BARREN OF ITSELF.

Wilhelm Tell, v. 1. 189.

So trägt die Unthat ihnen keine Frucht!
Rache trägt keine Frucht! Sich selbst ist sie

Die fürchterliche Nahrung, ihr Genuß
Ist Mord, und ihre Sättigung das Grauen.

Their crime has brought no fruit! Revenge is barren of itself!
Itself is the dreadful food it feeds on ; its delight is murder, and
its satiety despair.

THE HOME OF THE BRAVE.

The Bride of Messina, p. 394 (ed. Stuttgard, 1847).

Nicht wo die goldene Ceres lacht
Und der friedliche Pan, der Flurenbehüter,
Wo das Eisen wächst in der Berge Schacht,
Da entspringen der Erde Gebieter.

It is not where the golden-eared Ceres laughs, and the peaceful
Pan, lord of the flowery plains, but where the iron lies hid in the
mountain-cave, that the lords of the earth spring up.

THE CURSE OF THE GREAT.

The Bride of Messina, p. 404.

Es ist der Fluch der Hohen, daß die Niedern
Sich ihres offnen Ohr's bemächtigen.

It is the curse of the great that the low possess themselves of
their open ears.

AN ANGRY WORD.

The Bride of Messina, p. 409.

Nicht Wurzeln auf der Lippe schlägt das Wort,
Das unbedacht dem schnellen Zorn entflohen,
Doch von dem Ohr des Argwohns aufgefangen,
Kriecht es wie Schlingkraut endlos treibend fort,
Und hängt an's Herz sich an mit tausend Aesten
So trennen endlich in Verworrenheit
Unheilbar sich die Guten und die Besten!

The word of passion, that has escaped without intention, strikes
not roots from the lips, yet, swallowed by suspicion's ears, it creeps
like a rank poisonous weed, and hangs about the heart with thousand shoots, separating at last in sad perplexity the good and best
without a chance of reconciliation!

Mortal Joy ever on the Wing.

The Bride of Messina, p. 411.

Geflügelt ist das Glück und schwer zu binden,
Nur in verschloßner Lade wird's bewahrt,
Das Schweigen ist zum Hüter ihm gesetzt,
Und rasch entfliegt es, wenn Geschwätzigkeit
Voreilig wagt die Decke zu erheben.

Mortal joy is ever on the wing and hard to bind ; it can only be
kept in a closed box ; with silence we best guard the fickle good,
and swift it vanishes if a flippant tongue haste to raise the lid.

Man's Life.

The Bride of Messina, p. 419.

Etwas fürchten und hoffen und sorgen,
Muß der Mensch für den kommenden Morgen.

Man must fill the coming morning with fears and hopes and cares.

The Delights of Peace.

The Bride of Messina, p. 419.

Schön ist der Friede! Ein lieblicher Knabe
Liegt er gelagert am ruhigen Bach,
Und die hüpfenden Lämmer grasen
Lustig um ihn auf dem sonnigten Rasen
Süßes Tönen entlockt er der Flöte,
Und das Echo des Berges wird wach,
Oder im Schimmer der Abendröthe
Wiegt ihn in Schlummer der murmelnde Bach.

Peace is lovely ! a beauteous boy he lies couched by the tranquil
brook, where the skipping lambkins feed joyfully around him in
the sunny meadow ! His flute discourses sweet music, waking up
the echoes of the hills, or else the murmurs of the streamlet lull
him to sleep in the sunset's ruddy sheen.

Gentle Humility.

The Bride of Messina, p. **430.**

Schamhafte Demuth ist der Reize Krone,

Denn ein Verborgenes ist sich das Schöne,
Und es erschrickt vor seiner eignen Macht.

Modest humility is beauty's crown, for the beautiful is a **hidden**
thing and shrinks from its own power.

Moore says—

" Humility, that low, sweet root,
From which all heavenly virtues shoot."

TIME IS A BLOOMING FIELD.

The Bride of Messina, p. 467.

Leicht verschwindet der Thaten Spur
Von der sonnebeleuchteten Erde,
Wie aus dem Antlitz die leichte Geberde —
Aber nichts ist verloren und verschwunden,
Was die geheimnißvoll waltenden Stunden
In den dunkel schaffenden Schooß aufnahmen —
Die Zeit ist eine blühende Flur,
Ein großes Lebendiges ist die Natur,
Und alles ist Frucht, und alles ist Samen.

The traces of human deeds fade swiftly away from the sun-
lighted earth, as the transient shade of thought from the brow,
but nothing is lost and dissipated, which the rolling hours, replete
with secrets, have received into their dark creative bosom.   Time
is a blooming field; nature is ever teeming with life, and all is
seed, and all is fruit.

PATIENCE IS OUR BEST LESSON.

The Bride of Messina, p. 481.

Wenn die Wolken gethürmt den Himmel schwärzen,
Wenn dumpftosend der Donner hallt,
Da, da fühlen sich alle Herzen
In des furchtbaren Schicksals Gewalt.
Aber auch aus entwölkter Höhe
Kann der zündende Donner schlagen.
Darum in deinen fröhlichen Tagen
Fürchte des Unglücks tückische Nähe!
Nicht an die Güter hänge dein Herz,
Die das Leben vergänglich zieren!

Wer befitzt, der lerne verlieren,
Wer im Glück ist, der lerne den Schmerz!

When the clouds piled up aloft darken the sky; when the thunder's loud peal echoes around—then, then our trembling bosoms own the night of awful destiny. But also from the cloudless air can the lightning's glare dart forth. Therefore in thy joyous days fear the approach of sad fate! set not thy heart on the goods of this life, flowers that bloom but to decay! Let him who is in possession of a good, learn to be content to lose it ; let him who is in the lap of prosperity, learn to endure pains!

HID IS THE WOMB OF TIME.

The Bride of Messina, p. 484.

Vermauert ist dem Sterblichen die Zukunft,
Und kein Gebet durchbohrt den ehrnen Himmel.
Ob rechts die Vögel fliegen oder links,
Die Sterne so sich oder anders fügen,
Nicht Sinn ist in dem Buche der Natur,
Die Traumkunst träumt, und alle Zeichen trügen.

Futurity is impregnable to mortal ken : no prayer pierces through heaven's adamantine walls. Whether the birds fly right or left, whatever be the aspect of the stars, the book of Nature is a maze, dreams are a lie, and every sign a falsehood.

PRUDENT FORETHOUGHT.

The Bride of Messina, p. 489.

Und wer sich vermißt es flüglich zu wenden,
Der muß es selber erbauend vollenden.

Whoever fails to turn aside the ills of life by prudent forethought must submit to fulfil the course of destiny.

NATURE'S QUIET JOYS.

The Bride of Messina, p. 492.

Wohl dem! Selig muß ich ihn preisen,
Der in der Stille der ländlichen Flur,
Fern von des Lebens verworrenen Kreisen,
Kindlich liegt an der Brust der Natur.

Denn das Herz wird mir schwer in der Fürsten Palästen,
Wenn ich herab vom Gipfel des Glücks
Stürzen sehe die Höchsten, die Besten
In der Schnelle des Augenblicks!

Happy must I regard him, who, amidst the stillness of the country, far from the turmoil and pomps of life, childlike lies on Nature's bosom. For my heart is sad in the princely hall, when I see the good and great hurled from their towering pride of state in the twinkling of an eye!

FREEDOM ON THE MOUNTAINS.

The Bride of Messina, p. 493.

Auf den Bergen ist Freiheit! Der Hauch der Grüfte
Steigt nicht hinauf in die reinen Lüfte;
Die Welt ist vollkommen überall,
Wo der Mensch nicht hinkommt mit seiner Qual.

On the mountains is freedom! the breath of decay never sullies the pure blowing air; nature is perfect, wherever we stray, if man did not come in to deform it with care!

DEATH IS A MIGHTY MEDIATOR.

The Bride of Messina, p. 498.

Ein mächtiger Vermittler ist der Tod.
Da löschen alle Zornesflammen aus,
Der Haß versöhnt sich, und das schöne Mitleid
Neigt sich, ein weinend Schwesterbild, mit sanft
Anschmiegender Umarmung auf die Urne.

Death is a mighty mediator. There all the flames of rage are extinguished, hatred is appeased, and angelic pity, like a weeping sister, bends with gentle and close embrace over the funeral urn.

DEATH SUBLIMES THE MORTAL.

The Bride of Messina, p. 499.

Der Tod hat eine reinigende Kraft,
In seinem unvergänglichen Palaste
Zu echter Tugend reinem Diamant
Das Sterbliche zu läutern und die Flecken
Der mangelhaften Menschheit zu verzehren.

Death has a purifying power in his undecaying palace to sublime the mortal to the pure diamond of perfect virtue, and purge away the stains of frail humanity.

LIFE IS NOT THE HIGHEST GOOD.

The Bride of Messina, p. 504.

Das Leben ist der Güter höchstes nicht,
Der Uebel größtes aber ist die Schuld.

Life is not the supreme good : but of all earthly ills the chief is—guilt.

FAREWELL TO BELOVED SCENES.

The Maid of Orleans : Prologue, 4.

Lebt wohl ihr Berge, ihr geliebten Triften,
Ihr traulich stillen Thäler lebet wohl!
Johanna wird nun nicht mehr auf euch wandeln,
Johanna sagt euch ewig Lebewohl!
Ihr Wiesen, die ich wässerte, ihr Bäume,
Die ich gepflanzet, grünet fröhlich fort!
Lebt wohl ihr Grotten und ihr kühlen Brunnen!
Du Echo, holde Stimme dieses Thals,
Die oft mir Antwort gab auf meine Lieder,
Johanna geht, und nimmer kehrt sie wieder!

Farewell, ye mountains, ye beloved glades, ye truly tranquil valleys, fare ye well! Joanna will never more wander through you. Joanna bids you an eternal farewell! Ye meads which I have watered, ye trees which I have planted, bloom still in beauty! Farewell, ye grottoes and ye crystal springs! Thou echo, sacred voice of this vale, that hast often responded to my songs, Joanna goes and never returns!

THE POWER OF THE BARD.

The Maid of Orleans, I. 2. 24.

So schaffe welches. — Edle Sänger dürfen
Nicht ungeehrt von meinem Hofe ziehn.
Sie machen uns den dürren Scepter blühn,
Sie flechten den unsterblich grünen Zweig
Des Lebens in die unfruchtbare Krone,
Sie stellen herrschend sich den Herrschern gleich,

Aus leichten Wünschen bauen sie sich Throne,
Und nicht im Raume liegt ihr harmlos Reich;
Drum soll der Sänger mit dem König gehen,
Sie beide wohnen auf der Menschheit Höhen!

Gold must be procured. Noble bards must not go unhonoured from our court. It is they who make our barren sceptre bloom, it is they who twine the never-fading green of life around our fruitless crown. Reigning, they rank themselves as kings, erect their throne of gentle wishes, and their harmless realm exists not in space ; therefore should the bard accompany the king, they both dwell in the higher sphere of life !

IMPOSSIBILITIES.

The Maid of Orleans, I. 3. 48.

Kann ich Armeen aus der Erde stampfen?
Wächst mir ein Kornfeld in der flachen Hand?

Can I with a stamp summon armies from the earth? or grow a cornfield in my open palm ?

A NATION'S HONOUR.

The Maid of Orleans, I. 5. 81.

Nichtswürdig ist die Nation, die nicht
Ihr Alles freudig setzt an ihre Ehre.

Worthless is the nation that does not with pleasure venture its all for honour.

FIGHTING FOR RELIGION.

The Maid of Orleans, I. 5. 170.

Nichts schont er selber und erwartet sich
Nicht Schonung, wenn die Ehre ruft, wenn er
Für seine Götter oder seine Götzen kämpft.

Men show no mercy and expect no mercy, when honour calls, or when they fight for their idols or their gods.

A SLAUGHTER RATHER THAN A FIGHT.

The Maid of Orleans, I. 9. 50.

Ein Schlachten war's, nicht eine Schlacht zu nennen.

It was a slaughter rather than a fight !

Britain.

The Maid of Orleans, II. 1. 79.

Nie war der Ruhm des Britten glänzender,
Als da er, seinem guten Schwert allein
Vertrauend, ohne Helfershelfer focht.
Es kämpfe jeder seine Schlacht allein,
Denn ewig bleibt es wahr: französisch Blut
Und englisch kann sich redlich nie vermischen.

Never did Britain's fame shine more brightly than when, trusting to her own good sword, she fought alone. Let each one fight his battle for himself ; for it is an eternal truth that French and English blood can never blend together.

Day follows the Blackest Night.

The Maid of Orleans, III. 2. 60.

Tag wird es auf die dickste Nacht, und kommt
Die Zeit so reifen auch die spät'sten Früchte!

Day follows the murkiest night, and when the time comes, the latest fruits also ripen !

Mercy.

The Maid of Orleans, III. 4. 33.

Frei wie das Firmament die Welt umspannt,
So muß die Gnade Freund und Feind umschließen.
Es schickt die Sonne ihre Strahlen gleich
Nach allen Räumen der Unendlichkeit,
Gleichmessend gießt der Himmel seinen Thau
Auf alle dürstenden Gewächse aus.
Was irgend gut ist und von oben kommt,
Ist allgemein und ohne Vorbehalt,
Doch in den Falten wohnt die Finsterniß!

As freely as the firmament embraces the world, so mercy must encircle friend and foe. The sun pours forth impartially his beams through all the regions of infinity ; Heaven bestows the dew equally on every thirsty plant. Whatever is good and comes from on high is universal and without reserve ; but in the heart's recesses darkness dwells.

The Mighty Present.

The Maid of Orleans, III. 4. 54.

Der Menſch iſt, der lebendig fühlende,
Der leichte Raub des mächt'gen Augenblicks.

Man, living, feeling man, is the easy sport of the overmastering present.

Folly.

The Maid of Orleans, III. 6. 27.

Unſinn, du ſiegſt, und ich muß untergehn!
Mit der Dummheit kämpfen Götter ſelbſt vergebens.
Erhabene Vernunft, lichthelle Tochter
Des göttlichen Hauptes, weiſe Gründerin
Des Weltgebäudes, Führerin der Sterne,
Wer biſt du denn, wenn du, dem tollen Roß
Des Aberwitzes an den Schweif gebunden,
Ohnmächtig rufend, mit dem Trunkenen
Dich ſehend in den Abgrund ſtürzen mußt!
Verflucht ſey, wer ſein Leben an das Große
Und Würd'ge wendet und bedachte Pläne
Mit weiſem Geiſt entwirft! Dem Narrenkönig
Gehört die Welt.

Folly, thou conquerest, and I must yield! Against stupidity the very gods fight in vain. Exalted Reason, refulgent daughter of the divine head—wise foundress of the world's system—guide of the stars, who art thou then, if thou, bound to the tail of Folly's untamed steed, vainly shrieking, with the drunken crowd must plunge down headlong, with eyes open, in the abyss? Accursed who directs his life to great and noble ends, and forms his well-considered plans with deliberate wisdom! To the fool-king belongs the world.

Sorrow Brief, Joy Endless.

The Maid of Orleans, V. 14. 44.

Kurz iſt der Schmerz, und ewig iſt die Freude!

Brief is sorrow, and endless is joy!

F. SCHLEGEL.

Born A.D. 1772. Died A.D. 1829.

Friedrich Carl Wilhelm von Schlegel, an eminent German critic and philosophical writer, was born at Hanover in 1772; being at first intended for the mercantile profession, but having received a classical education, he prevailed on his father to allow him to devote himself to literature. He studied at Göttingen and Leipsic, commencing his career in 1794 by a short essay on the different schools of Greek poetry. In 1800 he established himself as a private teacher at Jena, where he delivered a course of philosophical lectures with success. In 1805 he joined the Roman Catholic Church, and from 1812 he was much occupied with diplomatic and political employments. Having acquired the friendship and confidence of Prince Metternich, he was employed by him as one of the representatives of the court of Vienna at Frankfort. He died at Dresden in 1829.

The Power of Thought.

Im Walde.

Windes Rauschen, Gottes Flügel,
Tief in kühler Waldesnacht,
Wie der Held in Rosses Bügel,
Schwingt sich des Gedankens Macht.
Wie die alten Tannen sausen,
Hört man Geistes Wogen brausen.

Wings of God, rustling breezes, deep in the cool night of the forest, like the hero on his charger, springs forth the might of thought. As the old pines whistle, one hears the surges of the mind roar.

SCHLEIERMACHER.

Born A.D. 1768. Died A.D. 1835.

Friedrich Daniel Ernst Schleiermacher, a philosophic theologian of great eminence, was born at Breslau, 21st November 1768. He was the son of a poor army chaplain in Silesia, who belonged to the Calvinistic communion, and was educated by the Moravians at Niesky. Soon tiring of the Moravians, he entered the University of Halle, and here he studied with great distinction. After various changes he was appointed to the pulpit of the Charité, the chief hospital in the Prussian capital. He began his literary career in 1799 by publishing his "Discourses on Religion," which F. Schlegel pronounced to be the first of their kind in the German language. He removed to Stolpe as court-preacher in 1802, and in 1809 was chosen at Trinity Church, Berlin; next year he was appointed Professor of Theology in the new university of the same city. In 1817 he was chosen President of the Synod of Berlin, and in 1833 he visited England, opening the German chapel at the Savoy. He died 12th February 1835.

How Man may best employ himself.
Collected Works.

Was kann der Mensch thun, als daß er nur seine eigene Natur durch den Geist immermehr reinigt und ausbildet? Gewalt braucht er nur dann, wenn er vorher sich hat Gewalt anthun lassen durch irgend ein Verderben. Sonst ist das Werk der göttlichen Gnade in dem Menschen ein stilles, ruhiges Werk, und je vollständiger es von statten geht, um desto natürlicher scheint es und ist auch wirklich so. Nur die Tugend ist ein Kampf, durch die man Fehler besiegt; die, durch welche jeder seine eigenthümliche Vollkommenheit im Sinne und Geiste Gottes erweiset, ist nur ein ruhiges Handeln.

In what way can man better employ himself than in purifying and cultivating his peculiar nature by his spiritual powers? He requires restraint only when he has given loose to his passions through some corruption of his nature. Otherwise the working of God's grace in man is a silent and noiseless operation, and the more successful it is the more natural it appears, and is so in reality. Virtue is only a conflict by which we get the mastery of our failings; that by which every man proves his peculiar power of understanding the will and spirit of God, is only a silent working of the inner man.

A Strong Will necessary in Man.
Collected Works.

Wenn es einem Menschen an dem lebendigen und kräftigen Willen fehlt, der auf das Gute allein gerichtet ist, der jedes innere Vermögen in Bewegung setzt, jedes äußere Verhältniß nützt, jeden Augenblick des Lebens auskauft, um auf eine dem Willen Gottes und den gerechten Forderungen der Gesellschaft angemessene Art thätig zu sein: so ist er entweder ein Spiel

2 D

ſinnlicher Begierden, deren Ausartung in heftige Leidenſchaften er nicht immer verhüten kann, oder ſein Trieb zu wirken wird durch keinen Gegenſtand in die gehörige Bewegung geſetzt, und er verbringt ſein Leben in unwürdiger Trägheit.

If a man possesses not a living and strong will that leads the way to good, rousing every inner faculty—seizing on every external circumstance—employing every moment of life that he may work in a way suitable to the will of God and the just requirements of society, then is he either a plaything of sensual desires, which he cannot always prevent from sinking into vehement passions, or his impulse for active life is not properly excited, and he passes a life of shameful indolence.

TRUE PLEASURE.

Collected Works.

Das Vergnügen iſt eine Blume, die zwar von ſelbſt, aber nur in fruchtbaren Gärten und in wohlangebauten Feldern wächſt. Nicht daß wir unſer Gemüth bearbeiten ſollten, um ſie zu gewinnen: aber wer es nicht bearbeitet hat, bei dem wird ſie nicht gedeihen; wer nicht etwas Nützliches und Würdiges in ſich hervorgebracht hat, der würde ſie vergeblich ausſäen. Auch derjenige, der es am beſten verſteht, kann zum Vergnügen eines andern nichts weiter beitragen, als daß er ihm dasjenige mittheilt, was die Grundlage des ſeinigen iſt. Wer nun gleichſam dieſen rohen Stoff nicht für ſich zu bear= beiten und ſich anzueignen weiß, wer nicht ſeine Sinne ver= feinert, ſeinen Geſchmack ausgebildet, ſich einen Schatz von Gedanken, eine Mannichfaltigkeit von Beziehungen, eine eigene Anſicht der Welt und der menſchlichen Dinge erworben hat, der weiß keine Gelegenheit zum Vergnügen zu benutzen, und gerade das Vorzüglichſte geht am ſicherſten für ihn verloren. Oder ſind es nicht etwa die Trägen, denen ſelbſt die zur Erholung beſtimmte Zeit ſo ſchwer auszufüllen iſt? die überall den Verdruß und die Langeweile wiederfinden? von denen wir die ewigen Klagen über die Dürftigkeit und Einförmigkeit des Lebens hören müſſen? die ſich über die geringen Talente der Menſchen zum geſelligen Umgang und über die Unzulänglichkeit aller Anſtalten zur Freude am bitterſten beſchweren? Es geſchieht ihnen aber recht: denn der Menſch ſoll nicht ernten, wo er nicht geſäet hat.

Pleasure is a flower, which grows indeed of itself, but only in fruitful gardens and well-cultivated fields. Not that we should labour in our mind to gain it ; but yet he who has not laboured for it, with him it will not grow : whoever has not brought out in his own character something profitable and praiseworthy, it is vain for him to sow. Even he who understands it best can do nothing better for the pleasure of another than that he should communicate to him what is the foundation of his own. Whosoever does not know to work up the rough stuff for himself, and thereby make it his own, whosoever does not refine his disposition, has not secured for himself a treasure of thoughts, a many-sidedness of relations, a view of the world and human things peculiar to himself—such a man knows not how to seize the proper occasion for pleasure, and the most important is assuredly lost for him. Is it not the indolent who find so much difficulty in filling up the time set aside for repose, who find vexation and ennui in everything?— from whom we are hearing never-ending complaints about the poverty and dull uniformity of life?—who are most bitter in their lamentations over the slender powers of men for social intercourse, and over the insufficiency of all measures to obtain joy? But this is only what they deserve ; for man cannot reap where he has not sown.

The Esteem of the World is a Great Good.
Collected Works.

Die Achtung unserer Brüder halten wir alle auch in Beziehung auf unser Wohlbefinden für ein großes Gut. Das Vertrauen auf unsere Rechtschaffenheit, der Glaube an unsere Talente, der daraus entspringende Wunsch, näher mit uns ver= bunden zu sein und unser Wohlwollen zu gewinnen, das ist oft ein besserer Schatz als vieler Reichthum. Das erkennt auch der Träge. Wenn nur die Menschen an seine Geschicklichkeit glauben wollten, ohne daß er nöthig hätte, irgend etwas Mühsames und Vollkommenes hervorzubringen! Wenn sie sich nur andere Beweise seiner Redlichkeit und Menschenliebe gefallen ließen als Thaten! Wenn sie nur eine andere Bürgschaft für seine Weisheit annehmen wollten, als verständige Reden, guten Rath und ein gesundes eigenes Urtheil über die Vollkommenheiten des Lebens! Statt sich zu einer wahren Ehrliebe zu erheben, friecht er in kindischer Eitelkeit umher, die durch erbärmliche Kleinigkeiten die Aufmerksamkeit der Menschen fesseln und durch leeren Schein glänzen will; statt etwas Tüchtiges zu erreichen, hält er nur mit Genauigkeit über äußern Gebräuchen; die hergebrachte Sitte ist seine Tugend und die herrschende Meinung ist sein Verstand.

We all consider what is thought of us by those around us as a substantial good. Trust in our uprightness of character, belief in our abilities, and the desire that arises from this to be more intimately connected with us, and to gain our good opinion, everything of this kind is often a more valuable treasure than great riches. Of this the indolent are quite aware. If men would only believe in their capacity without the necessity of producing anything painstaking and really praiseworthy! If they would only agree to take any other proof of their probity and love of mankind than deeds! If they would only accept some other security for their wisdom than prudent language, good counsel, and a sound judgment on the proper mode of conducting the affairs of life! Instead of rising to a true love of honour, such men creep amidst childish vanity, which tries to fix the attention of mankind by pitiful trifles and to glitter by shadowy appearances; instead of attempting to reach something really noble, they rest only on external customs; the mental disposition that arises from this is their virtue, and their governing passion is what they regard as understanding.

THE INDOLENT.

Collected Works.

In den wichtigsten Angelegenheiten des Menschen hat der Träge nur nichtige Wünsche, denen nichts entsprechen kann; und ehe diese erfüllt werden, beharrt er sorglos und freiwillig in seiner Rohheit, gibt seine Seele ohne Widerstand dem Einfluß aller Umstände hin, geht gleichgültig vorüber vor allen Gelegenheiten zu edeln, aber mühevollen Handlungen, und beweist seinen Eifer für diese wichtigen Theile der menschlichen Bestimmung nur dadurch, daß er sich oft und gern einen Zustand ausmalt, wo er sie ohne Arbeit würde erreichen können. Und indem er wünscht, ergeht das gerechteste Gericht über ihn: „Wer nicht hat, dem wird auch das genommen, was er hat."

In the weightiest concerns of life the indolent offers only vain wishes, to which nothing can correspond; and before these wishes are fulfilled he lives void of care, and willingly in his rudeness gives up his soul without opposition to the impression of surrounding circumstances, passes indifferently in the presence of occurrences to noble deeds but full of trouble, and shows his zeal for these weighty concerns of man only thus far, that he represents to himself often and with pleasure a position which he would like to reach without labour. And while he is wishing, the righteous sentence is passed on him: "Who has nothing, from him will be taken even that which he has."

It is not good for Man to be alone.
Collected Works.

Jeder Mensch muß schlechterdings in einem Zustande mora= lischer Gesellschaft stehen; er muß einen oder mehrere Menschen haben, denen er das Innerste seines Wesens, seines Herzens und seiner Führungen kund thut, nichts muß in ihm sein, wo möglich, was nicht noch irgend einem außer ihm mitgetheilt würde. Das liegt in dem göttlichen Ausspruche: Es ist nicht gut, daß der Mensch allein sei, mehr als irgend etwas anderes.

It is well that every man should be in a state of moral union with others; he must have one or more men to whom he can communicate the inmost feelings of his being, heart, and the reasons of his conduct; there should be nothing in him which is not known to some one else. That is the true meaning of the divine saying, "It is not good that man should be alone."

The Present.
Collected Works.

Die Gegenwart ist ein gar schönes Mittel, jedes Band fester zu knüpfen und jedes theure Andenken lebendiger zu machen.

The present is a beautiful medium to knit every bond closer, and to make every dear remembrance still more precious.

Intimate Friends.
Collected Works.

Nichts Aeußeres kann mir ein Recht geben, mich den Men= schen, mit denen ich einmal in Wechselwirkung gesetzt bin, und dem Mitempfinden für sie zu entziehen.

Nothing external can give me a right to withdraw myself from men with whom I have once been in close intercourse, and with whom I have had a feeling of sympathy.

The most Intimate Friendship.
Collected Works.

Die genaueste Freundschaft soll ja und muß auch die genaueste

Kenntniß geben, und der schönste Vorzug liegt ja darin, daß der Freund den Freund mit seinen Fehlern liebt, andere ihn aber oft nur lieben, weil sie sie nicht sehen.

The closest friendship should and must also give the most intimate acquaintance with our character ; and the highest advantage lies in this—that a friend loves his friend with all his failings ; but others often only love him because they do not see them.

No Despotism in Friendship.

Collected Works.

Es muß keine Art Despotismus in unserm freundschaftlichen Umgange sein; was wir den Menschen sein wollen, muß ganz nach ihrem Sinne sein, nämlich nach ihrem besten Sinne, mit und für sich selbst.

There must be no kind of despotism in our friendly intercourse ; what we wish to be to men must be precisely according to their own mode of thinking, but in their best moods.

No Friend can be replaced.

Collected Works.

Nie kann man die Stelle eines Freundes ersetzen; wer glücklich genug ist, deren mehrere zu haben, dem ist jeder einzelne etwas anderes ; eine Doublette in der Freundschaft hat gewiß niemand.

We can never replace a friend ; when a man is fortunate enough to have several, he finds that they are all different ; no one has a double in friendship.

No Friend can be replaced.

Collected Works.

Es ist doch im Menschen nicht so wie in der Welt, wo jede Stelle besetzt wird, die sich erledigt. Wenn uns jemand stirbt, bleibt immer eine leere Stelle. Es fehlen uns Mittheilungen und Empfindungen, die so nicht wieder erregt werden, eine Saite unsers Wesens hat ihren Resonanzboden verloren, und

das geht so fort, bis endlich das ganze Ding in die Polter=
kammer geworfen wird, aus welcher nur der große Musikmeister
alle diese veralteten Instrumente zu einem himmlischen und
ewigen Concert wieder hervorzieht und erneuert.

It is certainly not among men as in the world, where every place
is filled up as soon as it is vacant. If any one dies to us, his place
remains for ever empty : we feel that we have lost a companion—
that there are feelings which can never again be called up : a string
of our being has lost its sounding-board : and that continues to increase, till at last the whole thing is thrown into the lumber-room,
out of which only the greatest music-master can draw out and
renew all these ancient instruments, so as to create a heavenly
and never-ending concert.

Difference between Men and Women.

Collected Works.

Freilich sind die Frauen auch darin glücklicher als wir; ihre
Geschäfte begnügen sich mit einem Theil ihrer Gedanken, und
die Sehnsucht des Herzens, das innere schöne Leben der
Phantasie, beherrscht immer den größern Theil. Wenn ich
mich hingegen zu meiner Arbeit hinsetze, so muß ich ordentlich
von meinen Lieben Abschied nehmen, wie der Hausvater, der
seine Geschäfte auswärts hat, und wenn mir während derselben
ein Gedanke an sie mit Bewußtsein durch die Seele geht, so
kann ich ihm eben nur freundlich zunicken, wie der Vater den
Kindern, die ihn umspielen, mit denen er sich doch aber jetzt
nicht abgeben kann. Mir geht es aber überall so, wohin ich
sehe, daß mir die Natur der Frauen edler erscheint und ihr
Leben glücklicher, und wenn ich je mit einem unmöglichen
Wunsch spiele, so ist es mit dem, eine Frau zu sein.

Women are certainly more happy in this than we men ; their
employments occupy a smaller portion of their thoughts, and the
earnest longing of the heart, the beautiful inner life of the fancy,
always command the greater part. If I, on the other hand, set
myself to my work, I must in general take leave of my love, as
the master of the house who has his affairs elsewhere ; and if in
the midst of my daily labours a thought is turned homewards, **I**
can only nod in a friendly way to it, as the father to his children
who play around him, but to whom he cannot now give himself
up. But it appears to me, so far as I can judge, that the nature

of women seems more noble, and their life more happy; and if ever I toyed with an impossible thought, it is with the idea that I should like to be a woman.

WOMEN ARE EXCELLENT LETTER-WRITERS.

Collected Works.

Ueberhaupt sind die Weiber die eigentlichen Briefschreiberinnen, und wir Männer sind nur Stümper. Und nun gar Liebe schreiben, das kann kein Mann so, wie ihr es könnt.

Women are especially first-rate letter-writers, and we men are only bunglers. To write of love, that can no man do, as they can with their grandiloquent language.

FATHERS AND CHILDREN.

Collected Works.

Ihr Väter, erbittert euere Kinder nicht, daß sie nicht scheu werden. Wenn die Kinder im Leben erbittert werden und aus der Erbitterung Scheu entsteht und verhaltener Widerwille, so ist das das Unnatürlichste von allem. Das ganze Wesen der Kinder ist den Aeltern auf das Ursprünglichste verwandt und angehörig; tausend Aehnlichkeiten sprechen uns daraus an auf das Auffallendste, und mit jeder solchen Entwickelung scheinen Einverständniß und Liebe sich mehren zu müssen. In der unmittelbaren Nähe der Aeltern wachsen die Kinder heran; der erste Blick des Kindes fällt auf das liebende Auge der Mutter; sie ist es, von der das erste frohe Lächeln des Säuglings gleichsam bemerkt zu werden wünscht, und das Erste, was die Mutter es mittheilend lehrt, ist den Vater kennen und lieben; und je mehr die jungen Seelen sich entfalten, um desto mehr müssen sie fühlen, wie ihnen alles von den Aeltern und durch sie kommt. Hier ist also das innigste ungestörteste Heiligthum der Liebe, und wenn hier dennoch in den Kindern, die ja ursprünglich ganz Liebe und Anhänglichkeit sind, Entfernung, Zorn, Unwillen entsteht; wenn die Liebe, die nie auszurotten ist in ihrem Gemüth, statt sich denen zuzuwenden, die ihnen von Gottes und der Natur wegen die nächßen sind, eher auf frembere Gegenstände ablenkt, sobaß sie irgend von andern ertragen können, was von den Aeltern sie erbittert: so ist das gewiß das Unnatürlichste, was erfolgen kann. Und ebenso ist es auch verhältnißmäßig unnatürlich, wenn sich die Kinder gegen andere Erwachsene erbittern, welche auf ihr Leben einwirken und an ihrer Entwickelung mit= arbeiten. Haben sich die Herzen der Kinder gegen uns er= bittert und sind sie dadurch scheu geworden; hat sich das natürliche Vertrauen in einen dumpfen Argwohn verkehrt, als ob wir überall das Unserige suchten und nicht das Ihrige; ist die Liebe erloschen und das Vertrauen erblichen: wo ist dann der Schlüssel, mit dem wir uns die Herzen wieder öffnen können? wo ist der Zügel, an dem wir die jungen Gemüther von dem Wege des Verderbens ablenken wollen?

"Fathers, provoke not your children to wrath, lest they be discouraged." If the life of a child be embittered, and the result be shyness and secret aversion, that is the most unnatural state of all. The whole being of a child is from the very beginning linked to and dependent on those who are older than himself; there are thousands of resemblances between them that prove this in a surprising way, and as they are developed harmony and love must be the necessary result. Children grow up in the closest intimacy with their parents: the first glance of the child falls on the loving eye of the mother—she it is who watches the first joyous laugh of the babe, and teaches it first to know and love its father; and the more that the young souls are developed, the more do they feel that everything comes from and through their parents. Here, therefore, is the inmost and tranquil shrine of love, and if this be a spring for children who are originally all love and dependence, whence flow aversion, wrath, and evil feelings; if the love which can never be uprooted from their young hearts, instead of being turned to those who are placed near them by God and nature, be rather directed to strange objects, so that perhaps they have to bear from others the very same things which provoked their wrath in their parents— that certainly is the most unnatural state of things that can be imagined. And so also it is proportionably unnatural if children show dislike to those who are placed beside them to influence their lives and labour for the development of their characters. If the hearts of children be embittered towards us, making them timid in our presence—if their natural trustfulness be turned to hollow suspicion, as if we were seeking our own and not their interests— if love be extinguished and the feeling of confidence lost, where shall we again find the key with which we can open their hearts? where shall we find the bit by which we can direct their young minds from the road that is leading them to ruin?

ARTHUR SCHOPENHAUER.

Born A.D. 1788. Died A.D. 1860.

Arthur Schopenhauer was born, 22d February 1788, at Dantzic, where his father was an eminent merchant. In his youth he spent many years in England and France, thereby becoming intimately acquainted with the literature of both countries. In 1809 he attended the University of Göttingen, and in 1811 visited Berlin to make the acquaintance of Fichte. In 1818 he travelled in Italy, and again in 1822, remaining for three years in that country. His private means made him independent. At last he took up his residence at Frankfort, where he lived, a retired student of misanthropical habits, for thirty years. There he died 21st September 1860.

HIGH INTELLECTUAL QUALITIES IN ALL CLASSES.

Willen in der Natur, II. 84.

Unter allen Ständen finden wir Menschen von intellektueller Ueberlegenheit, und oft ohne alle Gelehrsamkeit. Denn natürlicher Verstand kann fast jeden Grad von Bildung ersetzen, aber keine Bildung den natürlichen Verstand.

In all classes we find men possessed of high intellectual qualities, though often without mental cultivation. For natural abilities can almost compensate for the want of every kind of cultivation, but no cultivation of the mind can make up for the want of natural abilities.

See (Lat.) Nature without learning.

WHAT POWER THE DOCTRINES OF RELIGION EXERCISE ON MAN.

Grundprobleme der Ethik, 234.

Wenn man die vortreffliche Moral, welche die Christliche und mehr oder weniger jede Religion predigt, vergleicht mit der Praxis ihrer Bekenner, und sich vorstellt, wohin es mit dieser kommen würde, wenn nicht der weltliche Arm die Verbrechen verhinderte, ja, was wir zu befürchten hätten, wenn auch nur auf Einen Tag alle Gesetze aufgehoben würden; so wird man bekennen müssen, daß die Wirkung aller Religion auf die Moralität eigentlich sehr geringe ist. Hieran ist freilich die Glaubensschwäche Schuld. Theoretisch und so lange es bei der frommen Betrachtung bleibt, scheint Jedem sein Glaube fest. Allein die That ist der harte Probierstein aller unserer Ueberzeugungen: wenn es zu ihr kommt und nun der Glaube durch große Entsagungen und schwere Opfer bewährt werden soll; da zeigt sich die Schwäche desselben. Wenn ein Mensch ein Verbrechen ernstlich meditirt; so hat er die Schranken der ächten reinen Moralität bereits durchbrochen; darnach aber ist das Erste, was ihn aufhält, alle Mal der Gedanke an Justiz und Polizei. Entschlägt er sich dessen, durch die Hoffnung diesen zu entgehen; so ist die zweite Schranke, die sich ihm ent= gegenstellt, die Rücksicht auf seine Ehre. Kommt er nun aber auch über diese Schutzwehr hinweg; so ist sehr viel dagegen zu wetten, daß, nach Ueberwindung dieser zwei mächtigen Wider= stände, jetzt noch irgend ein Religionsdogma Macht genug über ihn haben werde, um ihn von der That zurückzuhalten. Denn wen nahe und gewisse Gefahren nicht abschrecken, den werden die entfernten und bloß auf Glauben beruhenden schwerlich im Zaum halten.

If we compare the high moral doctrines, which the Christian and more or less all religions preach, with the practice of their professors, and consider what would be the result if the laws of our country did not forbid the commission of crimes under severe penalties, nay, what would be our state if all laws were annulled even for a single day, it is vain to deny that the effect of religion on the conduct of mankind is very slight ; the weakness of our faith is doubtless to be blamed for this. Theoretically, and so long as it remains merely in pious fancies, a man's faith appears to him to be impregnable. But deeds are the stern touchstone of our convictions ; when it comes to this point, and our faith has to be proved by great self-denial and severe sacrifices, then it is that the weakness of our faith is shown. If a man is meditating the commission of a crime, he has already broken down the fence of lofty morality, for the thought of justice and what is right is the first barrier that is raised against evil. If he is able to get rid of this, then the second barrier presents itself—a regard to personal honour. If he clears at a leap this bar, you may safely wager that by getting rid of these two powerful obstacles no religious dogma will have sufficient power over him to keep him from the performance of the deed. For the man who is not frightened by dangers which he sees near and almost certain, will scarcely be curbed by those that are remote and dependent on religious belief.

FAITH AND LOVE.

Parerga und Paralipomena, II. 326.

Der Glaube ist wie die Liebe: er läßt sich nicht erzwingen. Daher ist es ein mißliches Unternehmen, ihn durch Staats= maaßregeln einführen, oder befestigen zu wollen: denn, wie der Versuch, Liebe zu erzwingen, Haß erzeugt; so der, Glauben zu erzwingen, erst rechten Unglauben.

Faith is like love : it cannot be forced. Therefore it is a danger-ous operation if an attempt is made to introduce or bind it by state regulations; for as the attempt to force love begets hatred, so also to compel religious belief produces rank unbelief.

RELIGION IN THE EARLY AGES.

Parerga und Paralipomena, II. 326.

In frühern Jahrhunderten war die Religion ein Wald, hinter welchem Heere halten und sich decken konnten. Aber nach so vielen Fällungen ist sie nur noch ein Buschwerk, hinter welchem gelegentlich Gauner sich verstecken. Man hat dieser= halb sich vor Denen zu hüten, die sie in Alles hineinziehen möchten, und begegne ihnen mit dem spanischen Sprichwort: Detras de la cruz está el Diablo. (Hinterm Kreuze steht der Teufel.)

In the early ages religion was a thick forest, behind which armies could be drawn up and completely covered. But after so much felling of the timber, it is now only a shrubbery, behind which sharpers occasionally conceal themselves. We must, there-fore, guard ourselves against those who will insinuate themselves into everything, and meet them with the Spanish proverb, "Be-hind the cross stands the devil."

AUTHORITY AND EXAMPLE LEAD THE WORLD.

Grundprobleme der Ethif, 28.

Urtheilen aus eigenen Mitteln ist das Vorrecht Weniger: die Uebrigen leitet Autorität und Beispiel. Sie sehen mit fremden Augen und hören mit fremden Ohren. Daher ist es gar leicht, zu denken, wie jetzt alle Welt denkt; aber zu denken,

wie alle Welt über dreißig Jahre denken wird, ist nicht Jeder=
manns Sache.

To form a judgment intuitively is the privilege of few ; authority
and example lead the rest of the world. They see with the eyes
of others, they hear with the ears of others. Therefore it is very
easy to think as all the world now think ; but to think as all the
world will think thirty years hence, is not in the power of every
one.

ORIGINAL THINKERS AND THE OPPOSITE.

Parerga und Paralipomena, I. 143.

Man kann die Denker eintheilen in solche, die für sich
selbst, und solche, die für Andere denken : diese sind die
Regel, jene die Ausnahmen. Erstere sind demnach Selbstdenker
im zwiefachen, und Egoisten im edelsten Sinne des Worts : sie
allein sind es, von denen die Welt Belehrung empfängt. Denn
nur das Licht, welches Einer sich selber angezündet hat, leuchtet
nachmals auch Andern.

We may divide thinkers into those who think for themselves,
and those who think through others : the latter are the rule, the
former the exception. The first, therefore, are original thinkers
in a double sense, and egoists in the noblest meaning of the word ;
it is from them alone that the world learns wisdom. For only
the light, which we have kindled in ourselves, can illuminate
others.

TRUTH DERIVED FROM OTHERS.

Parerga und Paralipomena, II. 413.

Die bloß erlernte Wahrheit klebt uns nur an, wie ein
angesetztes Glied, ein falscher Zahn, eine wächserne Nase, oder
höchstens wie eine rhinoplastische aus fremdem Fleische. Die
durch eigenes Denken erworbene Wahrheit aber gleicht dem
natürlichen Gliede : sie allein gehört uns wirklich an. Darauf
beruht der Unterschied zwischen dem Denker und dem bloßen
Gelehrten.

A truth that is merely acquired from others only clings to us,
much in the same way as a limb that is added to our body, a false
tooth, a wax nose, or at most a nose that is made up of the flesh
of another. A truth which we have acquired by our own mental

exertions is like our natural limbs ; they alone really belong to **us.**
This is exactly the difference between an original thinker and **the**
mere learned man.

THE REAL MAN OF SCIENCE.
Die Welt als Wille, II. 87.

Dem, der studirt, um Einsicht zu erlangen, sind die Bücher
und Studien bloß Sprossen der Leiter, auf der er zum Gipfel
der Erkenntniß steigt: sobald eine Sprosse ihn um einen
Schritt gehoben hat, läßt er sie liegen. Die Vielen hingegen,
welche studiren, um ihr Gedächtniß zu füllen, benutzen nicht die
Sprossen der Leiter zum Steigen, sondern nehmen sie ab und
laden sie sich auf, um sie mitzunehmen, sich freuend an der
zunehmenden Schwere der Last. Sie bleiben ewig unten, da
sie Das tragen, was sie hätte tragen sollen.

To the man who studies to gain an insight into science, books
and study are merely the steps of the ladder by which he climbs
to the summit; as soon as a step has been advanced he leaves it
behind. The majority of mankind, however, who study to fill
their memory with facts, do not make use of the steps of the
ladder to mount upwards, but take them off and lay them on
their shoulders in order that they may take them along, delight-
ing in the weight of the burden they are carrying. They remain
ever below, as they carry what they should cause to carry them.

HOW CHILDREN SHOULD BE EDUCATED.
Parerga und Paralipomena, II. 505.

Kinder sollten das Leben, in jeder Hinsicht, nicht früher aus
der Kopie kennen lernen, als aus dem Original. Statt daher
zu eilen, ihnen nur Bücher in die Hände zu geben, mache man
sie stufenweise mit den Dingen und den menschlichen Verhält=
nissen bekannt. Vor allem sei man darauf bedacht, sie zu einer
reinen Auffassung der Wirklichkeit anzuleiten und sie dahin zu
bringen, daß sie ihre Begriffe stets unmittelbar aus der wirk=
lichen Welt schöpfen und sie nach der Wirklichkeit bilden, nicht
aber sie anderswo herholen, aus Büchern, Mährchen oder
Reden Anderer, und solche Begriffe nachher schon fertig zur
Wirklichkeit hinzubringen, welche letztere sie alsdann, den Kopf
voll Chimären, theils falsch auffassen, theils nach jenen

Chimären umzumodeln fruchtlos sich bemühen, und so durch
Beides auf Irrwege gerathen. Denn es ist unglaublich, wie
viel Nachtheil früh eingepflanzte Chimären und daraus ent-
standene Vorurtheile bringen: die spätere Erziehung, welche
die Welt und das wirkliche Leben uns geben, muß alsdann
hauptsächlich auf Ausmerzung jener verwendet werden.

Children, for many reasons, should not learn life from a copy
sooner than from the original. Instead, therefore, of being in a
hurry to put books only in their hands, we should make them
gradually acquainted with things and human relations. Especially
we should direct their minds to a clear apprehension of real
existence, and make them form their ideas from the real world,
and not from books, stories, and such like things, lest their heads
should be full of chimeras, and they should be led into a false
path. For it is scarcely to be believed how much mischief early
implanted chimeras and the mischief arising therefrom cause;
the latter training which the world and real life give us must be
principally employed in their removal.

THREE DIFFERENT KINDS OF AUTHORS.

Parerga und Paralipomena, II. 377.

Die Schriftsteller kann man eintheilen in Sternschnuppen,
Planeten und Firsterne. — Die Ersteren liefern die momentanen
Knall-Effekte: man schauet auf, ruft: „siehe da!" und auf
immer sind sie verschwunden. — Die Zweiten, also die Irr- und
Wandelsterne, haben viel mehr Bestand. Sie glänzen, wiewohl bloß vermöge ihrer Nähe, oft heller, als die Firsterne,
und werden von Nichtkennern mit diesen verwechselt. Inzwischen müssen auch sie ihren Platz bald räumen, haben zudem
nur geborgtes Licht und eine auf ihre Bahngenossen (Zeit-
genossen) beschränkte Wirkungssphäre. Sie wandeln und
wechseln: ein Umlauf von einigen Jahren Dauer ist ihre Sache.
Die Dritten allein sind unwandelbar, stehen fest am Firmament,
haben eigenes Licht, wirken zu Einer Zeit, wie zur Andern,
indem sie ihr Ansehen nicht durch die Veränderung unseres
Standpunktes ändern, da sie keine Parallaxe haben. Sie
gehören nicht, wie jene Andern, einem Systeme (Nation) allein
an; sondern der Welt. Aber eben wegen der Höhe ihrer

Stelle, braucht ihr Licht meistens viele Jahre, ehe es dem Erdbewohner sichtbar wird.

Authors may be divided into falling stars, planets, and fixed stars : the first have a momentary effect—we look up, call out, "See there ! " and in a moment they vanish for ever. The second, the wandering stars, have a much longer duration. They shine, though only by virtue of their nearness, often more clearly than the fixed stars, and are confounded with them by the ignorant. Meanwhile they quickly vacate their place ; have, besides, only borrowed light and a confined sphere of working on their contemporaries. They wander about and change their position ; an orbit of a few years is their utmost duration. But the third are unchangeable—possess their own light—work for all time, never changing their aspect by any change of our point of view—for they have no parallax. They do not belong as the others to one system alone, but to the whole universe. But even on account of the height of their position, their light generally requires many years before it is visible to the dwellers on earth.

STYLE IS THE PHYSIOGNOMY OF THE MIND.

Parerga und Paralipomena, II. 429.

Der Stil ist die Physiognomie des Geistes. Sie ist untrüglicher, als die des Leibes. Fremden Stil nachahmen heißt eine Maske tragen. Wäre diese auch noch so schön, so wird sie, durch das Leblose, bald insipid und unerträglich; so daß selbst das häßlichste lebendige Gesicht besser ist.

Style is the physiognomy of the mind. It is more infallible than that of the body. To imitate the style of another is said to be wearing a mask. However beautiful it may be, it is through its lifelessness insipid and intolerable, so that even the most ugly living face is more engaging.

HOW THE GREATNESS OF A MAN IS TO BE ESTIMATED.

Parerga und Paralipomena, II. 523.

In Hinsicht auf die Schätzung der Größe eines Menschen gilt für die geistige das umgekehrte Gesetz der physischen : diese wird durch die Ferne verkleinert, jene vergrößert.

In respect to the mode that a man's greatness ought to be estimated, the inverted law of the physical stands for the spiritual nature—the former is lessened by distance, the latter increased.

Lower Creation contrasted with Man.

Die Welt als Wille, I. 44.

Das Thier lernt den Tod erst im Tode kennen: der Mensch geht mit Bewußtseyn in jeder Stunde seinem Tode näher, und dies macht selbst Dem das Leben bisweilen bedenklich, der nicht schon am ganzen Leben selbst diesen Charakter der steten Vernichtung erkannt hat. Hauptsächlich dieserhalb hat der Mensch Philosophien und Religionen.

The lower creation learns death first in the moment of death ; man proceeds onward with the knowledge that he is every hour approaching nearer to death, and this throws a feeling of uncertainty over life, even to the man who forgets in the busy scenes of life that annihilation is awaiting him. It is for this reason chiefly that we have philosophies and religions.

The Brain.

Die Welt als Wille, II. 278.

Wie gute Verdauung einen gesunden starken Magen, wie Athletenkraft muskulöse, sehnige Arme erfordert; so erfordert außerordentliche Intelligenz ein ungewöhnlich entwickeltes, schön gebautes, durch feine Textur ausgezeichnetes und durch energischen Pulsschlag belebtes Gehirn. Hingegen ist die Beschaffenheit des Willens von keinem Organ abhängig und aus keinem zu prognosticiren. Der größte Irrthum in Gall's Schädellehre ist, daß er auch für moralische Eigenschaften Organe des Gehirns aufstellt.

As good digestion requires a sound and strong stomach—as athletic power requires muscular and sinewy arms—so extraordinary intelligence requires a brain uncommonly developed, well formed, distinguished by its peculiar texture, and animated by a vigorous pulse. On the other hand, the quality of the will is dependent on no organ, and its proceedings can be prognosticated by none. The great mistake of Gall's phrenological theory is that he also makes use of the organs of the brain for moral qualities.

Ennui.

Die Welt als Wille, I. 369.

Die Langeweile ist nichts weniger, als ein gering zu achtendes

2 E

Uebel: fie malt zuletzt wahre Verzweiflung auf das Geficht. Sie macht, daß Wesen, welche einander fo wenig lieben, wie die Menfchen, doch fo fehr einander fuchen, und wird dadurch die Quelle der Gefelligkeit. Auch werden überall gegen fie, wie gegen andere allgemeine Kalamitäten, öffentliche Vorkehrungen getroffen, fchon aus Staatsklugheit; weil diefes Uebel fo gut als fein entgegengefetztes Ertrem, die Hungersnoth, die Men= fchen zu den größten Zügellofigkeiten treiben kann: panem et circenses braucht das Volk. Das firenge Philadelphifche Pönitenziarfyftem macht, mittelft Einfamkeit und Unthätigkeit bloß die Langeweile zum Strafwerkzeug; und es ift ein fo fürchterliches, daß es fchon die Züchtlinge zum Selbftmord geführt hat. Wie die Noth die beftändige Geiffel des Volkes ift, fo die Langeweile die der vornehmen Welt. Im bürger= lichen Leben ift fie durch den Sonntag, wie die Noth durch die fechs Wochentage repräfentirt.

Ennui is an evil to which only too little attention is paid, though it at last paints despair on the face. It causes beings who have so little kindly feeling for each other, as men, to seek each other's company, and is thereby the origin of social inter-course. Open precautions are taken against it, as against other general calamities, by state policy; for this evil, like its very opposite extreme—hunger—can drive men to the greatest license; the people require "*panem et circenses.*" The strict penitentiary system of Philadelphia, through the medium of isolation and inactivity, makes mere ennui to be a punishment, and it is so terrible that it drives convicts to self-destruction. Necessity is the constant scourge of the lower orders, ennui that of the higher classes. In middle life it is represented by Sunday, as want is by the six week-days.

THE HISTORY OF MANKIND.

Parerga und Paralipomena, II. 248.

Die Gefchichte zeigt uns das Leben der Völker, und findet nichts, als Krieg und Empörungen zu erzählen; die friedlichen Jahre erfcheinen nur als kurze Paufen, Zwifchenakte, dann und wann ein Mal. Und ebenfo ift das Leben des Einzelnen ein fortwährender Kampf, nicht etwa bloß metaphorifch mit der Noth, oder mit der Langeweile; fondern auch wirklich mit Andern. Er findet überall den Widerfacher, lebt in beftän= digem Kampfe und ftirbt, die Waffen in der Hand.

Jedoch, wie unser Leib auseinanderplatzen müßte, wenn der Druck der Atmosphäre von ihm genommen wäre; — so würde, wenn der Druck der Noth, Mühseligkeit, Widerwärtigkeit und Vereitlung der Bestrebungen vom Leben der Menschen weggenommen wäre, ihr Uebermuth sich steigern, wenn auch nicht bis zum Platzen, doch bis zu den Erscheinungen der zügellosesten Narrheit, ja, Raserei. — Sogar bedarf Jeder allezeit eines gewissen Quantums Sorge, oder Schmerz, oder Noth, wie das Schiff des Ballastes, um fest und gerade zu gehn.

History presents to us the life of nations, and finds nothing to write about except wars and popular tumults : the years of peace appear only as short pauses, interludes, a mark here and there. And just so is the life of individuals a continued course of warfare, not at all in a metaphorical way of speaking, with want or ennui, but in reality too with his fellowmen. He finds everywhere adversaries—lives in continual struggles—and dies at last with arms in his hands.

Yet, after all, as our body must burst asunder if the weight of the atmosphere were to be withdrawn from it, so too, if the heavy burden of want, misery, calamities, and the non-success of our exertions, were taken away from the life of men, their arrogance would swell out, if not to the length of explosion, at all events to the exhibition of the most unbridled folly—nay, to madness. So that every man at all times requires a certain *quantum* of cares and sorrows, or necessities, as a ship does ballast, to enable him to go forward steadily and in a direct line.

Feeling of Immortality.
Parerga und Paralipomena, II. 231.

Jeder fühlt, daß er etwas Anderes ist, als ein von einem Andern einst belebtes Nichts. Daraus entsteht ihm die Zuversicht, daß der Tod wohl seinem Leben, jedoch nicht seinem Daseyn ein Ende machen kann.

Every one feels that he is something else than a nothing which has been animated by another. From this arises the confidence that death, though it may put an end to life, does not close man's existence.

Sleep and Death.
Die Welt als Wille, II. 572.

Was für das Individuum der Schlaf, das ist für den Willen

als Ding an ſich der Tod. Er würde es nicht aushalten, eine Unendlichkeit hindurch daſſelbe Treiben und Leiden, ohne wahren Gewinn, fortzuſeßen, wenn ihm Erinnerung und Individualität bliebe. Er wirft ſie ab, dies iſt der Lethe, und tritt, durch dieſen Todesſchlaf erfriſcht und mit einem andern Intellekt ausgeſtattet, als ein neues Weſen wieder auf: „zu neuen Ufern lockt ein neuer Tag!‟

What sleep is to the individual death is to the will as a thing in itself. Man could not continue for an eternity the same bustling habits and anxious scenes, without any gain from them, if his memory and individuality continued to exist. He throws them behind him (this is Lethe), and refreshed by this death-sleep, and endued with another intellect, he steps out as a new being: "a new day calls him to new shores."

Life and Death.

Parerga und Paralipomena, II. 232.

Das Leben kann allerdings angeſehen werden als ein **Traum**, und der Tod als das Erwachen. Dann aber gehört die Perſönlichkeit, das Individuum, dem träumenden und nicht dem wachen Bewußtſeyn an: weshalb denn jenem der Tod ſich als Vernichtung darſtellt. Jedenfalls jedoch iſt er, von dieſem Geſichtspunkt aus, nicht zu betrachten als der Uebergang zu einem uns ganz neuen und fremden Zuſtande, vielmehr nur als der Rücktritt zu dem uns urſprünglich eigenen, als von welchem das Leben nur eine kurze Epiſode war.

Life may be regarded as a dream, and death as an awakening. But in that case the personality, the individuality, belongs to the dreaming and not to the waking consciousness, and therefore death presents itself to the former as an annihilation. Yet from this point of view it is not to be regarded as the transition to an entirely new and strange state, rather as a return to what we were originally, and from which life is only a short episode.

The Useful and the Fine Arts.

Die Welt als Wille, II. 466.

Die Mutter der nützlichen Künſte iſt die Noth; die der ſchönen der Ueberfluß. Zum Vater haben jene den Verſtand, dieſe das Genie, welches ſelbſt eine Art Ueberfluß iſt.

The mother of useful arts is necessity ; that of the fine arts is luxury. For father the former have intellect, the latter genius, which itself is a kind of luxury.

Man is a Wild Beast.

Parerga und Paralipomena, II. 178.

Der Mensch ist im Grunde ein wildes entsetzliches Thier. Wir kennen es blos im Zustande der Bändigung und Zähmung, welche Civilisation heißt: daher erschrecken uns die gelegentlichen Ausbrüche seiner Natur. Aber wo und wann einmal Schloß und Kette der gesetzlichen Ordnung abfallen, und Anarchie eintritt, da zeigt sich was er ist. — Wer inzwischen auch ohne solche Gelegenheit sich darüber aufklären möchte, der kann die Ueberzeugung, daß der Mensch an Grausamkeit und Unerbittlichkeit keinem Tiger und keiner Hyäne nachsteht, aus hundert alten und neuen Berichten schöpfen.

Man is at bottom a wild, terrific animal. We know him only in connection with the taming and training, which is called civilisation ; hence the occasional outbreaks of his nature terrify us. But where and when the locks and bonds of legal order are loosened, and anarchy steps in, then he shows himself what he is. Even without such an opportunity, whoever can exhibit his real disposition can convince us, by a hundred old and new tales, that man is little inferior to any tiger or hyæna in cruelty and savageness.

The Sovereignty of the People is an Absurdity.

Parerga und Paralipomena, II. 210.

Die Frage nach der Souveränität des Volkes läuft im Grunde darauf hinaus, ob irgend Jemand ursprünglich das Recht haben könne, ein Volk wider seinen Willen zu beherrschen. Wie sich das vernünftigerweise behaupten lasse, sehe ich nicht ab. Allerdings also ist das Volk souverän: jedoch ist es ein ewig unmündiger Souverän, welcher daher unter bleibender Vormundschaft stehen muß und nie seine Rechte selbst verwalten kann, ohne gränzenlose Gefahren herbeizuführen; zumal er, wie alle Unmündigen, gar leicht das Spiel hinterlistiger Gauner wird, welche deshalb Demagogen heißen.

The question as to the sovereignty of the people depends very much on this, whether any one has an original right to command a people against its will. I see not how this can be rationally maintained. Therefore the people is at all times and in every way supreme ; yet it is a sovereign always in his minority, who must therefore ever remain in tutelage, and can never of himself exercise his rights, without incurring infinite dangers ; more especially, like all minors, he becomes easily the sport of crafty knaves, whom we call demagogues.

The Monarchical Form of Government.

Parerga und Paralipomena, II. 216.

Die monarchische Regierungsform ist die dem Menschen natürliche; fast so, wie sie es den Bienen und Ameisen, den reisenden Kranichen, den wandernden Elephanten, den zu Raubzügen vereinigten Wölfen und andern Thieren mehr ist, welche alle Einen an die Spitze ihrer Unternehmung stellen. Auch muß jede menschliche, mit Gefahr verknüpfte Unternehmung, jeder Heereszug, jedes Schiff seinem Oberbefehlshaber gehorchen: überall muß Ein Wille der leitende seyn. Sogar der thierische Organismus ist monarchisch construirt: das Gehirn allein ist der Lenker und Regierer, das Hegemonikon. Wenn gleich Herz, Lunge und Magen zum Bestande des Ganzen viel mehr beitragen; so können diese Spießbürger darum doch nicht lenken und leiten: dies ist Sache des Gehirns allein und muß von Einem Punkte ausgehen. Selbst das Planetensystem ist monarchisch. Hingegen ist das republikanische System dem Menschen so widernatürlich, wie es dem höhern Geistesleben, also Künsten und Wissenschaften ungünstig ist.

The monarchical form of government is natural to men, as it is to bees, ants, migrating cranes, wandering elephants, wolves in predatory expeditions, and other animals, who all appoint one to conduct their expeditions. Every expedition, too, of man attended by danger, every march of an army, every ship, must obey its leader ; above all there must be a leading mind. It seems thus that the organisation of animal nature is monarchical ; the brain alone is the leader and director. If the heart, lungs, and stomach contribute greatly to the maintenance of the system, they can neither direct nor guide : this is the act of the brain alone, and must issue from one point. Even the planetary system is monarchical. On the other hand, the republican system is as unnatural to man as to the higher spiritual life, therefore it is unfavourable to arts and sciences.

VIRTUE NOT TO BE LEARNED.

Die Welt als Wille, I. 320.

Die Tugend wird nicht gelehrt, so wenig wie der Genius: ja, für sie ist der Begriff so unfruchtbar und nur als Werkzeug zu gebrauchen, wie er es für die Kunst ist. Wir würden daher eben so thöricht seyn, zu erwarten, daß unsere Moralsysteme und Ethiken Tugendhafte, Edle und Heilige, als daß unsere Aesthetiken Dichter, Bildner und Musiker erweckten.

Virtue is as little to be acquired by learning as genius; nay, the idea is barren, and is only to be employed as an instrument, in the same way as genius in respect to art. It would be as foolish to expect that our moral and ethical systems would turn out virtuous, noble, and holy beings, as that our æsthetic systems would produce poets, painters, and musicians.

HIDDEN POWER IN MAN.

Parerga und Paralipomena, II. 481.

Welche Kräfte, zum Leiden und Thun, Jeder in sich trägt, weiß er nicht, bis ein Anlaß sie in Thätigkeit setzt; wie man dem im Teiche ruhenden Wasser, mit glattem Spiegel, nicht ansieht, mit welchem Toben und Brausen es vom Felsen un= versehrt herabzustürzen, oder wie hoch es als Springbrunnen sich zu erheben fähig ist; — oder auch, wie man die im eiskalten Wasser latente Wärme nicht ahndet.

What a man can do and suffer is unknown to himself till some occasion presents itself which draws out the hidden power; just as one sees not in the water of an unruffled pond the fury and the roar with which it can dash down a steep rock without injury to itself, or how high it is capable of rising; or as little as one can suspect the latent heat in the ice-cold water.

CHARACTER IS BEST SHOWN IN LITTLE THINGS.

Parerga und Paralipomena, I. 428.

Gerade in Kleinigkeiten, als bei welchen der Mensch sich nicht zusammennimmt, zeigt er seinen Charakter, und da kann man oft, an geringfügigen Handlungen, an bloßen Manieren, den gränzenlosen, nicht die mindeste Rücksicht auf Andere ken=

nenden Egoismus beobachten, der sich nachher im Großen nicht verleugnet, wiewohl verlarvt.

Man shows his character best in small trifles, where he is not on his guard, and it is in insignificant matters and the simplest habits that we may often be able to note the boundless egotism which pays not the slightest regard to the feelings of others, and which denies itself nothing in great things, though he may contrive to conceal it.

WE DECEIVE OURSELVES.

Die Welt als Wille, I. 350.

Wir betrügen und schmeicheln Niemanden durch so feine Kunstgriffe, als uns selbst.

We deceive and flatter no one by such delicate artifices as we do ourselves.

THE EXPRESSION OF THE FACE SPEAKS.

Parerga und Paralipomena, II. 509.

Das Gesicht eines Menschen sagt in der Regel mehr und Interessanteres als sein Mund: denn es ist das Kompendium alles Dessen, was dieser je sagen wird; indem es das Monogramm alles Denkens und Trachtens dieses Menschen ist. Auch spricht der Mund nur Gedanken eines Menschen, das Gesicht einen Gedanken der Natur aus. Daher ist Jeder werth, daß man ihn aufmerksam betrachte; wenn auch nicht Jeder, daß man mit ihm rede.

The face of a man, as a rule, speaks more eloquently and in a more interesting manner than his mouth; for it is the compendium of everything which the latter has to say; since it is the monogram of the thinking and acting of the man. Besides the mouth only utters the thoughts of the man, whereas the face expresses the thoughts of nature. Wherefore every man is worth being closely observed, though every man is not worth being talked to.

HOW A MAN'S REAL CHARACTER IS TO BE DISCOVERED.

Parerga und Paralipomena, II. 513.

Um die wahre Physiognomie eines Menschen rein und tief zu erfassen, muß man ihn beobachten, wenn er allein und sich selbst überlassen dasitzt. Schon jede Gesellschaft und sein Gespräch

mit einem Andern wirft einen fremden Reflex auf ihn, meiſtens
zu ſeinem Vortheil, indem er durch die Aktion und Reaktion in
Thätigkeit geſetzt und dadurch gehoben wird.   Hingegen allein
und ſich ſelber überlaſſen, in der Brühe ſeiner eigenen Gedanken
und Empfindungen ſchwimmend, — nur da iſt er ganz und gar
er ſelbſt.   Da kann ein tief eindringender phyſiognomiſcher
Blick ſein ganzes Weſen, im Allgemeinen, auf Ein Mal erfaſſen.
Denn auf ſeinem Geſichte, an und für ſich, iſt der Grundton
aller ſeiner Gedanken und Beſtrebungen ausgeprägt, der arrêt
irrévocable Deſſen, was er zu ſeyn hat und als was er ſich
nur dann ganz empfindet, wann er allein iſt.

To catch the true physiognomy of a man purely and thoroughly,
we must observe him when he is alone and given up to his own
thoughts.   The society and conversation of others throws upon
him an abnormal echo, mostly to his advantage, while he is by
the action and reaction roused to activity, and thereby lifted
beyond himself.   On the other hand, alone and given up to himself, swimming in the sea of his own thoughts and feelings—there
only is he quite and entirely himself.   Then can a single penetrating glance catch up his whole being, generally, at once.   For in
his face the key-note of all his thoughts and labours is deeply
engraved, the *arrêt irrévocable* of what he has to be and what he
feels himself to be, when he is alone.

Youth and Age.

Parerga und Paralipomena, I. 454.

Die Heiterkeit und der Lebensmuth unſerer Jugend beruht
zum Theil darauf, daß wir, bergauf gehend, den Tod nicht
ſehen; weil er am Fuße der andern Seite des Berges liegt.
Haben wir aber den Gipfel überſchritten, dann werden wir
den Tod, welchen wir bis dahin nur vom Hörenſagen kannten,
wirklich anſichtig, wodurch, da zu derſelben Zeit die Lebenskraft
zu ebben beginnt, auch der Lebensmuth ſinkt; ſo daß jetzt ein
trüber Ernſt den jugendlichen Uebermuth verdrängt und auch
dem Geſichte ſich aufdrückt.

Denn vom Standpunkte der Jugend aus geſehen, iſt das
Leben eine unendlich lange Zukunft; vom Standpunkte des
Alters aus, eine ſehr kurze Vergangenheit; ſo daß es Anfangs
ſich uns darſtellt wie die Dinge, wenn wir das Objektiv-
glas des Opernkuckers an's Auge legen, zuletzt aber wie wann

das Okular. Man muß alt geworden seyn, also lange gelebt haben, um zu erkennen, wie ephemer das Leben ist.

The calmness and courage of youth partly arise from this, that we are climbing up and see not death, because he lies on the other side of the mountain. But when we have passed over the summit, then we find death, of which we have only hitherto heard speak, stare us in the face, when our bodily strength begins to ebb and our courage to sink : then a sad earnestness takes the place of our youthful courage, and even impresses itself upon our countenance. From the standpoint of our youth life seems to be a never-ending long future ; from the standpoint of age a short past : so that in the beginning it presents itself to us, as things do if we place the object-glass of the opera to our eyes, but in the end as when we use the eye-glass. One must have become old, therefore lived long, to become satisfied how short life is.

Youth and Old Age contrasted.

Parerga und Paralipomena, I. 461.

Die ersten vierzig Jahre unsers Lebens liefern den Text, die folgenden dreißig den Kommentar dazu, der uns den wahren Sinn und Zusammenhang des Textes, nebst der Moral und allen Feinheiten desselben erst recht verstehen lehrt.

Gegen das Ende des Lebens nun gar geht es wie gegen das Ende eines Maskenballs, wenn die Masken abgenommen werden. Man sieht jetzt, wer Diejenigen, mit denen man, während seines Lebenslaufs, in Berührung gekommen war, eigentlich gewesen sind. Denn die Charaktere haben sich an den Tag gelegt, die Thaten haben ihre Früchte getragen, die Leistungen ihre gerechte Würdigung erhalten und alle Trugbilder sind zerfallen. Zu diesem Allen nämlich war Zeit erfordert.

The first forty years of our life give the text, the next thirty furnish the commentary upon it, which enables us rightly to understand the true meaning and connection of the text with its moral and its beauties.

Towards the end of life we move as towards the end of a mask-ball, when the masks are dropped. We see now what kind of persons those have really been with whom we have been connected during our life. For now the real characters of each are clearly revealed, their deeds have borne their fruit, their performances have got their true value, and anything false has fallen away. For all this time was required.

SCHUBART.

Born A.D. 1739. Died A.D. 1791.

Christian Frederick Daniel Schubart was born at Obersontheim, March 26, 1739, and died at Stuttgard, October 10, 1791, in the service of the Duke of Wirtemberg as poet for the theatre.

FOLLY.

Der Bettler.

Noth und Jammer sind die Gaben,
So die Thorheit ernten kann.

Want and sorrow are the gifts which folly earns for itself.

SEUME.

THE WHITE-WASHED COURTESY OF EUROPE.

Der Wilde.

Ein Kanabier, der noch Europens
Uebertünchte Höflichkeit nicht kannte.

A Canadian, who did not yet know the white-washed courtesy of Europe.

F. L. STOLBERG.

Born A.D. 1750. Died A.D. 1819.

Frederick Leopold, Count of Stolberg, distinguished as a poet and writer, was born, 1750, at Bramstedt in Holstein. His father was chamberlain to the King of Denmark. He was educated at the University of Göttingen, and was afterwards in various high employments in his country. In 1789 we find him ambassador in Berlin, where he married the Countess Sophia von Redern, with whom he made a tour through Switzerland, Italy, and Sicily, and wrote an interesting account of his travels. In 1800 he divested himself of his public employments and passed with all his family into the bosom of the Roman Catholic Church. He died at Söndermuhler near Osnabrück, 5th December 1819.

Nature.

An die Natur.

Süße, heilige Natur,
Laß mich gehn auf deiner Spur,
Leite mich an deiner Hand,
Wie ein Kind am Gängelband!

Wenn ich dann ermüdet bin,
Sink' ich dir am Busen hin,
Athme süße Himmelsluft
Hangend an der Mutterbrust.

Ach! wie wohl ist mir bei dir!
Will dich lieben für und für;
Laß mich gehn auf deiner Spur,
Süße, heilige Natur!

Sweet, holy Nature, let me ever follow thee, guide me with thy
hand as in leading-strings a child!
And when weary, then will I on thy bosom lie, breathing the
sweet joys of heaven, clinging to a mother's breast.
Ah! how sweet it is to dwell with thee! ever will I love thee
well; let me ever follow thee, holy Nature, sweet and free!

STURZ.

Born A.D. 1736.   Died A.D. 1779.

Helfrich Peter Sturz was born at Darmstadt in 1736. He
studied law at the Universities of Göttingen, Jena, and Giessen.
In 1759 he was appointed Secretary to the Austrian Embassy in
Munich, and later became private secretary to Count Bernstorf,
Prime Minister of Denmark. In 1768 he accompanied the king to
England and France, and was employed for many years in that
country in various capacities. He died in 1779.

A Statesman.

Erinnerungen aus Bernstorf's Leben.

Ein Staatsmann, der zu mißfallen anfängt, wandelt immer
an Abgründen hin, und thut keinen gleichgültigen Schritt
mehr. Ist er gelassen, so ist es ein Stolz, der gedemüthigt zu
werden verdient; verbirgt er seine Unruhe und seine Empfind=

lichkeit nicht, so ist es Bewußtseyn der Schuld; entschließt er sich, sein Amt niederzulegen, so wartet vielleicht eine Kränkung auf ihn, wozu nur der Anlaß gefehlt hat; und harrt er zu lange, reizt er die Ungeduld seiner Verfolger, so ist es ungewiß, zu welchem heftigen Ausbruch ihr Unwillen endlich verleitet werden mag. Wenn alle Zugänge des Throns von Rathgebern umringt sind, die ihre gemeinschaftliche Sicherheit vereinigt, so ist kein Fürst der Erde mächtig genug, den Eingebungen der Wahrheit, die zurückgescheucht wird, oder den Empfindungen eines unaufhörlich bestürmten Herzens zu folgen.

A statesman who begins to displease is ever walking on a precipice, and is no longer able to take a step which shall be of no importance. If he is calm, it is pride, which must be humbled ; if he does not conceal his anxiety and irritability, his feelings are his crime ; if he determines to lay down his office, he is anticipating an illness of which the opportunity was only wanting ; and if he continues too long, he excites the impatience of his followers, and it is uncertain to what length their displeasure may at last lead. If all the approaches to the throne are closed by counsellors which secure their common safety, no prince on earth is powerful enough to follow up the suggestions of truth, which is driven away, or the feelings of his heart, that is attacked without ceasing.

LUDWIG TIECK.

Born A.D. 1773.   Died A.D. 1853.

Ludwig Tieck, one of the most eminent writers of Germany, was born at Berlin in 1773. He studied at Halle, Göttingen, and Erlangen, beginning his literary career at the early age of twenty-two by publishing three novels. In 1795 he visited Jena, where he formed a lasting friendship with the Schlegels, Novalis, and Schelling. At Weimar he became acquainted with Herder. His long life was passed in literary persuits. In 1840 he was invited to Berlin by the King of Prussia, where he was made a privy-councillor, and passed the remainder of his life in his native city and at Potsdam, chiefly employed in revising his numerous works. He died, after a long period of suffering, heroically endured, in Berlin, 1853.

TRUE LOVE FEARS NO WINTER.

Herbstlied.

Die Liebe wintert nicht,

Nein, nein,
Ist und bleibt Frühlingsschein.

True love fears no winter. No, no! its spring is and ever remains.

THE ENERGETIC AND THE LAZY.

Denkspruch.

Wer lust'gen Muth zur Arbeit trägt
Und rasch die Arme stets bewegt,
Sich durch die Welt noch immer schlägt.
Der Träge sitzt, weiß nicht, wo aus,
Und über ihm stürzt ein das Haus.
Mit frohen Segeln munter
Fährt der Frohe das Leben hinunter.

Whoever brings cheerfulness to his work, and is ever active, dashes through this world's labours. The lazy sit, know not when their house is tumbling about their ears. The cheerful with full sails pass joyfully through life.

FLIGHT OF TIME.

Octavian, p. 1.

Wie flüchtig ist die Zeit! und wie beharrend,
Wenn uns die Gegenwart mit Qual umgiebt,
Wie träge dann zu scheiden, Platz zu machen.

How swift time flies! and yet how slow when we are overwhelmed with sorrow, how tardy then do the hours depart and pass away!

THE NOBLE AND IGNOBLE.

Octavian, p. 1.

Der ist nicht todt,
Der rühmlich schließt; gestorben ist noch lebend,
Wes Stirn die Schande brandmalt.

He is not dead who departs this life with high fame; dead is he, though still living, whose brow is branded with infamy.

The Troubled Life of Man.

Octavian, p. 1.

O Gott! wie bin ich glücklich! — Aber nein,
Kein Glück darf ungetrübt dem Menschen werden,
Er muß es fühlen, daß er lebt auf Erden,
Die harte Erde mischt sich mit der Sonne,
Und Trübsal dunkelt uns jedwede Wonne.

O God! how happy am I! But no, no happiness is unmixed to man, he must feel that he lives on earth ; the hard earth mingles itself with the sun, and affliction darkens every pleasure.

All is not Gold that glitters.

Octavian, p. 1.

O mein Monarch, ich darf es dir nicht sagen,
Wie nicht jedwedes Ding ist, was es scheint.
Das Laster trägt zu oft der Tugend Mantel,
Die Dürftigkeit erscheint als Reichthum oft,
Und Einfalt brüstet sich als Weisheit häufig,
Daß nur der Unerfahrne, Niegetäuschte,
In heiliger Miene Tugend sieht, und Schätze
Beim Bettel-Armen und Vernunft beim Thoren.

O your Majesty, I cannot tell you how different everything is from what it seems. Vice too oft wears the mask of virtue, poverty appears as riches, and folly often holds its head aloft like wisdom, so that it is only the inexperienced and deluded that see virtue in a holy exterior, treasures in a beggar, and wisdom in a fool.

The Noble.

Genoveva.

Der edle Mensch ist nur ein Bild von Gott.

The noble is only an image of God.

What distinguishes the Noble from the Ignoble.

Genoveva.

Wir alle kommen gleich geformt zur Welt,
Doch unterscheidet das den edlen Mann

Vom Pöbel, daß er seiner Meister wird,
Daß er den Ruhm die höchste Würde achtet
Und ihm die niedern Lüste unterwirft,
Ja, daß er auch den Ruhm vergessen kann,
Wenn Pflicht die strengen Worte zu ihm spricht.

We all come formed alike into the world, yet this distinguishes the noble from the low-minded—that he is his own master—that he pays the highest honour to glory, bringing the lower appetites in subjection to it—yea, that he can even forget glory if duty speaks to him its stern commands.

A Tide in the Affairs of Man.

Genoveva.

Ja wer so manchmal könnte sehn, wie seltsam
Die Fäden unsers ganzen Schicksals laufen!
Oft ist es nur ein Augenblick, versäumt
Man ihn, sind Mond' und Jahr' verloren.

Yes, who cannot but see sometimes how strange the threads of our whole destiny run! Oft it is only a moment, we miss it, and months and years are lost.

Time.

Genoveva.

Wird es nicht alle Tage Abend? Kommt der Morgen nicht nach der fürchterlichsten Nacht wieder? Schon einigemal dacht' ich: die Sonne kann nun nicht mehr aufgehn; und dennoch kam sie mit ihrer ersten Klarheit wieder. So geht die Zeit kalt und gleichgültig an uns vorüber, sie weiß von unsern Schmerzen, sie weiß von unsern Freuden nichts, sie führt uns mit eiskalter Hand tiefer und tiefer in das Labyrinth hinein, endlich läßt sie uns stehn, und wir sehn uns um und können nicht errathen, wo wir sind.

Is there not an evening to every day? Comes not the morning back again after the most terrific night? Sometimes I have thought—the sun can never rise again; and yet it came back again with its early dawn. Thus time passes cold and indifferent over us—it knows nothing of our sorrows—it knows nothing of our joys; it leads us with ice-cold hand deeper and deeper into the labyrinth; at last allows us to stand still—we look around and cannot guess where we are.

Chance.

Fortunat.

Er spricht Unsinn, für den vernünftigen
Menschen giebt es gar keinen Zufall.

He speaks nonsense, for sensible men there is no chance.

Different Ways of telling a Story.

Fortunat.

Ei, man lügt

Nicht eben immer grade zu, und findet
Doch Fußsteig', die nicht laufen wie die Straße;
Man kann ein Ding auf hundert Art erzählen,
Verschieden immer, und doch immer wahr,
Der Kluge nimmt davon so viel ihm nützt.

Well, people tell lies not precisely in a straightforward way,
and find paths that do not run like the high-road; one can tell
a story a hundred ways, all different, and yet always true; the
wise man takes as much of it as suits him.

To place Confidence in an Enemy.

Fortunat.

Denn das hab' ich im Leben oft gesehn:
Leichtsinniges Vertraun dem Feinde leihn
Ist schlimmer, als mit gift'gen Nattern spielen.

For I have often seen in life, to place thoughtless confidence in
an enemy is more dangerous than to play with poisonous vipers.

The Very Wise.

Fortunat.

Wer sich für den allerklügsten hält, muß immer die aller-
dummsten Streiche machen. Das ist der Gang der Natur.

He who considers himself a paragon of wisdom is sure to commit
some superlatively stupid act. That is the course of nature.

More Things in Heaven and Earth.
Fortunat.

Ja, mein Freund,
Kennt Ihr nicht die Sentenz: es giebt manch' Ding
Im Himmel und auf Erden, wovon Eure
Schulweisheit sich nicht träumen läßt?

Yes, my friend, know you not the saying—There are many
things in heaven and earth of which your philosophy cannot
dream?

So Shakespeare (*Hamlet*, i. 5) :—

" There are more things in heaven and earth, **Horatio,**
Than are dreamt of in your philosophy."

ANDREAS TSCHERNING.
Born A.D. 1611.   Died A.D. 1659.

Children.
Elternglück.

Lustig ist das Meer zu sehen,
Wenn nicht Aeols Brüder wehen,
Und das Schiff geht ohne Fahr:
Aber nichts von allen Dingen
Kann mehr Lust den Eltern bringen,
Als der Kinder muntre Schaar.

Kinder sind des Lebens Pfande,
Kinder sind die starken Bande,
Und die Säulen, so ein Haus
Vor dem Einfall aufrecht halten,
Wenn nunmehr die Eltern alten
Oder ziehn von hinnen aus.

Kinder sind auch allen Schätzen,
Allem Golde vorzusetzen;
Kinder sind der Liebe Lohn;
Die sich fromm zu seyn befleißen,
Denen hat Gott selbst verheißen
Manche Tochter, manchen Sohn.

It is pleasant to look on the ocean when the brothers of Æolus blow not, and the ship sails in safety ; but nothing can bring more delight to parents than a sprightly band of children.

Children are the pledges of life—children are the firmest bonds —the pillars which support a house when the parents are frail or go hence.

Children are to be preferred to precious treasures and gold ; children are the rewards of love ; to those who exert themselves to be pious God has promised to give many sons and daughters.

WEISSE.

Born A.D. 1726. Died A.D. 1804.

Christian Felix Weisse was born, 1726, at Annaberg, where he died, 1804, in the office of Receiver of Taxes.

DELAY.

Der Aufschub.

Morgen, morgen, nur nicht heute !
Sprechen immer träge Leute,
Morgen ! heute will ich ruh'n ;
Morgen jene Lehre fassen,
Morgen diesen Fehler lassen,
Morgen dies und jenes thun.

Und warum nicht heute? morgen
Kannst du für was And'res sorgen.
Jeder Tag hat seine Pflicht.
Was gescheh'n ist, ist geschehen ;
Dies nur kann ich übersehen,
Was gescheh'n kann, weiß ich nicht.

Jeder Tag, ist er vergebens,
Ist im Buche meines Lebens
Nichts, ein unbeschriebenes Blatt!
Wohl denn ! Morgen, so wie heute,
Steh' darin auf jeder Seite
Von mir eine gute That.

To-morrow, morrow, only not to-day ! Thus idle people ever say, To-morrow ! to-day I shall rest ! to-morrow learn that lesson, to-morrow forsake that sin, to-morrow do this and that.

And wherefore not to-day? to-morrow thou canst attend to something else ; every day has its allotted duty. Whatever has happened has happened—this only can I know ; but what may hap to-morrow I know not.

Every day if it vainly flies is in the volume of my life a page unwritten—blank and void. Well then, to-morrow, as well as to-day, place therein on every side a deed to be read by coming ages.

WIELAND.

Born A.D. 1733.   Died A.D. 1813.

Christopher Martin Wieland, born near Biberach in Swabia, in 1733, was carefully educated by his father, who was a Protestant clergyman. He attended the University of Tübingen to study law, though his whole thoughts were given up to literature. Abandoning his legal studies, he became amanuensis to Bodmer, a German poet of some eminence. His best novel, called "Agathon," appeared in 1766, and in 1772 he was appointed by the Duchess cf Weimar to superintend the education of her two sons. At Weimar he devoted himself with ardour to literary pursuits ; he wrote tragedies, he composed poetry, and compiled histories. Of his poems the best is the "Oberon ;" in his "History of the Abderites" he satirises, in imitation of Swift, the follies and foibles of mankind. He died at Weimar in 1813.

EARLY FEELINGS OF YOUTH.

Agathon.

Diese Blüthe der Empfindlichkeit, diese zärtliche Sympathie, mit allem, was lebt oder zu leben scheint, dieser Geist der Freude, der uns aus allen Gegenständen entgegenathmet, dieser magische Firniß, der sie überzieht, und uns über einen Anblick, von dem wir zehn Jahre später noch kaum flüchtig gerührt werden, in stillem Entzücken zerfliessen macht, dieses beneidenswürdige Vorrecht der ersten Jugend verliert sich unvermerkt mit dem Anwachs unserer Jahre, und kann nicht wieder gefunden werden.

This first bloom of sensibility, this tender sympathy with every living thing, or what appears to have life, this spirit of joy, which breathes upon us from things and makes us melt in quiet rapture at the sight of some objects, by which ten years later we would not be in the least moved—this enviable privilege of the first years of youth, is imperceptibly lost with the increase of years, and can never be again found.

Readers.

Abderiten, I. 1.

Beſchäftigte Leſer ſind ſelten gute Leſer. Bald gefällt ihnen alles, bald nichts; bald verſtehen ſie uns bald, bald gar nicht, bald (was noch ſchlimmer iſt) unrecht. Wer mit Vergnügen und Nutzen leſen will, muß gerade ſonſt nichts andres zu thun noch zu denken haben.

Busy readers are seldom good readers; sometimes everything pleases them, sometimes nothing; sometimes they half understand us—sometimes not at all—and sometimes (which is still worse) they misunderstand us. He who would read with pleasure or with profit, must have nothing else to do, nothing else to think of.

Nature and Education.

Abderiten, I. 2.

Die Natur, wenn man ſie nur ungeſtört arbeiten läßt, macht meiſtens alle weitere Fürſorge für das Gerathen ihrer Werke überflüſſig. Aber wiewohl ſie ſelten vergißt, ihr Lieblingswerk mit allen den Fähigkeiten auszurüſten, durch welche ein vollkommner Menſch ausgebildet werden könnte; ſo iſt doch eben dieſe Ausbildung das, was ſie der Kunſt überläßt: und es bleibt alſo jedem Staate noch Gelegenheit genug übrig, ſich ein Recht an die Vorzüge und Verdienſte ſeiner Mitbürger zu erwerben.

Nature, when left to herself, generally renders all extra care for the success of her works superfluous. But although she rarely forgets to endow her favourites with all those qualities by which accomplished men are distinguished, still education—the drawing out and developing of those qualities—is exactly the task she leaves to art, and therefore every state must seek for itself the opportunity of affording that instruction which its citizens require.

The Formation of Taste.

Abderiten, I. 2.

Die Bildung des Geſchmacks, d. i. eines feinen, richtigen und gelehrten Gefühls alles Schönen, iſt die beſte Grundlage zu jener berühmten Sokratiſchen Kalokagathie oder innerlichen Schönheit und Güte der Seele, welche den liebenswürdigen, edelmüthigen, wohlthätigen und glücklichen Menschen macht. Und nichts ist geschickter, dieses richtige Gefühl für uns zu bilden, als — wenn alles, was wir von Kindheit an sehen und hören, schön ist. In einer Stadt, wo die Künste der Musen in der größten Vollkommenheit getrieben werden, in einer mit Meisterstücken der bildenden Künste angefüllten Stadt, in einem Athen geboren zu seyn, ist daher allerdings kein geringer Vortheil.

The formation of the taste arises from a keen and true perception of the beautiful, and is the best groundwork of the celebrated "Kalogathia" of Socrates, making internal beauty and goodness of soul to constitute the noble-minded, beneficent, and happy man ; and nothing is easier than to form in us this correct feeling of beauty, if all that we see and hear from our childhood be beautiful. It is no small advantage to be born in a place where the arts and the sciences are cultivated in the greatest perfection —in a well-built town, filled with masterpieces of art, as in Athens.

To be Silent.

Abderiten, I. 4.

Schweigen — ist zuweilen eine Kunst! aber doch nie eine so große, als uns gewisse Leute glauben machen wollen, die dann am klügsten sind, wenn sie schweigen.

To be silent is sometimes an art, yet not so great a one as certain people would have us believe, who are wisest when they are most silent.

Dangerous to have more Sense than our Neighbours.

Abderiten, I. 9.

Es ist ordentlicher Weise eine gefährliche Sache, mehr Verstand zu haben als seine Mitbürger. Sokrates mußt' es mit dem Leben bezahlen ; und wenn Aristoteles noch mit heiler Haut davon kam, als ihn der Oberpriester Eurymedon zu Athen der Ketzerei anklagte, so kam es bloß daher, weil er sich in Zeiten aus dem Staube machte.

It is commonly a dangerous thing for a man to have more sense than his neighbours. Socrates paid for his superiority with his life ; and if Aristotle saved his skin, accused as he was of heresy by the chief priest Eurymedon, it was because he took to his heels in time (Ælian, *V. H.* iii. 36).

A Poet or Painter not made by Rules.

Abderiten, I. 12.

Denn so wie noch keiner durch die bloße Wissenschaft der Regeln ein guter Dichter oder Künstler geworden sey, und nur derjenige, welchen angebornes Genie, emsiges Studium, hartnäckiger Fleiß und lange Uebung zum Dichter oder Künstler gemacht, geschickt sey, die Regeln seiner Kunst recht zu verstehen und anzuwenden : so sey auch die Theorie der Kunst, aus dem Aeußerlichen des Menschen auf das Innerliche zu schließen, nur für Leute von großer Fertigkeit im Beobachten und Unterscheiden brauchbar, für jeden andern hingegen eine höchst ungewisse und betrügliche Sache.

For as nobody can become a good poet or painter by the knowledge of rules alone, but only those who, by native genius, long study, determined application, and continued practice, have learned how to apply them ; so the art of judging by the physiognomy, of a man's interior qualities, can be useful only to those who possess great experience, observation, and discernment ; to all others it can but be uncertain and deceptive.

The Wise are sometimes Foolish.

Abderiten, II. 1.

Die besten Menschen haben ihre Anomalien, und die Weisesten leiden zuweilen eine vorüber gehende Verfinsterung; aber dieß hindert nicht, daß man nicht mit hinlänglicher Sicherheit von einem verständigen Manne sollte behaupten können ; daß er gewöhnlich, und besonders bei solchen Gelegenheiten, wo auch die Dümmsten allen den ihrigen zusammen raffen, wie ein Mann von Verstand verfahren werde.

The best men have their anomalies, and the wisest of human beings may suffer sometimes a momentary eclipse ; but we may, notwithstanding this, assert with tolerable security, that he will in all ordinary cases act and speak as a man of intellect may be expected to do, and that especially when and where blockheads are collected together.

The Weak or Wicked.

Abderiten, II. 3.

Es giebt eine Art von Menschen, die man viele Jahre lang kennen und beobachten kann, ohne mit sich selbst einig zu werden, ob man sie in die Klasse der schwachen oder der bösen Leute setzen soll. Kaum haben sie einen Streich gemacht, dessen kein Mensch von einiger Ueberlegung fähig zu seyn scheint, so überraschen sie uns durch eine so wohl ausgedachte Bosheit, daß wir, mit allem guten Willen von ihrem Herzen das Beste zu denken, uns in der Unmöglichkeit befinden, die Schuld auf ihren Kopf zu legen.

There is a kind of men who may be known and observed for many years without its being determined whether they are wicked or merely weak. Scarcely have they committed an action of which a man with a little reflection would be incapable, when they astonish us with such an elaborate piece of malice, that with all goodwill on our parts to form the best opinion of their hearts, we feel compelled to bring them in guilty.

Reasoning Fools.

Abderiten, II. 4.

Die größten, die gefährlichsten, die unerträglichsten aller Narren (sagte er), sind die räsonirenden Narren. Ohne weniger Narren zu seyn als andre, verbergen sie dem unbenkenden Haufen die Zerrüttung ihres Kopfes durch die Fertigkeit ihrer Zunge, und werden für weise gehalten, weil sie zusammenhängender rasen als ihre Mitbrüder im Tollhause. Ein ungelehrter Narr ist verloren, so bald es so weit mit ihm gekommen ist, daß er Unsinn spricht. Bei dem gelehrten Narren hingegen sehen wir gerade das Widerspiel. Sein Glück ist gemacht und sein Ruhm befestiget, so bald er Unsinn zu reden oder zu schreiben anfängt. Denn die meisten, wiewohl sie sich ganz eigentlich bewußt sind, daß sie nichts davon verstehen, sind entweder zu mißtrauisch gegen ihren eigenen Verstand, um gewahr zu werden, daß die Schuld nicht an ihnen liegt; oder zu dumm, um es zu merken, und also zu eitel, um zu gestehen, daß sie nichts verstanden haben.

The greatest, the most dangerous, the most insupportable of all fools are reasoning fools ; without being the less foolish, they conceal from the unreflecting crowd the disorder of their heads by the dexterity of their tongues, and are reputed wise because they rave more coherently than their fellows in the asylum. An unlearned fool is lost if he happens to speak nonsense. But with the learned fool it is just the contrary—his fortune is made as soon as he begins to speak or to write absurdly ; for the greater part of mankind, though aware that they understand nothing of what is thus said or written, either are too suspicious of their own intellect to perceive that the fault does not lie in themselves, or too stupid to remark, and too vain to confess, that they are so entirely in the dark on the subject.

Stupidity.

Abderiten, III. 8.

Die Dummheit hat ihr Sublimes so gut als der Verstand, und wer darin bis zum Absurden gehen kann, hat das Erhabne in dieser Art erreicht, welches für gescheute Leute immer eine Quelle von Vergnügen ist.

Stupidity has its sublime as well as genius, and he who carries that quality to absurdity has reached it, which is always a source of pleasure to sensible people.

Authors and the Public.

Abderiten, III. 11.

In der That haben Dichter, Tonkünstler, Maler, einem aufgeklärten und verfeinerten Publikum gegenüber, schlimmes Spiel ; und gerade die eingebildeten Kenner, die unter einem solchen Publikum immer den größten Haufen ausmachen, sind am schwersten zu befriedigen. Anstatt der Einwirkung still zu halten, thut man alles, was man kann, um sie zu verhindern. Anstatt zu genießen was da ist, räsonirt man darüber was da seyn könnte. Anstatt sich zur Illusion zu bequemen, wo die Vernichtung des Zaubers zu nichts dienen kann als uns eines Vergnügens zu berauben, setzt man, ich weiß nicht welche kindische Ehre darein, den Filosofen zur Unzeit zu machen ; zwingt sich zu lachen, wo Leute, die sich ihrem natürlichen Gefühl über= lassen, Thränen im Auge haben, und, wo diese lachen, die Nase zu rümpfen, um sich das Ansehen zu geben, als ob man zu stark, ober zu fein, ober zu gelehrt fey, um sich von so was aus seinem Gleichgewicht setzen zu lassen.

In fact, authors, musicians, and painters have a difficult game to play before a scientific and refined public ; and the conceited connoisseurs, who compose a great part of such public, are the most difficult to satisfy ; instead of receiving impressions quietly, they do all they can to hinder them ; instead of giving way to an illusion, where the destruction of the charm can only rob us of a pleasure, they make it a point of honour, I do not know why, to act the philosopher out of season ; they force themselves to laugh when people with their natural feelings about them would have tears in their eyes ; and when others would laugh they turn up their noses and give themselves airs of being too strong-minded or too refined to be moved by anything.

The Wise and the Foolish.

Abderiten, iv. 10.

Es ist eine alte Bemerkung, daß verständige Leute durch's Alter gewöhnlich weiser, und Narren mit den Jahren immer alberner werden.

It is an old observation, that wise men grow usually wiser as they grow older and fools more foolish.

Despair not.

Oberon, c. i. *st.* 27.

Verzweifle keiner je, dem in der trübsten Nacht
Der Hoffnung letzte Sterne schwinden!

Let no one despair to whom in the murkiest night hope's last glimmer vanishes!

The Lightnings do not always Sleep.

Oberon, c. i. *st.* 50.

Du spottest noch? Erzittre! immer schlafen
Des Rächers Blitze nicht.

Mockest thou? Tremble! the avenging lightning does not always sleep.

What Man has are Gifts.

Oberon, c. II. *st.* 19.

Denn was ein Menſch auch hat, ſo ſind's am Ende Gaben.

Whatever a man has I call mere gifts from Heaven.

Experience.

Oberon, c. II. *st.* 24.

Da dacht' ich oft: ſchwaҍt noch ſo hoch gelehrt,
Man weiß doch nichts, als was man ſelbſt erfährt!

Oft have I thought—jabber as he will, how learned soever, man
knows nothing but what he has learned from experience!

Woes spring from Transient Lust.

Oberon, c. II. *st.* 52.

Zu oft iſt kurze Luſt die Quelle langer Schmerzen!

Too oft is transient pleasure the spring of lengthened woes!

Courtesies of Ancient Days.

Oberon, c. III. *st.* 39.

Mit aller Höflichkeit
Der guten alten Ritterszeit,
Die zwar ſo fein, wie unſre, nicht geweben,
Doch deſto derber war, und beſſer Farbe hielt.

With all the courtesies of the good old knightly times, which
were of a texture not so fine as ours, but more thickly twined and
of a better colour.

Soft Music.

Oberon, c. III. *st.* 57.

Allmählich ſank die ſüße Harmonie,
Gleich voll, doch ſchwächer ſtets, herunter bis zum Säuſeln
Der ſanftſten Sommerluft, wenn kaum ſich je und je
Ein Blatt bewegt, und um der Nymphe Knie
Im ſtillen Bache ſich die Silberwellen träuſeln.

Gradually the sweet melody declined, full as at first, but sinking in its close down to the whisperings of the softest summer wind, when scarce a leaf trembles on the spray, and round the Naiad's knee the silvery waves scarce curl in the still lake.

A Fair Lady.

Oberon, c. IV. *st.* 6.

Denk' dir ein Weib im reinsten Jugendlicht,
Nach einem Urbild von dort oben
Aus Rosengluth und Lilienschnee geweben;
Gieb ihrem Bau das feinste Gleichgewicht;
Ein stilles Lächeln schweb' auf ihrem Angesicht,
Und jeder Reiz, von Majestät erhoben,
Erweck' und schreck' zugleich die lüsterne Begier:
Denk' alles, und du hast den Schatten kaum von ihr!

Paint to thyself a woman in the bright light of youth, traced from the original above—woven of the ruddy rose and snow-white lily ; give the finest proportion to her form—let a soft smile play around her lips, and every charm tempered with majesty awake, and at the same time repress, voluptuous desire ; paint all this, and yet thou hast scarcely a shadow of her.

Hope.

Oberon, c. IV. *st.* 10.

Inzwischen, lieber Herr, thut euch die Hoffnung gut,
So hofft! Man macht dabei zum mind'sten rothes Blut.

Meanwhile, good sir, if hope your spirits cheer, hope on! Her dreams, at least, make the blood run red.

Our Early Days.

Oberon, c. IV. *st.* 21.

Sieht unvermerkt an's Ufer der Garonne,
Wo er als Kind den ersten Strauß gepflückt,
Von Eufrats Ufern weg der Alte sich verzückt.
Nein, denkt er, nirgends scheint doch unser's Herrgotts Sonne
So mild als da, wo sie zuerst mir schien,
So lachend keine Flur, so frisch kein andres Grün!

The old man strays imperceptibly in thought to the banks of the Garonne, where in childhood he plucked the first floweret; from the banks of the Euphrates he wanders away enraptured. Nowhere, he thinks, the sun so mildly gleams as there where he first drank its beams—so laughing no other mead, so fresh no other green!

MAN BLINDLY WORKS FATE'S COMMAND.

Oberon, c. IV. *st.* 59.

Blindlings thut er bloß den Willen des Geschickes.

Man but blindly works the will of fate.

YOUNG MAY.

Oberon, c. V. *st.* 25.

Frisch, wie der junge Mai sich an den Reihen stellt,
Wenn mit den Grazien di Nymphen Tänze halten.

Fresh as the lovely form of youthful May, when nymphs and graces in the dance unite.

FATE.

Oberon, c. V. *st.* 60.

Des Schicksals Zwang ist bitter.

The power of fate is bitter.

THE EYE OF LOVE NEVER DARKENED.

Oberon, c. V. *st.* 85.

Vergebens hüllt die Nacht mit dunstbeladnen Flügeln
Den Luftkreis ein; dieß hemmt der Liebe Sehkraft nicht
Aus ihren Augen strahlt ein überirdisch Licht,
Worin die Seelen selbst sich in einander spiegeln.
Nacht ist nicht Nacht für sie; Elysium
Und Himmelreich ist alles um und um;
Ihr Sonnenschein ergießet sich von innen,
Und jeder Augenblick entfaltet neue Sinnen.

In vain the night with vapour-laden wings enwraps the canopy of heaven; this dims not the all-seeing power of love: from their eyes rays of celestial light beam forth, by which their souls behold each other. Night is not night to them ; Elysium and heaven are round and round them : their sunshine comes from within, and every moment unfolds new feelings.

An Honest Woman.

Oberon, c. VI. *st.* 87.

Ein einz'ler Biedermann wird immer noch gesehen;
Doch wandre einer mir um's weite Erdenrund
Nach einem frommen Weib, er wird vergebens gehen!

One single honest man may yet be seen ; but wander all the world round to find one honest woman, he will search in vain !

Love.

Oberon, c. VII. *st.* 41.

O Liebe, süßes Labsal aller Leiden
Der Sterblichen, du wonnevoller Rausch
Vermählter Seelen! welche Freuden
Sind deinen gleich?

O love ! thou sweet balm of every woe that preys on man, thou intoxicating draught of wedded souls ! what joys can be compared to thine ?

What is the World ?

Oberon, c. VIII. *st.* 20.

Was ist ihm nun die Welt? Ein weiter leerer Raum,
Fortunen's Spielraum, frei ihr Rad herum zu rollen!

What is now the world to him ? a vast and vacant space, for Fortune's wheel to roll around at will !

The Power of Nature to soothe the Soul.

Oberon, c. VIII. *st.* 22.

Allmählig hob sein Herz sich aus der trüben Fluth
Des Grams empor; die Nüchternheit, die Stille,
Die reine freie Luft, durchläuterten sein Blut,
Entwölkten seinen Sinn, belebten seinen Muth.

Er ſpürte nun, daß aus der ew'gen Fülle
Des Lebens, Balſam auch für ſeine Wunden quille,
Oft brachte die Magie von einem Sonnenblick
Auf einmal aus der Gruft der Schwermuth ihn zurück.

By degrees his heart rose out of the troubled flood of grief; temperance, stillness, the pure free air, purified his blood, unclouded his mind, and reanimated his soul. He now perceived that, from the exhaustless store of life, a balm flowed even for wounds like his. Oft the magic of a sunbeam brought him at once back from the pit of despair.

LABOUR.

Oberon, c. VIII. *st.* 40.

Nichts unterhält ſo gut (verſichert ihn der Greis)
Die Sinne mit der Pflicht im Frieden,
Als fleiſſig ſie durch Arbeit zu ermüden;
Nichts bringt ſie leichter aus dem Gleis
Als müß'ge Träumerei.

The old man says: "Nothing maintains so well each sense in peace with duty as to weary ourselves unceasingly with work; nothing takes us more easily from the rut of virtue than dreamy idleness."

BEAUTIFUL THOUGHTS

FROM SPANISH AUTHORS.

———♦♦———

CALDERON.

Born A.D. 1601. Died A.D. 1681.

Calderon de la Barca, a celebrated dramatic author, was born of noble parentage at Madrid in 1601. After he completed his studies, he enlisted as a common soldier, and made several campaigns in Italy and Flanders. During this time, however, he cultivated a taste for dramatic poetry, and attracting the notice of Philip IV., he was invited to Madrid in 1636, and became the king's adviser in all matters connected with the theatricals of the court. In 1652 he devoted himself to the Church, and became a canon at Toledo. From this period till his death on the 25th May 1681, he abandoned dramatic composition except on sacred subjects.

No Captive sings willingly.

The Constant Prince, Act I. *sc.* **1.**

> Pues solo un rudo animal
> Sin discurso racional
> Canta alegre en la prision.

For it is only a soulless bird without reason that sings joyfully in its cage.

Age does not respect the Noble.

The Constant Prince, Act I. *sc.* **1.**

> Al peso de los años
> Lo eminente se rinde ;
> Que á lo fácil del tiempo
> No hay conquista dificil.

The noble yields to the weight of years, for conquest is not difficult for time.

What is Beauty without Happiness?

The Constant Prince, Act i. *sc.* 1.

De qué sirve la hermosura,
(Cuando lo fuese la mia)
Si me falta la alegría ?
Si me falta la ventura ?

What does loveliness avail (if indeed it is mine), if joy of heart fail me, if good fortune fail me ?

The Love-Sick Mind.

The Constant Prince, Act i. *sc.* 1.

Si yo supiera,
Ay Celima, lo que siento,
De mi mismo sentimiento
Lisonja al dolor hiciera ;
Pero de la pena mia
No sé la naturaleza ;
Que entonces fuera tristeza
Lo que hoy es melancolía,
Solo que sé sentir no sé,
Que ilusion del alma fue.

Ah, my Zelima, if I did but know what I feel, that certain knowledge would be a cure of my grief ; but I know not the nature of my pain, for now it seemeth tearful sadness, and now it is pensive melancholy ; I only know, I know I feel, though I know not what I feel, the illusions of my soul mock me so.

Comparison of Waves with Flowers.

The Constant Prince, Act i. *sc.* 1.

Pues no me puedo alegrar,
Formando sombras y lejos,
La emulacion, que en reflejos
Tienen la tierra y el mar ;
Cuando con grandezas sumas
Compiten entre esplendores

Las espumas á las flores,
Las flores á las espumas ;
Porque el jardin, envidioso
De ver las ondas del mar,
Su curso quiere imitar ;
Y asi el zéfiro amoroso
Matices rinde, y olores
Que soplando en ellas bebe,
Y hacen las hojas que mueve
Un océano de flores ;
Cuando el mar, triste de ver
La natural compostura
Del jardin, tambien procura
Adornar y componer
Su playa, la pompa pierde,
Y á segunda ley sujeto,
Compite con dulce efeto
Campo azul y golfo verde,
Siendo, ya con rizas plumas,
Ya con mezclados colores,
El jardin un mar de flores,
Y el mar un jardin de espumas :
Sin duda mi pena es mucha,
No la pueden lisonjear
Campo, cielo, tierra y mar.

Certainly, no more am I gladdened by the emulous reflections which the earth and sea with dark shades and distant projections form; when alike in charms and powers the sparkling foam competes with snow-white flowers, for the garden, envious of the curling waves of ocean, loves to imitate their motion, and the amorous zephyr gives back the perfumes which it drinks in by blowing over the shining waters, and makes the waving leaves an ocean of bright flowers ; when the sea, sad to view the natural beauties of the garden, while it tries to adorn its own realm, destroys its majestic mien, and subject to second laws, blends with sweet effect fields of blue with waves of green : coloured now like heaven's blue dome, now plumed with various hues, the garden seems a sea of flowers, and the sea a garden of bright foam. How deep my pain must be, since nothing delights me, nor earth, nor air, nor sea, nor sky !

A FIRM AND CONSTANT MIND.

The Constant Prince, Act I. *sc.* 1.

Que en un ánimo constante
Siempre se halla igual semblante
Para el bien y el mal.

For in a firm mind there is always found an unchanged countenance for good and evil.

THE RISING SUN.

The Constant Prince, Act I. *sc.* 1.

Una mañana, á la hora
Que, medio dormido el sol,
Atropellando las sombras
Del ocaso, desmaraña
Sobre jazmines y rosas
Rubios cabellos, que enjuga
Con paños de oro á la aurora
Lagrimas de fuego y nieve,
Que el sol convirtió en aljófar.

One morning, at the hour when the half-awakened sun, trampl-
ing down the lingering shadows of the west, spreads his ruby-
tinted tresses over jessamines and roses, drying with cloths of gold
Aurora's tears of mingled fire and snow, which the snow's rays
converted into pearls.

POWER OF THE ARTIST.

The Constant Prince, Act I. *sc.* 1.

Porque como en los matices
Sútiles pinceles logran
Unos visos, unos lejos,
Que en perspectiva dudosa
Parecen montes tal vez,
Y tal ciudades famosas
Porque la distancia siempre
Monstruos imposibles forma :
Asi en paises azules
Hicieron luces y sombras,

> Confundiendo mar y cielo
> Con las nubes y las ondas,
> Mil engaños á la vista.

For as on the canvas subtle pencils blend dark and bright in such proportions, that in dim perspective now appear mountains, now famous cities, for remoteness ever forms monstrous shapes ; thus athwart the fields of azure lights and shades alternate fly, intermingling sea and sky with clouds and the waves, mocking the sight with a thousand delusions.

COMPANIONSHIP IN WOES.

The Constant Prince, Act I. *sc.* 1.

> Que el tener en las desdichas
> Campañia de tal forma
> Consuela, que el enemigo
> Suele servir de lisonja.

For companionship in woes gives alleviation, even though it be that of an enemy.

WHAT IS LIFE?

The Constant Prince, Act I. *sc.* 1.

> El vivir
> Eterno es viver con honra.

Life is but to live with honour.

A STORM.

The Constant Prince, Act I. *sc.* 2.

> Cuando de un parasismo el mismo **Apolo,**
> Amortajado en nubes, la dorada
> Faz escondió, y el mar sañudo y fiero
> Deshizo con tormentas nuestra armada.

When in a paroxysm the sun, shrouded in clouds, concealed his golden face, and the fierce and fiery sea wrecked our fleet in foaming madness.

ARAB HORSE.

The Constant Prince, Act I. *sc.* **3.**

> En efecto, mi valor,
> Sujetando tus valientes

Brios, de tantos perdidos
Un suelto caballo prende,
Tan monstruo, que siendo hijo
Del viento, adopcion pretende
Del fuego, y entre los dos
Lo desdice y lo desmiente
El color, pues siendo blanco,
Dice el agua : parto es este
De mi esfera, sola yo
Pude cuajarle de nieve.
En fin en lo veloz viento,
Rayo en fin en lo eminente,
Era por lo blanco cisne
Por lo sangriento era sierpe,
Por lo hermoso era soberbio,
Por lo atrevido valiente,
Por los relinchos lozano,
Y por las cernejas fuerte.

In **effect, my** arm, subduing your courageous **strength, amid the** horses loosely flying seizes one, such a prodigy **that, though being the son of the wind,** it claimed adoption of the fire, but its hue shows it falsely denied its origin, for being white the water said, "It is the offspring of my sphere, I alone could have moulded such a form of curdled snow." Like the wind he flew in swiftness, lightning-like he flashed to and fro ; he was a swan in dazzling whiteness, speckled like the snake with blood, proud of his beauty, full of spirit in his neighing, firm and strong in his fetlocks.

A Good Action never wholly Lost.
The Constant Prince, Act I. *sc.* 3.

Porque al fin,
Hacer bien nunca se pierde.

For a good action is never wholly lost.

A Fountain.
The Constant Prince, Act II. *sc.* 1.

Lisonjera, libre, ingrata,
Dulce y suave una fuente

Hizo apacible corriente
De cristal y undosa plata ;
Lisonjera se desata,
Porque hablaba, y no sentia ;
Suave, porque fingia ;
Libre, porque claro hablaba ;
Dulce, porque murmuraba ;
É ingrata, porque corria.

Flattering, free, ungrateful, glides sweet and smooth a fountain with peaceful waters and crystal waves ; flattering, for it uttereth sound enough, and does not feel ; soft, because it feigneth ; free, for loud it runs ; sweet, because it murmureth ; and ungrateful, for it flies.

Every Fortune overcome by Patience.

The Constant Prince, Act II. *sc.* 1

Mas pensad,
Que favor del cielo fue
Esta piadosa sentencia ;
El mejorará la suerte ;
Que á la desdicha mas fuerte
Sabe vencer la prudencia.
Sufrid con ella el rigor
Del tiempo y de la fortuna,
Deidad bárbara importuna,
Hoy cadáver y ayer flor,
No permanece jamas,
Y asi os mudará de estado.

But think that this hard sentence may be given us as a favour by Heaven ; fortune will change it for the better ; for prudence knows how to subdue misfortune, however heavy. Bear with patience whatever sorrow time or fortune brings upon you—that barbarous fickle deity—now a corpse, now a flower, ever changing, and thus it may change our lot.

Sorrow follows Sorrow.

The Constant Prince, Act II. *sc.* 1.

Un dia llama á otro diá,
Y asi llama y encadena
Llanto á llanto, y pena á pena.

One day calls to another, and thus sorrow follows sorrow, and pains with pains intertwine.

The Fortunes of Men like Flowers.

The Constant Prince, Act II. *sc.* 2.

Estas, que fueron pompa y alegría,
   Despertando al albor de la mañana,
   Á la tarde serán lástima vana,
   Durmiendo en brazos de la noche fria.
Este matiz, que el cielo desafia,
   Iris listado de oro, nieve y grana,
   Será escarmiento de la vida humana,
   Tanto se emprenda en término de un dia
Á florecer las rosas madrugaron,
   Y para envejecerse flore cieron,
   Cuna y sepulcro en un boton hallaron.
Tales los hombres sus fortunas vieron,
   En un dia nacieron y espiraron ;
   Que pasados los siglos, horas fueron.

These flowers, which were beautiful, unfolding at the early dawn, will leave us vainly regretted at eve, locked in the cold embraces of the night. These shades, that shame the rainbow's arch of gold, snow, and purple, will be an example of human life--- so much is taught by one brief day ; roses bloom and bear flowers but to grow old, finding a cradle and a tomb in one crimson bud. Such are men's fortunes in this world of ours ; they are born and die in one day, for ages past seem to us like hours.

The Last Rays of the Sun.

The Constant Prince, Act II. *sc.* 2.

Esos vasgos de luz, esas centellas,
   Que cobran con amagos superiores
   Alimentos del sol en resplandores.
Aquello viven, que se duelen dellas,
Flores nocturnas son, aunque tan bellas,
   Efímeras padecen sus ardores ;
   Pues si un dia es el siglo de las flores,
   Una noche es la edad de las estrellas,

De esa pues primavera fugitiva
  Ya nuestro mal, ya nuestro bien se infiere,
  Registro es nuestro, ó muera el sol, ó viva.
Qué duracion habrá, qué el hombre espere?
  Ó qué mudanza habrá, que no reciba
  De astro, que cada noche nace y muere?

These points of light, these sparks of fire, torn boldly from the sun's departing ray, live when the beam has mournfully retired : these are the flowers of night ; though beautiful, their brightness passes swiftly away, for if the life of flowers is but one day, in one short night the brightest star expires, but still we ask from this fleeting spring tide of the sky now our good, now our ill ; it is the register of our fate, whether the sun die or live. Oh ! what duration is there that men should hope ? What change can be hoped from a star, that every night is born again and dies?

A Good Deed.

The Constant Prince, Act II. *sc.* 2.

Que hacer bien
Es tesoro, que se guarda
Para cuando es menester.

For indeed a good action is a treasure guarded for the doer's need.

Loyalty and Honour.

The Constant Prince, Act II. *sc.* 2.

Amor y amistad
En grado inferior se ven
Con la lealted y el honor.

Both love and friendship are inferior to loyalty and honour.

Kings should be Merciful.

The Constant Prince, Act III. *sc.* 2

Es tan augusta
De los reyes la deidad,
Tan fuerte, y tan absoluta,
Que engendra ánimo piadoso ;

Y asi es forzoso que acudas
Á la sangre generosa
Con piedad y con cordura.

So august is the divinity of monarchs, so strong and absolute, that it must ever engender pitying mind, and force noble blood to display pity and wisdom.

CRUELTY CONDEMNED BY EVERY LAW.

The Constant Prince, Act III. *sc.* 2.

La crueldad
En cualquiera ley es una.

To be cruel is condemned by every law

THE CRADLE AND THE COFFIN.

The Constant Prince, Act III. *sc.* 2.

Y por eso dió una forma
Con una materia en una
Semejanza la razon
Al ataud y á la cuna.
Accion nuestra es natural,
Cuando recibir procura
Algo un hombre, alzar las manos
En esta manera juntas ;
Mas cuando quiere arrojarlo,
De aquella misma accion usa,
Pues las vuelve boca abajo,
Porque asi las desocupa.
El mundo, cuando nacemos,
En señal de que nos busca,
En la cuna nos recibe
Y en ella nos asegura
Boca arriba ; pero cuando,
Ó con desden, ó con furia
Quiere arrojarnos de sí,
Vuelve las manos que junta,
Y aquel instrumento mismo

Forma esta materia muda ;
Pues fue cuna boca arriba
Lo que boca abajo es tumba
Tan cerca **vivimus** pues
De nuestra **muerte,** tan juntas
Tenemos, cuando nacemos,
El lecho, como la cuna.

And it is doubtless to exhibit life and death's divided power that
the cradle and coffin are so like to each other.   For it is our
natural action when a man receives anything that he raises his
hands upwards, joined together in this way ; but when he intends
refusal, by a similar action, only by turning them down, he makes
his intent known.   So the world, when we are born, as a proof it
seeks us, receives us in a cradle, with our face lying upwards ;
but should it, whether through disdain or fury, wish to drive us
forth, it turns back her hands to show that the coffin's mute
material be of that same instrument ; for an upturned open
cradle becomes a tomb when reversed.   Since we live so sure of
our death, we hold thus united our last bed and our cradle.

Bishop Hall in his *Epistles* (dec. iii. ep. 2) says—" Death borders
upon our birth, and our cradles stand in the grave."

No Virtue is Real that has not been Tried.

The Physician of his own Honour, Act I. *sc.* **2.**

Pues no hay virtud
Sin experiencia.   Perfecto
Está el oro en el crisol,
El iman en el acero,
El diamante en el diamante,
Los metales en el fuego.

Since no virtue can be real that has not been tried.   The gold
in the crucible alone is perfect ; the loadstone tests the steel, and
the diamond is tried by the diamond, while metals gleam the
brighter in the furnace.

The Sun.

The Physician of his own Honour, Act I. *sc.* **2.**

Porque el sol no se desdeña,
Despues que ilustró un palacio,

> De iluminar el topacio
> De algun pajizo arrebol.

For the sun, though it light a palace, does not disdain to fall
with its golden woof on the straw-thatched cottage-roof.

A WOMAN'S COUNSEL.

The Physician of his own Honour, Act I. *sc.* 2.

> Dicen, que el primer consejo
> Ha de ser de la muger.

They say that the best counsel is that of woman.

THE CLOSING DAY.

The Physician of his own Honour, Act I. *sc.* 2.

> Que el dia
> Ya en la tumba helada y fria,
> Huésped del undoso Dios,
> Hace noche.

As the day sinks cool and fresh into the tomb, to be the guest of
the sea-god, good-night to you.

HOW MEN ACT.

The Physician of his own Honour, Act I. *sc.* 2.

> O qué tales sois los hombres :
> Hoy olvido, ayer amor,
> Ayer gusto, y hoy rigor.

Oh ! it is thus with men : to-day forgetfulness, to-morrow love ;
to-morrow desire, and to-day hate.

A LITTLE SPARK KINDLETH A GREAT FLAME.

The Physician of his own Honour, Act I. *sc.* 3.

> Poca centella incita mucho fuego,
> Poco viento movió mucha tormenta,
> Poca nube al principio arroja luego
> Mucho diluvio, poca luz alienta

Mucho rayo despues, poco amor ciego
Descubre mucho engaño ; y asi intenta,
Siendo centella, viento, nube, ensayo,
Ser tormenta, diluvio, incendio **y** rayo.

A little spark kindleth a great flame—a little wind excites **a**
whirlwind's crash—a little cloud produces a great deluge—a little
light can feed the lightning's flash—a little love, though blind,
finds out many wiles ; and thus spark, wind, cloud, delights **to** be
storm, rain, burning, and lightning.

THE FOOL.

The Physician of his own Honour, *Act* I. *sc.* 3.

Soy cofrade del contento ;
El pesar no sé quien es,
Ni aun para servirle.   El fin
Soy, aqui donde me veis,
Mayordomo de la risa,
Gentilhombre del placer
Y camerero del gusto
Pues que me visto con él

I am a brother of contentment ; grief, I know not what it is,
nor have ever been servant to it.   Briefly, I am what you see
me : major-domo unto laughter, gentleman-in-waiting to pleasure,
and the chamberlain of frolic—which a glance, indeed, might
show you.

LOVE.

The Physician of his own Honour, *Act* II. *sc.* 4.

Sabed, Don Arias, que quien
Una vez le quiso bien,
No se vengará en su mal.

Know, Don Arias, that who has loved well will never seek the
loved one's ill.

DARK IMAGININGS.

The Physician of his own Honour, *Act* III. *sc.* 1.

Nada ; que hombres como **yo**
No ven, basta que imaginen,

Que sospechen, que prevengan,
Que rezelen, que adivénen,
Que . . . no sé como lo diga ;
Que no hay voz, que signifique
Una cosa, que aun no sea
Un atomo indivisible.

Nothing—since men formed as I am do not see, enough they fancy, suspect, foreshadow, feel some instinct—some divining— some . . . I know not what to say ; for there is no word that can give the meaning—feelings that resemble atoms that cannot be divided.

Honour.

The Physician of his own Honour, Act III. *sc.* 1.

El honor es reservado
Lugar, donde el alma asiste.

Honour is a sacred place, which the soul alone inhabits.

A Ship.

The Purgatory of St. Patrick, Act I. *sc.* 1.

Pues hay cosa á la vista mas suave,
Que ver quebrando vidrios una nave,
Siendo en su azul esfera,
Del viento pez, y de las ondas ave,
Cuando corre veloz, sulca ligera,
Y de los elementos amparada,
Vuela en las ondas, y en los vientos nada ?
Aunque ahora no fuera
Su vista á nuestros ojos lisonjera ;
Porque el mar alterado,
En piélagos de montes levantado,
Riza la altiva frente,
Y sañudo Neptuno,
Parece que importuno
Turbó la faz, y sacudió el tridente,
Tormenta el marinero se presuma ;
Que se atreven al cielo

> Montes de sal, pirámides de hielo,
> Torres de nieve, alcázares de espuma.

Is there anything more fair to the sight than to see a ship softly gliding, dividing the azure field, like a fish within the yielding air, or a bird upon the waves, when it runs swiftly, making a slight furrow, and, favourite of sea and sky, flies over the waves and swims through the wind? But now the sight could not be pleasing to our eyes, for the sea is altered, raised in huge billows, all deeply wrinkled in its lordly brow: dreadful Neptune has assumed an angry visage, and shaking his trident, affrights the sailor, even if he is daring; since mountainous waves, pyramids of ice, towers of snow, palaces of foam, all are dashed against the heaven.

Everything proclaims the Glory of God.

The Purgatory of St. Patrick, Act i. *sc.* 2.

> Causa primera de todo
> Sois, Señor, y en todo estais.
> Esos cristalinos velos,
> Que constan de luces bellas,
> Con el sol, luna y estrellas,
> No son cortinas y velos
> Del empireo soberano ?
> Los discordes elementos,
> Mares, fuego, tierra y vientos
> No son rasgos de esa mano ?
> No publican vuestros loores
> Y el poder, que en vos se encierra,
> Todos ? No escribe la tierra
> Con caractéres de flores
> Grandezas vuestras ? El viento.
> En los ecos repetido,
> No publica, que habeis sido
> Autor de su movimiento ?
> El fuego y el agua luego
> Alabanzas no os previenen,
> Y para este efecto tienen
> Lengua el agua, y lengua el fuego ?

Thou art the first cause of old, O Lord, and existest in every thing. These crystalline veils, woven of beautiful rays of the sun, moon, and stars, are they not the curtains between the heavenly world and this? The discordant elements, sea, fire, earth, and air, are they not shadows of thy hand? Do they not all proclaim thy praise, and the mighty power that encompasses thee? Does not the earth mark thy grandeur in the beauty of its flowers? Does not the wind, repeated in the echoes, proclaim by its accents that thou didst give it birth? The fire and the water fail not in thy praise; in every flame there is a tongue, in every wave there is a tongue to sound thy praise.

See the "Sacred Song" of Moore, beginning—

> "Thou art, O God, the life and light
> Of all this wondrous world we see."

MISFORTUNE AND BEAUTY UNITED.

The Purgatory of St. Patrick, Act II. *sc.* **2.**

> Polonia desdichada,
> Pension de la hermosura celebrada
> Fue siempre la desdicha ;
> Que no se avienen bien belleza y dicha.

Luckless Polonia, the dower of great beauty has always been misfortune ; since happiness and beauty do not agree together.

THE RISING SUN.

The Purgatory of St. Patrick, Act II. *sc.* **3.**

> Ya el sol las doradas trenzas
> Estiende desmarañadas
> Sobre los montes y selvas,
> Para que te informe el dia.

See, the sun spreads his golden tresses, disentangling them over the mountains and woods that it may warn thee of the day.

A HANGING ROCK.

The Purgatory of St. Patrick, Act II. *sc.* 4.

> No ves ese peñasco, que parece
> Que se está sustendando con trabajo,
> Y con el ansia misma que padece,
> Ha tantos siglos que se viene abajo ?

Pues mordaza es, que sella y enmudece
El aliento á una boca, que debajo
Abierta está, por donde con pereza
El monte melancolico bosteza.

See you not this rock suspended, so that it appears with difficulty kept up? and still it hangs as it has hung for un-numbered ages ; for it is a gag which checks and interferes with the breath that escapes from the cave, wherewith the melancholy mountain yawns.

Shelley in *The Cenci* has copied this idea :—

" But I remember,
Two miles on this side of the fort, the road
Crosses a deep ravine ; 'tis rough and narrow,
And winds with short turns down the precipice ;
And in its depth there is a mighty rock
Which has from unimaginable years
Sustained itself with terror and with toil
Over the gulf, and with the agony
With which it clings seems slowly coming down ;
Even as a wretched soul, hour after hour,
Clings to the mass of life ; yet clinging, leans,
And leaning, makes more dark the dread abyss
In which it fears to fall ; beneath this crag,
Huge as despair, as if in weariness,
The melancholy mountain yawns."

THE SUFFERINGS OF THE LOST.

The Purgatory of St. Patrick, Act II. *sc.* 4.

Apenas en la cueva entrar queria,
Cuando escucho en sus concavos feroces,
Como de quien se queja y desconfia
De su dolor, desesperadas voces ;
Blasfemias, maldiciones solo oia,
Y repetir delitos tan atroces,
Que pienso que los cielos, per no oillos,
Quisieron á esa cárcel reducillos.

Scarcely had I entered into the cavern when I heard in its sad bounds how each complained and lamented in accents of despair ; blasphemies, curses, alone I heard, crimes avowed, that I believe Heaven, in order not to hear them, had placed them in this prison.

See (**Fr.**) Lost, sufferings of.

A Woman should marry.

The Purgatory of St. Patrick, Act III. *sc.* 4.

Una muger no tiene
Valor para el consejo, y la conviene
Casarse.

A woman needs a stronger head than is her own for counsel—
she should marry.

Occupation makes Time Short.

The Secret in Words, Act I. *sc.* 2.

Que tal vez
Hacer ocupadas suele,
Si no mas breves las horas,
Que nos parezcan mas breves.

Since often occupation, if it does not make the hours less short,
makes their flight appear the shorter.

An Eternal Spring.

The Secret in Words, Act I. *sc.* 2.

O tú, hermoso jardin bello,
Cuya república verde
Patria es del Abril, pues solo
Al Abril conoce, y tiene
Por Dios de su primavera,
Por rey de sus doce meses.

O thou fair and beauteous garden, whose green republic is the
chosen clime of April; for it alone knows April, and makes it the
god of its spring-time—it the king of its twelve months.

The Conqueror that is unresisted.

The Secret in Words, Act I. *sc.* 2.

Pues quien vence sin contrario,
No puede decir que vence.

For he, who wins without resistance, can scarcely be said to win.

A Lover.

The Secret in Words, Act II. *sc.* 2.

> No es accion cuerda
> Dar á entender al amante
> Mas firme, que hay quien le quiera ;
> Porque el mas humilde cobra
> Querido tanta soberbia,
> Que la dádiva del gusto
> Ya desde alli la hace deuda.

It is not a prudent act to inform the firmest lover that there is one that loves him well ; for the humblest heart has so much vanity, that what it once thought to be a favour soon becomes a thankless debt.

The Conversation of a Friend.

The Secret in Words, Act III. *sc.* 3.

> Los cuerdos amigos son
> Il libro mas entendido
> De la vida, si porque
> Deleitan aprovechando.

Wise friends are the best book of life, because they teach with voice and looks.

Time and Fortune Twins.

Love after Death, Act I. *sc.* 1.

> Qué bien
> Pareja del tiempo llaman
> A la fortuna, pues ambos
> Sobre una rueda y dos alas
> Para el bien ó para el ma
> Corren siempre y nunca paran !

How truly call they Time and Fortune twins, since both, on one wheel and with two wings for good or evil, ever move and never stop !

Wounds heal before a Word.

Love after Death, Act I. *sc.* 1.

Pues una herida mejor
Se cura, que una palabra!

Since a wound is healed more easily than a word!

Joy followed by Grief.

Love after Death, Act II. *sc.* 2.

Porque es tal
De la fortuna el desden,
Que apenas nos hace un bien,
Cuando le desquita un mal.

For such is Fortune, that scarcely has she done a good when an evil follows.

The Fickle Crowd.

Love after Death, Act III. *sc.* 6.

Tal
Es de un vulgo la inconstancia,
Que los designios de hoy
Intentan borrar mañana.

Such is the fickleness of the crowd, that the designs of to-day they proceed to abandon on the morrow.

The Dawn.

The Scarf and the Flower, Act I. *sc.* 1.

No hagais, señora,
Ese desprecio al aurora
Que es dama, y soy muy cortes;
Y no dejaré agraviar
Una hermosura, á quien deben
Todo cuanto aliento beben
El clavel, jazmin y azar.
Su luz, deidad singular,
Es breve imperio del dia,

De los campos alegrìa,
Pulimento de las flores,
Estacion de los amores
De las aves harmonìa.

Do not such despite to the Aurora, a lady like thyself—be more courteous ; thou shouldst not wrong a beauty, in whose every breath we drink the odour of the pink and jessamine. Its brightness, mighty divinity, has a fleeting empire over the day—giving gladness to the fields, colour to the flowers, the season of the loves, harmonious hour of wakening birds.

PHILIP'S HORSEMANSHIP.

The Scarf and the Flower, Act I. **sc.** **1.**

Y aparte la alegoría,
Permjite, que me detenga
En pintarte de Filipo
La gala, el brio y destreza,
Con que iba puesto á caballo ;
Que como este afecto sea
Verdad en mi, y no lisonja,
No importa que lo parezca.
Era un alazan tostado
De foroz naturaleza
El monarca irracional,
En cuyo color se muestra
La cólera disculpando
Del sol, que la tez le tuesta,
Que hay estudio en lo voraz,
Y en lo bárbaro hay belleza.
Tan soberbio se miraba,
Que dió con sola soberbia
Á entender, que conocia
Ser, con todo un cielo acuestas.
Monte vivo de los brutos,
Vivo Atlante de las fieras.
Como te sabré decir
Con el desprecio y la fuerza,
Que, sin hacer dellas caso

Iba quebrando las piedras,
Sino con decirte solo
Que entonces conocí, que era
Centro de fuego Madrid?
Pues donde quiera que llega
El pie ó la mano, levanta,
Un abismo de centellas.
Y como quien toca el fuego
Huye la mano, que acerca,
Asi el valiente caballo
Retira con tanto priesa
El pie ó la mano del fuego,
Que la mano ó el pie engendra,
Que hecha gala del temor,
Ni el uno ni el otro asienta,
Deteniéndose en el aire
Con brincas y con corbetas.
Con tanto imperio en lo bruto,
Como en lo racional, vieras
Al Rey regir tanto monstruo
Al arbitrio de la rienda.

But, all allegory being laid aside, allow me to describe to you Philip, with what skill and noble daring he managed his steed: and as the description springs from truth and not from flattery, it is of no consequence if it seems so. The irrational brute was a bright-brown sorrel, fierce in nature, in whose colour shone the fury of the sun, with smooth skin, so that beauty and wildness were united in the noble beast. With such mettled pride he bounded that he proclaimed he could bear a whole heaven on his shoulders; among brutes a living mountain—Atlas turned to life among beasts. How can I find words to tell thee of the strong proud disregard with which he, unmindful of it, ground to dust the stony highway, but by saying this alone, that I only then discovered what a fire was beneath Madrid? For wherever his hoof descended, there seemed to open an abyss of fiery sparkles; and as he who touches fire suddenly withdraws his hand, so the noble steed drew back, with the same instinctive quickness, his hoof from out the fire which his hoof itself had kindled, making fear itself so graceful that his feet did not uphold him, cleverly upraised in air with his boundings and curvetings. As with man, so in the brute world must a firm hand guide and manage it; thus the king controlled the monster by the light touch of the reins.

This may be compared with Shakespeare's treatment of the same subject (*Richard II.*, act v. sc. 2) :—

> "Then, as I said, the duke, great Bolingbroke,
> Mounted upon a hot and fiery steed,
> Which his aspiring rider seemed to know,
> With slow but stately pace kept on his course,
> While all tongues cried, God save thee, Bolingbroke !
> You would have thought the very windows spake,
> So many greedy looks of young and old
> Through casements darted their desiring eyes
> Upon his visage ; and that all the walls,
> With painted imag'ry, had said at once,
> Jesu preserve thee ! welcome, Bolingbroke !
> Whilst he, from one side to the other turning,
> Bareheaded, lower than his proud steed's neck,
> Bespake them thus : I thank you, countrymen ;
> And thus still doing, thus he passed along."

And Fletcher (*The Two Noble Kinsmen*, act v. sc. 4) :—

> " List then ! your cousin
> Mounted upon a steed that Emily
> Did first bestow upon him, a black one, owning
> Not a hairworth of white, which some will say
> Weakens his price, and many will not buy
> His goodness with this note : which superstition
> Here finds allowance : on this horse is Arcite,
> Trotting the stones of Athens, which the calkias
> Did rather tell than trample, for the horse
> Would make his length a mile if't pleased his rider
> To put pride in him. As thus he went, counting
> The flinty pavement, dancing as 'twere to the music
> His own hoofs made (for as they say, from iron
> Came music's origin), what envious flint,
> Cold as old Saturn, and like him possessed
> With fire malevolent, darted a spark,
> Or what fierce sulphur else to this end made,
> I comment not ; the hot horse, hot as fire,
> Took toy at this, and fell to what disorder
> His power could give his will ; bounds, comes on end,
> Forgets school-doing, being therein trained,
> And of kind manage ; pig-like he whines
> At the sharp rowel, which he frets at rather
> Than any jot obeys ; seeks all foul means
> Of boisterous and rough jadery to disseat
> His lord, that kept it bravely. When nought served ;
> When neither curb would crack, girth break, nor diff'ring plunges
> Disroot his rider whence he grew, but that

> He kept him 'tween his legs, on his hind hoofs
> On end he stands,
> That Arcite's legs being higher than his head,
> Seemed with strange art to hang; his victor's wreath
> Even then fell off his head, and presently
> Backward the jade comes o'er, and his full poise
> Becomes the rider's load."

The Chase.

The Scarf and the Flower, Act I. sc. 1.

> Es tan ágil en la caza,
> Viva imágen de la guerra.

He is active in the chase, lively portraiture of warfare.

Sir Walter Scott speaks of the chase as being "a noble mimicry of war."

Passion portrayed in the Face.

The Scarf and the Flower, Act I. sc. 1.

> En los embates de amante,
> Al viento que corre, el pecho
> Se descubre en el semblante.

In the reverses of the lover, by the lightest winds that blow, the breast is often confessed in the face.

Green is the Colour which God flings on the World.

The Scarf and the Flower, Act I. sc. 2.

Lisida.—La verde es color primera
> Del mundo, y en quien consiste
> Su hermosura, pues se viste
> De verde la primevera.
> La vista mas lisonjera
> Es aquel verde ornamento,
> Pues sin voz y con aliento
> Nacen de varios colores.
> En cuna verde las flores,
> Que son estrellas del viento.

Chloris.—Al fin es color del suelo,
  Que se marchita y se pierde ;
  Y cuando el suelo de verde
  Se vista, de azul el cielo.
  Primavera es su azul velo,
  Donde son las flores bellas
  Vivas luces ; mira en ellas,
  Qué trofeos son mayores,
  Un campo cielo de flores,
  Ó un cielo campo de estrellas.

Lisida.—Ese es color aparente,
  Que la vista para objeto
  Finge ; que el cielo en efeto
  Color ninguno consiente.
  Con azul fingido miente
  La hermosura de su esfera :
  Luego en esa parte espera
  Ser la tierra preferida,
  Pues la una es beldad fingida
  Y otra es pompa verdadera.

Chloris.—Confieso, que no es color
  Lo azul del cielo, y confieso,
  Que es mucho mejor por eso ;
  Porque, si fuera en rigor
  Propio, no fuera favor
  La eleccion ; y de aqui infiero,
  Que, si le eligió primero,
  Fue, porque lo azul ha sido
  Aun mejor para fingido,
  Que otro para verdadero.

Lisida.—Lo verde dice esperanza,
  Que es el mas immenso bien
  Del amor. Digalo quien
  Ni la tiene ni la alcanza.
  Lo azul zelos y mudanza
  Dice, que es tormento eterno,
  Sin paz, quietud ni gobierno.
  Qué importa pues, que el amor

Tenga del cielo el color,
Si tiene el mal del infierno ?

Chloris.—Quien con esperanza vive,
Poco le debe su dama ;
Pero quien con zelos ama,
En bronce su amor escribe ;
Luego aquel que se apercibe
Á amar zeloso, hace mas,
En cuya razon verás,
Cuanto alcanzan sus dusvelos ;
Pues el infierno de zelos
No espera favor jamas.

Lisida.—Green is the prime colour of the world, and that from which its loveliness arises ; it is the colour of the spring ; the fairest sight is that green ornament that sees, voiceless and breathless, the many-tinted flowers take their birth in their green cradle – the trembling stars of every breeze.

Chloris.—In short, it is the colour of the earth, which fades and vanishes ; and when the earth is clothed with green, the heaven is azure. Spring hangs her azure veil on high, for the living lights are beauteous flowers ; see which is the richest dower of nature—an earthly heaven covered with flowers, or heaven's bright field strewn with stars.

Lisida.—It is a seeming colour, which mocks our eyes : for the sky in reality has no colour ; the heaven with this azure fiction tells a falsehood ; for this reason the earth should be preferred. One boasts a fictitious beauty, the other is a real verdant hue.

Chloris.—I confess that the azure of the sky is no colour, and I know that it is better for not being so ; if it were its actual dress, there would be no difficulty to prove its greater beauty. And hence I infer that if he chose the azure, it was because the azure is even of greater beauty than the other, however true is its green.

Lisida.—The green speaks hope, which we always prize as the most precious offering of love. Let her say so who neither possesses nor can obtain it. Azure speaks of jealousy and change, a never-ending torment, without peace, quiet, or control. What matters it, then, that love wears the hue of heaven, if it must feel the pains of hell ?

Chloris.—He who lives on hope, to him his lady owes little ; but he who loves with jealousy inscribes his love on bronze : he who loves jealously shows what a faithful heart he has, since in the hell of jealousy he can hope for favour no more.

The Spirit of Contentment.

The Scarf and the Flower, Act II. *sc.* 1.

Del color de la dicha
Se viste siempre el contento.

The spirit of contentment ever wears the hues of **joy.**

Simple Truth.

The Scarf and the Flower, Act II. *sc.* 1.

Desnuda la verdad vive,
Á imitacion del silencio.

Simple truth should live naked in imitation of honest silence.

The Vengeful Power of Love.

The Scarf and the Flower, Act II. *sc.* 2.

Bien el amor hoy del poder se venga,
Dando á entender ufano,
Que es rayo cada flecha de su mano,
Pues como rayo, que violento pasa,
Lo altivo hiere y lo eminente abrasa.

To-day love shows his vengeful power, making us proudly to understand that his arrows can fall from his hand like heaven's bolts ; for, like the lightning passing wildly by, he wounds the proud and lays low the high.

CERVANTES.

Born A.D. 1547. Died A.D. 1616.

Cervantes Saavedra, Miguel de, was born of noble parents at Alcala de Henares, New Castile, 9th October 1547. From his earliest years he was devoted to literature, more particularly to poetry ; but his productions were not favourably received by his countrymen, and in 1569 he set out for Rome, where he entered the service of the Cardinal Aquiviva, to whom he had been introduced at Madrid. He then joined the expedition to assist the Cyprians against Selim II., and was present at the battle of Lepanto, where he behaved with great bravery, losing the use of his left hand. In 1575, on his way back to Madrid, he was taken by the **Algerines** and carried to Algiers, where he remained in slavery for four years. After many unsuccessful attempts on the part of the Spaniards to relieve the captives, Cervantes and his companions were redeemed from slavery by the Trinitarian fathers, Juan Gil and Antonio de la Bella. On his return to Spain he again resumed his arms, and went in three successive expeditions to the Azores. From this period he was for ten years employed in writing plays for the Spanish stage. The first part of "Don **Quixote**" was published in 1605, and eight years afterwards appeared the "Novelas Esemplares." In 1615 he published the the continuation of "Don Quixote." He died at Madrid 23d April 1616, the same day which deprived the world of Shakespeare.

Every Man is the Son of his own Works.
Don Quixote, I. 4.

Quanto mas que cada uno es hijo de sus obras.

The rather since every man is the son of his own works.

Historians.
Don Quixote, II. 1.

Aviendo **y** deviendo ser los Historiodores puntuales, verdaderos, y no nada apassionados, y ni el interés, ni el miedo, el rancor, ni la aficion, no les haga torcer del camino de la verdad, cuya madre es la Historia emula del tiempo, deposito de las acciones, testigo de lo passado, exemplo **y** aviso de lo presente, advertencia de lo par venir.

For historians ought to be precise, truthful, and quite unprejudiced, and neither interest nor fear, hatred nor affection, should cause them to swerve from the path of truth whose mother is history, the rival of time, the depository of great actions, the witness of what is past, the example and instruction to the present, and monitor to the future.

To dine at Home.
Don Quixote, II. 3.

Y aun si và à dezir verdad, mucho mejor me sabe lo que como en mi rincon, sin melindres, ni respetos, aunque sea pan y cebolla, que los gallipavos de otras mesas donde me sea forçoso mascar de espacio, bever poco ; limpiarme **à menudo**, no estornudar, ni toser si me viene **gana, ni**

hazer otras cosas que la soledad y la libertad traen con
sigo.

And, besides, to tell you the truth, what I eat in my corner
without compliments or ceremonies, though it were nothing but
bread and an onion, relishes better than turkeys at other people's
tables, where I am forced to chew leisurely, drink little, wipe my
mouth often, neither sneeze nor cough when I have a mind, nor
do other things which follow the being alone and at liberty.

GOLDEN AGE.

Don Quixote, II. 3.

Eran en aquella santa edad todas las cosas comunes, à
nadie le era necessario para alcançár su ordinario sustento
tomar otro trabajo, que alçar la mano, y alcançarle de las
robustas enzinas, que liberalmente les estavan combinando
con su dulce y sazonado fruto. Las claras fuentes, y corrientes rios, en magnifica abundancia, sabrosas y tras-
parentes aguas les ofrecian. En las quiebras de las peñas,
y en lo hueco de los arboles, formavan su Republica las
solicitas y discretas abejas, ofreciendo à qualquiera mano,
sin interés alguno, la fértil cosecha de su dulcissimo trabajo. Los valientes alcornoques despedían de si, sin otro
artificio que el de su cortesia, sus anchas y livianes cortezas,
con que se començaron à cubrir las casas sobre rusticas
estacas sustentadas, no mas que para defensa de las in-
clemencias del cielo. Todo era paz entonces, todo amistad,
todo concordia ; aun no se avía atrevido la pesada reja del
corbo arado à abrir, ni visitar las entrañas piadosas de
nuestra primera madre, que ella sin ser forçada, ofrecía
por todas las partes de su fértil y espacioso seno, lo que
pudiesse hartar, sustentar y deleytar à los hijos que entonces la posseian. Entonces si, que andavan las simples
y hermosas çagaleias de valle en valle, y de otero en otero,
en trença y en cabello, sin mas vestidos de aquellos que
eran menester para cubrir honestamente, lo que la honesti-
dad quiere, y a querido siempre que se cubra, y no eran
sus adornos de los que aora se usan, à quien la purpura de
Tyro, y la por tantos modos martirizada seda encarecen,

sino de algunas hojas de verdes lampazos, y yedra, entre-
texidas, coñ lo que quiça ívan tan pomposas, y compuestas
como van aora nuestras cortesanas con las raras y pere-
grinas invenciones, que la curiosidad ociosa les a mostrado.
Entonces se decoravan los conceptos amorosos del alma,
simple, y sencillamente, del mesmo modo, y manera que
ella los concebía, sin buscar artificioso rodeo de palabras
para encarecerlos. No avía el fraude, el engaño, ni la
malicia, mezclandosose con la verdad y llaneza. La justicia
se estava en sus proprios terminos, sin que la osassen
turbar, ni ofender los del favor, y los del interesse, que
tanto aora la menoscaban, turban, y persiguen. La ley
del encaje, aun no se avía sentado en el entendimiento del
juez, porque entonces no avía que juzgar, ni quien fuesse
juzgado.

In that age of innocence all things were in common : no one
required to make any further exertion for his ordinary sustenance
than to raise his hand and pluck it from the sturdy oaks which
stood inviting him liberally to taste of their sweet and relishing
fruit. The limpid fountains and running streams offered them in
magnificent abundance their delicious and transparent waters.
In the clefts of rocks, in the hollow of trees, did the industrious
añd provident bees form their commonwealths, offering to every
hand, without usury, the rich produce of their most delicious
toil. The stout cork-trees, without any other inducement than
that of their own courtesy, divested themselves of their light and
expanded bark, with which men began to cover their houses,
supported by rough poles, only for a defence against the in-
clemency of the seasons. All then was peace, all amity, all
concord ; as yet the heavy culter of the crooked plough had not
dared to force open and search into the tender bowels of our first
mother, who, unconstrained, offered from every part of her fertile
and spacious bosom whatever might feed, sustain, and delight
those her children, who then had her in possession. Then did
the simple and beauteous young shepherdesses trip it from dale
to dale, and from hill to hill, their tresses sometimes plaited,
sometimes loosely flowing, with no more clothing than was
necessary modestly to cover what modesty has always required to
be concealed ; nor were their ornaments like those nowadays in
fashion, to which the Tyrian purple and the so-many-ways
martyred silk give a value, but composed of green dock-leaves
and ivy interwoven, with which, perhaps, they went as splendidly
and elegantly decked as our court ladies do now with all those
rare and foreign inventions which idle curiosity hath taught them.

Then were the amorous conceptions of the soul clothed in simple and sincere expressions; in the same way and manner they were conceived without seeking artificial phrases to set them off. Nor as yet were fraud, deceit, and malice intermixed with truth and plain dealing. Justice kept within her proper bounds—favour and interest, which now so much depreciate, confound, and persecute her, not daring then to disturb or offend her. As yet the judge did not make his own will the measure of justice, for then there was neither cause nor person to be judged.

Every One as God made him.
Don Quixote, II. 5.

Cada uno es como Dios le hijó, y aun peor muchas vezes.

Every one is as God made him, and oftentimes a great deal worse.

Different Kinds of Beauty.
Don Quixote, II. 6.

No todas hermosuras enamoran, que algunas alegran la vista, y no rinden la voluntad.

All kinds of beauty do not inspire love; there is a kind of it which only pleases the sight, but does not captivate the affections.

Beauty.
Don Quixote, II. 6.

La hermosura en la muger honesta, es como el fuego apartado, ò como la espada aguda, que ni èl quema, ni ella corta à quien à ellos no se acerca.

Beauty in a modest woman is like fire at a distance, or like a sharp sword : neither doth the one burn, not the other wound, those that come not too near them.

Remembrance.
Don Quixote, III. 1.

No ay memoria à quien el tiempo no acabe, ni dolor que muerte no le consuma.

There is no remembrance which time does not obliterate nor pain which death does not put an end to

Fear.

Don Quixote, III. 6.

El miedo tiene muchos **ojos.**

Fear has many eyes.

Misfortune.

Don Quixote, III. 10.

Para remediar desdichas del cielo, poco suelan valer los bienes de fortuna.

The goods of fortune seldom avail anything towards the relief of misfortunes sent from heaven.

Misfortunes sent by Heaven.

Don Quixote, III. 13.

Quando traen las desgracias la corriente de las estrellas, como vienen de alto à baxo despeñandose con furor, y con violencia, no ay fuerça en la tierra que las detenga, ni industria humana que prevenir las pueda.

When the strong influences of the stars pour down misfortunes upon us, they fall from on high with such violence and fury that no human force can stop them nor human address prevent them.

The Feelings of Women.

Don Quixote, IV. 1.

Por feas que seamos las mugeres, me parece à mi, que siempre nos dà gusto el óir que nos llamen hermosas.

For let us women be never so ill-favoured, I imagine that we are always delighted to hear ourselves called handsome.

Generous Minds betrayed into a Fault.

Don Quixote, IV. 6.

Que à un magnanimo pecho, à verguença
No solo a de moverle el ser mirado,
Que de si se averguenza quando yerra,
Si bien otro no vee que cielo, y tierra.

For generous minds, betrayed into a fault,
No witness want, but self-condemning thought;
To such the conscious earth alone and skies
Supply the place of thousand prying eyes.

The Hardships of the Scholar.

Don Quixote, IV. 10.

Digo pues, que los trabajos del estudiante son estos : Principalmente pobreza (no porque todos sean pobres, sino por poner este caso en todo el estremo que pueda ser) y en aver dicho que padece pobreza, me parece que no avía que dezir mas de su mala ventura. Porque quien es pobre, no tiene cosa buena, esta pobreza la padece por sus partes, ya en hambre, ya en frio, ya en desnudez, ya en todo junto. Pero con todo esso no es tanta que no coma, aunque sea un poco mas tarde de lo que se usa, aunque sea de las sobras de los ricos, que es la mayor miseria del estudiante, este que entre ellos llaman andar à la sopa, y no les falta algun ageno brasero, ò chimenea, que si no calienta, à los menos entibiè su frio, y en fin la noche duermen debaxo de cubierta.

I say, then, that the hardships of the scholar are these : in the first place, poverty (not that they are all poor, but I would put the case in the strongest manner possible), and when I have said that he endures poverty, methinks no more need be said to show his misery. For he who is poor is destitute of every good thing, he endures poverty in all its parts—sometimes in hunger and cold, and sometimes in nakedness, and sometimes in all these together. But, notwithstanding all this, it is not so great but that still he eats, though somewhat later than usual, or of the rich man's scraps and leavings, or, which is the scholar's greatest misery, by what is called among them, going a-*sopping*. Neither do they always want a fireside or chimney-corner of some charitable person, which, if it does not quite warm them, at least abates their extreme cold ; and lastly, they sleep somewhere under cover.

The Army.

Don Quixote, IV. 12.

Que es escuela la soldatesca, donde el mezquino se haze

franco, y el franco prodigo, y si algunos soldados se hallan miserabiles, son como monstruos, que se vèn raras vezes.

For the army is a school in which the niggardly become generous, and the generous prodigal ; and if there are some soldiers misers, they are a kind of monsters, but very rarely seen.

The Beauty of some Women.

Don Quixote, IV. 14.

Porque ya se sabe, que la hermosura de algunas mugeres tiene dias, y sazones, y requiere acidentes para diminuyrse, ò acrecentarse : y es natural cosa, que las passiones del animo la levanten, ò baxen, puesto, que las mas vezes la destruyen.

For it is well known that the beauty of some women has days and seasons, and depends upon accidents which diminish or increase it ; nay, the very passions of the mind naturally improve or impair it, and very often utterly destroy it.

Envy.

Don Quixote, IV. 20.

En fin donde reyna la embidia no puede vivir la virtud, ni adonde ay escaseza, la liberalidad.

In short, virtue cannot live where envy reigns, nor liberality subsist with niggardliness.

The Unwise.

Don Quixote, IV. 21.

Como por vér, que es mas el numero de los simples, que de los prudentes : y que puesto que es mejor ser loado de los pocos sabios, que burlado de los muchos necios, no quiero sujetarme al confuso juyzio del desvanecido vulgo, à quien por la mayor parte toca léer semejantes libros.

I regard it as true that the number of the unwise is greater than that of the prudent ; and though it is better to be praised by the few wise than mocked by a multitude of fools, yet I am unwilling to expose myself to the confused judgment of the giddy vulgar, to whose lot the reading of such books for most part falls.

RECREATION NECESSARY.

Don Quixote, IV. 21.

Pues no es possibile que estè continuo el arco armado, ni la condicion, y flaqueza humana se pueda sustentar sin alguna licita recreacion.

For the bow cannot possibly stand always bent, nor can human nature or human frailty subsist without some lawful recreation.

THE POET AND THE HISTORIAN.

Don Quixote, V. 3.

El poëta puede cantar ò cantar las cosas, no como fueron, sino como devían ser : y el historiador las a de escrivir, no como devían ser, sino como fueron, sin añadir, ni quitar à la verdad cosa alguna.

The poet may say or sing, not as things were, but as they ought to have been ; but the historian must pen them, not as they ought to have been, but as they really were, without adding to or diminishing anything from the truth.

THE FOOL IN COMEDY.

Don Quixote, V. 3.

La mas discreta figura de la comedia es la del bobo, porque no lo a de 'ser el que quiere dar à entender, que es simple.

The most difficult character in comedy is that of the fool, and he must be no simpleton that plays that part.

HISTORY.

Don Quixote, V. 3.

La historia es como cosa sagrada, porque a de ser verdadera, y donde està la verdad, està Dios en quanto à verdad.

History is a sacred kind of writing, because truth is essential to it, and where truth is, there God himself is, so far as truth is concerned.

CRITICS.

Don Quixote, v. 3.

Los hombres famosos por sus ingenios, los grandes poëtas, los ilustres historiadores siempre, ò las mas vezes, son embidiados de aquellos que tienen por gusto, y por particular entretenimiento, juzgar los escritos agenos, sin aver dado algunos proprios à la luz del mundo.

Men famous for their abilities, great poets and celebrated historians, are always envied by those who take a pleasure and make it their particular delight to criticise other men's writings, without ever having published any of their own.

TRUE VALOUR.

Don Quixote, v. 4.

En los estrémos de cobarde, y de temerario està el medio de la valencia.

The mean of true valour lies between the extremes of cowardice and rashness.

WOMEN.

Don Quixote, v. 5.

Nacemos las mugeres de ester obedientes à sus maridos, aunque sean unos porros.

We women are born to be obedient to our husbands, be they never such blockheads.

THE PEDIGREES OF PEOPLE.

Don Quixote, v. 6.

Mirad amigas, à quatro suertes de linages (y estad me atentas) se pueden reduzir todos los que ay en el mundo, que son estos. Unos que tuvieron principios humildes, y se fueron estendiendo, y dilatando hasta llegar à una suma grandeza. Otros que tuvieron principios grandes, y los fueron conservando, y los conservan, y mantienen en el ser que començaron. Otros que aunque tuvieron principios grandes acabaron en punta como piramide, aviendo disminuydo, y aniquilado su principio hasta parar en nonada, como los es la punta de la piramide, que respeto de su bassa, ò assiento. no es nada. Otros ay (y estos son los mas) que ni tuvieron principio bueno, ni razonable medio, y assi tendràn el fin sin nombre, como el linage de la gente plebeya y ordinaria.

Hear me, friends, with attention : all the genealogies in the world may be reduced to four sorts, which are these : —First, of those, who, having had a humble origin, have gone on extending and dilating themselves till they have reached the utmost grandeur. Secondly, of those, who, having had great beginnings, have preserved and continue to preserve them in the same condition they were at first. Thirdly, of those, who, though they had great beginnings, have ended in a small point like a pyramid, having gone on diminishing and decreasing continually, till they have come almost to nothing like the point of the pyramid, which, in respect of its base or pedestal, is next to nothing. Lastly, of those (and they are the most numerous), who, having had neither a good beginning nor a tolerable middle, will therefore end without a name, like the families of common and ordinary people.

VIRTUE AND VICE.
Don Quixote, v. 6.

Y sè que la senda de la virtud es muy estrecha, y el camino del vicio ancho y espacioso. Y sè, que sus fines y paraderos son diferentes, porque el del vicio dilatado y espacioso acaba en muerte, y el de la virtud estrecho y trabaioso acaba en vida, y no en vida que acaba, sino en la que no tendrà fin.

I know that the path of virtue is straight and narrow, and the road of vice broad and spacious. I know also that their ends and resting-places are different ; for those of vice, large and open, end in death ; and those of virtue, narrow and intricate, end in life, and not in life that has an end, but in that which is eternal.

TRUTH.
Don Quixote, v. 10.

La verdad adelgaza, y no quiebra, y siempre anda sobre la mentira, como el azeyte sobre el agua.

Truth may be stretched, but cannot be broken, and always gets above falsehood, as oil does above water.

LETTERS WITHOUT VIRTUE.

Don Quixote.

Letras sin virtud son perlas en el muladar.

Letters without virtue are pearls in a dunghill.

POETRY.

Don Quixote, v. 16.

La poësia, Señor Hidalgo, à mi parecer, es como **una** donzella tierna, y de poca edad, y en todo estremo hermosa, à quien tienen cuydado de enriquecer, pulir, y adornar otras muchas donzellas, que son todas las otras ciencias, **y** ella se a de servir de todas, y todas se an de autorizar con ella : pero esta tal donzella no quiere ser manoseada, ni trayda por las calles, ni publicada por las esquinas de **las** plaças ni por los rincones de los palacios. Ella es hecha de una alquimia de tal virtud, que quien la sabe tratar, la bolverà en oro purissimo de inestimable precio, a la de tener él que la tuviere à raya, no dexandola correr en tordes satyras, ni en desalmados sonetos, no a de ser vendible en ninguna manera, si ya no fuéra en poëmas heroicas, en lamentables tragedias, ò en comedias alegres y artificiosas : no se a de dexar tratar de los truhanes, ni del ignorante vulgo, incapaz de conocer ni estimar los tesóros que en ella se encierran.

Poetry, good sir, in my opinion, is like a tender virgin, **very** young, and extremely beautiful, whom divers other virgins— namely, all the other sciences—make it their business to enrich, polish, and adorn ; and to her it belongs to make use of them all, and on her part to give a lustre to them all. But this same virgin is not to be rudely handled, nor dragged through the streets, nor exposed in the turnings of the market-place, nor posted on the corners **or** gates of palaces. She is formed of an alchemy of such virtue, that he who knows how to manage her will convert her into the purest gold of inestimable price. He who possesses her should keep a strict hand over her, not suffering her to make excursions in obscene satires or lifeless sonnets. She must in no way be **venal ;** though she need not reject the profits arising from heroic **poems, mournful tragedies, or pleasant and artful comedies. She** must not be meddled with by buffoons, or by the ignorant vulgar, incapable of knowing or esteeming the treasures locked up in her.

THE PEN IS THE TONGUE OF THE MIND.

Don Quixote, v. 16.

La pluma es lengua del alma.

The pen is the tongue of the mind.

NO CHILDREN UGLY TO THEIR PARENTS.

Don Quixote, VI. 18.

Porque no ay padre, ni madre à quien sus hijos le parezcan féos : y en los que lo son del entendimiento, corre mas este engaño.

For no fathers or mothers think their own children ugly ; and this self-deceit is yet stronger with respect to the offspring of the mind.

A WIFE.

Don Quixote, VI. 19.

La de la propria muger no es mercaduría que una vez comprada se buelve ò se trueca ò cambia ; porque es acidente inseparable, que dura lo que dura la vida.

The wife is not a commodity, which, once bought, you can exchange or swap or return, but is an inseparable accessory, which lasts as long as life itself.

THE BEST PREACHER.

Don Quixote, VI. 20.

Bien predica quien bien vive.

He who lives well is the best preacher.

COMPARISONS ARE ODIOUS.

Don Quixote, VI. 23.

Yà sabe que toda comparacion es odiosa.

You know that all comparisons are odious.

LIBERTY.

Don Quixote, VIII. 58.

La libertad, Sancho, es uno de sos mas preciosos dones que à los hombres dieron los cielos, con ella no pueden igualarse los tesóros que encierra la tierra ni el mar encubre : por la libertad, assi como per la honra, se puede y deve aventurar la vida ; y por el contrario el cautiverio es el mayor mal que puede venir à los hombres.

Liberty, Sancho, is one of the most precious gifts which Heaven has bestowed on man ; with it we cannot compare the treasures which the earth contains or the sea conceals ; for liberty, as for honour, we can and ought to risk our lives ; and, on the other hand, captivity is the greatest evil that can befall man.

BLESSINGS TO HIM WHO INVENTED SLEEP.

Don Quixote, VIII. 68.

Bien aya el que inventò el sueño, capa que cubre todos los humanos pensamientos, manjar que quita la hambre, agua que ahuyenta la sed, fuego que calienta el frio, frio que templa el ardor, y finalmente moneda general, con que todas las cosas se compran, balança, y peso que iguala al pastor con el rey, y al simple con el discreto ; solo una cosa tiene mala el sueño, segun he oido dezir, y es que se parece à la muerte, pués de un dormido à un muerto, ay muy poco diferencia.

Blessings light on him that first invented sleep ! it covers a man all over, thoughts and all, like a cloak ; it is meat for the hungry, drink for the thirsty, heat for the cold, and cold for the hot ; in short, money that buys everything, balance and weights that make the shepherd equal to the monarch, and the fool to the wise ; there is only one evil in sleep, as I have heard, and it is that it resembles death, since between a dead and sleeping man there is but little difference.

WOMAN CAN MAKE HERSELF RESPECTED.

La Gitanilla.

La muger que se determina á ser honrada, entre un ejército de soldados lo puede ser.

The woman who is resolved to be respected can make herself to be so even amidst an army of soldiers.

HEART IS WAX TO RECEIVE AND MARBLE TO RETAIN.

La Gitanilla.

Para con elle es de cera mi alma, donde podrá imprimir lo que quisiere : y para conservarlo y guardarlo, no será como impreso en cera, sino como esculpido en mármoles, cuya dacreza se opone á la duracion de los tiempos.

For with her my heart is as wax, to be moulded as she pleases; and to keep it, it will not be as impressed on wax, but enduring as marble, to retain whatever impression she shall make upon it.

Byron (*Beppo*, st. 34) says —

" His heart was one of those which most enamour us:
Wax to receive, and marble to retain."

POESY.

La Gitanilla.

La poesía es una bellíssima doncella, casta, honesta, discreta, aguda, retirada, y que se contiene en los limites de la discrecion mas alta ; es amiga de la soledad, las fuentes la entretienen, los prados la consuelan, los árboles la desenojan, las flores la alegran ; y finalmente deleita y enseña à cuantos con elle comunican.

Poesy is a beauteous young lady, chaste, honourable, discreet, witty, retired, and who keeps herself within the limits of the strictest discretion ; she is the friend of solitude, fountains entertain her, meadows console her, woods free her from ennui, flowers delight her ; and, in short, she gives pleasure and instruction to all with whom she communicates.

THE MOB.

Illustre Fregona.

Como la mala bestia del vulgo por la mayor parte es mala, maldita, y maldiciente.

As the vile mob generally are vicious, worthless, and unprincipled.

To do Ill.

Coloquio de los Perros.

Como el hacer mal viene de natural cosecha, fácilmente
se aprende el hacerle.

As to do ill springs up as a spontaneous crop, it is easy to learn.

THE CID.

The poem of *The Cid* gives an account of the adventures of the
Cid, the great popular hero of Spain, and consists of three thousand lines. It is supposed to have been composed not later than
the year 1200, by whom is not known. The Cid himself was born
in the north-western part of Spain about the year 1040, and died
in 1099 at Valencia, which he had rescued from the Moors. He
passed almost the whole of his life fighting against the Moors,
suffering, so far as we know, scarcely a single defeat from the
enemy. The poem develops the character and glory of the Cid,
giving at the same time living pictures of the age it represents
with Homeric simplicity.

The Miseries of a Siege.

L. 1183.

Mal se aquexan los de Valencia, que not sabent ques' far ;
De ninguna part que sea no les viene pan
Nin da consejo padre à fijo, nin fijo à padre :
Nin amigo à amigo nos pueden consolar.
Mala cuenta es, Señores, aver mengua de pan,
Fijos e mugieres verlo morir de fambre.

Valencian men doubt what to do, and bitterly complain,
That whereso'er they look for bread, they look for it in vain ,
No father help can give his child, no son can help his sire,
Nor friend to friend assistance lend, or cheerfulness inspire.
A grievous story, sirs, it is, when fails the needed bread,
And women fair and children young in hunger join the dead.

Hookham Frere.

A Challenge.

Sanchez, tom. I. *p.* 359.

Azur Gonzalez entraba por el palacio ;
Manto armino è un brial rastrando :
Bermeio viene, ca era almorzado.
En lo que fablò avie poco recabdo.
"Hya varones, quien vió nunca tal mal ?
Quien nos darie nuevas de Mio Cid, el de Bibar ?
Fues' à Riodouirna los molinos picar,
E prender maquilas como lo suele far' ;
Quil' darie con los de Carrion à casar' ? "
Esora Muno Gustioz en pie se levantó :
"Cala, alevoso, malo è traydor :
Antes almuerzas, que bayas à oracion :
A los que das paz, fartas los aderredor.
Nos dices verdad amigo ni à Señor,
Falso à todos è mas al Criador.
En tu amistad non quiero aver racion.
Facertelo decir, que tal eres qual digo yo."

Assur Gonzalez was entering at the door,
With his ermine mantle trailing along the floor,
With his sauntering pace and his hardy look,
Of manners or of courtesy little heed he took ;
He was flushed and hot with breakfast and with drink.
"What ho ! my masters, your spirits seem to sink !
Have we no news stirring from the Cid, Ruy Diaz of Bivar?
Has he been to Riodivirna to besiege the windmills there ?
Does he tax the millers for their toil ? or is that practice past?
Will he make a match for his daughters, another like the last ? '
Munio Gustioz rose and made reply—
"Traitor ! wilt thou never cease to slander and to lie ?
You breakfast before mass, you drink before you pray ;
There is no honour in your heart, nor truth in what you say ;
You cheat your comrade, and your lord you flatter to betray ;
Your hatred I despise, your friendship I defy !
False to all mankind, and most to God on high,
I shall force you to confess that what I say is true."
Thus was ended the parley and challenge betwixt these two.

RODRIGO COTA.

Flourished A.D. 1470.

LOVE.

A Dialogue between Love and the Old Man.

> Ninguno cierre las puertas ;
> Si Amor viniese a llamar,
> Que no le ha aprovechar.

Let no man shut the door if Love should come to call, as it will do no good at all.

THE DANCE OF DEATH.

All must come.

> A esta mi Danza traye de presente
> Estas dos donçellas que vedes fermosas ;
> Ellas vinieron de muy mala mente
> A oyr mis canciones que son dolorosas.
> Mas non les valdran flores my rosas,
> Nin las composturas que poner solian.
> De mi si pudiesen partir se querrian,
> Mas non puede ser, que son mis esposas.

Bring to my dance without delay these two damsels whom you see so fair; they have come with very bad grace to hear my songs that are so dolorous. But neither flowers nor roses will avail them, nor the attire that they are wont to wear ; from me they may depart if they can, but it cannot be, they are my wedded brides.

BENITO FEYJOO.

Born A.D. 1676. Died A.D. 1764.

Benito Feyjoo was the son of respectable parents in the north-western part of Spain, and at an early age devoted himself to the Church, living for forty-seven years in a Benedictine convent at Oviedo. He introduced to his countrymen a knowledge of the labours of Galileo, Bacon, Newton, Pascal, and Gassendi, and when he died in 1764, was able to console himself with the thought that he had given a right direction to the intellectual life of his country, having done more than had been accomplished for a century.

THE ADVANTAGES OF VIRTUE OVER VICE.

Comunmente se concibe la virtud toda asperezas, el vicio
todo dulzuras ; la virtud metida entree spinas, el vicio
reposando en lecho de flores. Pero si pudiésemos ver los
corazones de los hombres entregados al vicio, presto se
quitaria la duda. Mas por reflexîon podremos verlos en
los espejos de las almas, que son semblantes, palabras, y
acciones. Atiéndase bien á estos infelices, y se hallará que
ninguno otro iguala la turbacion de sus semblantes, la
inquietud de sus acciones, la desazon de sus palabras. No
hay que estrañar ; son muchos los torcedores que los éstan
conturbando en el goce de sus adorados placeres. Su
propia conciencia, domestico enemigo, huesped inevitable,
pero ingrato, les está continuamente mezclando con el
nectar que beben.

Con enérgica propiedad dixo Tulio, que las culpas de los
impios, representados en en su imaginacion, son para ellos
continuas y domesticas furias : "hæ sunt impiis assiduæ
domesticæque furiæ." Estas son las serpientes, o los
buytres que despedazan las entrañas de el malvado Ticio ;
estas las aguilas que razgan el corazon de el atrevido
Prometheo ; estas los tormentos de un Cain, fugitivo de
todos, y aun, si pudiese, de si mismo, errante por montes y
selvas, sin poder jamas arrancar la flecha que la atravesaba
el pecho.

Generally, virtue is imagined to be all asperity, vice all delight ;
virtue to be placed amidst thorns, vice to be reclining on a bed of
flowers. Yet if we were able to look into the hearts of men, im-
mersed in vicious indulgence, our doubts would speedily vanish.
By reflection we shall be able to see them in the mirrors of the
soul—that is in the countenance, the speech, and actions. Only
look at those unhappy beings, and it will be found that nothing
can equal the agitation of their countenance, the frenzy of their
actions, and the inconsistency of their speech. You need not be
surprised ; many are the torments that disturb the enjoyment of
their pleasures. Their own conscience, a domestic enemy, an
unavoidable guest, though ungrateful, is always there, mingling
with the nectar which they are drinking.

With what power does Cicero declare that the vices of the

wicked pictured by the imagination are for them never-ending and domestic furies! These are the serpents or vultures which gnaw the entrails of the wicked Typhœus; these the eagles which tear the heart of the bold Prometheus; these the torments of Cain, a fugitive from all, and even, if it were possible, from himself, wandering over mountains and woods, without even being able to pull out the arrow which pierced his heart.

PERO FERNANDEZ DE VILLEGAS.

Flourished A.D. 1515.

Pero Fernandez was Archdeacon of Burgos, and wrote a poem entitled " Aversion del Mundo y Conversion á Dios."

THE VANITY OF THIS LIFE

Quedate, mundo malino,
Lleno de mal y dolor,
Que me vo tras el dulçor
Del bien eterno divino.
Tu tosigo, tu venino,
Vevemos açucarado,
Y la sierpo esta en el prado
De tu tan falso camino.

Quedate con tus engaños,
Maguera te dexo tarde,
Que te segui de cobarde
Fasta mis postreros años.
Mas ya tus males estraños
De ti me alançan forçoso,
Vome a buscar el reposo
De tus trabajosos daños.

Quedate con tu maldad
Con tu trabajo inhumano,
Donde el hermano al hermano
No guarda fe ni verdad.
Muerta es toda caridad;
Todo bien en ti es ya muerto :—
Acojome para el puerto,
Fuyendo tu tempestad.

Away, thou malignant world full of sin and sorrow, for I wish to enjoy the sweetness of the heavenly life. Your fatal poison here we drink, charmed by its sweets ; the serpent lurks in the meadow on thy path.

Away with thy snares, which I fly too late—I who, a coward, followed thee to my latest years ; but thy strange sins drive me from thee, wishing to seek repose from thy sorrowful service.

Away with thy wickedness, with thy inhuman toil, when brother to brother keeps not faith nor truth. All charity is dead in thee ; all good is dead in thee ; I look for a harbour, flying from thy storms.

GARCILASSO DE LA VEGA.

Born A.D. 1503. Died A.D. 1536.

Garcilasso was born at Toledo, and devoted himself to a military life, being constantly in the wars which the Emperor was carrying on in all directions. He distinguished himself in the defeat of the Turkish expedition of Soliman, and was at the siege of Turin when Charles the Fifth attempted to crush the Barbary powers. He was killed at the siege of Frejus, A.D. 1536, in the thirty-third year of his age.

An Unfaithful Mistress.

Por ti el silencio de la selva umbrosa,
    Por ti la esquividad y apartimiento
    Del solitario monte me agradaba :
    Por ti la verde hierba, el fresco viento,
El blanco lirio y colorada rosa,
    Y dulce primavera deseaba.
    Ay ! quento me engañaba,
    Ay ! quan diferente era,
    Y quan de otra manera
Lo que en tu falso pecho se escondia.

For thee I loved the silence of the shady wood, for thee the solitude and retirement of the lonely mountain ; for thee I loved the verdant grass, the cool wind, the pale lily, and blushing rose and sweet spring. Ah ! how much I was deceived ! ah ! how different I thought thee from that which was concealed in thy treacherous breast.

The Melody of the Nightingale.

Qual suele el ruyseñor, con triste canto,

Quexarse, entre las hojas encondido,
Del duro laborador, que cantamente
Le despojo su caro y dulce nido
De los tiernos hijuelos, entre tanto
Que del amado ramo estaua ausente ;
Y aquel dolor que siente,
Con diferencia tanta,
Por la dulce garganta
Despide, y a su canto el ayre suena ;
Y la callada noche no refrena
Sa lamentable oficio y sus querellas,
Trayendo de su pena
El cielo por testigo y las estrellas :

Desta manera suelto yo la rienda
A mi dolor, y aussi me quejo en vano
De la dureza de la muerte ayrada :
Ella en mi coraçon metyó la mano,
Y d'alli me llenò mi dulçe prenda,
Que aquel era su nido y su morada.

As the nightingale is wont to utter its griefs, concealed amidst the leaves, because the cruel hind has craftily stolen from her dear nest her tender young, while she was absent from her beloved bough ; and the grief which she feels she sends from her throat, filling the air with passionate complaint, and during the silent night does not cease her melancholy song, calling on heaven and stars to bear witness to her wrongs :—in the same way I am given up to misery, and thus I mourn in vain of the cruelty of death ; death thrusts his hand into my heart, and bears away, as from its nest and home, the love with which I was filled.

This is an imitation of Homer (*Odyss.* xix. 518) :—

" ὡς δ' ὅτε Πανδαρέου κούρη, χλωρηὶς Ἀηδών,
καλὸν ἀείδῃσιν ἔαρος νέον ἱσταμένοιο,
δενδρέων ἐν πετάλοισι καθεζομένη πυκινοῖσιν,
ἥτε θαμὰ τρωπῶσα χέει πολυηχέα φωνὴν,
παῖδ' ὀλοφυρομένη Ἴτυλον φίλον, ὅν ποτε χαλκῷ
κτεῖνε δι' ἀφραδίας, κοῦρον Ζήθοιο ἄνακτος."

As when the pale green nightingale, daughter of Pandareus, warbles sweetly in the very beginning of spring, sitting amidst the thick foliage of the branches ; changing her position, she pours forth long-drawn notes, bewailing the loss of her son Itylos, whom she once upon a time slew accidentally, thinking him to be the son of Zethus.

Virgil (*Georg.* iv. 510) says—

> "Qualis populeâ mœrens Philomela sub umbrâ
> Amissos queritur fetus, quos durus arator
> Observans nido implumes detraxit : at illa
> Flet noctem, ramoque sedens miserabile carmen
> Integrat, et mœstis late loca questibus implet."

As Philomela, wailing under the shade of the poplar, laments the loss of her young ones, when the cruel hind, watching, has stolen them still unfledged; but she mourns the livelong night, and sitting on a bough renews her piteous song, and fills the country far and near with her sorrowing complaints.

Milton, perhaps still more beautifully, says—

> "The wakeful bird
> Sings darkling, and in shadiest covert hid,
> Tunes her nocturnal notes."

THE PLEASURES OF A COUNTRY LIFE.

Ecloga II.

Quán bienaventurado
Aquel puede llamarse,
Que con la dulce soledad se abraza,
Y vive descuidado,
Y lejos de empacharse
En lo que al alma impide y embaraza !
No vé llena la plaza,
Ni la soberbia puerta
De los grandes Señores,
Ni los aduladores,
Á quien la hambre del favor despierta :
No le será forzoso
Rogar, fingir, temer, y estar quejoso.

   A la sombra holgando
De un alto pino, ó robre,
Ó de alguna robusta y verde encina,
El ganado contando
De su manada pobre,
Que por la verde selva se avecina;

2 K

Plata cendrada y fina,
Oro luciente y puro
Bajo y vil le parece ;
Y tanto lo aborece,
Que aun no piensa que dello está seguro ;
Y como esta en su seso,
Rehuye la cerviz del grave peso.
    Convida á un dulce sueño,
Aquel manso ruido
Del agua, que la clara fuente envia ;
Y las aves sin dueño,
Con canto no aprendido
Hinchen el ayre de dulce harmonía :
Háceles compañia,
Á la sombra volando,
Y entre varios olores,
Gustando tiernas flores
La solícita abeja susurrando :
Los arboles, el viento,
Al sueño ayudan con su movimiento.

How happy he may be called who is encompassed by the delights of solitude, and lives away from care, and far from being embarrassed with the anxieties which disturb and annoy the mind! He sees not the crowds of the streets, nor the proud portals of the noble senators, nor the flatterers whom hunger excites ; he is not forced to beg, to lie, to fear, and complain.

Reclining under the shade of some lofty pine or oak, or of some wide-spreading and green holm-oak, counting the lambs of his poor flock as they approach through the greenwood ; the finest silver-plate, bright and burnished gold, appear to him vile and of no account, and so much does he abhor it, that even he does not think that he can be sufficiently guarded from it, and throws it from him as a heavy weight.

He is invited to sweet sleep by a gentle murmuring stream which issues from a limpid fountain ; the wild birds with untaught music fill the air with their melodious notes ; the busy bee, humming, accompanies them, flying in the shade, and 'midst various odours sips the tender flowers ; the trees and the breeze assist by their movements to lull him to sleep.

This is an imitation of Horace (*Epod.* ii. 1).

GONZALO DE BERCEO.

Flourished from A.D. 1220 to A.D. 1246.

Gonzalo, a secular priest of the monastery of San Millan or Saint Emilianus in the territory of Galahorra, is commonly called Berceo from the place of his birth. Of his personal history we know little ; his works amount to above thirteen thousand lines, principally on religious subjects. They are found in the second volume of Sanchez's *Poesias Anteriores*.

THE SIGNS OF THE JUDGMENT-DAY.

Sanchez, tom. II. *p.* 274.

Esti sera el uno de los signos dubdados :
Subira a los nubes el mar muchos estados,
Mas alto que las sierras è mas que los collados,
Tanto que en sequero fincaran los pescados.

.   .   .   .   .   .

Las aves esso mesmo menudas è granadas
Andaran dando gritos todas mal espantadas ;
Assi faran las bestias por domar è domadas,
Non podran à la noche tornar à sus posadas.

This will be one of the signs that fill the mind with doubts and fear : the sea shall rise to the clouds, in height far above the sierras and hills, leaving the fishes on dry land.
The birds also, small and great, shall screaming fly and wheel about, all in great terror ; the beasts, too, both untamed and tame, will not be able at night to find their dens.

BEAUTIFUL ARBOUR.

Sanchez, tom. II. *p.* 285.

Yo Maestro Gonzalvo de Berceo nomnado
Iendo en Romeria caeci en un prado,
Verde è bien sencido, de flores bien poblado
Logar cobdiciaduero pora ome cansado.

Daban oler sobeio las flores bien olientes,
Refrescaban en ome las caras e las mientes,

Manaban cada canto fuentes claras corrientes,
En verano bien frias, en yvierno calientes.

Avie hy grand abondo de buenas arboledas,
Milgranos è figueras, peros è mazanedas,
E muchas otras fructas de diversas monedas ;
Mas non avie ningunas podridas nin acedas.

La verdura del prado, la olor de las flores,
Las sombras de los arbores de temprados sabores
Refrescaronme todo, è perdi los sudores :
Podrie vevir el ome con aquellos olores.

I, Master Gonzalo de Berceo, wandering as a pilgrim, found a
meadow, green, sweet-scented, and peopled full of flowers, a spot
where a weary man might rest with delight.

The flowers gave forth a sweet perfume, refreshing the senses
and the soul in man ; there flowed on every side clear and pure
fountains, very cool in summer and warm in winter.

There was a boundless maze of goodly trees—apples of Granada,
figs, pears, and many other fruits of various worth, but none that
decayed or turned sour.

The verdure of the meadow, the sweetness of the flowers, the
shadow of the trees, with temperate coolness refreshed man
wholly, and removed the heat ; a man might have lived on the
very odours.

GREGORIO SILVESTRE.

Born A.D. 1520.   Died A.D. 1570.

Gregorio Silvestre, a Portuguese who came in his childhood to
Spain, passed his time chiefly in Granada, of whose cathedral he
was the principal musician ; he wrote in pure and idiomatic
Castilian.

THE HAIR OF A LADY.

Señora, vuestros cabellos
De ora son,
Y de azero el coraçon
Que no se muere por ellos.
No quieren ser de oro, no,
Señora, vuestros cabellos,
Quel oro quiere ser dellos.

My lady, your locks are all of gold, and of steel is the heart
which does not die for you.
Not of gold would be your hair, my lady, that gold would be
your hair.

JUAN DE LA ENZINA.

Born about A.D. 1468. Died A.D. 1534.

Juan was born at Enzina, educated at the university of Salamanca, went to Rome, where he became a priest, and from his
skill in music, rose to be head of Leo the Tenth's chapel. He
made a pilgrimage to Jerusalem A.D. 1519, and returning to his
native country died at Salamanca A.D. 1534.

THE HAPPINESS OF A COUNTRY LIFE.

Ed. 1509, 6. 90.

Cata, Gil, que las mañanas,
  En el campo hay gran frescor,
  Y tiene muy gran sabor
  La sombra de las cabañas.
Quien es ducho de dormir
  Con el ganado de noche,
  No creas que no reproche
  El palaciego vivir.
Oh ! que gassajo es oir
  El sonido de los grillos,
  Y el tañar los caramillos ;
No hay quien lo pueda decir !
Ya sabes que gozo siente
  El pastor muy caluroso
  En beber con gran reposo,
De bruzas, agua en la fuente
O de la que va corriente
  Por el cascajal corriendo
  Que se va todo riendo ;
  Oh ! que prazer tan valiente !

Look ye, Gil, that in the morning the fields are fresh, and the
shade of the cabin has savoury coolness. He who is accustomed

to sleep amidst his flocks the livelong night, you cannot believe can find delight to dwell in a palace. Oh! what pleasure it is to hear the chirping of the cricket and the music of the flageolet : it is impossible to say what great pleasure it is! Thou knowest what luxury it is for the shepherd overcome by heat, in great stillness, to drink with his mouth touching the edge of some spring, or where the streamlet, hurrying on, rushes and frolics down its pebbly bed. Oh! what delight to drink from its merry gush!

LOPE DE VEGA.

Born A.D. 1562. Died A.D. 1638.

COWARDS DIE MANY TIMES.

Corona Tragica.

La muerte es menos pena que esperarla ;
Una vez quien la sufre la recibe ;
Pero por mucho que en valor se extreme
Muchas veces le passa quien la teme.

Comfort's in death, where 'tis in life unknown ;
Who death expects feels more than he who dies ;
Though too much valour may our fortune try,
To live in fear of death is many times to die.

So Shakespeare (*Julius Cæsar*, act ii. sc. 2) says—

"Cowards die many deaths before their deaths :
The valiant never taste of death but once."

VARIETY.

Arte de hacer Comedias.

Que aquesta variedad deleyta mucho ;
Buen exemplo nos dá natureleza,
Que por tal variedad tiene belleza.

But sweet variety must still delight ;
And spite of rules, Dame Nature says we're right,
Who throughout all her works the example gives,
And from variety her charms derives.

Envy.

La Necedad del Discreto.

Bien dizes, y assi vemos que la fama
No se despega de la propia embidia,
Si no es que muera el dueño que la tiene.
Dixo un discreto que era matrimonio,
Polibis, el de la embidia y de la fama.
Que se apartava solo con la muerte ;
De suerte que al que nace en alguna arte
Insigne, le esta bien de morirse presto :
Y si la vida ha de costar la fama
Famoso en todo á mi enemigo llama.

'Tis true—thus envy living worth attends ;
The hero dies, and then all envy ends.
Envy was honour's wife, a wise man said,
Ne'er to be parted till the man was dead.
Yes ; who excels may gain the glorious prize
Of endless fame, provided first he dies.
If such indeed must be the price of fame,
Let others seek it, I resign my claim :
On these conditions I will gladly grant,
E'en to my foes, what portion they may want.

PEDRO LOPEZ DE AYALA.

Flourished from A.D. 1370 to A.D. 1407.

Lopez held many distinguished offices under Peter the Cruel. He was a prisoner in England after the defeat of Henry of Trastamara by the Duke of Lancaster in 1367. He wrote a poem, " El Rimado de Palacio," on the duties of kings and nobles in the government of the state.

True Justice.

Justicia que es virtud atan noble e loada,
Que castiga los malos e ha la tierra poblada,
Deven la guardar Reyes, é la tien olvidada,
Siendo piedra preciosa de su corona onrrada.
Muchos ha que por cruesa cuydan justicia fer ;
Mas pecan en la maña, ca justicia ha de ser
Con todo piedat, e la verdat bien saber :
Al fer la execucion siempre se han de doler.

Justice, which is a virtue at once noble and renowned, which checks the guilty, and fills the land with people, ought to guard kings, and yet is forgotten, though it is the most precious stone of their honoured crown. Many think by cruelty to fulfil its duties, but their wisdom is nought, for justice has to dwell with pity, and to be with truth ; it always grieves to proceed to execution.

LUIS DE GRANADA.

Born A.D. 1504. Died A.D. 1588.

Luis de Granada, head of the Dominican Order, was distinguished for his eloquence in the pulpit, often preaching extemporaneously with great power and unction. His discourses have been published, written with remarkable purity of diction.

How Changeable the Life of Man.

Grande defecto tiene nuestra vida, que es ser mudable y nunca permancer en un mismo ser. "El hombre," dice Job, "nace de muger, vive pocos dias, es lleno de muchas miserias, sale como una flor, y luego se marchita, huyen sus dias así como sombra, y nunca permanece en un mismo estado." Qué cosa pues hay mas mudable ? Dicen que el camaleon muda en una hora muchos colores ; el mar Euripo es infamado de muchas mudanzas y la luna tiene para cada dia su figura. Mas ! qué es todo esto para las mudanzas del hombre ? Qué Prothéo mudó jamás tantas figuras, como muda el hombre á cada hora ? Ya enferno, ya sano ; ya contento, ya descontento ; ya triste, ya alegre ; ya temeroso, ya confiado ; ya sospechoso, ya seguro ; ya pacifico, ya airado ; ya quiere, ya no quiere ; y muchas veces él á si mismo no sé entiende. Finalmente tantas son sus mudanzas, quantos accidentes se levantan á cada hora, porque cada uno lo trastorna de su manera. Lo pasado le da pena ; lo presente le turba ; y lo venidero la congoia.

This is the great misfortune of life, that it is changeable, and never remains in the same state. "Man," says Job (xiv. 1), "that is born of woman, is of few days, and full of trouble. He cometh forth like a flower, and is cut down ; he fleeth also as a shadow, and continueth not." What is more changeable ? We are told that the chameleon assumes in an hour many colours; the sea of the Euripus has an evil name for its many changes, and the moon takes every day its own peculiar form. But what is all this compared to the changes of man? What Proteus ever assumed so many different forms as man does every hour? Now sick, now in health; now content, now discontent; now sad, now joyous; now timid, now hopeful; now suspicious, now credulous; now peaceful, now recalcitrant; now he wishes, now he wishes not; and many times he knows not what he wants. In short, the changes are as numerous as the accidents in an hour, so that every one of them turns him upside down. The past gives him pain, the present disturbs him, and the future causes him agony.

HOW MISERABLE IS THE LIFE OF MAN.

Qué será pues, si discurrimos por las miserias de todas las edades y estados de esta vida? Quan llena de ignorancia es la niñez! Quan liviana la mocedad! Quan arrebatada la juventud, y quan pesada la vejez! Qué es el niño, sino un animal bruto en figura de hombre? Qué el mozo, sino un caballo desbocado y sin freno? Qué el viejo ya pesado, sino un saco de enfermedades y dolores? El mayor deseo que tienen los hombres es de llegar á esta edad, donde el hombre está mas necesitado, que en toda la vida, y aun ménos socorrido. Pues al viejo desampara el mundo, desamparan sus deudos, desamparan hasta sus miembros y sentidos, y él mismo se desampara á si; pues ya le falta el uso de la razon, y solamente le accompañan enfermedades. Este es 'el blanco adonde tiene puestos los ojos la felicidad humana y la ambicion de la vida.

What will it be if we run over the miseries of all the ages and states of this life? How full of ignorance is childhood! how light-headed is boyhood! how rash is youth, and how cross is old age! What is a child but a brute animal in the form of a human being? What is youth but a steed with the bit in his mouth and without reins? What the old man, weighed down by years, but a bundle of infirmities and pains? The greatest desire that men have is to reach this age, where man is only more subject to necessities than in the other parts of his life, and even less assisted. For the old is abandoned by the world, by his relations, even his limbs and senses fail him, and himself too; for the use of his reason leaves him, and infirmities alone attend him. This is the goal on which human felicity and the ambition of life fixes its eyes.

Death.

O muerte, quan amarga es tu memoria! Quan presta
tu venida! Quan secretos tus caminos! Quan dudosa tu
hora! Quan universal tu señorio! Los poderosos no te
pueden huir; los sabios no te saben evitar; los fuertes
contigo pierden las fuerzas; para contigo ninguno hay
rico; pues ninguno puede comprar la vida, ni aun por
tesoros. Todo lo andas, todo lo cercas, y en todo lugar te
hallas. Todas las cosas tienen sus crecientes y mengu-
antes: mas tú, siempre permaneces en un mismo ser.
Eres un martillo que siempre hiere; espada que nunca se
embota; lazo en que todos caen; carcel en que todos
entran; mar donde todos peligran; pena que todos pada-
cen; y tributo que todos pagan: O muerte cruel! Robas
en una hora, en un minuto, lo que se ganó en muchos
años; cortas la sucesion de los linages; dejas los reynos
sin herederos: hinches el mundo de orfandades; cortas el
hilo de los estudios; haces malogrados los buenos ingenios;
juntas el fin con el principio, sin dar lugar á los medios.
O muerte, muerte! O implacable enemiga del genero
humano! Porque tuviste entrada en el mundo?

O death, how bitter is the thought of thee! how speedy thy
approach! how stealthy thy steps! how uncertain thy hour! how
universal thy sway! The powerful cannot escape thee; the wise
know not how to avoid thee; the strong have no strength to
oppose thee; there is no one rich for thee, since none can buy life
with treasures. Everywhere thou goest, every place thou
besettest, in every spot thou art found. All things have their
waxing and waning, but thou remainest ever the same. Thou art
a hammer that always strikes—a sword that is never blunt—a net
into which all fall—a prison into which all enter—a sea on which
all must venture—a penalty which all must suffer—and a tribute
which all must pay. O cruel death! thou carriest off in an hour,
in a moment, that which has been acquired with the labour of
many years; thou cuttest short the succession of the high-born;
thou leavest kingdoms without heirs; thou fillest the world with
orphans; thou cuttest short the thread of studies; makest of no
use the noblest genius; joinest the end to the beginning without
allowing any intermediate space. O death, death! O implacable
enemy of the human race! Why hast thou entered into the
world?

MANUEL.

Born about A.D. 1320.   Died A.D. 1362.

Don Juan Manuel, a Castilian prince, was one of the most distinguished men of his age. He was descended from the reigning family of Castile, from King Ferdinand III., usually called the Saint. He served his sovereign, Alphonso XI., with chivalrous fidelity, and was appointed by him governor of the country bordering on the Moorish kingdom of Granada. He made an irruption into Granada, and defeated the Moorish king in a great battle. He died in 1362, leaving behind him some of the ripest fruits of his experience in his "Count Lucanor."

THE GOOD WILL NEVER DIE.

Conde Lucanor.

Si algun bien fizieres, que chico assaz fuere,
Fazlo granado : que el bien nunca muere.

If you have done something good in little, do it also in great, as the good will never die.

TO BE RESERVED TO OUR FRIENDS.

Conde Lucanor.

Quien te conseja encobrir de tus amigos,
Engañar te quiere assaz, y sin testigos.

He who advises you to be reserved to your friends wishes to betray you without witnesses.

A POOR MAN'S ADVICE.

Conde Lucanor.

No aventures mucho tu riqueza
Por consejo de ome que ha pobreza.

Hazard not your wealth on a poor man's advice.

HE WHO HAS A GOOD SEAT.

Conde Lucanor.

Quien bien see, non se lieve.

He who has got a good seat should not leave it.

PRAISE.

Conde Lucanor.

Quien te alabare con lo que non has en ti
Sabe, que quiere relever lo que has de ti.

He who praises you for what you have not, wishes to take from
you what you have.

This last axiom is deduced from the well-known fable of the
Fox and the Raven.

RABBI SANTOB.

Flourished A.D. 1350.

Rabbi de Santob was a Jew of Carrion, who addressed a poem
to Peter the Cruel on his accession to the throne, but of his
personal history nothing is known. The poem consists of four
hundred and seventy-six stanzas.

GOOD ADVICE MAY BE GOT FROM THE HUMBLEST.

Por nascer en el espino,
La rosa ya non siento,
Que pierde ; ni el buen vino,
Por salir del sarmiento.
Non vale el açor menos
Porque en vil nido siga ;
Nin los enxemplos buenos
Porque Judio los diga.

Though the rose grows on a thorn, it does not thereby lose its
perfume ; nor is the wine less good because it flows from the vine-
stock. Nor is the goshawk less worth because it is hatched in a
humble nest ; nor do moral precepts lose their value because they
come from the mouth of a Jew.

YRIARTE.

Born A.D. 1750.   Died A.D. 1791.

MAXIM FOR AN AUTHOR.

Fab. 3.

Guarde para su regalo
Esta sentencia un autor ;

Si el sabio no aprueba, malo !
Si el necio aplaude, peor !

Let every author regard this maxim for a rule : If the wise do
not express their approbation, it is bad ; if the fool applaud, it is
worse.

LET YOUR MEANING BE CLEAR.

Fab. 6.

Perdonadme, sutiles y altas Musas,
Las que hacéis vanidad de ser confusas.
Os puedo yo decir con mejor modo
Que sin la claridad os falta todo ?

Thus, might I drop into an author's ear
A piece of counsel, I would say, " Be sure,
Whate'er you write, to keep your meaning clear ;
For dulness only ever is obscure."—*Rockliff.*

GRAVITY GIVES THE APPEARANCE OF CAPACITY.

Fab. 7.

Muy verosimil es ; pues que la gravedad
Suple en múchos así por la capacidad.
Dignanse rara vez de despegar sus labios,
Y piensan que con esto imitan á los sabios.

The moral of this is that gravity of demeanour supplies the
place in many of capacity. They seldom deign to open their lips,
and think that in this way they imitate the wise.

A FOOL.

Fab. 8.

Sin reglas del arte
Borriquitos hai
Que una vez aciertan
Por casualidad.

A fool, in spite of nature's bent,
May shine for once—by accident.

SCHOLIASTS.
Fab. 10.

Quando veo yo algunos que de otros escritores
A la sombra se arriman, y piensan ser autores
Con poner quatro notas, ó hacer un prologuillo,
Estói por aplicarles lo que dixo el tomillo.

When I see some who link themselves to other writers, and
think to be authors by adding notes or making a small prologue,
I am inclined to apply to them what the thyme said to the ivy.

To shine in an Inferior Line.
Fab. 13.

Y asi tenga sabido
Que lo importante y raro
No es entender de tódo,
Sinó ser diestro en algo.

So authors often estimate
Their talents at too high a rate ;
For, barely qualified to shine,
Perhaps in some inferior line,
They aim at all, instead of one,
And, like the goose, excel in none.—*Rockliff.*

To seek to understand Everything.
Fab. 14.

Si querer entender de tódo
Es ridícula presuncion,
Servir sólo para una cosa
Suele ser falta no menor.

To pretend to understand everything is ridiculous presumption,
to limit oneself to one trifling acquisition is wont to be a no less
fault.

To gain Fame without Knowledge.
Fab. 17.

Gran cosa ! ganar crédito sin ciencia,
Y perderle en llegando á la experiencia.

Mighty thing ! to gain credit without knowledge. and to lose it on reaching to experience.

The Youthful Bard.
Fab. 18.

Despues de este lance, en viendo
Que un autor ha principiado
Con altisonante estruendo,
　Al punto digo : cuidado !
Tente, hombre ; que te has de ver
En el vergonzoso estado
De la mula de alquiler.

The youthful bard may try in vain
　The path of poesy, unless,
Instead of urging, he restrain
　His winged courser's eagerness ;
For Pegasus, if ridden hard,
　Will sink at last from sheer excess,
And fling to earth the luckless bard.—*Rockliff.*

Men praise or blame as Interest sways.
Fab. 21.

La alabanza que muchos creen justa
Injusta les parece,
Si ven que su contrario lo merece.

The praise which many think just appears to others unjust, if it happens that its opposite deserves it.

Critics.
Fab. 22.

Cobardes son y traidores
Ciertos críticos que esperan,
Para impugnar, á que mueran
Los infelices autores,
Porque vivos respondieran.

Certain critics are cowards and traitors, who wait to attack till unhappy authors are dead, because alive they would answer.

Merchant-Authors.

Fab. 26.

Murciélagos literarios
    Que hacéis á pluma y á pelo,
Si queréis vivir con tódos,
    Miráos en este espejo.

So merchant-authors—they who range
Between Parnassus and the 'Change—
    Sole denizens of neither :
Who seek to play a double game,
To grub for gold and fly at fame,
    Are seldom bless'd with either.—*Rockliff.*

Dress.

Fab. 27.

La ropa no da ciencia.

Dress does not give knowledge.

The Vulgar have no Taste.

Fab. 28.

Siempre acostumbra hacer el vulgo necio
De lo bueno y lo malo igual aprecio.

The foolish vulgar is always accustomed to value equally the
good and the bad.

Fashionable Authors.

Fab. 32.

Y ahora digo yo ; Llene un volúmen
De disparates un autor famoso,
Y si no le alebaren, que me emplumen.

And now I say, "Let a famous author fill a volume with
nonsense, and if the public does not praise it, let me be tarred
and feathered."

Love of Country.

Fab. 32.

Sabéis por qué motivo el uno al altra ótro
Tánto se alaban? Porque son paisanos.

Do you know why the one praises the other so highly? Because
they are compatriots.

So Ovid (*Ex Pont. Ep.* i. 3) :—" Amor patriæ ratione valentior
omni."

The Critic.

Fab. 34.

Quando en las obras del sabio
No encuentra defectos
Contra la persona cargos
Suele hacer el necio.

When the works of the wise are free from faults, the fool
attacks the author's person.

Outside Appearance.

Fab. 36.

A fe que este lance
No echaré en olvido ;
Pues viene de molde
A un amigo mio,
El qual à buen precio
Ha comprado un libro
Bien enquadernado,
Que no vale un pito.

Thus, to end my fable, for all
Apologues must have a moral ;
Many a blockhead merely looks
To the covers of his books ;
In their purchase never minding,
If the gilding and the binding
Please his eye, though all within
Be not worth a single pin ;
Buying, like a foolish fellow,
" Nought but leather and prunella."—*Rockliff.*

WRITERS.

Fab. 43.

Así permitiera el cielo
Que sucediera otro tanto
Quando, trabajando à escote
Tres escritores, ó quatro,
Cada qual quiere la gloria,
Si es bueno el libro ó mediano ;
Y los compañeros tienen
La cúlpa si sale malo !

Thus, should Heaven permit that a work succeeds, when three
or four writers unite in contributing each one his mite, every one
arrogates all the success as his own if the book be good, or even
middling ; and his companions bear the blame if it turns out ill.

A CONTEST.

Fab. 46.

Quién se meta en contienda,
    Verbi-gracia de asunto literario,
A los años no atienda,
    Sinó á la habilidad de su adversario.

Let authors, ere they venture to engage
    In controversy, to this truth attend,
That on their rival's skill, and not his age,
    The issue of the contest must depend.

A MAN OF REAL LEARNING.

Fab. 48.

De aprender se desdeña
El literato grave ?
Pues mas debe estudiar el que mas sabe.

Thus every man of real learning
    Is anxious to increase his lore ;
And feels, in fact, a greater yearning,
    The more he knows, to know the more.

CHOICE OF BOOKS.

Fab. 50.

Que un tordo en aqueste **engaño**
Caiga, no lo dificulto ;
Pero es mucho mas estraño
Que hombre tenido por culto,
Aprecie por el tamaño
Los libros y por el vulto,
Grande es, si es buena, una obra ;
Si es mala, toda ella sobra.

That a thrush should fall into this mistake, I am not surprised ;
yet it is much more strange that an educated man should value
books for their size and outward appearance. A work is large
enough if it is good, if it is bad there is more than enough
of it.

See (Lat.) Books, not many.

STYLE.

Fab. 51.

Quien desprecie el estilo,
Y diga que á las cosas sólo atiende,
Advierta que si el hilo
Mas que el noble metal caro se **vende,**
Tambien de la elegancia
Su principal valor á la substancia.

Let the man who despises style, and says that he attends to the
matter, recollect that if the lace is sold at a higher price than the
noble metal, it owes its chief value to its elegance, and not to its
material.

AUTHORS.

Fab. 52.

Qualquiera pensaría
Que este aviso moral
Seguramente haría
Al cazador gran fuerza ; pues no hai tal.

Se quedó tan sereno
Como ingrato escritor
Que del auxilio ageno
Se aprovecha, y no cita al bien-hechor.

Thus many an author is disposed to draw
 His precepts from his practice, and impose
On others, who are juvenile and raw,
 His own peculiarities, as those
Which ought to form a precedent and law
 For all who would excel in verse or prose;
But genius teaches an unerring way,
While rules of art too often lead astray.—*Rockliff.*

ART AND GENIUS MUST COMBINE.

Fab. 54.

Este exemplo material
Todo escritor considere
Que el largo estudio no uniere
Al talento natural.
Ni da lumbre el pedernal
Sin auxilio de eslabon,
Ni hai buena disposicion
Que luzca faltando el arte.
Si obra cada quál aparte,
Ambos inútiles son.

Let every writer who does not unite deep study to natural
talents consider this example:—Neither does the flint give light
without the steel, nor, if you do not employ art, will your highest
ability shine forth. If anything separates these, both are useless.

CRITICS.

Fab. 56.

Los remendones, que escritos ajenos
Corregir piensan, acaso de errores
Suelen dexarlos die veces mas llenos . . .
Mas no haya miedo que de estos Señores

> Diga yo nada :
> Que se lo diga por mi la criada.

Botchers who think to amend classic writings are wont to make them ten times more full of errors. . . . There is no fear that I should say a single word about those gentlemen : let the house-maid say it for me.

No One willing to confess his Defects.
Fab. 59.

> Si el que es ciego y lo sabe,
> Aparenta que ve,
> Quien sabe que es idiota
> Confesará que los es ?

If he who is blind, and knows it, pretends that he sees, will he who knows that he is a fool confess that he is so?

The Best Portions of a Book disliked by the Critics.

> Que así como la reina de las flores
> Al sucio escarabajo desagrada,
> Así tambien á góticos doctores
> Toda invencion amena y delicada.

For as the queen of flowers is loathsome to the filthy beetle, so the best and brightest portions of a book are those which tasteless critics chide beyond the rest.

GERMAN INDEX.

GENERAL INDEX.

---

it is not good for him to be
alone, 421 ; is great or little
by his own will, 400 ; the good,
68 ; a happy, 152 ; has time
enough for everything, 128 ;
hidden powers in, 439 ; with
hopes realised, 105 ; how he
best portrays his character,
285 ; how he may best employ
himself, 417 ; how he must
act in life, 148 ; how he shows
his importance, 126 ; how his
greatness is to be estimated,
432 ; an imitative animal, 398 ;
immortality of, 8 ; the independent, 94 ; as individuals
and in the mass, 211, 315 ;
insignificance of, 375 ; an irresolute, 100 ; is easily forgotten,
274 ; is liable to error, 41 ; is
like a ball, 405 ; is made of
filth, 364 ; is a wild beast,
437 ; judges with his own preconceived ideas, 222 ; life of,
how miserable, 521 ; life of,
how changeable, 520 ; life of,
here has two and a half
minutes, 296 ; the lot of, 183 ;
lower creation contrasted with,
433 ; of merit patronised by a
blockhead, 120 ; the mind of,
is contracted within a narrow
circle, 382 ; nature of, cannot
be changed, 190 ; never returns, 261 ; no pang is permanent with, 401 ; powers of,
how they degenerate, 285 ;
the, regardless of law, 253 ;
a religious, 330 ; remains at
last alone, 204 ; renowned in
song, 67 ; sad fate of, 103 ;
selfishness of, 284 ; should not
be like a fungus, 140 ; two
souls in, 47 ; sentence-passing,

59 ; of the smallest mental
powers, 148 ; soul of, 173 ;
a strong will necessary in, 417 ;
tears of, 163 ; thoughts of,
grow by certain laws, 398 ; a
tide in the affairs of, 448 ;
troubled life of, 447 ; the, true
to himself, 160 ; the unthinking, 399 ; vain, 314 ; particular
vocation of, 18 ; a weak, 189 ;
what he reconciles himself to,
223 ; what he has are gifts,
459 ; what closes the heart of,
173 ; the, who has satisfied the
best of his time, 382 ; who
fears nothing, 361 ; the will of,
makes his fortune, 384 ; wisdom of, appears in his actions,
342 ; wishes of, 102 ; the wise,
143 ; the, with a great purpose
and fixed idea, 316 ; a, without
pretensions, 23

Mankind difficult to know, 375 ;
the destinies of, are balanced,
365 ; the history of, 434

Many, pleasing the, 350

Marriages are made in heaven, 141

Master, it is well to know the
whims of, 145

May of life only blooms once,
345 ; morning, 165, 461

Mean companions of youth, 102

Meaning, let it be clear, 525

Medicine not poison, 254

Men and women, difference of,
73, 114, 423 ; and gods, to
fight against, 196 ; the common race of, 52 ; deride what
they cannot understand, 48,
different feelings of, 155 ; different lives of, 14 ; earnest-
thinking, 150 ; employ, according to their gifts, 83 ; exertions of, 107 ; full of love and

gloomy night of life, 289 ; soft, 459

Mystifications, an amusement of idle people, 124

NATION, maturity of, 161 ; honour of a, 413

Nations blossom and fade, 172

Natural gifts, to enjoy in silence, 135

Nature, 444 ; all death in, is birth, 8 ; and rules, 89, 453 ; course of, 209 ; creation, days of, 277 ; discord of, 258 ; every, puts forth its own fruit, 288 ; the inner spirit of, 166 ; lovely as in days of old, 177 ; man's inmost, 75 ; man always returns to, 124 ; the maturity, 161 ; a musical instrument, 261 ; no one can lay aside his own, 70 ; a noble, 68 ; power of, to soothe the soul, 462 ; quiet joys of, 410 ; revives in spring, 348 ; richness of, 228 ; what it does for man, 263 ; what lies in, 203 ; what it has given, 361

Necessity commands with iron hand, 65 ; stern is the on-look, 393

New passion, a, 132 ; Testament, 49

Nest-life, the echo of the, 308

Night comes when no man can work, 162

Nightingale, melody of, 511

Night-life, immoral, 307

No rest in this world, 83

Nobility, factitious, 136 ; the soul's, 76 ; true, 19

Noble, the, to appreciate, 78 ; and ignoble, 446 ; the hope of, 401 ; how anything, can

be performed, 358 ; the, an image of God. 447 ; progenitors, 62 ; what distinguishes the, from the ignoble, 447

Noblest, what is, conceals itself, 304

Nothings, mere, 340

Novelty loses its zest, 368

Numbers give courage, 390

Numbered, our days are, 114

OCCUPATION makes time short, 482

Ocean, the swell of, 241

Oddities in the world, 57

Old, the, 150, 157

Old age, 213 ; of women, 270 ; characteristic of, 226

Old story but ever new, 167

Old thoughts in the newest books, 320

Old, the, what privilege they, lose, 157 ; one heart, one race, 404

Opinions, different, 119

Opportunity, the, is good, 405

Orator, good sense necessary to an, 43

Organisation much depends on our, 27

Original thinker, and the opposite, 429

Others, apt to compare ourselves with, 92

Our own, we love, 169

Ourselves, we deceive, 84, 159 ; the deepest gulf in, 84 ; to take too much care of, 127 ; not to think too much of, 152 ; what we cannot acknowledge to, 85

Outside appearance. 529

PAIN, we ought to resist, 188

THE END.